The
L/L Research
Channeling Archives

Transcripts of the Meditation Sessions

Volume 4
April 6, 1981 to February 14, 1982

Don
Elkins

Jim
McCarty

Carla L.
Rueckert

Copyright © 2009 L/L Research

All rights reserved. No part of this book may be reproduced or used in any form or by any means—graphic, electronic or mechanical, including photocopying or information storage and retrieval systems—without written permission from the copyright holder.

ISBN: 978-0-945007-78-4

Published by L/L Research
Box 5195
Louisville, Kentucky 40255-0195

E-mail: contact@llresearch.org
www.llresearch.org

About the cover photo: *This photograph of Jim McCarty and Carla L. Rueckert was taken during an L/L Research channeling session on August 4, 2009, in the living room of their Louisville, Kentucky home. Jim always holds hands with Carla when she channels, following the Ra group's advice on how she can avoid any possibility of astral travel.*

Dedication

These archive volumes are dedicated to Hal and Jo Price, who faithfully and lovingly hosted this group's weekly meditation meetings from 1962 to 1975,

to Walt Rogers, whose work with the research group Man, Consciousness and Understanding of Detroit offered the information needed to begin this ongoing channeling experiment,

and to the Confederation of Angels and Planets in the Service of the Infinite Creator, for sharing their love and wisdom with us so generously through the years.

Table of Contents

Introduction 7
Year 1981 9
    April 6, 1981 10
    April 12, 1981 13
    April 15, 1981 18
    April 15, 1981 20
    April 18, 1981 22
    April 19, 1981 26
    April 22, 1981 31
    April 22, 1981 35
    April 26, 1981 37
    April 27, 1981 40
    April 27, 1981 43
    May 3, 1981 45
    May 6, 1981 49
    May 6, 1981 53
    May 10, 1981 54
    May 13, 1981 59
    May 17, 1981 62
    May 19, 1981 67
    May 24, 1981 71
    May 25, 1981 76
    May 25, 1981 80
    May 29, 1981 82
    May 31, 1981 87
    June 5, 1981 91
    June 7, 1981 95
    June 8, 1981 99
    June 12, 1981 102
    June 14, 1981 107
    June 16, 1981 112
    June 21, 1981 116
    June 25, 1981 121
    June 25, 1981 125
    June 28, 1981 127
    July 1, 1981 131
    July 1, 1981 135
    July 5, 1981 139
    July 8, 1981 143

July 12, 1981	147
July 13, 1981	151
July 18, 1981	156
July 18, 1981	161
July 26, 1981	163
August 2, 1981	167
August 6, 1981	174
August 8, 1981	177
August 8, 1981	182
August 9, 1981	183
August 12, 1981	187
August 12, 1981	194
August 15, 1981	196
August 15, 1981	202
August 16, 1981	204
August 18, 1981	210
August 18, 1981	213
August 23, 1981	216
August 29, 1981	219
August 30, 1981	223
September 6, 1981	229
September 9, 1981	235
September 13, 1981	239
September 18, 1981	244
September 18, 1981	248
September 20, 1981	249
September 21, 1981	254
September 22, 1981	258
September 27, 1981	260
October 4, 1981	264
October 11, 1981	269
October 14, 1981	274
October 15, 1981	278
October 18, 1981	282
October 21, 1981	285
October 25, 1981	290
October 28, 1981	294
October 31, 1981	298
October 31, 1981	303
November 1, 1981	306
November 5, 1981	310
November 8, 1981	315

November 12, 1981 321
November 15, 1981 324
November 22, 1981 327
November 29, 1981 331
December 3, 1981 338
December 6, 1981 341
December 8, 1981 347
December 11, 1981 349
December 13, 1981 352
December 20, 1981 358

Year 1982 .... **364**
January 3, 1982 365
January 10, 1982 367
January 31, 1982 368
February 3, 1982 373
February 4, 1982 377
February 7, 1982 381
February 10, 1982 386
February 11, 1982 391
February 14, 1982 395

Introduction

Welcome to this volume of the *L/L Research Channeling Archives*. This series of publications represents the collection of channeling sessions recorded by L/L Research during the period from the early seventies to the present day. The sessions are also available on the L/L Research website, www.llresearch.org.

Starting in the mid-1950s, Don Elkins, a professor of physics and engineering at Speed Scientific School, had begun researching the paranormal in general and UFOs in particular. Elkins was a pilot as well as a professor and he flew his small plane to meet with many of the UFO contactees of the period.

Hal Price had been a part of a UFO-contactee channeling circle in Detroit called "The Detroit Group." When Price was transferred from Detroit's Ford plant to its Louisville truck plant, mutual friends discovered that Price also was a UFO researcher and put the two men together. Hal introduced Elkins to material called *The Brown Notebook* which contained instructions on how to create a group and receive UFO contactee information. In January of 1962 they decided to put the instructions to use and began holding silent meditation meetings on Sunday nights just across the Ohio River in the southern Indiana home of Hal and his wife, Jo. This was the beginning of what was called the "Louisville Group."

I was an original member of that group, along with a dozen of Elkins' physics students. However, I did not learn to channel until 1974. Before that date, almost none of our weekly channeling sessions were recorded or transcribed. After I began improving as a channel, Elkins decided for the first time to record all the sessions and transcribe them.

During the first eighteen months or so of my studying channeling and producing material, we tended to reuse the tapes as soon as the transcriptions were finished. Since those were typewriter days, we had no record of the work that could be reopened and used again, as we do now with computers. And I used up the original and the carbon copy of my transcriptions putting together a manuscript, *Voices of the Gods*, which has not yet been published. It remains as almost the only record of Don Elkins' and my channeling of that period.

We learned from this experience to retain the original tapes of all of our sessions, and during the remainder of the seventies and through the eighties, our "Louisville Group" was prolific. The "Louisville Group" became "L/L Research" after Elkins and I published a book in 1976, *Secrets of the UFO*, using that publishing name. At first we met almost every night. In later years, we met gradually less often, and the number of sessions recorded by our group in a year accordingly went down. Eventually, the group began taking three months off from channeling during the summer. And after 2000, we began having channeling meditations only twice a month. The volume of sessions dropped to its present output of eighteen or so each year.

These sessions feature channeling from sources which call themselves members of the Confederation of Planets in the Service of the Infinite Creator. At first we enjoyed hearing from many different voices: Hatonn, Laitos, Oxal, L/Leema and Yadda being just a few of them. As I improved my tuning techniques, and became the sole senior channel in L/L Research, the number of contacts dwindled. When I began asking for "the highest and best contact which I can receive of Jesus the Christ's vibration of unconditional love in a conscious and stable manner," the entity offering its thoughts through our group was almost always Q'uo. This remains true as our group continues to channel on an ongoing basis.

The channelings are always about love and unity, enunciating "The Law of One" in one aspect or another. Seekers who are working with spiritual principles often find the material a good resource. We hope that you will as well. As time has gone on the questions have shifted somewhat, but in general the content of the channeling is metaphysical and focused on helping seekers find the love in the moment and the Creator in the love.

At first, I transcribed our channeling sessions. I got busier, as our little group became more widely known, and got hopelessly behind on transcribing. Two early transcribers who took that job off my hands were Kim

Howard and Judy Dunn, both of whom masterfully transcribed literally hundreds of sessions through the eighties and early nineties.

Then Ian Jaffray volunteered to create a web site for these transcriptions, and single-handedly unified the many different formats that the transcripts were in at that time and made them available online. This additional exposure prompted more volunteers to join the ranks of our transcribers, and now there are a dozen or so who help with this. Our thanks go out to all of these kind volunteers, early and late, who have made it possible for our webguy to make these archives available.

Around the turn of the millennium, I decided to commit to editing each session after it had been transcribed. So the later transcripts have fewer errata than the earlier ones, which are quite imperfect in places. One day, perhaps, those earlier sessions will be revisited and corrections will be made to the transcripts. It would be a large task, since there are well over 1500 channeling sessions as of this date, and counting. We apologize for the imperfections in those transcripts, and trust that you can ascertain the sense of them regardless of a mistake here and there.

Blessings, dear reader! Enjoy these "humble thoughts" from the Confederation of Planets. May they prove good companions to your spiritual seeking.

For all of us at L/L Research,

Carla L. Rueckert

Louisville, Kentucky

July 16, 2009

Year 1981

April 6, 1981 to December 20, 1981

L/L Research

The Law of One, Book V, Session 45, Fragment 27
April 6, 1981

Jim: Session 45 was also a maintenance session with a few other minor areas of investigation included. The sessions were at their shortest at this time while Carla was regaining her vital energy level. At the end of the session Ra found the need to end the session somewhat prematurely. The fellows who delivered our water for our cistern had shown up and failed to read our notes on the door which said that we were not available, and that silence was required for the experiment in which we were engaged. Thus they proceeded to knock loudly on every door that they could find, including the door to the Ra session room. Needless to say, we blocked our driveway after that experience so that we would not again be disturbed by visitors while we were having a session with Ra.

Carla: This must have been a hilarious situation. I am sorry I missed it. We were so very careful in preparing our place of working, getting the various preparations done with care and grace, then my going off to sleep while Don and Jim walked the circle of One. And then, the exquisitely careful choice of questions, listening for Ra's very soft, very uninflected words—altogether a delicate operation. And then to have loud noises and the hurrying emotions behind them—I can just see the two men going quietly ballistic!

It is hard to read the constant reports of my failing energies, even now, because I remember so well the feelings of frustration and anger that I experienced as I offered myself, poor as I was, for contact. Inside, I felt a strength and power of self that was much different from my physical state, and I wondered why I had chosen such a limited physical body. Why had I not given myself a totally healthy body so I could be a better worker for the Light? And yet I knew, at least intellectually and consciously, that all is perfect, that this was the very best configuration of mind and body and energy balance, that this was precisely where I needed to be. Were I not a mystic, and able to access that part of me which is pure faith, I would have been tempted to give up.

In the time since Don's death and the end of the Ra contact, I have come to much more of a peace with this issue, seeing clearly the way my limitations worked to refine me, to hone my sense of purpose and make ever more substantial those joys of spirit that informed my awareness. I see them still at work, and can embrace now that fragility which has given me such fruits of consciousness, and hollowed me out so well. It is the empty instrument that is able to offer the purest substance through it, and it is limitation and loss that have refined and hollowed me, and given me that transparency of spirit that moves into simple joy. I am so very glad to see each new day, I cannot express it; and this is a gift given through suffering. So often, as we look at spiritual gifts, that is true: the gaining of them can be seen to involve tragedy and pain. Yet as we experience those depths of sorrow, we also find ourselves more able to move into joy in the everyday things that are so right and so precious.

Session 45, April 6, 1981

Ra: I am Ra. I greet you in the love and in the light of the one infinite Creator. We communicate now.

Questioner: Could you give us an estimate of the instrument's physical condition now that she is rested?

Ra: I am Ra. This instrument's condition as regards the bodily complex is extremely poor. This instrument is not rested. However, this instrument was eager for our contact.

Questioner: Did the period of abstinence from contact help the instrument's physical condition?

Ra: I am Ra. This is correct. The probability of this instrument's development of what you would call disease either of the pulmonary nature or the renal nature was quite significant at our previous contact. You have averted a possible serious physical malfunction of this instrument's bodily complex. It is to be noted that your prayerful support was helpful as was this instrument's unflagging determination to accept that which was best in the long run and thus maintain the exercises recommended without undue impatience. It is to be further noted that those things which aid this instrument are in some ways contradictory and require balance. Thus this instrument is aided by rest but also by diversions of an active nature. This makes it more difficult to aid this instrument. However, once this is known, the balancing may be more easily accomplished.

Questioner: Can you tell me if a large percentage of the Wanderers here now are those of Ra?

RA. I am Ra. I can.

Questioner: Are they?

Ra: I am Ra. A significant portion of sixth-density Wanderers are those of our social memory complex. Another large portion consists of those who aided those in South America; another portion, those aiding Atlantis. All are sixth density and all brother and sister groups due to the unified feeling that as we had been aided by shapes such as the pyramid, so we could aid your peoples.

Questioner: Can you say if any of the three of us are of Ra or any of the other groups?

Ra: I am Ra. Yes.

Questioner: Can you say which of us are of which group?

Ra: I am Ra. No.

Questioner: Are all of us of one of the groups that you mentioned?

Ra: I am Ra. We shall go to the limits of our attempts to refrain from infringement. Two are a sixth-density origin, one a fifth-density harvestable to sixth but choosing to return as a Wanderer due to a loving association between teacher and student. Thus you three form a greatly cohesive group.

Questioner: Can you explain the right and left ear tone and what I call touch contact that I continually get?

Ra: I am Ra. This has been covered previously. Please ask for specific further details.

Questioner: I get what I consider to be tickling in my right and my left ear at different times. Is this any different as far as meaning goes from the tone that I get in my right and left ear?

Ra: I am Ra. No.

Questioner: Why is the left ear of the service-to-self contact and the right service-to-others?

Ra: I am Ra. The nature of your physical vehicle is that there is a magnetic field positive and negative in complex patterns about the shells of your vehicle. The left portion of the head region of most entities is, upon the time/space continuum level, of a negative polarity.

QUESTIONER. Can you tell me what is the purpose or philosophy behind the fourth, fifth, and sixth-density positive and negative social memory complexes?

Ra: I am Ra. The basic purpose of a social memory complex is that of evolution. Beyond a certain point the evolution of spirit is quite dependent upon the understanding of self and other-self as Creator. This constitutes the basis for social complexes. When brought to maturity, they become social memory complexes. The fourth density and sixth density find these quite necessary. The fifth positive uses social memory in attaining wisdom, though this is done individually. In fifth negative much is done without aid of others. This is the last query as this instrument needs to be protected from depletion. Are there brief queries before we close?

Questioner: I just need to know if there is anything that we can do to make the instrument more comfortable or to improve the contact?

Ra: I am Ra. All is well, my brothers. *(Loud rapping at the door. Water truckers!)*

Questioner: What did you say?

Ra: I am Ra. All is well, my brothers. I leave you now in the love and in the light of the one infinite Creator. Go forth, then, rejoicing in the power and the peace of the one infinite Creator. Adonai. ☥

Sunday Meditation
April 12, 1981

(Jim channeling)

I am Hatonn, and I greet you in the love and the light of our infinite Creator. It is with great joy that we bring you our greetings this evening, for always it is an honor and a privilege to be able to share our simple thoughts with your group. Our thoughts, as always, are a humble reflection of the one original Thought of the Creator, that Thought that binds us all in unity, in love and in light.

It is for the purpose of sharing this one simple Thought that we feel the greatest of honors in addressing your group each session where it is possible for us to be with you. This evening we would speak a few words once again on the subject of love. This subject which is the focus of most of our communications with you is yet the subject which is not well understood by many of your people and, indeed, we would say that few really understand the concept of love, though many times have they heard the concept reviewed. It is for this reason that we speak again and again on this simple concept, for simple though it is, yet much seems to stand in the way of the peoples of your planet and their understanding of this simple concept.

There exists within the creation of the Father only one force, the force of love, which has created all that exists. The perceptions that your people have of the creation is one which sees many things; is one which looks and sees objects; which looks and sees interaction; which looks and sees ratios; which looks and sees the particles of existence broken down as though they were bricks, built back up as though they were buildings. It is, if you will pardon our expression, somewhat of a mechanical view of creation, a view which does not see far beyond the exterior appearance, a view which sees only that which is apparent with the physical senses.

We of Hatonn speak our simple words in order that the view of those who seek to see might be extended beyond the surface, beyond the exterior. For much there is, my friends, that does not meet the physical eye. Much there is that must be seen by other means. With this in mind, we present to you for your examination the simple concept that when you view the Father's creation, if you look with your heart, if you look with your inner eye, if you look with your interior perceptions, you might be made aware of a binding force which holds all of creation together, which serves as not only the binder, but also that which is bound, and yet not bound in a way which restricts to sight, or vision, but in a way which arranges that which is seen as a pattern of love that the Creator has arranged within all of Creation, an infinite variety of patterns of love, that these patterns might be seen in many, many ways.

But if, when seeing in any way, the realization is also kept in focus that that foundation upon which all is created is love, then that which is seen might be viewed in a clearer perspective. For if there is no binding force apparent to those who view the creation, is not all that is seen somewhat chaotic, somewhat disjointed, without rhyme or reason? For within the creation there is an ordering and that ordering of the Father is love, love which seeks to be known, love which seeks to know itself, love which calls, love which listens.

As you perceive that which is round about you, we suggest that you keep within your mind, within your heart, within your being, the consideration of what it is you see. Ask yourself, "Where is the love?" For surely, my friends, it surrounds you always.

At this time we would transfer our contact to another instrument. I am Hatonn.

(L channeling)

I am Hatonn, and again I greet you, my brothers, in the love and the light of the infinite Creator. We are pleased that you and your friends are seeking the light more readily in these days of approaching turmoil. My friends, it is difficult to perceive the approaching storm in that the vestiges of the season of tranquility that you are leaving tend to disguise the gradual formation of clouds that herald the thunder to come. Yet, my brothers, be attentive, for the thunder does come and the peace and tranquility that you are lulled into perceiving will not last.

My brothers, you are wise in that you listen when we speak, for there is always wisdom in listening. Yet, my brothers, you would be far wiser still if you chose to act upon the information that you have received. It is not within our grasp or our responsibility to advise each of you personally upon his or her future, for we all know, my brothers, that this is not possible and would violate your blessing of freedom of will. Yet, my brothers, we would encourage all of your race to be more attentive to the signs that surround you, for as the light shines from out of the east and covers all of the land in a gradual transformation of darkness into lightness, so also, my brothers, does the transformation come to your planet. It does and will continue to seem a gradual process that often appears to have ceased. Yet, my brothers, just as the sun, in climbing above the horizon, more and more rapidly erases the shadows, so also will the coming changes occur. It is, therefore, within your grasp to perceive these changes and to prepare yourselves accordingly.

The question [then] becomes not whether one should prepare, but rather how one should prepare oneself. It is possible to spend great lengths of your remaining time attempting to consolidate advantage on the physical plane in expectation that by accumulating what will become the riches of tomorrow one might find a way to purchase one's way through the impending future. My brothers, is this not what most of those beings upon your planetary surface are doing now and have done for thousands of years? Therefore, my brothers, is it not far wiser to ask oneself, "How may I prepare for my spiritual survival and advancement in this coming new age?"

The answer, my brothers, lies in the subject referred to through the aid of the instrument known as Jim, that subject being love. The riches that must be accumulated upon your planet and by its peoples are not those of property or gold or silver, but rather, my brothers, those riches of the soul that can only be received, not taken, and can only be given, not sold. My brothers, be strong in your goodness and fear not the impending struggle, for it is less wise to ask oneself, "Will I survive until tomorrow?" than to ask oneself, "Will I be able to love continuous until tomorrow?"

At this time, my brothers, we would ask if there are any questions that we may attempt to help you answer for yourselves, for is not that the true path of learning? Therefore, we will dispense with further rhetoric, for we love to answer what we are allowed to. I am Hatonn.

C: Yes, I have a question. It concerns my son, A. We've had troubles with A being afraid to be separated from us. But here in the last few weeks the fear is becoming more intense and it seems to have followed … of us trying to explain to him … to answer questions he had about death and about our coming to meditation and I'm afraid that somehow he's gotten the two equated with each other and I'm thinking he's afraid that we might not return from these meditations. I don't know if this is so, but if it is, how best can we explain to him what it is we're doing? But it's hard sometimes to communicate with a child, especially a very young child.

I am Hatonn. I understand your question. My brother, a child is much like a picture that has not been completed. Various forms have been sketched in and will later be endowed with color and substance. The picture is aware of its incompleteness, just as you are aware of your own incompleteness, being a somewhat more colorful picture. That was a pun—ha ha.

My brother, just as you sense directions in which your picture may further be completed, so also does your child, but being more recently returned from what you might call the spiritual aspect, he is less acquainted with the limitations imposed by your current physical plane. It is then understandable that he perceives your absence with the expressed intent of reestablishing your connection with the non-physical plane as a potentially permanent linkage, just as his more recent transition from the spiritual to the physical plane was relatively permanent.

Your child loves you greatly and realizes that he must maintain his contact with you upon this plane so as to achieve the situations necessary for his growth. As he is less than familiar with the multitude of rules and regulations governing the behavior of physical objects, such as your body, on this plane and concerning the necessary attachment of yourself to your body, he is concerned that an inadvertent and permanent separation might ensue. Furthermore, he realizes that your efforts toward growth and maturity are not characteristic of beings on your plane. And is not growth a departure from one locus with the intent of striving toward a non-existent, infinitely distant point?

Therefore, my brother, be assured that your child is not the victim of an external, malevolent force, but rather of his own affections for you as well as his own craving for those situations of the future which will enable him to grow at a considerable rate.

May we answer you further, my brother?

C: How can I better communicate with my child about what I'm doing, and what his mother is doing? Or is it really necessary to communicate with him verbally about it?

I am Hatonn. My brother, is experience not the best teacher? Verbal communication is a valuable tool in conveying abstract explanation and should be employed in conjunction with your other, more expressive forms of communication such as touching, holding and reassuring the young child of his value in your life. In addition, my brother, that [what] you would be well to consider would be the introduction of your child to the performance of brief meditation. It is not necessary nor is it advisable to make these introductory meditations of extensive time or of the purpose to convey messages, rather, my brother, we would suggest that occasionally you or your wife might stop, explain to your child that the present moment is an excellent opportunity for meditation and yourself or your wife briefly meditate while encouraging your child to join and share with you for a moment or two.

May we answer you further, my brother?

C: No, you've helped greatly. Thank you.

We thank you, my brother, for the opportunity of service. May we answer another question?

E: I have a question, Hatonn, and that is: in the Bible there are many references to the Kingdom of God or the Kingdom of Heaven and I've been mulling over in my own mind what is meant by these phrases, which seem to be used interchangeably. Could you tell me what is meant by the phrase "Kingdom of Heaven"?

I am Hatonn. Mull no longer, my friend. The Kingdom of Heaven is that place one reaches when one understands and shares the existence of oneness in this universe and all universes. Just as in a well exercised and cared for body on your plane, all cells work joyfully and share one set of vibrations, so also could be represented the Kingdom of Heaven.

Does this answer your question, my brother?

E: Yes. That's what I suspected, and may I ask further, does that then mean that entities such as you are part of the Kingdom of Heaven?

I am Hatonn. My brother, the answer to your question could be expressed as both yes and no. Yes, in that whether one realizes his perfection or not, he is a still a part of the Kingdom of Heaven, yet that heaviness which is within has not been allowed outward, and encompasses the individual's life. Regretfully, my brother, we of Hatonn have not yet attained that form of perfection which is responsible for the negative answer of the doubly answered question.

May we answer you further, my brother?

E: Yes. That makes me wonder how you have fallen short of attaining that Kingdom?

I am Hatonn. My brother, if we knew that answer—if we only knew. May we be of further service to you?

E: At some later time I'm sure you will be.

Thank you, my brother.

E: Thank you.

May we answer another question?

C: Yes. I know an individual who … one that I've spoken to before about things we have learned about meditation and this individual, when they're alone, feels a contact … had expressed to us he feels a contact, and the contact he feels—I get a very bad feeling about that he is being played with by influences other than the Confederation. Is this so?

I am Hatonn. My brother, we of Hatonn are not allowed to inform members of your race of the predilections of specific other members or of those from whom they seek learning. However, my brother, we would offer the advice that was carefully selected for your planet in reference to questions such as the one you have posed: "By their fruits ye shall know them."

May we answer you further, my brother?

C: No. Not at this time. Thank you

We thank you. May we answer another question?

E: I have one more concerning the Bible and that is the fairly frequent references to angels and my question is, what are angels?

I am Hatonn. My brother, you seek definitions which are functional to a mind which dwells in three-dimensional logic. To convey a three-dimensionally logical answer, we would respond that an angel is one who acts as the servant or messenger from God. Obviously, my brother, you are capable of perceiving the truth that extends beyond three-dimensional logic and this answer is not sufficient. Therefore, my brother, we would answer for you that an angel is one who acts in accordance with the flow of universal energy, for does not …

(Side one of tape ends.)

May we answer you further, my brother?

E: Yes. I'd like to know then … well, as my understanding of it is that angels must be very close to God, as we call it, and I would like to know if that's true.

My brother, God, or God-ness, is everywhere. What is more close than that? The angels to whom you refer were servants who performed specific tasks, not always realizing the service to which they were put, just as you yourself do not always realize the services you perform in other persons' lives simply by existing. For example, my brother, had you not encountered your recent accident and injury, the individual whose vehicle impacted your own might have more recently suffered a fatal accident through inattention to his driving performance. Obviously you were not a winged creature, although you did fly, yet you acted inadvertently in accordance with the will of the universe. The fact that you yourself were also in training, so to speak, does not alter your service, a service that you in your past contracted to perform.

Therefore, my brother, to reiterate, an angel is one who often unknowingly acts in such a manner as to be in attunement with the will of the universe.

May we answer you further, my brother?

E: I'll think on what you've said for now. Thank you.

We thank you, my brother. May we answer further questions?

(Pause)

I am Hatonn. We thank you for the opportunity to speak at such great lengths and upon so many interesting subjects. We of Hatonn do not always find interesting those subjects which are selected for discussion in that many are concerned with mechanical events and aspects of your three-dimensional illusion. We of Hatonn find more challenging and interesting the discussions of those subjects which are non-illusive, for these subjects are areas of our own enlightenment or lack thereof.

For this reason, my brothers, we are always grateful to you for your perceptive questions, for [is it] not the student who asks questions the real teacher of the class? Certainly the teacher—correction—instructor learns rapidly when faced with a question which had not previously incurred—correction—occurred to that instructor. Therefore, my brothers, we of Hatonn thank you both for the opportunity of being of service to yourselves and for your service in providing the stimuli for our further education.

At this time we would bid you adieu. I am Hatonn. ♣

L/L Research

L/L Research is a subsidiary of Rock Creek Research & Development Laboratories, Inc.

P.O. Box 5195
Louisville, KY 40255-0195

www.llresearch.org

Rock Creek is a non-profit corporation dedicated to discovering and sharing information which may aid in the spiritual evolution of humankind.

ABOUT THE CONTENTS OF THIS TRANSCRIPT: This telepathic channeling has been taken from transcriptions of the weekly study and meditation meetings of the Rock Creek Research & Development Laboratories and L/L Research. It is offered in the hope that it may be useful to you. As the Confederation entities always make a point of saying, please use your discrimination and judgment in assessing this material. If something rings true to you, fine. If something does not resonate, please leave it behind, for neither we nor those of the Confederation would wish to be a stumbling block for any.

© 2009 L/L Research

The Law of One, Book II, Session 46
April 15, 1981

Ra: I am Ra. I greet you in the love and in the light of the one infinite Creator. We communicate now.

Questioner: If an entity polarizes toward the service-to-self path, would anger have the same physical effect that it would have on the entity polarizing on the service-to-others path? Would it also cause cancer, or is it just a catalytic effect working in the positively polarizing entity?

Ra: I am Ra. The catalytic mechanisms are dependent, not upon the chosen polarity of a mind/body/spirit complex, but upon the use or purpose to which this catalyst is put. Thus the entity which uses the experience of anger to polarize consciously positively or negatively does not experience the bodily catalyst but rather uses the catalyst in mental configuration.

Questioner: I am not sure that I understand that. Let's take some examples: an entity polarizing toward the negative path becomes angry. Let's take the condition where he develops a cancer. What is the principle that is at work for him?

RA I am Ra. We see the thrust of your query and will respond at variance with the specific query if that meets with your approval.

Questioner: Certainly.

Ra: The entity polarizing positively perceives the anger. This entity, if using this catalyst mentally, blesses and loves this anger in itself. It then intensifies this anger consciously in mind alone until the folly of this red-ray energy is perceived not as folly in itself but as energy subject to spiritual entropy due to the randomness of energy being used.

Positive orientation then provides the will and faith to continue this mentally intense experience of letting the anger be understood, accepted, and integrated with the mind/body/spirit complex. The other-self which is the object of anger is thus transformed into an object of acceptance, understanding, and accommodation, all being reintegrated using the great energy which anger began.

The negatively oriented mind/body/spirit complex will use this anger in a similarly conscious fashion, refusing to accept the undirected or random energy of anger and instead, through will and faith, funneling this energy into a practical means of venting the negative aspect of this emotion so as to obtain control over other-self, or otherwise control the situation causing anger.

Control is the key to negatively polarized use of catalyst. Acceptance is the key to positively polarized use of catalyst. Between these polarities lies the potential for this random and undirected energy creating a bodily complex analog of what you call the cancerous growth of tissue.

Questioner: Then as I understand it you are saying that if the positively polarizing entity fails to accept the other-self or if the negatively polarizing entity fails to control the other-self, either of these conditions will cause cancer, possibly. Is this correct?

Ra: I am Ra. This is partially correct. The first acceptance, or control depending upon polarity, is of the self. Anger is one of many things to be accepted and loved as a part of self or controlled as a part of self, if the entity is to do work.

Questioner: Then are you saying that if a negatively polarizing entity is unable to control his own anger or unable to control himself in anger that he may cause cancer? Is this correct?

Ra: I am Ra. This is quite correct. The negative polarization contains a great requirement for control and repression.

Questioner: A repression of what?

Ra: I am Ra. Any mind complex distortion which you may call emotional which is of itself disorganized, needs, in order to be useful to the negatively oriented entity, to be repressed and then brought to the surface in an organized use. Thus you may find for instance, negatively polarized entities controlling and repressing such basic bodily complex needs as the sexual desire in order that in the practice thereof the will may be used to enforce itself upon the other-self with greater efficiency when the sexual behavior is allowed.

Questioner: Then the positively oriented entity, rather than attempting repression of emotion, would balance the emotion as stated in an earlier contact. Is this correct?

Ra: I am Ra. This is correct and illustrates the path of unity.

Questioner: Then cancer is a training catalyst operating for both polarities in approximately the same way but creating or attempting to create polarization in both directions, positive and negative, depending upon the orientation of the entity experiencing the catalyst. Is this correct?

Ra: I am Ra. This is incorrect in that catalyst is unconscious and does not work with intelligence but rather is part of the, shall we say, mechanism of learn/teaching set up by the sub-Logos before the beginning of your space/time.

Questioner: How does cancer do this learn/teaching when the entity developing cancer has no conscious idea of what is happening to him when he develops cancer?

Ra: I am Ra. In many cases catalyst is not used.

Questioner: What is the plan for use of the catalyst of cancer?

Ra: I am Ra. The catalyst, and all catalyst, is designed to offer experience. This experience in your density may be loved and accepted or it may be controlled. These are the two paths. When neither path is chosen the catalyst fails in its design and the entity proceeds until catalyst strikes it which causes it to form a bias towards acceptance and love or separation and control. There is no lack of space/time in which this catalyst may work.

Questioner: I am assuming that the plan of the Logos is for positively and negatively polarized social memory complexes in fourth density and above. Can you tell me the purpose of the plan for these two types of social memory complexes with respect to Coulomb's Law or negative and positive electrical polarity, or in any way that you can?

Ra: I am Ra. This instrument grows weary. We shall speak with you again. We may indicate the possibility, without further harm to this instrument, of approximately two sessions per your weekly period until these weeks of potential for attack and presence of very low physical energy are passed. May we say it is good to be with this group. We appreciate your fidelity. Are there any brief queries before the end of this work time?

Questioner: Only is there anything that we can do to make the instrument more comfortable or to improve the contact?

Ra: I am Ra. Each is supporting the instrument well and the instrument remains steady in its purpose. You are conscientious. All is well. We ward you ware of any laxity regarding the arrangement and orientation of appurtenances.

I am Ra. I leave you, my friends, in the love and in the light of the one infinite Creator. Go forth, therefore, rejoicing in the power and the peace of the one infinite Creator. Adonai.

L/L Research

L/L Research is a subsidiary of Rock Creek Research & Development Laboratories, Inc.

P.O. Box 5195
Louisville, KY 40255-0195

www.llresearch.org

Rock Creek is a non-profit corporation dedicated to discovering and sharing information which may aid in the spiritual evolution of humankind.

ABOUT THE CONTENTS OF THIS TRANSCRIPT: This telepathic channeling has been taken from transcriptions of the weekly study and meditation meetings of the Rock Creek Research & Development Laboratories and L/L Research. It is offered in the hope that it may be useful to you. As the Confederation entities always make a point of saying, please use your discrimination and judgment in assessing this material. If something rings true to you, fine. If something does not resonate, please leave it behind, for neither we nor those of the Confederation would wish to be a stumbling block for any.

© 2009 L/L RESEARCH

THE LAW OF ONE, BOOK V, SESSION 46, FRAGMENT 28
APRIL 15, 1981

Jim: In querying about how best to aid two of our cats as they were about to be put under anesthetic at the veterinarian's and how to reduce any negative influences that might have sought an inroad while the cats were being operated on, we discovered that when the investment of a second-density being has been successful, that second-density being attracts to it the spirit complex. And the presence of the spirit complex makes that being vulnerable to the same psychic greeting process that any third-density entity may experience, given the appropriate circumstances. The ritual sentences mentioned are taken from the Book Of Common Prayer of the Episcopal Church.

Carla: *When I was a young woman of 17, I thought I wanted a life full of children and home. But life never offered me that. Instead, I was drawn to follow a life of devotion, to Don and to the Creator. Instead of children, I have had the joy of being friend and/or counselor to many courageous and seeking souls. And cats!! Plenty of cats! I cannot remember being without a cat my whole life long! They delight me, and their company is always a pleasure. We relate to them as children, and they soak up a lot of my maternal feelings!*

Gandalf was an exceptionally devoted cat. He loved our laps, and would retrieve for Don, catching the peppermint candy wrappers that Don tossed and bringing them to deposit in Don's shoe. When he became old and full of years, he was more than ever devoted, and even after he could no longer walk, if I forgot to carry him with me, he would scrape along the floor little by little to come nearer again. Needless to say, we did not forget him often. And he still lives in loving memories.

Session 46, April 15, 1981

Questioner: The one question that is bothering us, which I got in meditation, may be an inappropriate question, but I feel it is my duty to ask it because it is central to the instrument's mental condition and ours. It has to do with the two cats which we were going to have worked upon today for teeth cleaning and for the removal of the small growth from Gandalf's leg. I got the impression that there might be an inroad there for the Orion group, and I was primarily concerned if there was anything that we could do for protection for these two cats. It may be out of line for me to ask this question, but I feel it my duty to ask it. Would you please give me any information that you can on that subject?

Ra: I am Ra. The entity, mind/body/spirit complex, Gandalf, being harvestable third density, is open to the same type of psychic attack to which you yourselves are vulnerable. Therefore, through the mechanism of images and dreams, it is potentially possible for negative concepts to be offered to this mind/body/spirit complex, thus having possible deleterious results. The entity, Fairchild, though harvestable through investment, does not have the vulnerability to attack in as great amount due to a lack of the mind complex activity in the distortion of conscious devotion.

For protection of these entities we might indicate two possibilities. Firstly, the meditation putting on the armor of light. Secondly, the repetition of short ritual sentences known to this instrument from the establishment which distorts spiritual oneness for this instrument. This instrument's knowledge will suffice. This will aid due to the alerting of many discarnate entities also aware of these ritual sentences. The meditation is appropriate at the time of the activity on behalf of these entities. The ritual may be repeated with efficacy from this time until the safe return, at convenient intervals.

Questioner: I am not familiar with the ritual sentences. If the instrument is familiar, you need not answer this but which sentences do you mean?

(Silence. No response from Ra.)

Questioner: I assume that the instrument is familiar with them then?

Ra: I am Ra. This is correct.

Questioner: Can you tell me something of the little growth on Gandalf's leg and if it is of danger to him?

Ra: I am Ra. The cause of such growths has been previously discussed. The danger to the physical body complex is slight given the lack of repeated stimulus to anger. ♣

The Law of One, Book II, Session 47
April 18, 1981

Ra: I am Ra. I greet you in the love and in the light of the one infinite Creator. We communicate now.

Questioner: Could you first give us an indication of the condition of the instrument?

Ra: I am Ra. It is as previously stated.

Questioner: The question that I was trying to ask at the end of the last session was: Of what value to evolution or experience with respect to the Creator knowing Itself are the positive and negative social memory complexes that form starting in fourth density, and why was this planned by the Logos?

Ra: I am Ra. There are inherent incorrectness in your query. However, we may answer the main point of it.

The incorrectness lies in the consideration that social memory complexes were planned by the Logos or sub-Logos. This is incorrect, as the unity of the Creator exists within the smallest portion of any material created by Love, much less in a self-aware being.

However, the distortion of free will causes the social memory complex to appear as a possibility at a certain stage of evolution of mind. The purpose, or consideration which causes entities to form such complexes, of these social memory complexes, is a very simple extension of the basic distortion towards the Creator's knowing of Itself, for when a group of mind/body/spirits becomes able to form a social memory complex, all experience of each entity is available to the whole of the complex. Thus the Creator knows more of Its creation in each entity partaking of this communion of entities.

Questioner: You gave the values of better than 50% service-to-others for fourth-density positive and better than 95% service-to-self for fourth-density negative social memory complexes. Do these two values correspond to the same rate, shall I say, of vibration?

Ra: I am Ra. I perceive you have difficulty in expressing your query. We shall respond in an attempt to clarify your query.

The vibratory rates are not to be understood as the same in positive and negative orientations. They are to be understood as having the power to accept and work with intelligent infinity to a certain degree or intensity. Due to the fact that the primary color, shall we say, or energy blue is missing from the negatively oriented system of power, the green/blue vibratory energies are not seen in the vibratory schedules or patterns of negative fourth and fifth rates of vibration.

The positive on the other hand, shall we say, has the full spectrum of true color time/space vibratory patterns and thus contains a variant vibratory pattern or schedule. Each is capable of doing fourth-density work. This is the criterion for harvest.

Questioner: Did you say that blue was missing from fourth-density negative?

Ra: I am Ra. Let us clarify further. As we have previously stated, all beings have the potential for all possible vibratory rates. Thus the potential of the green and blue energy center activation is, of course, precisely where it must be in a creation of Love. However, the negatively polarized entity will have achieved harvest due to extremely efficient use of red and yellow/orange, moving directly to the gateway indigo bringing through this intelligent energy channel the in-streamings of intelligent infinity.

Questioner: Then at fourth-density graduation into fifth is there anything like that which you gave as the percentages necessary for third-density graduation into fourth in polarization?

Ra: I am Ra. There are, in your modes of thinking, responses we can make, which we shall make. However, the important point is that the graduations from density to density do occur. The positive/negative polarity is a thing which will, at the sixth level, simply become history. Therefore, we speak in an illusory time continuum when we discuss statistics of positive versus negative harvest into fifth. A large percentage of fourth-density negative entities continue the negative path from fourth to fifth-density experience, for without wisdom the compassion and desire to aid other-self is not extremely well informed. Thus though one loses approximately two percent moving from negative to positive during the fourth-density experience we find approximately eight percent of graduations into fifth density those of the negative.

Questioner: What I was actually asking was if 50% is required for graduation from third to fourth in the positive sense and 95% was required for graduation in the negative sense, does this have to more closely approach 100% for graduation in both cases for graduation from fourth to fifth density? Does an entity have to be 99% polarized for negative and maybe 80% polarized positive for graduation?

Ra: I am Ra. We perceive the query now.

To give this in your terms is misleading for there are, shall we say, visual aids or training aids available in fourth density which automatically aid the entity in polarization while cutting down extremely upon the quick effect of catalyst. Thus the density above yours must take up more space/time.

The percentage of service-to-others of positively oriented entities will harmoniously approach 98% in intention. The qualifications for fifth density, however, involve understanding. This then, becomes the primary qualification for graduation from fourth to fifth density. To achieve this graduation the entity must be able to understand the actions, the movements, and the dance. There is no percentage describable which measures this understanding. It is a measure of efficiency of perception. It may be measured by light. The ability to love, accept, and use a certain intensity of light thus creates the requirement for both positive and negative fourth to fifth harvesting.

Questioner: Can you define what you mean by a "crystallized entity"?

Ra: I am Ra. We have used this particular term because it has a fairly precise meaning in your language. When a crystalline structure is formed of your physical material the elements present in each molecule are bonded in a regularized fashion with elements in each other molecule. Thus the structure is regular and, when fully and perfectly crystallized, has certain properties. It will not splinter or break; it is very strong without effort; and it is radiant, traducing light into a beautiful refraction giving pleasure of the eye to many.

Questioner: In our esoteric literature numerous bodies are listed. I have listed here the physical body, the etheric, the emotional, the astral. Can you tell me if this listing is the proper number, and can you tell me the uses and purposes and effects etc. of each of these and any other bodies that may be in our mind/body/spirit complex?

Ra: I am Ra. To answer your query fully would be the work of many sessions such as this one, for the interrelationships of the various bodies and each body's effects in various situations is an enormous study. However, we shall begin by referring your minds back to the spectrum of true colors and the usage of this understanding in grasping the various densities of your octave.

We have the number seven repeated from the macrocosm to the microcosm in structure and experience. Therefore, it would only be expected that there would be seven basic bodies which we would perhaps be most lucid by stating as red-ray body, etc. However, we are aware that you wish to correspond these bodies mentioned with the color rays. This will be confusing, for various teachers have offered their teach/learning understanding in various terms. Thus one may name a subtle body one thing and another find a different name.

The red-ray body is your chemical body. However, it is not the body which you have as clothing in the physical. It is the unconstructed material of the body, the elemental body without form. This basic unformed material body is important to understand for there are healings which may be carried out by the simple understanding of the elements present in the physical vehicle.

The orange-ray body is the physical body complex. This body complex is still not the body you inhabit but rather the body formed without self-awareness, the body in the womb before the spirit/mind complex enters. This body may live without the inhabitation of the mind and spirit complexes. However, it seldom does so.

The yellow-ray body is your physical vehicle which you know of at this time and in which you experience catalyst. This body has the mind/body/spirit characteristics and is equal to the physical illusion, as you have called it.

The green-ray body is that body which may be seen in séance when what you call ectoplasm is furnished. This is a lighter body packed more densely with life. You may call this the astral body following some other teachings. Others have called this same body the etheric body. However, this is not correct in the sense that the etheric body is that body of gateway wherein intelligent energy is able to mold the mind/body/spirit complex.

The light body or blue-ray body may be called the devachanic body. There are many other names for this body especially in your so-called Indian Sutras or writings, for there are those among these peoples which have explored these regions and understand the various types of devachanic bodies. There are many, many types of bodies in each density, much like your own.

The indigo-ray body which we choose to call the etheric body is, as we have said, the gateway body. In this body form is substance and you may only see this body as that of light as it may mold itself as it desires.

The violet-ray body may perhaps be understood as what you might call the Buddha body or that body which is complete.

Each of these bodies has an effect upon your mind/body/spirit complex in your life being-ness. The interrelationships, as we have said, are many and complex

Perhaps one suggestion that may be indicated is this: The indigo-ray body may be used by the healer once the healer becomes able to place its consciousness in this etheric state. The violet-ray or Buddhic body is of equal efficacy to the healer for within it lies a sense of wholeness which is extremely close to unity with all that there is. These bodies are part of each entity and the proper use of them and understanding of them is, though far advanced from the standpoint of third-density harvest, nevertheless useful to the adept.

Questioner: Which bodies do we have immediately after physical death from this yellow-ray body that I now am in?

Ra: I am Ra. You have all bodies in potentiation.

Questioner: Then the yellow-ray body in potentiation is used to create this chemical arrangement that I have as a physical body now. Is this correct?

Ra: I am Ra. This is incorrect only in that in your present incarnation the yellow-ray body is not in potentiation but in activation, it being that body which is manifest.

Questioner: Then after death from this incarnation we still have the yellow-ray body in potentiation, but then in the general case of our planetary population after death, would they then normally have the green-ray body manifested?

Ra: I am Ra. Not immediately. The first body which activates itself upon death is the "form-maker" or the indigo-ray body. This body remains—you have called it the "ka"—until etherea has been penetrated and understanding has been gained by the mind/body/spirit totality. Once this is achieved, if the proper body to be activated is green-ray, then this will occur.

Questioner: Let me make a statement and you tell me if I am correct. After death then, if an entity is unaware, he may become what is called an Earthbound spirit until he is able to achieve the required awareness for activation of one of his bodies. Would it be possible then to activate any of the bodies from red through violet?

Ra: I am Ra. Given the proper stimulus, this is correct.

Questioner: What stimulus would create what we call an Earth-bound spirit or a lingering ghost?

Ra: I am Ra. The stimulus for this is the faculty of the will. If the will of yellow-ray mind/body/spirit is that which is stronger than the progressive impetus of the physical death towards realization of that which comes, that is, if the will is concentrated enough upon the previous experience, the entity's shell of yellow-ray, though no longer activated, cannot either be completely deactivated and, until the will is released, the mind/body/spirit complex is caught. This often occurs, as we see you are aware, in the case of sudden death as well as in the case of extreme concern for a thing or an other-self.

Questioner: Well then, does orange-ray activation after death occur very frequently with this planet?

Ra: I am Ra. Quite infrequently, due to the fact that this particular manifestation is without will. Occasionally an other-self will so demand the form of the one passing through the physical death that some semblance of the being will remain. This is orange-ray. This is rare, for normally if one entity desires another enough to call it, the entity will have the corresponding desire to be called. Thus the manifestation would be the shell of yellow-ray.

Questioner: What does the large percentage of the Earth's population, as they pass through the physical, activate?

Ra: I am Ra. This shall be the last full query of this working.

The normal procedure, given an harmonious passage from yellow-ray bodily manifestation, is for the mind and spirit complex to rest in the etheric or indigo body until such time as the entity begins its preparation for experience in an incarnated place which has a manifestation formed by the etheric energy molding it into activation and manifestation. This indigo body, being intelligent energy, is able to offer the newly dead, as you would term it, soul a perspective and a place from which to view the experience most recently manifested. Is there a short query we may answer at this time?

Questioner: I will only ask if there is anything that we may do to make the instrument more comfortable or to improve the contact?

Ra: I am Ra. The appurtenances are conscientiously measured by eye and spirit. You are conscientious. All is well. Observe this instrument to ensure continued building of the vital energies. It will have to work upon its own physical energies for this weakness was brought about by free will of the self.

I am Ra. We leave you now in the love and in the light of the one infinite Creator. Go forth, therefore, rejoicing in the power and in the peace of the one infinite Creator. Adonai. ☥

Sunday Meditation, Easter
April 19, 1981

(L channeling)

I am Hatonn, and I greet you, my brothers, in the love and in the light of the infinite Creator. My brothers, it is with great pleasure that we of the Federation are able to share with you once again our simple thoughts and aspirations for those of your planet and dimension. It in easy enough for us to see areas of improvement that you may strive towards, yet, my brothers, you must understand that your confusion is similar to the confusion that we experience on our own level. Therefore, my brothers, be not down-hearted at our seeming unwillingness to communicate to you those lessons which you are striving so hard to learn in your struggle for growth. We of Hatonn are pleased in that we are often sought by those of this group and other groups for our advice, yet we are reluctant often to communicate to you the answer to those questions you pose. For, my brothers, it is not our place to prevent your growth by handing you the answers as one schoolboy with a crib sheet to another.

At this time, my brothers, I would like to attempt to contact the one known as E. If he will be patient, relax and open his mind, we will attempt to speak through him. I am Hatonn.

(E channeling)

I am Hatonn, and I greet you again in the love and light of the infinite Creator. We are most delighted to be working with this entity. If he can relax he will find that it is not difficult. I am Hatonn, and I would transfer to the one known as Jim.

(Jim channeling)

I am Hatonn, and am with this instrument. It is our privilege to speak to you once again, and tonight it is an especial joy to be able to use one more new instrument in the sending of our simple message of love. We of Hatonn are most honored to be able to partake in this sharing of love—which is the Creator's love—with those of our brothers and sisters of your people and especially to this meditation group which we have long been associated with.

It is always a joy to speak of the communion with the one infinite Creator with those with ears, hearts and minds which are opened to the frequency of love. It is a message which one would think all would wish to hear, and in truth so it is, but many do not know consciously that this message is that which their hearts yearn to hear. Many have not been able to realize that that which is missing from their lives is the simple message of love. Many attempt to fill that empty place in their beings with many other messages, many other thoughts, many other things. Much time and effort is spent in accumulating those thoughts, things and ideas which it is hoped will fill that void.

Your reality, your everyday life, is filled with those substitutes, those items of a transient nature which are the catalysts for your growth but are not that substance that will fill that empty place. For within all of the creation of the Father there is the space which contains all of creation, the space between all things, the space within all things, that vacuum, as it were, that needs to be filled with love, and in fact is filled with love. Those entities upon your planet are not consciously aware, for the most part, of that love that surrounds each in every activity in which each engages. It is the plan of the Creator that each of those upon your planet shall eventually know that love is that which each seeks. It is the plan of the Creator that each shall consciously become aware that love is that which they have not realized as the foundation of their being. It is the plan that each shall so realize and shall travel upon that path of love which they have been unconsciously traveling for many eons of time.

The cycle of growth upon your planet Earth now draws to a close in its present state of being. Those who have learned the lessons of love, of service to the Creator, shall pass through the graduation, shall continue their growth on the upward spiraling arc of oneness that binds us all together. Those who have not yet learned the lessons of love shall have the honor of repeating once again that great cycle of growth with every opportunity made available to learn the lessons of love, for there is no other lesson within your density which can allow the student of life to pass on to the next grade, so to speak.

We of Hatonn feel the greatest of honors in being able to share in some small way our simple understanding of the Creator's love. We hope that we have been of some aid to you throughout these many years of meditation and messages we have brought to the best of our ability. Our message has been simple: the love of the Creator is within each being each moment and in each part of the creation, and through the simple act of meditation might this love be known.

At this time we would transfer this contact to the one known as Carla. I am Hatonn.

(Carla channeling)

I am Hatonn, and I greet you once again, my brethren, in the love and in the light. As we were saying, in your meditations dwell upon the simple yet deep lesson which you will need in order to move forward. In meditation, my friends, feel the roots of spirit growing deep, deep and deeper still to the ground of silence. Perceive your self, not as the willow whole celery green color is always the first to show in the spring and whose beauty is unparalleled, but as the mighty cedar or oak. Such trees have their own being, but there is one great difference. The willow has roots that move shallowly in the earth, drinking eagerly and quickly from the thirsty grounds, feeding and growing and ripening and bearing fruit in haste, yet the storm comes and the wind blows and the willow is torn from the ground. It takes a mighty wind indeed to topple a cedar, for the roots go deep. It takes a great wind, my friends, to fell an oak for the roots seek downward, ever downward, into the deeper sources of moisture, of life, of food.

In your meditation, my friends, know that you are a thing growing, growing quietly, nourished and nurtured from the earth of your silence. Do not be satisfied with your own quick results. Do not be fooled by the constant taking of your own spiritual temperature. Simply and patiently, seek ever deeper in silence for the waters of truth, that they may nourish you and lift you up, that your fruits may be strong and good and ready for the harvest time.

At this time we would attempt to contact the one known as N in order to say a few closing words. If this entity would relax and cease all analysis and request this contact, we will attempt to send our thoughts to him in such a way that they may be perceived. I am Hatonn.

(Pause)

(Carla channeling)

I am Hatonn, I am again with this instrument. We thank the one known as N for the privilege of working with this instrument. We have some difficulty in making the contact due to the interference of misperception as to the sensations surrounding contact. It will be in time that which may be worked with and we look forward to any opportunity which may be offered us.

We would close through this instrument at this time. My friends, many will come to you and ask you for answers and you, yourself will seek them. Remember the lesson of the willow. True answers come from deep within your being. The shallow ones may be moved by the storms of your illusion.

We meet with you when ere you meditate. We send you our love in every moment, and yet not ours but that of the Creator's We are those of Hatonn and we leave you in the love and in the light of our infinite Creator. Adonai, my friends. Adonai vasu borragus.

(Carla channeling)

I am Latwii, and I greet you in the love and in the light of the infinite Creator. It is our privilege to speak to your group, though we have an odd situation for we have an embarrassment of riches. We would be able to use each of three instruments and we are having difficulty at first scan in detecting any questions that you might have. Therefore we may speak, but do not know to which topic you may put us. Therefore we have chosen this instrument because she does not have any questions. May we ask if you at this time—if you would like to ask any questions? If so, please feel free.

L: I have several questions. First, I understand to some extent the significance of the entity Ra during our previous Egyptian culture. Is there any significance to the Egyptian god Osiris, or was Osiris primarily a creation of man at that time?

I am Latwii. This is a somewhat difficult question due to the fact that the answer is double in nature. The specific character Osiris is part of a system of belief in which there are many names for the same basic story. The name Osiris, then, is a type of thought-form. Further, the story itself has an extremely important meaning. If you will consider the various religions among your peoples—there are many crucified or dismembered entities which are then considered saviors or those which aid fertility of the earth. The understanding ranges from the crucifixion for the sake of the earth to that of sacrifice for the sake of the so-called soul. This general type of story you may see as the basic pattern of passion or intended love whereby the disharmonies and difficulties of existence are brought into a more helpful configuration due to the sacrificial act, whether it be intended or unintended of an entity, Osiris being one such entity. This, then, is another type of thought-form being, one which is quite integrated into the mass consciousness of your race and your planet. There is not an entity from the Confederation who was hacked to pieces and is now king of the underworld.

Is there another question?

L: Yes, I am interested in doing some work on a farm and wish to approach it in a manner that is more in balance with the universe than to do it in a destructive manner. For this reason I am interested in contacting some of the land spirits or devas as we call them for that area, if there is such. Could you give me some information on how to go about this?

I am Latwii. My brother, this information is most easily given. Remember that not all beings may speak. Therefore you may speak to them, though they speak not to you, yet they hear you. In this manner you may approach the devas, as you call them. These spirits will, to the less sensitive beings, be silent and unseen, yet you shall contact them if you sit in meditation and speak with them upon reaching the appropriate state, universal love and respect, of which you have spoken. In time, you may find that due to your faith you will be able to feel, hear or see these spirits. They will, in any case, respond to you and cooperate more and more, as you hope.

May we answer you further?

L: You've answered me completely. Thank you.

As always, your thanks are returned and doubled for we are most happy to communicate. We don't know where you were hiding these questions when we scanned, but we are most pleased.

Is there another question?

N: Did the Caucasian, Negroid, and Oriental people come from a common root being or did one or more of these groups originate on another planet?

I am Latwii. All of your beings originated either upon another planet or were those which manifested from another density of your own planet. You do not have any native Americans, as I believe you call them. Everyone moves in the search for truth. To be more specific the various races all have one great commonality, that being that they are the Creator. Some races are differentiated due to the climatic needs of various geographic regions of your planetary surface. Others did indeed come from other planetary spheres.

May we answer you further?

N: Where would the Orientals have come from?

I am Latwii. This instrument has this information in her conscious mind, however we will also speak to the subject. These entities are from a place which you would call Deneb.

May we answer you further, my brother?

N: What is Deneb?

This is a star system. May we answer you further, my brother?

N: No.

As we may say, if you have seen one star system you have seen them all, due to the fact that one love created this universe. We intend not only to joke with you but to make a point, that being that there is no alien-ness to the creation, no strangeness to the Creator, but rather an infinite variety of representations of love.

Is there another question at this time?

E: I would like to ask you a question, Latwii. First of all, I would like to say hello. My question is: I have been getting a picture of the universe as a place that is teeming with life like our oceans are and I also have gotten the impression that solar systems are common to stars, and my question first of all is, are solar systems common to stars and if so, how is it—what are the dynamics involved in their formation? Why do solar systems form around stars?

I am Latwii. Hello, my brother. You certainly ask zingers! In the first place, it is correct that the universe teems with life, for are not all things alive? Is not love available in each portion of light which forms the creation in whatever form that light may take? As to the query about planetary systems, they are, of course, common to suns since solar systems would have a difficult time being common to anything else.

The nature of the formation [is] the zinger. This takes some little thought and deliberate speech. If you can imagine a force which is expanding and another force, which you may consider that of the materialization of love, which are contracting into an ordered state due to a plan of love, you may see that from a great beginning of creation, first great things are created and then smaller and smaller still. Thus the sun coalescing sends forth radiations and emissions, which being thrown out themselves, coalesce and become the solar system, so-called.

May we answer you further, my brother?

E: Yes. Is the solar system that we live in more or less typical of solar systems in general in the number of the planets, the size of the planets, and the life on the planets?

I am Latwii. Your planet is typical of a planet of a certain type of star. There are quite a few different types of stars. Not all stars begin at the same point and evolution as you would perceive this in your density, thus we may say that for your type of star …

(Side one of tape ends.)

(Jim channeling)

… planetary system is fairly typical in the number of planets—perhaps a bit more than the average but one gets into trouble with statistics. So-called numbers always confuse. For instance, it is in this instrument's head that she has recently heard that each couple has 1.7 children. I ask you, my brother, of what meaning is this statistic? We will simply say that the solar system is typical of its particular type of radiant energy.

May we answer you further?

E: What color are you in tonight?

We are in a lovely color, my brother. Follow us in your mind. What do you see?

E: Nothing very clearly. I'm afraid I get a little bit of purple.

I am Latwii. We will have to get better contact with you, my brother. We are in a beautiful shade you would call tangerine. We are studying some of the effects of your earth magnetic field, as opposed to the planetary consciousness effects, verging into orange from the yellow. It is quite a beautiful shade, very rich and full of life.

May we answer you further, my brother?

E: No. Thank you Latwii.

We thank you also, my brother. Is there another question at this time?

L: When an entity who once lived on this planet known as C. S. Lewis authored several works, was he receiving any form of communication from any source that you are aware of as a stimulus for his writings?

I am Latwii. This information can be helpful to you, my brother, for it is sometimes thought by those who listen to us that everything useful on a planet such as yours was given by some extraterrestrial source. This is not so. The entity of whom you spoke found in his meditations a very rich vein of memory and vision made available by angelic guardians and his higher self. With these companions this entity was moved to speak in perhaps of some of the most persuasive prose on your planet to the subject of Christianity, love, peace and an understanding of the nature of good and evil.

May we answer you further, my brother?

L: I'll need to examine that before I can even come up with another question. I thank you for your answer.

You are most welcome. Is there another question?

E: Yes, I'd like to ask you one more question, Latwii. Does it make sense to use the sun as a light source for a color therapy device rather than using an artificial light source? The reason that I ask this is because it would be a lot more difficult to use the sun, so if an incandescent source would be as good, or nearly as good, it would make more sense to go with that. But if the sun were a lot better than an incandescent source it would make more sense to go with that and do the extra work that it would take to make it work.

I am Latwii. Although I am aware of your question I find an answer to your question bordering upon infringement of free will. May we say this: the calculations necessary to determine the difference between the one source and the other are readily available to the tutored mind, of which we see you have one. Therefore, the differences are known to you. Your query is involved in the question of healing. This is the area of free will upon which we feel we cannot infringe. We are sorry not to be of more aid, my brother.

Is there another question?

(Pause)

I am Latwii. May we thank you once again for the fascinating array of questions which you have given us to consider. We cannot thank you enough and are most grateful to you for providing us with the opportunity to again be of some small service to you, a part of the infinite Creator. We serve you. We love you. We send you our light. And in this Creator's love and this Creator's light we leave you now. I am known to you as Latwii. Adonai vasu borragus.

(Carla channels Nona singing for several minutes to end the meditation.) ☙

The Law of One, Book II, Session 48
April 22, 1981

Ra: I am Ra. I greet you in the love and in the light of the one infinite Creator. We communicate now.

Questioner: Could you tell us of the instrument's condition and if she is improving with time?

Ra: I am Ra. This instrument's vital energies are improving with time, as you measure it. This instrument's physical energies are less than your previous asking.

Questioner: Thank you. If you, Ra, as an individualized entity were incarnate on Earth now with full awareness and memory of what you know now, what would be your objective at this time on Earth as far as activities are concerned?

Ra: I am Ra. The query suggests that which has been learned to be impractical. However, were we to again be naive enough to think that our physical presence was any more effective than that love/light we send your peoples and the treasure of this contact, we would do as we did do. We would be, and we would offer our selves as teach/learners.

Questioner: My lecture yesterday was attended by only a few. If this had occurred during a UFO flap many more would have attended. Since Orion entities cause the flaps, what is Orion's reward for visibility in that they actually create greater opportunities for the dissemination of information such as this information at those times?

Ra: I am Ra. This assumption is incorrect. The flaps cause many fears among your peoples, many speakings, understandings concerning plots, cover-ups, mutilations, killings, and other negative impressions. Even those supposedly positive reports which gain public awareness speak of doom. You may understand yourself as one who will be in the minority due to the understandings which you wish to share, if we may use that misnomer.

We perceive there is a further point we may posit at this time. The audience brought about by Orion-type publicity is not seeded by seniority of vibration to a great extent. The audiences receiving teach/learnings without stimulus from publicity will be more greatly oriented towards illumination. Therefore, forget you the counting.

Questioner: Thank you. That clears up that point very well. Can you tell me how positive and negative polarizations in fourth and fifth density are used to cause working in consciousness?

Ra: I am Ra. There is very little work in consciousness in fourth and in fifth densities compared to the work done in third density. The work that is accomplished in positive fourth is that work whereby the positive social memory complex, having, through slow stages, harmoniously integrated itself, goes forth to aid those of less positive orientation which seek their aid. Thus their service is their work and through this dynamic between the societal self and the other-self, which is the object of love, greater and greater intensities of understanding or compassion are attained. This intensity continues until the appropriate intensity of the light may be welcomed. This is fourth-density harvest.

Within fourth-density positive there are minor amounts of catalyst of a spiritual and mental complex distortion. This occurs during the process of harmonizing to the extent of forming the social memory complex. This causes some small catalyst and work to occur, but the great work of fourth density lies in the contact betwixt the societal self and less polarized other-self.

In fourth-density negative much work is accomplished during the fighting for position which precedes the period of the social memory complex. There are opportunities to polarize negatively by control of other-selves. During the social memory complex period of fourth-density negative the situation is the same. The work takes place through the societal reaching out to less polarized otherself in order to aid in negative polarization.

In fifth-density positive and negative the concept of work done through a potential difference is not particularly helpful as fifth-density entities are, again, intensifying rather than potentiating.

In positive, the fifth-density complex uses sixth-density teach/learners to study the more illuminated understandings of unity thus becoming more and more wise. Fifth-density positive social memory complexes will choose to divide their service to others in two ways: first, the beaming of light to creation; second, the sending of groups to be of aid as instruments of light such as those whom you are familiar with through channels.

In fifth-density negative, service to self has become extremely intense and the self has shrunk or compacted so that the dialogues with the teach/learners are used exclusively in order to intensify wisdom. There are very, very few fifth-density negative Wanderers for they fear the forgetting. There are very, very few fifth-density Orion members for they do not any longer perceive any virtue in other-selves.

Questioner: Thank you. I would like to take as an example an entity, starting before birth, who is roughly high on the seniority list for positive polarization and possible harvestability at the end of this cycle and follow a full cycle of his experience starting before his incarnation—which body is activated, the process of becoming incarnate, the activation of the third-density physical body, the process as the body moves through this density and is acted upon by catalysts, the process of death, and the activation of the various bodies so that we make a full circuit from a point prior to incarnation back around through incarnation and death; you might say one cycle of incarnation in this density. Could you do that for me?

Ra: I am Ra. Your query is most distorted for it assumes that creations are alike. Each mind/body/spirit complex has its own patterns of activation and its own rhythms of awakening. The important thing for harvest is the harmonious balance between the various energy centers of the mind/body/spirit complex. This is to be noted as of relative import. We grasp the thrust of your query and will make a most general answer stressing the unimportance of such arbitrary generalizations.

The entity, before incarnation, dwells in the appropriate, shall we say, place in time/space. The true color type of this location will be dependent upon the entity's needs. Those entities for instance which, being Wanderers, have the green, blue, or indigo true color core of mind/body/spirit complex will have rested therein.

Entrance into incarnation requires the investment or activation of the indigo-ray or etheric body for this is the "formmaker." The young or small physical mind/body/spirit complex has the seven energy centers potentiated before the birthing process. There are also analogs in time/space of these energy centers corresponding to the seven energy centers in each of the seven true color densities. Thus in the microcosm exists all the experience that is prepared. It is as though the infant contains the universe.

The patterns of activation of an entity of high seniority will undoubtedly move with some rapidity to the green-ray level which is the springboard to primary blue. There is always some difficulty in penetrating blue primary energy for it requires that which your people have in great paucity; that is, honesty. Blue ray is the ray of free communication with self and with otherself. Having accepted that an harvestable or nearly harvestable entity will be working from this green-ray springboard one may then posit that the experiences in the remainder of the incarnation will be focused upon activation of the primary blue-ray of freely given communication, of indigo ray, that of freely shared intelligent energy, and if possible, moving through this gateway, the penetration of violet-ray intelligent infinity. This may be seen to be manifested by a sense of the consecrate or hallowed nature of everyday creations and activities.

Upon the bodily complex death, as you call this transition, the entity will immediately, upon realization of its state, return to the indigo form-maker body and rest therein until the proper future placement is made.

Here we have the anomaly of harvest. In harvest the entity will then transfer its indigo body into violet-ray manifestation as seen in true color yellow. This is for the purpose of gauging the harvestability of the entity. After this anomalous activity has been carefully completed, the entity will move into indigo body again and be placed in the correct true color locus in space/time and time/space at which time the healings and learn/teachings necessary shall be completed and further incarnation needs determined.

Questioner: Who supervises the determination of further incarnation needs and sets up the seniority list for incarnation?

Ra: I am Ra. This is a query with two answers.

Firstly, there are those directly under the Guardians who are responsible for the incarnation patterns of those incarnating automatically, that is, without conscious self-awareness of the process of spiritual evolution. You may call these beings angelic if you prefer. They are, shall we say, "local" or of your planetary sphere.

The seniority of vibration is to be likened unto placing various grades of liquids in the same glass. Some will rise to the top; others will sink to the bottom. Layers and layers of entities will ensue. As harvest draws near, those filled with the most light and love will naturally, and without supervision, be in line, shall we say, for the experience of incarnation.

When the entity becomes aware in its mind/body/spirit complex totality of the mechanism for spiritual evolution it, itself, will arrange and place those lessons and entities necessary for maximum growth and expression of polarity in the incarnative experience before the forgetting process occurs. The only disadvantage of this total free will of those senior entities choosing the manner of incarnation experiences is that some entities attempt to learn so much during one incarnative experience that the intensity of catalyst disarranges the polarized entity and the experience thus is not maximally useful as intended.

Questioner: An analogy to that would be a student in college signing up for more courses than he could possibly assimilate in the time they were given. Is this correct?

Ra: I am Ra. This is correct.

Questioner: Could you tell me how the various bodies, red through violet, are linked to the energy centers, red through violet? Are they linked in some way?

Ra: I am Ra. This shall be the last full query of this working.

As we have noted, each of the true color densities has the seven energy centers and each entity contains all this in potentiation. The activation, while in yellow-ray, of violet-ray intelligent infinity is a passport to the next octave of experience. There are adepts who have penetrated many, many of the energy centers and several of the true colors. This must be done with utmost care while in the physical body for as we noted when speaking of the dangers of linking red/orange/yellow circuitry with true color blue circuitry the potential for disarrangement of the mind/body/spirit complex is great. However, the entity who penetrates intelligent infinity is basically capable of walking the universe with unfettered tread.

Is there any brief query before we leave this instrument?

Questioner: Just if there is anything that we can do to make the instrument more comfortable or to improve the contact?

Ra: I am Ra. All is well. As we have said, this instrument is weak physically and continued work times will lengthen this weakness. The continued contact also aids in the continued climb in vital energy of the instrument as well as the integration and vital energy of the group as an unit. The choice is yours. We are pleased. All is well. You are conscientious. Continue so.

I am Ra. I leave you in the love and in the light of the one infinite Creator. Go forth, then, my friends, rejoicing in the power and in the peace of the one infinite Creator. Adonai.

L/L Research

L/L Research is a subsidiary of Rock Creek Research & Development Laboratories, Inc.

P.O. Box 5195
Louisville, KY 40255-0195

www.llresearch.org

Rock Creek is a non-profit corporation dedicated to discovering and sharing information which may aid in the spiritual evolution of humankind.

ABOUT THE CONTENTS OF THIS TRANSCRIPT: This telepathic channeling has been taken from transcriptions of the weekly study and meditation meetings of the Rock Creek Research & Development Laboratories and L/L Research. It is offered in the hope that it may be useful to you. As the Confederation entities always make a point of saying, please use your discrimination and judgment in assessing this material. If something rings true to you, fine. If something does not resonate, please leave it behind, for neither we nor those of the Confederation would wish to be a stumbling block for any.

© 2009 L/L Research

The Law of One, Book V, Session 48, Fragment 29
April 22, 1981

Jim: The spiritual transfer of energy is apparently possible for Carla in any sexual energy transfer. It happens without any particular effort on her part and seems due, primarily, to her nature as one who considers all of her actions, first, in the light of how she may be of service to another. This kind of spiritual energy transfer, however, is possible for anyone to achieve through a conscious mental dedication of the shared sexual intercourse for the purpose of achieving such a transfer. With that dedication consciously made, the male will transfer the physical energy, which he has in abundance, to the female and refresh her, and the female will transfer the mental/emotional and spiritual energies, that she has in abundance, and inspire the male. The kinds of energy transferred by each biological sex are determined by the nature that is unique to each. The biological male tends to express the male principle of that quality which reaches. The biological female tends to express the female principle of that quality which awaits the reaching. The orgasm is the point at which the transfer takes place although well-mated partners do not necessarily need to experience the orgasm in order to achieve the transfer.

Carla: Since these sessions were recorded, I have continued to study the sexual part of red-ray activity, with the hope of finding ways to share the beauty and joy I have found in my sexuality with other people who wish to move into the experience of sacramental sex. More and more, I am convinced that we all have the ability to move into this vibratory level, where intercourse becomes ever more deeply a Holy Eucharist of red ray. I think that this orgasmic energy is pure love, and that as we experience this ecstasy, we are simply knowing the creator's vibration at rest. I suspect that the universe dwells in a state of orgasm, a timeless ecstasy. So much of our culture's training is bent on blunting the power of passion so that social strictures may be observed that the spontaneity of the act itself is lost. And the constant bombardment of sexual images in commercials and advertisements of every kind sharpen the desire for more and more: more partners, more unorthodox experiences, more thrills, more novelty.

In contrast to this, there is the red-ray part of self and its natural functions, natural and right and, like all other natural functions, something to fulfill in privacy, and with an eye to grace and purity of form in the doing. Once a man has found the wisdom to fix his desire upon Woman, the Goddess, as incarnate in his mate, and the woman has opened her heart to Man, as incarnate in her mate, there is laid the stage for an ever deeper practice of this glorious natural sharing of energy. It has been a blessing to me, certainly, as I apparently ran out of energy some years ago—but am still alive and kicking! Thanks in no small part to the truly fine natural functions of one James McCarty, a man most lovingly sensitive to the Goddess within.

Session 48, April 22, 1981

Questioner: I have a question from the instrument that I will read. "You have suggested several times that sexual energy transfers aid the instrument's vital energy and this contact. It seems that this is not true for all people; that the sexual circuitry and the spiritual circuitry are not the same. Is this instrument an anomaly, or is the positive effect of sexual activity on spiritual energy normal for all third-density beings?"

Ra: I am Ra. This instrument, though not anomalous, is somewhat less distorted towards the separation of mind, body, and spirit than many of your third-density entities. The energies of sexual transfer would, if run through the undeveloped spiritual electrical or magnetic complex which you call circuitry, effectually blow out that particular circuit. Contrarily, the full spiritual energies run through bodily complex circuitry will also adversely effect the undeveloped circuit of the bodily complex. Some there are, such as this instrument, who have not in the particular incarnation chosen at any time to express sexual energy through the bodily circuitry. Thus from the beginning of such an entity's experience the body and spirit express together in any sexual action. Therefore, to transfer sexual energy for this instrument is to transfer spiritually as well as physically. This instrument's magnetic field, if scrutinized by one sensitive, will show these unusual configurations. This is not unique to one entity but is common to a reasonable number of entities who, having lost the desire for orange and yellow-ray sexual experiences, have strengthened the combined circuitry of spirit, mind, and body to express the totality of beingness in each action. It is for this reason also that the social intercourse and companionship is very beneficial to this instrument, it being sensitive to the more subtle energy transfers.

♣

Sunday Meditation
April 26, 1981

(Carla channeling)

I am Oxal, and I greet you in the love and in the light of the infinite Creator. It is a great privilege to speak to this group and to use this instrument, whom we have not used for some time. We are very grateful for this opportunity.

We would speak to you this evening, my friends, about dissatisfaction. In your illusion dissatisfaction is the watchword. There are few indeed among your peoples who can be said to be satisfied with their condition, either physically, mentally, emotionally or spiritually. The reaction of your peoples is to attempt to eliminate dissatisfaction by correcting those items which cause dissatisfaction. If a consumer is dissatisfied with a product, the consumer attempts to cause the producer to correct the defect that is causing dissatisfaction. If two entities are dissatisfied with their relationship, one to the other, they will attempt to communicate through intermediaries, quite often in an attempt to correct the defects of that relationship. If there is dissatisfaction between the individual and the society, many individuals will attempt to correct the defects by correcting the societal bias causing this defect which dissatisfies the individual. If an entity is dissatisfied with himself, he will purchase volumes purporting to give advice and counsel upon correcting the defect within the self!

The mechanisms for erasing dissatisfaction abound and are considered appropriate and normal. My friends, let us consider the function of dissatisfaction. Were we to ask you what the primary reason for your existence is, the answer would not be satisfaction. Of this we are certain, for those who seek will never be satisfied. What then is your goal? We shall not say it for you, but as you may, then reevaluate the virtues of dissatisfaction. When an unthinking being such as an horse or a donkey does not wish to move forward, it is goaded. Consider your sources of dissatisfaction and look within yourselves for the causes, for the defects, for the stimulus to seeking.

Observe, from the standpoint of the self outside of time, that you are both responsible for your actions and quite without responsibility for these actions. You are responsible in the illusion for each and every moment, for each analysis of each stimulus to growth, but to be dissatisfied with the state of your dissatisfaction is to carry dissatisfaction beyond the function for which it was intended. When you find yourself dissatisfied, know that the source is your self. Without condemning the self, clear the mind, step away from the illusion of time and limitations, and do your work, not to seek satisfaction but to understand the stimulus, asking yourself the question: What do you seek? Patiently, humbly, quietly, dwell in this question, accepting your dissatisfaction. The combination you will find most fruitful. As always, we of Oxal join our brothers in recommending that this and all spiritual exercises be accompanied by meditation.

I am a sister of light known to you as one of Oxal. I leave this instrument, that another may speak to your group at this time. I leave you in the love and the light of the infinite Creator. Adonai.

(Don channeling)

I am Hatonn, and am with this instrument. I greet you, my friends, in the love and in the light of the infinite Creator. It is a very great privilege to speak with you once more and a privilege to once more use this instrument. Please bear with me while I condition the instrument.

(Pause)

I am Hatonn, and am with this instrument. As I was saying, it is a very great privilege to once more be with you and speak through this instrument. We have been watching this group progress and we are happy to see the harmonious progression taking place in the understanding of what we of the Confederation have to offer. We are always very privileged to work with any group that will receive our contact, and we are very appreciative when groups such as this one are able to put to use that which we have to offer.

My friends, our words have been heard by many upon your planet, but very few have put these words to use. They hear the words, they understand the words, but there is more to our communication than the hearing and the understanding. The important step, my friends, is the next step: putting into action that which we bring to you. That, my friends, is the only important step. The first two are necessary; the third produces the result.

We have been watching the people of your planet many, many of your years, as you well know. We have been concerned about their development and yet it seems that there is little that we can do, other than to attempt to contact groups such as yours to simply give to those who would seek our love and our light. My friends, in your future there will be more and more of your peoples seeking answers to questions that become apparent to them. At that time it will be necessary for you to have become very practiced in living and understanding that which we offer. We suggest that you practice at this time living the understanding that you receive from us. It is not an understanding that you are receiving in an original or a new manner, but it is simply an understanding that we remind you of. If you are able to live in every waking moment the understanding which we offer, you will then be able to effectively offer that understanding to those who will shortly be seeking it in much greater numbers.

This way of life and attitude, shall I say, my friends, will be your only credentials, for this is the way of the Creator. We suggest time spent in meditation and contemplation of this principle be allocated, for, my friends, this is the great work. This is the true service. We are always available to aid you in every way we can, to aid you so that you in turn may aid others. Shortly, you will have, shall I say, a golden opportunity that does not come too often.

I will transfer this contact at this time to another instrument. I am Hatonn.

(Pause)

(Carla channeling)

I am Hatonn. I am again with this instrument. As you know, my friends, to live each moment in the full realization of the Creator's love and light, of the original Truth, is beyond the capabilities of even the most gifted monk of your peoples and often among ours as well. Many are the moments in each of your experiences when the presence of the Creator seems far and distant and the love that surrounds you seems hidden, as though a great cloud had removed it from your environment. Illumination seems to take place not in a steady stream but in flashes, as if lightening had struck, and for just one moment the presence of the Creator is felt.

If you climbed into a cave and walked into the depths of the Earth you could travel patiently and long among the labyrinthian corridors of the caverns seeking and searching for a shaft of light. This is your situation in your heavy chemical illusion. The shafts of light, however, do appear, and the memory of them is seared upon your brain and upon your being. Do not hesitate, then, to attempt to live your life in memory of these past experiences and in watchful expectation of those in the future, for the rest of your experience is the illusion caused by the heaviness of the earth betwixt you and the light. Ready yourselves for the work at hand, not as a student for a test, not as a vain woman before a glass preparing for the evening, but as one who, knowing and accepting the illusion that experience offers, yet knows too that the sudden illuminations are the reality and it is no hypocrisy to practice according to the light gained in those moments of comprehension.

We thank you, my brothers, for our association has been long and as we have said, we are always available to you. Before we leave this instrument we would open the meeting to any questions that you may have at this time.

(Pause)

I am Hatonn. There is an unverbalized question at this time to which we will give a very brief answer: love.

I am with this instrument. I leave you in the love and in the light of our infinite Creator and in the freedom of His service. Join us, my friends. Adonai vasu borragus. ✻

L/L Research

L/L Research is a subsidiary of Rock Creek Research & Development Laboratories, Inc.

P.O. Box 5195
Louisville, KY 40255-0195

www.llresearch.org

Rock Creek is a non-profit corporation dedicated to discovering and sharing information which may aid in the spiritual evolution of humankind.

ABOUT THE CONTENTS OF THIS TRANSCRIPT: This telepathic channeling has been taken from transcriptions of the weekly study and meditation meetings of the Rock Creek Research & Development Laboratories and L/L Research. It is offered in the hope that it may be useful to you. As the Confederation entities always make a point of saying, please use your discrimination and judgment in assessing this material. If something rings true to you, fine. If something does not resonate, please leave it behind, for neither we nor those of the Confederation would wish to be a stumbling block for any.

© 2009 L/L Research

The Law of One, Book II, Session 49
April 27, 1981

Ra: I am Ra. I greet you in the love and in the light of the one infinite Creator. We communicate now.

Questioner: Would you please give us a reading on the instrument's condition?

Ra: I am Ra. It is as previously stated.

Questioner: I was wondering; in a previous session you had mentioned the left and right ear tones, the left and the right brain somehow being related to the polarities of service-to-self and service-to-others. Could you comment on this?

Ra: I am Ra. We may comment on this.

Questioner: Will you go ahead and comment on this?

Ra: I am Ra. The lobes of your physical complex brain are alike in their use of weak electrical energy. The entity ruled by intuition and impulse is equal to the entity governed by rational analysis when polarity is considered. The lobes may both be used for service to self or service-to-others. It may seem that the rational or analytical mind might have more of a possibility of successfully pursuing the negative orientation due to the fact that in our understanding too much order is by its essence negative. However, this same ability to structure abstract concepts and to analyze experiential data may be the key to rapid positive polarization. It may be said that those whose analytical capacities are predominant have somewhat more to work with in polarizing.

The function of intuition is to inform intelligence. In your illusion the unbridled predominance of intuition will tend to keep an entity from the greater polarizations due to the vagaries of intuitive perception. As you may see, these two types of brain structure need to be balanced in order that the net sum of experiential catalyst will be polarization and illumination, for without the acceptance by the rational mind of the worth of the intuitive faculty the creative aspects which aid in illumination will be stifled.

There is one correspondence between right and left and positive and negative. The web of energy which surrounds your bodies contains somewhat complex polarizations. The left area of the head and upper shoulder is most generally seen to be of a negative polarization whereas the right is of positive polarization, magnetically speaking. This is the cause of the tone's meaning for you.

Questioner: Will you expand on the positive and negative polarizations in general and how they apply to individuals and planets, etc.? I think there is a correlation here, but I'm not sure.

Ra: I am Ra. It is correct that there is a correlation between the energy field of an entity of your nature and planetary bodies, for all material is constructed by means of the dynamic tension of the magnetic field. The lines of force in both cases may be seen to be much like the interweaving spirals of the braided hair. Thus positive and negative wind and

40

interweave forming geometric relationships in the energy fields of both persons, as you would call a mind/body/spirit complex, and planets.

The negative pole is the south pole or the lower pole. The north or upper pole is positive. The crisscrossing of these spiraling energies form primary, secondary, and tertiary energy centers. You are familiar with the primary energy centers of the physical, mental, and spiritual body complex. Secondary points of the crisscrossing of positive and negative center orientation revolve about several of your centers. The yellow-ray center may be seen to have secondary energy centers in elbow, in knee, and in the subtle bodies at a slight spacing from the physical vehicle at points describing diamonds about the entity's naval area surrounding the body.

One may examine each of the energy centers for such secondary centers. Some of your peoples work with these energy centers, and you call this acupuncture. However, it is to be noted that there are most often anomalies in the placement of the energy centers so that the scientific precision of this practice is brought into question. Like most scientific attempts at precision, it fails to take into account the unique qualities of each creation.

The most important concept to grasp about the energy field is that the lower or negative pole will draw the universal energy into itself from the cosmos. Therefrom it will move upward to be met and reacted to by the positive spiraling energy moving downward from within. The measure of an entity's level of ray activity is the locus wherein the south pole outer energy has been met by the inner spiraling positive energy.

As an entity grows more polarized this locus will move upwards. This phenomenon has been called by your peoples the kundalini. However, it may better be thought of as the meeting place of cosmic and inner, shall we say, vibratory understanding. To attempt to raise the locus of this meeting without realizing the metaphysical principles of magnetism upon which this depends is to invite great imbalance.

Questioner: What process would be the recommended process for correctly awakening the kundalini and of what value would that be?

Ra: I am Ra. The metaphor of the coiled serpent being called upwards is vastly appropriate for consideration by your peoples. This is what you are attempting when you seek. There are, as we have stated, great misapprehensions concerning this metaphor and the nature of pursuing its goal. We must generalize and ask that you grasp the fact that this in effect renders far less useful that which we share. However, as each entity is unique, generalities are our lot when communicating for your possible edification.

We have two types of energy. We are attempting then, as entities in any true color of this octave, to move the meeting place of inner and outer natures further and further along or upward along the energy centers. The two methods of approaching this with sensible method are first, the seating within one's self of those experiences which are attracted to the entity through the south pole. Each experience will need to be observed, experienced, balanced, accepted, and seated within the individual. As the entity grows in self-acceptance and awareness of catalyst the location of the comfortable seating of these experiences will rise to the new true color entity. The experience, whatever it may be, will be seated in red ray and considered as to its survival content and so forth.

Each experience will be sequentially understood by the growing and seeking mind/body/spirit complex in terms of survival, then in terms of personal identity, then in terms of social relations, then in terms of universal love, then in terms of how the experience may beget free communication, then in terms of how the experience may be linked to universal energies, and finally in terms of the sacramental nature of each experience.

Meanwhile the Creator lies within. In the north pole the crown is already upon the head and the entity is potentially a god. This energy is brought into being by the humble and trusting acceptance of this energy through meditation and contemplation of the self and of the Creator.

Where these energies meet is where the serpent will have achieved its height. When this uncoiled energy approaches universal love and radiant being the entity is in a state whereby the harvestability of the entity comes nigh.

Questioner: Will you recommend a technique of meditation?

Ra: I am Ra. No.

Questioner: Is it better, or shall I say, does it produce more useable results in meditation to leave the mind as blank as possible and let it run down, so to speak, or is it better to focus in meditation on some object or some thing for concentration?

Ra: I am Ra. This shall be the last full query of this work time.

Each of the two types of meditation is useful for a particular reason. The passive meditation involving the clearing of the mind, the emptying of the mental jumble which is characteristic of mind complex activity among your peoples, is efficacious for those whose goal is to achieve an inner silence as a base from which to listen to the Creator. This is an useful and helpful tool and is by far the most generally useful type of meditation as opposed to contemplation or prayer.

The type of meditation which may be called visualization has as its goal not that which is contained in the meditation itself. Visualization is the tool of the adept. Those who learn to hold visual images in mind are developing an inner concentrative power that can transcend boredom and discomfort. When this ability has become crystallized in an adept the adept may then do polarizing in consciousness without external action which can effect the planetary consciousness. This is the reason for the existence of the so-called White Magician. Only those wishing to pursue the conscious raising of planetary vibration will find visualization to be a particularly satisfying type of meditation.

Contemplation or the consideration in a meditative state of an inspiring image or text is extremely useful also among your peoples, and the faculty of will called praying is also of a potentially helpful nature. Whether it is indeed an helpful activity depends quite totally upon the intentions and objects of the one who prays.

May we ask if there are any brief queries at this time?

Questioner: I will just ask if there is anything that we may do to make the instrument more comfortable or to improve the contact and if the two periods per week are still appropriate?

Ra: I am Ra. We request your care in the placement of the neck support for this entity as it is too often careless. You are conscientious and your alignments are well. The timing, if we may use that expression, of the sessions is basically correct. However, you are to be commended for observing fatigue in the circle and refraining from a working until all were in love, harmony, and vital energy as one being. This is, and will continue to be, most helpful.

I am Ra. I leave you in the love and in the light of the one infinite Creator. Go forth, therefore, rejoicing in the power and in the peace of the one infinite Creator. Adonai.

L/L Research

L/L Research is a subsidiary of Rock Creek Research & Development Laboratories, Inc.

P.O. Box 5195
Louisville, KY 40255-0195

www.llresearch.org

Rock Creek is a non-profit corporation dedicated to discovering and sharing information which may aid in the spiritual evolution of humankind.

ABOUT THE CONTENTS OF THIS TRANSCRIPT: This telepathic channeling has been taken from transcriptions of the weekly study and meditation meetings of the Rock Creek Research & Development Laboratories and L/L Research. It is offered in the hope that it may be useful to you. As the Confederation entities always make a point of saying, please use your discrimination and judgment in assessing this material. If something rings true to you, fine. If something does not resonate, please leave it behind, for neither we nor those of the Confederation would wish to be a stumbling block for any.

© 2009 L/L RESEARCH

THE LAW OF ONE, BOOK V, SESSION 49, FRAGMENT 30
APRIL 27, 1981

Jim: I was the one of the three of us most interested in querying about my own experiences. Having once also been a conspiracy buff this may be understandable as the result of an over-active and over-dramatic curiosity. Questions about Carla were always of a maintenance nature, trying to figure out the best way to keep her physical vehicle running smoothly or at least running in some cases, and Don seldom queried about himself at all. The following comments by Ra amplify the sacramental function that sexual intercourse can fulfill in one's journey of seeking the truth. With the proper balance of mind and body, uniquely determined for each entity, the orgasm can serve as a kind of triggering mechanism that activates the spirit complex and serves as a kind of shuttle, and which then can allow the entity to contact what Ra calls intelligent infinity.

The "pertinent information" concerning the frontal lobes portion of the brain that Ra speaks of concerns the fact that no one knows for sure what that part of the brain is for. All of the qualities that make us human beings are accounted for in the rear five-eighths of the reptilian and mammalian brain. Pioneer thinkers studying this portion of the brain have posited the possibility that the frontal lobes are dormant in most people and may be activated by removing the various blockages in the lower energy centers which childhood experiences have placed there, in accordance with pre-incarnative choices of lessons for the incarnation. When these blockages have been removed—i.e. lessons have been learned—then the frontal lobes may in some degree be activated and a quantum leap in consciousness may be experienced for various lengths of time, usually quite short except in the cases of genuine yogis, saints, and mystics. This is the theory. However, Jim is still "looking forward," shall we say.

Carla: Jim's fascination, early on, about possible conspiracies of political, economic and metaphysical nature, was one he had in common with a large number of people interested in UFOs and UFO messages. Somehow, the mind that revolved around to the mystery of UFOs was also vulnerable to the sensational and elaborate theories which involved secret governmental and international corporate powers. When I first began to channel in 1974, such questions were very common. It took me several years of experience in channeling and watching how the group energy felt to me, to determine to my own satisfaction that asking questions about this sort of fear-based specific material was substantially detrimental to the tuning of the contact, and therefore to the virtue of the information received. In recent years, I allow and even welcome questions that may touch on specific issues for a questioner—but I also offer caveat that the answer will not be specific. I value highly the good contact we continue to be able to sustain, and guard its tuning carefully.

Jim's whole experience with frontal lobe research was a life-changing thing. It seemed to be the thing that opened up for him the life-style of homesteader, certainly an unusually retiring and abstemious way of life, but one which suited Jim to a tee. So without understanding much of the research, I can see that it was very helpful to Jim. The man who created and promulgated this research, however, was a person increasingly devoted to specific questions, when his students began channeling. So I think Jim learned the hard way that any channel can be tainted when the questioning gets too specific, and focuses on worldly things rather than eternal values.

Session 49, April 27, 1981

Questioner: I have a question here from Jim first. He says: "For the past nine years I have had what I call frontal lobes experiences in the pre-conscious state of sleep when I wake up in the morning. They are a combination of pleasure and pressure which begins in the frontal lobes and spreads in pulses through the whole brain and feels like an orgasm in the brain. I have had over 200 of these experiences and often they are accompanied by voices and visions which seldom make much sense to me. What is the source of these frontal lobes experiences?"

Ra: I am Ra. We scan the questioner and find some pertinent information already available which regards the physiological disposition of this particular part of the brain. The experiences described and experienced are those distillations which may be experienced after a concentration of effort upon the opening of the gateway or indigo mind complex so that experience of a sacramental or violet ray may occur. These experiences are the beginnings of that which, as the body, the mind, and the spirit become integrated at the gateway or indigo level, may then yield not only the experience of joy but the comprehension of intelligent infinity which accompanies it. Thus the body complex orgasm and mind complex orgasm becoming integrated may then set forth the proper gateway for the spiritual complex integration and its use as a shuttle for the sacrament of the fully experienced presence of the one infinite Creator. Thus there is much to which the questioner may look forward.

Sunday Meditation
May 3, 1981

(Don channeling)

I greet you, my friends, in the love and the light of our infinite Creator. It's a very great privilege to be with you this evening. We are always privileged to speak with this group and any new members that join this group. I am Hatonn. I am, as you now know, what you call a social memory complex. This information has recently been given to you. I am of the planet, Hatonn. This instrument has spoken to the planet itself and received its thoughts. When you speak to us of Hatonn, you may speak to an individualized portion or, in some instances, the entire memory complex, depending on the particular tuning, shall we say, the particular purpose for the communication.

At this time, I, an individualized portion of that social memory complex, impress my thoughts upon this instrument, who then repeats them as he receives them. It is possible for any of you here tonight to receive my thoughts in the same manner that this instrument receives them. It is not necessary that you verbalize them as he does at this time. All that is necessary for you to receive our thoughts is for you first to desire that reception, and then, second, to make yourself available to that reception. Availability is accomplished simply by removing from the conscious mind the clutter of thinking that normally involves the mind in mundane daily activities. The removal of this clutter can be done by the simple process of meditation. For this reason, and for other reasons, we suggest that daily meditation be accomplished if our contact is desired.

We of the planet Hatonn are here and have been here for many of your years. The purpose: bringing to those who desire our contact a very simple message. That message is of what you would call universal love, for this, my friends, is what the people of your planet need at this time. If they were able to realize truth contained within this very simple message, all of the problems that they now are faced with would very rapidly dissolve to nothingness. We, and many other members of the Confederation, have been actively beaming to [the] population of planet Earth for many of your years that simple message of universal love; not so much in an intellectual sense, but in, what you might call, a subliminal way, a way that has brought about an increase in awareness of universal love with a portion of your population.

Unfortunately, the vast majority of the population of your planet at this time is unaware of the truth of concept of universal love. For this reason, you find yourselves immersed, shall I say, in the sea of troubles. These troubles are the creation of the individual members of your planet. They are manufactured by the thinking that is engaged in by those who dwell upon your surface. This has created some difficulty for those who seek awareness of love and then attempt to put that awareness into practice, for all about them they find the continuing problems created by those who have blocked, shall I say, the truth of universal love which is every being, every thing, every experience in the entire creation. For this reason, you will find [it] sometimes very difficult to look about you and see the re-expression of the planetary population, an expression of the love generated through manifestations of our infinite Creator. However, if you are able to accomplish this under the conditions which you now experience, you will have passed, shall I say, a rather stern test.

My friends, you look upon each of the problems generated by those who do not seem to be aware of the universality of the Creator's love as simply a small test of your awareness and if you successfully pass that small test in each and every day, in each and every way, you will have then learned the very simple lesson, a very simple lesson that will open to you that gateway to your Creator.

It has been a privilege speaking through this instrument. I am Hatonn. I shall now transfer this contact to another instrument.

(L channeling)

I am Hatonn, and I greet you again, my brothers, in the love and the light of our Creator. It is difficult to select a channel when offered a group of such willing candidates. However, as so many are both available and willing, we will attempt to speak through each if possible.

We of Hatonn are engaged at this time in a study of your manifestations, for we find them to be often confusing. It is not that they are confusing in their substance, but rather in their contradiction, for we do not understand sometimes how you are able, as a people, to pursue that which you simultaneously deplore. My brothers, the lessons of your dimension are many and can be difficult, therefore, we urge you to maintain an awareness whenever possible of the fact that you exist within an illusion of your own creation. If your creation, your illusion, is contradictory, then you will find that your growth is impeded in that you expend your energy praying for and rejecting at the same time.

For example, if you choose to desire a car of a specific type and year, you have only to voice your prayer, or creative form, and follow it with a conscious creative effort. If you then follow this prayer, this creative effort, with an evaluation of people who seek new cars instead of growth, your energy—your creative ability—has been superseded by itself. You are living, my brothers, in a world of illusions, yet you must remember that it is the individual who creates the illusion within which he lives, not the illusion forming the individual. It is therefore wise, my brothers, to examine your world constantly as if through the eyeglasses of another whose visual acuity is dissimilar from your own, for just as your physical reality would be grossly distorted by such an act, it would simultaneously be made more real to you as its actual existence is displayed in wavy lines and hazy forms. The image is but an image, the form is simply a bottle which you fill or empty at will.

At this time we would transfer our contact to another instrument. I am Hatonn.

(Jim channeling)

I am Hatonn, and greet you once again in the love and the light of our infinite Creator. It is a measure, as we have said before, to have so many instruments from which to choose. Our only sorrow, if it could be called that, is that all are in the same room this evening. It is our wish, as you know, to develop as many instruments as possible upon the surface of your planet. And it is not surprising to see that many have grown from the same seed pit. We would hope that it would not appear too greedy on our part to have more instruments to spread about the surface of your planet, but certainly we rejoice in the abundance of instruments that has appeared within the grouping that has gathered this evening.

We of Hatonn have spoken for many years to those of your people who have sought our messages and that is the important factor in the delivering of the simple message which we have to offer. We are unable to present any kind of communication other than the simple sending of love and light to your peoples unless there is a calling—a calling for that service which we have to offer. And we are overjoyed to report that the calling upon your planet, though still of a relatively small degree, is yet increasing and as that illusion which is called time goes on, the calling appears to be increasing.

This, my friends, is, as most of you know, a result of the illusion and its course which it has been taking for many, many of your years. Those of you who have taken time to observe the events upon the planet of your Earth, in the realms called political and the realms called military, in the realms of geophysical events, in those interpersonal relationships between the entities upon your plane, in each segment of the illusion in which you partake, those of you who have looked, have seen that much of what may be called catalyst of experience is intensifying, that each energy which is inverted in any area is magnified and the results of actions seem now to be increasing in their intensity and their numbers and in the learning that is available. This is a natural progression of events upon your planet.

For many of your years the people of your planet have sought valiantly to make sense of the illusion. Many of their efforts to make sense of this illusion have only caused greater confusion, greater confusion it would seem, but to those who look from the heart of love, of universal love, it may be seen that there is more than meets the eye. For the confusion which seems so rampant upon your planet today is the logical outgrowth of an illusion pursued to its ultimate completion, for my friends, as you know, this illusion in which you live is just that: it is an illusion. It is not that which sustains, it is not that which is the goal of evolution, the goal of the Creator, or the goal of any of the entities which partake in it. It is simply the means, it is simply the catalyst. It is simply the opportunities presented time and again for each of the entities partaking in it to learn, to seek in another direction, to learn to seek within, to seek from within the center of their own being the love of the Creator, to seek to know the unity that binds all things, all beings, all life.

The illusion in which you live has this simple purpose: to teach you that it is not real, that the reality which is the center of your being, the source of your life and the goal of your learning is found within your own being, is found in what might be called the form of love. We of Hatonn have through these many years attempted to bring this simple message to your peoples. We have advised that each entity partake in meditation on a daily basis, for we have found in our own seeking that meditation is the surest way to discover the love of the Creator within all that exists.

We would now transfer this contact to another instrument. I am Hatonn.

(Carla channeling)

I am Hatonn. We would like to take this opportunity to once again invoke the light and the love of the Creator as we work with a new channel, the one known as C. Our brothers and sisters of Laitos are with us at this time and we of Hatonn would like to speak a few words through this channel at this time, if he would relax and speak without hesitation as thoughts come into his mind. We now transfer this contact. I am Hatonn.

(C channeling)

I am Hatonn. I am with this instrument. It is a pleasure to speak …

(Carla channeling)

I am Hatonn. I am again with this instrument. It is indeed a great pleasure to work with new channels. We have made great progress with the one known as C and it will continue such, for this instrument is desirous of learning this particular service. We always stress that this is but one kind of service and that each of you may be of service one way or the other channeling the love and the peace of the infinite Creator. However, as these times proceed that have already begun, as confusion springs within the hearts, in the minds, of those peoples whom you personally know, there will come times when perhaps you may wish to be able to channel philosophy of love in such a way that it is less overlaid by the dogma and the theology of those structured spiritual disciplines which you call religions. It is unfortunate but true that many of those who seek the hardest are those who do not wish or need the bones, the hard skeleton of churches, ashrams, or synagogues, but rather need the soft heart of a living and loving Creator. Therefore, each new channel is cause for rejoicing.

We would share our vibrations with all of you present if you will open your minds at this time. We will make our presence known especially to the one known as H and the one known as D. I am Hatonn.

(Pause)

I am Hatonn, and am again with this instrument. I thank you for your patience as we work with new instruments. Before we leave this group, we would like to ask if you have any questions at this time.

L: I have a question. Are you familiar with two entities who call themselves *(name)* and *(name)*?

I am Hatonn. My brother, we are aware of your question and we suggest that you do not repeat the names which you have just pronounced. We will say no more.

Is there another question at this time?

L: No, thank you.

We suggest in general, my friends, the removal, by neglect, of those vocalizations which embody unneeded or unwanted thought forms.

Is there another question at this time, my friends?

(Pause)

I am Hatonn. We feel there is a question that is on the tip of the tongue, yet we do not wish to infringe on free will. Thus, we will ask once more and then move on, if you have a question at this time.

L: I would ask one other question. Of the entities previously mentioned, is there a negative facet to their existence and to dealing with them. Should I be warned against them?

I am Hatonn, and am joined by two in the Confederation, Laitos and Nona. Nona will speak as we finish. Laitos is with you, as are we. You understand that there are many things which we cannot detail due to our desire and our necessity of non-infringement on free will. It is written, "By their fruits ye shall know them." The warnings are always within the discrimination of the entity. My brother, you are more wise and more powerful than you know. You have help, you have love, and above all you have a universe within you. We cannot make a judgment, give a warning or speak ill in the context in which you ask this question, for it is of some importance in your future. Accept our apology, but we are unable to lessen our own polarity by infringing upon your free will. We feel that we have, shall we say, tripped about the edges of the question with every ounce, if you will, of verbiage that can be given.

May we answer you in another fashion, my brother?

L: I thank you for your answers. I find them sufficient at this time.

Very well. Is there another question at this time?

(Pause)

If there are no more questions at this time, my friends, I leave you naked, yet strong; alone, yet full of love; pilgrims, yet accompanied by the hosts of heaven. You trod a path that is rocky, steep, and difficult and yet your vistas could not be more beautiful. As you seek the truth, you experience a greater range of what you would call catalysts than those who do not seek, and this is for a reason. There is much in the illusion. As we have said, it is well not to fight the self. It is well not to praise and condemn the same thing. It is well to understand the illusion, to feel comfortable, to feel free in the self, unreconstructed—unperfected, as you would say—just as you are in the illusion. This is you. This is the Creator. Experience yourself, my friends, as part of the illusion. This is …

(Side one of tape ends.)

(Carla channeling)

… perfection can be overshadowed by any error, any stumbling, any blockage, whatever the problem, the difficulty, the limitation, the mistake, there is love enough inside you to cause creation to be radiant, from one infinite realm to another, and to another, forever. Seek the Creator and we shall be with you as you meditate, as you live.

I am one of those known to you as Hatonn. We are sorry we need to use words with you. We wish we could share with you the love of the Creator without these masks. We do not mean to deceive you, but we cannot give you the power of love with these weak tools called words. Nevertheless, with all of our hearts we reach out to you with them in the hopes that some inspiration may send you searching more and more for the larger life that awaits you. Adonai, my friends. We leave you in the love and the light of the infinite Creator. Adonai.

(Carla channels Nona until the end of the tape.)

L/L Research

The Law of One, Book II, Session 50
May 6, 1981

Ra: I am Ra. I greet you in the love and in the light of the one infinite Creator. We communicate now.

Questioner: Could you please give me an indication of the instrument's condition now?

Ra: I am Ra. It is as previously stated.

Questioner: In the last session you made the statement that experiences are attracted into the entity through the south pole. Could you expand on that and give us a definition of what you mean?

Ra: I am Ra. It takes some consideration to accomplish the proper perspective for grasping the sense of the above information. The south or negative pole is one which attracts. It pulls unto itself those things magnetized to it. So with the mind/body/spirit complex. The in-flow of experience is of the south pole influx. You may consider this a simplistic statement.

The only specific part of this correctness is that the red-ray or foundation energy center, being the lowest or root energy center of the physical vehicle, will have the first opportunity to react to any experience. In this way only, you may see a physical locus of the south pole being identified with the root energy center. In every facet of mind and body the root or foundation will be given the opportunity to function first.

What is this opportunity but survival? This is the root possibility of response and may be found to be characteristic of the basic functions of both mind and body. You will find this instinct the strongest, and once this is balanced much is open to the seeker. The south pole then ceases blocking the experiential data and higher energy centers of mind and body become availed of the opportunity to use the experience drawn to it.

Questioner: Why do you say the experience is drawn to or attracted to the entity?

Ra: I am Ra. We say this due to our understanding that this is the nature of the phenomenon of experiential catalyst and its entry into the mind/body/spirit complex's awareness.

Questioner: Could you give an example of how an entity sets up a condition for attracting a particular experiential catalyst and how that catalyst then is provided or is learned.

Ra: I am Ra. Such an example may be given.

Questioner: Will you give that?

Ra: I am Ra. We paused to scan *(name's)* consciousness to use its experiential catalyst as example. We may proceed.

This is one instance and extrapolation may be made to other entities which are aware of the process of evolution. This entity chose, before incarnation, the means whereby catalyst had great probability of being obtained. This entity desired the process of expressing love and light without expecting any return. This entity programmed also to endeavor to accomplish spiritual work and to comfort itself with companionship in the doing of this work.

Agreements were made prior to incarnation; the first, with the so-called parents and siblings of this entity. This provided the experiential catalyst for the situation of offering radiance of being without expectation of return. The second program involved agreements with several entities. These agreements provided and will provide, in your time/space and space/time continuum, opportunities for the experiential catalyst of work and comradeship.

There are events which were part of a program for this entity only in that they were possibility/probability vortices having to do with your societal culture. These events include the nature of the living or standard of living, the type of relationships entered into in your legal framework, and the social climate during the incarnation. The incarnation was understood to be one which would take place at harvest.

These givens, shall we say, apply to millions of your peoples. Those aware of evolution and desirous in the very extreme of attaining the heart of love and the radiance which gives understanding no matter what the lessons programmed: they have to do with other-selves, not with events: they have to do with giving, not receiving, for the lessons of love are of this nature both for positive and negative. Those negatively harvestable will be found at this time endeavoring to share their love of self.

There are those whose lessons are more random due to their present inability to comprehend the nature and mechanism of the evolution of mind, body, and spirit. Of these we may say that the process is guarded by those who never cease their watchful expectation of being of service. There is no entity without help, either through self-awareness of the unity of creation or through guardians of the self which protect the less sophisticated mind/body/spirit from any permanent separation from unity while the lessons of your density continue.

Questioner: Could you give an example of negative polarization sharing love of self? It would seem to me that that would deplete negative polarization. Could you expand on the concept?

Ra: I am Ra. We may not use examples of known beings due to the infringement this would cause. Thus we must be general.

The negatively oriented being will be one who feels that it has found power that gives meaning to its existence precisely as the positive polarization does feel. This negative entity will strive to offer these understandings to other-selves, most usually by the process of forming the elite, the disciples, and teaching the need and rightness of the enslavement of other-selves for their own good. These other-selves are conceived to be dependent upon the self and in need of the guidance and the wisdom of the self.

Questioner: Thank you. How does the ability to hold visual images in mind allow the adept to do polarization in consciousness without external action?

Ra: I am Ra. This is not a simple query, for the adept is one which will go beyond the green-ray which signals entry into harvestability. The adept will not simply be tapping into intelligent energy as a means of readiness for harvest but tapping into both intelligent energy and intelligent infinity for the purpose of transmuting planetary harvestability and consciousness.

The means of this working lie within. The key is first, silence, and secondly, singleness of thought. Thusly a visualization which can be held steady to the inward eye for several of your minutes, as you measure time, will signal the adept's increase in singleness of thought. This singleness of thought then can be used by the positive adept to work in group ritual visualizations for the raising of positive energy, by negative adepts for the increase in personal power.

Questioner: Can you tell me what the adept, after being able to hold the image for several minutes, does to affect planetary consciousness or affect positive polarity?

Ra: I am Ra. When the positive adept touches intelligent infinity from within, this is the most powerful of connections for it is the connection of the whole mind/body/spirit complex microcosm with the macrocosm. This connection enables the, shall we say, green-ray true color in time/space to manifest in your space/time. In green ray thoughts are beings. In your illusion this is normally not so.

The adepts then become living channels for love and light and are able to channel this radiance directly into the planetary web of energy nexi. The ritual will always end by the grounding of this energy in praise and thanksgiving and the release of this energy into the planetary whole.

Questioner: Could you give me more information on the energy fields of the body as related to the right and left brain and if this is somehow related to the pyramid shape as far as energy focusing goes? I am at a loss as to how to get into this line of questioning, so I will ask that question.

Ra: I am Ra. We are similarly at a loss at this line of answering. We may say that the pyramid shape is but one which focuses the in-streamings of energy for use by entities which may become aware of these in-streamings. We may say further that the shape of your physical brain is not significant as a shape for concentrating in-streamings of energy. Please ask more specifically if you may that which you seek.

Questioner: Each of us feels, in meditation, energy upon the head in various places. Could you tell me what this is, what it signifies, and what the various places in which we feel it signify?

Ra: I am Ra. Forgetting the pyramid will be of aid to you in the study of these experiences. The in-streamings of energy are felt by the energy centers which need, and are prepared for, activation. Thus those who feel the stimulation at violet-ray level are getting just that. Those feeling it within the forehead between the brows are experiencing indigo ray and so forth. Those experiencing tingling and visual images are having some blockage in the energy center being activated and thus the electrical body spreads this energy out and its effect is diffused.

Those not truly sincerely requesting this energy may yet feel it if the entities are not well-trained in psychic defense. Those not desirous of experiencing these sensations and activations and changes even upon the subconscious level will not experience anything due to their abilities at defense and armoring against change.

Questioner: Is it normal to get two simultaneous stimulations at once?

Ra: I am Ra. The most normal for the adept is the following: the indigo stimulation activating that great gateway into healing, magical work, prayerful attention, and the radiance of being; and the stimulation of the violet ray which is the spiritual giving and taking from and to Creator, from Creator to Creator.

This is a desirable configuration.

Please ask one more full query at this working.

Questioner: Can you expand on the concept which is that it is necessary for an entity, during incarnation in the physical as we know it, to become polarized or interact properly with other entities and why this isn't possible in between incarnations when the entity is aware of what he wants to do. Why must he come into an incarnation and lose conscious memory of what he wants to do and then act in a way in which he hopes to act?

Ra: I am Ra. Let us give the example of the man who sees all the poker hands. He then knows the game. It is but child's play to gamble, for it is no risk. The other hands are known. The possibilities are known and the hand will be played correctly but with no interest.

In time/space and in the true color green density, the hands of all are open to the eye. The thoughts, the feelings, the troubles, all these may be seen. There is no deception and no desire for deception. Thus much may be accomplished in harmony but the mind/body/spirit gains little polarity from this interaction.

Let us re-examine this metaphor and multiply it into the longest poker game you can imagine, a lifetime. The cards are love, dislike, limitation, unhappiness, pleasure, etc. They are dealt and re-dealt and re-dealt continuously. You may, during this incarnation begin—and we stress begin—to know your own cards. You may begin to find the love within you. You may begin to balance your pleasure, your limitations, etc. However, your only indication of other-selves' cards is to look into the eyes.

You cannot remember your hand, their hands, perhaps even the rules of this game. This game can only be won by those who lose their cards in the melting influence of love, can only be won by those who lay their pleasures, their limitations, their all upon the table face up and say inwardly: "All, all of you players, each other-self, whatever your hand, I love you." This is the game: to know, to accept, to forgive, to balance, and to open the self in love. This cannot be done without the forgetting, for it would carry no weight in the life of the mind/body/spirit being-ness totality.

Is there a brief query before we leave this instrument?

Questioner: Is there anything that we can do to make the instrument more comfortable or to improve the contact?

Ra: I am Ra. You are conscientious and your alignments are careful. It would be well to take care that this instrument's neck is placed carefully upon its support.

I am Ra. I leave you, my friends, in the love and the light of the one infinite Creator. Go forth, then, rejoicing in the power and in the peace of the one infinite Creator. Adonai. ✣

L/L Research

L/L Research is a subsidiary of Rock Creek Research & Development Laboratories, Inc.

P.O. Box 5195
Louisville, KY 40255-0195

www.llresearch.org

Rock Creek is a non-profit corporation dedicated to discovering and sharing information which may aid in the spiritual evolution of humankind.

ABOUT THE CONTENTS OF THIS TRANSCRIPT: This telepathic channeling has been taken from transcriptions of the weekly study and meditation meetings of the Rock Creek Research & Development Laboratories and L/L Research. It is offered in the hope that it may be useful to you. As the Confederation entities always make a point of saying, please use your discrimination and judgment in assessing this material. If something rings true to you, fine. If something does not resonate, please leave it behind, for neither we nor those of the Confederation would wish to be a stumbling block for any.

© 2009 L/L Research

The Law of One, Book V, Session 50, Fragment 31
May 6, 1981

Jim: When I was in the process of cutting trees with which to build my cabin in the woods of central Kentucky in the spring of 1973, I was quite unsure of how or if I would be able to survive alone in that remote environment. Though subdued most of the time, my nervousness about this whole project was obvious. One night, in my tent, I was awakened by the sound of a friend's dog eating dog food from its plastic bowl. I mentally heard the message that is spoken of in the following material and wrote it down by flashlight. It appears that each of us has at least three guides to aid us, and aid is usually given in a symbolic manner in order to give us clues that will stimulate our own thinking and seeking abilities rather than by laying out answers in a plain and unquestionable fashion.

Carla: I have experienced Jim's nervousness through our long association, and found that his quickness and alertness are preternatural. The trait seems to be a mixed blessing, however, for if the objects he is manipulating have the temerity to be balky, the tension can escalate. I suppose virtues always have their shadows! I have come to find that level of trust with Jim where one accepts another without regard for anything but complete support, and would not change him to be one iota less fiery. That race-horse temperament is simply the shadow of so many wonderful traits that make him the extremely efficient and ever-resourceful good judge of men and situations that he is.

Session 50, May 6, 1981

Questioner: I have a question from Jim about an experience which he had when he first moved to his land in which he was told, "The key to your survival comes indirect, through nervousness." The entity was Angelica. Could you give him information with respect to this?

Ra: I am Ra. Yes.

Questioner: Would you please do that?

Ra: I am Ra. As we have noted, each mind/body/spirit complex has several guides available to it. The persona of two of these guides is the polarity of male and female. The third is androgynous and represents a more unified conceptualization faculty.

The guide speaking as sound vibration complex, Angelica, was the female polarized persona. The message may not be fully explicated due to the Law of Confusion. We may suggest that in order to progress, a state of some dissatisfaction will be present, thus giving the entity the stimulus for further seeking. This dissatisfaction, nervousness, or angst, if you will, is not of itself useful. Thus its use is indirect.

Sunday Meditation
May 10, 1981

(L channeling)

[I am Hatonn,] and I greet you again, my friends, in the love and the light of our infinite Creator. It is with great pleasure, my brothers, that we greet again the one known as M, for it has been a great time, in your conception of time passage, since we have been able to welcome her presence in this group. It is also a great honor that we feel in speaking to this group, for you honor us by consistently and faithfully tuning yourselves to the meager advice we are capable of offering. It is the love of the Creator that motivates both yourselves and ourselves, therefore, my brothers, let us rejoice in the love and light that the Creator has blessed us with.

My brothers, this night is one of calm, for although there is much strife in your world, there is also a peace in the hearts of many who have been blessed this day. It is a custom on your planet and your world as you know it, to honor those receptive entities that you term mothers, on this day and the effect—correction—the cumulative effect of this vibration is one of the creation of a state of receptivity upon an area of your planet that is often responsible for much of the strife that exists on the surface of your world. Therefore, the result has been an increase in the receptivity and in the quantity of peace, if you will, within the hearts of many of the entities of your planet, not only in the geographic area in which you reside, but across the surface, for peace has a cumulative effect that increases beyond its original numbers.

Therefore, my brothers we greet you once again in the love and the light and in the peace of your infinite Creator. At this time we would transfer our contact to another instrument that we may give further experience to those present who desire to channel our voices. I am Hatonn.

(Jim channeling)

I am Hatonn, and I greet you once again in the love and the light of our infinite Creator. It is our special privilege to be speaking to you this evening. It is always a privilege to be able to address groups such as yourselves who have gathered with a common quest: the seeking of truth, the seeking of love. We of Hatonn have attempted to aid such seekers for many of your years. We attempt this aid because it is our understanding of the plan of the Creator that all of the creation is one Thought; that all of the creation, whether it is conscious of its oneness with the Creator or not, all of the creation is part of the Creator, and those entities who have been privileged to travel the trail of conscious evolution, such as we of Hatonn have been so privileged, such entities as ourselves by the traveling of that trail do incur a certain responsibility that is a privilege as well. And that privilege and that responsibility is to serve those who have not traveled quite so far, but who seek to travel the trail of awareness and who choose to seek, each in their own way, the truth and the love of the Creator. By such service we not only aid those who seek our service, but we aid ourselves, for are we not all one? And in this service, is not all of the Creation advanced yet one tiny step further? For as one becomes illumined, the All shines just a bit brighter, and every particle and being of the creation of the Father has a full understanding of its unity with the Creator.

Not until this time, my friends, may any rest in their service to others, for if one remains in the darkness, does not the darkness fall upon all? Therefore, we of Hatonn deem it a great privilege to be able to share our meager understandings with all who ask for our assistance and we wish at this time to assure each entity within this gathering that we are always with you; that should you ever request our assistance in any of your ponderings, of your meditations, of your spiritual endeavors, we shall be most honored to respond and, indeed, many times have we responded, even though you may not have known it was those of Hatonn who went to their aid. We do not seek recognition for this service, for the service is its own reward. For as we have said many times in our messages, we are all one and as any gains in understanding, all gain thereby.

We would at this time pause for a moment so that our brother of Laitos might pass among those in this group and might aid each in their meditation as the request is made. We will pause for a moment and then resume. I am Hatonn.

(Pause)

(Jim channeling)

I am Hatonn, and am with this instrument once again. We have been speaking thus far this evening about the honor of service. We would ask that each entity within this group consider carefully the concept of service. Consider the unity that binds each of you with each person that you meet, with each activity which you undertake, with each thought that you think. We would ask that as you go your ways over the days and the months ahead, that as you face the various difficulties, the various joys, the various experiences, we ask that you consider your response to each as an act of service. We will not explain completely what we wish for you to consider by seeing each action as a service, but will leave a majority of that understanding to come as a result of your ponderings, for we of Hatonn are not able to give full understanding, for we do not have full understanding. And even if that full understanding was within our possession, still we would not give it, for it cannot be given but may only be received by each entity's own effort. Therefore, we would once again ask that you look through the lens of service as you travel your ways and encounter the experiences which await you.

We would, at this time, transfer our contact to another instrument. I am Hatonn.

(Carla channeling)

I am Hatonn, and I greet you once again in the love and the light of the infinite Creator. At this time, my friends, we would like to open the meeting to questions.

L: Hatonn, I have in my hand several pieces of paper on which are written a series of questions—correction—series of statements that I directed to your attention earlier this evening. Without violating the Law of Confusion, can you tell me [if] these statements are correct or false?

I am Hatonn. I accept your questions, my friend, but find that I cannot answer you with such a simple reply. I shall spend some time with the questions and at that time will allow you as much time, as you call it, as you need to decide what more you would wish to know upon this particular subject. The knowledge which has been offered you is the knowledge of an adept. This has been offered you because of past experiences which enable you in this particular experience to avail yourself of a state of consciousness in which this level of information is appropriate.

It is correct and to be understood fully that such an ability is companioned by an explicit and fastidious responsibility. Any power has the tendency, as you say among your peoples, to corrupt, and it is the work of an adept to be radiant, to shine, and to aid with the power. The power which you ask was inadvertently asked in such a way that you received an understanding of what you may call names of power, having to do with certain elements of your natural creation. As you know, all things live and may be commended.

We ask that you guard yourself against any lightly held commands and that you preface any use of the abilities instinctive to your nature with careful and conscientious preparation in this life experience in the area of compassion and acceptance, for the creation of the Father is interrelated by webs of love and service. The power to disrupt this web is within your being. You would not inadvertently wish to do this. Ponder this and seek harmony in all that you attempt in your service to the creation.

May we answer you further, my brother?

L: Yes. There was one statement in my series of statements in my list that would be particularly significant in my further seeking of advice from you in this area. For that reason I would like to reiterate those statements to assure myself of their accuracy. Those statements are as follows.

First, I may assign names to these entities that will enable me to discuss them with you or another such as yourself without summoning them; second, the entities have the potential to assume characteristics associated with those assigned names unless this is specifically forbidden at the time the names are assigned; third, I may at this time assign those names and forbid the entities from assuming any characteristics associated with those names; and fourth, knowledge of those names that I have assigned the entities will not enable another person to summon those entities. Are these statements correct?

I am Hatonn. My brother, we have attempted in general terms to answer these questions for you by warning you against the hasty use of that which is not developed in this incarnation, but which has been developed previously. Your assumptions, although not totally incorrect, are basically misapprehensions due to the fact that behind the name is the thought and in the area in which you are working, the thought is that which has power. The name is the symbol of that power. New names are simply new symbols for the same power and in the perception of another not so positively oriented, the name to which you have given authority, bound or unbound, may then be used if the second entity has power to bind or unbind that entity by whatever name you have assigned.

Let us give an example. Your own vibration contains several names to which you answer. Some of these have great power over you. For instance, the name, "Daddy," has great power over you. Yet, you are not called by that name. You are in a position where an entity, given the right to use this name, will then command your complete attention. So it is with the entities of which you speak. These entities are your brethren, and are to be valued. However, like yourself, they may be commanded. It is well to know how and what to ask and to have the full understanding of the essence of their nature. Before work is begun, we suggest that no names be used. You, of course, may do as you wish.

May we answer you further, my brother?

L: Yes. I am reluctant to command, having no command that I desire to make or request beyond the simple ones I have already made to my brethren. However, it has been my experience on this plane that one gains ability through practice and dealing with the magnitude that you describe I am extremely hesitant to practice and I would seek further learning that I feel will accompany the ability. Is there any advice you could offer to assist me in achieving that end?

I am Hatonn. My brother, this answer may have grown rusty and creaky with overuse, yet, it is our answer. Meditate, and in that state allow those questions which you may have to be sent out into the inner planes of your great being. There are resources available to you which will have their fruits, first upon planes of thought which may not offer you words, but which will bring understanding, and then the plane of the physical illusion will aid you as it reflects to you that which you have attracted by your seeking.

Is there another question at this time?

L: No. I think any further questions on this subject need to be directed inward. I thank you for your assistance.

We are humbly grateful for the opportunity to serve. Is there another question at this time?

L: I have one more question, if I may interrupt. Do these entities desire to be channeled at any time?

I am Hatonn. These entities are channels, my brother. You will understand this after some meditation.

L: Thank you.

Is there another question at this time?

M: Yes, I have a question. In our new area we have been undecided as to whether to seek out a new group or to try to just wait for the right time. We go back and forth on what to do. Are you aware of another group that … are you in contact with, in that area in Colorado?

I am Hatonn. Yes, my sister, we are aware of a group that has had some communication with us. However, it is our feeling that your understanding is enough advanced, if we may use this term, that the experience of working with your own group would be of more aid than the contact with a group which is somewhat interested in specific information almost to the exclusion of philosophy, as you may call it. This is not as helpful for your seeking as that which you may, through your own channels, receive, whether in silent meditation or through a channel such as this one.

Be aware, as we have said, that our love is with you and we of the Confederation are never apart from any member of this group, no matter what the so-called geographical distance between this meeting place and your domicile, for all is one place, for all is the creation. Thus, if we may be so bold, we would gladly accept your seeking in any way you may wish, but would not speak through this instrument of any other groups, for the vibrations within your own small group are somewhat, as we have said, more advanced.

Does this answer your question, my sister?

M: Yes, thank you.

Is there another question at this time?

(Side one of tape ends.)

(Carla channeling)

… simple thoughts. We have spoken with peace and yet, surely you know by now that the peace of which we speak is not the peace of your peoples, for your peoples have no true peace, but only destruction and the numbing of the senses. It is written in one of your holy works that the one known as Jesus said, "I come to bring not peace, but a sword." And so will this peace seem in your life. As you become able to view your experiences in a conscious and loving manner, multiplying the true peace of your existence, that vision will cut through the feelings and the preferences of those about you who do not prefer true peace, but rather the illusion.

If you seek peace, know this: it is truly worth that which is paid for, and yet it may sometime seem like loss. Rest, then in your meditation, in the true peace of love, and as you find your understanding causing you to act in such a way as to cause those about you to observe a difference in your actions, understand that those who radiate love may also be counted as fools.

We have spoken also this evening of service. A great part of the peace that is true peace is service to others. Moment by moment you have unending opportunities to view your situations as opportunities to be of service, to sow a seed of calm, of love, of kindness. Again, many times you may be countered as a fool, but my friends, it is the fools of this world who shall be in salvation. Only a fool can love without judging. Only a foolish person can desire to serve those who are unlovable, can pray for those who are unattractive and cold in their misery.

Be fools, then. And join a joyful host of such fools, for those who love will always be such. It is to be remembered that those ways of judging among your peoples are greatly various. It is to be remembered that it is impossible to judge, but through the grace of the inner light and love available to you, it is possible, indeed, to love.

We hold out our hands to you in great joy and leave you in the love and in the light of our infinite Creator. I am known to you as Hatonn. Adonai, my friends. Adonai, vasu

I am Nona, and I greet you, my friends, in the love and in the light of the infinite Creator. We are called to this meeting to aid in the healing vibrations for the one known as P. We would attempt to channel this healing through the one known as C. I am Nona.

(C channeling)

Aahhhhhhhh …

(Carla channeling)

I am Oxal, and I greet this group in the love and light of the infinite Creator. It is a great privilege to be able to address you briefly. We wish to be with you to greet the one known as M, for we have been with this entity and wish to assure this entity of our continued love and light.

We ask you, my friends, to remember the great cross and circle of being: the mouth, the heart, and the hands—the great cross of being. If these four points of your physical illusion may be coordinated, you may begin to flow in the great circle of the ever-present moment. You may strive and strive and never find that great circle of being, and so we say to you, my friends, strive with your heart and release with great freedom the lock upon your heart so that your hands and your lips may show forth the love and the light that your heart so strives to encompass.

I leave you, my friends, through this instrument, but am always with you. I am Oxal. Adonai, my friends. ♣

L/L Research

L/L Research is a subsidiary of Rock Creek Research & Development Laboratories, Inc.

P.O. Box 5195
Louisville, KY 40255-0195

www.llresearch.org

Rock Creek is a non-profit corporation dedicated to discovering and sharing information which may aid in the spiritual evolution of humankind.

ABOUT THE CONTENTS OF THIS TRANSCRIPT: This telepathic channeling has been taken from transcriptions of the weekly study and meditation meetings of the Rock Creek Research & Development Laboratories and L/L Research. It is offered in the hope that it may be useful to you. As the Confederation entities always make a point of saying, please use your discrimination and judgment in assessing this material. If something rings true to you, fine. If something does not resonate, please leave it behind, for neither we nor those of the Confederation would wish to be a stumbling block for any.

© 2009 L/L RESEARCH

THE LAW OF ONE, BOOK III, SESSION 51
MAY 13, 1981

Ra: I am Ra. I greet you in the love and in the light of the one infinite Creator. We communicate now.

Questioner: As we begin Book Three of *The Law Of One* there are a couple of questions of fairly non-transient importance that I have and one that I consider to be of a transient nature that I feel obligated to ask.

The first is clearing up the final point about harvest. I was wondering if there is a supervision over the harvest and if so, why this supervision is necessary and how it works since an entity's harvestability is determined by the violet ray? Is it necessary for entities to supervise the harvest, or is it automatic?

Ra: I am Ra. In time of harvest there are always harvesters. The fruit is formed as it will be, but there is some supervision necessary to ensure that this bounty is placed as it should be without the bruise or the blemish.

There are those of three levels watching over harvest.

The first level is planetary and that which may be called angelic. This type of guardian includes the mind/body/spirit complex totality or higher self of an entity and those inner plane entities which have been attracted to this entity through its inner seeking.

The second class of those who ward this process are those of the Confederation who have the honor/duty of standing in the small places at the edge of the steps of light/love so that those entities being harvested will not, no matter how confused or unable to make contact with their higher self, stumble and fall away for any reason other than the strength of the light. These Confederation entities catch those who stumble and set them aright so that they may continue into the light.

The third group watching over this process is that group you call the Guardians. This group is from the octave above our own and serves in this manner as light bringers. These Guardians provide the precise emissions of light/love in exquisitely fastidious disseminations of discrimination so that the precise light/love vibration of each entity may be ascertained.

Thus the harvest is automatic in that those harvested will respond according to that which is unchangeable during harvest. That is the violet ray emanation. However, these helpers are around to ensure a proper harvesting so that each entity may have the fullest opportunity to express its violet ray selfhood.

Questioner: This next question I feel to be a transient type of question; however, it has been asked me by one whom I have communicated with who has been involved intensely in the UFO portion of the phenomenon. If you deem it too transient or unimportant we'll skip it, but I have been asked how it is possible for the craft of the fourth-density to get here since it seems that as you approach the velocity of light the mass approaches infinity. My question would be why craft would be necessary at all?

Ra: I am Ra. You have asked several questions. We shall respond in turn.

Firstly, we agree that this material is transient.

Secondly, those for the most part coming from distant points, as you term them, do not need craft as you know them. The query itself requires understanding which you do not possess. We shall attempt to state what may be stated.

Firstly, there are a few third-density entities who have learned how to use craft to travel between star systems while experiencing the limitations you now understand. However, such entities have learned to use hydrogen in a way different from your understanding now. These entities still take quite long durations of time, as you measure it, to move about. However, these entities are able to use hypothermia to slow the physical and mental complex processes in order to withstand the duration of flight. Those such as are from Sirius are of this type. There are two other types.

One is the type which, coming from fourth, fifth, or sixth density in your own galaxy, has access to a type of energy system which uses the speed of light as a slingshot and thus arrives where it wishes without any perceptible time elapsed in your view.

The other type of experience is that of fourth, fifth, and sixth densities of other galaxies and some within your own galaxy which have learned the necessary disciplines of personality to view the universe as one being and, therefore, are able to proceed from locus to locus by thought alone, materializing the necessary craft, if you will, to enclose the light body of the entity.

Questioner: I assume that that latter type is the type we experience with the landings of the Orion group. Is this correct?

Ra: I am Ra. The Orion group is mixed between the penultimate and the latter groups.

Questioner: Why is a vehicle necessary for this transition? When you, as Ra, went to Egypt earlier you used bell-shaped craft, but you did this by thought. Can you tell me why you used a vehicle rather than just materializing the body?

Ra: I am Ra. The vehicle or craft is that thought-form upon which our concentration may function as motivator. We would not choose to use our mind/body/spirit complexes as the focus for such a working.

Questioner: Thank you. It seems to me, and you can tell me where I am going wrong with this statement, that we have seven bodies each corresponding to one of the seven colors of the spectrum and that energy that creates these seven bodies is a universal type of energy that streams into our planetary environment and comes in through the seven energy centers that we have called chakras to develop and perfect these bodies. Each of these bodies is somehow related to the mental configuration that we have and the perfection of these bodies and the total in-streaming of this energy is a function of this mental configuration, and through this mental configuration we may block, to some extent, the in-streamings of energy that created these seven bodies. Could you comment on where I am wrong and correct that which I have stated?

Ra: I am Ra. Your statement is substantially correct. To use the term "mental configuration" is to oversimplify the manners of blockage of in-streaming which occur in your density. The mind complex has a relationship to the spirit and body complexes which is not fixed. Thus blockages may occur betwixt spirit and mind, or body and mind, upon many different levels. We reiterate that each energy center has seven sub-colors, let us say, for convenience. Thus spiritual/mental blockages combined with mental/bodily blockages may affect each of the energy centers in several differing ways. Thus you may see the subtle nature of the balancing and evolutionary process.

Questioner: I am unsure as to whether this will provide an avenue of questioning that will be fruitful, but I will ask this question since it seems to me that there is a connection here.

On the back of the book, *Secrets Of The Great Pyramid*, there are several reproductions of Egyptian drawings or works, some showing birds flying over horizontal entities. Could you tell me what this is and if it has any relationship to Ra?

Ra: I am Ra. These drawings of which you speak are some of many which distort the teaching of our perception of death as the gateway to further experience. The distortions concern those considerations of specific nature as to processes of the so-called "dead" mind/body/spirit complex. This may be termed, in your philosophy, the distortion of Gnosticism: that is, the belief that one may achieve knowledge and a proper position by means of carefully perceived and accentuated movements, concepts, and symbols. In fact, the process of the physical death is as we have described before: one in which there is aid available and the only need at death is the releasing of that entity from its body by those around it and the praising of the process by those who grieve. By these means may the mind/body/spirit which has experienced physical death be aided, not by the various perceptions of careful and repeated rituals.

Questioner: You spoke at an earlier time of rotational speeds of energy centers. Am I correct in assuming that this is a function of the blockage of the energy center so that when it is less blocked, the speed of rotation is higher and the energy instreaming is greater?

Ra: I am Ra. You are partially correct. In the first three energy centers a full unblocking of this energy will create speeds of rotation. As the entity develops the higher energy centers, however, these centers will then begin to express their nature by forming crystal structures. This is the higher or more balanced form of activation of energy centers as the space/time nature of this energy is transmuted to the time/space nature of regularization and balance.

Questioner: What do you mean by crystal structures?

Ra: I am Ra. Each of the energy centers of the physical complex may be seen to have a distinctive crystalline structure in the more developed entity. Each will be somewhat different just as in your world no two snowflakes are alike. However, each is regular. The red energy center often is in the shape of the spoked wheel. The orange energy center in the flower shape containing three petals.

The yellow center again in a rounded shape, many faceted, as a star.

The green energy center sometimes called the lotus-shape, the number of points of crystalline structure dependent upon the strength of this center.

The blue energy center capable of having perhaps one hundred facets and capable of great flashing brilliance.

The indigo center a more quiet center which has the basic triangular or three-petalled shape in many, although some adepts who have balanced the lower energies may create more faceted forms.

The violet energy center is the least variable and is sometimes described in your philosophy as thousand-petalled as it is the sum of the mind/body/spirit complex distortion totality.

Questioner: Right now I feel a feeling at the indigo center. If this center were totally activated and not blocked at all, would I then feel nothing there?

Ra: I am Ra. This query, if answered, would infringe upon the Law of Confusion.

Questioner: Immediately after the death of the physical body you have stated that the primary activated body is the indigo, and you stated that it is the form-maker. Why is this so?

Ra: I am Ra. This will be the last full query of this session of working.

The indigo body may be seen to be an analog for intelligent energy. It is, in microcosm, the Logos. The intelligent energy of the mind/body/spirit complex totality draws its existence from intelligent infinity or the Creator. This Creator is to be understood, both in macrocosm and microcosm, to have, as we have said, two natures: the unpotentiated infinity which is intelligent; this is all that there is.

Free will has potentiated, both the Creator of us all and our selves as co-Creators with intelligent infinity which has will. This will may be drawn upon by the indigo or form-making body and its wisdom used to then choose the appropriate locus and type of experience which this co-Creator or sub-sub-Logos you call so carelessly a person will take.

I am Ra. This is the time for any brief queries.

Questioner: Is there anything that we can do to make the instrument more comfortable or to improve the contact?

Ra: I am Ra. All is well. You are conscientious. I leave you now, my brothers, in the love and in the light of the one infinite Creator. Go forth, then, rejoicing in the power and the peace of the one infinite Creator. Adonai.

Sunday Meditation
May 17, 1981

(Carla channeling)

[I am Hatonn,] and I greet you, my friends, in the love and in the light of our infinite Creator. It is a great privilege to speak with this group once again and we greet each of you.

We feel that it is not only our privilege, but also that which we must do in order to be of most service to you as you seek the truth, to speak to you about some of the aspects of love which are not recognized by your peoples and, therefore, which in many people's minds blur the image of love past all recognition in the cosmic sense of the word, if you would term it such. We speak to you, my friends, of the freedom of love. Many, many times it comes to the attention of all of those who seek that there is a concept called right and wrong, virtue or sin. This concept is much like one who willingly builds a jail house and locks himself within it.

My friends, we are not suggesting in any way that lawlessness prevails or that nihilism is an appropriate stance for those who seek the truth. We suggest only that that which is appropriate for each being is known to some portion of that being—is known within, my friends, and the entity which seeks the counsel of society, of accepted modes of conduct and behavior without discrimination, is like unto the willing prisoner.

Perfect love is perfect freedom. Perfect love is an entrance into a fresh field of flowers from the dark dungeon of fear. Love does not bind or unbind according to one man-made law. We speak to you in this wise, because we understand your desire to go further than the surface of seeking. Therefore, it is time, if you will allow us to use this term, for each to take the responsibility for the use of discrimination in the ascertaining of those actions which are appropriate, not in the eyes of others, or of a society which is faceless, but in the eyes of the self facing itself in meditation.

This is the law of love that binds and unbinds. This is the law, which when used correctly causes the entity to take upon itself the raiment of the co-creator that each of you really is. Only when you choose the responsibility of seeking in love your own answers, your own formulations of questions, can you become one who acts rather than one who reads. The abilities of one who allows the original Thought to energize his being are many. The ability to serve others is immensely enhanced when the seeker ceases pondering the rightness and wrongness of action, but rather takes it to meditation and releases it, allowing then the original Thought of love to have a clear channel through which to work.

My friends, as the new vibrations mount about you and you see both the very beautiful new things and those most disturbing of the older things occurring about you, it is very advantageous for you, if you would be of service, to take these thoughts into meditation with you, to seek what virtue there may be in them.

At this time, we would transfer this contact to the one known as L. I am Hatonn.

(L channeling)

I am Hatonn, and I greet you again, my brothers, in the love and light of our Creator. It is said that we are also very unsure of ourselves at times, yet we continue to speak on various subjects in an attempt to enlighten your selves. This, my brothers, is due to the fact that we also are continuing to grow, and although we continue to share what we have learned with you, so as to stimulate through service our own growth, we sometimes find that we have misconstrued or have acquired additional learning upon a particular subject, so we, in your [channeling] meditations, return to those subjects so as to clarify these new details. This, my brothers, is why we often seem to be repetitive and that as we discover additional nuances pertaining to a particular subject, such as love, or because we acquire new information concerning your selves, we assimilate the new data and in your [channeling] meditations return once again to what sometimes must seem a tedious subject.

My brothers, it is only that we deeply care for you and are concerned that you be given as much as is allowed to assist your growth prior to the impending events which we have already also discussed at great length and possibly to the point of tedium. We of Hatonn are grateful to you for the opportunity—correction—opportunities that you have presented to us for growth in service and we are aware that your motivation is very often on a subconscious level, partially the motive of service in return for us.

In your world there is a saying, "I'll scratch your back if you'll scratch mine." So it is with service. He who serves is served in turn by he who provides the opportunity for service, thus multiplying any goodness many times beyond the actual performance. When one loves another person, one performs a service in consciously defining the polarity of thought images referenced to the subject individual. The individual being loved has the opportunity for service in return, for if one is capable of stepping outside of the traditional love roles of your illusion and simply seeing love for the gift that it is, one realizes that the receiving of love can function in a manner so as to facilitate the growth and health of both entities involved.

For example, the person who consciously loves another without attempting to restrict the other or define areas of performance to assure themselves of a correct behavior pattern, directs his or her conscious mind to emit a force that produces beneficial energy vibrations, both in himself and the object of his or her affection. The one who receives this energy, if he or she receives it in a consciously non-judgmental fashion is allowed both to benefit himself from the quality of these vibrations, but also to benefit the original person in not resisting this flow of beneficial energy.

My brothers, on your planet, in your illusion, love has been construed as a system of barter for the accomplishment of selective reproduction. It is necessary to achieve an understanding that this is only a facet of your illusion, somewhat like a bad dream to one who has awakened. My brothers, we ask you to awaken to see that each individual on your planet and each entity throughout all dimensions and all universes is capable and deserving of loving and being loved, for this is the path which must be followed to attain the state of an illumined soul, as you would call it.

At this time we would transfer our contact to the instrument known as Jim. I am Hatonn.

(Jim channeling)

I am Hatonn, and am with this instrument and greet you once again in love and light. We would exercise this instrument at this time in the manner of offering ourselves for any questions which you might have to ask us. Are there any questions that we might attempt to answer?

Carla: Hatonn, in our prayers and meditations, is there any particular part of the planet that we should direct light to at this time?

I am Hatonn, and am aware of your question. We would suggest for those who wish to be of service in aiding the vibrations of your planet to simply visualize the entire planet in a state, initially, of darkness, seeing the planet as a blackened void. After a few moments in this visualization, then we would suggest that you begin to see points of light in different locations upon your planet beginning to shine. Continue this process until you see the light growing in size and in brilliance until finally you see the light completely encompassing your planet, until it glows as though it were a sun.

We suggest this simple method of meditation and visualization, for it is simple and accessible and also because it recognizes the unity of all peoples upon your planet, for those same areas of your planet are in great turmoil and other areas appear to be less tumultuous. Yet, each being upon your planet has those areas of darkness. Each area of your planet has those areas of darkness; each being and each location has those areas of light. For each particle of your creation is composed of polarities of the light and the dark; the positive, the negative; that which is called good and that which is called evil, and if all are indeed one, then all must be treated the same. Therefore, we would suggest this simple meditation for those who wish to increase the vibrations and be of service to the planet which you inhabit.

May we answer you further, my sister?

Carla: No thank you. That's fine.

We thank you for this opportunity to serve. May we attempt another answer to another question?

L: I have a question I'd like to ask, Hatonn. I have noticed in channeling that more and more often now I seem to receive pictures or concepts instead of words. I am interested in why I'm experiencing this effect. I'm also concerned as to whether I'm translating correctly what you're attempting to convey. Could you give me some information on that, please?

I am Hatonn, and am aware of your question. We of Hatonn, in transmitting our thoughts to those of your planet who are able to receive them, use the means by which we might be most effective. There are various means we use to achieve this contact. For some we use a word by word, or perhaps grouping of words, transmitted one or two at a time, which when spoken create what might be called a vacuum, which draws yet more of our word transmissions into the mind of the instrument.

There is another method of which you speak in which we transmit concepts, images or pictures into the mind of the instrument. In this way we short circuit, or shall we say to be more precise, we make a shortcut in the transmission of our concept, for we present it in a more holistic fashion and leave to the instrument the task of forming the words which will transmit the concept which we have projected to the instrument's mind.

In any method which we might use of making contact with an instrument, there is a possibility of distortion of concepts. In the method of which you have spoken and shown an interest and an ability, the chances, shall we say, to distort are greater than in the word by word transmission. Yet, we feel that for certain instruments [it] is more advantageous to use the concept method, for it gives a greater feeling of confidence to the instrument to have within his or her mind the parameters, shall we say, of the concepts that are being transmitted in the message which we intend.

We would assure you that though there is a greater possibility of distortion in this method, the distortion is not so as to detract from the message, for within your own being is the very same message which we seek to transmit, for we are all as one and within your being and the being of each entity upon your planet there is the connection which we of Hatonn have realized on a conscious level, the connection that brings us all together, as do the spokes of a wheel connect the rim to the hub. And this connection is that which might be called a channel which might convey information.

We of Hatonn consider that each who serves as instrument will provide part of the message which we convey. This might be looked upon, and correctly so, as a distortion. But it is a distortion which we consider to be beneficial, for it recognizes the divinity within each being and each being has something of value to offer each other being, and we of Hatonn, in transmitting these messages wish to recognize that fact. So we would suggest, my brother, that you not be concerned about distortions, for there will be distortions no matter what method is used.

May we answer you further?

L: No. You've answered my question. Thank you.

And we thank you. May we answer another question?

Carla: I have a question, but I'm not sure if you can answer it. Just say so if you can't. We've been receiving some material from a Confederation member named Ra, and I've noticed that the viewpoint of that material, being as they say, from sixth density, is somewhat different than your viewpoint, taking into account your viewpoint and adding to it. I wondered if you have access to the information of the higher densities than yourself or if you yourself are attempting, say as a fourth-density planetary being, to attempt to learn lessons that lie between your state of mind and the state of mind of Ra. Do you have teachers of sixth density, and is this information available to you?

I am Hatonn, and we shall attempt to answer in the best way possible for us to express this concept. We of Hatonn have achieved what you have called a social memory complex. This means that each of the individuals within our complex has at his disposal the complete knowledge of each other entity. But there are, shall we say, limits to what the entities within our complex have learned. We of Hatonn are of the density of love. This is the density which is directly above, shall we say, your own. We have available to us information from densities yet beyond our own, in manners similar to the method by which you now receive our contact.

We of Hatonn have, as a social memory complex and as individuals, we have teachers in densities advanced to our own, therefore, we have available to us information similar to that which you now receive through the contact known to you as Ra. We of Hatonn do not attempt in our contact with you to pass on the concepts which the entity known as Ra shares in its contact with you, for those concepts are to us lessons yet to be learned. When we make contact with your group, we attempt to share those lessons which we have learned by experience and therefore feel somewhat more able and confident in sharing. Were we to share information which has been transmitted to us by our teachers, we would be, so to speak, only telling tales, for these lessons we have yet to learn, but are being prepared in the learning by our teachers.

May we answer you further, my sister?

Carla: Yes, Hatonn. I understand completely and I'd like to make a statement and you tell me if it is true. The lesson that we would then draw from what you say is that we should not tell tales, but only speak of those things which we have experienced as true, not simply thought of as true. Is that correct?

I am Hatonn. In this area, my sister, we would agree with you in general and to be more specific we would also add that the sharing of any information, whether it be that which has been experienced and seated within your own being or that which you consider as possibilities, the sharing of any information must be on the level whereby those with whom you share it seek it, for any information shared of spiritual nature which has not been sought is as the pearl cast before the swine. And we do not mean by using this terminology from your holy works to denigrate those who do not seek the information which you share, but mean to create in your minds the image of the situation which you would be placing yourself in if you should share information which has not been sought, for those whom you would share this with would not understand it, would not seek it, and very likely would not appreciate it. And in this situation there can be the danger of what might be called alienation of affections or the reduction of the polarity of those who would share, whether sharing …

(Side one of tape ends.)

(Jim channeling)

I am Hatonn, and am once again with this instrument. Is there another question which we might attempt to answer?

L: I have two more questions, Hatonn. There are two entities that I have discussed with you to whom I have been bonded in some manner. I would like to know what density these entities are and what it is that they channel.

I am Hatonn, and am aware of your question, but we must suggest, my brother, that information of this type is not that which we might pass on, but we would suggest instead that if this be of value to you and of interest to you, it might best be sought as you meditate and then when the timing, shall we say, is correct, this information might be known from within and thereby the rights of free will might not be abridged, so to speak.

May we answer you further, my brother?

L: Yes. I have begun to believe that there is a timing necessary for the proper perception on my part of this information on this general subject. I have begun to feel that in striving, and possibly striving too early and too hard to learn, that I'm in effect trying to push a river upstream. Would you be willing to comment on this?

I am Hatonn. We would say only that which you have discovered yourself and that is that you are correct. The timing which you have begun to experience is that which will continue to make itself known to you. And though it might seem that you attempt to, as you put it, push the river upstream, that you will progress as your abilities allow and though you may seem, in your own thinking and feeling, to be somewhat out of kilter in your seeking from time to time, these are but the adjustments which are made from the inside out, shall we say, of your being. And as you continue in your seeking these adjustments, or ripples upon the pond of your mind, shall smooth and make room for more learning, for more experience, for more what is called catalyst upon your plane, and you shall progress as you are ready to progress.

May we answer you further, my brother?

L: No, you've answered me fully. I thank you.

Again, we thank you. Is there another question which we might attempt to answer?

(Pause)

I am Hatonn. Before we would leave this group we would pause for a moment so that our brother, Laitos, might pass among those gathered here and aid the deepening of the meditative state of any who would request this aid. We would pause at this time. I am Hatonn.

(Pause)

I am Hatonn. We feel a very great privilege to have been able to speak a few simple words to your group this evening. It is always a great honor when we are asked to speak with you. We hope in our simple sharing that we have helped you within your being to uncover yet one more aspect of that message which we so often bring, the message of love. Though we have spoken upon this message many, many times to this group, we feel it is a message which cannot be overdone, shall we say, for it is a message that upon you planet has seldom been clearly understood, and this we feel we understand, for always do we learn more about this concept and this message of love. And as we learn more, we feel it is an honor, but also a duty, shall we say, to share what we have learned with those who ask for what we have to share. Therefore, we hope that we will be asked in your future to share yet more of our understanding, for in such sharing all might increase the opportunity for growth.

We thank you many times over for allowing us the opportunity to share those few learnings and teachings which we have gained through our own experience. We are known to you as Hatonn and we leave you now in the love and in the light of the infinite Creator. Adonai.

(Carla channeling)

I am Oxal, and I greet this group also in the love and in the light of our infinite Creator. It is a distinct pleasure to speak with you and we come to exhort you, my brothers and my sisters, to exhort you as a parent a child. We have watched your peoples living the illusion as if it were reality and ignoring the brevity of this illusion. But you, my friends, do you wish to live like children? We come to ask you to meditate and seek as your higher self surely knows to do. We ask you, my friends, to avoid becoming so involved in this illusion. It is good to be a child. It is well to play, but it is well also, my friends, for beings which are infinite to look to that side of their nature. We cannot be eloquent, for only silence is eloquent. We can only urge you to see yourselves as those who take themselves seriously enough to do the work you came to do. Your illusion is beautiful my friends, and the work you came to do may seem to be a burden, but as the illusion lifts, which it will, my friends, you will discover that your true joy has always lain in the fullest knowledge possible of your infinite self.

It is said in your holy works, "Seek ye first the kingdom of heaven and all else shall be added unto you." What seek ye, my friends? I am with you at any time, and send you love and the light that we channel that is truly that of the Creator and in this love and this light and this infinity, we leave you. I am called Oxal. Adonai, my friends. Adonai vasu borragus. ☙

L/L Research

The Law of One, Book III, Session 52
May 19, 1981

Ra: I am Ra. I greet you in the love and in the light of the one infinite Creator. We communicate now.

Questioner: In the previous session you stated: "The other type of experience is the fourth, fifth, and sixth densities of other galaxies and some within your own galaxy which have learned necessary disciplines of personality to view the universe as one being are able to proceed from locus to locus by thought alone, materializing the necessary craft." I would like to ask you when you say fourth, fifth, and sixth densities of other galaxies, some within your own galaxy, are you stating here that more of the entities in other galaxies have developed the abilities of personality than have those in this galaxy for this type of travel? I am using the term galaxy with respect to the lenticular shape of billions of stars.

Ra: I am Ra. We have once again used a meaning for this term, galaxy, that does not lie within your vocabulary at this time, if you will call it so. We referred to your star system.

It is incorrect to assume that other star systems are more able to manipulate the dimensions than your own. It is merely that there are many other systems besides your own.

Questioner: Thank you. I think that possibly I am on an important point here because it seems to me that the great work in evolution is the discipline of personality, and it seems that we have two types of entities moving around the universe, one stemming from disciplines of personality, and the other stemming from what you call the slingshot effect. I won't even get into the sub-light speeds because I don't consider that too important. I only consider this material important because of the fact that we are considering disciplines of the personality.

Is the use of the slingshot effect for travel what you might call an intellectual or a left brain type of involvement of understanding rather than a right brain type?

Ra: I am Ra. Your perception on this point is extensive. You penetrate the outer teaching. We prefer not to utilize the terminology of right and left brain due to the inaccuracies of this terminology. Some functions are repetitive or redundant in both lobes, and further, to some entities the functions of the right and left are reversed. However, the heart of the query is worth some consideration.

The technology of which you, as a social complex, are so enamored at this time is but the birthing of the manipulation of the intelligent energy of the sub-Logos which, when carried much further, may evolve into technology capable of using the gravitic effects of which we spoke.

We note that this term is not accurate but there is no closer term. Therefore, the use of technology to manipulate that outside the self is far, far less of an aid to personal evolution than the disciplines of the mind/body/spirit complex resulting in the whole knowledge of the self in the microcosm and macrocosm.

To the disciplined entity, all things are open and free. The discipline which opens the universes opens also the gateways to evolution. The difference is that of choosing either to hitchhike to a place where beauty may be seen or to walk, step by step, independent and free in this independence to praise the strength to walk and the opportunity for the awareness of beauty.

The hitchhiker, instead, is distracted by conversation and the vagaries of the road and, dependent upon the whims of others, is concerned to make the appointment in time. The hitchhiker sees the same beauty but has not prepared itself for the establishment, in the roots of mind, of the experience.

Questioner: I would ask this question in order to understand the mental disciplines and how they evolve. Does fourth, fifth, and sixth-density positive or service-to-others orientation of social memory complexes use both the slingshot and the personality disciplines type of effect for travel or do they use only one?

Ra: I am Ra. The positively oriented social memory complex will be attempting to learn the disciplines of mind, body, and spirit. However, there are some which, having the technology available to use intelligent energy forces to accomplish travel, do so while learning the more appropriate disciplines.

Questioner: Then I am assuming that in the more positively oriented social memory complexes a much higher percentage of them use the personality disciplines for this travel. Is this correct?

Ra: I am Ra. This is correct. As positive fifth-density moves into sixth there are virtually no entities which any longer use outer technology for travel or communication.

Questioner: Could you give me the same information on the negatively oriented social memory complexes as to the ratios and as to how they use the slingshot effect or the disciplines of the personality for travel?

Ra: I am Ra. The fourth-density negative uses the slingshot gravitic light effect, perhaps 80% of its membership being unable to master the disciplines necessary for alternate methods of travel. In fifth-density negative approximately 50% at some point gain the necessary discipline to use thought to accomplish travel. As the sixth-density approaches, the negative orientation is thrown into confusion and little travel is attempted. What travel is done is perhaps 73% of light/thought.

Questioner: Is there any difference close to the end of fifth-density in the disciplines of personality between positive and negative orientation?

Ra: I am Ra. There are patent differences between the polarities but no difference whatsoever in the completion of the knowledge of the self necessary to accomplish this discipline.

Questioner: Am I correct, then, in assuming that discipline of the personality, knowledge of self, and control in strengthening of the will would be what any fifth-density entity would see as those things of importance?

Ra: I am Ra. In actuality these things are of importance in third through early seventh densities. The only correction in nuance that we would make is your use of the word, control. It is paramount that it be understood that it is not desirable or helpful to the growth of the understanding, may we say, of an entity by itself to control thought processes or impulses except where they may result in actions not consonant with the Law of One. Control may seem to be a short-cut to discipline, peace, and illumination. However, this very control potentiates and necessitates the further incarnative experience in order to balance this control or repression of that self which is perfect.

Instead, we appreciate and recommend the use of your second verb in regard to the use of the will. Acceptance of self, forgiveness of self, and the direction of the will; this is the path towards the disciplined personality. Your faculty of will is that which is powerful within you as co-Creator. You cannot ascribe to this faculty too much importance. Thus it must be carefully used and directed in service-to-others for those upon the positively oriented path.

There is great danger in the use of the will as the personality becomes stronger, for it may be used even subconsciously in ways reducing the polarity of the entity.

Questioner: I sense, possibly, a connection between what you just said and why so many Wanderers have selected the harvest time on this planet to incarnate. Am I correct?

Ra: I am Ra. It is correct that in the chance to remember that which has been lost in the forgetting there is a nimiety of opportunity for positive polarization. We believe this is the specific thrust of your query. Please ask further if it is not.

Questioner: I would just include the question as to why the time of harvest is selected by so many Wanderers as time for incarnation?

Ra: I am Ra. There are several reasons for incarnation during harvest. They may be divided by the terms self and other-self.

The overriding reason for the offering of these Brothers and Sisters of Sorrow in incarnative states is the possibility of aiding other-selves by the lightening of the planetary consciousness distortions and the probability of offering catalyst to other-selves which will increase the harvest.

There are two other reasons for choosing this service which have to do with the self.

The Wanderer, if it remembers and dedicates itself to service, will polarize much more rapidly than is possible in the far more etiolated realms of higher density catalyst.

The final reason is within the mind/body/spirit totality or the social memory complex totality which may judge that an entity or members of a societal entity can make use of third-density catalyst to recapitulate a learning/teaching which is adjudged to be less than perfect. This especially applies to those entering into and proceeding through sixth-density wherein the balance between compassion and wisdom is perfected.

Questioner: Thank you. Just as something that I am a little inquisitive about, but which is not of much importance, I would like to make a statement which I intuitively hunch. I may be wrong.

You were speaking of the slingshot effect and that term has puzzled me.

The only thing that I can see is that you must put energy into a craft until it approaches the velocity of light and this of course requires more and more energy. The time dilation occurs and it seems to me that it would be possible to, by moving at 90° to the direction of travel, somehow change this stored energy in its application of direction or sense so that you move out of space/time into time/space with a 90° deflection. Then the energy would be taken out in time/space and you would re-enter space/time at the end of this energy burst. Am I in any way correct on this?

Ra: I am Ra. You are quite correct as far as your language may take you and, due to your training, more able than we to express the concept. Our only correction, if you will, would be to suggest that the 90° of which you speak are an angle which may best be understood as a portion of a tesseract.

Questioner: Thank you. Just a little point that was bothering me of no real importance.

Is there then, from the point of view of an individual who wishes to follow the service-to-others path, anything of importance other than disciplines of personality, knowledge of self, and strengthening of will?

Ra: I am Ra. This is technique. This is not the heart. Let us examine the heart of evolution.

Let us remember that we are all one. This is the great learning/teaching. In this unity lies love. This is a great learn/teaching. In this unity lies light. This is the fundamental teaching of all planes of existence in materialization. Unity, love, light, and joy; this is the heart of evolution of the spirit.

The second-ranking lessons are learn/taught in meditation and in service. At some point the mind/body/spirit complex is so smoothly activated and balanced by these central thoughts or distortions that the techniques you have mentioned become quite significant. However, the universe, its mystery unbroken, is one. Always begin and end in the Creator, not in technique.

Questioner: In the previous session you mentioned the lightbringers from the octave. Am I to understand that those who provide the light for the graduation are of an octave above the one we experience? Could you tell me more about these lightbringers, who they are, etc.?

Ra: I am Ra. This will be the last full query of this working.

This octave density of which we have spoken is both omega and alpha, the spiritual mass of the infinite universes becoming one central sun or Creator once again. Then is born a new universe, a new infinity, a new Logos which incorporates all that the Creator has experienced of Itself. In this new octave there are also those who wander. We know very little across the boundary of octave except that these beings come to aid our octave in its Logos completion. Is there any brief query which you have at this time?

Questioner: Only is there anything that we can do to make the instrument more comfortable or to improve the contact?

Ra: I am Ra. This instrument has some distortion in the area of the lungs which has been well compensated for by the position of the physical complex.

All is well.

We leave you, my friends, in the love and in the light of the one infinite Creator. Go forth, therefore, rejoicing in the power and in the peace of the one infinite Creator. Adonai.

Sunday Meditation
May 24, 1981

(L channeling)

I am Hatonn, and I greet you in the love and light of the infinite Creator. My brothers, it is with great pleasure that we welcome here this night those of you who are new to these communications or have not been in communication with us for some time. It is always a pleasure to encounter again or for the first time our beloved friends. We of Hatonn are grateful for the opportunity to speak to this assembly, for it is so seldom on your planet that we are capable of reaching the minds and hearts of its inhabitants. The message we bring you is not our own, but rather a reflection of that message which springs from your own hearts, for it is merely a repetition of the knowledge within your own souls that one might refer to as having been misplaced or mislaid. Therefore, my brothers, although we are grateful for the love with which you greet us, be aware that we are not teachers or doers but rather beloved friends who would assist you, if allowed, to regain and recover the knowledge within your own beings.

It is frequent that we are called upon to express our messages, but the calling is often erratic in that those beings who summon our message often do not care for the content and draw away from us, seeking instead the pleasures of the illusion within which you all function to a greater or lesser extent. We therefore, my brothers, encourage that you seek further contact, that you may both develop your own perceptive abilities and also affect more greatly the polarity of your planetary sphere. Your actions, my brothers, affect your planetary sphere more strongly than those of the group whom we may describe as undecided, in that they have not selected yet a polarity of striving. Therefore, your own striving in meditation and service-oriented living is a further service to your planetary brothers in and of itself, as it affects their lives.

It is important that you be aware of this in that the coming events affecting your planet will tend to dismay and panic those beings of your race who are not aware of the causes or intentions behind the cataclysmic events that cast them as twigs into the maul of a maelstrom. As they seek frantically for a point of security or stability within the whirlpool of their lives, they will more and more readily perceive yourselves as steadfast and will hopefully seek to understand and emulate your own efforts toward spiritual growth. Your example, my brothers, has always been pointed out to you as the most efficient teacher, yet in the times to come this will be more and more significant, for events will occur that will tend to encourage more and more of your race to polarize in one direction or the other, thus, hopefully enabling them to achieve inclusion in the harvest.

Sunday Meditation, May 24, 1981

At this time we would attempt to continue through another instrument. I am Hatonn.

(Carla channeling)

I am Hatonn, and I am now with this instrument. Again I greet you, my friends, in the love and light of the infinite Creator. To continue, my friends, how often have you acted and thought, on the basis of the illusion, that there is such a thing as being justified? How many times have you condemned yourself because you were not justified in your own mind? When one has not sufficiently sought to know the self, sought to know the Creator and the Creator within themselves, one is liable to accept what might be called a belief that those ethics and dogmas of your peoples have an independent propriety. How much sadness, my friends, guilt, grief and consternation has been caused because your peoples do not go within to seek for what is right for them, because the events of the days act upon them, the only measuring stick is the degree of justification in terms of ethics or religion which is accepted outwardly by your peoples.

My friends, to the best of our understanding, there is no justification. You are never justified. You cannot ever be justified, nor can you be wronged, nor can you wrong except intentionally. When you think to yourself, "Ah yes, I shall drink a toast to myself. Such and such an action was justified," step back, my friends, and see the perfection that created both yourself and whatever else seems to be in conflict with yourself. What is it, my friends, that requires that you be justified? What is it but a lack of seeking to know the truth, that in reality disharmony is not necessary, that in reality those things about you are perfect as they are, without justification.

Within your illusion, my friends, there is and there will be much that has no justification. But you, my friends, may transcend that illusion by seeking within yourself a wider perspective, a deeper realization. There will be, just as there have been in the past, times when in moments of decision there is no guideline for action; times when that which your society labels justified does not seem appropriate; times when your religious teachings, as sincerely and earnestly meant to help as they have been, do not seem appropriate; times when there is no outward source for peace and for the feeling that you as a spirit, as a soul, have done as well as you can.

The one known as Jesus said, in your holy works, "I am the way, the truth, the life. No one comes to the Father but by me." This saying, my friends, has been much misunderstood and is very central to that which we have to say. This entity known to you as Jesus often went to be by himself, to seek within himself that knowledge which is not justification, but rather the knowledge of love, and when he became one with that love he also became one with the knowledge of what creative actions he might take to be in harmony with the rhythms of his particular way of existence, his particular means of sharing that love among your peoples in what you call your life. And when this entity was in that state of love, he was one in consciousness with the Creator, with love itself. And you also, my friends, when you find that consciousness, when you find that selfhood, that "I" which is beyond justification, concerns and worries, that "I" which may move mountains, you too will be the way, for love is the way, the truth. For is not love the truth? And the life? And you will be one with the Father, for there is no road to the Father but by love.

As you move from moment to moment, we hope that you may in your day never be far from the realization of this love, never be too far from the means to find the gateway to this paradise. For never will others find justice in all that you do and never will you find justice in those things that others do. This is not the way of the illusion, but in the knowledge of love there comes a peace of the feeling that all things are love and that all things are of one Creation …

(A telephone rings.)

I am Hatonn. We are sorry for the delay, but this instrument's concentration was somewhat disturbed by her realization that she had forgotten to do some duties to make this meditation more smooth. My friends, it is this kind of thinking of which we are speaking. For a disturbance to occur may not be justified, but that it does occur is a perfect part of a creation of love. When these things occur, when you feel that you have failed, when you feel that you are not justified, step back, my friends, and know that it does not matter. Failure; success; justification. These are illusions and dreams within a dream. Know yourself, then, as one who is learning from failure, from success, from striving and from not striving, and accept all those things in yourself and in others.

At this time we would pause that the one known as Laitos may pass among you and offer you the conditioning wave that will enable you to become somewhat more aware of our presence. Merely mentally request that we be with you, for we would not interfere with free will, but are always happy to aid in the deepening of the meditative state. We shall resume through another channel. I am Hatonn.

(Jim channeling)

I am Hatonn, and am with this instrument and I greet you once again in the love and the light of our infinite Creator. It is our privilege at this time to offer ourselves in the manner of answering questions which you may have. Are there any questions which we might attempt to answer through this instrument?

L: I have a question, Hatonn. Earlier this morning while sleeping I had a rather unusual dream. Would you care to comment on that?

I am Hatonn, and am aware of your question. We would suggest that in dreams of this nature that you consider carefully the message which you feel through your own feelings in response to the dream. Your dreams are often ways in which another part of yourself chooses to express self to you, to gain an avenue of your attention which normally is not open to it while you are in your waking state. In this general way, we are able to respond to such a question. To speak to the specific nature and content of the dream we feel would be an infringement upon your free will, but wish to say that the significance in your dream is as you perceive it.

May we answer you further, my brother?

L: No, that answers it well. Thank you.

We thank you. Is there another question which we might attempt to answer?

Carla: Could you give some sort of probability for the Mt. St. Helen and that chain of volcanic openings in the earth having problems again in the next few months? I've been having some intuitive feelings about that. And if so, would it aid if we meditated?

I am Hatonn, and we would suggest, my sister, that in instances such as the eruptions of volcanoes, the occurrence of earthquakes and other natural phenomena which might be viewed as catastrophic in nature, all these are but repercussions or reflections, you might say, of the consciousness of your peoples which has been expressed upon your planet for many centuries, for the friction which has occurred between your peoples has, in its very being, and is in its very being, a vibration of a nature which penetrates the planet on which you live. And as you approach the time which has been called the time of harvest, the energies which have been invested in your planetary sphere will be coming full circle, so to speak, and be returning, so that those who inhabit your planet at this time might experience the culmination of this cycle in every degree.

The likelihood of such occurrences to continue is very great; to state when such might occur is very difficult. For those, such as yourself, who are interested in alleviating some of the difficulties that ensue when such occurrences happen, we would suggest the healing meditation which we have mentioned in other sessions. To simply restate, we might say, that in your state of meditation you might see your planet as it is, with many fissures and openings, scars, and wounds, that there might be seen here and there darkness and ignorance, that this might be held in your vision for a few moments and then you might see your planet beginning to shine with a light emanating from various locations and continue to see the light spreading until your planet glows as a sun. In this way you will lend the healing energies of your visualization to the healing of the energies which have so long been festering within the material part of your planet.

May we answer you further, my sister?

Carla: No, thanks, Hatonn. I think I got it this time.

Again, we thank you. Is there another question which we might attempt to answer?

L: Yes. I have a question concerning healing, especially in light of your previous discussion of justification. It would seem to me that some lessons I've been receiving recently concerning healing would indicate that there are instances where it is appropriate to either heal or refrain from healing and that an individual would intuitively know when it would be appropriate, but that my previously held concept that healing impartially without perception of the results of the healing is less correct. Let's see if I can rephrase my question. Could you consider that an accurate interpretation of the lesson that has been presented to me lately? Am I perceiving it correctly?

I am Hatonn. And we would say, my brother that, in general, you have perceived the process of healing, to the best of our understanding, in a correct manner. To further explicate, we may say that to heal without the permission of the one to be healed is not permitted, or shall we say, advisable, and we may further add that in many cases, most cases, not possible, for the one who is to be healed must not only give permission to be healed, but must also take part in the process by opening the self to the energies of a healing nature which are being prepared for that entity and which will be transmitted through the channel known as the healer.

Because each entity is part of a Oneness, each entity participates in the transfer of energy from one part of the Oneness to another. The healer, so called, is the means by which this energy is transmitted. The one to be healed must recognize that there is, within its own being, that part which is not in balance. This part must be accepted, this part must be recognized, and this part must be forgiven for its imbalance. Then, with this state of openness created within the one to be healed, then may the energy from the infinite Creator flow through the channel to the one to be healed, and then may the healing process occur.

May we answer you further, my brother?

L: Yes. There are two other areas I would like for you to address on that subject, if you will please. …

(Side one of tape ends.)

L: … First is the area of healing on second-dimensional beings, for instance, an injured animal. Second area I would ask you to address is the area of attempting to channel healing for an unconscious human being.

I am Hatonn, and we may answer you, my brother, by saying that in both cases, since conscious consent cannot be given, then the abilities of the healer must include being able to communicate with the higher self of each entity. This is especially true in the case of the second-density being, for it is not usually the case that clear communication can be achieved with those entities who do not have the, shall we say, complex of mind functioning or activated for communication, but in both cases it is necessary for the healer to communicate, preferably in the state of meditation or prayer, with the higher self of the entity to be healed and when the confirmation from the higher self is received, then may the healing process proceed.

May we answer you further, my brother?

L: No. You've clarified the areas that I needed [clarified]. Thank you.

Again, we thank you. Is there another question which we might attempt to answer?

Carla: Well, I had one but now I have two. The first one was just—I was kind of curious—it seems to me that some people have a touch with plants or animals that quiets the animal or plants grow well for that person and not for other people. And it's almost an instantaneous state of communication between them and I was wondering if perhaps this meditative state didn't have to be formal, but perhaps in some healers that are just gifted that way, could almost be communicated, almost … through the fingers—instantaneously.

I am Hatonn, and we would answer you, my sister, by saying that in some instances, rare though they be, such entities exist, that by their very presence and their very being, they heal those who are round about them who may not consciously ask to be healed, but who subconsciously, shall we say, recognize the presence of one who can heal.

May we answer you further, my sister?

Carla: Yes. The other question was considerably different. I have been watching with some passing interest the downfall of the world and really glad it's happening so slowly because otherwise I'd kind of get lost, but anyway, the news keeps being very bad and you haven't been gone for quite awhile and I was pondering why it was that the Confederation and you hadn't pow-wowed and sent you off to send love to some world leader or another because so many of them seem bloody-minded right now. And it occurred to me that it was possible that you had done, or perhaps people in the Confederation in general, had worked enough with the people on Earth that they were beginning to lose some of their polarity, because so much had been rejected, so much love had been rejected. I was wondering if this was true and if this was why you'd given up this tactic and just fallen back on talking with groups like ours.

I am Hatonn, and to this matter we would say that fortunately within the Confederation there are many entities, many planetary entities such as ourselves, who are able to perform the tasks which many times, as you know, we of Hatonn have been asked to perform, that being the sending of love to certain areas and leaders of your planet to lessen the intensities and reduce the likelihood of the outbreak of war or hostilities. It is unfortunate that we observe that there are no fewer intense areas upon your planet than there have been in the recent past. At the present there are many areas which present the likelihood of the outbreak of hostilities. These areas are receiving aid from other entities within the Confederation. We of Hatonn have served in this capacity many times and we anticipate, without being pessimistic, that we shall be asked once again at some point in the future to serve in this capacity.

May we answer you further, my sister?

Carla: Just to clear up the part of the query, do you lose polarity when the love is sent back to you without being used or is it just a service that you're not attached to the outcome of and therefore you don't lose any positive polarity, no matter what happens?

I am Hatonn, and your assumption is correct that we of Hatonn do not lose our polarity when we, shall we say in your terms, may fail at the attempt to send love and experience its reflection instead, but we may also say, in greater terms, that there is no such thing as failure, for in the attempt to be of service there are still many who are served, for love is not particular in whom it seeks for its resting, shall we say. And though the entities whom we have, shall we say, targeted for our love may not accept it, still the love is sent and still some part of the Creator receives.

May we answer you further, my sister?

Carla: No, thank you.

We thank you. Is there another question which we might attempt to answer?

(Pause)

I am Hatonn. Once again may we say it has been a great privilege to be able to address your group this evening. We hope that in some small way our simple message has made a spot or a place of love a bit larger in your being. We feel it is a great privilege to be asked to join you in your meditations. We of Hatonn are beings of service; to serve another part of the Creator we view as the only reason for being, for the Creator is all that there is. We leave you now in the love and the light of the infinite Creator. We are known to you as Hatonn. Adonai vasu borragus. ☥

The Law of One, Book III, Session 53
May 25, 1981

Ra: I am Ra. I greet you in the love and in the light of the one infinite Creator. We communicate now.

Questioner: I would first like to ask what is the instrument's condition and then ask two questions for her. She would like to know if she can now do one exercise period per day, and also is the pain she feels prior to doing a session due to an Orion attack?

Ra: I am Ra. The instrument's condition is as previously stated. In answer to the question of exercise, now that the intensive period is over, this instrument may, if it chooses, exercise one period rather than two. In scanning this instrument's physical complex distortions we find the current period of exercise at the limit of this instrument's strength. This is well in the long run due to a cumulative building up of the vital energies. In the short run it is wearying to this entity. Thus we suggest the entity be aware of our previous admonitions regarding other aids to appropriate bodily distortions. In answer to the second query we may say that the physical complex difficulties prior to contact with our social memory complex are due to the action of the subconscious will of the instrument. This will is extremely strong and requires the mind/body/spirit complex to reserve all available physical and vital energies for the contact. Thus the discomforts are experienced due to the dramatic distortion towards physical weakness while this energy is diverted. The entity is, it may be noted, also under psychic attack, and this intensifies pre-existing conditions and is responsible for the cramping and the dizziness as well as mind complex distortions.

Questioner: Thank you. I would like to know if *(name)* may attend one of these sessions in the very near future?

Ra: I am Ra. The mind/body/spirit complex, *(name)*, belongs with this group in the spirit and is welcome. You may request that special meditative periods be set aside until the entity sits with this working. We might suggest that a photograph of the one known as *(name)* be sent to this entity with his writing upon it indicating love and light. This held while meditating will bring the entity into peaceful harmony with each of you so that there be no extraneous waste of energy while greetings are exchanged between two entities, both of whom have a distortion towards solitude and shyness, as you would call it. The same might be done with a photograph of the entity, *(name)*, for the one known as *(name)*.

Questioner: Thank you. During my trip to Laramie certain things became apparent to me with respect to dissemination of the first book of the Law of One to those who have had experiences with UFOs and other Wanderers, and I will have to ask some questions now that I may have to include in Book One to eliminate a misunderstanding that I am perceiving as a possibility in Book One. Therefore, these questions, although for the most part transient, are aimed at eliminating certain distortions with respect to the understanding of the material in Book One. I hope that I am using the correct approach here. You may not be able to answer some of them, but that's all right. We'll just go on to others then if you can't answer the ones I ask.

Can you tell me of the various techniques used by the service-to-others positively oriented Confederation contacts with the people of this planet, the various forms and techniques of making contact?

Ra: I am Ra. We could.

Questioner: Would you do this please?

Ra: I am Ra. The most efficient mode of contact is that which you experience at this space/time. The infringement upon free will is greatly undesired. Therefore, those entities which are Wanderers upon your plane of illusion will be the only subjects for the thought projections which make up the so-called "close encounters" and meetings between positively oriented social memory complexes and Wanderers.

Questioner: Could you give me an example of one of these meetings between a social memory complex and a Wanderer as to what the Wanderer would experience?

Ra: I am Ra. One such example of which you are familiar is that of the one known as Morris.[1] In this case the previous contact which other entities in this entity's circle of friends experienced was negatively oriented. However, you will recall that the entity, Morris, was impervious to this contact and could not see, with the physical optical apparatus, this contact.

However, the inner voice alerted the one known as Morris to go by itself to another place and there an entity with the thought-form shape and appearance of the other contact appeared and gazed at this entity, thus awakening in it the desire to seek the truth of this occurrence and of the experiences of its incarnation in general.

The feeling of being awakened or activated is the goal of this type of contact. The duration and imagery used varies depending upon the subconscious expectations of the Wanderer which is experiencing this opportunity for activation.

Questioner: In a "close encounter" by a Confederation type of craft I am assuming that this "close encounter" is with a thought-form type of craft. Have Wanderers within the past few years had "close encounters" with landed thought-form type of craft?

Ra: I am Ra. This has occurred although it is much less common than the Orion type of so-called "close encounter." We may note that in a universe of unending unity the concept of a "close encounter" is humorous, for are not all encounters of a nature of self with self? Therefore, how can any encounter be less than very, very close?

Questioner: Well, talking about this type of encounter of self to self, have any Wanderers of a positive polarization ever had a so-called "close encounter" with the Orion or negatively oriented polarization?

Ra: I am Ra. This is correct.

Questioner: Why does this occur?

Ra: I am Ra. When it occurs it is quite rare and occurs either due to the Orion entities' lack of perception of the depth of positivity to be encountered or due to the Orion entities' desire to, shall we say, attempt to remove this positivity from this plane of existence. Orion tactics normally are those which choose the simple distortions of mind which indicate less mental and spiritual complex activity.

Questioner: I have become aware of a very large variation in the contact with individuals. Could you give me general examples of the methods used by the Confederation to awaken or partially awaken the Wanderers they contact?

Ra: I am Ra. The methods used to awaken Wanderers are varied. The center of each approach is the entrance into the conscious and subconscious in such a way as to avoid causing fear and to maximize the potential for an understandable subjective experience which has meaning for the entity. Many such occur in sleep; others in the midst of many activities during the waking hours. The approach is flexible and does not necessarily include the "close encounter" syndrome as you are aware.

---

[1] This refers to Case #1 in *Secrets of the UFO*, by D. T. Elkins with Carla L. Rueckert, Louisville, KY, L/L Research, 1976, p. 10-11.

Questioner: What about the physical examination syndrome. How does that relate to Wanderers and Confederation and Orion contacts?

Ra: I am Ra. The subconscious expectations of entities cause the nature and detail of thought-form experience offered by Confederation thought-form entities. Thus if a Wanderer expects a physical examination, it will perforce be experienced with as little distortion towards alarm or discomfort as is allowable by the nature of the expectations of the subconscious distortions of the Wanderer.

Questioner: Well, are those who are taken on both Confederation and Orion craft then experiencing a seeming physical examination?

Ra: I am Ra. Your query indicates incorrect thinking. The Orion group uses the physical examination as a means of terrifying the individual and causing it to feel the feelings of an advanced second-density being such as a laboratory animal. The sexual experiences of some are a sub-type of this experience. The intent is to demonstrate the control of the Orion entities over the Terran inhabitant.

The thought-form experiences are subjective and, for the most part, do not occur in this density.

Questioner: Well, we have a large spectrum of entities on Earth with respect to harvestability, both positively oriented and negatively oriented. Would the Orion group target in on the ends of this spectrum, both positively and negatively oriented, for contact with Earth entities?

Ra: I am Ra. This query is somewhat difficult to accurately answer. However, we shall attempt to do so.

The most typical approach of Orion entities is to choose what you might call the weaker-minded entity that it might suggest a greater amount of Orion philosophy to be disseminated.

Some few Orion entities are called by more highly polarized negative entities of your space/time nexus. In this case they share information just as we are now doing. However, this is a risk for the Orion entities due to the frequency with which the harvestable negative planetary entities then attempt to bid and order the Orion contact just as these entities bid planetary negative contacts. The resulting struggle for mastery, if lost, is damaging to the polarity of the Orion group.

Similarly, a mistaken Orion contact with highly polarized positive entities can wreak havoc with Orion troops unless these Crusaders are able to depolarize the entity mistakenly contacted. This occurrence is almost unheard of. Therefore, the Orion group prefers to make physical contact only with the weaker-minded entity.

Questioner: Then in general we could say that if an individual has a "close encounter" with a UFO or any other type experience that seems to be UFO-related, he must look to the heart of the encounter and the effect upon him to determine whether it was Orion or Confederation contact. Is this correct?

Ra: I am Ra. This is correct. If there is fear and doom, the contact was quite likely of a negative nature. If the result is hope, friendly feelings, and the awakening of a positive feeling of purposeful service-to-others, the marks of Confederation contact are evident.

Questioner: Thank you. I did not wish to create the wrong impression with the material that we are including in Book One. I may find it necessary to add some of this material. As I say, I know that it is transient, but I believe it is necessary for a full understanding or, shall I say, a correct approach to the material.

I'll ask a few questions here, but if you do not care to answer them we'll save them. I would like to ask, however, if you can tell me what, for the most part, the Confederation entities look like?

Ra: I am Ra. The fourth-density Confederation entity looks variously depending upon the, shall we say, derivation of its physical vehicle.

Questioner: Do some of them look just like us? Could they pass for Earth people?

Ra: I am Ra. Those of this nature are most often fifth-density.

Questioner: I assume that the same answer would apply to the Orion group. Is this correct?

Ra: I am Ra. This is correct.

Is there any other query of a brief nature we may answer?

Questioner: I apologize for asking many transient questions during this session. I felt it necessary to include some of this material so that those Wanderers and others reading the first book of THE

LAW OF ONE would not get the wrong impression with respect to their experiences in contacts. I am sorry for any problems that I might have caused.

I will just ask if there is anything that we can do to aid the contact or to aid the instrument?

Ra: I am Ra. The instrument is well. Please guard your alignments carefully. We leave you now, my friends, in the love and in the light of the one infinite Creator. Go forth, therefore, rejoicing in the power and the peace of the infinite Creator. Adonai.

L/L Research is a subsidiary of Rock Creek Research & Development Laboratories, Inc.

P.O. Box 5195
Louisville, KY 40255-0195

L/L Research

www.llresearch.org

Rock Creek is a non-profit corporation dedicated to discovering and sharing information which may aid in the spiritual evolution of humankind.

ABOUT THE CONTENTS OF THIS TRANSCRIPT: This telepathic channeling has been taken from transcriptions of the weekly study and meditation meetings of the Rock Creek Research & Development Laboratories and L/L Research. It is offered in the hope that it may be useful to you. As the Confederation entities always make a point of saying, please use your discrimination and judgment in assessing this material. If something rings true to you, fine. If something does not resonate, please leave it behind, for neither we nor those of the Confederation would wish to be a stumbling block for any.

© 2009 L/L Research

The Law of One, Book V, Session 53, Fragment 32
May 25, 1981

Jim: We have omitted the name of the person contacted in this query in Session 53 because we still would not want to be part of reducing the polarity of those of Ra. We would, however, like to share the rest of the question and answer because it seems to us to be a good illustration of the general principles that extraterrestrials of the positive polarity utilize in their face-to-face encounters with the population of our planet.

In the spring of 1981 Don traveled by himself to Laramie, Wyoming to give a talk on the Law of One at one of Leo Sprinkle's UFO contactee conferences. The cause of his sickness during that conference and the aid of a support group are interesting points gleaned from that experience. Again, we see the desire not to abridge free will paramount in Ra's answer. The answer was possible because Don had already reached the same general conclusion in his own thinking.

The last question and answer in this section give an interesting perspective on the phenomenon of ball lightning. When Carla was a small child a ball of what looked to be lightning came in through the window, rolled around her crib and left through the same window. When Don was a young child, he had a similar experience.

Carla: It would seem that once any seeker dedicates herself to following the path towards the Creator that has opened before her awakening gaze, odd coincidences and events mount up rapidly. The silver flecks were first noticed by Andrija Puharich, as he and Uri Geller worked together. They might be strewn around a hotel room's rug, showing up overnight. After Don and I made contact with Puharich in 1974, and began working with him from time to time, I began getting them on my face and upper body. We got glitter of all the kinds we could find and compared them. The sparkles on my face were not the shape of any of the manufactured kinds. When the contact with those of Ra began, silver flecks started showing up much more frequently. This little phenomenon ended when Donald died in 1984. However, we do continue to be blessed frequently with Ra's other form of saying hello: the hawk. We actually have a family of hawks nesting in our trees for the second year! And often, when Jim and I are discussing something, we will get a hawk sighting just when we come to a decision. It always feels great to see this sign of Love.

Everyone will have his own set of these little signals that say "you are on the beam" or "perhaps not." As illogical as this sounds, we encourage you to note these coincidences when they begin to repeat. They are a definite form of communication with spirit energies that are benign and loving, as far as we can tell.

Our association with Leo Sprinkle is long-standing. This courageous researcher became interested in UFO phenomena when asked to participate as hypnotist in the research being done on a UFO contactee. He worked with many such contactees through the years, and eventually founded a research organization which holds a yearly Rocky Mountain Conference for UFO contactees. It is a good support group for these witnesses to the unusual. In 1975, we spent an hilarious weekend at a UFO convention held in Fort Smith, Arkansas, working on a movie together. (The movie, The Force Beyond, turned out so badly that Don renamed it The Farce Beyond) Leo was hypnotizing a UFO witness, Don and I were consultants on the script and he obtained most of the psychics and witnesses that were in the film. When Leo did the actual hypnosis, things went wrong repeatedly with equipment and so forth, and it was midnight before we sat down to eat. I asked him how he was holding up. Completely deadpan, he dropped his head on the table in front of him as though poleaxed. It was a delightful moment after a long day.

Since Don and I began talking about these experiences with light coming to greet us, seemingly, we have heard from many others to whom this has also occurred. It is a marvelous thing to ponder. Are these the bodies we shall use to experience a higher density? They are most fair and pure.

Session 53, May 25, 1981

Questioner: First I will ask if you could tell me the affiliation of the entities who contacted. (name).

Ra: I am Ra. This query is marginal. We will make the concession towards information with some loss of polarity due to free will being abridged. We request that questions of this nature be kept to a minimum.

The entities in this and some other vividly remembered cases are those who, feeling the need to plant Confederation imagery in such a way as not to abrogate free will, use the symbols of death, resurrection, love, and peace as a means of creating, upon the thought level, the time/space illusion of a systematic train of events which give the message of love and hope. This type of contact is chosen by careful consideration of Confederation members which are contacting an entity of like home vibration, if you will. This project then goes before the Council of Saturn and, if approved, is completed. The characteristics of this type of contact include the nonpainful nature of thoughts experienced and the message content which speaks not of doom but of the new dawning age.

Questioner: It is not necessary that I include the information that you just gave in the book to accomplish my purpose. In order to save your polarity, shall we say, I can keep that as private material if you wish. Do you wish for me to keep it unpublished?

Ra: I am Ra. That which we offer you is freely given and subject only to your discretion.

Questioner: I thought you would say that. In that case can you tell me anything of the "blue book" mentioned by (name) in that case?

Ra: I am Ra. No.

Questioner: Can you tell me why (name) has so many silver flecks on her?

Ra: I am Ra. This is infringement. No.

Questioner: Thank you. Can you tell me why I got sick during Carl Rushkey's talk?

Ra: I am Ra. We scan your thoughts. They are correct and therefore we do not infringe by confirming them. The space/time of your allotted speaking was drawing near and you came under Orion attack due to the great desire of some positively oriented entities to become aware of the Law of One. This may be expected especially when you are not in a group lending strength to each other.

Questioner: Thank you. Can you comment on my and the instrument's, if she approves, so-called ball of lightening experiences as a child?

Ra: I am Ra. This will be the last query of this working.

You were being visited by your people to be wished well. ❧

The Law of One, Book III, Session 54
May 29, 1981

Ra: I am Ra. I greet you in the love and in the light of the one infinite Creator. We communicate now.

Questioner: I would like to trace the energy that I assume comes from the Logos. I will make a statement and let you correct me and expand on my concept.

From the Logos comes all frequencies of radiation of light. These frequencies of radiation make up all of the densities of experience that are created by that Logos. I am assuming that the planetary system of our sun, in all of its densities, is the total of the experience created by our sun as a Logos. Is this correct?

Ra: I am Ra. This is correct.

Questioner: I am assuming that the different frequencies are separated, as we have said, into the seven colors, and I am assuming that each of these colors may be the basic frequency for a sub-Logos of our sun Logos and that a sub-Logos or, shall we say, an individual may activate any one of these basic frequencies or colors and use the body that is generated from the activation of the frequency or color. Is this correct?

Ra: I am Ra. If we grasp your query correctly this is not correct in that the sub-sub-Logos resides, not in dimensionalities, but only in co-Creators, or mind/body/spirit complexes.

Questioner: What I meant was that a mind/body/spirit complex can then have any body activated that is one of the seven rays. Is this correct?

Ra: I am Ra. This is correct in the same sense as it is correct to state that any one may play a complex instrument which develops an euphonious harmonic vibration complex such as your piano and can play this so well that it might offer concerts to the public, as you would say. In other words, although it is true that each true color vehicle is available potentially there is skill and discipline needed in order to avail the self of the more advanced or lighter vehicles.

Questioner: I have made these statements to get to the basic question which I wish to ask. It is a difficult question to ask.

We have, coming from the sub-Logos we call our sun, intelligent energy. This intelligent energy is somehow modulated or distorted so that it ends up as a mind/body/spirit complex with certain distortions of personality which are necessary for the mind/body/spirit complex or mental portion of that complex to undistort in order to conform once more with the original intelligent energy.

First, I want to know if my statement on that is correct, and, secondly, I want to know why this is the way that it is and if there is any answer other than the first distortion of the Law of One for this?

Ra: I am Ra. This statement is substantially correct. If you will penetrate the nature of the first distortion in its application of self knowing self, you may begin to distinguish the hallmark of an infinite Creator, variety. Were there no potentials for misunderstanding and, therefore, understanding, there would be no experience.

Questioner: OK. Once a mind/body/spirit complex becomes aware of this process it then decides that in order to have the full abilities of the Creator it is necessary to reharmonize its thinking with the Original Creative Thought in precise vibration or frequency of vibration. In order to do this it is necessary to discipline the personality so that it precisely conforms to the Original Thought, and this is broken into seven areas of discipline each corresponding to one of the colors of the spectrum. Is this correct?

Ra: I am Ra. This statement, though correct, bears great potential for being misunderstood. The precision with which each energy center matches the Original Thought lies not in the systematic placement of each energy nexus but rather in the fluid and plastic placement of the balanced blending of these energy centers in such a way that intelligent energy is able to channel itself with minimal distortion.

The mind/body/spirit complex is not a machine. It is rather what you might call a tone poem.

Questioner: Do all mind/body/spirit complexes in the entire creation have seven energy centers?

Ra: I am Ra. These energy centers are in potential in macrocosm from the beginning of creation by the Logos. Coming out of timelessness, all is prepared. This is so of the infinite creation.

Questioner: Then I will assume that the Creator in its intelligent appraisal of the ways of knowing Itself, created the concept of the seven areas of knowing. Is this correct?

Ra: I am Ra. This is partially incorrect. The Logos creates light. The nature of this light thus creates the nature of the catalytic and energetic levels of experience in the creation. Thus it is that the highest of all honor/duties, that given to those of the next octave, is the supervision of light in its manifestations during the experiential times, if you will, of your cycles.

Questioner: I will make another statement. The mind/body/spirit complex may choose, because of the first distortion, the mental configuration that is sufficiently displaced from the configuration of the intelligent energy in a particular frequency or color of in-streaming energy so as to block a portion of instreaming energy in that particular frequency or color. Is this correct?

Ra: I am Ra. Yes.

Questioner: Can you give me an idea of the maximum percentage of this energy it is possible to block in any one color?

Ra: I am Ra. There may be, in an entity's pattern of in-streaming energy, a complete blockage in any energy or color or combination of energies or colors.

Questioner: OK. Then I assume that the first distortion is the motivator or what allows this blockage. Is this correct?

Ra: I am Ra. We wish no quibbling but prefer to avoid the use of terms such as the verb, to allow. Free will does not allow, nor would predetermination disallow, experiential distortions. Rather the Law of Confusion offers a free reach for the energies of each mind/body/spirit complex. The verb, to allow, would be considered pejorative in that it suggests a polarity between right and wrong or allowed and not allowed. This may seem a minuscule point. However, to our best way of thinking it bears some weight.

Questioner: Thank you. It bears weight to my own way of thinking also. I appreciate what you have told me.

Now, I would like to then consider the origin of catalyst. First we have the condition of mind/body/spirit complex which, as a function of the first distortion, has reached a condition of blockage or partial blockage of one or more energy centers. I will assume that catalyst is necessary only if there is at least partial blockage of one energy center. Is this correct?

Ra: I am Ra. No.

Questioner: Could you tell me why?

Ra: I am Ra. While it is a primary priority to activate or unblock each energy center, it is also a primary priority at that point to begin to refine the balances between the energies so that each tone of the chord of total vibratory being-ness resonates in clarity, tune, and harmony with each other energy.

This balancing, tuning, and harmonizing of the self is most central to the more advanced or adept mind/body/spirit complex. Each energy may be activated without the beauty that is possible through the disciplines and appreciations of personal energies or what you might call the deeper personality or soul identity.

Questioner: Let me make an analogy that I have just thought of. A seven-stringed musical instrument may be played by deflecting each string a full deflection and releasing it producing notes. instead of producing the notes this way the individual creative personality could deflect each string the proper amount in the proper sequence producing music. Is this correct?

Ra: I am Ra. This is correct. In the balanced individual the energies lie waiting for the hand of the Creator to pluck harmony.

Questioner: I would like then to trace the evolution of catalyst upon the mind/body/spirit complexes and how it comes into use and is fully used to create this tuning. I assume that the sub-Logos that formed our tiny part of the creation using the intelligence of the Logos of which it is a part, provides the base catalyst that will act upon mind/body complexes and mind/body/spirit complexes before they have reached a state of development where they can begin to program their own catalyst. Is this correct?

Ra: I am Ra. This is partially correct. The sub-Logos offers the catalyst at the lower levels of energy, the first triad; these have to do with the survival of the physical complex. The higher centers gain catalyst from the biases of the mind/body/spirit complex itself in response to all random and directed experiences.

Thus the less developed entity will perceive the catalyst about it in terms of survival of the physical complex with the distortions which are preferred. The more conscious entity being conscious of the catalytic process will begin to transform the catalyst offered by the sub-Logos into catalyst which may act upon the higher energy nexi. Thus the sub-Logos can offer only a basic skeleton, shall we say, of catalyst. The muscles and flesh having to do with the, shall we say, survival of wisdom, love, compassion, and service are brought about by the action of the mind/body/spirit complex on basic catalyst so as to create a more complex catalyst which may in turn be used to form distortions within these higher energy centers.

The more advanced the entity, the more tenuous the connection between the sub-Logos and the perceived catalyst until, finally, all catalyst is chosen, generated, and manufactured by the self, for the self.

Questioner: Which entities incarnate at this time on this planet would be in that category of manufacturing all of their catalyst?

Ra: I am Ra. We find your query indeterminate but can respond that the number of those which have mastered outer catalyst completely is quite small.

Most of those harvestable at this space/time nexus have partial control over the outer illusion and are using the outer catalyst to work upon some bias which is not yet in balance.

Questioner: In the case of service-to-self polarization, what type of catalyst would entities following this path program when they reach the level of programming their own catalyst?

Ra: I am Ra. The negatively oriented entity will program for maximal separation from and control over all those things and conscious entities which it perceives as being other than the self.

Questioner: A positively oriented entity may select a certain narrow path of thinking and activities during an incarnation and program conditions that would create physical pain if this were not followed. Is this correct?

Ra: I am Ra. This is correct.

Questioner: Would a negatively oriented entity do anything like this? Could you give me an example?

Ra: I am Ra. A negatively oriented individual mind/body/spirit complex will ordinarily program for wealth, ease of existence, and the utmost opportunity for power. Thus many negative entities burst with the physical complex distortion you call health.

However, a negatively oriented entity may choose a painful condition in order to improve the distortion toward the so-called negative emotive mentations such as anger, hatred, and frustration. Such an entity may use an entire incarnative experience honing a blunt edge of hatred or anger so that it may polarize more towards the negative or separated pole.

Questioner: Prior to incarnation, as an entity becomes more aware of the process of evolution and has selected a path whether it be positive or negative, at some point the entity becomes aware of what it wants to do with respect to unblocking and balancing its energy centers. At that point it is able to program for the life experience those catalytic experiences that will aid it in its process of unblocking and balancing. Is that correct?

Ra: I am Ra. That is correct.

Questioner: The purpose then, of what we call the incarnate physical state, seems to be wholly or almost wholly that of experiencing the programmed catalyst and then evolving as a function of that catalyst. Is that correct?

Ra: I am Ra. We shall restate for clarity the purpose of incarnative existence is evolution of mind, body, and spirit. In order to do this it is not strictly necessary to have catalyst. However, without catalyst the desire to evolve and the faith in the process do not normally manifest and thus evolution occurs not. Therefore, catalyst is programmed and the program is designed for the mind/body/spirit complex for its unique requirements. Thus it is desirable that a mind/body/spirit complex be aware of and hearken to the voice of its experiential catalyst, gleaning from it that which it incarnated to glean.

Questioner: Then it seems that those upon the positive path as opposed to those on the negative path would have precisely the reciprocal objective in the first three rays; red, orange, and yellow. Each path would be attempting to utilize the rays in precisely the opposite manners. Is this correct?

Ra: I am Ra. It is partially and even substantially correct. There is an energy in each of the centers needed to keep the mind/body/spirit complex, which is the vehicle for experience, in correct conformation and composition. Both negative and positive entities do well to reserve this small portion of each center for the maintenance of the integrity of the mind/body/spirit complex. After this point, however, it is correct that the negative will use the three lower centers for separation from and control over others by sexual means, by personal assertion, and by action in your societies.

Contrary-wise, the positively oriented entity will be transmuting strong red-ray sexual energy into green-ray energy transfers and radiation in blue and indigo and will be similarly transmuting selfhood and place in society into energy transfer situations in which the entity may merge with and serve others and then, finally, radiate unto others without expecting any transfer in return.

Questioner: Can you describe the energy that enters these energy centers? Can you describe its path from its origin, its form, and its effect? I don't know if this is possible.

Ra: I am Ra. This is partially possible.

Questioner: Would you please do that?

Ra: The origin of all energy is the action of free will upon love. The nature of all energy is light. The means of its ingress into the mind/body/spirit complex is duple.

Firstly, there is the inner light which is Polaris of the self, the guiding star. This is the birthright and true nature of all entities. This energy dwells within.

The second point of ingress is the polar opposite of the North Star, shall we say, and may be seen, if you wish to use the physical body as an analog for the magnetic field, as coming through the feet from the earth and through the lower point of the spine. This point of ingress of the universal light energy is undifferentiated until it begins its filtering process through the energy centers. The requirements of each center and the efficiency with which the individual has learned to tap into the inner light determine the nature of the use made by the entity of these in-streamings.

Questioner: Does experiential catalyst follow the same path? This may be a dumb question.

Ra: I am Ra. This is not a pointless question, for catalyst and the requirements or distortions of the energy centers are two concepts linked as tightly as two strands of rope.

Questioner: You mentioned in an earlier session that the experiential catalyst was first experienced by the south pole and appraised with respect to its survival value. That's why I asked the question. Would you expand on this concept?

Ra: I am Ra. We have addressed the filtering process by which in-coming energies are pulled upwards according to the distortions of each energy center and the strength of will or desire emanating from the awareness of inner light. If we may be more specific, please query with specificity.

Questioner: I'll make this statement which may be somewhat distorted and then let you correct it. We have, coming through the feet and base of the spine, the total energy that the mind/body/spirit complex will receive in the way of what we call light. Each energy center then filters out and uses a portion of this energy, red through violet. Is this correct?

Ra: I am Ra. This is largely correct. The exceptions are as follows: The energy ingress ends with indigo. The violet ray is a thermometer or indicator of the whole.

Questioner: As this energy is absorbed by the energy centers at some point it is not only absorbed into the being but radiates through the energy center outwardly. I believe this begins at the blue center and also occurs in the indigo and violet? Is this correct?

Ra: I am Ra. Firstly, we would state that we had not finished answering the previous query and may thus answer both in part by stating that in the fully activated entity, only that small portion of in-streaming light needed to tune the energy center is used, the great remainder being free to be channeled and attracted upwards.

To answer your second question more fully we may say that it is correct that radiation without the necessity of response begins with blue ray although the green ray, being the great transitional ray, must be given all careful consideration, for until transfer of energy of all types has been experienced and mastered to a great extent, there will be blockages in the blue and indigo radiations.

Again, the violet emanation is, in this context, a resource from which, through indigo, intelligent infinity may be contacted. The radiation thereof will not be violet ray but rather green, blue, or indigo depending upon the nature of the type of intelligence which infinity has brought through into discernible energy.

The green ray type of radiation in this case is the healing, the blue ray the communication and inspiration, the indigo that energy of the adept which has its place in faith.

Questioner: What if a mind/body/spirit complex feels a feeling in meditation at the indigo center, what is he feeling?

Ra: I am Ra. This will be the last full query of this working.

One who feels this activation is one experiencing in-streamings at that energy center to be used either for the unblocking of this center, for its tuning to match the harmonics of its other energy centers, or to activate the gateway to intelligent infinity.

We cannot be specific for each of these three workings is experienced by the entity which feels this physical complex distortion.

Is there a brief query before we leave this instrument?

Questioner: I just would ask if there is anything that we can do to make the instrument more comfortable or to improve the contact?

Ra: I am Ra. Please be aware of the need for the support of the instrument's neck. All is well. I leave you, my friends, in the love and in the light of the one infinite Creator. Go forth, then, rejoicing in the power and the peace of the one infinite Creator. Adonai.

L/L Research

Sunday Meditation
May 31, 1981

(Carla channeling)

I am Hatonn, and I greet you, my friends, in the love and the light of the infinite Creator. It is a very great privilege to speak with you this evening and we especially wish to greet the one known as B. We have not had the pleasure of sitting with him in this group for some of your time and it is an honor that we cherish, although, of course, we are always with each of you if you call upon us and we have indeed been with the one known as B.

My friends, we would speak to you in parables. Once there was a young man. This young man roamed the highways. He was homeless and carried that little which he had upon his back and in his arms. This young man was consumed with the knowledge of his imperfection. From time to time when he was not hungry and not sleepy, he would take the guitar from his pack and play it in what little way he could and attempt to distract himself, for he was a most troubled young man. When he looked upon himself, he saw nothing but error, mistakes, imperfections and faults. With his ears he could hear much beauty, for bird call and the rustle of the wind are the friends of those who live by the road. With his eyes he witnessed an unending panorama of the creation of the Father. His skin was touched with sun and welcomed rain from the heat. And the flowers greeted his nose with that beauty that is so careless that it gives itself regardless of the witnesses it may have.

One day, my friends, this young man caught a ride upon one of your freight trains and found that he was not alone but rather was joined by another young man much like himself. This man, however, dirty and ragged and poor though he was, was radiant. A light shone from his eyes. "My friend," he said. "What is wrong with you? Are you hungry? May I help you?"

"No," the young man replied. "It is hopeless. I cannot help myself, for I have done many things of which I am ashamed."

"What are they?" queried the other. "Have you raped? Have you killed? Have you stolen?"

"Oh no," said the young man, startled. "But I have lied and I have run, and I have hidden and I am not clean and there is no hope of my overcoming these faults in character."

"Is that right?" said the other. "Now let us examine this." He made a gesture. "Sit up my friend. You were made in the image of the Creator. Where is the fault in that?"

"Why, no fault!" replied the young man. "But you do not understand."

The other made another gesture. "Now see here. Has your Father not told you to be perfect?"

"Yes!" cried the young man in anguish. "That is what I cannot be."

"Ha!" said the other. "How foolish. To think that the Creator would ask you to be perfect, unless He thought you could be." The radiant eyes seemed to burn into the young man's very soul.

"Touch the places within yourself that you feel are at fault and know that the Creator is waiting confidently for you to be perfect."

With a shudder the young man closed his eyes and prayed. Finally, he spoke. "Whoever you are, I cannot find the truth that you give me, for I have touched my iniquities, my harsh words, my ill feelings, my half truths. I can find no health in them, much less perfection."

"Aha!" said the other, radiant one. "But you have touched them. You know them. Now let us proceed into the importance of the matter. Open your eyes, my friend. Do you not love me?"

The young man opened his eyes, quite startled. "Yes, of course I do." The radiant one smiled. "There, you see?" said he. "Is that not perfection? Continue, then, to love."

I am Hatonn.

After a brief pause, we will transfer this contact.

(Jim channeling)

I am Hatonn, and I greet you once again in the love and light of our infinite Creator. We have been attempting to contact the one known as Don but find that our vibration is not in harmony with the vibration which the one known as Don is using, shall we may, as his tuning this evening. We shall proceed through this instrument. We would, at this time, offer ourselves in the role of answering or attempting to answer, should we say, any questions that you might have to ask. Are there any questions at this time?

Carla: I have a question from S. She wanted to know if the inner feelings which she had about her true personality and its magical working in this life were accurate and if you had any comments on her feelings.

I am Hatonn, and am aware of the question from the one known as S. We might answer by saying that the feelings which the one known as S has expressed within its being are those feelings which come from the depth of being that is her source and her knowing. These feelings, we might say, are of a nature which can only be confirmed from within her own being, for it is within her that they arise. We of Hatonn can only go so far, shall we say, in expressing our feelings about her own, for as you know, the concept of free will prohibits us from being too specific. We would assure the one known as S that those feelings which have made an impression upon her are from the heart of her being and always we would advise each entity to follow the feelings that come from the heart, for the lesson of your plane of existence is to follow the ways of the heart, to know from the depth of your being that love is your source and love is your path in whatever way you choose to manifest love.

May we answer you further, my sister?

Carla: No. I thank you for S.

[I am Hatonn.] And of course we are thankful for the opportunity of being of this service. May we ask if there is another question which we might attempt to answer?

C: Yes. In the parable, the young man expressed love for the radiant one. But at the same time he seemed so negative and unloving of himself. Can you truly love others without a love for the self?

I am Hatonn, and would answer you, my brother, by saying that the answer is not simple, for of course it is true that one cannot truly love another until the self knows love for itself, but we must also say in this case, did not the young man love a portion of himself when he expressed love for the radiant one? What is the self, if it is not all that is?

May we answer you further, my brother?

C: I'm not sure. I don't see his acceptance of himself. Is the loving of another … I'm not sure how I want to word this … Is an ability to love another a first step toward an acceptance of loving and loving of oneself? Or is it necessary to learn to love oneself as one is before we can love another?

I am Hatonn and we would answer you by saying that the process of loving the self may begin at any point, for all is one. And when an entity can truly love any other entity or any other idea that seems to be other than self, then the entity has made a start in loving the self which will, shall we say, become as a chain of reactions, each feeding the other—the love of the self for the other for the self for the other for the self, and so on until the channel of love is open within the entity and flows freely, the waters of love touching all.

May we answer you further, my brother?

C: No, thank you very much.

We thank you. Is there another question which we might attempt to answer?

C: Yes, I think I have one more question. I have interaction with people at work and one [in] particular seems [to have] a very negative opinion of himself—seemingly very loving and giving toward others and we talked not long ago about love. And he was expressing disappointment and even resentment because in his mind he never seemed to receive love in kind for what he'd given and to me—I expressed that I thought love was not a thing that is bartered with, but given freely without thought of compensation. Was this a wise thing to say to someone in such a situation?

I am Hatonn. To answer, my brother, we would say that such a response or any response given with love and concern for the other is a response which is of great value. For it is a response truly exhibiting the ideals of love, for as you have said yourself, love can only be given freely. Many, though, while learning this lesson, attempt what we might call the lesser lessons of loving and that is what might be described as the bartering: giving what is perceived as love in hopes of receiving that which will be perceived as love. When this process has run its course, finally the entity will discover that love is free, and that when one gives freely, one receives freely, for all indeed is part of a oneness and many are the attempts of such as your friend, before this lesson is realized.

May we answer you further, my brother?

C: No, but I do have a request—for you to be with me in my further dealings with my friends.

I am Hatonn. As always, we are honored to be with each of you whenever it is asked of us, for freely do we wish to serve the one infinite Creator that resides within all beings. And we are honored and privileged to be invited by any of your group or any of your people, to be of whatever service we can be. Rest assured, my brother, we shall be with you.

C: Thank you.

We thank you. Is there another question which we might attempt to answer?

C: Yes. I have one more. It's in regard to meditation last week. And I have a question to ask on the subject of healing, and it was that for one to heal another, that the one to be healed must really want to be healed and aid the other. How does that affect the case where as we at the end of these meditations send light to people of the planet. Where they—you don't actually tell them that we are sending them light, but we send it. Does that not help even though they're not consciously asking for the help that we seek to give?

I am Hatonn, and we would answer by saying that when you send your love, your light, and your healing energies at the end of your meditations, those to whom you send these energies must ask on some level of their being, whether it be conscious or unconscious, that they be healed in order to receive the healing energy. Otherwise, the healing aspects of your sendings will be reflected and will not be received, for it is, what might be said, a law of the universe that only those energies which are sought may be found. But we may also say that the love and the light which you send may serve its purpose and find its mark within those entities whom you seek to heal and will aid them in a general uplifting of their being and will aid them in their receptivity, though not directly aid them in the healing.

May we answer you further, my brother?

C: No, thank you.

Again, we thank you. Is there another question which we might attempt to answer?

(Pause)

I am Hatonn. We are most honored to have been able to join you this evening. Before we leave this group, we would pause for a moment so that the one known as Laitos may pass among those in this group and aid any who ask for assistance [in] meditation, in their meditation. We will pause now for a moment. I am Hatonn.

(Pause)

I am Hatonn. We have been very pleased to be able to join you this evening and to take part in your meditation. It is always a great honor to be with you.

We hope we shall have this opportunity many times in what you call your future and we hope that each of you will know that as you go your own individual ways in your daily life that we are always with you, that at any time should you need our assistance, we would be most honored to join you in whatever effort you are engaged and to lend our love and light to that effort so that it might result in a learning of love of the Creator. It is always present and available for your use. We are known to you as Hatonn, and we leave you in the love and the light of the infinite Creator. Adonai vasu borragus. ☙

L/L Research

The Law of One, Book III, Session 55
June 5, 1981

Ra: I am Ra. I greet you in the love and in the light of the one infinite Creator. I communicate now.

Questioner: I would first like to ask as to the condition of the instrument, please?

Ra: I am Ra. This instrument is experiencing physical distortions toward weakness of the bodily complex occurring due to psychic attack. This instrument's vital energies have not been affected, however, due to the aid of those present in healing work. This instrument will apparently be subject to such weakness distortions due to incarnative processes which predispose the body complex towards weakness distortions.

Questioner: Is there any specific thing that we can do that you have already told us or otherwise to alleviate this psychic attack or to help the instrument the most?

Ra: I am Ra. We scan this instrument and find its distortion towards appreciation of each entity and each entity's caring, as you may call it. This atmosphere, shall we say, offers the greatest contrast to the discomfort of such psychic attacks, being the reciprocal, that is, the atmosphere of psychic support.

This each of you do as a subconscious function of true attitudinal, mental, emotional, and spiritual distortions towards this instrument. There is no magic greater than honest distortion toward love.

Questioner: Thank you. I want to ask a couple questions about previous material that I didn't understand. I am hoping that this will clear up my understanding somewhat with respect to the mental configurations with which we have been dealing.

In the session before last you stated, "However, this is a risk for the Orion entities due to the frequency with which the harvestable negative planetary entities attempt to bid and order the Orion contact just as these entities bid planetary negative contacts." Can you explain the mechanisms that affect polarization in consciousness with respect to this statement?

Ra. I am Ra. The negative polarization is greatly aided by the subjugation or enslavement of other-selves. The potential between two negatively polarized entities is such that the entity which enslaves the other or bids the other gains in negative polarity.

The entity so bidden or enslaved, in serving an other-self, will necessarily lose negative polarity although it will gain in desire for further negative polarization. This desire will then tend to create opportunities to regain negative polarity.

Questioner: Am I to understand then that just the fact that the third-density entity calls or bids an Orion Crusader is a polarizing type of action that affects both entities?

Ra: I am Ra. This is incorrect. The calling mechanism is not congruent in the slightest degree with the bidding mechanism. In the calling, the entity which calls is a suppliant neophyte asking for aid in negative understanding, if you may excuse this misnomer. The Orion response increases its negative polarity as it is disseminating the negative philosophy, thereby enslaving or bidding the entity calling.

There are instances, however, when the contact becomes contest which is prototypical of negativity. In this contest, the caller will attempt, not to ask for aid, but to demand results. Since the third-density negatively oriented harvestable entity has at its disposal an incarnative experiential nexus and since Orion Crusaders are, in a great extent, bound by the first distortion in order to progress, the Orion entity is vulnerable to such bidding if properly done. In this case, the third-density entity becomes master and the Orion Crusader becomes entrapped and can be bid. This is rare. However, when it has occurred, the Orion entity or social memory complex involved has experienced loss of negative polarity in proportion to the strength of the bidding third-density entity.

Questioner: You mentioned that this will work when the bidding is properly done. What did you mean by "when the bidding is properly done"?

Ra: I am Ra. To properly bid is to be properly negative. The percentage of thought and behavior involving service to self must approach 99% in order for a third-density negative entity to be properly configured for such a contest of bidding.

Questioner: What method of communication with the Orion entity would a bidder of this type use?

Ra: I am Ra. The two most usual types of bidding are: One, the use of perversions of sexual magic; two, the use of perversions of ritual magic. In each case the key to success is the purity of the will of the bidder. The concentration upon victory over the servant must be nearly perfect.

Questioner: Can you tell me, in the polarizations in consciousness, if there is any analogy with respect to what you just said in this type of contact with respect to what we are doing right now in communicating with Ra?

Ra: I am Ra. There is no relationship between this type of contact and the bidding process. This contact may be characterized as one typical of the Brothers and Sisters of Sorrow wherein those receiving the contact have attempted to prepare for such contact by sacrificing extraneous, self-oriented distortions in order to be of service.

The Ra social memory complex offers itself also as a function of its desire to serve. Both the caller and the contact are filled with gratitude at the opportunity of serving others.

We may note that this in no way presupposes that either the callers or those of our group in any way approach a perfection or purity such as was described in the bidding process. The calling group may have many distortions and the working with much catalyst, as may those of Ra. The overriding desire to serve others, bonded with the unique harmonics of this group's vibratory complexes, gives us the opportunity to serve as one channel for the one infinite Creator.

Things come not to those positively oriented but through such beings.

Questioner: Thank you. You have stated in an earlier session that "until transfers of energy of all types have been experienced and mastered to a great extent, there will be blockages in the blue and in the indigo radiations." Could you explain that more fully?

Ra: I am Ra. At this space/time we have not covered the appropriate intermediate material. Please requestion at a more appropriate space/time nexus.

Questioner: I'm sort of hunting around here for an entry into some information. I may not be looking in a productive area.

You had stated that "as we *(Ra)* had been aided by shapes such as the pyramid, so we could aid your people." These shapes have been mentioned many, many times and you have also stated that the shapes themselves aren't of too much consequence. I see a relation between these shapes and the energies that we have been studying with respect to the body, and I would like to ask a few questions on the pyramids to see if we might get an entry into some of this understanding.

You stated, "You will find the intersection of the triangle which is at the first level on each of the four sides forms a diamond in a plane which is horizontal." Can you tell me what you meant by the word, intersection?

Ra: I am Ra. Your mathematics and arithmetic have a paucity of configurative descriptions which we might use. Without intending to be obscure, we may note that the purpose of the shapes is to work with time/space portions of the mind/body/spirit complex. Therefore, the intersection is both space/time and time/space oriented and thus is expressed in three dimensional geometry by two intersections which, when projected in both time/space and space/time, form one point.

Questioner: I have calculated this point to be one-sixth of the height of the triangle that forms the side of the pyramid. Is this correct?

Ra: I am Ra. Your calculations are substantially correct and we are pleased at your perspicacity.

Questioner: This would indicate to me that in the Great Pyramid at Giza, the Queen's Chamber, as it is called, would be the chamber used for initiation. Is this correct?

Ra: I am Ra. Again, you penetrate the outer teaching.

The Queen's Chamber would not be appropriate or useful for healing work as that work involves the use of energy in a more synergic configuration rather than the configuration of the centered being.

Questioner: Then would the healing work be done in the King's Chamber?

Ra: I am Ra. This is correct. We may note that such terminology is not our own.

Questioner: Yes, I understand that. It is just that it is the common naming of the two chambers of the Great Pyramid. I don't know whether this line of questioning is going to take me to a better understanding of the energies, but until I have explored the concepts there is nothing much that I can do but to ask a few questions.

There is a chamber below the bottom level of the pyramid, down below ground, that appears to be roughly in line with the King's Chamber. What is that chamber?

Ra: I am Ra. We may say that there is information to be gained from this line of querying. The chamber you request to be informed about is a resonating chamber. The bottom of such a structure, in order to cause the appropriate distortions for healing catalyst, shall be open.

Questioner: The book, *The Life Force Of The Great Pyramid*, has related the ankh shape with a resonance in the pyramid. Is this a correct analysis?

Ra: I am Ra. We have scanned your mind and find the phrase "working with crayons." This would be applicable. There is only one significance to these shapes such as the crux ansata; that is the placing in coded form of mathematical relationships.

Questioner: Is the 76° and 18' angle at the apex of the pyramid a critical angle?

Ra: I am Ra. For the healing work intended, this angle is appropriate.

Questioner: Why does the King's Chamber have the various small chambers above it?

Ra: I am Ra. This will be the last full query of this working.

We must address this query more generally in order to explicate your specific question. The positioning of the entity to be healed is such that the life energies, if you will, are in a position to be briefly interrupted or intersected by light. This light then may, by the catalyst of the healer with the crystal, manipulate the aural forces, as you may call the various energy centers, in such a way that if the entity to be healed wills it so, corrections may take place. Then the entity is reprotected by its own, now less distorted, energy field and is able to go its way.

The process by which this is done involves bringing the entity to be healed to an equilibrium. This involves temperature, barometric pressure, and the electrical charged atmosphere. The first two requirements are controlled by the system of chimneys.

Questioner: Does this healing work by affecting the energy centers in such a way that they are unblocked so as to perfect the seven bodies that they generate and, therefore, bring the entity to be healed into proper balance?

Ra: I am Ra. This entity tires. We must answer in brief and state simply that the distorted configuration of the energy centers is intended to be temporarily interrupted and the opportunity is then presented to the one to be healed to grasp the baton, to take the balanced route and to walk thence with the distortions towards disease of mind, body, and spirit greatly lessened.

The catalytic effect of the charged atmosphere and the crystal directed by the healer must be taken into consideration as integral portions of this process, for the bringing back of the entity to a configuration of conscious awareness would not be accomplished after the reorganization possibilities are offered without the healer's presence and directed will. Are there any brief queries before we leave this instrument?

Questioner: Only is there anything that we can do to make the instrument more comfortable or to improve this contact?

Ra: I am Ra. All is well. You are conscientious. I now leave this working. I am Ra. I leave you, my friends, in the love and in the light of the one infinite Creator. Go forth, then, rejoicing in the power and in the peace of the one infinite Creator. Adonai. ✣

Sunday Meditation
June 7, 1981

(L channeling)

[I am Hatonn.] … brothers, in the love and light of the infinite Creator. It is with great pleasure that we of Hatonn are able once again to communicate with this group. We are especially pleased to greet those from whom we have been separated, so to speak, for such a long time. It is always our pleasure to renew contact with those who have for some time followed other paths.

Tonight we would like to tell you a small story concerning one of our brethren who was, a long time ago and in a distant place, a seeker. He felt as though his efforts were not sufficient, yet was unable to arrive at a decision or realization of the next step upon his path of awareness. It seemed to him that the more often he tried to establish a foothold upon his next slope of climb, so to speak, the more often his outstretched foot would simply pass through his illusive goal and land him once again upon the all too solid earth upon which he trod.

He began to despair ever being able to develop further. It seemed that all of his efforts were futile and he became despondent, not realizing that the source of growth is not solely in trying. In his depression he decided to give up and attempt to retrace his steps of growth so that he could once again become the person he once was, a simple, half-conscious being, lost among a crowd of other half-conscious beings. In this, however, he was unsuccessful, for the way of the lonely one is not the path of the blind.

Finally he could stand it no longer and painfully, arduously he again retraced his path of growth, feeling that to be alone and trying was better than the company of the blind. When he arrived at his metaphysical destination, he found his path no longer blocked. He was able to continue and to once again initiate a spiritual ascent.

My brothers, there are times in your lives, in our lives, when the path appears to be blocked, when the harder one tries the less one seems to accomplish. It is necessary, my brothers, to realize that one does not grow by attempting to force change, rather one must wait until the flow of the universe guides one into his proper path. There are many experiences that are necessary upon the plane you now occupy, before you are ready and able to ascend to the next plane. Therefore, my brothers, do not be hasty. Welcome and cherish the experiences before you, for it is on this plane that you will establish the necessary growth to attain the next and it is each of you, my brothers, who is and was and will be that striving being that we have described in our little tale.

At this time we would like to exercise another channel. Therefore, we shall continue to another. I am Hatonn.

(H channeling)

I am Hatonn. Greeting once again, my friends. It is a pleasure to speak through this instrument as it has been quite a spell of time. We of the Confederation of Planets in Service to the Infinite Creator, have come to your planet and we have communicated with many of your peoples. Many have heard our words, many have shared this experience. Many have come and listened and gone away with the feeling that what they have heard is of value. But, my friends, the value is not what you hear, it is in what you do with that which you have received. We could speak to you and reveal to you a great deal of knowledge, but unless you have the initiative to employ that knowledge into your everyday actions, then our mission has been of no use.

Within this group we have seen a great deal of growth and we have seen many setbacks come upon the people with whom you associate, and for the most part we smile upon this group of people, for they have overcome the difficulties and they have maintained spiritual goals. Though it may not be evident at all times, the people with whom you associate is a very special group to us. We are aware of the difficulty upon your planet of continued associations, one with the other, due to your needs and your desires. We believe what has come about in this day is only another step in the growth of all concerned, and we are pleased.

I shall now transfer this communication to another instrument. I am Hatonn.

(Carla channeling)

I am Hatonn, and am now with this instrument. At this time we would pause and with our brother, Laitos, move about this group so that each of you who request it may experience a deepening of our contact. I am Hatonn.

(Pause)

I am again with this instrument. I am Hatonn, and again I greet you in love and light. It is a privilege at this time to open the meeting to questions.

L: Hatonn, do you have any information concerning E and why we have not heard from him?

I am Hatonn. My brother, as you probably know, this type of query is not the type which we may answer due to infringement upon free will. We would, however, use this opportunity to speak to you of the place which those dear to you may have in your existence. It is apparently difficult not to be concerned about the disposition of a brother about whom you have no information. Nevertheless, it is well to remember that each entity is infinitely present and that there is no end to the perfect condition of the one known as E.

In this particular case we believe that your phrase is, "All is well," however, were this loved one to vanish from your ken, yet still would your brother be in the creation of the Father. It is well to take comfort in this perspective, for there is an inevitable rise and fall to the physical illusion of any one entity and many are the times in your incarnation that all will not be well with a loved one, yet you must remember that all is indeed perfect. It is the illusion that may fail, as illusions always do.

Is there another question, my friend?

L: No, thank you.

S: I have a question. I had a dream that I related to Don and Carla by mail and I was wondering if you could, since it was a lengthy dream, if you know of the dream that I am talking about and if my interpretation of it was correct, because it involved several people in it.

I am Hatonn. My sister, our ability to answer you is limited due to the level upon which you dreamed. We may confirm the substantial interpretation of this dream and suggest to you that the level upon which you dreamed was one wherein those forgotten abilities prior to incarnation, those alliances and shared ideals, were brought into realization in the dream state.

May we answer you further, my sister?

S: No, just to get it straight, then, that it was more of a symbolic exercise of power and unity than an actual event on another plane.

I am Hatonn. That which occurred in what seemed to be dreaming consciousness was occurring in another time and another dimension in actuality and was not of the nature of contest, so much as the nature of unity, the love and wisdom of the group being shared or given in such a way as to unify all darkness into light. The level of this work is such that we are not able to speak well about it, as we ourselves are attempting to study such matters. This was a dream state which was not, as you might say, ordinary.

May we answer you further, my sister?

S: Just as a curiosity, if for some reason I had not done the right thing, would there have been any harm to me in this plane?

I am Hatonn. We are not able to speak to this, for we would infringe upon free will. However, we may suggest consideration of our story told earlier. There would have been the retracing of steps.

Is there another question at this time, my friend?

S: No. Thank you very much.

May we answer another question?

L: Hatonn, I've noticed that it seems more and more frequently the answers to questions placed before you are refusals to answer, based upon free will, and I consider this … I surmise that this is a condition based upon the type of questions being asked, rather than any change in your restrictions. Therefore, it would seem to me that there is possibly a level of learning that one can attain to contact with you and then one must go, in some manner, beyond that contact. I'm reluctant to abandon good counsel, yet I suppose my question is, is there a point reached in contact with the Confederation where one has a requirement to move on, so to speak, to grow further?

I am Hatonn. We cannot say, my brother, what requirement there shall be for an individual entity, for each has his own path, and one path may require such a separation from a source in order to find another.

The reason for a seeming frequency of, shall we say, half answers in this particular group at this particular time, is, as you surmise, that this group has attained a certain level of discrimination and has begun asking questions which it is not the purpose of our group, or any positively-oriented spiritual counsel to answer, for we cannot smell flowers for you; we cannot feel the air for you; we cannot inform your senses nor can we offer you predigested enlightenment or assurances of a specific nature, without losing our ability to speak clearly upon matters that we consider of importance.

The questions that we may answer in any degree of detail to any length and at any cost are questions of love, of light, of the Creator. This is the message we have come to share. Questions of a personal nature are examined by us for information which will aid in the spiritual journey and give to you whatever gifts we may, whatever understanding we have, that may aid you. We do not wish to stunt your growth by telling you, only to spur your growth by inspiring you.

Thus, when questions of a specific nature are asked and we cannot find a spiritual bone to chew, shall we say, we do not speak. There are many entities in the Confederation of Planets and there is virtually no end to the information to be gained. However, we of the Confederation, being oriented solely towards the desire to serve you, would far rather that you sought elsewhere if we cannot serve you. If your need for information is specific, dogmatic or even trivial, we urge any to move onward and seek out that which is literal, that which is theological, that which is prophetic.

May we answer you further, my brother?

L: Only a clarification. The problem is not so much the questions, as the direction of the question—that I'm basically asking questions that are in an area you're not allowed to answer, rather than reaching the limits of your answering ability. Is that correct?

I am Hatonn. It is both incorrect and correct. It is incorrect in that there are limits to our own understanding and as your understanding improves, you will draw those to you who will be able to speak specifically to your needs for philosophy. However, the substance of your assumption is quite correct. We must examine each question for the thrust of the question, for to interfere in any way with the freedom of your own thought processes, to give you information that can be proven in any way, to make for you a case that we exist, that we are right, that we can be proven, is completely against the Law of Free Will which guarantees that each entity has the complete and total right to choose subjectively for himself the path which he may walk. If you seek love, seek it then because we have perhaps inspired or given you pause for thought, not because something which we have said has proven miraculously to be true, or has seemed to be good advice on a particular matter.

Have we explained the Law of Free Will sufficiently for you, my brother?

L: Yes, and I thank you. I have one other question on a different subject that I would like to offer. I am, from past experiences, past meditations, of the impression that you are capable of reading minds but that there are limitations to your capability. Is this correct and would you be willing to discuss the matter in some detail so that I can gain a better understanding of communication with you in this fashion?

I am Hatonn. We are capable of sharing your thoughts. Those who do not think are not capable of sharing their thoughts with us. We are capable, then, only of sharing the feelings with many of your peoples. The sharing of which we are capable is largely upon this level. The well-developed intellect with clear-cut thought patterns is not altogether common among your peoples. This is our greatest limitation.

May we answer you further?

L: Yes. Beings who have clear-cut thought patterns—there are those thoughts which you might refer to as private and others which might be referred to as directed toward you. Is my assumption correct that you are capable of perceiving both but, perhaps out of good manners, ignore the former?

I am Hatonn. …

(Side one of tape ends.)

(Carla channeling)

… one other person at a party, we only hear our own names. Much conversation may go on about us, but it does not concern us. The concept of good manners exists among your peoples where there is also a concept of the ill-mannered behavior. Within our society such a concept does not exist since all thoughts are open to all, yet we take only that which is sent to us. It would not occur to us to scan all minds at all times, for the energy needed would be quite large and it would not be interesting to know a great deal about so many. Thus, when you call us we hear. This you may rely upon. When you do not call us, and most of your peoples do not call us a great portion of the time, we do not hear, for we cannot be of service.

May we answer you further?

L: Yes, one last question. The description you've given of your own ability to listen and respond is comparable to that of other members of the Confederation who contact us. Is this correct?

I am Hatonn. This is correct.

L: Thank you.

We thank you, my brother. Is there another question before we leave this instrument?

(Pause)

I am Hatonn. It has been a pleasure to speak through this instrument and each instrument this evening. We would, if we may, close through another instrument at this time. I am Hatonn.

(Don channeling)

I am Hatonn. It's been a very great privilege to be with this group this evening. We are always aware of any call for our service, for this, my friends, is what we do. We serve those who call, for in giving this service, we serve ourselves. Each service which any entity performs, no matter to whom, how small or how large it may be, that service is simply to himself, for all of us are one being, all of us are growing in the very same way. As we serve you through contacts such as this one, we grow in awareness just as you grow in awareness. That growth, my friends, is the growth of one being. That growth is the experience of the one infinite Creator. Rejoice in the knowledge that you are a part of this great experiment—the experiment which you call the creation, the universe, the Creator.

I leave you now in the love and the light that is your love and your light, the love and the light of the infinite Creator. Adonai vasu borragus.

L/L Research is a subsidiary of Rock Creek Research & Development Laboratories, Inc.

P.O. Box 5195
Louisville, KY 40255-0195

www.llresearch.org

Rock Creek is a non-profit corporation dedicated to discovering and sharing information which may aid in the spiritual evolution of humankind.

ABOUT THE CONTENTS OF THIS TRANSCRIPT: This telepathic channeling has been taken from transcriptions of the weekly study and meditation meetings of the Rock Creek Research & Development Laboratories and L/L Research. It is offered in the hope that it may be useful to you. As the Confederation entities always make a point of saying, please use your discrimination and judgment in assessing this material. If something rings true to you, fine. If something does not resonate, please leave it behind, for neither we nor those of the Confederation would wish to be a stumbling block for any.

© 2009 L/L Research

The Law of One, Book III, Session 56
June 8, 1981

Ra: I am Ra. I greet you in the love and in the light of the one infinite Creator. We communicate now.

Questioner: Would you first please give me an indication of the instrument's condition?

Ra: I am Ra. This instrument is severely distorted towards weakness of the mental and physical complexes at this time and is under psychic attack due to this opportunity.

Questioner: Would it be better to discontinue the contact at this time?

Ra: I am Ra. This is entirely at your discretion. This instrument has some energy transferred which is available. However, it is not great due to the effects as previously stated.

We, if you desire to question us further at this working, will as always attempt to safeguard this instrument. We feel that you are aware of the parameters without further elaboration.

Questioner: In that case, I will ask how does the pyramid shape work?

Ra: I am Ra. We are assuming that you wish to know the principle of the shapes, angles, and intersections of the pyramid at what you call Giza.

In reality, the pyramid shape does no work. It does not work. It is an arrangement for the centralization as well as the diffraction of the spiraling upward light energy as it is being used by the mind/body/spirit complex.

The spiraling nature of light is such that the magnetic fields of an individual are affected by spiraling energy. Certain shapes offer an echo chamber, shall we say, or an intensifier for spiraling prana, as some have called this all-present, primal distortion of the one infinite Creator.

If the intent is to intensify the necessity for the entity's own will to call forth the inner light in order to match the intensification of the spiraling light energy, the entity will be placed in what you have called the Queen's Chamber position in this particular shaped object. This is the initiatory place and is the place of resurrection.

The off-set place, representing the spiral as it is in motion, is the appropriate position for one to be healed as in this position an entity's vibratory magnetic nexi are interrupted in their normal flux. Thus a possibility/probability vortex ensues; a new beginning, shall we say, is offered for the entity in which the entity may choose a less distorted, weak, or blocked configuration of energy center magnetic distortions.

The function of the healer and crystal may not be over-emphasized, for this power of interruption must needs be controlled, shall we say, with incarnate intelligence; the intelligence being that of one which recognizes energy patterns which, without judging, recognizes blockage, weakness, and other distortion and which is capable of visualizing, through the regularity of self and of crystal, the less distorted other-self to be healed.

Other shapes which are arched, groined, vaulted, conical, or as your tipis are also shapes with this type of intensification of spiraling light. Your caves, being rounded, are places of power due to this shaping.

It is to be noted that these shapes are dangerous. We are quite pleased to have the opportunity to enlarge upon the subject of shapes such as the pyramid for we wish, as part of our honor/duty, to state that there are many wrong uses for these curved shapes; for with improper placement, improper intentions, or lack of the crystallized being functioning as channel for healing the sensitive entity will be distorted more rather than less in some cases.

It is to be noted that your peoples build, for the most part, the cornered or square habitations, for they do not concentrate power. It is further to be noted that the spiritual seeker has, for many of your time periods of years, sought the rounded, arched, and peaked forms as an expression of the power of the Creator

Questioner: Is there an apex angle that is the angle for maximum efficiency in the pyramid?

Ra: I am Ra. Again, to conserve this instrument's energy, I am assuming that you intend to indicate the most appropriate angle of apex for healing work. If the shape is such that it is large enough to contain an individual mind/body/spirit complex at the appropriate off-set position within it, the 76° 18', approximate, angle is useful and appropriate. If the position varies, the angle may vary. Further, if the healer has the ability to perceive distortions with enough discrimination, the position within any pyramid shape may be moved about until results are effected. However, we found this particular angle to be useful. Other social memory complexes, or portions thereof, have determined different apex angles for different uses, not having to do with healing but with learning. When one works with the cone, or shall we say, the silo type of shape, the energy for healing may be found to be in a general circular pattern unique to each shape as a function of its particular height and width and in the cone shape, the angle of apex. In these cases, there are no corner angles. Thus the spiraling energy works in circular motion.

Questioner: I will make a statement which you can correct. I intuitively see the spiraling energy of the Giza pyramid being spread out as it moves through the so-called King's Chamber and refocusing in the so-called Queen's Chamber. I am guessing that the spread of energy in the so-called King's Chamber is seen in the spectrum of colors, red through violet, and that the energy centers of the entity to be healed should be aligned with this spread of the spectrum so that the spectrum matches his various energy centers. Will you correct this statement?

Ra: I am Ra. We can correct this statement.

Questioner: Will you please do that?

Ra: The spiraling energy is beginning to be diffused at the point where it goes through the King's Chamber position. However, although the spirals continue to intersect, closing and opening in double spiral fashion through the apex angle, the diffusion or strength of the spiraling energies, red through violet color values, lessens if we speak of strength, and gains, if we speak of diffusion, until at the peak of the pyramid you have a very weak color resolution useful for healing purposes. Thus the King's Chamber position is chosen as the first spiral after the centered beginning through the Queen's Chamber position. You may visualize the diffusion angle as the opposite of the pyramid angle but the angle being less wide than the apex angle of the pyramid, being somewhere between 33 and 54°, depending upon the various rhythms of the planet itself.

Questioner: Then I assume that if I start my angle at the bottom of the Queen's Chamber and make a 33 to 54° angle from that point, so that half of that angle falls on the side of the centerline that the King's Chamber is on, that will indicate the diffusion of the spectrum, starting from the point at the bottom of the Queen's Chamber; let's say, if we were using a 40° angle, we would have a 20° diffusion to the left of the centerline, passing through the King's Chamber. Is that correct?

Ra: I am Ra. This will be the last full question of this session. It is correct that half of the aforementioned angle passes through the King's Chamber position. It is incorrect to assume that the Queen's Chamber is the foundation of the angle. The angle will begin somewhere between the Queen's Chamber position and thence downward towards the level of the resonating chamber, off-set for the healing work.

This variation is dependent upon various magnetic fluxes of the planet. The King's Chamber position is designed to intersect the strongest spiral of the energy flow regardless of where the angle begins. However, as it passes through the Queen's Chamber position, this spiraling energy is always centered and at its strongest point.

May we answer any brief queries at this time?

Questioner: I will just ask if there is anything that we can do to make the instrument more comfortable or to improve the contact?

Ra: I am Ra. All is well, my friends. It is well, however, to be conscious of the limitations of this instrument. We feel the alignments are excellent at this time. I am Ra. I leave you in the love and in the light of the one infinite Creator. Go forth, therefore, rejoicing in the power and in the peace of the one infinite Creator. Adonai.

L/L Research

The Law of One, Book III, Session 57
June 12, 1981

Ra: I am Ra. I greet you in the love and in the light of the one infinite Creator. We communicate now.

Questioner: First, could you give me an indication of the instrument's condition, please?

Ra: I am Ra. This instrument is under a most severe psychic attack. This instrument is bearing up well due to replenished vital energies and a distortion towards a sense of proportion which your peoples call a sense of humor.

This attack is potentially disruptive to this contact for a brief period of your space/time.

Questioner: Is there anything in particular that we can do in addition to what we are doing to alleviate this attack?

Ra: I am Ra. There is nothing you can do to alleviate the attack. The understanding of its mechanism might be of aid.

Questioner: Could you tell us its mechanism?

Ra: I am Ra. The Orion group cannot interfere directly but only through preexisting distortions of mind/body/spirit complexes.

Thus in this case, this entity reached for an heavy object with one hand and this miscalculated action caused a deformation or distortion of the skeletal/muscular structure of one of this instrument's appendages.

Your aid may be helpful in supporting this instrument in the proper care of this distortion which is equivalent to what you call your post-operative state when bones are not firmly knit. This instrument needs to be aware of care necessary to avoid such miscalculated actions and your support in this state of awareness is noted and encouraged.

Questioner: Is there anything that we can specifically do to alleviate this problem that is already existing?

Ra: I am Ra. This information is harmless, thus we share it though it is transient, lacking the principle but only offering a specific transient effect.

The wrist area should be wrapped as in the sprained configuration, as you call this distortion, and what you call a sling may be used on this distorted right side of the body complex for one diurnal period. At that time symptoms, as you call these distortions, shall be reviewed and such repeated until the distortion is alleviated.

The healing work to which each is apprentice may be used as desired.

It is to be noted that a crystal is available.

Questioner: Which crystal is that?

Ra: I am Ra. The flawed but sufficient crystal which rests upon the digit of this instrument's right hand.

Questioner: Would you tell me how to use that crystal for this purpose?

Ra: I am Ra. This is a large question.

You first, as a mind/body/spirit complex, balance and polarize the self, connecting the inner light with the upward spiraling in-pourings of the universal light. You have done exercises to regularize the processes involved. Look to them for the preparation of the crystallized being.

Take then the crystal and feel your polarized and potentiated balanced energy channeled in green ray healing through your being, going into and activating the crystalline regularity of frozen light which is the crystal. The crystal will resound with the charged light of incarnative love, and light energy will begin to radiate in specified fashion, beaming, in required light vibrations, healing energy, focused and intensified towards the magnetic field of the mind/body/spirit complex which is to be healed. This entity requesting such healing will then open the armor of the overall violet/red ray protective vibratory shield. Thus the inner vibratory fields, from center to center in mind, body, and spirit, may be interrupted and adjusted momentarily, thus offering the one to be healed the opportunity to choose a less distorted inner complex of energy fields and vibratory relationships.

Questioner: Should the crystal be held in the right hand of the healer?

Ra: I am Ra. This is incorrect. There are two recommended configurations.

The first, the chain about the neck to place the crystal in the physical position of the green-ray energy center. Second, the chain hung from the right hand, out-stretched, wound about the hand in such a way that the crystal may be swung so as to affect sensitive adjustments.

We offer this information realizing that much practice is needed to efficiently use these energies of self. However, each has the capability of doing so, and this information is not information which, if followed accurately, can be deleterious.

Questioner: Would an unflawed crystal be considerably more effective than the flawed one that we have now?

Ra: I am Ra. Without attempting to deem the priorities you may choose, we may note that the regularized or crystallized entity, in its configuration, is as critical as the perfection of the crystal used.

Questioner: Does the physical size of the crystal have any relationship to the effectiveness in the healing?

Ra: I am Ra. In some applications concerning planetary healing, this is a consideration. In working with an individual mind/body/spirit complex, the only requirement is that the crystal be in harmony with the crystallized being. There is perhaps a lower limit to the size of what you may call a faceted crystal, for light coming through this crystal needs to be spread the complete width of the spectrum of the one to be healed. It may further be noted that water is a type of crystal which is efficacious also although not as easy to hang from a chain in your density.

Questioner: Placing the end of this pencil on my naval, would the point of it then represent the place where the crystal should hang for proper green ray? Is this position correct?

Ra: I am Ra. We attempt your measurements. From 2 to 5.4 centimeters towards your heart is optimal.

Questioner: Using this piece of wood then, I would determine, from my naval, the position to be at the top of the piece of wood. Is this correct?

Ra: I am Ra. This is correct.

Questioner: How does the healing that you just told us about relate to the healing done in the King's Chamber in the Giza pyramid?

Ra: I am Ra. There are two advantages to doing this working in such a configuration of shapes and dimensions.

Firstly, the disruption or interruption of the violet/red armoring or protective shell is automatic.

In the second place, the light is configured by the very placement of this position in the seven distinctive color or energy vibratory rates, thus allowing the energy through the crystallized being, focused with the crystal, to manipulate with great ease the undisturbed and, shall we say, carefully delineated palate of energies or colors, both in space/time and in time/space. Thus the unarmored being may be adjusted rapidly. This is desirable in some cases, especially when the armoring is the largest moiety of the possibility of continued function of body complex activity in this density. The trauma of the interruption of this armoring vibration is then seen to be lessened.

We take this opportunity to pursue our honor/duty, as some of those creating the pyramid shape, to note that it is in no way necessary to use this shape in order to achieve healings, for seniority of vibration has caused the vibratory complexes of mind/body/spirit complexes to be healed to be less vulnerable to the trauma of the interrupted armoring.

Furthermore, as we have said, the powerful effect of the pyramid, with its mandatory disruption of the armoring, if used without the crystallized being, used with the wrong intention, or in the wrong configuration, can result in further distortions of entities which are perhaps the equal of some of your chemicals which cause disruptions in the energy fields in like manner.

Questioner: Is there currently any use for the pyramid shape at all that is beneficial?

Ra: I am Ra. This is in the affirmative if carefully used.

The pyramid may be used for the improvement of the meditative state as long as the shape is such that the entity is in Queen's Chamber position or entities are in balanced configuration about this central point.

The small pyramid shape, placed beneath a portion of the body complex may energize this body complex. This should be done for brief periods only, not to exceed 30 of your minutes.

The use of the pyramid to balance planetary energies still functions to a slight extent, but due to earth changes, the pyramids are no longer aligned properly for this work.

Questioner: What is the aid or the mechanism of the aid received for meditation by an entity who would be positioned in the so-called Queen's Chamber position?

Ra: I am Ra. Consider the polarity of mind/body/spirit complexes. The inner light is that which is your heart of being. Its strength equals your strength of will to seek the light. The position or balanced position of a group intensifies the amount of this will, the amount of awareness of the inner light necessary to attract the in-streaming light upward spiraling from the south magnetic pole of being.

Thus this is the place of the initiate, for many extraneous items or distortions will leave the entity as it intensifies its seeking, so that it may become one with this centralized and purified in-coming light.

Questioner: Then if a pyramid shape is used, it would seem to me that it would be necessary to make it large enough so that the Queen's Chamber position would be far enough from the King's Chamber position so that you could use that energy position and not be harmed by the energy position of the King's Chamber position. Is this correct?

Ra: I am Ra. In this application a pyramid shape may be smaller if the apex angle is less, thus not allowing the formation of the King's Chamber position. Also efficacious for this application are the following shapes: the silo, the cone, the dome, and the tipi.

Questioner: Do these shapes that you just mentioned have any of the effect of the King's Chamber at all, or do they have only the Queen's Chamber effect?

Ra: I am Ra. These shapes have the Queen's Chamber effect. It is to be noted that a strongly crystallized entity is, in effect, a portable King's Chamber position.

Questioner: Then are you saying that there is absolutely no need, use, or good in having the King's Chamber effect at this time in our planetary evolution?

Ra: I am Ra. If those who desired to be healers were of a crystallized nature and were all supplicants, those wishing less distortion, the pyramid would be, as always, a carefully designed set of parameters to distribute light and its energy so as to aid in healing catalyst.

However, we found that your peoples are not distorted towards the desire for purity to a great enough extent to be given this powerful and potentially dangerous gift. We, therefore, would suggest it not be used for healing in the traditional, shall we say, King's Chamber configuration which we naively gave to your peoples only to see its use grossly distorted and our teachings lost.

Questioner: What would be an appropriate apex angle for a tipi shape for our uses?

Ra: I am Ra. This is at your discretion. The principle of circular, rounded, or peaked shapes is that the center acts as an invisible inductive coil. Thus the energy patterns are spiraling and circular. Thus the choice of the most pleasant configuration is yours. The effect is relatively fixed.

Questioner: Is there any variation in the effect with respect to the material of construction, the thickness of the material? Is it simply the geometry of the shape, or is it related to some other factors?

Ra: I am Ra. The geometry, as you call it, or relationships of these shapes in their configuration is the great consideration. It is well to avoid stannous material or that of lead or other baser metals. Wood, plastic, glass, and other materials may all be considered to be appropriate.

Questioner: If a pyramid shape were placed below an entity, how would this be done? Would it be placed beneath the bed? I'm not quite sure about how to energize the entity by "placing it below." Could you tell me how to do that?

Ra: I am Ra. Your assumption is correct. If the shape is of appropriate size it may be placed directly beneath the cushion of the head or the pallet upon which the body complex rests.

We again caution that the third spiral of upward lining light, that which is emitted from the apex of this shape, is most deleterious to an entity in overdose and should not be used over-long.

Questioner: What would the height be, in centimeters, of one of these pyramids for best functioning?

Ra: I am Ra. It matters not. Only the proportion of the height of the pyramid from base to apex to the perimeter of the base is at all important.

Questioner: What should that proportion be?

Ra: I am Ra. This proportion should be the 1.16 which you may observe.

Questioner: Do you mean that the sum of the four base sides should be 1.16 of the height of the pyramid?

Ra: I am Ra. This is correct.

Questioner: By saying that the Queen's Chamber was the initiatory place, could you tell me what you mean by that?

Ra: I am Ra. This question is a large one. We cannot describe initiation in its specific sense due to our distortion towards the belief/understanding that the process which we offered so many of your years ago was not a balanced one.

However, you are aware of the concept of initiation and realize that it demands the centering of the being upon the seeking of the Creator. We have hoped to balance this understanding by enunciating the Law of One, that is, that all things are one Creator. Thus seeking the Creator is done not just in meditation and in the work of an adept but in the experiential nexus of each moment.

The initiation of the Queen's Chamber has to do with the abandoning of self to such desire to know the Creator in full that the purified in-streaming light is drawn in balanced fashion through all energy centers, meeting in indigo and opening the gate to intelligent infinity. Thus the entity experiences true life or, as your people call it, resurrection.

Questioner: You also mentioned that the pyramid was used for learning. Was this the same process or is there a difference?

Ra: I am Ra. There is a difference.

Questioner: What is the difference?

Ra: I am Ra. The difference is the presence of other-selves manifesting in space/time and after some study, in time/space, for the purpose of teach/learning. In the system created by us, schools were apart from the pyramid, the experiences being solitary.

Questioner: I didn't quite understand what you meant by that. Could you tell me more of what you are talking about?

Ra: I am Ra. This is a wide subject. Please restate for specificity.

Questioner: Did you mean that teachers from your vibration or density were manifest in the Queen's Chamber to teach those initiates, or did you mean something else?

Ra: I am Ra. In our system experiences in the Queen's Chamber position were solitary. In Atlantis and in South America teachers shared the pyramid experiences.

Questioner: How did this learning process take place—learning or teaching—in the pyramid?

Ra: I am Ra. How does teach/learning and learn/teaching ever take place?

Questioner: The dangerous pyramid shape for use today would be a four-sided pyramid that was large enough to create the King's Chamber effect. Is that statement correct?

Ra: I am Ra. This statement is correct with the additional understanding that the 76° apex angle is that characteristic of the powerful shape.

Questioner: Then I am assuming that we should not use a pyramid of 76° at the apex angle under any circumstances. Is that correct?

Ra: I am Ra. This is at your discretion.

Questioner: I will restate the question. I am assuming then that it might be dangerous to use a 76° angle pyramid, and I will ask what angle less than 76° would be roughly the first angle that would not produce this dangerous effect?

Ra: I am Ra. Your assumption is correct. The lesser angle may be any angle less than 70°.

Questioner: Thank you. I want to go on with more questioning on the pyramid, but I want to ask a question that *(name)* has here. I'll throw it in at this point. Could you please expand on the concept of space/time and time/space and how to get past this concept and what density level do these concepts no longer affect the individual?

Ra: I am Ra. This will be the last full query of this working. This instrument has some vital energy left. However, we become concerned with the increasing distortions of the body complex towards pain.

The space/time and time/space concepts are those concepts describing as mathematically as possible the relationships of your illusion, that which is seen to that which is unseen. These descriptive terms are clumsy. They, however, suffice for this work.

In the experiences of the mystical search for unity, these need never be considered, for they are but part of an illusory system. The seeker seeks the One. The One is to be sought, as we have said, by the balanced and self-accepting self aware, both of its apparent distortions and its total perfection. Resting in this balanced awareness, the entity then opens the self to the universe which it is. The light energy of all things may then be attracted by this intense seeking, and wherever the inner seeking meets the attracted cosmic prana, realization of the One takes place.

The purpose of clearing each energy center is to allow that meeting place to occur at the indigo ray vibration, thus making contact with intelligent infinity and dissolving all illusions. Service-to-others is automatic at the released energy generated by this state of consciousness.

The space/time and time/space distinctions, as you understand them, do not hold sway except in third-density. However, fourth, fifth, and to some extent, sixth, work within some system of polarized space/time and time/space.

The calculation necessary to move from one system to another through the dimensions are somewhat difficult. Therefore, we have the most difficulty sharing numerical concepts with you and take this opportunity to repeat our request that you monitor our numbers and query any that seem questionable.

Is there a brief query that we may answer before we leave this instrument?

Questioner: Is there anything that we can do to make the instrument more comfortable or to improve the contact?

Ra: I am Ra. All is harmonious. We greet you all in joy. The adjustments are satisfactory.

I am Ra. I leave you in the love and in the light of the one infinite Creator. Go forth, therefore, rejoicing in the power and in the peace of the one infinite Creator. Adonai.

Sunday Meditation
June 14, 1981

(Carla channeling)

[I am Hatonn,] and I greet you, my friends, in the love and in the light of our infinite Creator. It gives us great pleasure to greet each of you, and especially do we welcome the one new to our group and assure this entity that we are most honored to be able to share our thoughts with her at this time.

My friends, we have always spoken to you of one very simple Thought that is the original Thought of the Creator. This original Thought is love. Thus, we bring to your peoples the love of the Creator. All that you see about you that is material, is made of the material of love, which is light, and it is for this reason that we greet you in love and in light. We speak always to that point and attempt in many different ways to approach it according to your various circumstances.

Tonight we would approach this understanding of love by speaking to you of a concept which is generated by your peoples. That concept is security. Among your peoples, my friends, it is understood that security is desirable, and yet rare is the person that feels secure. Where is security to be found, my friends? Is it to be found in the accumulation of your worldly goods? It would seem that this is not the case, for there are many among your peoples who have amassed a comfortable amount of worldly goods, and yet are painfully insecure. Is it the occupation of your hours, of what you call work, that gives you security? This seems to be a widespread concept among your peoples, that what an entity does lends to that entity reality, which the entity alone does not have. To do, then, is to be, and to do represents security.

And, yet, if an entity is at all thoughtful, this security too will pall, for it will become clear as experiences accumulate for an entity, that he is more than what he does, and thus this security too will vanish. We have often asked you to meditate, my friends, and we suggest it once again in this regard, for there is only one security: that is the knowledge of the nature of yourself. To know that you are not a transient being is to be secure. To know that this is an illusion and that though you participate in it and play your part, that there is an infinite which is part of your makeup, is to feel secure.

This knowledge of the self may come spontaneously to a few, but for the most part it is a hard won knowledge. Serenity, long sought after, is seldom won permanently and so, day by day, you must seek knowledge of your true nature, of your true oneness with love in meditation. It does not matter what the technique may be for your meditation. It matters only that you desire to seek the truth of your own nature and of the nature of the creation. As you look about you, you may see great evidence, my friends, of your peoples striving for security. As you sit within this domicile, you sit within a location which has been carefully planned to increase security of entities and so it shall do for a brief period of your time.

One day, my friends, these entities will be in this dimension no more. They will leave their shell, their securities, their misconceptions of what security is, and they will embark upon a very interesting journey, my friends. In meditation you may begin that journey now. You may become aware of the infinite nature of yourself while in this illusion and, knowing this, your behavior may be such that the Creator's love may find its way through the channel of your being with more ease.

At this time I would transfer this contact. I am Hatonn.

(L channeling)

I am Hatonn, and I greet you, my brothers, in the love and the light of our Creator.

The concept of security in its reality is not difficult to understand, my brothers, for true security lies not in that which one possesses, but rather in that which one gives away. If you would seek security, seek it in service, for service is the path upon which the soul, as you call it, rises through the planes of the universe. As one performs service, either in the path of service to oneself or in service to other, his act functions as a sort of solvent which reduces his density just as water, for example, will dissolve away crystalline forms that might be adhering to a less solid formation, thus freeing it of unnecessary weight and rigidity which might be holding it back.

Consider, if you will, how a spring might be pressed and then coated with a solid substance that, if allowed to remain, would keep the spring forever compressed, never allowed to release its pent energy to grow and expand. Service, for the individual, is that which dissolves away the more dense actions, the more dense perceptions and prejudices that we use to force ourselves to retain a form which needs to be dissolved away, allowing us to use the energy contained within us and release ourselves from our self-imposed bondage.

Therefore, my brothers, if you would be secure, then be secure in your striving. Find your contentment in accelerated growth. Hitch your wagon, as the saying goes, to the nearest star and let it bear you where it will, as ever onward and ever upward. And that, my brothers, is the objective of your striving.

At this time I would transfer this contact to another instrument, I am Hatonn.

(Jim channeling)

I am Hatonn. I am with this instrument. We would now offer ourselves in the service of answering questions—or attempting them, to be more precise. Are there any questions which we might attempt to answer?

Carla: I have a very minor one. I was just wondering if the reason that there was a pause there was because two of our numbers were asleep and I woke them up and as soon as I woke them up you were able to come through. Was that the blockage? Is there a drain on the energy of the group if there is someone asleep?

I am Hatonn, and we would answer you, my sister, by saying that, in part, you are correct, For the most efficient contact to be made, as you know, your tuning device, whichever you may use for the evening, serves the purpose of making each of the entities within your circle as one, each with the other, and it is to this total entity that we communicate. There was also another problem, shall we say, and that was this instrument was not concentrating as precisely as necessary, for his attention was also drawn to those who had, shall we say, momentarily departed our group.

May we answer you further, my sister?

Carla: That does it except I was also interested in whether the children that were with us were content that we were meditating and that was why the contact was such a good one tonight.

I am Hatonn. We would say in this answer that the young entities which are resting now in the upper part of this dwelling are a, shall we say, gentling influence upon the group if they are not within the earshot, shall we say, of the group and the message, for if they are located too closely, then they may serve the opposite purpose of keeping the contact from occurring, for they are not yet of the age of decision, whereby they may decide that they wish to participate in this group, and as you know, each person within the circle must, of their own free will, choose to be within the circle and to experience the message which we have to offer. Thus, entities such as the young children may play either role and on this occasion they are, what might be called, a gentling influence, helping each within the circle to find that openness of child within the self which wishes to hear a message such as the humble and simple message which we of Hatonn have to share with your group.

May we answer you further, my sister?

Carla: No. Thank you, Hatonn.

We thank you, as always. May we answer another question?

C: I don't know if it's so much a question as just me wanting to talk. I work at a … we have grocery stores … and I see a lot of food and things just wasted because of laws that have been established by our lawmakers. But, this past week there was an incidence in which I was a part, and which afterwards I was kind of regretting having done to begin with. I remember before the incident happened, I thought what a waste it was going to be that we had to destroy all this food and then I got to thinking—according to the laws made by our lawmakers to protect people, since this food was not exactly as it should have been according to guidelines that have been established, that perhaps it was the best thing to get rid of it, but I didn't really want to have a part in it, but then when it came down to the time to destroy the food, instead of … I did not have to do it, but something in me made me want to do it. I don't know what it was, how or what … to destroy this stuff, and like I say, after it all occurred it was just … at first it didn't hit me … the waste. I didn't think anything about me doing it, then later I couldn't figure out why I had done this … why I even enjoyed doing this, I mean, in this particular case I knew the exact nature of [the] problem with the food stuff was nothing serious. It was nothing major. It was nothing to hurt anyone. It was just a little too much of water in the product. But the fact that I did it and really almost felt compelled to, just wanted to do it, bothered me.

It was not the first time it's happened. It's happened other times with things they throw away which are really still useful, but I don't know. I just … in this instance it just hit me. I'm just wondering, as we progress, will we gain enough sense not to destroy just because some law says we should or we grow out of need for an established code of laws. What can we expect as we leave this density?

I am Hatonn. My brother, we would answer you by saying, as we have spoken earlier this evening concerning security, that those laws which your culture has conceived are laws which deal with your material world and deal with matters which are not the heart of your being. You may concern yourselves with them as much or as little as you like, for they are, if we may say, of little consequence in the overall picture of your life, the journey which you are making, and the goal towards which each of you move.

When you leave this density you will, for a greater or shorter period of what you call time, depending upon your own individual need and place, shall we say, be able to tune into the universal laws which govern all creation. These laws are based upon the foundation of the love of the infinite Creator. These laws are those which shall guide you as surely as the stars have guided your sailors for centuries. These laws are those which are, at this moment, available to each of those upon your planet. Available for the seeking; available to the seeker. We would suggest that you use each of the instances, such as the one which you have spoken of this evening, as what might be called a catalyst to discover the underlying or greater law, the law greater than the one on the surface, greater than appearance, greater than rules, regulations in the amount of water in a product. We would suggest that you use each puzzling circumstance as a riddle in your own mind and let your consideration of it take you deeper and deeper until you discover for yourself the true law at its foundation.

May we answer you further, my brother?

C: Something that's beyond this last instance was brought forward in my mind. I don't know. It just seems like for years now it's been little power games going on in my mind, rethinking situations, having hindsight of what I should have done, what I will do so that I'll have the upper hand, I won't be the one under the other person. I don't believe that I physically manifest them to a great extent, as far as physical actions to carry things out, but sometimes I worry because it seems like they just keep reoccurring, reoccurring, just like a steady stream. It's not so much here and there, but just isolated situations—seems like a constant thing.

Then I get situations like this week we had a chance to just let out this thing, that I had all this power to destroy all this stuff, exhilarating for the moment but really, it really made me feel bad. Should I just spend more time in meditation, why these things are occurring?

I am Hatonn. Again, my brother, we would say that you have discovered for yourself the necessary step to take. Indeed, meditation might be that procedure which would aid you in your balancing as you go about your daily activities, for most of the activities of the people of your planet do not have balance, do not have harmony. It is as if there is disease and those who participate within the daily activities of your planet are susceptible to this disease, or imbalance, and by using the technique of meditation you will find within yourself the ability to balance, so that the activities [in] which you participate during the day might become part of a larger understanding within your own being and might become, for you, catalysts to learn and to grow further and further into the understanding and the oneness of the infinite Creator. We cannot urge too often for you people to consider meditation as the opportunity to find any answers to the puzzles which are presented daily in your lives.

May we answer you further, my brother?

C: No. I think I just felt like talking a little bit tonight, thank you. Thank you for your answers.

We thank you. It is always a privilege and an honor to be able, not only to share our simple thoughts with your group, but to listen to those thoughts which are of concern to you. Is there another question at this time?

L: I have a question I'd like to ask, Hatonn. I have a small child that I'm responsible for and I find that this service to him of being a parent frequently conflicts with my desire to attend these meditations. He is, as yet, too young to be able to converse or understand your advice and the teachings you convey to us, therefore, would it be proper to bring him along to the meditations or would this interfere with the meditations?

I am Hatonn. My brother, as we have mentioned earlier this evening, each entity which joins this circle must join of their own free will and in most cases this means that entities must be able to decide and be of the age of decision whereby they may decide to join this group. We have, on some occasions, spoken to groups which contained entities who were of, what might be called, a young age. But these instances have been few and we have on those instances been required by the decision of the group and of the young entities to speak in much more general terms than we are able to speak on this occasion, for instance.

We would, in your case, suggest that as an alternative to bringing your young child to this meditation that you attempt through your own words to explain to your child those concepts which have meaning to you, that you have derived from this meditation. And when your child is of an age whereby through this dialogue with you he is able to choose for himself to come to a meditation such as this and partake, then that shall be the time when it is proper to include your child.

May we answer you further, my brother?

L: Yes. I have two questions. One is, could you define more fully the age at which a child is capable of making that decision and second, to the best of my understanding, my child is not yet able to understand even single sentence explanations. He's still functioning on the basis of communication through single words and very limited word associations. I find it difficult to believe that I could explain any concepts to him at this time. Is there any further advice you could offer in that area?

I am Hatonn. In this instance, my brother, we would say that it is difficult to determine precisely the age at which a child …

(Side one of tape ends.)

(Jim channeling)

I am Hatonn, and am with this instrument once again. As we were saying, it is not easy to determine the age at which a child may be able to decide for itself, but we might suggest that the age of decision-making for most children, a range, shall we say, for those of your peoples, is somewhere between the ages of approximately four to the age of seven. It varies according to individual circumstances. We would suggest further that in the case of your own child that you might proceed first, if he is unable to understand complete sentences, that you explain words or concepts individually by actions which have meaning for your child.

In this area you will, of necessity, need to rely upon your own creativity, a type of communication which your child is able to understand and which you are aware through experience with your child that he is able to understand and to connect with words and phrases.

We would suggest as a next step that when your child is able to understand sentences, that you continue as we previously suggested, to provide, may we say, your child with those concepts which are of value to you, and in this way begin the education on a spiritual level which will enable your child to understand those concepts which we present here. For when your child is able to understand those concepts spoken from your lips, as we speak to you, then he will also be able to understand what it is we have to share with each who attends these meditations, for we are none other than your other selves, or should we say, your brothers and sisters, who speak to you as brothers and sisters. Therefore, when your child is able to understand through dialogue with you, then you will know that he is also able to understand that which we have to share with those in your group.

May we answer you further, my brother?

L: No. I feel you've answered my question. Thank you.

We thank you. Is there another question at this time?

(Pause)

I am Hatonn. It has been a great privilege and an honor to be able to speak a few of our simple thoughts with your group this evening. We greatly appreciate each opportunity to join you in your meditations. It is a source of great joy for we of Hatonn to be able to join any group or any entity as their meditations are conducted. We would assure each in this circle tonight that we would be most happy to join them in meditation at any time, whether they are with this group or alone, meditating. We would be most happy to join you and your request is all that is needed. We are known to you as those of Hatonn, simple messengers of the love and the light of the infinite Creator, and in that love and light we leave you now. I am Hatonn. Adonai. ✣

The Law of One, Book III, Session 58
June 16, 1981

Ra: I am Ra. I greet you in the love and in the light of the one infinite Creator. We communicate now.

Questioner: Would you please give me an indication of the instrument's condition?

Ra: I am Ra. This condition is as previously noted except that the physical distortions mentioned have somewhat increased.

Questioner: Could you tell me the cause of the increase of the physical distortions.

Ra: I am Ra. Physical distortions of this nature are begun, as we have said, due to overactivity of weak, as you call this distortion, portions of the body complex. The worsening is due to the nature of the distortion itself which you call arthritis. Once begun, the distortion will unpredictably remain and unpredictably worsen or lessen.

Questioner: We have tried healing with the diamond crystal. I have tried both using the crystal around my neck and dangling it from a chain held in my right hand. I think that possibly that to do the best work on the wrist I should dangle the crystal just below my right hand from a distance of just a centimeter or two, holding it directly above the wrist. Is this correct?

Ra: I am Ra. This would be appropriate if you were practiced at your healing art. To work with a powerful crystal such as you have, while unable to perceive the magnetic flux of the subtle bodies, is perhaps the same as recommending that the beginner, with saw and nail, create the Vatican.

There is great art in the use of the swung crystal. At this point in your development, you would do well to work with the unpowerful crystals in ascertaining, not only the physical major energy centers, but also the physical secondary and tertiary energy centers and then begin to find the corresponding subtle body energy centers. In this way, you may activate your own inner vision.

Questioner: What type of crystal should be used for that?

Ra: I am Ra. You may use any dangling weight of symmetrical form, for your purpose is not to disturb or manipulate these energy centers but merely to locate them and become aware of what they feel like when in a balanced state and when in an unbalanced or blocked state.

Questioner: Am I correct in assuming that what I am to do is to dangle a weight approximately two feet below my hand and place it over the body, and when the weight starts moving in a clockwise rotational direction it would indicate an unblocked energy center. Is this correct?

Ra: I am Ra. The measurement from hand to weight is unimportant and at your discretion. The circular motion shows an unblocked energy center. However, some entities are polarized the reverse of others and, therefore, it is well to test the form of normal energy spirals before beginning the procedure.

Questioner: How would you test?

Ra: I am Ra. Test is done by first holding the weight over your own hand and observing your particular configuration. Then using the other-self's hand, repeat the procedure.

Questioner: In the case of the instrument we are concerned with the healing of the wrists and hands. Would I then test the energy center of the instrument's wrist area? Is this correct?

Ra: I am Ra. We have given you general information regarding this form of healing and have explicated the instrument's condition. There is a line beyond which information is an intrusion upon the Law of Confusion.

Questioner: I would like to trace the energy patterns and what is actually happening in these patterns and flow of energy in a couple of instances. I would first take the pyramid shape and trace the energy that is focused somehow by this shape. I will make a statement and let you correct it.

I think that the pyramid can be in any orientation and provide some focusing of spiraling energy, but the greatest focusing of it occurs when one side of it is precisely parallel to magnetic north. Is this correct?

Ra: I am Ra. This is substantially correct with one addition. If one corner is oriented to the magnetic north, the energy will be enhanced in its focus also.

Questioner: Do you mean that if I drew a line through two opposite corners of the pyramid at the base and aimed that at magnetic north—that would be precisely 45° out of the orientation of one side aimed at magnetic north—that it would work just as well? Is that what you are saying?

Ra: I am Ra. It would work much better than if the pyramid shape were quite unaligned. It would not work quite as efficiently as the aforementioned configuration.

Questioner: Would the pyramid shape work just as well right side up as upside down with respect to the surface of the Earth, assuming the magnetic alignment was the same in both cases?

Ra: I am Ra. We do not penetrate your query. The reversed shape of the pyramid reverses the effects of the pyramid. Further, it is difficult to build such a structure, point down. Perhaps we have misinterpreted your query.

Questioner: I used this question only to understand the way the pyramid focuses light, not for the purpose of using one. I was just saying if we did build a pyramid point down, would it focus at the Queen's Chamber position or just below it the same way as if it were point up?

Ra: I am Ra. It would only work thusly if an entity's polarity were, for some reason, reversed.

Questioner: Then the lines of spiraling light energy—do they originate from a position towards the center of the Earth and radiate outward from that point?

Ra: I am Ra. The pyramid shape is a collector which draws the in-streaming energy from what you would term, the bottom or base, and allows this energy to spiral upward in a line with the apex of this shape. This is also true if a pyramid shape is upended. The energy is not Earth energy, as we understand your question, but is light energy which is omni-present.

Questioner: Does it matter if the pyramid is solid or is made of four thin sides, or is there a difference in effect between those two makes?

Ra: I am Ra. As an energy collector, the shape itself is the only requirement. From the standpoint of the practical needs of your body complexes, if one is to house one's self in such a shape, it is well that this shape be solid sided in order to avoid being inundated by outer stimuli.

Questioner: Then if I just used a wire frame that was four pieces of wire joined at the apex running down to the base, and the pyramid were totally open, this would do the same thing to the spiraling light energy? Is this correct?

Ra: I am Ra. The concept of the frame as equal to the solid form is correct. However, there are many metals not recommended for use in pyramid shapes designed to aid the meditative process. Those that are recommended are, in your system of barter, what you call expensive. The wood, or other natural materials, or the man-made plastic rods will also be of service.

Questioner: Why is the spiraling light focused by something as open and simple as four wooden rods joined at an apex angle?

Ra: I am Ra. If you pictured light in the metaphysical sense, as water, and the pyramid shape as a funnel, this concept might become self-evident.

Questioner: Thank you. I do not wish to get into subject matter of no importance. I had assumed that questions about the pyramid were desired by you due to the fact that some danger was involved to some who had misused the pyramid, etc.

I am trying to understand the way light works and am trying to get a grasp of how everything works together, and I was hoping that questions on the pyramid would help me understand the third distortion, which is light. As I understand it, the pyramid shape acts as a funnel increasing the density of energy so that the individual may have a greater intensity of actually the third distortion. Is this correct?

Ra: I am Ra. In general, this is correct.

Questioner: Then the pure crystalline shape, such as the diamond, you mentioned as being frozen light—it seems that this third-density physical manifestation of light is somehow a window or focusing mechanism for the third distortion in a general sense. Is this correct?

Ra: I am Ra. This is basically correct. However, it may be noted that only the will of the crystallized entity may cause interdimensional light to flow through this material. The more regularized the entity, and the more regularized the crystal, the more profound the effect.

Questioner: There are many people who are now bending metal, doing other things like that by mentally requesting this happen. What is happening in that case?

Ra: I am Ra. That which occurs in this instance may be likened to the influence of the second spiral of light in a pyramid being used by an entity. As this second spiral ends at the apex, the light may be likened unto a laser beam in the metaphysical sense and when intelligently directed may cause bending not only in the pyramid, but this is the type of energy which is tapped into by those capable of this focusing of the upward spiraling light. This is made possible through contact in indigo ray with intelligent energy.

Questioner: Why are these people able to do this? They seem to have no training; they are just able to do it.

Ra: I am Ra. They remember the disciplines necessary for this activity which is merely useful upon other true color vibratory experiential nexi.

Questioner: Then you are saying that this wouldn't be useful in our present density. Will it be useful in fourth-density on this planet in the very near future?

Ra: I am Ra. The end of such energy focusing is to build, not to destroy, and it does become quite useful as, shall we say, an alternative to third-density building methods.

Questioner: Is it also used for healing?

Ra: I am Ra. No.

Questioner: Is there any advantage in attempting to develop these characteristics or in being able to bend metal, etc.? What I am trying to say is, are these characteristics a signpost of the development of an entity, or is it merely something else? For instance, as an entity develops through his indigo would a signpost of his development be this bending ability?

Ra: I am Ra. This will be the last full query of this working.

Let us specify the three spirals of light energy which the pyramid exemplifies. Firstly, the fundamental spiral which is used for study and for healing. Second, the spiral to the apex which is used for building. Thirdly, the spiral spreading from the apex which is used for energizing.

Contact with indigo ray need not necessarily show itself in any certain gift or guidepost, as you have said. There are some whose indigo energy is that of pure being and never is manifested, yet all are aware of such an entity's progress. Others may teach or share in many ways contact with intelligent energy. Others continue in unmanifested form, seeking intelligent infinity.

Thus the manifestation is lesser signpost than that which is sensed or intuited about a mind/body/spirit complex. This violet ray being-ness is far more indicative of true self.

Are there any brief queries or small matters we may clear up, if we can, before we leave this instrument?

Questioner: I did have a question on what you meant by the "third spiral" and if that is too long I would just ask if there is anything that we can do to make the instrument more comfortable or to improve the contact?

Ra: I am Ra. We may answer briefly. You may query in more detail if you deem it desirable at another session.

If you picture the candle flame, you may see the third spiral.

This instrument is well balanced. The accoutrements are aligned well. You are conscientious.

I am Ra. I leave you, my friends, in the love and in the light of the one infinite Creator. Go forth, therefore, rejoicing in the power and the peace of the one infinite Creator. Adonai.

Sunday Meditation
June 21, 1981

(Jim channeling)

I am Hatonn. I am with this instrument. I greet you, my friends, in the love and the light of the infinite Creator. We have had some difficulty initiating contact this evening. The difficulty has to do with our pleasant problem, shall we say, of an abundance of instruments from which to choose. This instrument was finally able to speak our contact after doing a bit of manipulating with the machine.

As always, it is a great honor and privilege to be asked by your group to share a few of our thoughts with you. We of Hatonn strive through such meetings as this to share a simple, but, we feel, profound message with your people, with those who are willing to open their hearts and their minds to new experiences and new understanding of the one infinite Creator. The new understandings are always built upon the never changing original Thought which the Creator used to create all of the creation. This thought, my friends, as you know, is based on the concept of love and the concept of unity. Throughout all of the creation, the creation is unified by love. Love is the moving force, the foundation upon which all is built.

We of Hatonn have the simple task, it would seem—though it has not always proven simple in our past—we have the task of sharing our insights and our understandings of how love works within the density which you inhabit at this time. We hope through these communications that we are able to provide means whereby you might see love in action in each of your waking moments, for that is the task of your density. That is the learning which each must, to a certain degree, master before passing on to the next lesson, shall we say. We have not always been able to find means whereby we might be able to explain love to those who seek our guidance in every manner, but through continued communications with your people we have learned much in the realm of explaining and experiencing that concept of love, whichever is sought by those of your people.

This evening we would speak a few words upon the concept of confusion and its relationship to love. It might not seem, at first glance, as an area which could be connected to love, but consider, my friends, the state of confusion. Surely, each of you can remember many times when you found yourself in such a state. Look at the response which is confusion. Confusion is, as you know, a state whereby there is little activity, for activity has been brought to a halt because certain messages do not, shall we say, jibe with your ideas or your preconceived notions about what should be. We would suggest that in such a situation described as confusion that it is most beneficial to rest within that position for a few of, what you might call, your moments of time.

Consider now and place yourself now in such a state for a few moments, if you will. Look within the boundaries of confusion. See? There appears to be no exit. Within the confusion you have a status of motionless—motionless being. You have traveled a path up to that point and the path leads no further. You are unsure of which way you should go. Look now at the directions which present themselves, most usually in a multitude, so that you are yet more confused. Each path a possibility, yet each path an impossibility. Confusion.

Consider carefully, now, what response will take you yet further in clear understanding of your journey. At this particular time, how shall you approach the problem, the predicament? Shall you blindly go forward upon the first path which presents itself? And if this path is the incorrect choice? More confusion. Shall you wait and shall you assess the many paths that present themselves? Still you find yourself in confusion. Shall you do nothing? The confusion persists. What must you do to move from confusion and to the proper path for your next step of growth?

Consider this for a few moments, if you will. As the confusion fills your being, what shall you do? Look within your being, my friends. Can you find an openness and acceptance of your state of confusion? It is, after all, your state at the moment. Could you not perhaps claim it? It is no sin, shall we say, to be confused. Indeed, perhaps it is of great benefit, for if you can accept the situation in which you know that you do not know, then might there be the openness, the acceptance, the love within your being of this state of confusion; the openness that will allow the proper course of action of thought to be drawn to you as a magnet draws the filings of iron.

For if you are open as an empty cup, then more can be added, or poured into your being, but if you persist in believing that you know exactly what you need to do to keep up the image, shall we say, and to bull ahead with any plan simply to have a plan of action, then you are likened unto the cup that is full and no more may be added until the cup is empty.

Within this state of confusion, when the state of confusion can be accepted as a part of the being that is yourself, then, through this acceptance you may find within yourself the openness to draw wisdom unto your being. Wisdom is much likened unto the forces which fill a vacuum. It is all about you. It is always available; available for the learning; available to those who make a place within their being for it; available to those who seek it, seek it, perhaps, by realizing that they do not know all the answers that they need at any moment, though at every moment most entities console themselves by thinking that they know much.

We of Hatonn would counsel foolishness, my friends. We would counsel that you know very little, that we ourselves know very little, but that this state of confusion, shall we say, is a state of infinite possibilities to those who accept it as part of their being and who use it as a method of drawing wisdom unto then.

We would at this time pause for a few moments so that our brother of Laitos may pass among you, and to those who request assistance in their meditation, our brother Laitos will contact each and deepen the meditative state. We would pause now for a few moments. I am Hatonn.

(Pause)

I am Hatonn, and am with this instrument once again. We would at this time transfer this contact to another instrument. I am Hatonn.

(Carla channeling)

I am now with this instrument. I am Hatonn and I greet you, my friends, again in the love and in the light of our infinite Creator. Yes, my friends, there is much in your illusion which seems to you to be inconvenient and which does bring confusion, and yet, we suggest to you that without some disorder there is no creation. Perhaps you have known entities or perhaps you have even found within yourself some tendency towards the desire for the ultimate orderliness of existence. And perhaps you have noted the sterility which this brings. Just as that which is fruitful multiplies—does so with a minimum of neatness and an excess of enthusiasm—so does confusion offer you a minimum of neatness.

It is to you, my friends, that the decision is handed: enthusiasm, or its opposite. It is often difficult to be enthusiastic about the unknown. It is difficult to be enthusiastic when you truly do not know what to do. It is difficult to count oneself lucky when one seems to be lost in a sea with no shore in sight. But this is the breeding ground of new beginnings, of transformations, and of wisdoms. Where are you, my friends? Where do you see yourselves at this moment? Do you see yourselves in a room or in a dwelling or in a city or a nation? Can you pull away and see yourself upon the surface of the planet, sitting in darkness? Can you pull further, further away and lose sight of the planet altogether as you view the galaxy in which you have your being at this time? Is there any meaning to so small a piece of consciousness as one entity—you—seated in darkness on a small planet in a minor solar system in a reasonable-sized galaxy among billions of other galaxies? Or is it all confusion?

We suggest to you, my friends, that confusion is balanced by meaning and meaning by confusion. You will not find the meaning within each moment of your existence without the acceptance of the confusion, of the foolishness of the limitations of our understanding as entities which are part of a vast and mysterious universe. The meaning is there, my friends. We have seen the laws of creation and their working never falters, to the best of our understanding. Yet, from moment to moment, the great laws disappear and confusion often reigns. If you can remain conscious both of how small a part of creation you are and of how perfect a part of it you are, you will have achieved a great deal.

And this, my friends, as you know, cannot be done without meditation. We offer these thoughts to you at this time, for we know your desire to be of service to others, but we suggest to you that you first must align yourself with the original Thought of the Creator in whatever situation you may find yourself, including the greatest confusion. Then and only then, can you be of maximum aid to those about you.

At this time we would open the meeting to questions.

C: Yes, I have a question. We were discussing before the meditation about entities sort of getting together before their incarnation here to set up the lessons that they need to learn and to work with each other, but it seems that many times second-density creatures aid us in our lessons. And I was wondering, is there some coordinating force who coordinates the second-density creatures to aid in the lessons of third-density creatures, referring to an event like what happened this week with the turtle?

I am Hatonn. The cart is basically before the horse in your question in that third-density entities may be of great service to second-density entities by offering them love. The second-density entity then mirrors that emotion and develops the responses which it is taught by the third-density entity.

May we answer you further?

C: Then, so our expression of love toward second-density creatures aids them in their evolution. I can see that, but it seems they're also a reinforcement for us and it seems like many times more than a coincidence that situations arise where we serve them or they serve us.

I am Hatonn. We had to keep this instrument quiet while the machine was being changed.

We understand your question and find it slightly difficult to respond to, for there are random events which, when responded to, are invested with meaning according to the response given. Thus, if a second-density creature, whether it be a tree or an animal or some other second-density entity, is aided voluntarily by a third-density entity, this may well be a random choice and yet, it is catalyst for growth for the third-density entity as well as the second-density entity. The greatest help that can be given is that of the pet, as you may call a domestic animal or plant, whereby love is shared and the second-density entity invested with love. This second-density entity then becomes a mirror reflecting the third-density entity, both in good and bad habits, as you may call them, according to your own judgment.

May we answer you further, my brother?

C: No, I guess not. Thank you.

We thank you. Is there another question at this time?

M: How does one get in touch with the infinite intelligence? Ra has spoken of the infinite intelligence at length, but how do we get in touch?

I am Hatonn. My brother, the answer to this question would be impossible to share except in a joking manner. We may say to you, to get to Carnegie Hall you must rehearse, and yet that does not give you all the information which you need to know. To follow the path of love is to achieve unity with infinite intelligence, as you call it, or the one infinite Creator. There is no other possibility in the end, for it is the ultimate attraction towards which we all are drawn. To achieve this contact within your present illusion it is necessary to achieve within the self a serenity and love of self, a peaceful love of others, and an overriding desire to seek the truth.

There are many avenues to intelligent infinity, all having to do with the use of the creative force of love. Meditation, healing, communication, what you may call ritual and ceremony, the proper use of the body, the mind, and the spirit, all these are ways and keys of achieving intelligent infinity contact, as you call it. We would simply say love and serve and seek to know. This has been our simple message always.

May we answer you further, my brother?

M: Yes. Ra has spoken of several entities, both positive and negative, that were able to be of great service to others or to themselves because they were in touch with this cosmic consciousness, yet, how did they reach that point in this particular plane and with all its confusion?

I am Hatonn. As we said, my brother, there is a great amount of discipline involved in this seeking. This is the seeking of the adept. It cannot be achieved quickly or lightly, for the most part, but must be sought fruitlessly and seemingly without any achievement in all patience, through all confusion, through all self-doubt, through all tribulation, constantly seeking, constantly asking, constantly waiting, constantly knowing that that which is sought will be found and at some moment, when all is completed within your being, at some moment unknown it will occur and in that moment you will know the joy of love and light and infinity. This will happen to you and to each. This is your destiny. If you consciously seek it, it will simply occur more quickly in your time measurement.

May we answer you further, my brother?

M: No, thank you.

We thank you also. Is there another question at this time?

L: Could you speak to us on the subject of relationships between men and women on this plane? The proper state, as opposed to a number of rituals and games we've developed for interrelating?

I am Hatonn. My brother, in your question lies the answer. The relationship between any two entities among your peoples would hopefully be that of love freely given and freely received, of aid and service freely given and freely received. There are difficulties inherent in your cultural or societal structure having to do with possession of property and this causes entities to consider other entities much as one business would consider another when contemplating a merger. This is not an appropriate method of polarizing towards the love and the light of the infinite Creator, nor does it give the greatest opportunity for freely given service, each to the other.

It is not necessary to participate in such ritualized activities in order to form deep and lasting relationships. It is, in fact, possible, and we have seen it among your peoples, for entities to engage in what you call the marriage bond and remain in free and open love and service one to the other. This, however, takes a great amount of conscious awareness of the dangers of impersonal thinking on the part of each entity involved in such a relationship. In any relationship, the key is to consider service to the other entity above all things.

May we answer you further?

L: Yes. You made the phrase, "the dangers of impersonal living." I believe I quoted you correctly. Could you expand upon that please?

I am Hatonn. When there are contracts between business entities, the contract gives each entity rights and privileges and duties. This contract then binds the entities in an agreement. This is an impersonal arrangement which dehumanizes a relationship if it be between two entities on a personal level, and causes each to think of his or her rights and privileges and how to minimize the responsibilities. It is difficult not to succumb from time to time to thinking of these rights and privileges due to one who has so carefully written out this agreement and signed it, for much is given by one who signs such an agreement. These contracts between entities are of a serious nature, and this seriousness is felt by both and often becomes burdensome, thus entities begin dealing with each other in an impersonal way, working for their rights and privileges and forgetting that the entire source of the relationship was the boundless joy of the other company and a great desire to serve that entity.

May we answer you further, my brother?

L: No, thank you.

It is a pleasure to share our thoughts with you. Is there another question at this time?

(Pause)

I am Hatonn. If there are no more questions at this time we would close the meeting through another instrument. We will contact him now. I am Hatonn.

(L channeling)

I am Hatonn, and I greet you once again, my brothers. It has been a great pleasure for us in that, by performing this insignificant service for you we have been able, ever so slightly, *(inaudible)* the light of the universe, to further illumine an area which has, shall we say, drawn its blinds in the past. It is our wish, my brothers, that we be allowed, at any place or time in your lives, to assist you in whatever manner possible, for it is through you and others such as yourselves that the blind may once again be raised and the light allowed to permeate your sphere. Again, my brothers, we thank you. I am Hatonn.

(Carla channels Nona until the end of the meditation.)

The Law of One, Book III, Session 59
June 25, 1981

Ra: I am Ra. I greet you in the love and in the light of the one infinite Creator. We communicate now.

Questioner: Could you first tell me the instrument's condition and why she feels so tired?

Ra: I am Ra. This instrument's condition is as previously stated. We cannot infringe upon your free will by discussing the latter query.

Questioner: Would it be any greater protection for the instrument if *(name)* changed his sitting position to the other side of the bed?

Ra: I am Ra. No.

Questioner: At the end of the second major cycle there were a few hundred thousand people on Earth. There are over four billion people on Earth today. Were the over four billion people that are incarnate today in the Earth planes and not incarnate at that time, or did they come in from elsewhere during the last 25,000 years?

Ra: I am Ra. There were three basic divisions of origin of these entities.

Firstly, and primarily, those of the planetary sphere you call Maldek, having become able to take up third-density once again, were gradually loosed from self-imposed limitations of form.

Secondly, there were those of other third-density entrance or neophytes whose vibratory patterns matched the Terran experiential nexus. These then filtered in through incarnative processes.

Thirdly, in the past approximate 200 of your years you have experienced much visiting of the Wanderers. It may be noted that all possible opportunities for incarnation are being taken at this time due to your harvesting process and the opportunities which this offers.

Questioner: Just to clarify that could you tell me approximately how many mind/body/spirit complexes were transferred to Earth at the beginning of this last 75,000 year period?

Ra: I am Ra. The transfer, as you call it, has been gradual. Over two billion souls are those of Maldek which have successfully made the transition.

Approximately 1.9 billion souls have, from many portions of the creation, entered into this experience at various times. The remainder are those who have experienced the first two cycles upon this sphere or who have come in at some point as Wanderers; some Wanderers having been in this sphere for many thousands of your years; others having come far more recently.

Questioner: I'm trying to understand the three spirals of light in the pyramid shape. I would like to question on each.

The first spiral starts below the Queen's Chamber and ends in the Queen's Chamber? Is that correct?

Ra: I am Ra. This is incorrect. The first notion of upward spiraling light is as that of the scoop, the light energy being scooped in through the attraction of the pyramid shape through the bottom or base. Thus the first configuration is a semi-spiral.

Questioner: Would this be similar to the vortex you get when you release water from a bathtub?

Ra: I am Ra. This is correct except that in the case of this action the cause is gravitic whereas in the case of the pyramid the vortex is that of upward spiraling light being attracted by the electro-magnetic fields engendered by the shape of the pyramid.

Questioner: Then the first spiral after this semi-spiral is the spiral used for study and healing. Relative to the Queen's Chamber position, where does this first spiral begin and end?

Ra: I am Ra. The spiral which is used for study and healing begins at or slightly below the Queen's Chamber position depending upon your Earth and cosmic rhythms. It moves through the King's Chamber position in a sharply delineated form and ends at the point whereby the top approximate third of the pyramid may be seen to be intensifying the energy.

Questioner: The first spiral is obviously different somehow from the second and third spirals since they have different uses and different properties. The second spiral then starts at the end of the first spiral and goes up to the apex. Is that correct?

Ra: I am Ra. This is partially correct. The large spiral is drawn into the vortex of the apex of the pyramid. However, some light energy which is of the more intense nature of the red, shall we say, end of the spectrum is spiraled once again causing an enormous strengthening and focusing of energy which is then of use for building.

Questioner: And then the third spiral radiates from the top of the pyramid. Is this correct?

Ra: I am Ra. The third complete spiral does so. This is correct. It is well to reckon with the foundation semi-spiral which supplies the prana for all that may be affected by the three following upward spirals of light.

Questioner: Now I am trying to understand what happens in this process. I'll call the first semi-spiral zero position and the other three spirals one, two, and three, the first spiral being a study in healing. What change takes place in light from zero position to the first spiral that makes that first spiral available for healing?

Ra: I am Ra. The prana scooped in by the pyramid shape gains coherence of energetic direction. The term "upward spiraling light" is an indication, not of your up and down concept, but an indication of the concept of that which reaches towards the source of love and light.

Thus all light or prana is upward spiraling but its direction, as you understand this term, is unregimented and not useful for work.

Questioner: Could I assume then that from all points in space light radiates in our illusion outward in a 360° solid angle and this scoop shape with the pyramid then creates the coherence to this radiation as a focusing mechanism? Is this correct?

Ra: I am Ra. This is precisely correct.

Questioner: Then the first spiral has a different factor of cohesion, you might say, than the second. What is the difference between this first and second spiral?

Ra: I am Ra. As the light is funneled into what you term the zero position, it reaches the point of turning. This acts as a compression of the light multiplying tremendously its coherence and organization.

Questioner: Then is the coherence and organization multiplied once more at the start of the second spiral? Is there just a doubling effect or an increasing effect?

Ra: I am Ra. This is difficult to discuss in your language. There is no doubling effect but a transformation across boundaries of dimension so that light which was working for those using it in space/time—time/space configuration becomes light working in what you might consider an inter-dimensional time/space—space/time configuration. This causes an apparent diffusion and weakness of the spiraling energy. However, in position two, as you have called it, much work may be done inter-dimensionally.

Questioner: In the Giza pyramid there was no chamber at position two. Do you ever make use of position two by putting a chamber in that position on other planets or in other pyramids?

Ra: I am Ra. This position is useful only to those whose abilities are such that they are capable of serving as conductors of this type of focused spiral.

One would not wish to attempt to train third-density entities in such disciplines.

Questioner: Then the third spiral radiating from the top of the pyramid you say is used for energizing. Can you tell me what you mean by "energizing"?

Ra: I am Ra. The third spiral is extremely full of the positive effects of directed prana and that which is placed over such a shape will receive shocks energizing the electro-magnetic fields. This can be most stimulating in third-density applications of mental and bodily configurations. However, if allowed to be in place over-long such shocks may traumatize the entity.

Questioner: Are there any other effects of the pyramid shape beside the spirals that we have just discussed?

Ra: I am Ra. There are several. However, their uses are limited. The use of the resonating chamber position is one which challenges the ability of an adept to face the self. This is one type of mental test which may be used. It is powerful and quite dangerous.

The outer shell of the pyramid shape contains small vortices of light energy which, in the hands of capable crystallized beings, are useful for various subtle workings upon the healing of invisible bodies affecting the physical body.

Other of these places are those wherein perfect sleep may be obtained and age reversed. These characteristics are not important.

Questioner: What position would be the age reversal position?

Ra: I am Ra. Approximately 5 to 10° above and below the Queen's Chamber position in ovoid shapes on each face of the four-sided pyramid extending into the solid shape approximately one-quarter of the way to the Queen's Chamber position.

Questioner: In other words, if I went just inside the wall of the pyramid a quarter of the way but still remained three-quarters of the way from the center at approximately the level above the base of the Queen's Chamber I would find that position?

Ra: I am Ra. This is approximately so. You must picture the double teardrop extending in both the plane of the pyramid face and in half towards the Queen's Chamber extending above and below it. You may see this as the position where the light has been scooped into the spiral and then is expanding again. This position is what you may call a prana vacuum.

Questioner: Why would this reverse aging?

Ra: I am Ra. Aging is a function of the effects of various electro-magnetic fields upon the electromagnetic fields of the mind/body/spirit complex. In this position there is no input or disturbance of the fields, nor is any activity within the electro-magnetic field complex of the mind/body/spirit complex allowed full sway. The vacuum sucks any such disturbance away. Thus the entity feels nothing and is suspended.

Questioner: Is the pyramid shape constructed in our yard functioning properly? Is it aligned properly and built properly?

Ra: I am Ra. It is built within good tolerances though not perfect. However, its alignment should be as this resting place for maximum efficacy.

Questioner: Do you mean that one of the base sides should be aligned 20° east of north?

Ra: I am Ra. That alignment would be efficacious.

Questioner: Previously you stated that one of the base sides should be aligned with magnetic north. Which is better, to align with magnetic north or to align with 20° east of magnetic north?

Ra: I am Ra. This is at your discretion. The proper alignment for you of this sphere at this time is magnetic north. However, in your query you asked specifically about a structure which has been used by specific entities whose energy vortices are more consonant with the, shall we say, true color green orientation. This would be the 20° east of north.

There are advantages to each orientation. The effect is stronger at magnetic north and can be felt more clearly. The energy, though weak, coming from the now distant, but soon to be paramount, direction is more helpful.

The choice is yours. It is the choice between quantity and quality or wide band and narrow band aid in meditation.

Questioner: When the planetary axis realigns, will it realign 20° east of north to conform to the green vibration?

Ra: I am Ra. We fear this shall be the last question as this entity rapidly increases its distortion towards what you call pain of the body complex.

There is every indication that this will occur. We cannot speak of certainties but are aware that the grosser or less dense materials will be pulled into conformation with the denser and lighter energies which give your Logos its proceedings through the realms of experience.

May we answer any brief queries at this time?

Questioner: Only if there is anything that we can do to make the instrument more comfortable or to improve the contact?

Ra: I am Ra. All is well. We are aware that you experience difficulties at this time, but they are not due to your lack of conscientiousness or dedication. I am Ra. I leave you in the love and in the light of the one infinite Creator. Go forth, then, rejoicing the power and the peace of the one infinite Creator. Adonai.

The Law of One, Book V, Session 59, Fragment 33
June 25, 1981

Jim: When it becomes known to a seeker that there are negative entities of an unseen nature that may present one with psychic greetings that, in general, tend to intensify difficulties that the seeker has freely chosen, it is often easy for the seeker totally to blame the negative entities for difficulties that appear in the life pattern rather than continuing to trace the line of responsibility to its source within the free will choices of the self. I illustrated this trait in the following question.

I had known very well from an early age that I had a well-exercised temper. In Ra's response to my question about that temper it is interesting to see one possible source for such anger and the potential for balancing that such anger can provide. A future query in this same general area elicits another facet of this quality of anger.

Carla: *When one feels she has a fault, it is very easy to focus on eliminating the fault. Yet Ra encourages us not to erase faults but to balance them. I think this to be a key concept. All of us dwelling in this veil of flesh have biases and opinions that seem distorted to some degree. Of course, if one has a fault that involves infringing on the free will of another, then the fault does need to be addressed by eliminating that behavior. One does not find ways to balance thieving or murder. But Jim's anger, my eternal vagueness and forgetfulness, all of people's little quirks, can be seen to be energies that need balancing, rather than removal. One tries to behave completely without error, yet errors occur. This should not be an excuse for the self to judge the self, but rather a chance for the self to offer love and support to the self, while gently bringing the behavior into balance. Unless we get this principle solidly under our metaphysical belts, we will be self-judgmental people who are petty in complaint and grudging with praise, not just for the self, but for others.*

Session 59, June 25, 1981

Questioner: I have a question from Jim and it states: "I think that I have penetrated my lifelong mystery of my anger at making mistakes. I think that I have always been aware subconsciously of my ability to master new learning, but my desire to successfully complete my work on Earth has been energized by the Orion group into irrational and destructive anger when I fail. Could you comment on this observation?

Ra: I am Ra. We would suggest that as this entity is aware of its position as a Wanderer, it may also consider what pre-incarnative decisions it undertook to make regarding the personal or self-oriented portion of the choosing to be here at this particular time/space. This entity is aware, as stated, that it has great potential, but potential for what? This is the pre-incarnative question. The work of sixth density is to unify wisdom and compassion. This entity abounds in wisdom. The compassion it is desirous of balancing has, as its antithesis, lack of compassion. In the more conscious being this expresses or manifests itself as lack of compassion for self. We feel this is the sum of suggested concepts for thought which we may offer at this time without infringement. ❧

L/L Research

L/L Research is a subsidiary of Rock Creek Research & Development Laboratories, Inc.

P.O. Box 5195
Louisville, KY 40255-0195

www.llresearch.org

Rock Creek is a non-profit corporation dedicated to discovering and sharing information which may aid in the spiritual evolution of humankind.

ABOUT THE CONTENTS OF THIS TRANSCRIPT: This telepathic channeling has been taken from transcriptions of the weekly study and meditation meetings of the Rock Creek Research & Development Laboratories and L/L Research. It is offered in the hope that it may be useful to you. As the Confederation entities always make a point of saying, please use your discrimination and judgment in assessing this material. If something rings true to you, fine. If something does not resonate, please leave it behind, for neither we nor those of the Confederation would wish to be a stumbling block for any.

CAVEAT: This transcript is being published by L/L Research in a not yet final form. It has, however, been edited and any obvious errors have been corrected. When it is in a final form, this caveat will be removed.

© 2009 L/L Research

Sunday Meditation
June 28, 1981

(Carla channeling)

I am Hatonn, and I greet you my friends, in the love and in the light of our infinite Creator. It is with great pleasure that I speak with each of you and send you our love.

We have spoken to you very often, my friends, about how love can be realized and manifested between yourself and the other persons who are your fellow travelers in this your life experience at this time. Tonight we would like to say a few words about love, the original Thought and how you may manifest and realize this in relation to the world of things.

Each of you has been taught by those who mean very well that is a good and proper thing for people to gather about them an amount of useful or decorative items—what you would call your furniture, your clothing, your transport, and many other items with which you may decorate your domicile or use in your daily life, and each of you has, to same extent, performed and manifested this understanding, that it is good to have these things. When one begins to tread in an earnest manner the path of the pilgrim, one becomes immediately aware that there is too much emphasis placed upon things, and there is, in many cases, a great reaction against things, as if things were intrinsically not spiritual or conducive to spirituality.

You, my friends, are one portion of the original Thought. The first thing which you possess is your physical vehicle. The important entity is yourself, but without this vehicle you would not be manifested in this density. Therefore, this vehicle has a justification and deserves appropriate, loving care. So it is, my friends, with your possessions. If you are able, as part of the original Thought, to view your things as those things invested by you with love, you are then able to create in them the vibrations of peace, harmony, love and light, which will touch all who come within the vicinity of your possessions.

Perhaps you have experienced entering the domicile of one whose heart is serene and whose mind is placed upon the will of the Father. In that place each thing seems comforting and comfortable and there is an atmosphere which is exuded from the very walls. It is in this light that you may observe your relationship to your possessions. In and of themselves they have no importance. If within you there is a love of them greater than the love of the Creator, they are an unfortunate influence upon your spiritual path. If you may imbue your possessions with love while remaining unattached to them, it does not matter what the amount of your possessions may be, for through them, as through everything else in the radiant Being, you are being of service.

(Pause)

I am Hatonn. We are aware of the weariness of the one known as C and would attempt to keep this communication fairly short. We would at this time wish to extend our gratitude to this entity for the sharing of his seeking for the truth that brings him to this circle in spite of this weariness. It is a privilege to share our thoughts with those who seek. I would, at this time, transfer this contact. I am Hatonn.

(L channeling)

I am Hatonn, and I greet you again, my brothers, in the love and the light of our Creator. My brothers, is it not strange that we who are on a path of development seem to spend so much time combating the path with all of our skill and daring? We use those tools which have been provided for our advancement to prevent that very act. Our minds, the complex and infinitely wonderful tool that we have created to serve our needs in the embodied state, have became the master instead of the servant, and must be constantly subdued in order to even set foot on the path, much less advance upon it. My brothers, the choice is ours.

We have made what we have made and only we can undo that which, with more wisdom, we would have not made. Each of you, my brothers, must experience again and again a very individualized Armageddon, an end of the world, for it is in ending your personal world, your concepts, your treasures, the physical illusion to which you so dramatically cling, in the ending of all this, my brothers, comes growth. For just as an eagle cannot rise to the heights and soar through the heavens while chained to a perch or clinging to an overly large prey that has been conquered, you also, my brothers, must release that to which you cling so fervently.

The value or lack of value in the physical object lies not in its existence, for that is part of the illusion, but rather in the use to which one puts it. If one uses a chair as a tool, a means of supporting one comfortably, while at rest or at work, then that chair acts in service and is used as a tool toward advancement, but, my brothers, that same chair used as a throne becomes a different matter altogether. In the first case, the chair releases. In the second, the chair, through your will, restrains. Therefore, my brothers, be not overly concerned with the quality or the quantity of possessions. Be concerned, rather, with the service accomplished through the use of those tools which have been given you.

At this time, we of Hatonn would seek to be of service in answering those questions which we are able to answer. I am Hatonn.

Carla: Hatonn, I have a question for S. She says: "I feel that the increase of negative influence or path of service to self in the various media arenas—that is, movies, books and music—is having a very, very subtle effect on people individually and as a whole. I am referring to a far more subliminal level or door that has been found and used by the Orion Confederation. Am I correct, and could you expand on this concern?"

I am Hatonn. To our sister S—you are correct, my sister, in your assumption. As the time grows near in which each member of your race must decide his direction, a battle, a very subliminal battle is being fought. The battle, however, is not a tug of war in which the negative and positive polarities seek to drag the individual to their own polarity. Rather, the struggle is within the seeking of the individual. He or she is torn between seeking for self and seeking for others. Just as we are capable of providing information, suggestion and advice, so also are those which we term of negative polarity, capable, in their own manner, of providing service.

One must be careful to perceive them as a goodness in their own right and not an evil to be avoided. One such as this instrument would shrink from contact with that herb referred to as poison ivy, but would not regard it as an evil. Rather, as a goodness that must be avoided so that it might continue to perform its service without interference. In the examples provided it is true there are many subliminal suggestions, as you call them, toward polarization, but it is important to realize that those suggestions are toward polarization and not toward a single polarity, for just as many of those suggestions encourage one to gravitate toward a negative or self-serving polarity, there are also many suggestions to gravitate toward a positive or other-serving polarity. We of Hatonn know that if you seek, you shall find. This applies also to those areas of your concern. If we may be of further service on this subject, we would encourage you, our sister, to question us further. I am Hatonn.

Carla: Thank you, Hatonn, for S. I'll see that she gets it soon as D is kind enough to type it up.

We thank you, my sister. May we be of further service?

Carla: I have a couple of questions of my own. Hopefully they will be brief for C's sake. I found myself with the necessity of dealing with a person whom I conceive to be a negatively-oriented person. I have no trouble loving him at all, none whatsoever. I can love him with all my heart and see him as part of myself. However, there's a necessity for not only dealing with him, but possibly entering into contracts with him and I have not been able to find myself feeling completely free of the desire to avoid this person and his contracts. Is this an acceptable reaction to negative polarity or should I strive more to balance that reaction with indifference or is even that not enough?

I am Hatonn. We understand your question. My sister, all reactions are acceptable. It is a misconception to regard any honest reaction as insufficient, in that these reactions, as you so accurately term then, are guideposts on your personal path, telling you your mileage, so to speak. My sister, each person who enters your life is your teacher, for a true teacher is one who stimulates or prompts his student to teach himself. Therefore, we might suggest that you attempt to perceive this individual as one who, on a non-physical level, chose to enter your life at this time to assist you in your growth. The fact of his consciousness or lack of consciousness concerning his role in your life is not significant. What is significant, my sister, is your choice of words. You speak not of action freely undertaken, consciously chosen, but rather reaction which seems to imply a non-conscious response to a stimulus.

My sister, emotions are simply tools. Some serve to teach, others serve to warn and correct or advise. If you were to attempt to serve a meal, my sister, the preparation of that meal might entail the use of a pan known as a skillet. The skillet would serve to warm a certain type of food, but would you continue to cling to the skillet after it has served this purpose, even to the point of retaining your hold on the skillet throughout the meal? My sister, your reactions serve a purpose of warning and preparing you, but if we were to advise you on this matter we would say that you should consider releasing the skillet once it has served its purpose. Your actions are yours and can be consciously chosen. Your reactions are a conscious choice to place your actions before the whims and will of another. We would ask you to consider this in dealing with the teachers who surround you, my sister.

May we answer you further?

Carla: Just one sub-question. In my dealings with this person, in all the actions I've ever had with him I have, as far as I know, carefully chosen a blameless path, which is my normal way of dealing with people, no matter what I think. What I'm concerned about is my thoughts. I take it, then, that what you are speaking of is mental action rather than physical action.

I am Hatonn. My sister, the mind is your tool. You may use it as you wish. If you wish to retain an image of the individual and create within your mind additions to the illusion before you, those things which are termed daydreams or suppositions, then you are protecting yourself from that which does not exist even within your illusion. My sister, there is no wrong nor imbalance in perceiving a warning when dealing with individuals of questionable intent. It is our suggestion, however, that if you would seek a course of action, follow this one: perceive the warning less within your mind and heart, both the source of the warning and the individual against whom you are warned, and as soon as possible put both from your mind.

May we answer you further, my sister?

Carla: No, thank you Hatonn.

We thank you for this service that you do us, my sister. Is there another question?

Carla: I had one more. Just a comment I wondered if you wanted to make. Up until this time in my life I had always thought that the most aid one could be to another was to be as clear a communicator as possible and I feel that I have been discovering lately that there is a kind of restraint which is in some cases more helpful than seemingly clear communication which ends up just being words. Do you have a comment on this?

My sister, within your heart a comment exists concerning pearls and swine. May we answer you further?

Carla: No, I really don't think I know any pigs but I think I know what you mean. Thank you.

My sister, we would further advise you, if we might.

Carla: Please.

The pig referred to is a blessed creature, equal in standing in the eyes of the Creator with us all. Is there another question at this time?

Carla: No, thank you Hatonn.

Thank you. I am Hatonn. Although it is pleasant to listen through the ears of this instrument to the night creatures sing, we are aware that darkness is also a time for rest of many of those present. Therefore, at this time we bid you all good night, in the love and the light of our Creator. Adieu, my friends. I am Hatonn.

The Law of One, Book III, Session 60
July 1, 1981

Ra: I am Ra. I greet you in the love and in the light of the one infinite Creator. We communicate now.

Questioner: When you spoke in the last session of "energizing shocks" coming from the top of the pyramid, did you mean that these came at intervals rather than steadily?

Ra: I am Ra. These energizing shocks come at discrete intervals but come very, very close together in a properly functioning pyramid shape. In one whose dimensions have gone awry the energy will not be released with regularity or in quanta, as you may perhaps better understand our meaning.

Questioner: The next statement that I will make may or may not be enlightening to me in my investigation of the pyramid energy, but it has occurred to me that the effect of the so-called Bermuda Triangle could be possibly due to a large pyramid beneath the water which releases this third spiral in discrete and varying intervals. Entities or craft that are in the vicinity may change their space/time continuum in some way. Is this correct?

Ra: I am Ra. Yes.

Questioner: Then this third spiral has an energizing effect that, if strong enough, will actually change the space/time continuum. Is there a use or value to this type of change?

Ra: I am Ra. In the hands of one of fifth-density or above this particular energy may be tapped in order to communicate information, love, or light across what you would consider vast distances but which with this energy may be considered transdimensional leaps. Also, there is the possibility of travel using this formation of energy.

Questioner: Would this travel be the instantaneous type used primarily by sixth-density entities, or is it the sling-shot effect that you are talking about?

Ra: I am Ra. The former effect is that of which we speak. You may note that as one learns the, shall we say, understandings or disciplines of the personality each of these configurations of prana is available to the entity without the aid of this shape. One may view the pyramid at Giza as metaphysical training wheels.

Questioner: Then is the large underwater pyramid off the Florida coast one of the balancing pyramids that Ra constructed or did some other social memory complex construct it and if so, which one?

Ra: I am Ra. That pyramid of which you speak was one whose construction was aided by sixth-density entities of a social memory complex working with Atlanteans prior to our working with the, as you call them, Egyptians.

Questioner: You mentioned working with one other group other than the Egyptians. Who were they?

Ra: I am Ra. These entities were those of South America. We divided our forces to work within these two cultures.

Questioner: The pyramid shape then, as I understand it, was deemed by your social memory complex to be at that time of paramount importance as the physical training aid for spiritual development. At this particular time in the evolution of our planet it seems that you place little or no emphasis on this shape. Is this correct?

Ra: I am Ra. This is correct. it is our honor/duty to attempt to remove the distortions that the use of this shape has caused in the thinking of your peoples and in the activities of some of your entities. We do not deny that such shapes are efficacious, nor do we withhold the general gist of this efficacy. However, we wish to offer our understanding, limited though it is, that contrary to our naive beliefs many thousands of your years ago the optimum shape for initiation does not exist.

Let us expand upon this point. When we were aided by sixth-density entities during our own third-density experiences we, being less bellicose in the extreme, found this teaching to be of help. In our naiveté in third-density we had not developed the interrelationships of your barter or money system and power. We were, in fact, a more philosophical third-density planet than your own and our choices of polarity were much more centered about the, shall we say, understanding of sexual energy transfers and the appropriate relationships between self and other-self.

We spent a much larger portion of our space/time working with the unmanifested being. In this less complex atmosphere it was quite instructive to have this learn/teaching device and we benefited without the distortions we found occurring among your peoples.

We have recorded these differences meticulously in the Great Record of Creation that such naiveté shall not be necessary again.

At this space/time we may best serve you, we believe, by stating that the pyramid for meditation along with other rounded and arched or pointed circular shapes is of help to you. However, it is our observation that due to the complexity of influences upon the unmanifested being at this space/time nexus among your planetary peoples it is best that the progress of the mind/body/spirit complex take place without, as you call them, training aids because when using a training aid an entity then takes upon itself the Law of Responsibility for the quickened or increased rate of learn/teaching. If this greater understanding, if we may use this misnomer, is not put into practice in the moment by moment experience of the entity, then the usefulness of the training aid becomes negative.

Questioner: Thank you. I don't know if this question will result in any useful information, but I feel that I must ask it. What was the ark of the covenant, and what was its use?

Ra: I am Ra. The ark of the covenant was that place wherein those things most holy, according to the understanding of the one called Moishe, were placed. The article placed therein has been called by your peoples two tablets called the Ten Commandments. There were not two tablets. There was one writing in scroll. This was placed along with the most carefully written accounts by various entities of their beliefs concerning the creation by the one Creator.

This ark was designed to constitute the place wherefrom the priests, as you call those distorted towards the desire to serve their brothers, could draw their power and feel the presence of the one Creator. However, it is to be noted that this entire arrangement was designed, not by the one known to the Confederation as Yahweh, but rather was designed by negative entities preferring this method of creating an elite called the Sons of Levi.

Questioner: Was this a device for communication then? You also said that they drew power from it. What sort of power? How did this work?

Ra: I am Ra. This was charged by means of the materials with which it was built being given an electromagnetic field. It became an object of power in this way and, to those whose faith became that untarnished by unrighteousness or separation, this power designed for negativity became positive and is so, to those truly in harmony with the experience of service, to this day. Thus the negative forces were partially successful but the positively oriented Moishe, as this entity was called, gave to your planetary peoples the possibility of a path to the one infinite Creator which is completely positive.

This is in common with each of your orthodox religious systems which have all become somewhat mixed in orientation, yet offer a pure path to the one Creator which is seen by the pure seeker.

Questioner: Where is the ark of the covenant now? Where is it located?

Ra: I am Ra. We refrain from answering this query due to the fact that it does still exist and is not that which we would infringe upon your peoples by locating.

Questioner: In trying to understand the creative energies, it has occurred to me that I really do not understand why unusable heat is generated as our Earth moves from third into fourth density. I know it has to do with disharmony between the vibrations of third and fourth density but why this would show up as a physical heating within the Earth is beyond me. Can you enlighten me on that?

Ra: I am Ra. The concepts are somewhat difficult to penetrate in your language. However, we shall attempt to speak to the subject. If an entity is not in harmony with its circumstances it feels a burning within. The temperature of the physical vehicle does not yet rise, only the heat of the temper or the tears, as we may describe this disharmony. However, if an entity persists for a long period of your space/time in feeling this emotive heat and disharmony, the entire body complex will begin to resonate to this disharmony, and the disharmony will then show up as the cancer or other degenerative distortions from what you call health.

When an entire planetary system of peoples and cultures repeatedly experiences disharmony on a great scale the earth under the feet of these entities shall begin to resonate with this disharmony. Due to the nature of the physical vehicle, disharmony shows up as a blockage of growth or an uncontrolled growth since the primary function of a mind/body/spirit complex's bodily complex is growth and maintenance. In the case of your planet the purpose of the planet is the maintenance of orbit and the proper location or orientation with regards to other cosmic influences. In order to have this occurring properly the interior of your sphere is hot in your physical terms. Thus instead of uncontrolled growth you begin to experience uncontrolled heat and its expansive consequences.

Questioner: Is the Earth solid all the way through from one side to the other?

Ra: I am Ra. You may say that your sphere is of an honey-comb nature. The center is, however, solid if you would so call that which is molten.

Questioner: Are there third-density entities living in the honey-comb areas? Is this correct?

Ra: I am Ra. This was at one time correct. This is not correct at this present space/time.

Questioner: Are there any inner civilizations or entities living in these areas other than physically incarnate who do come and materialize on the Earth's surface at some times?

Ra: I am Ra. As we have noted, there are some which do as you say. Further, there are some inner plane entities of this planet which prefer to do some materialization into third-density visible in these areas. There are also bases, shall we say, in these areas of those from elsewhere, both positive and negative. There are abandoned cities.

Questioner: What are these bases used for by those from elsewhere?

Ra: I am Ra. These bases are used for the work of materialization of needed equipment for communication with third-density entities and for resting places for some equipment which you might call small craft. These are used for surveillance when it is requested by entities.

Thus some of the, shall we say, teachers of the Confederation speak partially through these surveillance instruments along computerized lines, and when information is desired and those requesting it are of the proper vibratory level the Confederation entity itself will then speak.

Questioner: I understand then that the Confederation entity needs communication equipment and craft to communicate with the third-density incarnate entity requesting the information?

Ra: I am Ra. This is incorrect. However, many of your peoples request the same basic information in enormous repetition, and for a social memory complex to speak ad infinitum about the need to meditate is a waste of the considerable abilities of such social memory complexes.

Thus some entities have had approved by the Council of Saturn the placement and maintenance of these message givers for those whose needs are simple, thus reserving the abilities of the Confederation members for those already meditating and absorbing information which are then ready for additional information.

Questioner: There has been, for the past 30 years, a lot of information and a lot of confusion, and in fact, I would say that the Law of Confusion has been working overtime—to make a small joke—in bringing information for spiritual catalysis to groups requesting it, and we know that both the positively and the negatively oriented social memory complexes have been adding to this information as they can. This has led to a condition of apathy in a lot of cases with respect to the information. Many who are truly seeking have been thwarted by what I might call spiritual entropy in this information. Can you comment on this and the mechanisms of alleviating these problems?

Ra: I am Ra. We can comment on this.

Questioner: Only if you deem it of importance would I request a comment.

If you deem it of no importance we'll skip it.

Ra: I am Ra. This information is significant to some degree as it bears upon our own mission at this time.

We of the Confederation are at the call of those upon your planet. If the call, though sincere, is fairly low in consciousness of the, shall we say, system whereby spiritual evolution may be precipitated, then we may only offer that information useful to that particular caller. This is the basic difficulty. Entities receive the basic information about the Original Thought and the means, that is meditation and service-to-others, whereby this Original Thought may be obtained.

Please note that as Confederation members we are speaking for positively oriented entities. We believe the Orion group has precisely the same difficulty.

Once this basic information is received it is not put into practice in the heart and in the life experience but instead rattles about within the mind complex distortions as would a building block which has lost its place and simply rolls from side to side uselessly, yet still the entity calls. Therefore, the same basic information is repeated. Ultimately the entity decides that it is weary of this repetitive information. However, if an entity puts into practice that which it is given, it will not find repetition except when needed.

Questioner: Thank you. Are the chakras or bodily energy centers related to or do they operate like the pyramid energy funnel?

Ra: I am Ra. No.

Questioner: Was there a purpose for mummification having to do with anything other than bodily burial?

Ra: I am Ra. Much as we would like to speak to you of this distortion of our designs in constructing the pyramid, we can say very little for the intent was quite mixed and the uses, though many felt them to be positive, were of a nonpositive order of generation. We cannot speak upon this subject without infringement upon some basic energy balances between the positive and negative forces upon your planet. It may be said that those offering themselves felt they were offering themselves in service-to-others.

Questioner: What civilization was it that helped Ra using the pyramid shape while Ra was in third-density?

Ra: I am Ra. Your people have a fondness for the naming. These entities have begun their travel back to the Creator and are no longer experiencing time.

Questioner: The instrument wished to know, when using the pendulum in discovering energy centers, what the back and forth motion meant instead of the circular motion?

Ra: I am Ra. This shall have to be the final question although this entity is still providing us with energy. It is experiencing the distortion towards pain.

The rotations having been discussed, we shall simply say that the weak back and forth motion indicates a partial blockage although not a complete blockage. The strong back and forth motion indicates the reverse of blockage which is over-stimulation of a chakra or energy center which is occurring in order to attempt to balance some difficulty in body or mind complex activity. This condition is not helpful to the entity as it is unbalanced. Are there any brief queries before we leave this instrument?

Questioner: Only is there anything that we can do to make the instrument more comfortable or to improve the contact?

Ra: I am Ra. Be merry, my friends. All is well and your conscientiousness is to be recommended. We leave you in the love and the light of the one infinite Creator. Rejoice, then, and go forth in the peace and in the glory of the one infinite Creator. I am Ra. Adonai.

L/L Research is a subsidiary of
Rock Creek Research &
Development Laboratories, Inc.

P.O. Box 5195
Louisville, KY 40255-0195

L/L Research

www.llresearch.org

Rock Creek is a non-profit
corporation dedicated to
discovering and sharing
information which may aid in
the spiritual evolution of
humankind.

ABOUT THE CONTENTS OF THIS TRANSCRIPT: This telepathic channeling has been taken from transcriptions of the weekly study and meditation meetings of the Rock Creek Research & Development Laboratories and L/L Research. It is offered in the hope that it may be useful to you. As the Confederation entities always make a point of saying, please use your discrimination and judgment in assessing this material. If something rings true to you, fine. If something does not resonate, please leave it behind, for neither we nor those of the Confederation would wish to be a stumbling block for any.

© 2009 L/L RESEARCH

THE LAW OF ONE, BOOK V, SESSION 60, FRAGMENT 34
JULY 1, 1981

Jim: The first two questions in this portion of Session 60 touch upon Carla's tendency towards martyrdom in general terms; that is, in the case of the Ra contact Carla's desire to be of service in this contact was strong enough that she would open herself completely to the contact until there was no vital energy left for her own ease of transition back to the waking state. Ra's suggestion in this regard was that if she were to reserve some vital energy, it would be possible that the contact could continue over a longer period of time. Ra recognized that her basic incarnational lesson was to generate as much compassion as possible and was the root of the unreserved opening to the contact, but Ra also suggested that a little addition of wisdom in the reserving some small amount of vital energy might enhance her service.

In fact, our entire group was then in the process of exercising more caution regarding the frequency of sessions. We had begun to travel the martyr's path in having sessions too frequently and giving of the self—of the instrument—until there was nothing left. As we continued to hold sessions when she was not in good shape, it was also suggested to us by Ra that overly to stress caution in scheduling sessions further apart and in resting Carla was as deleterious to retaining the contact as our martyring behavior was at the beginning of the sessions. In having the sessions, in distributing the material to others, and in living the daily life in general we found that there is a basic kind of dedication to serving others that is helpful. But when that dedication becomes focused on a strong desire that a specific outcome be the result of any effort to serve others, then one is distorting the service with preconceived ideas. "Not my will, but Thy will" is the attitude offering the most efficient service.

And once again we see the beneficial role that a physical limitation can play in one's incarnation. In this case, Carla's arthritis is seen to be the means by which she pre-incarnatively determined to focus her attention, not on the usual activities of the world, but on the inner life, the life of meditation and contemplation which her physical limitation offered her. This same limitation has also been used to carry out other pre-incarnatively chosen lessons, as mentioned by Ra in the last two responses. Such pre-incarnatively chosen limitations confound many healers who have the opinion that no disease is ever necessary. However, it seems that some people choose lessons that will utilize the entire incarnation and not just a portion of it. Thus the distortions needed to present the opportunities for these kinds of lessons are not meant to yield to healing efforts.

Carla: It may seem as though I have had a life ruled by disease and limitation. In actuality, that just isn't so. At one time, when Donald had died and I had not yet fully decided to survive him, my condition worsened to the point where I had to stay horizontal all the time. But even then I was able to make letter tapes and to channel, until the very end of that dark period, the month or so before going to the hospital in January of 1992. And I can honestly say that even in that extremity, I wanted to stay.

Today, I simply do not think very much about my aches and pains, and I don't think other people notice anything out of the ordinary about me. I don't appear ill, and do not act that way either, so people just assume I am healthy. Having done everything I could to better my condition, and failed to make any dent by any means, I have concluded that the symptoms of pain which I experience are not signal but noise. This is the basic pain management theory I learned in rehab that fateful year of 1992. Something that has no message is a useless thing, no matter how irritating. I was riding one of those electric buggies airline employees use to transport the elderly and feeble, and remarked on the constant **bee-baw, bee-baw, bee-baw** as the cart wended its way through the pedestrian traffic in the huge corridor. The driver said she didn't even notice it any more, she was so used to it. Exactly. I don't do this perfectly: I complain at least daily to my mate, who has identified listening to the daily report as a service to the weary! It really helps to gripe a bit. As long as the griper doesn't take it too seriously.

I know this is not easy, and I spent months during that period thinking that I might not make the cut! It is difficult to face pain, especially ancient, blade-keen pain that has crippled, and to work through the crystallizations that kept the arms down and the back separated from the neck. What saved me was love. I have a real passion for cooking. I love to play with tastes, to mix herbs and spices and all the kinds of food there are. The fact that the result of this playtime is meals that people enjoy is icing on the cake! I'd been banned from the kitchen 12 years ago. After thorough testing to be sure I would not harm my condition, I was OK'd to take up cooking again. I loved being in the kitchen to the point where I would just hang on to the stove and cook long past the point where I would have given up if I'd just been sitting or standing and doing nothing. And then there was the love I had for Jesus—I promised Him that I would get better, and give praise and thanksgiving and glory to His holy Name. Which I do, frequently! Between the two, a miracle occurred for me, given by Love to love for Love's sake. And I pray to be able to share my story of being a Wanderer and one who wishes to serve, with all those who are awakening to their spiritual identity at this time.

Yes, I am still limited by my physical restrictions. I have spent literally years refining a schedule that I can live with, that has the most things in it that I want in my life, without overstressing my frail body. At this point, Jim and I have things worked out very well, and I have been fortunate to escape difficulty this last year or so. It is a first! I just take things at the speed I know is safe for me.

Needless to say, when this contact was ongoing, I had no such concept of caution. I adored Don, he wanted this contact more than anything I'd ever seen him go after; during this time he was actually a happy man. These were golden moments for me: I had had but one goal for a long time from 1968 onwards, and that was to make a real home, both physical and metaphysical, for Don. I knew he was comforted by being with me, so I felt I always helped. But this state he was in was unique. Here was my star-crossed love, peaceful and completely satisfied with his life for the first and only time I ever saw. I couldn't wait to do the next session, just so I could wake up to see him grinning with delight.

It is fairly easy to see from the questions he was asking that Don felt my best chance for healing lay in mental work along the lines of his Church Of Christ Scientist Mother's faith. He was accustomed, when a family member got a cold or illness, to calling the Practitioner, who would spend time in prayer and meditation, affirming the perfection of whatever seemed to be imperfect. This method of thinking is extremely valuable, and I do want to give credit to this marvelous practice of affirming perfection. For that is the overriding truth—behind all of this seeming imperfection there is utter perfection beyond telling or measure. I have sensed and felt it, but have never been able to bring back words. However I believe those experiences to be true.

As to the idea of my pre-incarnatively choosing the limitations, and the lesson of loving without expectation of a return, both of these topics had been covered in a past-life regression done by Larry Allison in 1975, and I felt sure that this was the case. It rang true with that depth of resonance I have come to associate with personal truth. I felt and feel fortunate to be alive, and if I have to pay some dues, that's OK. I'm glad to be at the party! When I do die to this world, I hope that I will be satisfied I've done all I can—and I don't feel that way yet. One thing I know I still have ahead is to write some sort of witness to those truths that have been *shared with me at dear cost. When I have written all I know about the devotional life lived in the midst of it all, then I will be fairly satisfied that I have served my part. But we never really know what the sum of service is, do we? I don't presume to think that I know all that is slated for me to experience. And am satisfied to let it surprise me.*

Session 60, July 1, 1981

Questioner: It is my opinion that the best way for the instrument to improve her condition is through periods of meditation followed by periods of contemplation with respect to the condition and its improvement. Could you tell me if I am correct and expand on this?

Ra: I am Ra. Meditation and contemplation are never untoward activities. However, this activity will in all probability, in our opinion, not significantly alter the predispositions of this instrument which cause the fundamental distortions which we, as well as you, have found disconcerting.

Questioner: Can you tell me the best approach for altering, to a more acceptable condition, the distortions that the instrument is experiencing?

Ra: I am Ra. There is some small amount of work which the instrument may do concerning its pre-incarnative decisions regarding service to the infinite Creator in this experience. However, the decision to open without reservation to the offering of self when service is perceived is such a fundamental choice that it is not open to significant alteration, nor would we wish to interfere with the balancing process which is taking place with this particular entity. The wisdom and compassion being so balanced by this recapitulation of fourth density is helpful to this particular mind/body/spirit complex. It is not an entity much given to quibbling with the purity with which it carries out that which it feels it is best to do. We may say this due to the instrument's knowledge of its self which is clear upon this point. However, this very discussion may give rise to a slightly less fully unstopped dedication to service in any one working so that the service may be continued over a greater period of your space/time.

Questioner: You are saying, then, that the physical distortions that the instrument experiences are part of a balancing process? Is this correct?

Ra: I am Ra. This is incorrect. The physical distortions are a result of the instrument's not accepting fully the limitations placed prior to incarnation upon the activities of the entity once it had begun the working. The distortions caused by this working, which are inevitable given the plan chosen by this entity, are limitation and to a degree, consonant with the amount of vital and physical energy expended, weariness, due to that which is the equivalent in this instrument of many, many hours of harsh physical labor.

This is why we suggested the instrument's thoughts dwelling upon the possibility of its suggesting to its higher self the possibility of some slight reservation of energy at a working. This instrument at this time is quite open until all resources are quite exhausted. This is well if desired. However, it will, shall we say, shorten the number of workings in what you may call the long run.

Questioner: Will spreading the workings out over greater intervals of time so that we have more time between workings help?

Ra: I am Ra. This you have already done. It is not helpful to your group to become unbalanced by concern for one portion of the work above another. If this instrument is, in your judgment, capable and if the support group is functioning well, if all is harmonious and if the questions to be asked have been considered well, the working is well begun. To overly stress the condition of the instrument is as deleterious to the efficiency of this contact as the antithetical behavior was in your past.

Questioner: Aside from the workings I am concerned about the physical distortions of the instrument in the area of her hands and arms. Is there a, shall we say, mental exercise or something else that the instrument could work on to help to alleviate the extreme problems that she has at this time with her hands, etc.?

Ra: I am Ra. Yes.

Questioner: Would this be an exercise of meditation and contemplation upon the alleviation of these problems?

Ra: I am Ra. No.

Questioner: What would she do then in order to alleviate these problems?

Ra: I am Ra. As we have said, this instrument, feeling that it lacked compassion to balance wisdom, chose an incarnative experience whereby it was of necessity placed in situations of accepting self in the absence of other-selves' acceptance and the acceptance of other-self without expecting a return or energy transfer. This is not an easy program for an incarnation but was deemed proper by this entity. This entity therefore must needs meditate and consciously, moment by moment, accept the self in its limitations which have been placed for the very purpose of bringing this entity to the precise tuning we are using. Further, having learned to radiate acceptance and love without expecting return, this entity now must balance this by learning to accept the gifts of love and acceptance of others which this instrument feels some discomfort in accepting. These two balanced workings will aid this entity in the release from the distortion called pain. The limitations are, to a great extent, fixed.

Questioner: Is the fact that the instrument was already consciously aware of this the reason that the first distortion was not in force in making it impossible for you to communicate this to us?

Ra: I am Ra. This is not only correct for this entity which has been consciously aware of these learn/teachings for some of your years, but also true of each of the support group. The possibility of some of this information being offered was not there until this session.

Sunday Meditation
July 5, 1981

(Carla channeling)

[I am Hatonn,] and I greet you, my friends, in the love and light of the infinite Creator. It is a great joy and privilege to be with you and we welcome and greet each of you, especially the one known as K, whom we have not seen for some time and the one known as E, who is always with us, yet we have not seen this entity either for some time in this group. We welcome each of you and wish you to know that we are always with you at any time that you may request our aid in your meditation.

Outside your domicile, my friends, it rains upon the earth and the great cycles of your nature move in their stately cycles through the many ways of service which the Creator offers in His creation and in yourselves, too. The rains come and moisten the surfaces of your thoughts and yet, my friends, as inspiration falls to you from the Creator it does much more than simply moisten your daily thoughts and emotions. It goes deep within the surface of your mind and your heart. This rain, which you may call grace or love, feeds the deepest rivers which flow at the very heart of the being. These rivers are never dry, no matter what the outer surface of your reality may seem at any time. These rivers of your deepest heart and your deepest mind are always enriched and forever full of the waters of love, and in each meditation you may come to these waters and be bathed and cleansed in their sweetness.

We speak to you of love, for it is the original Thought and it is the cause of our being with you this evening. In the difficulties and the hurly-burly of your daily existence, how easy it is to mistake the surface weather of your moods and your emotions and your thoughts for the deeper sources of the being, and to think that you are as you feel. Indeed, my friends, it is good to know just how you do feel and how you do think at all times, that you may be careful to use the experiences of your daily life, yet it is well also to realize that that which is deep within you is the true reality of your being and often bears no resemblance whatsoever to your thinking or your feeling on the outer planes. For your true self, my friends, is one which is beyond the human joys and sorrows that you experience in this illusion. Your true self, my friends, is one which is part of the creation of the Father and as such, experiences the entire creation outside of time, outside of space, outside of all things but the unity of the eternal present of the creation.

Many there are upon your sphere who have dabbled their toes in these underground rivers of consciousness and, finding them too deep, have turned back. We realize that each of you seeks these deep rivers of love within your being. We ask that you imagine where this rain, that you now experience upon the roof of your domicile, is coming from. Does it come from elsewhere, from some outside source? No, my friends. This rain that falls from your sky was once a part of the deepest underground waterways, surfacing in sea and lake and stream, to be taken up into the air, to fall once again in service upon the good earth. So it is with love, my friends. It is not something that you need seek upon the outer planes, for it is within you. And as it comes to you so it has flowed from you. Thus, to seek love is to give love in the unending cycle of service.

At this time we would transfer this contact. I am Hatonn.

(Jim channeling)

I am Hatonn, and I greet you once again in the love and the light of our infinite Creator. We would at this time offer ourselves in the service of answering questions which might be upon your minds. Are there any questions that we might attempt to answer?

Carla: I would like to take this opportunity to thank you, Hatonn, for being with me in my meditations in these last few days.

I am Hatonn. My sister, we may say it has been a great honor and privilege to join you in your meditations, for always do we seek to serve those who request our assistance. In this way we provide the means whereby we also progress. Those whom we serve, hopefully, are aided in their progression and the Creator is aided yet one more step further in the recognition of each entity as Creator. We thank you, my sister.

Is there a question which we might attempt to answer at this time?

C: Hatonn, could you talk to me a little bit about the value of solitude as an aid to growth?

I am Hatonn, and am aware of your question, my brother. We would answer by saying there are many ways which an entity may use for growth in this illusion which you now experience. The most common method is the everyday experience which you share with the entities round about you, for each entity is likened unto a mirror and reflects back to you that image which is the part of yourself which most needs attention and acceptance at that moment. For fewer numbers of entities, but for all from time to time, a method of experiencing solitude is also of great use. Solitude, though it does not provide the easy access of a mirror which the entities around you provide in your daily life, still provides a great mirroring for the entity who is alert and aware of the fact that each experience one encounters is part of your very being.

In the situation of solitude you must be aware that, though you do not have other entities around you, yet you are surrounded by the Creator, you are surrounded by yourself in forms not so easily recognizable. The experience of solitude has the effect of driving the attention of the entity deeper within the self of the entity, for your experience in solitude is a focus, a focus into your being which has the ability to show you that all about you is your being, that all about you is your experience, that you create your reality in your response to that which you experience.

Solitude must be carefully used, may we say, for it is a more powerful tool for the entity who wishes to progress in the growth and the realization of oneness with the Creator, for though many entities experience the reflecting of the part of themselves needing attention by other-selves in their daily lives, since this occurs so often it is easy to ignore, but when one experiences solitude, the experience of the self as all is much more profound and is harder to ignore.

Therefore, we would suggest for those who seek to progress upon the path of realization the use of solitude as a tool upon this path, but the use of this tool with discretion, for it is one of the more powerful tools which entities upon your plane have at their disposal.

May we answer you further, my brother?

C: No, thank you very much.

We thank you. May we answer another question at this time?

Carla: My friend B just wrote a letter and said that she thought that a lot of new age babies were being born right now. Is this perhaps the reason that some of my friends, say that who didn't expect to start families and then later in life did start families, are experiencing childbirth and the beginning of families at this time? Are there many new souls, or are these souls trying for graduation?

I am Hatonn. And we would answer you, my sister, by saying many are the ways in which service may be provided, and at this time upon your planet, as your peoples approach graduation in the great harvesting of souls in your near future, many of the entities upon your plane are providing a service for souls wishing to incarnate upon this planet and this dimension at this time. Since the harvest grows near, those who have but a short distance to travel or a few lessons to learn, those able with a small amount, shall we say, of experience needed, do now wish to incarnate upon your plane. Those who have a chance for graduation realize that chance is now.

Many are the souls which knock upon the door of your plane. Many are the entities who now open themselves to this service, providing a channel, shall we say, for these souls to enter upon your plane. Those entities being born now and for the last few years, shall we say, as you measure time, are those souls which are old, as time is reckoned, and which have experienced enough of the catalysts of your dimension that graduation is near at hand for them, and many are the souls which seek this graduation. Yes, my sister, we would say that the service of providing that which is called by your peoples parenthood, many are those which shall provide this service in these days approaching the harvest.

May we answer you further, my sister?

Carla: No, thank you, Hatonn. That's fine.

We thank you, as always. May we attempt to answer another question at this time?

E: When one feels that one has not accomplished that which they came here to do and feels that the time, perhaps, is short, what would be your advice?

I am Hatonn. My sister, we would answer you by saying that to seek the love of the infinite Creator in each moment of your life is the greatest service and the greatest learning that can be accomplished upon your plane, for it is the lesson of this dimension to discover the love of the Creator within all that is experienced within the self, within the life, within the family, within the community, within each activity, each experience and there is, shall we say, an infinite amount of time to discover this love.

May we answer you further, my sister?

E: No, thank you.

We thank you. Is there another question at this time?

Carla: This is really off the wall, but I would just like to know if, in this density, in this cycle, in this particular universe, were there ever dragons? Where did that come from? Is it a parallel universe or is it a deep thought form in our being, or what? It must be real somewhere—dragons and magic.

I am Hatonn, and we would answer you, my sister, by saying that thousands of years ago, in the measure of time as your people measure time, as the circumstances and the level of living and understanding was much simpler, there were seen by the entities upon your planet many dangers and many threats, not only of the world of survival from day-to-day and of what you would call neighboring tribes and entities and of animals of various natures of temperament, but the weather, the very world itself, appeared to the simpler understanding as a great threat to existence. Many were the means by which the simpler entities imagined the world about them and many were the deities and powers and gods and beings which these entities beseeched for assistance and worshipped for power.

It is difficult to separate the group or mass mind of your peoples from these times, the many influences and forces which shaped the images of fear and power which your people have contained within their collective consciousness. But we might say in relation to your question about dragons, there have been many types of images or powers which your people have experienced in their past. Many of these have taken the forms of dragons or serpents or monsters as explanations for the unknown powers which ruled the world these people experienced. There have not been, to the best of our understanding, the types of dragons which are commonly portrayed in your comic books and upon your movie screens, though there have been many types of beasts, shall we say, that have walked your planet and have come quite close in their effect upon the population of your planet.

May we answer you further, my sister?

Carla: Yes, just to follow it through. I was, of course, referring to the movie, "Dragon Slayer," which I just saw and I was pondering why it is that something within me responds to a certain fineness and goodness in bravery, or whatever myth it is, that is the "dragon slayer," like St. George or like some fine sorcerer of old that has the ability to slay the dragon. I was wondering why I respond so deeply to that image. Is it possible that it's just a part of the mass mind that I'm aware of or that it's a strong image?

I am Hatonn. We would answer, my sister, by saying that the imagery of the dragon, of the force which threatens, is an old image upon your planet. As we said before, many are the images and the feelings of fear which your people have experienced. There has been, in your illusion, the illusion of separation, of having to contend or compete against another entity, another nation or another force to win the survival, to win the day. Many have been the forces which have been seen as being in opposition; many have been the unknown threats. It is the conquering of the unknown, the winning of the day by one means or another, that has been the allegorical story for your people throughout their history.

For each entity, in his or her life faces many unknowns, many dragons, many threats, and many are the opportunities, therefore, for each entity to confront, to face and to slay the dragon by one means or another and thereby pass yet one more test, shall we say, in this course of learning within this density. It is an old and noble image and story, that of the dragon, that of the unknown, that of the one who slays the dragon and frees people and frees the self.

May we answer you further, my sister?

Carla: No, thank you Hatonn. The answer was a lot better than the question. Thank you very much.

Again, we thank you. Is there another question at this time?

M: Hatonn, about the new births coming in close to the harvest [that] are many souls that are ready to go into the next density. Will their physical bodies be able to go into the next density, [for those that make it?]

I am Hatonn. My brother, we would answer you simply by saying there shall be, as it appears at this time, a remnant that shall remain with your planet, as even at this time your planet has begun movement into the fourth density, and there are, as you know quite well, many entities upon your planet now experiencing this transition. As the harvest grows near and the various signs of the transition take place, there shall be yet remaining with each transition and each difficulty, a remnant, and many shall pass to the fourth density inhabiting that which is known as a physical body complex.

May we answer you further?

M: No, thank you.

Is there another question at this time?

(Pause)

I am Hatonn. May we say it has been a great privilege to be with you this evening in your meditation. We hope that in some small way our simple message has been able to shine a bit of light upon your understanding, and we have been able, hopefully, to share the love that we feel, the love of the infinite Creator, with your group this evening.

We would say once again that should at any time you request that we be with you in your meditations or in your daily life, we would be most honored to join you at that time. Always, we are with you, for always we are one in the love and in the light of the infinite Creator. We are known to you as those of Hatonn and we leave you now in the love and in the light of the infinite Creator. Adonai. ☥

The Law of One, Book III, Session 61
July 8, 1981

Ra: I am Ra. I greet you, my friends, in the love and in the light of the infinite Creator. We communicate now.

Questioner: Could you give me an indication of the instrument's condition?

Ra: I am Ra. This instrument's vital energies are improving. The physical complex distortions are quite marked at this space/time and there is a decrease in physical complex energies.

Questioner: Is there anything in particular that the instrument could do to improve the physical condition?

Ra: I am Ra. This instrument has two factors affecting its bodily distortions. This is in common with all those which by seniority of vibration have reached the green-ray level of vibratory consciousness complexes.

The first is the given in-streamings which vary from cycle to cycle in predictable manner. In this particular entity the cyclical complexes at this space/time nexus are not favorable for the physical energy levels.

The second ramification of condition is that which we might call the degree of mental efficiency in use of catalyst provided for the learning of programmed lessons in particular and the lessons of love in general.

This instrument, unlike some entities, has some further distortion due to the use of preincarnative conditions.

Questioner: Can you expand on what you meant by the "cycling in-streamings of energy"?

Ra: I am Ra. There are four types of cycles which are those given in the moment of entry into incarnation. There are in addition more cosmic and less regularized in-pourings which, from time to time, affect a sensitized mind/body/spirit complex. The four rhythms are, to some extent, known among your peoples and are called bio-rhythms.

There is a fourth cycle which we may call the cycle of gateway of magic of the adept or of the spirit. This is a cycle which is completed in approximately eighteen of your diurnal cycles.

The cosmic patterns are also a function of the moment of incarnative entrance and have to do with your satellite you call the moon, your planets of this galaxy, the galactic sun, and in some cases the in-streamings from the major galactic points of energy flow.

Questioner: Would it be helpful to plot these cycles for the instrument and attempt to have these sessions at the most favorable points with respect to the cycles?

Ra: I am Ra. To that specific query we have no response.

It may be noted that the three in this triad bring in this energy pattern which is Ra. Thus each energy input of the triad is of note.

We may say that while these information systems are interesting they are in sway only in so far as the entity or entities involved have not made totally efficient use of catalyst and, therefore, instead of accepting the, shall we say, negative or retrograde moments or periods without undue notice, have the distortion towards the retaining of these distortions in order to work out the unused catalyst.

It is to be noted that psychic attack continues upon this entity although it is only effective at this time in physical distortions towards discomfort.

We may suggest that it is always of some interest to observe the roadmap, both of the cycles and of the planetary and other cosmic influences, in that one may see certain wide roads or possibilities. However, we remind that this group is an unit.

Questioner: Is there some way that we could, as a unit then, do something to reduce the effect of the psychic attack on the instrument and optimize the communicative opportunity?

Ra: I am Ra. We have given you the information concerning that which aids this particular mind/body/spirit complex. We can speak no further. It is our opinion, which we humbly offer, that each is in remarkable harmony with each for this particular third-density illusion at this space/time nexus.

Questioner: I would like to ask questions about healing exercises. The first is, in the healing exercises concerning the body, what do you mean by the disciplines of the body having to do with the balance between love and wisdom in the use of the body in its natural functions?

Ra: I am Ra. We shall speak more briefly than usual due to this instrument's use of the transferred energy. We, therefore, request further queries if our reply is not sufficient.

The body complex has natural functions. Many of these have to do with the unmanifested self and are normally not subject to the need for balancing. There are natural functions which have to do with other-self. Among these are touching, loving, the sexual life, and those times when the company of another is craved to combat the type of loneliness which is the natural function of the body as opposed to those types of loneliness which are of the mind/emotion complex or of the spirit.

When these natural functions may be observed in the daily life they may be examined in order that the love of self and love of other-self versus the wisdom regarding the use of natural functions may be observed. There are many fantasies and stray thoughts which may be examined in most of your peoples in this balancing process.

Equally to be balanced is the withdrawal from the need for these natural functions with regard to other-self. On the one hand there is an excess of love. It must be determined whether this is love of self or other-self or both. On the other hand there is an over-balance towards wisdom.

It is well to know the body complex so that it is an ally, balanced and ready to be clearly used as a tool, for each bodily function may be used in higher and higher, if you will, complexes of energy with other-self. No matter what the behavior, the important balancing is the understanding of each interaction on this level with other-selves so that whether the balance may be love/wisdom or wisdom/love, the other-self is seen by the self in a balanced configuration and the self is thus freed for further work.

Questioner: Then the second question is, could you give an example of how feelings affect portions of the body and the sensations of the body?

Ra: I am Ra. It is nearly impossible to speak generally of these mechanisms, for each entity of proper seniority has its own programming. Of the less aware entities we may say that the connection will often seem random as the higher self continues producing catalyst until a bias occurs. In each programmed individual the sensitivities are far more active and, as we have said, that catalyst not used fully by the mind and spirit is given to the body.

Thus you may see in this entity the numbing of the arms and the hands signifying this entity's failure to surrender to the loss of control over the life. Thus this drama is enacted in the physical distortion complex.

In the questioner we may see the desire not to be carrying the load it carries given as physical manifestation of the soreness of those muscles for carrying used. That which is truly needed to be carried is a preincarnative responsibility which seems highly inconvenient.

In the case of the scribe we see a weariness and numbness of feelings ensuing from lack of using catalyst designed to sensitize this entity to quite significant influxes of unfamiliar distortion complexes of the mental, emotional, and spiritual level. As the numbness removes itself from the higher or more responsive complexes the bodily complex distortions will vanish. This is true also of the other examples.

We would note at this time that the totally efficient use of catalyst upon your plane is extremely rare.

Questioner: Could you tell me how you are able to give us information like this with respect to the first distortion or Law of Confusion?

Ra: I am Ra. Each of those is already aware of this information.

Any other reader may extract the heart of meaning from this discussion without interest as to the examples' sources. If each was not fully aware of these answers we could not speak.

It is interesting that in many of your queries you ask for confirmation rather information. This is acceptable to us.

Questioner: This brings out the point of the purpose of the physical incarnation, I believe. And that is to reach a conviction through your own thought processes as to a solution to problems and understandings in a totally free situation with no proof at all or anything that you would consider proof, proof being a very poor word in itself. Can you expand on my concept?

Ra: I am Ra. Your opinion is an eloquent one although somewhat confused in its connections between the freedom expressed by subjective knowing and the freedom expressed by subjective acceptance. There is a significant distinction between the two.

This is not a dimension of knowing, even subjectively, due to the lack of overview of cosmic and other in-pourings which affect each and every situation which produces catalyst. The subjective acceptance of that which is at the moment and the finding of love within that moment is the greater freedom.

That known as the subjective knowing without proof is, in some degree, a poor friend for there will be anomalies no matter how much information is garnered due to the distortions which form third-density.

Questioner: The third question that I have here is, could you give examples of bodily polarity?

Ra: I am Ra. Within the body there are many polarities which relate to the balancing of the energy centers of the various bodies of the unmanifested entity. It is well to explore these polarities for work in healing.

Each entity is, of course, a potential polarized portion of an other-self.

Questioner: The last question here says that it would seem the proper balancing exercises for all the sensations of the body would be some sort of inactivity such as meditation or contemplation. Is this correct?

Ra: I am Ra. This is largely incorrect. The balancing requires a meditative state in order for the work to be done. However, the balancing of sensation has to do with an analysis of the sensation with especial respect to any unbalanced leaning between the love and the wisdom or the positive and the negative. Then whatever is lacking in the balanced sensation is, as in all balancing, allowed to come into the being after the sensation is remembered and recalled in such detail as to overwhelm the senses.

Questioner: Could you tell me why it is important for the appurtenances and other things to be so carefully aligned with respect to the instrument and why just a small ruffle in the sheet by the instrument causes a problem with the reception of Ra?

Ra: I am Ra. We may attempt an explanation. This contact is narrow-band. The instrument is highly sensitive. Thus we have good entry into it and can use it to an increasingly satisfactory level.

However, the trance condition is, shall we say, not one which is without toll upon this instrument. Therefore, the area above the entrance into the physical complex of this instrument must be kept clear to avoid discomfort to the instrument especially as it re-enters the body complex. The appurtenances give to the instrument's sensory input mental visualizations which aid in the trance beginning. The careful alignment of these is important for the energizing group in that it is a reminder to that support group that it is time for a working. The ritualistic behaviors are triggers for many energies of the support group. You may have noticed more energy being used in workings as the number has increased due to the long-term, shall we say, effect of such ritualistic actions.

This would not aid another group as it was designed for this particular system of mind/body/spirit complexes and especially the instrument.

There is enough energy transferred for one more long query. We do not wish to deplete this instrument.

Questioner: Then I will ask this question. Could you tell us the purpose of the frontal lobes of the brain and the conditions necessary for their activation?

Ra: I am Ra. The frontal lobes of the brain will, shall we say, have much more use in fourth density.

The primary mental/emotive condition of this large area of the so-called brain is joy or love in its creative sense. Thus the energies which we have discussed in relationship to the pyramids: all of the healing, the learning, the building, and the energizing are to be found in this area. This is the area tapped by the adept. This is the area which, working through the trunk and root of mind, makes contact with intelligent energy and through this gateway, intelligent infinity.

Are there any queries before we leave this instrument?

Questioner: Only is there anything that we can do to make the instrument more comfortable or to improve the contact?

Ra: I am Ra. This instrument is somewhat distorted but each is doing well. You are conscientious. We thank you for continuing to observe the alignments and request that on each level you continue to be this fastidious as this will maintain the contact.

I am Ra. I leave you in the love and the light of the one infinite Creator. Go forth my friends, rejoicing in the power and the peace of the one infinite Creator. Adonai.

Sunday Meditation
July 12, 1981

(Carla channeling)

[I am Hatonn,] and I greet you, my friends, in the love and in the light of our infinite Creator. It is a great privilege to greet each of you and we do so with love and with joy.

We would speak to you this evening about the process of allowing that channel which is within you to flow without blockage, that channel for the original Thought which, when blocked, can cause such great misery and confusion among your peoples. When we observe the belief systems of your particular societal patterns, we find a frightening situation. In each area of the common social life and in each personal area there is the concept of failure or success. In your cultural patterns there is a strong drive to succeed. Thus, those who, by the standards of your society, garner great amounts of that which you call money, power or prestige, are admired simply because they have succeeded and those whose accomplishments are modest in the eyes of the society are looked upon with kindness or with pity, but not with admiration, in spite of the fact, my friends, that this is all an illusion. You cannot know whether the work that you are doing in order to garner your money is succeeding. You can only do it with love. You cannot judge yourself, nor can anyone judge you with any accuracy whatsoever. For it is the love in your work, not the remuneration, that will affect your eternal self.

In your peoples at this time there is tremendous turmoil and many people feel the pressure to succeed by means of relationships. Those who have many friends or a devoted spouse are considered great successes in their personal lives. Those whose relationships end in separation or who, because they are loners, have not gathered about themselves a great many of acquaintances are considered—with kindness or with pity—as those who simply somehow failed to make a personal success of the personal side of life, and yet again, my friends, it is not the length of relationships, the number of relationships; it is the love given and received between yourself and strangers, enemies, acquaintances, friends, lovers, mates, family, any self whatsoever, that accounts for the true value of your personal channel of love, for it is in giving that you receive. Not in this illusion, my friends, but in that which remains your eternal spirit.

In your religious lives you may have been familiar as children and some yet abide in a system which states that there is a judgment and that some will succeed and some will fail. What are the conditions for that judgment? In your holy works the answer is not clear, for the master known as Jesus erased the concept of morality, as you would call it, as the prerequisite for success, by the forgiveness which he showed to sinners, as your holy works called those who for some reason were not serving others to the best of their ability.

This is frightening, my friends. This illusion places upon you a desire to succeed in that which is the most infinitely important of all areas, the spiritual. How does one know if one is among those who will be with the Creator? How can one monitor one's behavior so as to be sure of this eventuality? It is easy for us to say to you that you can monitor your behavior, but we must at this point stop and say to you, my friends, there is no success or failure. There is no judgment. There is, in each of you, the Creator. This Creator seeks to express Itself through you in whatever way that It may, to a world much unused to the original Thought.

Thus, my friends, many, many values which are subjectively clear to you seem ineffectual or even perverted when offered freely, gladly and lovingly to a world that does not believe that there are those who wish to love without gain of any kind, who wish to love without succeeding, who would be glad to fail in the eyes of the world if, through that mechanism, love could best be channeled.

As you find the blockages in your minds and in your hearts, turn within to the original Thought, for it, my friends, is simple, unlike your paradoxical illusion with its great ideas of success and its poor ideas of failure. There is a comfort in knowing that you cannot run out of spiritual food. You cannot be hungry; you cannot be thirsty, for you have only to turn within. To you can be opened the secrets of your birthright—the fire of love, its joy, and its power and the radiance of the whole creation as it echoes the praises of the one unity which is all of us, my friends.

Let your hearts be soothed, and when you hear the thoughts of others or the thoughts of yourself regarding the success or failure of an enterprise, of a relationship, of your own behavior, seek the comfort of the original Thought. There is work for you to do. The world may think it poor. That is nothing. It is what you feel in your heart that is all-important, for the heart is informed in meditation of many, many things far too mysterious for words, and the attempt to speak them can be but a paltry one.

What a treasure you have, my friends. What a wonderful treasure room is locked within you. There is no limitation and no difficulty that can remove the key to that treasure room from your hand. Feel merry then, my friends, and with utmost gladness seek the original Thought, that fire that blew upon creation and formed the planets in their courses, the suns in all their brilliance, the galaxies in their splendor and your tiny, delicate, island home, your Earth. You are inheritors of the splendor of creation. And as you channel that love and that light, you are co-creators with it. Be of good cheer. Understood or reviled, if your work is as it should be within your heart, there is nothing that can truly sway you to the quick, for you are covered in light.

We would leave this instrument at this time and after a brief pause, while our brothers and sisters of Laitos pass among you to offer their services to you in the deepening of the meditative state, we will transfer to another instrument. I am Hatonn.

(Pause)

(Carla channeling)

I am again with this instrument. I am Hatonn, and will speak a few more words through this instrument while we are conditioning the other instrument so that he may be in the proper state.

To observe those who are successes is not, by this token, to observe those who have somehow became derailed from the spiritual path, for those who have garnered your monies, your positions, and your prestige are in a position to share with many that which is their channel, that which is their way of expressing love. It is simply to say that, also, those who participate in the rearing of children, those who in their personal lives are kind to those some may find it difficult to show kindness to, those who serve in jobs considered lowly, with dedication and love, are creating for themselves the same bias, in the infinite sense. It is this thought that you may grasp and move forward using, no matter what your position, no matter what your thoughts about your life. It is an illusion designed to give you opportunities to find love in each experience and to freely give it forth. Again I will leave this instrument and transfer this contact. I am known to you as Hatonn.

(Jim channeling)

I am Hatonn. I am with this instrument. We have been having some difficulty contacting this instrument as well as the one known as Don. We shall proceed through this instrument at this time.

We would now like to offer ourselves in the attempt to answer any questions that you might have. Are there any questions at this time?

M: Can Hatonn give us any guidance on how we can recognize—with efforts toward success of one type or another, say success in society versus success spiritually—when they're conflicting with each other?

I am Hatonn. My brother, we would say to you that you recognize the success of the spiritual journey, if we will use that term and you will accept it, is the task of each entity upon your plane. The success of the spiritual journey has one mark and one mark only in this density, and that is the mark of love, the acceptance of all about you as part of the Creator, the giving and receiving of love as the gift of the Creator. When you see any part of this mark in your life, in whatever direction you are seeking at that time, know that you are achieving, what might be called upon your plane, a successful journey. When you do not find love in your life, in your endeavors, in your activities, you may take this as a sign that you are, perhaps shall we say, embarking upon an empty journey or goal. It is not difficult, my friends, to recognize love, for when you, yourself, come in contact with that which is love you shall know it, for it shall enlarge your field of perception. Within your mind it shall enlarge your capacity to feel the glory of the creation within your heart and it shall be unmistakable to the depths of your very being.

May we answer you further, my brother?

M: No, thank you.

We, as always, thank you. May we ask if there is another question at this time?

Carla: Yes. Just following up what M said—if there seemed to be a clear cut problem, where a job seemed to be requiring a great deal of time and the harmonies in the job were such as to seemingly drain one of the love—of the channel of love—is this necessarily in conflict with the spiritual path or is this a challenge for more opening of the channel in that difficult situation?

I am Hatonn. My sister, we would answer by saying that in truth, there are no conflicts on the path of love, for as you have correctly surmised yourself, each activity or each supposed conflict is but a further opportunity to find love, to express love, to share love, to be the heart of love. Those situations which appear to be the most, in what you may call, conflict with this seeking, the sharing of love, are those situations which offer the most opportunity for the finding and the sharing of love, for there are no accidents or mistakes upon your plane, no truly misdirected avenues. Each path that any entity might take has the possibility of providing love. There is nothing but love, whatever density an entity may inhabit, and this, my sister, is most certainly true of this density which each of you inhabit at this time.

May we answer you further, my sister?

Carla: No thank you, Hatonn. That was very eloquent and most satisfactory.

Again, we thank you. May we be of assistance in any other queries at this time?

Carla: I have a question which you probably can't answer but I have been attempting to surrender the control over my life totally to the Creator and I have found it difficult because my personality is one which is much given to arrangements and control over circumstance and in the past I have been good at it, which adds to the difficulty of letting go. Is there any specific exercise or visualization that I might do in addition to the meditations I am already doing, with which you are helping, to my great gratitude?

I am Hatonn. My sister, we would say to you that this journey which you have chosen for yourself in this life is not what might be called an easy one. As we have said before in the previous answer, difficulties, as they are known to your people, are merely opportunities offering greater service to others in a sharing of love. The service which you perform at this time in your working is a service which requires a great surrendering. We know that this surrendering is not easy for any among your peoples, for upon your planet the control of the situation round about each entity is most sought, and control is the concept which pervades your planet most fully at this time.

For yourself as an individual entity upon this planet attempting to be of service, you have achieved, as you know, a great deal of surrender, yet there is more surrender which you seek and which shall be of aid to you in the work that you are now undertaking. In this effort to surrender we would simply suggest to you—the most we are able to suggest—that is, that in each moment you attempt to be totally conscious of your efforts as a channel, your efforts to open completely to remove control, to be completely free of obstructions, of thoughts of busyness, of thoughts of doing anything but what you at the moment feel the Creator would wish you to do. We can say no more, for as you know, we are most desirous of maintaining free will among each of your peoples at this time.

May we answer you further in any other way, my sister?

Carla: No, thank you Hatonn.

Again, we thank you. May we attempt to answer any other questions at this time?

Carla: Is Latwii off on assignment or was he called to this group by a certain individual like E? I was wondering why he had been absent for some time? He and she.

I am Hatonn. Our brothers and sisters of Latwii are of the vibration of light and have a specific purpose, as each in the Confederation has, and their sharings with those of your peoples who call in a certain way for their services. We of Hatonn are of the vibration of love and at this time in your group it has been assessed that love is the vibration which is most called, that which is most needed, and that which would be of the most service to each of the entities of your group and to your group as a unit. For this reason we have remained with your group. We would also say that those of Latwii are in the wings, so to speak, and it is correct that when certain entities, such as the one known as E, are with this group, it is from time to time enough of a change in the calling, shall we say, so that those of Latwii might blend their vibrations with this group in addition to those which we offer as our sharing of love.

May we answer you further, my sister?

Carla: No. Thank you. That's really interesting.

Again, we thank you. May we answer any other questions at this time?

(Pause)

I am Hatonn. Once again, my friends, may we say it has been the greatest of privileges, the greatest of pleasures to join you this evening in your meditation. We would remind each of you that we are most willing to be with each of you in your meditation at any time which you should choose to call us. We of Hatonn seek in every way possible to share that understanding which we have gained through our own seeking of the one Creator, that understanding which is known to your peoples as love. We are known to you as Hatonn, and we leave you now in that love and in the light of the one infinite Creator. Adonai. ☙

The Law of One, Book III, Session 62
July 13, 1981

Ra: I am Ra. I greet you in the love and in the light of the one infinite Creator.

Before we begin may we request that a circle be walked about this instrument and that then each of the supporting group expel breath forcibly, approximately two and one-half feet above the instrument's head, the circle then again being walked about the instrument.

(This was done as directed.)

Ra: I am Ra. We appreciate your kind cooperation. Please recheck the alignment of perpendicularity and we will begin.

(This was done as directed.)

Ra: I am Ra. We communicate now.

Questioner: Could you tell me what was wrong or what caused the necessity for the rewalking of the circle and the purpose for the expelling of the breath?

Ra: I am Ra. This instrument was under specific psychic attack at the time of the beginning of the working. There was a slight irregularity in the words verbalized by your sound complex vibratory mechanisms in the protective walking of the circle. Into this opening came this entity and began to work upon the instrument now in trance state, as you would call it. This instrument was being quite adversely affected in physical complex distortions. Thus the circle was properly walked. The breath of righteousness expelled the thought-form and the circle again was walked.

Questioner: What was the nature of the thought-form or its affiliation?

Ra: I am Ra. This thought-form was of Orion affiliation.

Questioner: Was the attack successful in creating any further distortion in the instrument's physical complex?

Ra: I am Ra. This is correct.

Questioner: What is the nature of this distortion?

Ra: This thought-form sought to put an end to this instrument's incarnation by working with the renal distortions which, although corrected upon time/space, are vulnerable to one which knows the way to separate time/space molding and space/time distortions which are being unmolded, vulnerable as before the, shall we say, healing.

Questioner: What detrimental effect has been done?

Ra: I am Ra. There will be some discomfort. However, we were fortunate in that this instrument was very open to us and well-tuned. Had we not been able to reach this instrument and instruct you, the instrument's physical vehicle would soon be unviable.

Questioner: Will there be any lasting effect from this attack as far as the instrument's physical vehicle is concerned?

Ra: I am Ra. This is difficult to say. We are of the opinion that no lasting harm or distortion will occur.

The healer was strong and the bonds taking effect in the remolding of these renal distortions were effective. It is at this point a question of two forms of the leavings of what you may call a spell or a magic working; the healer's distortions versus the attempt at Orion distortions; the healer's distortions full of love; the Orion distortions also pure in separation. It seems that all is well except for some possible discomfort which shall be attended if persistent.

Questioner: Was the opening that was made in the protective circle planned to be made by the Orion entity? Was it a specific planned attempt to make an opening, or was this just something that happened by accident?

Ra: I am Ra. This entity was, as your people put it, looking for a target of opportunity. The missed word was a chance occurrence and not a planned one.

We might suggest in the, shall we say, future, as you measure space/time, as you begin a working be aware that this instrument is likely being watched for any opportunity. Thus if the circle is walked with some imperfection it is well to immediately repeat. The expelling of breath is also appropriate, always to the left.

Questioner: Would you expand on what you just said on the expelling of the breath? I'm not quite sure of what you mean.

Ra: I am Ra. The repetition of that performed well at this working is advisable if the circle is walked in less than the appropriate configuration.

Questioner: But you mentioned the expelling of the breath to the left, I believe. Would you tell me what you meant by that?

Ra: I am Ra. It is as you have just accomplished, the breath being sent above the instrument's head from its right side to its left.

Questioner: Is there anything that we can do for the instrument after she comes out of the trance to help her recover from this attack?

Ra: I am Ra. There is little to be done. You may watch to see if distortions persist and see that the appropriate healers are brought into contact with this mind/body/spirit complex in the event that difficulty persists. It may not. This battle is even now being accomplished. Each may counsel the instrument to continue its work as outlined previously.

Questioner: Who would the appropriate healers be, and how would we bring them in contact with the instrument?

Ra: I am Ra. There are four. The difficulty being at all noticed as bodily distortion, the one known as *(name of spiritual healer)* and the one known as *(name of spiritual healer)* may work upon the instrument's bodily complex by means of the practices which are developing in each entity. Given persistence of distortion, the one known as *(name of allopathic healer)* shall be seen. Given the continued difficulty past the point of one of your cycles called the fortnight, the one known as *(name of allopathic healer)* shall be seen.

Questioner: Does the instrument know who these people are, *(name)* and *(name)*? I don't know who they are?

Ra: I am Ra. This is correct.

Questioner: Is that the sum total of what we can do to aid the instrument?

Ra: I am Ra. This is correct. We may note that the harmonies and loving social intercourse which prevails habitually in this group create a favorable environment for each of you to do your work.

Questioner: What priority, shall I say, does the Orion group place on the reduction of effectiveness or elimination of effectiveness of this group with respect to activities on planet Earth at this time? Can you tell me that?

Ra: I am Ra. This group, as all positive channels and supporting groups, is a greatly high priority with the Orion group. This instrument's bodily distortions are its most easily unbound or unloosed distortion dissolving the mind/body/spirit complex if the Orion group is successful; this particular group, having learned to be without serious chinks, may we say, in mind and spirit complex vibratory patterns. In other channels other chinks may be more in evidence.

Questioner: I'll make this statement and you correct it. The Orion group has an objective of the bringing of the service-to-self polarized entities to harvest, as great a harvest as possible. This harvest will build their potential or their ability to do work in consciousness as given by the distortion of the Law of One called the Law of Squares or Doubling. Is this correct?

Ra: I am Ra. This is correct.

Questioner: Are there other groups of those who are on the service-to-self path joined with those of the Orion constellation, for instance those of Southern Cross, presently working for the same type of harvest with respect to Earth?

Ra: I am Ra. These you mention of Southern Cross are members of the Orion group. It is not, shall we say, according to understood wording that a group from various galaxies should be named by one. However, those planetary social memory complexes of the so-called Orion constellation have the upper hand and thus rule the other members. You must recall that in negative thinking there is always the pecking order, shall we say, and the power against power in separation.

Questioner: By creating as large a harvest as possible of negatively oriented entities from Earth, then, the social memory complex of the Orion group gains in strength. Am I correct in assuming that this strength then is in the total strength of the complex, the pecking order remaining approximately the same, and those at the top gaining in strength with respect to the total strength of the social memory complex? Is this correct?

Ra: I am Ra. This is correct. To the stronger go the greater shares of polarity.

Questioner: Is this the fourth-density group that we are talking about now?

Ra: I am Ra. There are fourth and a few fifth-density members of the Orion group.

Questioner: Then is the top of the pecking order fifth-density?

Ra: I am Ra. This is correct.

Questioner: What is the objective; what does the leader, the one at the very top of the pecking order in fifth-density of the Orion group, have as an objective? I would like to understand his philosophy with respect to his objectives and plans for what we might call the future or his future?

Ra: I am Ra. This thinking will not be so strange to you. Therefore, we may speak through the densities as your planet has some negatively oriented action in sway at this space/time nexus.

The early fifth-density negative entity, if oriented towards maintaining cohesion as a social memory complex, may in its free will determine that the path to wisdom lies in the manipulation in exquisite propriety of all other-selves. It then, by virtue of its abilities in wisdom, is able to be the leader of fourth-density beings which are upon the road to wisdom by exploring the dimensions of love of self and understanding of self. These fifth-density entities see the creation as that which shall be put in order.

Dealing with a plane such as this third-density at this harvesting, it will see the mechanism of the call more clearly and have much less distortion towards plunder or manipulation by thoughts which are given to negatively oriented entities although in allowing this to occur and sending less wise entities to do this work, any successes redound to the leaders.

The fifth-density sees the difficulties posed by the light and in this way directs entities of this vibration to the seeking of targets of opportunity such as this one. If fourth-density temptations, shall we say, towards distortion of ego, etc. are not successful the fifth-density entity then thinks in terms of the removal of light.

Questioner: When the Orion entity who waits us seeking the opportunity to attack is with us here can you describe his method of coming here, what he looks like, and what his signs are? I know that this isn't too important, but it might give me a little insight into what we are talking about.

Ra: I am Ra. Fifth-density entities are very light beings although they do have the type of physical vehicle which you understand. Fifth-density entities are very fair to look upon in your standard of beauty.

The thought is what is sent for a fifth-density entity is likely to have mastered this technique or discipline. There is little or no means of perceiving such an entity, for unlike fourth-density negative entities the fifth-density entity walks with light feet.

This instrument was aware of extreme coldness in the past diurnal cycle and spent much more time than your normal attitudes would imagine to be appropriate in what seemed to each of you an extremely warm climate. This was not perceived by the instrument, but the drop in subjective temperature is a sign of presence of a negative or nonpositive or draining entity.

This instrument did mention a feeling of discomfort but was nourished by this group and was able to dismiss it. Had it not been for a random mishap, all would have been well, for you have learned to live in love and light and do not neglect to remember the one infinite Creator.

Questioner: Then it was a fifth-density entity that made this particular attack upon the instrument?

Ra: I am Ra. This is correct.

Questioner: Isn't this unusual that a fifth-density entity then would bother to do this rather than sending a fourth-density servant, shall I say?

Ra: I am Ra. This is correct. Nearly all positive channels and groups may be lessened in their positivity or rendered quite useless by what we may call the temptations offered by the fourth-density negative thought-forms. They may suggest many distortions towards specific information, towards the aggrandizement of the self, towards the flowering of the organization in some political, social, or fiscal way.

These distortions remove the focus from the One Infinite Source of love and light of which we are all messengers, humble and knowing that we, of ourselves, are but the tiniest portion of the Creator, a small part of a magnificent entirety of infinite intelligence.

Questioner: Is there something that the instrument could do or we could do for the instrument to eliminate the problems that she has, that she continually experiences of the cold feeling of these attacks?

Ra: I am Ra. Yes.

Questioner: Would you tell me what we could do?

Ra: I am Ra. You could cease in your attempts to be channels for the love and the light of the one infinite Creator.

Questioner: Have I missed anything now that we can do at all to aid the instrument during, before, or after a session or at any time?

Ra: I am Ra. The love and devotion of this group misses nothing. Be at peace. There is some toll for this work. This instrument embraces this or we could not speak. Rest then in that peace and love and do as you will, as you wish, as you feel. Let there be an end to worry when this is accomplished. The great healer of distortions is love.

Questioner: I have a question that I didn't properly answer last night for *(name)*. It has to do with the vibrations of the densities. I understand that the first-density is composed of core atomic vibrations that are in the red spectrum, second in the orange, etc. Am I to understand that the core vibrations of our planet are still in the red and that second-density beings are still in the orange at this space/time right now and that each density as it exists on our planet right now has a different core vibration, or is this incorrect?

Ra: I am Ra. This is precisely correct.

Questioner: Then as the fourth-density vibrations come in this means that the planet can support entities of fourth-density core vibration. Will the planet then still be first-density core vibration and will there be second-density entities on it with second-density vibrations, and will there be third-density entities on it with third-density vibrations?

Ra: I am Ra. This will be the last full query of this working. There is energy but the distortions of the instrument suggest to us it would be well to shorten this working with your permission.

Questioner: Yes.

Ra: You must see the Earth, as you call it, as being seven Earths. There is red, orange, yellow, and there will soon be a completed green color vibratory locus for fourth-density entities which they will call Earth. During the fourth-density experience, due to the lack of development of fourth-density entities, the third-density planetary sphere is not useful for habitation since the early fourth-density entity will not know precisely how to maintain the illusion that fourth-density cannot be seen or determined from any instrumentation available to any third-density.

Thus in fourth-density the red, orange, and green energy nexi of your planet will be activated while the yellow is in potentiation along with the blue and the indigo.

May we ask at this time if there be any brief queries?

Questioner: Is there anything that we can do to make the instrument more comfortable or to improve the contact?

Ra: All is well. You have been most conscientious.

I am Ra. I leave you, my friends, in the glory of the love and the light of the one infinite Creator. Go forth, then, rejoicing in the power and the peace of the one infinite Creator. Adonai.

L/L Research

L/L Research is a subsidiary of Rock Creek Research & Development Laboratories, Inc.

P.O. Box 5195
Louisville, KY 40255-0195

www.llresearch.org

Rock Creek is a non-profit corporation dedicated to discovering and sharing information which may aid in the spiritual evolution of humankind.

ABOUT THE CONTENTS OF THIS TRANSCRIPT: This telepathic channeling has been taken from transcriptions of the weekly study and meditation meetings of the Rock Creek Research & Development Laboratories and L/L Research. It is offered in the hope that it may be useful to you. As the Confederation entities always make a point of saying, please use your discrimination and judgment in assessing this material. If something rings true to you, fine. If something does not resonate, please leave it behind, for neither we nor those of the Confederation would wish to be a stumbling block for any.

© 2009 L/L RESEARCH

THE LAW OF ONE, BOOK III, SESSION 63
JULY 18, 1981

Ra: I am Ra. I greet you in the love and in the light of the one infinite Creator. We communicate now.

Questioner: Could you give me an indication of the condition of the instrument?

Ra: I am Ra. This instrument's vital energies are at the distortion which is normal for this mind/body/spirit complex. The body complex is distorted due to psychic attack in the area of the kidneys and urinary tract. There is also distortion continuing due to the distortion called arthritis.

You may expect this psychic attack to be constant as this instrument has been under observation by negatively oriented force for some time.

Questioner: Is the necessity of the instrument to go to the bathroom several times before a session due to the psychic attack?

Ra: I am Ra. In general this is incorrect. The instrument is eliminating from the body complex the distortion leavings of the material which we use for contact. This occurs variably, sometimes beginning before contact, other workings this occurring after the contact.

In this particular working this entity is experiencing the aforementioned difficulties causing the intensification of that particular distortion/condition.

Questioner: I know that you have already answered this question, but I feel it my duty now to ask it each time in case there is some new development, and that is, is there anything that we can do that we aren't doing to lessen the effectiveness of the psychic attack upon the instrument?

Ra: I am Ra. Continue in love and praise and thanksgiving to the Creator. Examine previous material. Love is the great protector.

Questioner: Could you give me a definition of vital energy?

Ra: I am Ra. Vital energy is the complex of energy levels of mind, body, and spirit. Unlike physical energy, it requires the integrated complexes vibrating in an useful manner.

The faculty of will can, to a variable extent, replace missing vital energy and this has occurred in past workings, as you measure time, in this instrument. This is not recommended. At this time, however, the vital energies are well-nourished in mind and spirit although the physical energy level is, in and of itself, low at this time.

Questioner: Would I be correct in guessing that the vital energy is a function of the awareness or bias of the entity with respect to his polarity or general unity with the Creator or creation?

Ra: I am Ra. In a nonspecific sense we may affirm the correctness of your statement. The vital energy may be seen to be that deep love of life or life experiences such as the beauty of creation and the appreciation of other-selves and the distortions of your co-Creators' making which are of beauty.

Without this vital energy the least distorted physical complex will fail and perish. With this love or vital energy or élan the entity may continue though the physical complex is greatly distorted.

Questioner: I would like to continue with the questions about the fact that in fourth-density the red, orange, and green energies will be activated; yellow, blue, etc. being in potentiation. Right now, we have green energies activated. They have been activated for the last 45 years. I am wondering about the transition through this period so that the green is totally activated and the yellow is in potentiation. What will we lose as the yellow goes from activation into potentiation, and what will we gain as green comes into total activation, and what is the process?

Ra: I am Ra. It is misleading to speak of gains and losses when dealing with the subject of the cycle's ending and the green-ray cycle beginning upon your sphere. It is to be kept in the forefront of the faculties of intelligence that there is one creation in which there is no loss. There are progressive cycles for experiential use by entities. We may now address your query.

As the green-ray cycle or the density of love and understanding begins to take shape the yellow-ray plane or Earth which you now enjoy in your dance will cease to be inhabited for some period of your space/time as the space/time necessary for fourth-density entities to learn their ability to shield their density from that of third is learned. After this period there will come a time when third-density may again cycle on the yellow-ray sphere.

Meanwhile there is another sphere, congruent to a great extent with yellow ray, forming. This fourth-density sphere coexists with first, second, and third. It is of a denser nature due to the rotational core atomic aspects of its material. We have discussed this subject with you.

The fourth-density entities which incarnate at this space/time are fourth-density in the view of experience but are incarnating in less dense vehicles due to desire to experience and aid in the birth of fourth-density upon this plane.

You may note that fourth-density entities have a great abundance of compassion.

Questioner: At present we have, in third-density incarnation on this plane, those third-density entities of the planet Earth who have been here for some number of incarnations who will graduate in the three-way split, either positive polarity remaining for fourth-density experience on this planet, the negative polarity harvestable going to another planet, and the rest unharvestable third-density going to another third-density planet. In addition to these entities I am assuming that we have here some entities already harvestable from other third-density planets who have come here and have incarnated in third-density form to make the transition with this planet into fourth-density, plus Wanderers.

Is this correct?

Ra: I am Ra. This is correct except we may note a small point.

The positively oriented harvested entities will remain in this planetary influence but not upon this plane.

Questioner: I think you said there were 60 million Wanderers, approximately, here now. Am I correct in that memory?

Ra: I am Ra. This is approximately correct. There is some excess to that amount.

Questioner: Does that number include the harvestable entities who are coming to this planet for the fourth-density experience?

Ra: I am Ra. No.

Questioner: Approximately how many are here now who have come here from other planets who are third-density harvestable for fourth-density experience?

Ra: I am Ra. This is a recent, shall we say, phenomenon and the number is not yet in excess of 35,000 entities.

Questioner: Now these entities incarnate into a third-density vibratory body. I am trying to understand how this transition takes place from third to fourth-density. I will take the example of one of these entities of which we are speaking who is now in a third-density body. He will grow older and then will it be necessary that he die from the third-density physical body and reincarnate in a fourth-density body for that transition?

Ra: I am Ra. These entities are those incarnating with what you may call a double body in activation.

It will be noted that the entities birthing these fourth-density entities experience a great feeling of, shall we say, the connection and the use of spiritual energies during pregnancy. This is due to the necessity for manifesting the double body.

This transitional body is one which will be, shall we say, able to appreciate fourth-density vibratory complexes as the instreaming increases without the accompanying disruption of the third-density body. If a third-density entity were, shall we say, electrically aware of fourth-density in full, the third-density electrical fields would fail due to incompatibility.

To answer your query about death, these entities will die according to third-density necessities.

Questioner: You are saying, then, that for the transition from third to fourth-density for one of the entities with doubly activated bodies, in order to make the transition the third-density body will go through the process of what we call death. Is this correct?

Ra: I am Ra. The third and fourth, combination, density's body will die according to the necessity of third-density mind/body/spirit complex distortions.

We may respond to the heart of your question by noting that the purpose of such combined activation of mind/body/spirit complexes is that such entities, to some extent, conscientiously are aware of those fourth-density understandings which third-density is unable to remember due to the forgetting. Thus fourth-density experience may be begun with the added attraction to an entity oriented toward service-to-others of dwelling in a troubled third-density environment and offering its love and compassion.

Questioner: Would the purpose in transitioning to Earth prior to the complete changeover then be for the experience to be gained here before the harvesting process?

Ra: I am Ra. This is correct. These entities are not Wanderers in the sense that this planetary sphere is their fourth-density home planet. However, the experience of this service is earned only by those harvested third-density entities which have demonstrated a great deal of orientation towards service-to-others. It is a privilege to be allowed this early an incarnation as there is much experiential catalyst in service to other-selves at this harvesting.

Questioner: There are many children now who have demonstrated the ability to bend metal mentally which is a fourth-density phenomenon. Would most of these children, then, be the type of entity of which we speak?

Ra: I am Ra. This is correct.

Questioner: Is the reason that they can do this and the fifth-density Wanderers who are here cannot do it the fact that they have the fourth-density body in activation?

Ra: I am Ra. This is correct. Wanderers are third-density activated in mind/body/spirit and are subject to the forgetting which can only be penetrated with disciplined meditation and working.

Questioner: I am assuming that the reason for this is, first, since the entities of harvestable third-density who very recently have been coming here are coming here late enough so that they will not affect the polarization through their teachings. They are not infringing upon the first distortion because they are children now and they won't be old enough to really affect any of the polarization until the transition is well advanced. However, the Wanderers who have come here are older and have a greater ability to affect the polarization. They must do their affecting as a function of their ability to penetrate the forgetting process in order to be within the first distortion. Is this correct?

Ra: I am Ra. This is quite correct.

Questioner: It would seem to me that some of the harvestable third-density entities are, however, relatively old since I know of some individuals who can bend metal who are over 50 years old and some others over 30. Would there be other entities who could bend metal for other reasons than having dual activated bodies?

Ra: I am Ra. This is correct. Any entity who, by accident or by careful design, penetrates intelligent energy's gateway may use the shaping powers of this energy.

Questioner: Now as this transition continues into fourth-density activation, in order to inhabit this fourth-density sphere it will be necessary for all third-density physical bodies to go through the process which we refer to as death. Is this correct?

Ra: I am Ra. This is correct.

Questioner: Are there any inhabitants at this time of this fourth-density sphere who have already gone through this process. Is it now being populated?

Ra: I am Ra. This is correct only in the very, shall we say, recent past.

Questioner: I would assume that this population is from other planets since the harvesting has not yet occurred on this planet. It is from planets where the harvesting has already occurred. Is this correct?

Ra: I am Ra. This is correct.

Questioner: Then are these entities visible to us? Could I see one of them? Would he walk upon our surface?

Ra: I am Ra. We have discussed this. These entities are in dual bodies at this time.

Questioner: Sorry that I am so stupid on this, but this particular concept is very difficult for me to understand. It is something that I am afraid requires some rather dumb questions on my part to fully understand, and I don't think I will ever fully understand it or even get a good grasp of it.

Then as the fourth-density sphere is activated there is heat energy being generated. I assume that this heat energy is generated on the third-density sphere only. Is this correct?

Ra: I am Ra. This is quite correct. The experiential distortions of each dimension are discrete.

Questioner: Then at some time in the future the fourth-density sphere will be fully activated. What is the difference between full activation and partial activation for this sphere?

Ra: I am Ra. At this time the cosmic influxes are conducive to true color green core particles being formed and material of this nature thus being formed. However, there is a mixture of the yellow-ray and green-ray environments at this time necessitating the birthing of transitional mind/body/spirit complex types of energy distortions. At full activation of the true color green density of love the planetary sphere will be solid and inhabitable upon its own and the birthing that takes place will have been transformed through the process of time, shall we say, to the appropriate type of vehicle to appreciate in full the fourth-density planetary environment. At this nexus the green-ray environment exists to a far greater extent in time/space than in space/time.

Questioner: Could you describe the difference that you are speaking of with respect to time/space and space/time?

Ra: I am Ra. For the sake of your understanding we will use the working definition of inner planes. There is a great deal of subtlety invested in this sound vibration complex, but it, by itself, will perhaps fulfill your present need.

Questioner: I will make this statement and have you correct me. What we have is, as our planet is spiraled by the spiraling action of the entire major galaxy and our planetary system spirals into the new position, the fourth-density vibrations becoming more and more pronounced. These atomic core vibrations begin to create, more and more completely, the fourth-density sphere and the fourth-density bodily complexes for inhabitation of that sphere. Is this correct?

Ra: I am Ra. This is partially correct. To be corrected is the concept of the creation of green-ray density bodily complexes. This creation will be gradual and will take place beginning with your third-density type of physical vehicle and, through the means of bisexual reproduction, become by evolutionary processes, the fourth-density body complexes.

Questioner: Then are these entities of whom we have spoken, the third-density harvestable who have been transferred, the ones who then will, by bisexual reproduction, create the fourth-density complexes that are necessary?

Ra: I am Ra. The influxes of true color green energy complexes will more and more create the conditions in which the atomic structure of cells of bodily complexes is that of the density of love. The mind/body/spirit complexes inhabiting these physical vehicles will be, and to some extent, are, those of whom you spoke and, as harvest is completed, the harvested entities of this planetary influence.

Questioner: Is there a clock-like face, shall I say, associated with the entire major galaxy so that as it revolves it carries all of these stars and planetary systems through transitions from density to density? Is this how it works?

Ra: I am Ra. You are perceptive. You may see a three-dimensional clock face or spiral of endlessness which is planned by the Logos for this purpose.

Questioner: I understand that the Logos did not plan for the heating effect in our third-density transition into fourth. Is this correct?

Ra: I am Ra. This is correct except for the condition of free will which is, of course, planned by the Logos as It, Itself, is a creature of free will. In this climate an infinity of events or conditions may occur. They cannot be said to be planned by the Logos but can be said to have been freely allowed.

Questioner: It would seem to me that the heating effect that takes place on the planet is analogous to a disease in the body and would have as a root cause the same or analogous mental configuration. Is this correct?

Ra: I am Ra. This is correct except that the spiritual configuration as well as mental biases of your peoples has been responsible for these distortions of the body complex of your planetary sphere.

Questioner: When the third-density goes out of activation and into potentiation that will leave us with a planet that is first, second, and fourth-density. At that time there will be no activated third-density vibrations on this planet. Am I correct in assuming that all third-density vibrations on this planet now are those vibrations that compose the bodily complexes of entities such as we are; that that is the sum total of third-density vibrations on this planet at this time?

Ra: I am Ra. This will be the last full query of this working. This instrument has energy left due to transfer but there is discomfort. We do not wish to deplete this instrument. May we say that this instrument seems in better configuration despite attack than previous workings.

To answer your query, this is incorrect only in that in addition to the mind/body/spirit complexes of third-density there are the artifacts, thought-forms, and feelings which these co-Creators have produced. This is third-density.

May we answer any brief queries as we leave this instrument?

Questioner: Is there anything that we can do to make the instrument more comfortable or to improve the contact?

Ra: I am Ra. You are conscientious. All is well. We leave you now, my friends, in the glory of the love and the light of the one infinite Creator. Go forth, then, rejoicing in the power and the peace of the infinite Creator. Adonai. ☥

The Law of One, Book V, Session 63, Fragment 35
July 18, 1981

Jim: Carla's arthritis began just after her kidneys failed when she was thirteen years old. In her childhood she had the very strong desire to be of service to others, but after many difficult experiences as a child unable to fit well anywhere she felt so sure that she would never be able to really be of service that by the age of thirteen she prayed that she might die. When her kidney failure six months later provided her with an avenue for such an exit from the incarnation, her near-death experience was of the nature where she was told that she could go on if she chose to but that her work was not done. She immediately chose to return to this life, now feeling that there was indeed service to be provided, and the juvenile rheumatoid arthritis set in immediately.

You can also see here how the efforts of negative entities intensified the choice to die that she had made of free will, but by that same free will there was no force that could hinder her return to service once she had made that choice.

Carla: The concept of limitation, especially in the form of physical disease, being a benign thing can be disturbing to think upon at first. I asked myself why in heaven's name would I choose this particular condition? For it is as cunning in how it limits me as it could be. Although the rheumatoid disease has altered each joint in my body, it has focused on my hands, wrists and shoulders and back. I simply cannot do anything physical for too long a period, including typing at this very computer's keyboard. I cannot pick up heavy things, or do heavy cleaning around the house. In general, I must watch how long I work at anything, for I cannot do a good day's work and expect to rise the next day feeling well. I simply must write a lot of rest into the schedule. Any time I do overstep these unseen limitations, I reap the reward of having lots of quiet time while I recuperate.

Through the years, therefore, I have become very able to live in a world that is retired to the point of being a hermit's way. Even in the depths of illness, in the early '90's, I was still given work to do, in the channeling, and in correspondence with a wide variety of students, counsel-ees and friends. My voice, because it hurt to produce a tone, was faint, but my thoughts still flew with wings, and there was immense satisfaction in continuing to serve.

It has always been difficult for me to take things lightly. I am always the one so intensely riveted on whatever I am doing that there's no possibility of my being "cool." Forget it! So Ra's telling me I needed to reserve energy for myself during sessions did not sit well. However, given the way I was physically wasting away, I realized I would have to learn how to do that. I have come to appreciate this lesson greatly, and so pass the advice on to each who sees himself in these words. It is a worthwhile thing to preserve the physical shell; indeed, it is the kind of loving act that teaches as it aids.

Session 63, July 18, 1981

Questioner: Was the original problem with the kidneys some 25 years ago caused by psychic attack?

Ra: I am Ra. This is only partially correct. There were psychic attack components to the death of this body at that space/time. However, the guiding vibratory complex in this event was the will of the instrument. This instrument desired to leave this plane of existence as it did not feel it could be of service.

Questioner: You are saying then that the instrument itself created the kidney problem at that time?

Ra: I am Ra. The instrument's desire to leave this density lowered the defenses of an already predisposed weak body complex, and an allergic reaction was so intensified as to cause the complications which distorted the body complex towards unviability. The will of the instrument, when it found that there was indeed work to be done in service, was again the guiding factor or complex of vibratory patterns which kept the body complex from surrendering to dissolution of the ties which cause the vitality of life.

The Law of One, Book III, Session 64
July 26, 1981

Ra: I am Ra. I greet you in the love and in the light of the one infinite Creator. We communicate now.

Questioner: Could you first tell me the condition of the instrument?

Ra: I am Ra. It is as previously stated with the exception of a transitory distortion lessening the free flow of vital energy.

Questioner: Can you tell me what the transitory distortion is?

Ra: I am Ra. This is marginal information.

Questioner: Then we won't question on it.

Could you explain the basic principles behind the ritual which we perform to initiate the contact and what I would call the basic white magical principles of protection?

Ra: I am Ra. Due to your avenue of question we perceive the appropriateness of inclusion of the cause of this instrument's transitory vital energy distortion. The cause is a bias towards the yearning for expression of devotion to the one Creator in group worship.

This entity was yearning for this protection both consciously in that it responds to the accoutrements of this expression, the ritual, the colors and their meanings as given by the distortion system of what you call the church, the song of praise, and the combined prayers of thanksgiving and, most of all, that which may be seen to be most centrally magical, the intake of that food which is not of this dimension but has been transmuted into metaphysical nourishment in what this distortion of expression calls the holy communion.

The subconscious reason, it being the stronger for this yearning was the awareness that such expression is, when appreciated by an entity as the transmutation into the presence of the one Creator, a great protection of the entity as it moves in the path of service-to-others.

The principle behind any ritual of the white magical nature is to so configure the stimuli which reach down into the trunk of mind that this arrangement causes the generation of disciplined and purified emotion or love which then may be both protection and the key to the gateway to intelligent infinity.

Questioner: Can you tell me why the slight error made in the ritual starting this communication two sessions ago allowed the intrusion by an Orion affiliated entity?

Ra: I am Ra. This contact is narrow band and its preconditions precise. The other-self offering its service in the negative path also is possessed of the skill of the swordsman. You deal in this contact with, shall we say, forces of great intensity poured into a vessel as delicate as a snowflake and as crystalline.

The smallest of lapses may disturb the regularity of this pattern of energies which forms the channel for these transmissions.

We may note for your information that our pause was due to the necessity of being quite sure that the mind/body/spirit complex of the instrument was safely in the proper light configuration or density before we dealt with the situation. Far better would it be to allow the shell to become unviable than to allow the mind/body/spirit complex to be shall we say, misplaced.

Questioner: Could you describe or tell me of rituals or techniques used by Ra in seeking in the direction of service?

Ra: I am Ra. To speak of that which sixth-density social memory complexes labor within in order to advance is at best misprision of plain communication for much is lost in transmission of concept from density to density, and the discussion of sixth-density is inevitably distorted greatly.

However, we shall attempt to speak to your query for it is an helpful one in that it allows us to express once again the total unity of creation. We seek the Creator upon a level of shared experience to which you are not privy and rather than surrounding ourselves in light we have become light. Our understanding is that there is no other material except light. Our rituals, as you may call them, are an infinitely subtle continuation of the balancing processes which you are now beginning to experience.

We seek now without polarity. Thus we do not invoke any power from without, for our search has become internalized as we become light/love and love/light. These are the balances we seek, the balances between compassion and wisdom which more and more allow our understanding of experience to be informed that we may come closer to the unity with the one Creator which we so joyfully seek.

Your rituals at your level of progress contain the concept of polarization and this is most central at your particular space/time.

We may answer further if you have specific queries.

Questioner: Would it be helpful if Ra were to describe the techniques that Ra used while Ra was third-density to evolve in mind, body, and spirit?

Ra: I am Ra. This query lies beyond the Law of Confusion.

Questioner: What about fourth-density experience of Ra? Would that also be beyond the Law of Confusion?

Ra: I am Ra. This is correct. Let us express a thought. Ra is not elite. To speak of our specific experiences to a group which honors us is to guide to the point of a specific advising. Our work was that of your people, of experiencing the catalyst of joys and sorrows. Our circumstances were somewhat more harmonious. Let it be said that any entity or group may create the most splendid harmony in any outer atmosphere. Ra's experiences are no more than your own. Yours is the dance at this space/time in third-density harvest.

Questioner: The question was brought up recently having to do with possible records left near, in, or under the Great Pyramid at Giza. I have no idea whether this would be of benefit. I will just ask if there is any benefit in investigating in this area?

Ra: I am Ra. We apologize for seeming to be so shy of information. However, any words upon this particular subject create the possibility of infringement upon free will.

Questioner: In a previous session you mentioned the gateway of magic for the adept occurring in eighteen-day cycles. Could you expand on that information please?

Ra: I am Ra. The mind/body/spirit complex is born under a series of influences, both lunar, planetary, cosmic, and in some cases, karmic. The moment of the birthing into this illusion begins the cycles we have mentioned.

The spiritual or adept's cycle is an eighteen-day cycle and operates with the qualities of the sine wave. Thus there are a few excellent days on the positive side of the curve, that being the first nine days of the cycle—precisely the fourth, the fifth, and the sixth—when workings are most appropriately undertaken, given that the entity is still without total conscious control of its mind/body/spirit distortion/reality.

The most interesting portion of this information, like that of each cycle, is the noting of the critical point wherein passing from the ninth to the tenth and from the eighteenth to the first days the adept will experience some difficulty especially when there is a transition occurring in another cycle at the same time. At the nadir of each cycle the adept will be at its least powerful but will not be open to difficulties in nearly the degree that it experiences at critical times.

Questioner: Then to find the cycles we would take the instant of birth and the emerging of the infant from the mother into this density and start the cycle at that instant and continue it through the life. Is this correct?

Ra: I am Ra. This is mostly correct. It is not necessary to identify the instant of birthing. The diurnal cycle upon which this event occurs is satisfactory for all but the most fine workings.

Questioner: Am I correct in assuming that whatever magic the adept would perform at this time would be more successful or, shall we say, more to his design than that performed at less opportune times in the cycle?

Ra: I am Ra. This cycle is an helpful tool to the adept but as we said, as the adept becomes more balanced the workings designed will be dependent less and less upon these cycles of opportunity and more and more even in their efficacy.

Questioner: I have no ability to judge at what point the level of abilities of the adept would be reached to be independent of this cyclical action. Can you give me an indication of what level of "adeptness" that would be necessary in order to be so independent?

Ra: I am Ra. We are fettered from speaking specifically due to this group's work, for to speak would seem to be to judge. However, we may say that you may consider this cycle in the same light as the so-called astrological balances within your group; that is, they are interesting but not critical.

Questioner: Thank you. I read that recent research has indicated that the normal sleep cycle for entities on this planet occurs one hour later each diurnal period so that we have a 25 hour cycle instead of a 24 hour cycle. Is this correct, and if so, why is this?

Ra: I am Ra. This is in some cases correct. The planetary influences from which those of Mars experience memory have some effect upon these third-density physical bodily complexes. This race has given its genetic material to many bodies upon your plane.

Questioner: Thank you. Ra mentioned the ones *(name)* and *(name)* in a previous session. These are members of what we call our medical profession. What is the value of modern medical techniques in alleviating bodily distortions with respect to the purpose for these distortions and what we might call karma?

Ra: I am Ra. This query is convoluted. However, we shall make some observations in lieu of attempting one coherent answer, for that which is allopathic among your healing practices is somewhat two-sided.

Firstly, you must see the possibility/probability that each and every allopathic healer is in fact an healer. Within your cultural nexus this training is considered the appropriate means of perfecting the healing ability. In the most basic sense any allopathic healer may be seen to, perhaps, be one whose desire is service-to-others in alleviation of bodily complex and mental/emotional complex distortions so that the entity to be healed may experience further catalyst over a longer period of what you call the life. This is a great service-to-others when appropriate due to the accumulation of distortions toward wisdom and love which can be created through the use of the space/time continuum of your illusion.

In observing the allopathic concept of the body complex as a machine we may note the symptomology of a societal complex seemingly dedicated to the most intransigent desire for the distortions of distraction, anonymity, and sleep. This is the result rather than the cause of societal thinking upon your plane.

In turn this mechanical concept of the body complex has created the continuing proliferation of distortions towards what you would call ill-health due to the strong chemicals used to control and hide bodily distortions. There is a realization among many of your peoples that there are more efficacious systems of healing not excluding the allopathic but also including the many other avenues of healing.

Questioner: Let us assume that a bodily distortion occurs within a particular entity who then has a choice of seeking allopathic aid or experiencing the catalyst of the distortion and not seeking correction of the distortion. Can you comment on the two possibilities for this entity and his analysis of each path?

Ra: I am Ra. If the entity is polarized towards service-to-others, analysis properly proceeds along the lines of consideration of which path offers the most opportunity for service-to-others.

For the negatively polarized entity the antithesis is the case.

For the unpolarized entity the considerations are random and most likely in the direction of the distortion towards comfort.

Questioner: I understand *(name)* brought a four-toed Bigfoot cast by here the other day. Could you tell me which form of Bigfoot that cast was?

Ra: I am Ra. We can.

Questioner: I know that it is totally unimportant, but as a service to *(name)* I thought that I should ask that.

Ra: I am Ra. This entity was one of a small group of thought-forms.

Questioner: He also asked—I know this is also unimportant—why there were no Bigfoot remains found after the entities have died on our surface. Could you also answer this? I know this is of no importance but as a service to him I ask it.

Ra: I am Ra. You may suggest that exploration of the caves which underlie some of the western coastal mountain regions of your continent will one day offer such remains. They will not be generally understood if this culture survives in its present form long enough in your time measurement for this probability/possibility vortex to occur.

There is enough energy for one more full query at this time.

Questioner: In the healing exercises, when you say examine the sensations of the body, do you mean those sensations available to the body via the five senses or in relation to the natural functions of the body such as touching, loving, sexual sharing, and company, or are you speaking of something else altogether?

Ra: I am Ra. The questioner may perceive its body complex at this moment. It is experiencing sensations. Most of these sensations or in this case, nearly all of them, are transient and without interest. However, the body is the creature of the mind. Certain sensations carry importance due to the charge or power which is felt by the mind upon the experience of this sensation.

For instance, at this space/time nexus one sensation is carrying a powerful charge and may be examined. This is the sensation of what you call the distortion towards discomfort due to the cramped position of the body complex during this working. In balancing you would then explore this sensation. Why is this sensation powerful? Because it was chosen in order that the entity might be of service-to-others in energizing this contact.

Each sensation that leaves the aftertaste of meaning upon the mind, that leaves the taste within the memory shall be examined. These are the sensations of which we speak.

May we answer any brief queries before we leave this instrument?

Questioner: Is there anything that we could do to make the instrument more comfortable or to improve the contact?

Ra: I am Ra. Continue to consider the alignments. You are conscientious and aware of the means of caring for the instrument in its present distortions having to do with the wrists and hands. As always, love is the greatest protection.

I am Ra. I leave you, my friends, in the glorious love and joyful light of the infinite Creator. Go forth, then, rejoicing in the power and in the peace of the one infinite Creator. Adonai.

Sunday Meditation
August 2, 1981

(L channeling)

I am Hatonn, and I greet you, my brothers and sisters, in the love and the light of our infinite Creator. It was with great pleasure, my friends, that we listened to your song and to the joy with which you shared your singing. My brothers, it is always a wonder to us to be able to share this contact between your race and our races, yet on times—correction—occasions such as this there is such an overflowing abundance of loving and happiness that we feel in some manner fulfilled beyond any expectations that we might have formed concerning the potentials for sharing throughout the universe.

At this time we would like to share this contact with those of another planetary entity known as Orcas. If the instrument would relax and be patient, an attempt will be made to make contact. I am Hatonn.

(L channeling)

I am Orcas, and I greet you in the love and the light of the infinite Creator. It is a pleasure to be allowed to contact this group.

Carla: May I ask you two questions, Orcas?

I am Orcas.

Carla: Do you come in the name of Christ, whom we serve with all of our heart, all of our mind, and all of our soul?

I am Orcas. I come in the love and the light of the infinite Creator, the Is which was and is continuing to be served by that entity known to you as the Christ.

Carla: Are you a member of the Confederation of Planets in the Service of the Infinite Creator?

I am Orcas. That is correct.

Carla: We welcome you to our group.

I an Orcas. I thank you both for your welcome and your caution, my friend. It is somewhat difficult for this instrument to receive our signal, but with patience the channel of communication may be enhanced. Are there any questions?

M: Yes. You come through Hatonn to address us. What particular area is your expertise? Laitos is in conditioning and Hatonn in bringing love and other entities have particular areas of their talent. What do you bring our group?

I am Orcas. I have been allowed to contact this group due to an upswelling of emotional sharing between the members of your group and the subsequent reduction of residual animosities between members of your group and others of your race. To attempt to reduce this to a more understandable form, as you love one another more intensely, you overcome your residual irritation with others not in your group.

As to the purpose of my contact, I am one who may be of assistance in guidance in surviving future events on your planetary surface. There are limitations, my brother, to the amount of information that I can offer without receiving a specific request for that information. I am Orcas.

Carla: I personally am not interested at all in taking thought for physical survival. Why would such information be of use when, if we're needed on whatever level, the means for that will be provided?

I am Orcas. I am told that in your race is a saying that, "God helps those who help themselves." While it is indeed not necessary to become overwhelmed with attention to the physical future, it is also of a potential benefit to receive advice concerning the interaction between your physical vehicle and the realm within which it exists. The advice or information that I may provide at your request is not necessary, just as the information provided by other members of the Federation is not necessary. Does this answer your question?

Carla: Yes. My basic area of interest is the development of the evolution of my spirit and consequently I have no questions at all about survival. So I will wish you well and if any one else has any questions please go ahead.

C: Orcas? Is your contacting this group due to a need of our services in regards to our fellow members of this race or was there a specific calling for you …

(The microphone was dropped)

[I am] … Orcas. There has been a calling from your planet of sufficient quantity or value to allow the calling to meet response. As many on your planetary surface find a likelihood for a very difficult physical future in which to complete their incarnate lessons prior to the time of harvest, it was deemed a sufficient calling to allow response.

May I answer further?

C: Not at this moment, but I might have more questions later. Thank you.

Thank you. May I answer another in this group?

J: What is your advice on survival? What may entities do to best survive?

I am Orcas. While I am unable to provide a strategy, for such would infringe upon your rights, I am allowed to encourage an amount of identification of one's third-dimensional self with the Earth's second and third-dimensional realms within which the physical body resides. The awareness that the oneness exists, traversing those realms, can be of assistance in physical survival. In essence, this understanding may assist an individual in attaining a striven-for growth in this incarnation.

May I answer you further, my brother?

J: Since you have come to share information on survival, it would suggest that the times of cataclysms perhaps are close. Do you have information as to when we might expect the necessity for survival to be present, when these cataclysms might occur?

I am Orcas. It is not within my realm to provide announcement of events, but rather to assist in the attainment of that awareness that may serve both in personal growth and the survival of the events you describe. The timing of my arrival, so to speak, was dependent, not upon physical events, but rather on a level of desire emitted from your planetary surface.

May I answer further?

J: Not at this time. I may have some questions later. Thank you

I am Orcas. Is there another question?

C: Have you made contact with any other contact groups or is this the first for you?

I am Orcas. This is my initial contact.

C: Are there other Confederation members who would feel *(inaudible)* at this time?

I am Orcas. I am unaware of any entity performing my allotted task. However, my brother, as your question was somewhat vague, I am unable to answer definitively.

C: It's just that I'm curious as to the reasons why this group *(inaudible)*. In other words *(inaudible)* for us to aid your teaching.

I am Orcas. Rather than a need—for all are complete—the ability to receive, and in awareness and desire for more information in my area of service, for example, this group, although a stronger desire exists elsewhere upon your planetary surface, the ability for communication does not exist.

May I answer you further?

C: Could you possibly know which area it is you speak of?

I am Orcas. By area we assume you refer to our area of advising. If this is so, then our area concerns advising entities to accept their surroundings as a portion of themselves, to live in a manner in which a sharing exists between themselves and the first and second level entities—correction—first, second and third-level entities of their world.

C: *(Inaudible)* question, what particular area of our world was this need for the information *(inaudible)* that you were unable to contact due to a lack of a channel.

I am Orcas. The calling exists in a primarily scattered form throughout your race as more become convinced of an impending disaster and an awareness *(inaudible)* concerning each entity's lack of knowledge concerning their own planetary surface and their ability to coexist with what the Creator has placed upon that surface. The discomfort associated with this knowledge resulted in a calling sufficient to evoke a response.

May we answer further?

C: No thank you.

I am Orcas. Is there another question?

C: One more. Before you spoke of the actual probability of the cataclysms to come *(inaudible)* happen sooner will have increased?

I am Orcas. I am unable to answer your question, however, I would emphasize that my arrival, so to speak, results from a calling and not from impending physical conditions.

May I answer you further?

(Inaudible)

Is there another question?

J: What is your density?

I am Orcas. I am of fourth density, but feel compelled to add that I am of comparatively recent graduation to this density and have been allowed this contact …

(Side one of tape ends.)

(L channeling)

… opportunity to learn to service.

May I answer further?

J: On the third-density planet from which you have recently graduated, did you have similar cataclysms as those which appear upon the horizon of our planet?

I am Orcas. On our third-dimensional point of origin, so to speak, we attained an attunement with our third-dimensional realm, or planet, that *(inaudible)* the necessity of such events.

May we respond further?

J: Not at this time. Thank you.

We thank you. Is there another question?

(Pause)

I am Orcas. We thank you for this opportunity to serve and if called upon will respond with the best of our ability in service, my brothers. Adonai.

(Carla channeling)

I am Laitos, and I greet you, my friends, in the love and the light of our infinite Creator. We would like to take this opportunity to share with our brothers and sisters and would at this time pass among you. [If you] will make the request that we be with you we will work at deepening the meditative state *(inaudible)*.

(Pause)

I am again with this instrument. It is a pleasure to be with each of you. At this time we would like to exercise the instrument known as C. If he would relax, we would speak a few words through him. *(Inaudible)* any analysis and speak thoughts you think without hesitation and we shall speak a few words. I am Laitos.

(C channeling)

I am Laitos. *(Inaudible)*.

(Carla channeling)

I am Laitos. I am again with this instrument *(inaudible)*. It is a great pleasure to exercise *(inaudible)* there is a great deal of energy *(inaudible)* and we experience *(inaudible)*, however, the one known as C *(inaudible)*. We will continue to work with you, my brother, and we thank you for your service. *(Inaudible)* I am known to you as Laitos. Adonai.

Sunday Meditation, August 2, 1981

(Carla channeling)

I am Latwii, and I greet you in the love and the light of the infinite Creator. It has been some time since we used this instrument. We will have to step down our vibration, if you will be patient. We are working on it. We are getting better. We have good contact. We forget about this instrument in between times that we use *(inaudible)* this is better. This is more comfortable for the instrument.

We have been long away from your group due to the fact that the proper configuration of vibration was not present. There was a great desire for information of a certain nature that was best given you by the brothers and sisters of Hatonn and, therefore, we stayed close to you in our hearts, but did not speak *(inaudible)*. However, this evening we find the configuration which requests those small differences which we might offer, due to the fact that we have a certain variation in our understanding of the one simple truth of love and light. Since our perspective is that of light, rather than love, thus we see things with a slightly different point of view. It is sometimes proper to view things from this angle of total and ever joy.

The compassion with which you are so full is of great aid to those about you. And we can but encourage you to look in each moment of your daily life for opportunities to share that compassion which you have so dearly bought by many periods of thought, contemplation, meditation and *(inaudible)*. There is a dimension which it also *(inaudible)*. It is *(inaudible)* for there are few people whom you may serve by sharing with them the laughter and the energy of the light, yet with these *(inaudible)* which is the material of *(inaudible)* all that is beautiful, good and true is composed of one of the infinite complexes of vibration which you call light.

There is an infinite vibration. You may think of the universe as an infinite expression of joy and *(inaudible)* in an eternally moving and luminous form. In the shadow of your illusion when compassion itself is hard to remember and often nearly impossible to show, the thought of the *(inaudible)* joy laughing and ecstasy is the thought of the Creator, but we say to you, my friends, come and be the fools that we are, for there is a kingdom of such as we and in that kingdom there is not the darkness whereby compassion cannot *(inaudible)*. You may choose in each moment that which you *(inaudible)*. It is our wish to experience the beauty of the material of the various colors of your *(inaudible)* and our *(inaudible)* to share our joy and whatever love we may have saved up from our own experience with you, our brothers and sisters.

At this time we would like to change the instrument through which we speak. I am a brother of Latwii.

(Jim channeling)

I am Latwii, and I greet you once again in the love and the light of the infinite Creator. We had some small difficulty making contact with this instrument, but we are very pleased to once again be able to utilize this instrument in our speaking to this group.

As we said before, long has it been since we have spoken to this group and a pleasure it is to find a configuration proper this evening to once again be able to share our humble thoughts and feelings with your group.

At this time it is our pleasure and our priv— correction. This instrument is somewhat tongue-tied—it is our privilege, shall we say, to be able and to attempt to answer questions that you may have.

Might we answer a question at this time?

M: Yes, please. What was the exact configuration which you are speaking of that allows you to be here tonight?

I am Latwii. The configuration necessary for our contact contains not only a desire for the sharing of the compassion in love of our brothers and sisters of Hatonn, but also a calling for a desire for the sharing of wisdom to balance that love. Love is the moving force which creates all of creation. In the light of wisdom might the creation be clearly seen so that love might be used in a balanced fashion, so that one does not run, shall we say, headlong into difficulties with a completely and uninhibitedly open channel of love.

Might we answer you further, my brother?

M: What about this particular group creates that configuration?

I am Latwii. On this particular evening there is the addition of members who have not been with this group for quite some time which adds the necessary configuration for the seeking of the wisdom or light vibration. To those new additions, shall we say, or additions long absent from this group, we may thank for proper configuration for our speaking.

May we answer you further, my brother?

M: No, thank you.

We thank you, as always. Might we answer another question at this time?

Carla: May I say I'm glad to hear your cheery voice *(inaudible)*.

I am Latwii, and we thank you for your appreciation of our liveliness. We hope we did not overdo the liveliness when we first made contact with you. We are somewhat clumsy in our attempts, as you know from your experience with our contact. This evening, it is our pleasure to be basking in the color of what you would call a violet ray, quite beautiful by any standards, and we wish that we could share it with you, but as you know, it is quite difficult to share the exact true color of any vibration which we might experience.

Might we answer you further, my sister?

Carla: No, thank you.

We thank you, as always. Might we answer another question at this time?

C: Yes. I'm needing some advice. Here of late I haven't been very compassionate. I've been impatient. When I meditate, I get up with a drained, tired feeling, but I was wondering, is there something that I'm doing wrong or is it a physical deficiency? I don't think my diet is proper to keep my body properly maintained *(inaudible)*.

I am Latwii. My brother, we would suggest, as it is well known to you, that the work which you engage yourself in for your living, your daily existence, is quite draining upon you at almost every turn. This has been a problem for you in the past and continues to be so in your meditations. May we suggest that as you enter your meditation you perform a simple ritual in which you leave the cares of the day and the worries which may have come your way aside for these few moments of meditation. In the state of meditation you are, in effect, opening yourself to every possible energy which you have come in contact with, and an indiscriminate opening may allow such energy draining effects which you have experienced in your work to magnify in your meditation.

A simple ritual which has meaning for you in which you leave these cares by the door, shall we say, would be, may we suggest, of assistance to you as you enter the meditative state and will allow you to choose those energies or tune to those vibrations which are of an uplifting nature rather than carrying with you and magnifying those which tend to drain your energy.

May we answer you further, my brother?

C: Yes. When I do meditate there are times I have this vision of traveling at extreme speeds through space. And I almost have a feeling that I'm partially leaving my body. Is this happening or is it just a sensation of meditation?

I am Latwii. My brother, there are various explanations possible for this phenomenon which you are experiencing. A partial leaving of the body is one, but potential, may we say, explanation for this phenomenon. There are other possibilities which include your diet, which you mentioned before. Occasionally the chemical balances or imbalances within the brain may be affected by those ingredients which are ingested by your peoples as a normal part of your daily existence. Care in diet can often be of assistance in making the meditative state a clearer channel for the expressing of those vibrations which are attempting to be made manifest during your meditation.

In this particular case of which you speak, we may say that it is a combination of these two possible explanations which is acting and causing an imbalance in your experience of the meditative state. One is attempting to express as the leaving of the cares or the body as you experience. The other, the intake of certain chemicals or foods is inhibiting this expression.

May we be of further service, my brother?

C: Is this chemical that you speak of the ingestion of sugars?

I am Latwii. You are correct, my brother. We could not say this without your finding for yourself of this truth.

C: I guess I've known it for some time. Try to get off one, seems like I'm substituting one for the other. Thank you for your reassurance and information.

As always, we thank you. May we be of further service with another question at this time?

L: Yes. I'm a member of a communal farm. I notice that there seems to be a greater amount of friction between members recently. Is this the result of an effort from negatively polarized entities? If so, what information can you give me about it?

I am Latwii. My brother, in this case we may say that though it might be somewhat glamorous to consider the possibility of negative entities inviting themselves into the affairs of your community, it is more possibly the case that those in this community are having more or less success at using the catalyst of learning and from time to time will suffer falling back, shall we say, and at other times shall be more successful in the use of their catalyst. Might we answer you further, my brother?

L: Not at this time, thank you.

Again, we thank you. Might we answer another question?

Carla: You might. Recently the three of us that live in this house have been so inundated with a lot of scare talk about doom, imminent doom, and my reactions to it have been basic disinterest. I wonder if you might comment on the reason, the possible reason for my *(inaudible)*.

I am Latwii. And we might make an answer at this time and, indeed, we find we shall! And we also might say that we heartily enjoy the humor of this group and we have missed it greatly during the absence.

In answer to your question, may we say that speaking of doom which is so prevalent among your peoples at this time is most likely caused by the great possibility that such doom-filled cataclysms shall and, indeed, have begun occurring upon your planet. Of this there can be no denying, but we would suggest, as you have suggested yourself, that one's response to such doom-saying is what is of most importance. You must consider for yourself that which you wish to do. Do you wish to be swayed by prophecies of doom which comes your way? If so, you have your choice of many, for many there are at this time and many more shall there be, for indeed you shall continue to see more cataclysms upon your planet, but we of Latwii may or may not be able to be of assistance in this area for we are those who have what might be called a light touch upon this matter and do not see such things with the same gravity as many who speak of them. We are very pleased that you enjoy our humor and hope that you have received our message as well.

May we answer you further, my sister?

Carla: No, that happens to be completely with my own feelings. So I have no more questions whatsoever. Thank you very much.

Again, may we thank you. May we answer another question at this time?

L: I'd just like to make a comment that I think we all appreciate the punishment you've given us.

I am Latwii. And we have been outdone, and we yield the floor to the punster of rank among us.

May we answer another question?

M: It is my perception that many people of this group aren't particularly concerned about their physical well-being through the coming cataclysms which may befall us. Why is it that we had the new contact tonight? It does not seem to me that that is our particular call for information that *(inaudible)*.

I am Latwii, and, my brother, on this question we must, we are afraid, remain somewhat silent; though there is much that may be said at this time, it is not proper that it be said.

May we be of further service with another question?

Carla: May I make a statement and ask if you would confirm or deny it? Is it possible that the reason that Orcas spoke with this group is that there is a clear channel *(inaudible)* for information which caused this new social memory complex to find its *(inaudible)* in such a way that *(inaudible)*.

I am Latwii. It is possible. May we answer another question?

L: I'd like to formulate a hypothesis which requires that you confirm or deny it, if you would like to, that the entity Orcas is being given an initial opportunity to work through the Federation with a third-dimensional group—ourselves—and has been assigned an area with which it has greatest familiarity, as there was an area of considerable ability *(inaudible)*.

I am Latwii, and, my brother, at this time, that we are hindered by necessity of remaining silent for fear of infringement.

May we answer another question?

Carla: Are there still fourth-density planetary entities that are working with *(inaudible)*?

I am Latwii, and as you know, my sister, that is correct, for your own beloved teacher, Hatonn, is one of these entities who works with those leaders of your planet who have the power, shall we say—or shall we say, it seems have the power—to determine whether war occurs or does not occur upon your planet. Many are those from the Confederation who pour their light and love upon your planet at this time to each entity upon the surface of your planet, not only to the leaders, but to each entity that forms the entire mind complex of your planet. Many are those upon your planet who call for this service at this time and hopefully, it is the hope of our group, at least, of the Confederation, that these efforts of pouring light and love upon your planet shall be successful in averting the catastrophes of war which seem, at times, so imminent among your peoples.

May we answer you further, my sister?

Carla: No, thank you.

We thank you once again. May we answer another question?

L: I have one last question about Orcas. Is Orcas capable of exerting an influence on first or second-dimensional entities or is Orcas capable of instructing us in the accomplishment of *(inaudible)*?

I am Latwii. My brother, we do not mean to seem obscure, but again we must remain silent in this area. There is, as we said, much that could be said in this area, but at this time we do not deem it the proper time to say that which could be said.

May we answer another question?

M: Well, since we're getting the whole clan of contacts tonight, where's Oxal?

I am Latwii. The one known to you as Oxal is, shall we say, waiting in the wings and though it appears may not speak—we correct this instrument once again. We believe we are tiring his tongue—though it appears Oxal may not speak this evening, there is a good chance that Oxal may speak at a future date, in your near future.

May we answer you further, my brother?

(Inaudible)

May we answer another question at this time?

(Pause)

I am Latwii. And our thanks to your group, as always, for inviting us to share our humble thoughts and feelings and simple humor with your group. It is always a joy to be able to speak with those whose ears and minds and hearts are open to words of love and light, simple and humble though they be. We are known to you as Latwii and we leave you in the love and the light of the one infinite Creator. Adonai, my friends. ☙

Intensive Meditation
August 6, 1981

(Unknown channeling)

I am Laitos, and I am with this instrument. I greet you all, my friends, in the love and the light of the infinite Creator. It is an honor and a privilege once again to be called to your group for the purpose of exercising a new instrument. It is always a joy for us to join your meditations in whatever capacity possible. It is our special joy and privilege to join at this time, for it is our service as members of the Confederation of Planets in the Service of the Infinite Creator to serve as those who introduce new instruments to the conditioning vibration of the Confederation and the initial contacts. We of Laitos have long served in this role and find great meaning in sharing this service with those few of people who choose to seek.

Always *(inaudible)* for the opportunity to share the love and the light of the infinite Creator with yet one more entity, and to see that entity in turn become a beacon to share that light yet further with more of your people. Thusly, it is our hope that more and more people upon the surface of your planet might become aware of the philosophy of the Federation and, more importantly, of the love and the light of the infinite Creator that is found within. In this regard, we hope that this service that we now offer might be [arranged.]

At this time we will prepare the one known as C to receive our conditioning vibrations, if the one known as C would relax. We will now send a few words to the one known as C. They shall, as before, be the phrase, "I am Laitos." We shall repeat it a number of times before continuing further. I am Laitos.

(C channeling)

I am Laitos. I am Laitos. I am Laitos. I am Laitos. I am Laitos.

(Unknown channeling)

I am Laitos, and I am again with this instrument. We are very pleased with the progress the one known as C continues to make. At this time we will once again transfer this contact to the one known as C in order that we might speak a few sentences through this instrument. If he would relax and refrain from analysis, speak each word-thought as it appears in his mind. I am Laitos.

(C channeling)

I am Laitos, and I greet you once again in the love and the light of the Creator. *(inaudible)* simple thoughts is but one way in which *(inaudible)* can seek to serve *(inaudible)*. I am Laitos.

(Unknown channeling)

I am Laitos, and I greet you once again in love and light. We thank the one known as C for allowing us to use his instrument. And we say once again, it is a privilege and a pleasure and a great honor for us to be able to exercise a new instrument. And may we say that we are very pleased by the progress shown by the one known as C.

At this time we will transfer this contact to another instrument for the purpose of answering any questions which any gathered here might have. We now transfer this contact. I am Laitos.

(Unknown channeling)

I am Laitos. I am now with this instrument, and greet you once again in the love and the light of the infinite Creator. May we ask if we may have the privilege of attempting to share our thought with you on any subject?

Questioner: If I may, could you speak a few words on the relationship we call marriage and its role in responsibilities?

I am Laitos. The question that you ask is somewhat complex. The relationship known among your peoples as marriage is a vehicle for service. The polarity between two entities draws them together and forms within each a bias to be of service. This is the basis of the relationship. This relationship is heavily laden with heavy difficulties inherent in the non-flexible structure which is lacking in the bias toward service.

Thus, when dealing in the illusion with this relationship, it is well to clear from the mind all possible thoughts of the necessity which the marriage bond seems to suggest and to focus instead upon the bias toward service to another which caused the genesis of the relationship.

There are several responsibilities in this relationship. There is the responsibility of offering the self for service. There is the responsibility of expressing the self in as undistorted a manner as possible, so that [yours] may be to the other entity a clear self, a self that communicates and is therefore of service by teaching or by offering the ability of one in need of teaching.

There is the responsibility of being the friend and protector of those entities which may issue from the physical sexual reproductive activities of this relationship, in such a way that the self is offered to the so-called children in service in ways which the young entity may understand. These ways include the basic orientation of service to others, the familiarizing of the children with the concept of the Creator and their relationship to the Creator, the family remembrance of this relationship and, in general, the best guidance each in the relationship may possibly offer to these young ones, in whatever they may encounter as they progress in the illusion.

May we answer you further?

Questioner: No. Thank you very much.

We thank you. Is there another question?

Questioner: Can you give me some idea of the accuracy of my channeling?

I am Laitos. The accuracy of channeling is always imperfect. We assume you intend to discover the percentage of channeling which comes from your own resources and the percentages which come from the Confederation resources. This ratio of percentages varies widely but at present you are beginning to reach the level where your percentage remains within acceptable Confederation limits for clear contact. It is our intent in this type of contact to retain at least 25 percent of the contact for the use of the channel. This enables our message to find the unique expression in each and every instrument while maintaining the basic simple tenor of what our group has to offer—that is, the explication of the original Thought of love.

Thus, this channel, for instance, is normally approximately 30 percent using her own resources. In your case, you are beginning to stabilize at approximately 35 to 37 percent your own resources. This is a plateau which must be reached. Once stability is reached, it is then possible through experience to gradually approach the 25 percent which is considered by us to be the limit beyond we would not wish to go. The lower acceptable limit is 50 percent one's own resources. So you may see you have advanced in your own work to a great extent. Therefore, we thank you for your desire to be as pure a channel as possible and request that you never be concerned if you find some material from your own experience worked into the channeling, for it is our precise intention to use experiences which illustrate the basic love and light of the infinite Creator.

May we answer you further?

Questioner: No. Thank you for your answer.

We thank you greatly for your service and offer every encouragement. Is there another question?

(Pause)

I am Laitos. If there are no more questions at this time we shall close this meeting. We shall again transfer to the one known as C to bid you farewell. I am Laitos.

(C channeling)

I am Laitos, and I once again am with this instrument. It has been our pleasure to *(inaudible)* the ones who call us. I am Laitos. I leave you now in the love and the light of the infinite Creator. Adonai, my friends, *(inaudible)*. ❧

L/L Research

L/L Research is a subsidiary of Rock Creek Research & Development Laboratories, Inc.

P.O. Box 5195
Louisville, KY 40255-0195

www.llresearch.org

Rock Creek is a non-profit corporation dedicated to discovering and sharing information which may aid in the spiritual evolution of humankind.

ABOUT THE CONTENTS OF THIS TRANSCRIPT: This telepathic channeling has been taken from transcriptions of the weekly study and meditation meetings of the Rock Creek Research & Development Laboratories and L/L Research. It is offered in the hope that it may be useful to you. As the Confederation entities always make a point of saying, please use your discrimination and judgment in assessing this material. If something rings true to you, fine. If something does not resonate, please leave it behind, for neither we nor those of the Confederation would wish to be a stumbling block for any.

© 2009 L/L Research

The Law of One, Book III, Session 65
August 8, 1981

Ra: I am Ra. I greet you in the love and in the light of the one infinite Creator. We communicate now.

Questioner: Could you first please give us an indication of the instrument's condition and the level of vital and physical energies?

Ra: I am Ra. This instrument's vital energies are as previously stated. The physical energies are greatly distorted towards weakness at this space/time due to the distortion complexes symptomatic of that which you call the arthritic condition. The level of psychic attack is constant but is being dealt with by this instrument in such a way as to eliminate serious difficulties due to its fidelity and that of the support group.

Questioner: I may be recovering a little ground already covered today, but I am trying to get a more clear picture of some things that I don't understand and possibly develop a plan of my own for activity in the future.

I have the impression that in the near future the seeking will increase by many who now are incarnate in the physical on this planet. Their seeking will increase because they will become more aware of the creation as it is and as it is opposed, I might say, to the creation of man. Their orientation and their thinking will be, by catalyst of a unique nature, reoriented to thinking of more basic concepts, shall I say. Is this correct?

Ra: I am Ra. The generalities of expression can never be completely correct. However, we may note that when faced with a hole in the curtain, an entity's eyes may well peer for the first time through the window beyond. This tendency is probable given the possibility/probability vortices active within your space/time and time/space continua at this nexus.

Questioner: I have assumed that the reason that so many Wanderers and those harvested third-density entities who have been transferred here find it a privilege and an exceptionally beneficial time to be incarnate upon this planet is that the effect that I just spoke of gives them the opportunity to be more fully of service because of the increased seeking. Is this, in general, correct?

Ra: I am Ra. This is the intention which Wanderers had prior to incarnation. There are many Wanderers whose dysfunction with regard to the planetary ways of your peoples have caused, to some extent, a condition of being caught up in a configuration of mind complex activity which, to the corresponding extent, may prohibit the intended service.

Questioner: I noticed that you are speaking more slowly than usual. Is there a reason for this?

Ra: I am Ra. This instrument is somewhat weak and although strong in vital energy and well able to function at this time is somewhat more fragile than the usual condition we find. We may note a continuing bearing of the physical distortion called pain which has a weakening effect upon physical energy. In order to use the considerable store of available energy without harming the instrument we are attempting to channel even more narrow band than is our wont.

Questioner: Have I properly analyzed the condition that creates the possibility of greater service as follows: Seniority by vibration of incarnation has greatly polarized those upon the surface of the planet now, and the influx of Wanderers has greatly increased the mental configuration toward things of a more spiritual nature. This would be, I assume, one of the factors creating a better atmosphere for service. Is this correct?

Ra: I am Ra. This is correct.

Questioner: Would the coming changes as we progress into fourth-density such as changes in the physical third-density planet due to the heating effect and changes such as the ability of people to perform what we term paranormal activities act as catalyst to create a greater seeking?

Ra: I am Ra. This is partially correct. The paranormal events occurring are not designed to increase seeking but are manifestations of those whose vibratory configuration enables these entities to contact the gateway to intelligent infinity. These entities capable of paranormal service may determine to be of such service on a conscious level. This, however, is a function of the entity and its free will and not the paranormal ability.

The correct portion of your statements is the greater opportunity for service due to the many changes which will offer many challenges, difficulties, and seeming distresses within your illusion to many who then will seek to understand, if we may use this misnomer, the reason for the malfunctioning of the physical rhythms of their planet.

Moreover, there exists probability/possibility vortices which spiral towards your bellicose actions. Many of these vortices are not of the nuclear war but of the less annihilatory but more lengthy so-called "conventional" war. This situation, if formed in your illusion, would offer many opportunities for seeking and for service.

Questioner: How would conventional warfare offer the opportunities for seeking and service?

Ra: I am Ra. The possibility/probabilities exist for situations in which great portions of your continent and the globe in general might be involved in the type of warfare which you might liken to guerrilla warfare. The ideal of freedom from the so-called invading force of either the controlled fascism or the equally controlled social common ownership of all things would stimulate great quantities of contemplation upon the great polarization implicit in the contrast between freedom and control. In this scenario which is being considered at this time/space nexus the idea of obliterating valuable sites and personnel would not be considered an useful one. Other weapons would be used which do not destroy as your nuclear arms would. In this on-going struggle the light of freedom would burn within the mind/body/spirit complexes capable of such polarization. Lacking the opportunity for overt expression of the love of freedom, the seeking for inner knowledge would take root aided by those of the Brothers and Sisters of Sorrow which remember their calling upon this sphere.

Questioner: We would seem to have dual catalysts operating, and the question is which one is going to act first. The prophecies, I will call them, made by Edgar Cayce indicated many Earth changes and I am wondering about the mechanics describing the future. Ra, it has been stated, is not a part of time and yet we concern ourselves with possibility/probability vortices. It is very difficult for me to understand how the mechanism of prophecy operates. What is the value of such a prophesy such as Cayce made with respect to Earth changes and all of these scenarios?

Ra: I am Ra. Consider the shopper entering the store to purchase food with which to furnish the table for the time period you call a week. Some stores have some items, others a variant set of offerings. We speak of these possibility/probability vortices when asked with the understanding that such are as a can, jar, or portion of goods in your store.

It is unknown to us as we scan your time/space whether your peoples will shop hither or yon. We can only name some of the items available for the choosing. The, shall we say, record which the one you call Edgar read from is useful in that same manner. There is less knowledge in this material of other possibility/probability vortices and more attention paid to the strongest vortex. We see the same vortex but also see many others. Edgar's material could be likened unto one hundred boxes of your cold cereal, another vortex likened unto three, or six, or fifty of another product which is eaten by your peoples for breakfast. That you will breakfast is close to certain. The menu is your own choosing.

The value of prophecy must be realized to be only that of expressing possibilities. Moreover, it must be, in our humble opinion, carefully taken into consideration that any time/space viewing, whether by one of your time/space or by one such as we who view the time/space from a dimension, shall we say, exterior to it will have a quite difficult time expressing time measurement values. Thus prophesy given in specific terms is more interesting for the content or type of possibility predicted than for the space/time nexus of its supposed occurrence.

Questioner: So we have the distinct possibility of two different types of catalyst creating an atmosphere of seeking that is greater than that which we experience at present. There will be much confusion, especially in the scenario of Earth changes simply because there have been many predictions of these changes by many groups giving many and sundry reasons for the changes. Can you comment on the effectiveness of this type of catalyst and the rather wide pre-knowledge of the coming changes but also the wide variation in explanation for these changes?

Ra: I am Ra. Given the amount of strength of the possibility/probability vortex which posits the expression by the planet itself of the difficult birthing of the planetary self into fourth-density, it would be greatly surprising were not many which have some access to space/time able to perceive this vortex. The amount of this cold cereal in the grocery, to use our previous analogy, is disproportionately large. Each which prophesies does so from an unique level, position, or vibratory configuration. Thus biases and distortions will accompany much prophecy.

Questioner: This entire scenario for the next twenty years seems to be aimed at producing an increase in seeking and an increase in the awareness of the natural creation, but also a terrific amount of confusion. Was it the preincarnative objective of many of the Wanderers to attempt to reduce this confusion?

Ra: I am Ra. It was the aim of Wanderers to serve the entities of this planet in whatever way was requested and it was also the aim of Wanderers that their vibratory patterns might lighten the planetary vibration as a whole, thus ameliorating the effects of planetary disharmony and palliating any results of this disharmony.

Specific intentions such as aiding in a situation not yet manifest are not the aim of Wanderers. Light and love go where they are sought and needed, and their direction is not planned aforetimes.

Questioner: Then each of the Wanderers here acts as a function of the biases he has developed in any way he sees fit to communicate or simply be in his polarity to aid the total consciousness of the planet. Is there any physical way in which he aids, perhaps by his vibrations somehow just adding to the planet just as electrical polarity or charging a battery? Does that also aid the planet, just the physical presence of the Wanderers?

Ra: I am Ra. This is correct and the mechanism is precisely as you state. We intended this meaning in the second portion of our previous answer.

You may, at this time, note that as with any entities, each Wanderer has its unique abilities, biases, and specialities so that from each portion of each density represented among the Wanderers come an array of preincarnative talents which then may be expressed upon this plane which you now experience so that each Wanderer, in offering itself before incarnation, has some special service to offer in addition to the doubling effect of planetary love and light and the basic function of serving as beacon or shepherd.

Thus there are those of fifth-density whose abilities to express wisdom are great. There are fourth and sixth-density Wanderers whose ability to serve as, shall we say, passive radiators or broadcasters of love and love/light are immense. There are many others whose talents brought into this density are quite varied.

Thus Wanderers have three basic functions once the forgetting is penetrated, the first two being basic, the tertiary one being unique to that particular mind/body/spirit complex.

We may note at this point while you ponder the possibility/probability vortices that although you have many, many items which cause distress and thus offer seeking and service opportunities, there is always one container in that store of peace, love, light, and joy. This vortex may be very small, but to turn one's back upon it is to forget the infinite possibilities of the present moment. Could your planet polarize towards harmony in one fine, strong, moment of inspiration? Yes, my friends. It is not probable; but it is ever possible.

Questioner: How common in the universe is a mixed harvest from a planet of both positively and negatively oriented mind/body/spirit complexes?

Ra: I am Ra. Among planetary harvests which yield an harvest of mind/body/spirit complexes approximately 10% are negative; approximately 60% are positive; and approximately 30% are mixed with nearly all harvest being positive. In the event of mixed harvest it is almost unknown for the majority of the harvest to be negative. When a planet moves strongly towards the negative there is almost no opportunity for harvestable positive polarization.

Questioner: Can you tell me why there is almost no opportunity in that case?

Ra: The ability to polarize positively requires a certain degree of self determination.

Questioner: Then as these final days of the cycle transpire if the harvest were to occur now, today, it would have a certain number harvested positively and negatively and a certain number of repeaters. I am going to assume that because of the catalyst that will be experienced between now and the actual harvesting time these numbers of harvestable entities will increase.

Generally speaking, not particularly with respect to this planet but with respect to general experience in harvesting, how big an increase in harvestable entities can you logically assume will occur because of the catalyst that occurs in the final period such as this one, or am I making a mistake in assuming that other planets have added catalyst at the end of a harvesting period when they have a mixed harvest?

Ra: I am Ra. In the event of mixed harvest there is nearly always disharmony and, therefore, added catalyst in the form of your so-called "Earth changes." In this assumption you are correct.

It is the Confederation's desire to serve those who may indeed seek more intensely because of this added catalyst. We do not choose to attempt to project the success of added numbers to the harvest for this would not be appropriate. We are servants. If we are called, we shall serve with all our strength. To count the numbers is without virtue.

Questioner: Now the added catalyst at the end of the cycle is a function specifically of the orientation of the consciousness that inhabits the planet. The consciousness has provided the catalyst for itself in orienting its thinking in the way it has oriented it, thus acting upon itself the same as catalyst of bodily pain and disease act upon the single mind/body/spirit complex. I made this analogy once before but reiterate it at this time to clarify my own thinking in seeing the planetary entity as somewhat of a single entity made up of billions of mind/body/spirit complexes. Is my viewpoint correct?

Ra: I am Ra. You are quite correct.

Questioner: Then we deal with an entity that has not yet formed a social memory but is yet an entity just as one of us can be called a single entity. Can we continue this observation of the conglomerate entity through the galactic entity, or shall I say, planetary system type of entity? Let me try to phrase it this way. Could I look at a single sun in its planetary system as an entity and then look at a major galaxy with its billions of stars as an entity? Can I continue this extrapolation in this way?

Ra: I am Ra. You can but not within the framework of third-density space/time.

Let us attempt to speak upon this interesting subject. In your space/time you and your peoples are the parents of that which is in the womb. The Earth, as you call it, is ready to be born and the delivery is not going smoothly. When this entity has become born it will be instinct with the social memory complex of its parents which have become fourth-density positive. In this density there is a broader view.

You may begin to see your relationship to the Logos or sun with which you are most intimately associated. This is not the relationship of parent to child but of Creator, that is Logos, to Creator that is the mind/body/spirit complex, as Logos. When this realization occurs you may then widen the field of "eyeshot," if you will, infinitely recognizing parts of the Logos throughout the one infinite creation and feeling, with the roots of Mind informing the intuition, the parents aiding their planets in evolution in reaches vast and unknown in the creation, for this process occurs many, many times in the evolution of the creation as an whole.

Questioner: The Wanderer goes through a forgetting process. You mentioned that those who have both third-and fourth-density bodies activated now do not have the forgetting that the Wanderer has. I was just wondering if, say, a sixth-density Wanderer were here with a third-density body activated, would he have gone through a forgetting that was in sections, shall I say, a forgetting of fourth, fifth, and sixth-densities and if he were to have his fourth-density body activated then he would have a partial additional memory and then another partial memory if his fifth-density body were activated and full memory if he had his sixth-density body activated? Does this make any sense?

Ra: I am Ra. No.

Questioner: Thank you. The forgetting process was puzzling me because you said that the fourth-density activated people who were here who had been harvested did not have the same forgetting problem. Could you tell me why the Wanderer loses his memory?

Ra: I am Ra. The reason is twofold. First, the genetic properties of the connection between the mind/body/spirit complex and the cellular structure of the body is different for third-density than for third/fourth-density.

Secondly, the free will of third-density entities needs be preserved. Thus Wanderers volunteer for third-density genetic or DNA connections to the mind/body/spirit complex. The forgetting process can be penetrated to the extent of the Wanderer remembering what it is and why it is upon the planetary sphere. However, it would be an infringement if Wanderers penetrated the forgetting so far as to activate the more dense bodies and thus be able to live, shall we say, in a god-like manner. This would not be proper for those who have chosen to serve.

The new fourth-density entities which are becoming able to demonstrate various newer abilities are doing so as a result of the present experience, not as a result of memory. There are always a few exceptions, and we ask your forgiveness for constant barrages of over-generalization.

Questioner: I don't know if this question is related to what I am trying to get at or not. I'll ask it and see what results. You mentioned in speaking of the pyramids the resonating chamber was used so that the adept could meet the self. Would you explain what you meant by that?

Ra: I am Ra. One meets the self in the center or deeps of the being. The so-called resonating chamber may be likened unto the symbology of the burial and resurrection of the body wherein the entity dies to self and through this confrontation of apparent loss and realization of essential gain, is transmuted into a new and risen being.

Questioner: Could I make the analogy of in this apparent death of losing the desires that are the illusory, common desires of third-density and gaining desires of total service-to-others?

Ra: I am Ra. You are perceptive. This was the purpose and intent of this chamber as well as forming a necessary portion of the King's Chamber position's effectiveness.

Questioner: Can you tell me what this chamber did to the entity to create this awareness in him?

Ra: I am Ra. This chamber worked upon the mind and the body. The mind was affected by sensory deprivation and the archetypical reactions to being buried alive with no possibility of extricating the self. The body was affected both by the mind configuration and by the electrical and piezoelectrical properties of the materials which were used in the construction of the resonating chamber.

This will be the last full query of this working. May we ask if there are any brief queries at this time?

Questioner: Is there anything that we can do to make the instrument more comfortable or to improve the contact?

Ra: I am Ra. We feel that the instrument is well supported and that all is well. We caution each regarding this instrument's distortions towards pain, for it dislikes sharing these expressions but as support group this instrument subconsciously accepts each entity's aid. All is in alignment. You are conscientious. We thank you for this. I am Ra. I leave you, my friends, rejoicing in the love and the light of the one infinite Creator. Go forth, therefore, glorying in the power and in the peace of the one infinite Creator. Adonai.

L/L Research

L/L Research is a subsidiary of Rock Creek Research & Development Laboratories, Inc.

P.O. Box 5195
Louisville, KY 40255-0195

www.llresearch.org

Rock Creek is a non-profit corporation dedicated to discovering and sharing information which may aid in the spiritual evolution of humankind.

ABOUT THE CONTENTS OF THIS TRANSCRIPT: This telepathic channeling has been taken from transcriptions of the weekly study and meditation meetings of the Rock Creek Research & Development Laboratories and L/L Research. It is offered in the hope that it may be useful to you. As the Confederation entities always make a point of saying, please use your discrimination and judgment in assessing this material. If something rings true to you, fine. If something does not resonate, please leave it behind, for neither we nor those of the Confederation would wish to be a stumbling block for any.

© 2009 L/L RESEARCH

THE LAW OF ONE, BOOK V, SESSION 65, FRAGMENT 36
AUGUST 8, 1981

Jim: The following material returns to the realm of transient information in general—and a portion of the conspiracy theory specifically—as an outgrowth of our querying about prophesies, earth changes, probable futures, and their effect on seeking truth. You will notice that we didn't linger long here this time.

Carla: *I think it is important, in the context of this little volume of fragments we kept out of the first four volumes of* The Law Of One, *that we look straight and hard at the tendency of UFO researchers and people in general to see conspiracies and treachery behind every bush and gossip item. When I first started reading in this area, in the late sixties, there were prophets claiming a near future in which war, catastrophe and desolation would reign. In the years since, nothing has changed but the dates. Always this great trouble is seen to be coming a couple of years from now, and the call is to put all else aside except for preparing for this time of trial. I have known people of sound judgment who have basement walls lined with freeze-dried food, proof against disaster. Let's call it the bomb shelter syndrome.*

The thing I wish to emphasize is that these thoughts do harm to the innocent future. They take present energy away from the immediate happenings of the day, and sap it with chronic fear and fear-based planning. Disasters do occur, indubitably. And when they do come, we can hope simply to meet them with some grace. In that day, it will be the people who have learned to live from a loving heart that will be able to help the most, not the people who have barricaded themselves into a mind-set based on fear.

Session 65, August 8, 1981

Questioner: Are you saying then that this possible condition of war would be much more greatly spread across the surface of the globe than anything we have experienced in the past and therefore touch a larger percentage of the population in this form of catalyst?

Ra: I am Ra. This is correct. There are those now experimenting with one of the major weapons of this scenario, that is the so-called psychotronic group of devices which are being experimentally used to cause such alterations in wind and weather as will result In eventual famine. If this program is not countered and proves experimentally satisfactory, the methods in this scenario would be made public. There would then be what those whom you call Russians hope to be a bloodless invasion of their personnel in this and every land deemed valuable. However, the peoples of your culture have little propensity for bloodless surrender.

Sunday Meditation
August 9, 1981

(Carla channeling)

[I am Hatonn,] and I greet you, my friends, in the love and in the light of our infinite Creator. It is a great privilege to be with you this evening, and we especially greet those new to this group, and send to each the love and the light which we channel from the one infinite Creator. We would speak to you this evening of ships. You may see yourself, my friends, as one upon a ship. There are many different configurations in the sky and there is no land in sight. The ship is equipped with rudder and sail and the wind is keen and swift, yet there is much that needs to be done before you can set sail and move before the wind.

Each of you, my friends, is upon a path which, like the trackless seas, offers no apparent signpost. The daily experience of your peoples is one of great confusion. How, then, to get the bearings, how to read the skies. My friends, there is within you the ability to create the knowledge which you need in order to be master of your destiny. There is, shall we say, a knowledge of constellations and the sextant whereby to measure them. It is not hidden within you at any great depth. This ability to guide your path is separated by your conscious mind only through a veil which may be penetrated by meditation, contemplation, and the desire to seek.

There are many times when it does not even seem important to find the path through this ocean, for things occur which make one feel infinitely small and at the mercy of all those elements. In our analogy they would be weather, night, day, hunger and thirst, loneliness, despair in your daily life. You may see the vessel of your physical body as meeting far more complex elements as you deal with the many other persons with whom you may come in contact and the many societal pressures which may come to bear upon your situation.

How helpless can such a sailor feel, my friends? We would remind you of the story spoken of in one of your holy works wherein one the disciples of the one known to you as Jesus saw this entity walking towards his boat across the water. "If you truly be he," said the disciple, "bid me come and walk to you." "Come," said the one known as Jesus, and so the disciple did. As he doubted, he sank, and as he asked, he walked. In meditation, my friends, you find more than just the tools for plotting the course. You find a feeling, a sensitivity, an openness for what your course may be. This is the function of what some call faith. It is not necessary to have rigid beliefs in order to progress, in fact quite the opposite, for the path, like the ocean, is ever *(inaudible)* and ever changing.

It is important, however, to reach, to seek and to dare. To step out upon the water is not a sensible thing to do, and yet, in this story it was instructed for the disciple to do what he felt. Yes, my friends, many times you may begin to sink; many times you may clamber back into your boat and wonder if you will make error after error in your search for the truth. Nevertheless, if you seek and yet again seek to know the truth of who you are, how you came to be here and why you make this pilgrimage at this particular time in this particular way, you will find that your path opens more and more fair before you.

At this time I would leave this instrument that one of my sisters may speak through another instrument. We thank you with all of our hearts for allowing us to share our humble thoughts with you. It has been a great privilege to do so, and we ask you to consider what we say, not as the words of the wise, but as words to the wise, for we are your brothers and your sisters and can share in our imperfect way that which we have come to understand. I am known to you as Hatonn. I leave you in the love and the light of the infinite Creator. Adonai, my friends.

(L channeling)

I am Latwii, and I greet you, my brothers and sisters, in the love and the light of the Creator. It is a great pleasure to speak to a group as large, and may we say, as comfortable as this one. It is much easier to transmit messages to a group that has, for the time being, managed to lay aside its individual dramas, and, in the words of one who has occupied your planetary surface, "be here now." We would like to invite questions at this time for we are aware that there are a number of questions yet to be answered in the minds of those participating this night. Are there any questions that we may attempt to answer? I am Latwii.

(Pause)

I am Latwii. It is apparent that those who bear questions in their minds have not formulated those questions into the conscious thought patterns necessary to conversion into speech. Therefore, we shall again pause to enable those present to accomplish this magnificent task, if such is your individual desires. I am, patiently, Latwii.

Carla: I have laboriously come up with a question as to what color you are into tonight. What color are you into tonight?

I am Latwii. My sister, it is wonderful to hear your voice tonight. It is wonderful to hear any voice tonight. At this time we are experiencing a shade known as lavender, simply because we are relaxing and find this color conducive to relaxation without what would approximate to your sleep.

May we answer you further?

Carla: Well, that brings up an interesting point. I know that you're fifth density. Do you then have work periods rather than being in a state of conscious working all the time? Do you have some sort of time sense in that dimension?

I am Latwii. Time, as the occupants of your planetary sphere refer to, does not exist in our dimension, or for that matter, in yours, but enough of the puzzles. We find it necessary to recharge, as you might describe it, if a particularly strenuous effort has been made, such as our brother Hatonn's efforts at producing harmony in your planetary sphere. As you are aware, this sometimes has a deteriorative effect upon our brother Hatonn that requires some recuperation. However, we find that sleep, as you know it, is not necessary, as we have nothing to sleep with but find the state of mind, so to speak, that you refer to as meditation to be highly desirable.

May we answer you further?

Carla: You may. In other communications we've had some information about fifth-density beings having a much denser light body. I was wondering if you spend the entire experience in fifth density in one body or whether you go through a process of reincarnation as does third and fourth density?

I am Latwii. My sister, it is necessary to understand that the physical apparatus that you refer to as a body is merely a tool, and as you would use a screwdriver or spoon to accomplish a task, or a book to learn a lesson, so also do we create and use our tools, but cease to retain them upon completion of the task or learning necessary. This is also within the possibility of those in your plane, however, most are not aware of this potential and do not make use of it except in dreaming.

May we answer you further?

Carla: Well, just to clarify. I didn't quite understand. You said—are you saying that you only create or need one vehicle for the fifth-density experience or that you now use a fifth-density vehicle for each experience? In other words, do you reincarnate, or—I couldn't quite tell what you were saying. I know from other communications that the bisexual reproduction is the same although the vibrations are quite a bit different, obviously, but the function of this being to offer other entities fifth-density lessons. It isn't clear to me whether this would indicate reincarnation or whether you simply need one vehicle only for the entire working of the lessons of the learning of wisdom. I don't suppose it matters a lot. If this is not information that you can share just say so.

I am Latwii. I am prepared to speak now. We cannot describe the necessities for all of those entities in our dimension, for just as your awareness is lacking concerning your own, shall we say, field of endeavor, so also is our awareness less than total for our own educational facility that is our dimension. We can inform you that we find it unnecessary at some points in our education to possess a physical vehicle, yet at others the vehicle facilitates our learning experience. It is not, however, always necessary to enter the physical realm without the awareness of our lessons or knowledge prior to what you described as incarnating.

Does this answer your question?

Carla: Yes, indeed. I think I understand now what you were saying before. You do go through the process of reincarnation in a much more conscious way than we do, but what you were saying before was that we too go in and out of bodies and use time in between incarnations as well as the time during incarnations. We're just not as conscious of that while we're here in the illusion. Does that sum up what you were saying?

I am Latwii. Your answer is correct, and as this instrument would say, quite succinct, although we are not sure that the instrument knows the meaning of the term, as we cannot find the definition. We will simply accept his shot in the dark.

Carla: That's cool. Thank you, Latwii.

We thank you. Is there another question?

(Pause)

I am Latwii. As we are unable to answer the last comment we shall assume that your remaining questions shall be presented at another time. We therefore thank you for this opportunity of service and would encourage those present to continue to contact the members of the Federation at any time, however brief, for we are willing to respond at any opportunity that you will afford us. We leave you now and ask that you be aware that all who strive are beautiful points of balance within creation. With this puzzle, my friends, we bid you adieu. I am Latwii.

(Carla channeling)

I am Laitos, and I greet you, my friends. We will speak briefly for we realize this has been a somewhat lengthy meeting for you. We wish to offer to you an opportunity to experience the conditioning vibration which may aid you in deepening your meditative state, and for those who wish to experience the service known as vocal channeling, aid them in the perception of contact with the Confederation of Planets in the Service of the Infinite Creator. We would pass among you at this time. If you would wish us to work with you, please mentally request this and we would be most privileged to be of service.

While we are working with you, we will especially be conditioning the one known as C, and would say a few words through the one known as Jim before we close this meeting. I am Laitos, and will pause at this time, my friends.

(Jim channeling)

I am Laitos, and am with this instrument, and greet you all once again in love and light. We are aware that the one known as C is having some difficulty this evening dealing with the increase in energy attendant with our contact. We will pause once again. If the one known as C will relax, we will again attempt contact through his instrument and attempt to say a few words to this group. I am Laitos.

(C channeling)

I am Laitos, and I am with this instrument. It is again, as always, a pleasure to work with those who seek service as a vocal channel. We wish to assure this instrument that contact is good, but we ask that he relax and refrain from trying too hard, for we know that the words at first are hard to know and hard to discern from the entity's own thought patterns. We are happy with this contact and will continue to work with this instrument.

We would now transfer this contact back to the one known as Jim. I am Laitos.

(Jim channeling)

I am Laitos, and am again with this instrument. We thank the one known as C for his effort this evening. We are very pleased with his progress and very grateful for the opportunity to provide this service, for we of Laitos have the specific function of introducing entities upon your planet who wish to be vocal channels to the vibrations of the Confederation of Planets in Service of the Infinite Creator. We find far too few opportunities upon your planet to exercise this service, and each time another opportunity is presented to us, we cherish it as a treasure in our hearts, and we thank each of you for your patience in allowing us to work with yet one more new instrument that might serve as a beacon of the light and the love of the infinite Creator.

We are known to you as those of Laitos, and we leave you now in that love and in that light of the one infinite Creator. Rejoice with us each of the moments of your days as you travel in that love and light with all of the creation of the Father. Adonai, my friends. Adonai vasu borragus.

L/L Research is a subsidiary of Rock Creek Research & Development Laboratories, Inc.

P.O. Box 5195
Louisville, KY 40255-0195

www.llresearch.org

Rock Creek is a non-profit corporation dedicated to discovering and sharing information which may aid in the spiritual evolution of humankind.

ABOUT THE CONTENTS OF THIS TRANSCRIPT: This telepathic channeling has been taken from transcriptions of the weekly study and meditation meetings of the Rock Creek Research & Development Laboratories and L/L Research. It is offered in the hope that it may be useful to you. As the Confederation entities always make a point of saying, please use your discrimination and judgment in assessing this material. If something rings true to you, fine. If something does not resonate, please leave it behind, for neither we nor those of the Confederation would wish to be a stumbling block for any.

© 2009 L/L RESEARCH

The Law of One, Book III, Session 66
August 12, 1981

Ra: I am Ra. I greet you in the love and in the light of the one infinite Creator. We communicate now.

Questioner: I would like to investigate the mechanism of healing using the crystallized healer. I am going to make a statement, and I would appreciate it if you would correct my thinking.

It seems to me that once the healer has become properly balanced and unblocked with respect to energy centers, it is possible for him to act in some way as a collector and focuser of light in a way analogous to the way a pyramid works, collecting light through the left hand and emitting it through the right; this then, somehow, penetrating the first and seventh chakras' vibratory envelop of the body and allowing for the realignment of energy centers of the entity to be healed. I'm quite sure that I'm not completely correct on this and possibly considerably off. Could you rearrange my thinking so that it makes sense?

Ra: I am Ra. You are correct in your assumption that the crystallized healer is analogous to the pyramidal action of the King's Chamber position. There are a few adjustments we might suggest.

Firstly, the energy which is used is brought into the field complex of the healer by the outstretched hand used in a polarized sense. However, this energy circulates through the various points of energy to the base of the spine and, to a certain extent, the feet, thus coming through the main energy centers of the healer spiraling through the feet, turning at the red energy center towards a spiral at the yellow energy center and passing through the green energy center in a microcosm of the King's Chamber energy configuration of prana; this then continuing for the third spiral through the blue energy center and being sent therefrom through the gateway back to intelligent infinity.

It is from the green center that the healing prana moves into the polarized healing right hand and therefrom to the one to be healed.

We may note that there are some who use the yellow-ray configuration to transfer energy and this may be done but the effects are questionable and, with regard to the relationship between the healer, the healing energy, and the seeker, questionable due to the propensity for the seeker to continue requiring such energy transfers without any true healing taking place in the absence of the healer due to the lack of penetration of the armoring shell of which you spoke.

Questioner: A Wanderer who has an origin from fifth or sixth-density can attempt such a healing and have little or no results. Can you tell me what the Wanderer has lost and why it is necessary for him to regain certain balances and abilities for him to perfect his healing ability?

Ra: I am Ra. You may see the Wanderer as the infant attempting to verbalize the sound complexes of your peoples. The memory of the ability to communicate is within the infant's undeveloped mind complex, but the ability to practice or manifest this called speech is not immediately forthcoming due to the limitations of the mind/body/spirit complex it has chosen to be a part of in this experience.

So it is with the Wanderer which, remembering the ease with which adjustments can be made in the home density, yet still having entered third-density, cannot manifest that memory due to the limitation of the chosen experience. The chances of a Wanderer being able to heal in third-density are only more than those native to this density because the desire to serve may be stronger and this method of service chosen.

Questioner: What about the ones with the dual type of activated third and fourth-density bodies, harvested from other third-density planets? Are they able to heal using the techniques that we have discussed?

Ra: I am Ra. In many cases this is so, but as beginners of fourth-density, the desire may not be present.

Questioner: I'm assuming, then, that we have a Wanderer with the desire attempting to learn the techniques of healing while, shall I say, trapped in third-density. He then, it seems to me, is primarily concerned with the balancing and unblocking of the energy centers. Am I correct in this assumption?

Ra: I am Ra. This is correct. Only in so far as the healer has become balanced may it be a channel for the balancing of an other-self. The healing is first practiced upon the self, if we may say this, in another way.

Questioner: Now as the healer approaches an other-self to do the healing we have a situation where the other-self has, through programming of catalyst, possibly created a condition which is viewed as a condition needing healing. What is the situation and what are the ramifications of the healer acting upon the condition of programmed catalyst to bring about healing? Am I correct in assuming that in doing this healing, the programmed catalyst is useful to the one to be healed in that the one to be healed then becomes aware of what it wished to become aware of in programming the catalyst? Is this correct?

Ra: I am Ra. Your thinking cannot be said to be completely incorrect but shows a rigidity which is not apparent in the flow of the experiential use of catalyst.

The role of the healer is to offer an opportunity for realignment or aid in realignment of either energy centers or some connection between the energies of mind and body, spirit and mind, or spirit and body. This latter is very rare.

The seeker will then have the reciprocal opportunity to accept a novel view of the self, a variant arrangement of patterns of energy influx. If the entity, at any level, desires to remain in the configuration of distortion which seems to need healing it will do so. If, upon the other hand, the seeker chooses the novel configuration, it is done through free will.

This is one great difficulty with other forms of energy transfer in that they do not carry through the process of free will as this process is not native to yellow-ray.

Questioner: What is the difference, philosophically, between a mind/body/spirit complex healing itself through mental, shall I say, configuration and it being healed by an healer?

Ra: I am Ra. You have a misconception. The healer does not heal. The crystallized healer is a channel for intelligent energy which offers an opportunity to an entity that it might heal itself.

In no case is there an other description of healing. Therefore, there is no difference as long as the healer never approaches one whose request for aid has not come to it previously. This is also true of the more conventional healers of your culture and if these healers could but fully realize that they are responsible only for offering the opportunity of healing, and not for the healing, many of these entities would feel an enormous load of misconceived responsibility fall from them.

Questioner: Then in seeking healing a mind/body/spirit complex would then be seeking in some cases a source of gathered and focused light energy. This source could be another mind/body/spirit complex sufficiently crystallized for this purpose or the pyramid shape, or possibly something else. Is this correct?

Ra: I am Ra. These are some of the ways an entity may seek healing. Yes.

Questioner: Could you tell me the other ways an entity could seek healing?

Ra: I am Ra. Perhaps the greatest healer is within the self and may be tapped with continued meditation as we have suggested.

The many forms of healing available to your peoples … each have virtue and may be deemed appropriate by any seeker who wishes to alter the physical complex distortions or some connection between the various portions of the mind/body/spirit complex thereby.

Questioner: I have observed many activities known as psychic surgery in the area of the Philippine Islands. It was my assumption that these healers are providing what I would call a training aid or a way of creating a reconfiguration of the mind of the patient to be healed as the relatively naive patient observes the action of the healer in seeing the materialized blood, etc. and reconfigures the roots of mind to believe, you might say, the healing is done and, therefore, heals himself. Is this analysis that I have made correct?

Ra: I am Ra. This is correct. We may speak slightly further on the type of opportunity.

There are times when the malcondition to be altered is without emotional, mental, or spiritual interest to the entity and is merely that which has, perhaps by chance genetic arrangement, occurred. In these cases that which is apparently dematerialized will remain dematerialized and may be observed as so by any observer. The malcondition which has an emotional, mental, or spiritual charge is likely not to remain dematerialized in the sense of the showing of the objective referent to an observer. However, if the opportunity has been taken by the seeker the apparent malcondition of the physical complex will be at variance with the actual health, as you call this distortion, of the seeker and the lack of experiencing the distortions which the objective referent would suggest still held sway.

For instance, in this instrument the removal of three small cysts was the removal of material having no interest to the entity. Thus these growths remained dematerialized after the so-called psychic surgery experience. In other psychic surgery the kidneys of this instrument were carefully offered a new configuration of being-ness which the entity embraced. However, this particular portion of the mind/body/spirit complex carried a great deal of emotional, mental, and spiritual charge due to this distorted functioning being the cause of great illness in a certain configuration of events which culminated in this entity's conscious decision to be of service. Therefore, any objective scanning of this entity's renal complex would indicate the rather extreme dysfunctional aspect which it showed previous to the psychic surgery experience, as you call it.

The key is not in the continuation of the dematerialization of distortion to the eye of the beholder but rather lies in the choosing of the newly materialized configuration which exists in time/space.

Questioner: Would you explain that last comment about the configuration in time/space?

Ra: I am Ra. Healing is done in the time/space portion of the mind/body/spirit complex, is adopted by the form-making or etheric body, and is then given to the space/time physical illusion for use in the activated yellow mind/body/spirit complex. It is the adoption of the configuration which you call health by the etheric body in time/space which is the key to what you call health, not any event which occurs in space/time. In the process you may see the transdimensional aspect of what you call will, for it is the will, the seeking, the desire of the entity which causes the indigo body to use the novel configuration and to reform the body which exists in space/time. This is done in an instant and may be said to operate without regard to time. We may note that in the healing of very young children there is often an apparent healing by the healer in which the young entity has no part. This is never so, for the mind/body/spirit complex in time/space is always capable of willing the distortions it chooses for experience no matter what the apparent age, as you call it, of the entity.

Questioner: Is this desire and will that operates through to the time/space section a function only of the entity who is healed or is it also the function of the healer, the crystallized healer?

Ra: I am Ra. May we take this opportunity to say that this is the activity of the Creator. To specifically answer your query the crystallized healer has no will. It offers an opportunity without attachment to the outcome, for it is aware that all is one and that the Creator is knowing Itself.

Questioner: Then the desire must be strong in the mind/body/spirit complex who seeks healing to be healed in order for the healing to occur? Is this correct?

Ra: I am Ra. This is correct on one level or another. An entity may not consciously seek healing and yet subconsciously be aware of the need to experience the new set of distortions which result from healing. Similarly an entity may consciously desire healing greatly but within the being, at some level, find some cause whereby certain configurations which seem quite distorted are, in fact, at that level, considered appropriate.

Questioner: I assume that the reason for assuming the distortions appropriate would be that these distortions would aid the entity in its reaching its ultimate objective which is a movement along the path of evolution in the desired polarity. Is this correct?

Ra: I am Ra. This is correct.

Questioner: Then an entity who becomes aware of his polarization with respect to service-to-others might find a paradoxical situation in the case where it was unable to fully serve because of distortions chosen to reach the understanding it has reached. At this point it would seem that the entity who was aware of the mechanism might, through meditation, understand the necessary mental configuration for alleviating the physical distortion so that it could be of greater service-to-others. At this particular nexus am I correct in this thinking?

Ra: I am Ra. You are correct although we might note that there are often complex reasons for the programming of a distorted physical complex pattern. In any case, meditation is always an aid to knowing the self.

Questioner: Is a vertical positioning of the spine useful or helpful in the meditative procedure?

Ra: I am Ra. It is somewhat helpful.

Questioner: Would you please list the polarities within the body which are related to the balancing of the energy centers of the various bodies of the unmanifested entity?

Ra: I am Ra. In this question there lies a great deal of thought which we appreciate. It is possible that the question itself may serve to aid meditations upon this particular subject. Each unmanifested self is unique. The basic polarities have to do with the balanced vibratory rates and relationships between the first three energy centers and to a lesser extent, each of the other energy centers?

May we answer more specifically?

Questioner: Possibly in the next session we will expand on that.

I would like to ask the second question. What are the structure and contents of the archetypical mind, and how does the archetypical mind function in informing the intuition and conscious mind of an individual mind/body/spirit complex.

Ra: I am Ra. You must realize that we offered these concepts to you so that you might grow in your own knowledge of the self through the consideration of them. We would prefer, especially for this latter query, to listen to the observations upon this subject which the student of these exercises may make and then suggest further avenues of the refinement of these inquiries. We feel we might be of more aid in this way.

Questioner: You mentioned that an energizing spiral is emitted from the top of any pyramid and that you could benefit by placing this under the head for a period of thirty minutes or less. Can you tell me how this third spiral is helpful and what help it gives the entity who is receiving it?

Ra: I am Ra. There are substances which you may ingest which cause the physical vehicle to experience distortions towards an increase of energy. These substances are crude, working rather roughly upon the body complex increasing the flow of adrenaline.

The vibration offered by the energizing spiral of the pyramid is such that each cell, both in space/time and in time/space, is charged as if hooked to your electricity. The keenness of mind, the physical and sexual energy of body, and the attunement of will of spirit are all touched by this energizing influence. It may be used in any of these ways. It is possible to over-charge a battery, and this is the cause of our cautioning any who use such pyramidal energies to remove the pyramid after a charge has been received.

Questioner: Is there a best material or an optimal size for this small pyramid to go beneath the head?

Ra: I am Ra. Given that the proportions are such as to develop the spirals in the Giza pyramid, the most appropriate size for use beneath the head is an overall height small enough to make placing it under the cushion of the head a comfortable thing.

Questioner: There's no best material?

Ra: I am Ra. There are better materials which are, in your system of barter, quite dear. They are not that much better than substances which we have mentioned before. The only incorrect substances would be the baser metals.

Questioner: You mentioned the problems with the action in the King's Chamber of the Giza-type pyramid. I am assuming if we used the same geometrical configuration that is used in the pyramid at Giza this would be perfectly all right for the pyramid placed beneath the head since we wouldn't be using the King's Chamber radiations but only the third spiral from the top, and I'm also asking if it would be better to use a 60° apex angle than the larger apex angle? Would it provide a better energy source?

Ra: I am Ra. For energy through the apex angle the Giza pyramid offers an excellent model. Simply be sure the pyramid is so small that there is no entity small enough to crawl inside it.

Questioner: I assume that this energy then, this spiraling light energy, is somehow absorbed by the energy field of the body. Is this somehow connected to the indigo energy center? Am I correct in this guess?

Ra: I am Ra. This is incorrect. The properties of this energy are such as to move within the field of the physical complex and irradiate each cell of the space/time body and, as this is done, irradiate also the time/space equivalent which is closely aligned with the space/time yellow-ray body. This is not a function of the etheric body or of free will. This is a radiation much like your sun's rays. Thus it should be used with care.

Questioner: How many applications of thirty minutes or less during a diurnal time period would be appropriate?

Ra: I am Ra. In most cases, no more than one. In a few cases, especially where the energy will be used for spiritual work, experimentation with two shorter periods might be possible, but any feeling of sudden weariness would be a sure sign that the entity had been over-radiated.

Questioner: Can this energy help in any way as far as healing of physical distortions?

Ra: I am Ra. There is no application for direct healing using this energy although, if used in conjunction with meditation, it may offer to a certain percentage of entities some aid in meditation. In most cases it is most helpful in alleviating weariness and in the stimulation of physical or sexual activity.

Questioner: In a transition from third to fourth-density we have two other possibilities other than the type that we are experiencing now. We have the possibility of a totally positively polarized harvest and the possibility of a totally negatively polarized harvest that I understand have occurred elsewhere in the universe many times. When there is a totally negatively polarized harvest, the whole planet that has negatively polarized makes the transition from third to fourth-density. Does the planet have the experience of the distortion of disease that this planet now experiences prior to that transition?

Ra: I am Ra. You are perceptive. The negative harvest is one of intense disharmony and the planet will express this.

Questioner: The planet has a certain set of conditions in late third-density, and then the conditions are different in early fourth-density. Could you give me an example of a negatively polarized planet and the conditions in late third-density and early fourth-density so that I can see how they change?

Ra: I am Ra. The vibrations from third to fourth-density change on a negatively oriented planet precisely as they do upon a positively oriented planet. With fourth-density negative comes many abilities and possibilities of which you are familiar. The fourth-density is more dense and it is far more difficult to hide the true vibrations of the mind/body/spirit complex. This enables fourth-density negatives, as well as positives, the chance to form social memory complexes. It enables negatively oriented entities the opportunity for a different set of parameters with which to show their power over others and to be of service to the self. The conditions are the same as far as the vibrations are concerned.

Questioner: I was concerned about the amount of physical distortions, disease, and that sort of thing in third-density negative just before harvesting and in fourth-density negative just after harvesting or in transition. What are the conditions of the physical problems, disease, etc. in late third-density negative?

Ra: I am Ra. Each planetary experience is unique. The problems, shall we say, of bellicose actions are more likely to be of pressing concern to late third-density negative entities than the earth's reactions to negativity of the planetary mind, for it is often by such warlike attitudes on a global scale that the necessary negative polarization is achieved.

As fourth-density occurs there is a new planet and new physical vehicle system gradually expressing itself and the parameters of bellicose actions become those of thought rather than manifested weapons.

Questioner: Well then is physical disease and illness as we know it on this planet rather widespread on a third-density negative planet before harvest into fourth-density negative?

Ra: I am Ra. Physical complex distortions of which you speak are likely to be less found as fourth-density negative begins to be a probable choice of harvest due to the extreme interest in the self which characterizes the harvestable third-density negative entity. Much more care is taken of the physical body as well as much more discipline being offered to the self mentally. This is an orientation of great self-interest and self-discipline. There are still instances of the types of disease which are associated with the mind complex distortions of negative emotions such as anger. However, in an harvestable entity these emotional distortions are much more likely to be used as catalyst in an expressive and destructive sense as regards the object of anger.

Questioner: I am trying to understand the way that disease and bodily distortions are generated with respect to polarities, both positive and negative. It seems that they are generated in some way to create the split of polarization, that they have a function in creating the original polarization that occurs in third-density. Is this correct?

Ra: I am Ra. This is not precisely correct. Distortions of the bodily or mental complex are those distortions found in beings which have need of experiences which aid in polarization. These polarizations may be those of entities which have already chosen the path or polarization to be followed.

It is more likely for positively oriented individuals to be experiencing distortions within the physical complex due to the lack of consuming interest in the self and the emphasis on service-to-others. Moreover, in an unpolarized entity catalyst of the physical distortion nature will be generated at random. The hopeful result is, as you say, the original choice of polarity. Oftentimes this choice is not made but the catalyst continues to be generated. In the negatively oriented individual the physical body is likely to be more carefully tended and the mind disciplined against physical distortion.

Questioner: This planet, to me, seems to be what I would call a cesspool of distortions. This includes all diseases and malfunctions of the physical body in general. It would seem to me that, on the average, this planet would be very, very high on the list if we just took the overall amount of these problems. Am I correct in this assumption?

Ra: I am Ra. We will review previous material.

Catalyst is offered to the entity. If it is not used by the mind complex it will then filter through to the body complex and manifest as some form of physical distortion. The more efficient the use of catalyst, the less physical distortion to be found.

There are, in the case of those you call Wanderers, not only a congenital difficulty in dealing with the third-density vibratory patterns but also a recollection, however dim, that these distortions are not necessary or usual in the home vibration.

We over-generalize as always, for there are many cases of preincarnative decisions which result in physical or mental limitations and distortions, but we feel that you are addressing the question of widespread distortions towards misery of one form or another. Indeed, on some third-density planetary spheres catalyst has been used more efficiently. In the case of your planetary sphere there is much inefficient use of catalyst and, therefore, much physical distortion.

We have enough energy available for one query at this time.

Questioner: Then I will ask if there is anything that we can do to make the instrument more comfortable or to improve the contact?

Ra: I am Ra. Continue as always in love. All is well. You are conscientious.

I am Ra. I leave you in the love and in the light of the one infinite Creator. Go forth rejoicing in the power and the peace of the one infinite Creator. Adonai.

The Law of One, Book V, Session 66, Fragment 37
August 12, 1981

Jim: There were no great tricks or elaborate rituals employed to aid Carla in maintaining her physical health and her ability to serve as the instrument for this contact. Good foods, reasonable exercise, and a healthy and happy attitude are techniques that are within most people's reach.

Carla: It was not very much fun to be so scrutinized for estimation of my energy level in this way. I have always had tons of mental, emotional and spiritual energy, but low physical energy. In fact I would say my life has been lived mainly on nerve. To me, life has always seemed a marvelous celebration, a party of sun and moon and earth and sky, birdsong and green leaves and people of every sort and kind, doing various amazing things. This joy in life is a pure gift, and it has made my life a dream of love. It was no surprise to me when Ra spoke of my low energy! And I doubt any athlete worked harder to keep in shape than I did during this time.

Session 66, August 12, 1981

Questioner: Would you give me an indication of the instrument's condition?

Ra: I am Ra. The vital energies are somewhat depleted at this time but not seriously so. The physical energy level is extremely low. Otherwise, it is as previously stated.

Questioner: Is there anything that we can do, staying within the first distortion, to seek aid from the Confederation in order to alleviate the instrument's physical problems?

Ra: I am Ra. No.

Questioner: Can you tell me the most appropriate method in attempting to alleviate the instrument's physical problems?

Ra: I am Ra. The basic material has been covered before concerning the nurturing of this Instrument. We recapitulate: the exercise according to ability, not to exceed appropriate parameters, the nutrition, the social intercourse with companions, the sexual activity in green ray or above, and in general, the sharing of the distortions of this group's individual experiences in an helpful, loving manner.

These things are being accomplished with what we consider great harmony, given the density in which you dance. The specific attention and activities, with which those with physical complex distortions may alleviate these distortions, are known to this instrument.

Finally, it is well for this instrument to continue the practices it has lately begun.

Questioner: Which practices are those?

Ra: I am Ra. These practices concern exercises which we have outlined previously. We may say that the variety of experiences which this entity seeks is helpful as we have said before, but as this instrument works in these practices the distortion seems less mandatory.

The Law of One, Book III, Session 67
August 15, 1981

Ra: I am Ra and I greet you in the love and in the light of the one infinite Creator. I communicate now.

Questioner: Could you first give us the instrument's condition, please?

Ra: I am Ra. The vital energies are more closely aligned with the amount of distortion normal to this entity than previous asking showed. The physical complex energy levels are somewhat less strong than at the previous asking. The psychic attack component is exceptionally strong at this particular nexus.

Questioner: Can you describe what you call the psychic attack component and tell me why it is strong at this particular time?

Ra: I am Ra. We shall elect not to retrace previously given information but rather elect to note that the psychic attack upon this instrument is at a constant level as long as it continues in this particular service.

Variations towards the distortion of intensity of attack occur due to the opportunities presented by the entity in any weakness. At this particular nexus the entity has been dealing with the distortion which you call pain for some time, as you call this measurement, and this has a cumulatively weakening effect upon physical energy levels. This creates a particularly favorable target of opportunity, and the entity of which we have previously spoken has taken this opportunity to attempt to be of service in its own way. It is fortunate for the on-going vitality of this contact that the instrument is a strong-willed entity with little tendency towards the distortion, called among your peoples, hysteria, since the dizzying effects of this attack have been constant and at times disruptive for several of your diurnal periods.

However, this particular entity is adapting well to the situation without undue distortions towards fear. Thus the psychic attack is not successful but does have some draining influence upon the instrument.

Questioner: I will ask if I am correct in this analysis. We would consider that the entity making this so-called attack is offering its service with respect to its distortion in our polarized condition now so that we may more fully appreciate its polarity, and we are appreciative of the fact and thank this entity for its attempt to serve our one Creator in bringing to us knowledge in, shall I say, a more complete sense. Is this correct?

Ra: I am Ra. There is no correctness or incorrectness to your statement. It is an expression of a positively polarized and balanced view of negatively polarized actions which has the effect of debilitating the strength of the negatively polarized actions.

Questioner: We would welcome the services of the entity who uses, and I will use the misnomer attack, since I do not consider this an attack but an offering of service, and we welcome this offering of service, but we would be able, I believe, to make more full use of the services if they were not physically disabling the instrument in a minor way. For with a greater physical ability she would be able to more appreciate the service. We would greatly appreciate it if the service was carried on in some manner which we could welcome in even greater love than at present. This, I assume, would be some service that would not include the dizzying effect.

I am trying to understand the mechanism of this service of the entity that seems to be constantly with us, and I am trying to understand the origin of this entity and his mechanism of greeting us. I will make a statement that will probably be incorrect but is a function of my extreme limitation in understanding the other densities and how they work. I am guessing that this particular entity is a member of the Orion Confederation and is possibly incarnate in a body of the appropriate density, which I assume is the fifth, and by mental discipline he has been able to project a portion or all of his consciousness to our coordinates, you might say, here and it is possibly one of the seven bodies that make up his mind/body/spirit complex. Is any of this correct, and can you tell me what is correct or incorrect about this statement?

Ra: I am Ra. The statement is substantially correct.

Questioner: Would you rather not give me information as to the specifics of my statement?

Ra: I am Ra. We did not perceive a query in further detail. Please requestion.

Questioner: Which body in respect to the colors does the entity use to travel to us?

Ra: I am Ra. This query is not particularly simple to answer due to the transdimensional nature, not only of space/time to time/space, but from density to density. The time/space light or fifth-density body is used while the space/time fifth-density body remains in fifth-density. The assumption that the consciousness is projected thereby is correct. The assumption that this conscious vehicle attached to the space/time fifth-density physical complex is that vehicle which works in this particular service is correct.

Questioner: I undoubtedly will ask several uninformed questions. However, I was trying to understand certain concepts that have to do with the illusion, I shall say, of polarization that seems to exist at certain density levels in the creation and how the mechanism of the interaction of consciousness works. It seems to me that the fifth-density entity is attracted in some way to our group by the polarization of this group which acts somehow as a beacon to this entity. Am I correct?

Ra: I am Ra. This is, in substance, correct but the efforts of this entity are put forward only reluctantly. The usual attempts upon positively oriented entities or groups of entities are made, as we have said, by minions of the fifth-density Orion leaders; these are fourth-density. The normal gambit of such fourth-density attack is the tempting of the entity or group of entities away from total polarization towards service-to-others and toward the aggrandizement of self or of social organizations with which the self identifies. In the case of this particular group each was given a full range of temptations to cease being of service to each other and to the one infinite Creator. Each entity declined these choices and instead continued with no significant deviation from the desire for a purely other-self service orientation. At this point one of the fifth-density entities overseeing such detuning processes determined that it would be necessary to terminate the group by what you might call magical means, as you understand ritual magic. We have previously discussed the potential for the removal of one of this group by such attack and have noted that by far the most vulnerable is the instrument due to its preincarnative physical complex distortions.

Questioner: In order for this group to remain fully in service to the Creator, since we recognize this fifth-density entity as the Creator, we must also attempt to serve in any way we can, this entity. Is it possible for you to communicate to us the desires of this entity if there are any in addition to us simply ceasing the reception and dissemination of that which you provide?

Ra: I am Ra. This entity has two desires. The first and foremost is to, shall we say, misplace one or more of this group in a negative orientation so that it may choose to be of service along the path of service to self. The objective which must precede this is the termination of the physical complex viability of one of this group while the mind/body/spirit complex is within a controllable configuration. May we say that although we of Ra have limited understanding, it is our belief that sending this entity love and light, which each of the group is doing, is the most helpful catalyst which the group may offer to this entity.

Questioner: We find a—I'm sorry. Please continue.

Ra: I am Ra. We were about to note that this entity has been as neutralized as possible in our estimation by this love offering and thus its continued presence is perhaps the understandable limit for each polarity of the various views of service which each may render to the other.

Questioner: We have a paradoxical situation with respect to serving the Creator. We have requests, from those whom we serve in this density, for Ra's information. However, we have requests from another density not to disseminate this information. We have portions of the Creator requesting two seemingly opposite activities of this group. It would be very helpful if we could reach the condition of full service in such a way that we were by every thought and activity serving the Creator to the very best of our ability. Is it possible for you to solve, or for the fifth-density entity who offers its service to solve, this paradox which I have observed?

Ra: I am Ra. It is quite possible.

Questioner: Then how could we solve this paradox?

Ra: I am Ra. Consider, if you will, that you have no ability not to serve the Creator since all is the Creator. You do not have merely two opposite requests for information or lack of information from this source if you listen careful to those whose voices you may hear. This is all one voice to which you resonate upon a certain frequency. This frequency determines your choice of service to the one Creator. As it happens this group's vibratory patterns and those of Ra are compatible and enable us to speak through this instrument with your support. This is a function of free will.

A portion, seemingly of the Creator, rejoices at your choice to question us regarding the evolution of spirit. A seemingly separate portion would wish for multitudinous answers to a great range of queries of a specific nature. Another seemingly separate group of your peoples would wish this correspondence through this instrument to cease, feeling it to be of a negative nature. Upon the many other planes of existence there are those whose every fiber rejoices at your service and those such as the entity of whom you have been speaking which wish only to terminate the life upon the third-density plane of this instrument. All are the Creator. There is one vast panoply of biases and distortions, colors and hues, in an unending pattern. In the case of those with whom you, as entities and as a group, are not in resonance, you wish them love, light, peace, joy, and bid them well. No more than this can you do for your portion of the Creator is as it is and your experience and offering of experience, to be valuable, needs be more and more a perfect representation of who you truly are. Could you, then, serve a negative entity by offering the instrument's life? It is unlikely that you would find this a true service. Thus you may see in many cases the loving balance being achieved, the love being offered, light being sent, and the service of the service-to-self oriented entity gratefully acknowledged while being rejected as not being useful in your journey at this time. Thus you serve one Creator without paradox.

Questioner: This particular entity, by his service, is able to create a dizzying effect on the instrument. Could you describe the mechanics of such a service?

Ra: I am Ra. This instrument, in the small times of its incarnation, had the distortion in the area of the otic complex of many infections which caused great difficulties at this small age, as you would call it. The scars of these distortions remain and indeed that which you call the sinus system remains distorted. Thus the entity works with these distortions to produce a loss of the balance and a slight lack of ability to use the optic apparatus.

Questioner: I was wondering about the magical, shall I say, principles used by the fifth-density entity giving this service and his ability to give it. Why is he able to utilize these particular physical distortions from the philosophical or magical point of view?

Ra: I am Ra. This entity is able to, shall we say, penetrate in time/space configuration the field of this particular entity. It has moved through the quarantine without any vehicle and thus has been more able to escape detection by the net of the Guardians.

This is the great virtue of the magical working whereby consciousness is sent forth essentially without vehicle as light. The light would work instantly upon an untuned individual by suggestion, that is the stepping out in front of the traffic because the suggestion is that there is no traffic. This entity, as each in this group, is enough disciplined in the ways of love and light that it is not suggestible to any great extent. However, there is a predisposition of the physical complex which this entity is making maximal use of as regards the instrument, hoping for instance, by means of increasing dizziness, to cause the instrument to fall or to indeed walk in front of your traffic because of impaired vision.

The magical principles, shall we say, may be loosely translated into your system of magic whereby symbols are used and traced and visualized in order to develop the power of the light.

Questioner: Do you mean then that this fifth-density entity visualizes certain symbols? I am assuming that these symbols are of a nature where their continued use would have some power or charge. Am I correct?

Ra: I am Ra. You are correct. In fifth-density light is as visible a tool as your pencil's writing.

Questioner: Then am I correct in assuming that this entity configures the light into symbology, that is what we would call a physical presence? Is this correct?

Ra: I am Ra. This is incorrect. The light is used to create a sufficient purity of environment for the entity to place its consciousness in a carefully created light vehicle which then uses the tools of light to do its working. The will and presence are those of the entity doing the working.

Questioner: The fifth-density entity you mentioned penetrated the quarantine. Was this done through one of the windows or was this because of his, shall I say, magical ability?

Ra: I am Ra. This was done through a very slight window which less magically oriented entities or groups could not have used to advantage.

Questioner: The main point with this line of questioning has to do with the first distortion and the fact that this window exists. Was this a portion of the random effect and are we experiencing the same type of balancing in receiving the offerings of this entity as the planet in general receives because of the window effect?

Ra: I am Ra. This is precisely correct. As the planetary sphere accepts more highly evolved positive entities or groups with information to offer, the same opportunity must be offered to similarly wise negatively oriented entities or groups.

Questioner: Then we experience in this seeming difficulty the wisdom of the first distortion and for that reason must fully accept that which we experience. This is my personal view. Is it congruent with Ra's?

Ra: I am Ra. In our view we would perhaps go further in expressing appreciation of this opportunity. This is an intensive opportunity in that it is quite marked in its effects, both actual and potential, and as it affects the instrument's distortions towards pain and other difficulties such as the dizziness, it enables the instrument to continuously choose to serve others and to serve the Creator.

Similarly it offers a continual opportunity for each in the group to express support under more distorted or difficult circumstances of the other-self experiencing the brunt, shall we say, of this attack, thus being able to demonstrate the love and light of the infinite Creator and, furthermore, choosing working by working to continue to serve as messengers for this information which we attempt to offer and to serve the Creator thereby.

Thus the opportunities are quite noticeable as well as the distortions caused by this circumstance.

Questioner: Thank you. Is this so-called attack offered to myself and *(name)* as well as the instrument?

Ra: I am Ra. This is correct

Questioner: I personally have felt no effect that I am aware of. Is it possible for you to tell me how we are offered this service?

Ra: I am Ra. The questioner has been offered the service of doubting the self and of becoming disheartened over various distortions of the personal nature. This entity has not chosen to use these opportunities and the Orion entity has basically ceased to be interested in maintaining constant surveillance of this entity.

The scribe is under constant surveillance and has been offered numerous opportunities for the intensification of the mental/emotional distortions and in some cases the connection matrices between mental/emotional complexes and the physical complex counterpart. As this entity has become aware of these attacks it has become much less pervious to them. This is the particular cause of the great intensification and constancy of the surveillance of the instrument, for it is the weak link due to factors beyond its control within this incarnation.

Questioner: Is it within the first distortion to tell me why the instrument experienced so many physical distortions during the new times of its physical incarnation?

Ra: I am Ra. This is correct.

Questioner: In that case can you answer me as to why the instrument experienced so much during its early years?

Ra: I am Ra. We were affirming the correctness of your assumption that such answers would be breaking the Way of Confusion. It is not appropriate for such answers to be laid out as a table spread for dinner. It is appropriate that the complexes of opportunity involved be contemplated.

Questioner: Then there is no other service at this time that we can offer that fifth-density entity of the Orion group who is constantly with us. As I see it now from your point of view there is nothing that we can do for him? Is this correct?

Ra: I am Ra. This is correct. There is great humor in your attempt to be of polarized service to the opposite polarity. There is a natural difficulty in doing so since what you consider service is considered by this entity non-service. As you send this entity love and light and wish it well it loses its polarity and needs to regroup.

Thus it would not consider your service as such. On the other hand, if you allowed it to be of service by removing this instrument from your midst you might perhaps perceive this as not being of service. You have here a balanced and polarized view of the Creator; two services offered, mutually rejected, and in a state of equilibrium in which free will is preserved and each allowed to go upon its own path of experiencing the one infinite Creator.

Questioner: Thank you. In closing that part of the discussion I would just say that if there is anything that we can do that is within our ability—and I understand that there are many things such as the ones that you just mentioned that are not within our ability—that we could do for this particular entity, if you would in the future communicate its requests to us we will at least consider them because we would like to serve in every respect. Is this agreeable to you?

Ra: I am Ra. We perceive that we have not been able to clarify your service versus its desire for service. You need, in our humble opinion, to look at the humor of the situation and relinquish your desire to serve where no service is requested. The magnet will attract or repel. Glory in the strength of your polarization and allow others of opposite polarity to similarly do so, seeing the great humor of this polarity and its complications in view of the unification in sixth-density of these two paths.

Questioner: Thank you very much. I have a statement here that I will have you comment on for accuracy or inaccuracy. In general, the archetypical mind is a representation of facets of the One Infinite Creation. The Father archetype corresponds to the male or positive aspect of electromagnetic energy and is active, creative, and radiant as is our local sun. The Mother archetype corresponds to the female or negative aspect of electromagnetic energy and is receptive or magnetic as is our Earth as it receives the sun's rays and brings forth life via third-density fertility. The Prodigal Son or the Fool archetype corresponds to every entity who seems to have strayed from unity and seeks to return to the one infinite Creator. The Devil archetype represents the illusion of the material world and the appearance of evil but is more accurately the provider of catalyst for the growth of each entity within the third-density illusion. The Magician, Saint, Healer, or Adept corresponds to the higher self and, because of the balance within its energy centers, pierces the illusion to contact intelligent infinity and thereby demonstrates mastery of the catalyst of third-density. The archetype of Death symbolizes the transition of an entity from the yellow-ray body to the green-ray body either temporarily between incarnations or, more permanently, at harvest.

Each archetype presents an aspect of the One Infinite Creation to teach the individual mind/body/spirit complex according to the calling or the electromagnetic configuration of mind of the entity. Teaching is done via the intuition. With the proper seeking or mind configuration, the power of will uses the spirit as a shuttle to contact the appropriate archetypical aspect necessary for the teach/learning. In the same way each of the other informers of intuition are contacted. They are hierarchical and proceed from the entity's own subconscious mind to group or planetary mind, to guides, to higher self, to archetypical mind, to cosmic mind or intelligent infinity. Each is contacted by the spirit serving as shuttle according to the harmonized electromagnetic configuration of the seeker's mind and the information sought.

Would you please comment on the accuracy of these observations and correct any errors and fill in any omissions?

Ra: I am Ra. The entity has been using transferred energy for most of this session due to its depleted physical levels. We shall begin this rather complex answer which is interesting but do not expect to finish it. Those portions which we do not respond to we ask that you requestion us on at a working in your future.

Questioner: Perhaps it would be better to start the next session with the answer to this question. Would that be appropriate or is the energy already fixed?

Ra: I am Ra. The energy is as always allotted. The choice, as always, is yours.

Questioner: In that case, continue.

Ra: I am Ra. Perhaps the first item we shall address is the concept of the spirit used as a shuttle between the roots and the trunk of mind. This is a misapprehension and we shall allow the questioner to consider the function of the spirit further, for in working with the mind we are working within one complex and have not yet attempted to penetrate intelligent infinity. It is well said that archetypes are portions of the one infinite Creator or aspects of its face. It is, however, far better to realize that the archetypes, while constant in the complex of generative energies offered, do not give the same yield of these complexes to any two seekers. Each seeker will experience each archetype in the characteristics within the complex of the archetype which are most important to it. An example of this would be the observation of the questioner that the Fool is described in such and such a way. One great aspect of this archetype is the aspect of faith, the walking into space without regard for what is to come next. This is, of course, foolish but is part of the characteristic of the spiritual neophyte. That this aspect was not seen may be pondered by the questioner. At this time we shall again request that the query be restated at the next working and we shall at this time cease using this instrument. Before we leave may we ask if there may be any short questions?

Questioner: Only if there is anything that we can do to make the instrument more comfortable or to improve the contact?

Ra: I am Ra. Continue, my friends, in the strength of harmony, love, and light. All is well. The alignments are appreciated for their careful placement.

I am Ra. I leave you now, my friends, in the glory of the love and the light of the infinite Creator. Go forth, then, rejoicing in the power and the peace of the one infinite Creator. Adonai. ✣

L/L Research

The Law Of One, Book V, Session 67, Fragment 38
August 15, 1981

Jim: In the first question Don is asking Ra how we could resolve the seeming paradox of being able to serve various portions of the same Creator, some of which rejoiced at our service and some of which wished nothing less than to remove the instrument and the contact from the third density, i.e. our fifth-density, negative friend. We removed the sentence that you see in brackets because we did not wish for over attention to be given to our personalities. We include it now because it might be helpful for those who have the feeling that they may be here from elsewhere to know that there is a kind of momentum of serving others which adds its support to the individual's desire to learn and to serve well.

Those who have read *The Crucifixion Of Esmerelda Sweetwater* will recognize the last query of this section. This book was written by Don and Carla in 1968, when they first got together and formed L/L Research. It was their first project and was unusual in that seemed to be seen first and then recorded as a story. And it was also unusual in the fact that it seemed to anticipate many of the experiences that Don and Carla, and later I, would share in their work together.

Carla: *Into this first work of ours was poured all the love we had for each other and for the ideals and concerns of a purer, higher way, a way of love undefiled by any hint of the heaviness of earth. We were smitten with each other; it was a wonderful time. Mind you, Don was never verbal, but this time held our short-lived intimate physical relationship, which I treasure, and our time of that nearly trembling joy one has when one is in love. The story seemed to tell itself, and we saw the characters so clearly they might have been telling us the story over our shoulder. The only part of the book which was in error was the ending. The character that rather resembled me on a perfect day was killed off by the bad guys at the end of the book. In real life, my frail body was stronger than Don's due, I think, to my gifts of faith and élan vital. Don was never the least bit at home on this earth. He lived his life very defended and isolated, except for me and a very few close friends and relations. One thing is sure: his gifts have been well shared in the body of work that comprises the material Ra shared with us. His questions were marvels of sense and always game to head in a new direction. The romance ended badly, in the sense that Don has entered a larger life, and I have been left to become a whole different person than the one he groomed and appreciated. But the work has not ended at all, and will not until the world no longer has any need of our material.*

Session 67, August 15, 1981

Questioner: Then how could we solve this paradox? *(The sentence of personal material which was removed from Ra's answer is inserted in this paragraph which may be found on pg. 90 of Book III.)*

Ra: I am Ra. Consider, if you will, that you have no ability not to serve the Creator since all is the

Creator. In your individual growth patterns appear the basic third-density choice. [Further, there are overlaid memories of the positive polarizations of your home density.] Thus your particular orientation is strongly polarized towards service to others and has attained wisdom as well as compassion.

Questioner: Are you familiar with a book that the instrument and I wrote approximately twelve years ago called *The Crucifixion Of Esmerelda Sweetwater*, in particular the banishing ritual that we used to bring the entities to Earth?

Ra: I am Ra. This is correct.

Questioner: Were there any incorrectnesses in our writing with respect to the way this was performed?

Ra: I am Ra. The incorrectnesses occurred only due to the difficulty an author would have in describing the length of training necessary to enable the ones known in that particular writing as Theodore and Pablo in the necessary disciplines.

Questioner: It has seemed to me that that book has somehow, in its entirety, been a link to many of those whom we have met since we wrote it and to many of the activities we have experienced. Is this correct?

Ra: I am Ra. This is quite so.

Sunday Meditation
August 16, 1981

(Jim channeling)

I am Hatonn, and I greet you in the love and in the light of the one infinite Creator. We have been listening in great joy to the song and the vibrations of this group and it is a great privilege and an honor to join your group this evening. We of Hatonn have a simple mission and a simple service which we gladly offer to your group and that is sharing of the love, the vibration of love of the infinite Creator, with each of those who seek our service. We are old, shall we say in the way of the vibrations of love and in the speaking to groups such as this one.

Long have we sought to share our simple message with those people of your planet who call for our service. Many are there upon the surface of your planet who seek the experience of love. It is the lesson of your density which has escaped, shall we say, the notice of many of the students upon your planet, though everywhere is this lesson of love taught. You cannot walk your streets; you cannot recline in any seat; you cannot climb any mountain; you cannot experience any event upon your planet that does not contain within it one facet of the lesson of love, yet, so many upon your planet do not seem to be aware that it is this lesson they have chosen to learn at this time in your density.

Many seek other lessons, other goals. Many seek the ways of the world which seem to grant those rewards which are honored by most of your people. We speak of the positions of power, the positions of social eminence, the rewards of your monetary system, the recognition of your fellow beings for achievements of one kind or another. We do not say that these seekings are irrelevant, for each contain within the core of their being the lesson of love. We do suggest that when one seeks only the outer trappings, such as we have spoken of, that one might find the lesson learned somewhat hollow, and after due consideration, somewhat disappointing.

But this, my friends, is also an important lesson, for it points the seeker in yet another direction, for deep within the being of each of the entities upon your planet is the knowledge of why they are here, is the knowledge of their great desire to learn the lesson of love, and each seeker in time will turn in the direction of conscious seeking of love. How long it will take for many upon your planet, we cannot say, but always do we offer ourselves in whatever capacity we are asked to teach this lesson of love.

And what, my friends, is love? Many upon your planet have sought the answer to this question for years and for lifetimes. Poets have written volumes concerning the nature of love. My friends, we do not say that we can answer this riddle but we do say that we have traveled perhaps somewhat further down this trail than have most upon your planet, and we offer our meager understandings of love to your peoples when asked. Love, as we experience this vibration which is our density, is that unconditional acceptance by the infinite Creator of all that is [is].

My friends, this may seem a simple statement, but upon reflection we would suggest that you might find within it yet more mysteries, for Who is the Creator and what is the Creation? Many upon your planet have pondered these questions also for many years and lifetimes, seemingly without end. We of Hatonn are learning the lesson of love and it has taught us that there is nothing but the Creator. Each of you gathered this evening in this group are the Creator. Each of you are expressions of the original Thought of the one infinite Creator. Each of you have, as your foundation, the one infinite Creator and within your being you may discover your connection to each other being upon your planet, to each facet of your existence within this density, and to all parts of the creation throughout the universe.

We know this sounds to many like a much too simple description of the nature of love and to others sounds much too abstract. This is the nature of any search of any seeker, for the one infinite Creator begins and ends in mystery and each seeker on his path back to the Creator will experience the reality of love in an unique pattern. Each is a unique expression of the Creator and each shall ponder the mysteries of love of the creation and of one's own being and from this pondering you will find your own solutions to the mystery, and though your solutions may seem at odds with those of others, yet are they all the same, for all lead eventually to the unity, the oneness of the Creator.

For, my friends, you shall upon your journey into the depths of your own being discover for yourself which words of wisdom and of love ring true for you. This is the nature of the quest. This is the nature of your own being. This is the nature of love.

At this time we would pause so that our brother of Laitos might pass among you and to each who requests the service of our brother Laitos will be given an experience of a conditioning vibration of the Confederation. This is to help deepen your meditative state and to help relax your mind and your body. We would pause at this time so that our brother of Laitos might pass among you. I am Hatonn.

(Pause)

(Carla channeling)

I am Hatonn, and am now with this instrument. I greet you once again in the love and the light of the infinite Creator.

My brother of Laitos thanks each of you for the privilege of working with you and will be conditioning the one known as C as we speak through this instrument in a gentle manner. We shall continue through this instrument.

What, my friends, can you do to most efficiently seek for the nature of yourself, of the creation, or of love? Where can you go? What activity can you perform that will enable you to find those things that do ring true in the depths of your being? As you listen to the world about you and experience its distractions it is clear that the world in which you now live, the outer world with its jangling vibrations and its disturbed feelings, thoughts and activities, is not a place conducive to efficient seeking. My friends, there is one sanctuary which no man can bar you from, beside which no fence can be built. This is the sanctuary of your own inner self. This is the true tabernacle for there none may pass, none may distract, none may say you nay, nor discredit you in any way.

It is often among your peoples that as you begin to seek you wish to share your thoughts and your feelings, your amazement at the mysteries of the unknown. And you find in the reactions of those to whom you speak little or no support for understanding, no answers, but only the confused reaction of one who does not wish to be removed from the illusion in which he has placed himself. But each of you, my friends, has the capacity to seek within, in the sanctuary of your own silence, for within you lies a great knowing of great understanding, a great peace and a path that can guide you step-by-step through what seems to the outer eye to be more or less chaotic. To the inner eye there is a purpose, there is a learning, there is a blessedness about every circumstance that may befall you. None can take this capacity from you, nor discourage you from seeking it. You have only to meditate, to listen in silence and awaken with the echo of the still, small voice. You may hear nothing and yet, at the point at which you need to choose the way in which you must go, that love which you have sought will speak to you in the silence and your choice will be made simple.

For love—and by this we do not mean the love so confused by your peoples—is the great simplifier. As you seek, so you will find. The teacher known to you as Jesus was quoted in your holy works as saying, "My house shall be a house of prayer." Houses, my friends, can be shaken, blown and scattered. The winds of chance, the storms of happenstance may remove you from all those things which are now physically yours in this illusion. The one house which is yours, through whose lintels you may always pass, is the house of your own physical body, your mind and your spirit. Let, then, your house be habitually one in which there is meditation, silence and listening, for love waits within. The creation, of which love is the great ingredient, waits within.

As always, we ask that you listen to our words, not as if we were wise, for we are not, not as if we are perfect, for we are not, but as if we were your brothers and sisters, for this we are. We reach out our hands to you in love and in a desire to serve by offering this simple message. We would close through the one known as C. I am Hatonn.

(C channeling)

I am Hatonn, and I am with this instrument. Our simple message tonight is one that though [it] seems simple to us, we know that you in your world have great difficulty understanding. We can only, through our simple messages, hope that you shall continue to seek love and to live in such a way that you continue to grow and seek the love that is with you and surrounds you in all of your moments within this existence.

We of Hatonn are privileged to speak our humble words of love to such groups as this one, who seek and will listen. We will leave you now in the love and the light of the one infinite Creator. I am Hatonn. Adonai, my friends.

(Carla channeling)

I am Latwii. I greet you in the love and in the light of our infinite Creator. We were conditioning the one known as L, but we found that this instrument was somewhat distracted and so we shall use this instrument this evening with fond thanks to the one known as L.

If there are any questions at this time we would be positively thrilled to answer them. Please ask any questions that you may have at this time and we will do our poor best at framing some kind of answer.

C: Latwii, I have a question to ask about channeling. When Hatonn transferred to me tonight—I'm still new at this—as I was channeling I could feel a change in the vibration I was receiving. Do the members of the Confederation, when they are conditioning or channeling to an instrument, are they in a constant process of adjustment to ease the—to relax the instrument more or to find a more comfortable level? Do they just constantly, without pausing, or what was going on tonight?

I am Latwii. As you will notice, my brother, from the variations in the strength of the voice level which is proceeding from this instrument's vocal apparatus, we do indeed attempt constantly to adjust to an instrument's particular vibrations so that we may convey those thoughts which we have to offer without unduly causing discomfort of any kind due to the minor amount of control necessary for this type of contact.

There is an additional factor which is the constantly varying flow of energy in the group. As the group becomes more or less unified as one member perhaps becomes weary and somewhat less unified with the group, then returns to unification with the group, the energy of the group will be in flux and this energy is working with the instrument much like a battery. Consequently, you will from time to time feel an energy change. Since you do not have an ammeter, you cannot see this, however, this does occur.

May we answer you further, my brother?

C: No, thank you.

We thank you also. Is there another question at this time?

L: I have a question, Latwii. I seem to be on the verge of a recurrent growth cycle, initiating again, and I realize that you're forbidden to give specific information, however, if there are areas that you would suggest for my attention or for meditation, I would appreciate any advice you could offer.

I am Latwii. My brother, we appreciate your understanding of our complete compliance with the requirements of the Law of Free Will. We cannot speak in any specific areas which may cause changes in your future, for to do so would be a negative influence, may we say, upon your own growth. We would not have you depend upon a brother or a sister when you have yourself to depend upon, for you yourself are the greatest and strongest of your allies. There are many portions of yourself upon which you may call for aid. When you feel disheartened by your own growth cycles, we might suggest that you make use of these portions of yourself, which at this time might aid you, for there are portions of yourself which are not a part of these cycles and yet which are completely one with you and are you in your own unique vibratory configuration. Some have called this the higher self. There are other entities or guides which are with you and await your requests in order to serve as those who may support your requests for peace of mind and for confidence.

We may further suggest that you consider that the creation of the Father is one in which there is an infinite process of growth, and that this growth cannot be halted because one has become comfortable but must then go further into that which may be unknown. The conscious self may consider explorations of the self at a certain point as being disheartening, yet these uncertainties and discomforts of the mind and spirit are a necessary part of a growth pattern.

Finally, we might suggest that it is unwise to take one's spiritual temperature. The thermometer you are using is not accurate. You are a part of the Creator, whatever may seem to be your manifestation at this time. You must realize and ponder your basic nature and when you have come to some conclusion about this nature, you must than seek to see this nature as your true self and the behavior and manifestation as an ongoing experience in an illusion. One is real, one is a dream.

May we answer you further, my brother?

L: You've given me much to grow with. I have one other question concerning some specific detail of what you have just given me. In reference to supportive entities, at one time in the past a reference was made to other entities that I shall not name. Are these the same entities or some of the same entities?

I am Latwii. We scan this information and find that these entities are not connected with you personally, but are connected with geographical locations. The entities of which we speak have been termed by your peoples guardian angels or guides. They need have no particular introduction, however, if you seek within the reaches of your mind, you may find some feelings—we shall not say advice—coming to you which you may identify as being not a portion of your own intuition, but that of a supportive influence. It is almost as though within your own confluence of energy there lies a parental or mothering and fathering influence …

(Side one of tape ends.)

… listen to that which seems supportive, even if biased, and take the comfort that is intended by this energetic influence.

May we answer you further?

L: No, and I thank you for *(inaudible)*.

As always, we thank you, for without the questions we would not have the opportunity to share our thoughts with you. Is there another question at this time?

M: Yes, Latwii. Ra describes this planet as going into fourth density, and there will be a subsequent harvest as third-density entities cannot stand the light. Going into fourth density as a planet, will all spiritual entities be fourth density and above, and I ask this question in relation to the second and first-density life forms.

I am Latwii. You must realize that the one known as Ra has a density on us and therefore, has got straighter poop, however, we will attempt to share with you our own understanding, limited as it might be.

Each density is the density—a true color, as we see in your mind this terminology describes. Thus, first density will have the true color of red. The fourth density is one in which the beings of fourth density will have true color green core vibration. The environment which supports them, then, will also be a true color green. However, within this true color green density there will be the overlay of first-density red, second-density orange, and so forth, for there is no awareness beyond the appropriate density of the creatures of that density.

Thus, you have the basic vibratory patterns of fourth density enabling fourth-density creatures to experience incarnation. However, the second-density creatures, for instance the animals and the plant life, will have the characteristics of animals and of plant life without the enhancement of fourth density, just as in third density, as you have experienced, although there is true color yellow at the core of this density, still first and second-density creatures have the experiences and the overlay of colors of their densities.

May we answer you further, my brother?

M: So as Earth goes into fourth density, or green, the actual mineral expression which is normally first density—is the spiritual entity of the planet, being mineral essentially, first density or fourth? Or do they co-exist?

I am Latwii. Not only do they co-exist, but you have first, second, and fourth; the third density, at some point in your future, will cease being active. However, in the long run you have each density occurring concurrently, so that the planetary sphere has first, second, third, fourth, fifth, sixth and seventh. This is the mature planetary system of bodies. One is not discarded when another is activated; each functions concurrently with the others.

This is a difficult subject, for the mind perhaps is attempting to rationalize whether the second-density tree at third density is the same second-density tree in fourth density. Yes, my brother, it is the same tree, but in the fourth density of vibration it will [have] slightly different characteristics and will be able to have a more conscious relationship with the fourth-density being, for instance, being able to communicate the simple second-density feelings to the fourth-density entity. It remains the same tree, but as each density observes it, it grows in its ability to be understood in its essence.

May we answer you further?

M: Just one quick one. Okay. The tree. The second-density spiritual still would be fourth-density physical after the transition. Is that correct?

I am Ra. For a time it will be second density, overlaid third density and fourth density. May we answer you further?

M: No, thank you.

We thank you. May we ask if there may be another question at this time?

R: When a planet is fourth density, it will no longer support third density forever, or just for a temporary period?

I am Ra … We correct this instrument. We are attempting to retrieve this instrument from a trance state. Please have patience.

I am Latwii. We have this instrument. This instrument was going into a trance state due to the subject matter. We are now with this instrument. We will continue talking complete nonsense through this instrument for a moment, if you will have patience, so that we can gain good control of this instrument.

L: Is there any way we can assist?

We are achieving good control. Thank you for your offer. I am Latwii. Sometimes, my friends, we are less than careful with our contact with this instrument.

Now, to the question that was asked. The third density may be likened to a kind of body; the fourth density, a denser type of body. In fourth density there is a type of experience which goes with this type of body. This experience is new to this body and the body, like that of any child, must mature and grow. If the fourth density were visible to third density, the processes of third density would be those with whom it would greatly interfere, for in third density there are choices to be made and lessons to be learned, and if fourth-density positive or negative were visible to third density, the entire process of choice would be abrogated.

Consequently, while the fourth density of planetary complex is young, third density remains unactivated. This is normally so only for a limited amount of time, until fourth-density entities become able, through the process of maturing and forming the social memory complex, of removing their density from the view of third density. When this is possible without strain, third-density experience may once again become available for those who are graduating, shall we say, from second density.

May we answer you further?

R: Do the non-harvested third-density individuals remain in a state of limbo, if you will, or are they allowed to recycle on another third-density planet while this one is not proper for them?

I am Latwii. As this instrument would say, "What mean we, white man?" There is no particular virtue, as far as we know, in the concept of limbo, for the entity does not stop experiencing. If any entity does not find itself in the graduating class and therefore finds itself ready to repeat third density, it will, in good time, as one might say, be taken to another sphere where third-density experience is beginning its cycle.

The use of limbo might profitably be discussed, if you will allow us a moment. This concept is profitable if you consider it to be a form of healing. This indeed occurs upon the cessation of your physical vehicle at the end of your brief experience here in this illusion. There are, at times, healings which must take place before the entity can review its lifetime, as you would call it, and therefore make some judgment as to what it might need to do with its next opportunity for experience. These hearings could be called a Limbo, for they are periods of rest, but indeed they are not only rest, but also a readying for further experience.

May we answer you further?

R: No, thank you.

We thank you, and may we thank this group for supporting this instrument. We were afraid that we had lost her to trance which would have been most inconvenient for all concerned.

Is there another question at this time?

C: Yes, what color are you all experiencing tonight?

We are experiencing the red-violet color. This is a combination, a hue which we are examining. It is the shell of your planetary sphere and we are at work at this time attempting to assess the strength and purity of this shell.

May we answer you further, my brother?

C: No, thank you.

Is there another question at this time?

L: Yes. At the conclusion of Ra sessions there are some procedures undertaken for the benefit of the instrument. Due to the brief Ra contact here, is any of it advisable?

I am Latwii. We would ask that the instrument's name be mentioned before a light is turned on, however, it is our judgment that this instrument is with us, as you would say. We thank you for your concern, of course.

Is there another question?

(Pause)

I am Latwii. Please pardon us for yelling at you for the duration of this contact, but it was our method of retrieving this instrument to full consciousness and we have found it useful. Can we say to you that we greatly appreciate our turn at sharing some thoughts with you and feeling the sharing of love and light which each of you offers to the Creator. We join you in that happy state of unity with the Creator at this time. I leave you, my friends, in this love and this light. I am one of those known to you as Latwii. Adonai, my friends. Adonai vasu. ❧

L/L Research

L/L Research is a subsidiary of Rock Creek Research & Development Laboratories, Inc.

P.O. Box 5195
Louisville, KY 40255-0195

www.llresearch.org

Rock Creek is a non-profit corporation dedicated to discovering and sharing information which may aid in the spiritual evolution of humankind.

ABOUT THE CONTENTS OF THIS TRANSCRIPT: This telepathic channeling has been taken from transcriptions of the weekly study and meditation meetings of the Rock Creek Research & Development Laboratories and L/L Research. It is offered in the hope that it may be useful to you. As the Confederation entities always make a point of saying, please use your discrimination and judgment in assessing this material. If something rings true to you, fine. If something does not resonate, please leave it behind, for neither we nor those of the Confederation would wish to be a stumbling block for any.

© 2009 L/L RESEARCH

THE LAW OF ONE, BOOK III, SESSION 68
AUGUST 18, 1981

Ra: I am Ra. I greet you in the love and in the light of the one infinite Creator. We communicate now.

Questioner: The primary reason that we decided to have this session today is that I might not be around for a while and I had a pressing question about what happened Sunday night when, apparently, the instrument was slipping into a trance state during one of the normal Sunday night meditations, and I would like to question you on this. Can you give me information about what happened?

Ra: I am Ra. We can.

Questioner: Would you tell me what happened in that case?

Ra: I am Ra. We have instructed this instrument to refrain from calling us unless it is within this set of circumscribed circumstances. In the event of which you speak this instrument was asked a question which pertained to what you have been calling the Ra Material. This instrument was providing the voice for our brothers and sisters of the wisdom density known to you as Latwii.

This instrument thought to itself, "I do not know this answer. I wish I were channeling Ra." The ones of Latwii found themselves in the position of being approached by the Orion entity which seeks to be of service in its own way. The instrument began to prepare for Ra contact. Latwii knew that if this was completed the Orion entity would have an opportunity which Latwii wished to avoid.

It is fortunate for this instrument, firstly, that Latwii is of fifth-density and able to deal with that particular vibratory complex which the Orion entity was manifesting and, secondly, that there were those in the support group at that time which sent great amounts of support to the instrument in this crux. Thus what occurred was the ones of Latwii never let go of this instrument although this came perilously close to breaking the Way of Confusion. It continued to hold its connection with the mind/body/spirit complex of the instrument and to generate information through it even as the instrument began to slip out of its physical vehicle.

The act of continued communication caused the entity to be unable to grasp the instrument's mind/body/spirit complex and after but a small measure of your space/time Latwii recovered the now completely amalgamated instrument and gave it continued communication to steady it during the transition back into integration.

Questioner: Could you tell me what the plan of the fifth-density negatively oriented entity was and how it would have accomplished it and what the results would have been if it had worked?

Ra: I am Ra. The plan, which is on-going, was to take the mind/body/spirit complex while it was separated from its yellow body physical complex shell, to then place this mind/body/spirit complex within the negative portions of your time/space. The shell would then become that of the unknowing, unconscious entity and could be, shall we say, worked upon to cause malfunction which would end in coma and then in what you call the death of the body. At this point the higher self of the instrument would have the choice of leaving the mind/body/spirit complex in negative sp—we correct—time/space or of allowing incarnation in space/time of equivalent vibration and polarity distortions. Thus this entity would become a negatively polarized entity without the advantage of native negative polarization. It would find a long path to the Creator under these circumstances although the path would inevitably end well.

Questioner: Then you are saying that if this fifth-density negative entity is successful in its attempts to transfer the mind/body/spirit complex when that complex is in what we call the trance state to negatively polarized time/space, then the higher self has no choice but to allow incarnation in negatively polarized space/time? Is that correct?

Ra: I am Ra. This is incorrect. The higher self could allow the mind/body/spirit complex to remain in time/space. However, it is unlikely that the higher self would do so indefinitely due to its distortion towards the belief that the function of the mind/body/spirit complex is to experience and learn from other-selves thus experiencing the Creator. A highly polarized positive mind/body/spirit complex surrounded by negative portions of space/time will experience only darkness, for like the magnet, there is no, shall we say, likeness. Thus a barrier is automatically formed.

Questioner: Let me be sure that I understand you. Is that darkness experienced in negative space/time or in negative time/space?

Ra: I am Ra. Negative time/space.

Questioner: Incarnation in negative space/time then in a condition like that would result in incarnation into which density level for, let us take as an example, the instrument?

Ra: I am Ra. The answer to this query violates the first distortion.

Questioner: OK then, let's not take the instrument as an example. Let's assume that this was done to a Wanderer of sixth-density. If this answer violates the first distortion, don't answer. But let's say a sixth-density Wanderer had this happen and went into negative time/space. Would that be a sixth-density negative time/space, and would he incarnate into sixth-density negative space/time?

Ra: I am Ra. Your assumption is correct. The strength of the polarization would be matched as far as possible. In some positive sixth-density Wanderers the approximation would not quite be complete due to the paucity of negative sixth-density energy fields of the equivalent strength.

Questioner: Is the reason that this could be done the fact that the Wanderer's mind/body/spirit complex extracted in what we call the trance state, leaving the third-density physical, in this state the Wanderer does not have the full capability to magically defend itself? Is this correct?

Ra: I am Ra. In the case of this instrument, this is correct. This is also correct when applied almost without exception to those instruments working in trance which have not consciously experienced magical training in time/space in the, shall we say, present incarnation. The entities of your density capable of magical defense in this situation are extremely rare.

Questioner: It would seem to me that since I can't imagine anything worse than this particular result it would be very advisable to seek the magical training and defense for this situation. Could Ra and would Ra instruct us in this type of magical defense?

Ra: I am Ra. This request lies beyond the first distortion. The entity seeking magical ability must do so in a certain manner. We may give instructions of a general nature. This we have already done. The instrument has begun the process of balancing the self. This is a lengthy process.

To take an entity before it is ready and offer it the scepter of magical power is to infringe in an unbalanced manner. We may suggest with some asperity that the instrument never call upon Ra in any way while unprotected by the configuration which is at this time present.

Questioner: I think that it is important for me to investigate the techniques, if they are within the first distortion, of the fifth-density entity who wishes to displace the mind/body/spirit complexes of this group. Am I within the first distortion in asking you to describe how this entity goes about this working?

Ra: I am Ra. You are.

Questioner: Well, then, how does this fifth-density entity go about this working from the very start of being alerted to the fact that we exist?

Ra: I am Ra. The entity becomes aware of power. This power has the capacity of energizing those which may be available for harvest. This entity is desirous of disabling this power source. It sends its legions. Temptations are offered. They are ignored or rejected. The power source persists and indeed improves its inner connections of harmony and love of service.

The entity determines that it must needs attempt the disabling itself. By means of projection it enters the vicinity of this power source. It assesses the situation. It is bound by the first distortion but may take advantage of any free will distortion. The free will, preincarnative distortions of the instrument with regards to the physical vehicle seem the most promising target. Any distortion away from service-to-others is also appropriate.

When the instrument leaves its physical vehicle it does so freely. Thus the displacement of the mind/body/spirit complex of the instrument would not be a violation of its free will if it followed the entity freely. This is the process.

We are aware of your pressing desire to know how to become impervious as a group to any influences such as this. The processes which you seek are a matter of your free choice. You are aware of the principles of magical work. We cannot speak to advise but can only suggest, as we have before, that it would be appropriate for this group to embark upon such a path as a group, but not individually, for obvious reasons.

Questioner: I am interested as to how the first distortion applies to the negatively polarized entity misplacing the mind/body/spirit complex. Why is the negatively polarized entity followed to the place of negative time/space? Why would one of us freely follow the entity?

Ra: I am Ra. The positive polarity sees love in all things. The negative polarity is clever.

Questioner: Then I am assuming if the negative polarity used any other approach that did not use the free will of the other-self, he would lose polarization and magical power. This is correct, isn't it?

Ra: I am Ra. This is correct. The transferred energy grows low. We wish to close. Are there any short queries before we leave this instrument?

Questioner: Only if there is anything that we can do to make the instrument more comfortable or to improve the contact?

Ra: I am Ra. You are conscientious. We realize your necessity for these queries. All is well, my friends. We thank you and leave you in the love and in the light of the one infinite Creator. Go forth, therefore, rejoicing in the power and in the peace of the one infinite Creator. Adonai.

L/L Research

L/L Research is a subsidiary of Rock Creek Research & Development Laboratories, Inc.

P.O. Box 5195
Louisville, KY 40255-0195

www.llresearch.org

Rock Creek is a non-profit corporation dedicated to discovering and sharing information which may aid in the spiritual evolution of humankind.

ABOUT THE CONTENTS OF THIS TRANSCRIPT: This telepathic channeling has been taken from transcriptions of the weekly study and meditation meetings of the Rock Creek Research & Development Laboratories and L/L Research. It is offered in the hope that it may be useful to you. As the Confederation entities always make a point of saying, please use your discrimination and judgment in assessing this material. If something rings true to you, fine. If something does not resonate, please leave it behind, for neither we nor those of the Confederation would wish to be a stumbling block for any.

© 2009 L/L RESEARCH

THE LAW OF ONE, BOOK V, SESSION 68, FRAGMENT 39
AUGUST 18, 1981

Jim: In seeking advice from Ra on caring for Carla's condition and in scheduling sessions we again found that Ra constantly guarded our free will by providing loosely formed guidelines that offered us direction but which required that we continually exercise our ability and duty to make the decisions ourselves. Thus was the contact a function of our free will by the fact that information was given only in response to questions, that the kind of information was determined by the nature of our seeking being formed into such and such a question, and by the actual scheduling or timing of sessions. So it is necessary for each seeker of truth to decide what to seek, how to seek, and when to seek. Not everyone speaks so directly to Ra, but everyone speaks with the one Creator in one form or another. If the seeking is strong enough any portion of the Creator can teach you all that you wish to know. It is the seeking that determines the finding.

The last two questions and answers refer to a most unusual phenomenon which we discovered was a possibility in Session 68; that is, the misplacement of the mind/body/spirit complex of the instrument, under certain unprotected conditions, by the fifth-density negative entity which monitored our Ra sessions. This possibility was unusual enough, but to add to its extraordinary nature is the fact that Don and Carla wrote about an identical situation in *The Crucifixion Of Esmerelda Sweetwater* thirteen years earlier. The ending of the book was not seen as was the remainder of the book, and it had to be written in the usual way. Now this all makes sense to us, for it seems that the ending of that book was a symbolic description of Don's death in November of 1984.

Carla: Have you ever been put on the spot by someone asking how you were? Usually, the civil greeting "how are you?" is a meaningless murmur indicating respect and awareness of presence, rather than a true request for information. The last thing wanted is a laundry list of woes and ailments. So I was not accustomed to being so in touch with myself that I could tell my exact condition. When one is in pain all the time, as I have been for a long time now, the stimulus eventually becomes dulled and ignored simply because it is telling one nothing useful. When one has done all one can, one is far better off simply getting on with the life which is offered. This may sound extreme, but I know just how many chronic-pain patients there are out there, quietly dealing with life, usually very well indeed. So the last thing I would wish is to be constantly checking to see my energy level. My reaction, at that time, and at this one, is "Ya gotta be kidding!" I cannot remember ever having physical energy. Mental, emotional, spiritual energy oh YES! Tons of that I have, and a heart full of joy to be here, whatever my limitations. But I run on nerve alone, in my own perception. So this concern, while genuine and necessary, was a challenge to me. I really wanted to do sessions so much, also, which biased my response.

The matter of The Crucifixion Of Esmerelda Sweetwater *playing itself out in real life is to me a fascinating example of the liquidity and permeability of the supposed boundaries of space and time. We saw that story as if it were a movie running in our heads. We wrote it never knowing it had to do with us in the future. It was most unsettling when the more tragic parts of the book played themselves out with horrid accuracy. Life humbles one again and again, bringing us all to our knees and revealing self to self in utter fidelity. As always when I think on Don's death, I am warmed by the perfection of his opening to love and his nobility, as I am chilled by his absence from my side. One can do little except offer it all up to the Creator in thanksgiving and praise.*

Session 68, August 18, 1981

Questioner: Could you first please give me an indication of the instrument's condition?

Ra: I am Ra. This instrument's physical energies are depleted completely. The remainder is as previously stated.

Questioner: With the physical energies completely depleted should I continue with the session? I'm not sure exactly what that means?

Ra: I am Ra. We have available transferred energy which is due to the service offered by two of this group and, therefore, we are able to continue. Were it not for this transferred energy, the instrument whose will is strong would have depleted its vital energies by willing the available resources. Thus if there is no transfer of energy, and if the instrument seems depleted to the extent it now is, it is well to refrain from using the instrument. If there is energy transferred, this service may be accepted without damage to the distortion of normal vital energy.

We may note that the physical energy has been exhausted, not due to the distortion toward pain, although this is great at this space/time, but primarily due to the cumulative effects of continual experience of this distortion.

Questioner: Would you recommend a greater rest period between the end of this work period and the next work period? Would that help the instrument?

Ra: I am Ra. We might suggest, as always, that the support group watch the instrument with care and make the decision based upon observation. It is not within our capacity to specifically recommend a future decision. We would note that our previous recommendation of one working on alternate diurnal periods did not take into account the fragility of the instrument and thus we would ask your forgiveness for this suggestion.

At this nexus our distortion is towards a flexible scheduling of workings based upon, as we said, the support group's decisions concerning the instrument. We would again note that there is a fine line between the care of the instrument for continued use which we find acceptable and the proper understanding, if you will excuse this misnomer, of the entire group's need to work in service.

Thus if the instrument's condition is truly marginal, by all means let more rest occur between workings. However, if there is desire for the working and the instrument is at all able in your careful opinion, it is, shall we say, a well done action for this group to work. We cannot be more precise, for this contact is a function of your free will.

Questioner: We have been speaking almost precisely of a portion of the Esmerelda Sweetwater book which we wrote having to do with the character Trostrick's misplacement of the space girl's mind/body/spirit complex. What is the significance of that work which we did with respect to our lives? It has been confusing to me for some time as to how it meshes in. Can you tell me that?

Ra: I am Ra. We scan each and find we may speak.

Questioner: Would you please do so now?

Ra: I am Ra. We confirm the following which is already, shall we say, supposed or hypothesized.

When the commitment was made between two of this group to work for the betterment of the planetary sphere, this commitment activated a possibility/probability vortex of some strength. The experience of generating this volume was unusual in that it was visualized as if watching the moving picture.

Time had become available in its present-moment form. The scenario of the volume went smoothly until the ending of the volume. You could not end the volume, and the ending was not visualized as the entire body of the material but was written or authored.

This is due to the action of free will in all of the creation. However, the volume contains a view of significant events, both symbolically and specifically, which you saw under the influence of the magnetic attraction which was released when the commitment was made and full memory of the dedication of this, what you may call, mission restored. ☘

Sunday Meditation
August 23, 1981

(Jim channeling)

I am Hatonn, and I greet you, my friends, in the love and in the light of the infinite Creator. It is a great honor for us to join your group this evening. We especially greet those who are new to this group and add a special greeting to those who have joined our group once again after a long absence. We of Hatonn are members of the Confederation of Planets in the Service of the Infinite Creator. We have the honor and the privilege of addressing groups such as this one, those of your people who seek our service. It has been said in your holy works that as one seeks so shall one find. It is our honor and in joy we perform this honor to acquaint groups such as this one with our vibration of love.

We of Hatonn long have sought the love of the infinite Creator. We are no different than any of your people except, perhaps, we have journeyed that path of seeking love a little longer than have most of the entities upon you planet. Because we have so journeyed, our seeking also has been rewarded. We of Hatonn have been blessed by the Creator that is within us all with a small understanding of the love of the one infinite Creator. Because it is this love that we are learning, it is also our honor and our duty to teach this love to those who seek this learning. Only because we are students of the vibration of love may we also serve as teachers to others who seek this knowledge.

Long have we spent in the study and the teaching of love. Many of your peoples have heard our words. It has been our privilege to speak through the years to many groups such as this one. We have always felt the greatest of joys in this effort, but we also have other feelings, shall we say, for many of your peoples do not know of the love of the Creator. Many of your peoples are not aware that this density, this illusion which they inhabit and go about their daily existences within, is an illusion. Many do not know the lesson of this illusion is the recognition and experience of love. Many seek many other lessons. Many seek the rewards that your world has to offer. Many seek the positions of power, large or small, the rewards of money, large or small, the recognition of peers, large or small. Many seek in many directions, many goals. Few find that which truly fulfills their thirst, for though few among your people know what it is they seek, it is almost true without exception that each knows it seeks something. The power of the desire of the seeking cannot forever be denied; thus, the seeking goes on within each in many ways.

We of Hatonn feel the great calling of your people. We feel their sorrow. We feel their pain. We feel their frustration. We feel their desire, for we are your brothers and sisters. We are as one being and any feeling that any entity feels we feel as well, for we are as one. It is because we feel the calling of your peoples that we have come in the capacities which are open to us that do not infringe upon any entity's free will, for though each, in some way, consciously or subconsciously, seeks love, there may not be an infringement of any entity's free will by offering the knowledge of love without a calling for that knowledge.

Many we are able to serve in their dreams, by inspirations and intuitions, for within their minds in the manner in which they believe, this is the only method which they will accept. We come however we may. We serve wherever it is possible, but never may we infringe upon any entity's path back to the Creator, for we cannot learn lessons for an entity. That would be robbing the entity of experience and upon your planet and within this illusion all experience has one purpose; that is, to teach.

All experience teaches in some way the knowledge of love, the love of the one infinite Creator. Thusly, we of Hatonn respond to the callings that are made and respond in the manner in which is allowed. We have, in our own way, served long upon your planet and shall continue this service for as long as the calling exists, for we learn as we teach. You, my brothers and sisters, are teachers to us as well. We learn from you how to serve the Creator better and better, with more love and compassion and understanding and we thank you for allowing us to serve in this way. For, my friends, there is nothing but service—for there is nothing but the Creator. It has been truly said that all is one.

We would pause at this time so that our brothers and sisters of Laitos might pass among your group and give each who request it the conditioning vibration of the Confederation, the purpose being to deepen the meditative state. We shall pause at this time as our brothers and sisters of Laitos pass among you. I am Hatonn.

(Pause)

I am Hatonn, and am once again with this instrument and greet you all once again in the love and the light of the infinite Creator. At this time we shall transfer this contact to the one known as C so that, as a new instrument, we might speak a few words through his channel and exercise his ability to receive our thoughts. If he would relax and refrain from analysis we shall transfer this contact at this time. I am Hatonn.

(C channeling)

I am Hatonn, and I am with this instrument. It is always a pleasure to speak to groups such as these, for there are far too few. We of Hatonn will always answer any of those who call. We bring, as always, a simple message, a message of love, love that is within and surrounds each and every thing. We are privileged that we may work with this group and thank each of those who have gathered to hear our humble words.

We will transfer now to the entity known as L. We are known to you as Hatonn.

(L channeling)

I am Hatonn, and I greet you once again in the love and the light of our infinite Creator. It is said, my friends, that one must go blindly into the darkness to discover the significance of light. There is some truth to this statement, yet as analogy it has lost something in the translation, for although blindness and darkness are not necessary to ascertain the significance of light, they are beneficial tools toward that end. It would be more correct to say that once one has gone blindly through darkness, the value of light is more readily perceived.

In your lives, my friends, there is a borderline across which the majority of your people meander with little cognizance of its significance. That borderline signifies the division between awareness and non-awareness; between light and its absence, darkness. My friends, all illusions require a source of energy for their maintenance and such is also true of your own illusion, for in your world the illusion produced through the manipulation of the light energy can exist only with the presence of that power source. If we may examine, therefore, the consequences of a dominance of either polarity on your planet, that is, a totality of light or a total absence of light, we discover that in both instances, in the pursuit by the individual of either polarity until it is maximized within the individual, the illusion begins to disappear, for within darkness there is no light energy to maintain the illusion, yet within total lightness the illusion, as in a projector, can no longer be focused. The light penetrates and overwhelms the illusion until only that which is real stands in evidence.

My brothers, it is difficult for those minds which have been trained in terms of right or wrong, good or bad, to look with love and appreciation upon the efforts of those who struggle in efforts contrary to one's own, yet it is important to remember that even those who strive toward darkness, the absence of light, shall in their striving overcome the illusion. We of Hatonn would encourage you, my brothers, to increase the amount of light in your lives, for such is our path. And such is the tool which has benefited us so well, yet we would hasten to remind you that in doing so, in seeing beyond the illusion, you must learn also to see the value of your brother's struggle and appreciate your brother as one struggling for spiritual nourishment even though his path may not be your own. It is a blessing to follow either path, for no matter what the path, the blessing exists in the seeking and in seeking one will always find.

We, therefore, would encourage our brothers of this planet to perceive the advice of one of their own: to love the God-ness of the universe with their entirety, to make it an expression of their lives and themselves, and to love their brothers and sisters, to love their brothers and sisters with that same intensity.

At this time we would like to allow questions to be asked through this instrument. I am Hatonn.

R: Hatonn, when can I see your craft?

I am Hatonn. My brother, we find ourselves tempted to follow the example of our sister, Latwii, and perform what she refers to as a joke, in that the term "craft" is ambiguous. In one sense, it is our craft we are describing to you this evening, for is not our handiwork our craft?

However, my brother, to answer you more seriously, you yourself are all that stands between your eyes and the perception of our vehicle, for it is not visible to one within your density. When your attainment of higher densities occurs, so also will your visual experience, although we doubt it will be significant to you.

May we answer you further?

(Inaudible)

I am Hatonn. I am again with this instrument. Is there another whose question may be answered?

M: Yes. Back in the mid-sixties there were the so-called Ohio Valley sightings in which a great number of people, a great many places and times had sightings. Were these Confederation sightings or Orion sightings?

I am Hatonn. I am aware of your question. My brother, a majority of those sightings of actual vehicles were not of the Confederation, but rather of those who would seek to cause an imbalance resulting from fear and confusion. However, my brother, you must also remember that the power of Creation resides within the individual and, being aware of this, understand that a number of the sightings were generated by those who sighted the thought forms which appeared as vehicles.

May we answer you further?

M: No—well, yes. You're saying the people that saw a number of these sightings were creating the thought forms rather than other entities—aliens—creating these thought forms?

I am Hatonn. That is correct. There resides within the individual the ability to create shared perceptions, for as you well know, my brother, your existence is within a world of illusion and who but yourselves create the illusion? It is possible for others to add to your illusion, but as this instrument might choose to say, the flour in the cake is your own.

May we answer you further?

M: No.

Is there another question?

(Pause)

I am Hatonn. Although the beauty of the music caused by the night creatures of your world is pleasant to us, we would feel remiss in our duties should we remain for that reason. Therefore, my brothers, we bid you adieu. ☙

L/L Research

L/L Research is a subsidiary of Rock Creek Research & Development Laboratories, Inc.

P.O. Box 5195
Louisville, KY 40255-0195

www.llresearch.org

Rock Creek is a non-profit corporation dedicated to discovering and sharing information which may aid in the spiritual evolution of humankind.

ABOUT THE CONTENTS OF THIS TRANSCRIPT: This telepathic channeling has been taken from transcriptions of the weekly study and meditation meetings of the Rock Creek Research & Development Laboratories and L/L Research. It is offered in the hope that it may be useful to you. As the Confederation entities always make a point of saying, please use your discrimination and judgment in assessing this material. If something rings true to you, fine. If something does not resonate, please leave it behind, for neither we nor those of the Confederation would wish to be a stumbling block for any.

© 2009 L/L RESEARCH

THE LAW OF ONE, BOOK III, SESSION 69
AUGUST 29, 1981

Ra: I am RA. I greet you in the love and in the light of the one infinite Creator.

Before we proceed may we make a small request for future workings. At this particular working there is some slight interference with the contact due to the hair of the instrument. We may suggest the combing of this antenna-like material into a more orderly configuration prior to the working.

We communicate now.

Questioner: A question which I didn't get to ask at the previous session and which I will be forced to ask at this time is, is the trance state the only state in which a mind/body/spirit positive entity may be lured by a negative entity or adept to negative time/space configuration?

Ra: I am Ra. This is a misperceived concept. The mind/body/spirit complex which freely leaves the third-density physical complex is vulnerable when the appropriate protection is not at hand. You may perceive carefully that very few entities which choose to leave their physical complexes are doing work of such a nature as to attract the polarized attention of negatively oriented entities. The danger to most in trance state, as you term the physical complex being left, is the touching of the physical complex in such a manner as to attract the mind/body/spirit complex back thereunto or to damage the means by which that which you call ectoplasm is being recalled.

This instrument is an anomaly in that it is well that the instrument not be touched or artificial light thrown upon it while in the trance state. However, the ectoplasmic activity is interiorized. The main difficulty, as you are aware, is then the previously discussed negative removal of the entity under its free will.

That this can happen only in the trance state is not completely certain, but it is highly probable that in another out-of-body experience such as death the entity here examined would, as most positively polarized entities, have a great deal of protection from comrades, guides, and portions of the self which would be aware of the transfer you call the physical death.

Questioner: Then you are saying that the protective friends, we will call them, would be available in every condition except for what we call the trance state which seems to be anomalistic with respect to the others. Is this correct?

Ra: I am Ra. This is correct.

Questioner: Why is this trance state, as we call it, different? Why are there not entities available in this particular state?

Ra: I am Ra. The uniqueness of this situation is not the lack of friends, for this, as all entities, has its guides or angelic presences and, due to polarization, teachers and friends also. The unique characteristic of the workings which the social memory complex

Ra and your group have begun is the intent to serve others with the highest attempt at near purity which we as comrades may achieve.

This has alerted a much more determined friend of negative polarity which is interested in removing this particular opportunity.

We may say once again two notes: Firstly, we searched long to find an appropriate channel or instrument and an appropriate support group. If this opportunity is ended we shall be grateful for that which has been done, but the possibility/probability vortices indicating the location of this configuration again are slight. Secondly, we thank you for we know what you sacrifice in order to do that which you as a group wish to do.

We will not deplete this instrument in so far as we are able. We have attempted to speak of how the instrument may deplete itself through too great a dedication to the working. All these things and all else we have said has been heard. We are thankful. In the present situation we express thanks to the entities who call themselves Latwii.

Questioner: Do I understand, then, that death, whether it is by natural means or accidental means or suicide, that all deaths of this type would create the same after-death condition which would avail the entity to its protection from friends? Is this correct?

Ra: I am Ra. We presume you mean to inquire whether in the death experience, no matter what the cause, the negative friends are not able to remove an entity. This is correct largely because the entity without the attachment to the space/time physical complex is far more aware and without the gullibility which is somewhat the hallmark of those who love wholeheartedly.

However, the death, if natural, would undoubtedly be the more harmonious; the death by murder being confused and the entity needing some time/space in which to get its bearings, so to speak; the death by suicide causing the necessity for much healing work and, shall we say, the making of a dedication to the third-density for the renewed opportunity of learning the lessons set by the higher self.

Questioner: Is this also true of unconscious conditions due to accident, or medical anesthetic, or drugs?

Ra: I am Ra. Given that the entity is not attempting to be of service in this particular way which is proceeding now, the entities of negative orientation would not find it possible to remove the mind/body/spirit. The unique characteristic, as we have said, which is, shall we say, dangerous is the willing of the mind/body/spirit complex outward from the physical complex of third-density for the purpose of service-to-others. In any other situation this circumstance would not be in effect.

Questioner: Would this be a function of the balancing action of the first distortion?

Ra: I am Ra. Your query is somewhat opaque. Please restate for specificity.

Questioner: I was just guessing that since the mind/body/spirit complex's will from the third-density body for a particular duty or service-to-others would then create a situation primarily with respect to the first distortion where the opportunity for balancing this service by the negative service would be available and, therefore, magically possible for the intrusion of the other polarization. Is this thinking at all correct?

Ra: I am Ra. No. The free will of the instrument is indeed a necessary part of the opportunity afforded the Orion group. However, this free will and the first distortion applies only to the instrument. The entire hope of the Orion group is to infringe upon free will without losing polarity. Thus this group, if represented by a wise entity, attempts to be clever.

Questioner: Has a Wanderer ever been so infringed upon by a negative adept and then placed in negative time/space?

Ra: I am Ra. This is correct.

Questioner: Can you tell me the situation that the Wanderer finds himself in and the path back, why that path could not be the simple moving back into positive time/space?

Ra: I am Ra. The path back revolves, firstly, about the higher self's reluctance to enter negative space/time. This may be a significant part of the length of that path. Secondly, when a positively oriented entity incarnates in a thoroughly negative environment it must needs learn/teach the lessons of the love of self thus becoming one with its other-selves.

When this has been accomplished the entity may then choose to release the potential difference and change polarities.

However, the process of learning the accumulated lessons of love of self may be quite lengthy. Also the entity, in learning these lessons, may lose much positive orientation during the process and the choice of reversing polarities may be delayed until the mid-sixth-density. All of this is, in your way of measurement, time-consuming although the end result is well.

Questioner: Is it possible to tell me roughly how many Wanderers who have come to this planet during this master cycle have experienced this displacement into a negative time/space?

Ra: I am Ra. We can note the number of such occurrences. There has been only one. We cannot, due to the Law of Confusion, discuss the entity.

Questioner: You said that the higher self is reluctant to enter negative space/time. Is that correct?

Ra: I am Ra. The incarnative process involves being incarnated from time/space to space/time. This is correct.

Questioner: I will make this statement and see if I am correct. When first moved into time/space of a negative polarization the positive entity experiences nothing but darkness. Then, by incarnation into negative space/time by the higher self, it experiences a negative space/time environment with negatively polarized other-selves. Is this correct?

Ra: I am Ra. This is correct.

Questioner: It would seem to me that it would be an extremely difficult situation for the positively polarized entity and the learning process would be extremely traumatic. Is this correct?

Ra: I am Ra. Let us say that the positively polarized individual makes a poor student of the love of self and thus spends much more time, if you will, than those native to that pattern of vibrations.

Questioner: I am assuming that this displacement must be a function of his free will in some way. Is this correct?

Ra: I am Ra. This is absolutely correct.

Questioner: This is a point that I find quite confusing to me.

It is the function of the free will of the positively oriented entity to move into the negatively polarized time/space. However, it is also a function of his lack of understanding of what he is doing. I am sure that if the entity had full understanding of what he was doing he would not do it. It is a function of his negatively polarized other-self creating a situation where he is lured to that configuration. What is the principle with respect to the first distortion that allows this to occur since we have two portions of the Creator, each of equal value or of equal potential, but oppositely polarized and we have this situation resulting. Could you tell me the philosophical principle behind this particular act?

Ra: I am Ra. There are two important points in this regard. Firstly, we may note the situation wherein an entity gets a road-map which is poorly marked and in fact is quite incorrect. The entity sets out to its destination. It wishes only to reach the point of destination but, becoming confused by the faulty authority and not knowing the territory through which it drives, it becomes hopelessly lost.

Free will does not mean that there will be no circumstances when calculations will be awry. This is so in all aspects of the life experience. Although there are no mistakes, there are surprises.

Secondly, that which we and you do in workings such as this carries a magical charge, if you would use this much misunderstood term, perhaps we may say a metaphysical power. Those who do work of power are available for communication to and from entities of roughly similar power. It is fortunate that the Orion entity does not have the native power of this group. However, it is quite disciplined whereas this group lacks the finesse equivalent to its power. Each is working in consciousness but the group has not begun a work as a group. The individual work is helpful for the group is mutually an aid, one to another.

Questioner: This instrument performs services that involve channeling other members of the Confederation. We are reluctant to continue this because of the possibility of her slipping into trance and being offered the services of the negatively polarized entity or adept. Are there any safeguards to create a situation whereby she cannot go into trance other than at a protected working such as this one?

Ra: I am Ra. There are three. Firstly, the instrument must needs improve the disciplined subconscious taboo against requesting Ra. This would involve daily conscious and serious thought. The second safeguard is the refraining from the opening of the instrument to questions and answers for the present. The third is quite gross in its appearance but suffices to keep the instrument in its physical complex. The hand may be held.

Questioner: Are you saying, then, that just by holding the instrument's hand during the channeling sessions this would prevent trance?

Ra: I am Ra. This would prevent those levels of meditation which necessarily precede trance. Also in the event that, unlikely as it might seem, the entity grew able to leave the physical complex the auric infringement and tactile pressure would cause the mind/body/spirit complex to refrain from leaving.

We may note that long practice at the art which each intuits here would be helpful. We cannot speak of methodology for the infringement would be most great. However, to speak of group efforts is, as we scan each, merely confirmation of what is known. Therefore, this we may do.

We have the available energy for one fairly brief query.

Questioner: There are many techniques and ways of practicing so-called white magical arts. Are rituals designed by a particular group for their own particular use just as good or possibly better than those that have been practiced by groups such as the Order of the Golden Dawn and other magical groups?

Ra: I am Ra. Although we are unable to speak with precision on this query, we may note some gratification that the questioner has penetrated some of the gist of a formidable system of service and discipline.

I am Ra. May we thank you again, my friends, for your conscientiousness. All is well. We leave you rejoicing in the power and the peace of the one infinite Creator. Go forth with joy. Adonai.

L/L Research

Sunday Meditation
August 30, 1981

(L channeling)

I am Hatonn, and I greet you, my brothers and sisters, in the love and the light of the infinite Creator. We are happy to join this group, as much because of the opportunity to serve as the obvious joy and love in which we have gathered. It is, therefore, our pleasure not only to serve, but to share, and for this we thank you.

Tonight we would like to present to you a small story concerning a young child in a wilderness. The child, as the story goes, found himself abandoned in a wilderness in which the very milieu within which he found himself was antagonistic toward his own growth and survival, but being a child he was not aware of the circumstances surrounding him, for a child is much more aware of those circumstances which he wishes to see and to encounter and this being the actuality of his perceptions, he was unaffected by his surroundings and quite happily and successfully grew and learned in his hostile environment.

My brothers and sisters, the child is yourself, for is it not true that as a child you came to the life you now experience, a life, an illusion that is unquestionably hostile to your own spiritual growth and progression, for your illusion entitles you to a multitude of distractions and setbacks designed primarily to prevent your growth. My brothers, we encourage you to see through your illusion. You have within you the power of creation. Make use of your power. Create the garden that you so fervently desire to return to, for the only return to Eden that you will experience, my brothers, is a return through the development of your innate abilities to transform disorder and chaos into balance and beauty, and, as the child in the story, by seeing in your world and in your brothers and sisters only that which you wish to see, only beauty, only love.

In this manner, my brothers, will you grow and prosper and return to your Eden. It is very difficult we know, to receive what often seems vague, esoteric advice and attempt to incorporate it into the daily distractions of your illusion, for your hostile environment requires your active participation to insure the maintenance of your physical vehicles within the illusion. This in as it should be in that your education requires the development of your ability to simultaneously experience the illusion, playing by its rules, so to speak, yet also rising above the illusion and perceiving it as such. In your schools it is often required that you perform the mathematics necessary to sustain and resolve an illusory problem, referring to the mysterious appearance and disappearances of numbers of apples and oranges. In a like manner, the illusion in which you live has problems that require resolution, but not, my brothers, immersion.

Therefore, we encourage you to see beyond your daily apples and oranges, to view them as only problems to be resolved that you might hone your skills in dealing with illusory problems and identifying them as such, for in exerting your will in choosing to be conscious of the illusion as it exists and not immersed in it comes the awareness necessary for perception of that which actually is real within the universe. There is a reality in the realization that all is all, that one is all, that all is one. In your daily acts of service you achieve steps in redressing the imbalance between your race's perception of the illusion and the reality. In redressing this imbalance you serve not only yourself but bring more of the universe one step closer to their eventual progression to higher levels of consciousness and education.

At this time we would like to exercise another instrument. I am Hatonn.

(Carla channeling)

I am Hatonn. I am now with this instrument and am pleased to be speaking through this instrument. We would continue, my friends, greeting you once again in the love and in the light of our infinite Creator.

My friends, we speak to you this evening not of meditation, for this is not an introductory group. We speak to you of the fruits of that meditation. Those fruits are the manifestations and expressions of love. You would call that service. To be of service to those about you is a far more subtle thing than it would seem. Many there are among your peoples at this time that may be likened unto weeds. Those things which they offer may appear to be pretty, but they take the place of good growing things and give back neither fruit nor scent nor true beauty. Many there are among your peoples who, in attempting to serve, judge harshly their fellow creatures. We have seen many times those who truly wish to serve speak again and again believing that they are aiding their fellow beings and all the while judging, limiting and divorcing themselves from their fellow beings. Many of your so-called religions operate in this manner. We find it unfortunate, for there is a true service that, like the rose, not only blooms but has a sweet scent and when cut, wishes only to serve by growing again.

It is, as we have said, often difficult to feel as though the radiance of the Creator bloomed within you, for your illusion is powerful and its traps are intentionally dangerous. But it is not so difficult as you might think to remain, in many cases, conscious of the radiance and the beauty of that love which you channel.

We have only one thought to offer you before we leave this instrument. We ask that you recall the cheerfulness, the joy, which you may experience in good company. My friends, all creatures are good company for all are the Creator. On some the illusion may hang heavy and, like an Halloween mask, protect them from your sight so that you may think some of your brothers and sisters to be those with whom we could not be cheerful, could not be joyful, could not, in fact, share love. The essence of service, my friends, is an effortless cheerfulness, a lack of judgment, and a willingness to serve as others would have you serve them. Sometimes, my friends, this may mean you cannot serve them. Accept this with cheerfulness and let this very cheer be the service you offer to those who are not yet ready to seek whatever joy you may have, whatever gifts you may share.

At this time, my brother of Laitos will join us and we would move among you so that each in the group might experience our conditioning and contact. We will attempt to moderate our contact with the one known as R, as we discern that there has been some slight discomfort in the past due to this instrument's sensitivity.

We leave this instrument at this time in the love and light of the infinite Creator. We shall resume after this pause through another instrument with his kind permission. I am known to you as Hatonn.

(C channeling)

I am Hatonn, and I am with this instrument. We have been attempting to contact this instrument for a free chance for him to exercise, for he needed a bit of experience for it has been a while since his last attempt. We of Hatonn speak always of love and wish that each of your peoples could or would open themselves so that they may experience beauty that is around them and that as they serve they shall become more aware of love, for with service to your fellow beings you slowly, but steadily, grow yourselves and increasingly bask more so in the love around and in yourselves.

Sunday Meditation, August 30, 1981

We of the Confederation wish always to serve each of you in your process of growth toward a greater awareness of the infinite Creator. We will at any time be with any who wish our aid, for as we said, we seek to serve, for through service we may grow and as it is for us, so is it for you people. To serve is to grow. To serve is a great privilege and to serve is an honor, for through this service each grows.

We are known to you as Hatonn, and will at this time transfer this contact to another instrument for the purpose and privilege of answering any questions you might have, for through answering your questions we also gain greater understanding and deem it a great teaching aid, not only for you in your quest, but also for us. We transfer now. We are known to you as Hatonn.

(Jim channeling)

I am Hatonn, and am with this instrument and we greet you once again in love and light. We offer ourselves at this time for the purpose of answering questions which might be of aid to those who quest. Are there any questions at this time?

C: Yes. As I was channeling—toward the end—once again I felt myself drifting, looking for the words, the concepts, looking to complete those words which I'd begun. Is there some way that I can keep myself more within myself and channel? I tried to do some things that were suggested tonight. I had my hands crossed and one leg crossed over the other two to keep the energy field closed. Is there anything else that I can do to keep more control for myself?

I am Hatonn. My brother, in this case we feel we might best answer you by suggesting that it is simply a matter of increased practice that will be of most service at this stage of your channeling experience, for as you continue in your contact with our vibration, you have noticed that you look for the next phrase or thought or concept to complete the one begun. It is the free and clear opening of the self to our contact and not the seeking through the mind that allows our concepts to be transmitted through your instrument.

Therefore, we would suggest that in order to gain confidence and to open yourself more fully to our contact it is simply a matter of practice, so that you will learn by your own experience that you need not look for the next concept or word but need merely to open yourself and allow these to be transmitted through your instrument. We feel you have made great progress in this regard and we would reassure you that it is simply a matter of practice.

May we answer you further, my brother?

C: No, not at this time. Thank you.

As always, we thank you. Is there another question at this time?

Carla: I have a question which may not be proper, but I was wondering if you had any comment concerning …

(Side one of tape ends.)

(Jim channeling)

I am Hatonn, and am once again with this instrument. The advanced course in tape changing has just been completed. To answer you, my sister, most fully, we would say that we were quite pleased with our contact with you this evening. The precautions that you have taken to remain within your physical vehicle have worked, in our estimation, quite well and we commend the effort that is being made in this regard.

May we answer you further, my sister?

Carla: No. I just want to thank you for the judgment from your end. I felt that way too. I'm really pleased that I can continue to be of service. Thank you.

I am Hatonn. We thank you and look forward, as always, to future contacts through your channel. May we answer another question at this time?

D: Yes. You mentioned earlier that the distractions within this illusion that get in our way of radiating this love, these distractions are put here purposely and they're designed for the purpose of distraction. Can you explain that more fully, please?

I am Hatonn. My brother, we would say that it is well known to many upon your planet that each of the entities now incarnate on this planet have, before incarnation, taken part in designing at some level the experience which they encounter within their incarnation. In most cases it is what is called the higher self which designs the program that will be pursued and the lessons that will be learned. In an increasing number of cases upon your planet at this time the individuals who are called by our brothers and sisters of Ra the mind/body/spirit complex, itself designs the experience that it will encounter and the lessons it wishes to learn. The lessons are presented as what might be called obstacles, for when one exerts an energy in a certain direction seemingly against a problem or situation, there is an interaction that occurs which, if one is aware, results in learning.

It is necessary within your illusion that there be a forgetting after incarnation, or else the obstacles encountered and the lessons learned would carry no weight since they would not have been forgotten in their purpose, but when forgotten and encountered within the incarnation, present the opportunity for the learning of a specific lesson. The lesson may take many forms. Each entity has its own unique perceptions and needs and methods of experiencing this lesson. The basic lesson of your illusion is that all is one. There is nothing but the Creator and it is called an illusion that you dance within, for during your incarnation it seems time and again that there is nothing but opposition, separation, anxiety, frustration, hatred, even unto war. All of this illusion, all of these obstacles, are teaching devices determined by each of you before your incarnation as that which you shall experience so that you might overcome, so to speak, the perception that you have obstacles, that there is separation, that there is anything but the one infinite Creator.

The experience within your illusion is intense. It is intensified by the fact that there is forgetting by each who participates within the illusion. It is your task to remember. It is your task to discover that, in fact, there are no obstacles, that there is only the one infinite Creator, that there is only love and that this love might be found within each part of your experience of the illusion. Time and again you shall experience the opportunity to learn this simple lesson.

May we answer you further, my brother?

D: No, thank you.

We thank you. Is there another question at this time?

Carla: I have a question. I have a relative who is a fundamental Christian, so fundamental that it boggles the imagination, and I sort of felt like when you were channeling earlier that I really could identify a lot of the judgmental things that my brother has said with what you were talking about. I wonder what the best service one can be is to such a loved person who, on the other hand is so terribly judgmental? Is all one can do to be of good cheer and to love or is there some seed that one can plant?

I am Hatonn. My sister, in many cases such as this one of which you speak, there is very little that can be done in the way of overt teaching, shall we say, for all who experience this illusion, in whatever perception they may bask, each experiences a valid perception of the one infinite Creator, for there is nothing but the Creator. Each progresses through this illusion and hopefully refines the perception and the experience of the Creator. As this growth proceeds, many teachers are met, for there is nothing but teaching and learning within this illusion. Your brother and each entity upon this planet meets teachers each time he meets another human being or another experience or another thought or another moment within the Creation. You are one such teacher. As each teaches, so do you teach.

Your experience with your brother has been long and intense, so to speak. Many ways have you tried to share that which is of meaning to you, as each who becomes more conscious of the patterns of the evolution of the spirit attempts to share that perception with those about them. You may find after a period of time that your very being, that cheer of which you speak, is the best teacher, the best means of your teaching for your brother, for it has often been said that the actions speak much louder and clearer than do the words, and though your brother on a conscious level may seldom experience or express the learning that he gains from your being, yet within his heart and mind and being, your being will shine, for you do feel love for this entity and that is the greatest teaching device upon your planet.

May we answer you further, my sister?

Carla: Not unless you can think of a good answer to the question, "Have you accepted Christ into your heart today?"

I am Hatonn. May we suggest a simple "Yes"?

Carla: Thank you, Hatonn. Thank you very much.

Again, we thank you. Is there another question at this time?

F: Yes. I've been told that in your spiritual seeking, that by digging many holes, as with a well—digging shallow holes—that it would be better to dig one deep hole. In other words, choosing one path, or one so-called religion. Would you comment on this please?

I am Hatonn. My sister, to your query we might respond by saying that though it would appear that an entity, by digging many holes, as you call them, is digging many holes and dividing itself in its seeking, there is only one seeking and it is the desire for this seeking that shall result in the finding. The many holes, when added up, shall we say, shall result in the one path which the entity pursues, and from moment to moment it might appear that the entity is pursuing yet another path, digging yet another hole, but we might suggest that each entity pursues the path that feels to it to be of greatest benefit and learns from each the lessons therein, for many are the paths upon your planet and within your illusion.

Each has that which might be of aid to those who travel that path. In short, may we say, it is your choice to pursue your path and there is nothing but the one path that you pursue and we would suggest, if we might, that within the depths of your being you are quite aware of the path that you pursue, and in meditation you shall discover the path upon which you wish to tread. Do not be concerned if from time to time the path appears to change. We would suggest that the path is long and the path is one, and your journey on that path can yield nothing but success, for all paths lead to the one infinite Creator.

May we answer you further, my sister?

F: No, thank you.

We thank you. Is there another question at this time?

L: Hatonn, I notice that you seem to be developing a sense of humor. Would you care to comment on that?

I am Hatonn. During our lone experience with this group, we have found there are certain avenues of experience and expression which have been opened to us by the needs and the desires of those to whom we speak. It has been our honor and a great privilege to speak in whatever manner is allowed and called for. We find at this time within this group there is a certain lightness, shall we say, that has not been present in such quantity before. Because it is now more possible, shall we say, to utilize the tool of humor, we are exercising this ability which we have not been able to exercise before, and may we say that it is a great honor to find yet another path of service and it is with great fervor that we do our push-ups.

May we answer you further, my brother?

L: I would simply like to offer a comment that more and more the conversations with you are as pleasant as a cool drink of water and we're grateful for your presence.

I am Hatonn. We share your feeling of gratitude. This group has provided those whom you know of our people as Hatonn with many sips of nectar. Is there another question at this time?

F: May I ask for some advice on showing young children the light and love other than by example? Ways that they may be able to learn, maybe, faster?

I am Hatonn. My sister, in this regard we might say that there is no greater teacher for the young one of your peoples than the example which they see and which they experience themselves within their daily lives. To specifically guide your decision-making in this regard we cannot do, for this would infringe upon your free will, but we can say in general that to experience yourself the love of the one infinite Creator in a manner which your children can understand and to reflect this love through your behavior with those round about you is the greatest teaching which can be done. To find a means to daily express in some way your love of the Creator and your desire to serve the Creator will express to your children that which you value most.

If there might be some way in which you could, shall we say, regularize or ritualize this experience and expressing of devotion and love to the one Creator with your children partaking, this would be a most effective means of allowing them not only to see but to experience with you this love and desire.

May we answer you further, my sister?

F: I don't do any ritual myself other than meditation by myself. I guess maybe I don't understand or would ask you to go further on that *(inaudible)*.

I am Hatonn. Many there are among your people who praise the Creator in song. Many there are among your people who praise the Creator in dance. Many there are who praise the Creator in prayer or meditation or in certain spoken words which convey the feelings within. Many ways have your peoples found of praising the one Creator. Any way will be suite sufficient for the child to learn, if practiced regularly.

May we answer you further, my sister?

F: No. Thank you, Hatonn.

Again, we thank you. May we answer another question at this time?

(Pause)

I am Hatonn. May we say once again how great an honor it has been to join your group this evening. As always, we find ourselves immersed in joy when we are asked to join this group. We thank you with every fiber of our being for being allowed to partake in your meditations and for being asked to share our humble message with you. By this service do we learn more of the love of the Father. We would say once again that at any time should any request our aid in their daily meditations, it need only be asked that we join in meditation and we shall worship with each the one infinite Creator.

We are known to you as those of Hatonn. We shall now take our leave of this instrument and this group for this evening. We look forward to joining you in your meditations as you go about your daily lives. We leave you now in the love and in the light of the one infinite Creator. Adonai vasu borragus.

(Carla channeling)

I am Nona, and I greet you in the love and in the light of the infinite Creator. We come among you at this time as we have been called to share our healing vibrations at this time.

(Carla channels Nona until the end of the meditation.)

Sunday Meditation
September 6, 1981

(Carla channeling)

[I am Hatonn,] … and I greet you, my friends, in the love and the light of the infinite Creator. It is a great privilege, as always, to be with you this evening and we greet each of you.

We would like tonight to share with you a small story. There was once a very steep mountain. So precipitous were its heights that clouds formed across the face of the cliffs so that the valley never saw the sky and those who lived upon the heights never saw the valley. Those who lived in the valley were very jealous of the land and of the possessions, one of the other. Their methods of sharing experiences with each other was harsh in the extreme and disharmony reigned under the clouds.

Another group lived high among the peaks of this mountain. This society lived very meagerly, having far, far less than those in the valley, for game was scarce and little grew that could be eaten, but they survived and such was their society that their leaders whom they chose were wise and good and when judgment must needs be made t'was fair. Harmony reigned also between people, for all was offered as all had so little that it must be pooled to survive. Those who looked upon the stars, though they had little, dwelt in peace and harmony, and because they did not think of possessions; as they mated, each was content, one with the other, and harmony was given as an heirloom from generation to generation.

This was, my friends, one mountain, one location, and one illusion. The factors of existence varied. Under the cloud there was plenty and above there was little, and yet, which people bore like a shield and buckler the light of harmony and the seeking for the truth? My friends, sometimes it may seem as though your days stretch before you as a plain, vast and featureless and indistinguishable by any landmark, any signpost to which you may look to for inspiration or a new way of being. Actually, my friends, the terrain of your illusion is constantly precipitous. Your illusion has many levels. You, yourself, may choose the level at which you wish to experience the conditions of your existence.

When it seems that though you have plenty, that though all things should be harmonious, they are not, put yourself to the task of scaling a cliff within yourself. Move beyond a cloud which obscures the ever-present pinnacle that towers out of sight above the fog. At that level, my friends, you may experience certain losses and feel in these losses, which are only those needs which you have discarded as you see the illusory nature of them, a freedom to be joyful and in harmony, that you could not see dwelling under a cloud.

This cloud is part of the illusion and may be penetrated most easily by meditation. It is, however, possible at any moment to mentally climb the precipice, to, by an act of desire, move above the obscuring clouds and see the stars, the points of light and love and truth which are not visible from the lower points of viewing. There is one fine gift, perhaps above most, that such an overview may offer to you. That is a sense of the honor that it is to dwell with those about you, for each is a unique and beautiful part of the creation, which is vast, free, resplend—we correct this instrument—resplendently lovely.

This sense of honor in sharing experiences with others is so often lost among your peoples that it is quite rare to experience. However, my friends, you can perhaps cast your mind back to a point at which you met such an entity, an entity who honored the life within you, whether you yourself at that time honored it or not. What a gift has such a person given—the gift of recognition, for are we not all one being? One part of an infinite Creator? And is not each part full worthy of the utmost honor?

At this time we would transfer this contact. I am Hatonn.

(L channeling)

I am Hatonn, and I greet you again, my brothers and sisters, in the love and the light of the Creator. We of Hatonn desire to be of service to you for in so doing we accomplish the task of growth which we have set before ourselves. It is a privilege to serve you, for in doing so we find that we serve ourselves, as one self in a body serves itself through benefiting the entire body.

At this time we would like to exercise another instrument, so as to familiarize the instrument with the sensation of our contact. I am Hatonn.

(Carla channeling)

I am Hatonn, and am again with this instrument. We have been attempting to speak a few words through the one known as E. If he would relax and speak the words that are given at the moment to him without hesitation, we shall again transfer to the instrument known as E. I am Hatonn.

(E channeling)

I am Hatonn, and I great you once again in love and the light of the infinite Creator. It is a pleasure to work with a new instrument. We suggest that this instrument relax and allow the words to come without thinking or worrying about what is being said. We will return now to the one known as Carla. I am Hatonn.

(Carla channeling)

I am Hatonn, and am again with this instrument. May we thank each of you for the patience which it requires for you to offer energy to the group while we exercise new channels. It is enormously appreciated. We and our brothers and sisters of Laitos would like to take this opportunity while there is some pause for working with each of you who is not at the present time channeling, as this instrument calls this activity of service. We would not wish at this time to put words in your mouths, but merely to work with each of you to help deepen your state of meditation and to make some adjustments which are unique with each of your vibrations.

We would work at this time with the one known as D.

(Pause)

We would, at this time move to the one known as S, if she would relax.

(Pause)

I am Hatonn. May we say to the one known as S that we appreciate the effort that has been made by this entity and are with her.

As we move to the one known as R may we say we are attempting to be extremely cautious that we may disrupt as little as possible a somewhat sensitive energy field. We would work with this instrument at this time.

(Pause)

I am Hatonn. We move now to the one known as Don and offer our vibration.

(Pause)

I am Hatonn, and greet you once again in love and light. I and my brother Laitos thank you for the privilege of working with each of you. We would at this time move on, if we may, to another channel. I am Hatonn.

(L channeling)

I am Hatonn. I am again with this instrument. We thank you for your patience as we have had some difficulty in contacting this instrument. It is our privilege at this time to attempt to answer any questions that you may have. I am Hatonn.

C: Yes, Hatonn, I have a question. I asked earlier and was told that as third density we aid second density in their attempt to become third. I was wondering, as a second-density entity grows, does it seek out contact with third?

I am Hatonn. I am aware of your question. My brother, second density, like your own third density, has levels of development within it, for just as in your own density, not all who occupy that density are of simultaneous development. Also, my brother, we would remind you that not all seek the some experiences simultaneously in your dimension, therefore, we would answer your question by saying that, with these factors understood, some of second density will seek out the experience of contact with third-density entities such as yourself, while others will not seek out that contact.

May we answer you further, my brother?

C: No, not on that subject, but here of late I've been observing a friend who is experiencing extreme emotional difficulties and I was wondering if you could give me any advice about how best to aid this person in this difficult time.

I am Hatonn. My brother, your heart is open to sharing, for such is your nature, and you do not limit your sharing to joy, but also to sharing the pains and sorrows experienced by others because of the love that you feel for them. My brother, the saying exists on your planet that "time heals all wounds." Though we would not attempt to evaluate the accuracy of the terms used in this saying, we would make use of it to suggest that what you refer to as time with the sharing of a sincere loved one can be of great assistance in assimilating the experiences your friend has chosen to take on at this time. Therefore, my brother, to be more concise, we would suggest that your patient willingness to serve through sharing of experience is the most valuable form of assistance you can render your friend.

May we answer you further, my brother?

C: No, thank you very much.

We thank you. Is there another question?

E: I have a question, Hatonn, and that is during the recent flyby Saturn I heard on the radio that the camera of the satellite went out of order. There was also a period of ten to fifteen minutes of transmissions from three other sets of instruments that were described as being very strange, that is that for ten to fifteen minutes strange data was coming through three other sets of instruments, and my question is can you tell us what that incident means or what that strange data was?

I am Hatonn. My brother, you are aware that we of the Federation are unable to supply proof of our efforts for existence. Consequently, to passively allow any such event to occur would be a violation of our own morals, so to speak. To answer what we feel is your subsequent question, if we may be so presumptuous …

E: Certainly.

…We thank you. We cannot reveal to you …

(Side one of tape ends.)

… suggest that the variation and terminations of data could be construed as indicative of variations within the supposedly concrete universe within which many minds attempt to function. The statement made on your planet long ago, "Those who have eyes, let them see; those who have ears, let them hear," is very appropriate for the situation to which you have referred, my brother, for the perceptions must be selective for their growth value to be derived.

May we answer you further?

E: Not at this time. Thank you.

As always, we thank you, my brother. Is there another question?

E: Yeah. I'd like to ask one other question, and that is—and this just occurred to me—we are of the third density on a planet that is entering fourth density and on our planet there are beings of first, second and third density, and as we enter fourth density I would assume there would then be beings of first, second, third and fourth density, but as I understand it, when the planet becomes fourth density, then those of us that remain in the third density will have to go elsewhere. Is that correct? And why is it that we can't stay with the planet, if we don't become fourth density, because second-density creatures stay or are on this planet now, so why can't third-density creatures inhabit or be on a planet that is in fourth density?

I am Hatonn. I am aware of your question. It is appropriate, my brother, for a mixture of polarities to exist simultaneously when the opportunity exists for those polarities to achieve growth due to the potential produced by the presence of both polarities. However, the presence of both positive and negative fourth-dimensional polarities upon a planetary sphere that contains solely unpolarized third-dimensional entities would potentially result in the third-dimensional entities becoming a sort of battleground between the fourth-dimensional polarities.

To remove either of the two fourth-dimensional polarities would have a detrimental effect upon the remaining third-dimensional entities, therefore, my brother, we have a situation where it is not possible to allow all three to occupy the some planetary sphere, nor is it possible to allow either fourth-dimensional polarity along with the unpolarized third-dimensional entities. Finally, to cover all of the potential combinations, to allow the joint occupation of the planetary sphere by both fourth-dimensional polarities without the undecided third-dimensional polarities—correction—third-dimensional unpolarized entities would be simply to extend and aggravate the immediately pre-harvest third-dimensional condition. For these reasons, it is necessary to separate the groups.

In reference to your comparison with the simultaneous occupation of first, second and third densities, my brother, you must remember the significance of the third-dimensional existence, that is, a time of choice.

May we answer you further, my brother?

E: I think I understand. Thank you.

We thank you. Is there another question we may answer?

D: Yes, Hatonn. At the time you were attempting, that you were working with all of us in the room and you began to work with me, it seemed to me that you passed over rather quickly and I'd like to know if you can tell me why that was and for me specifically and, in general, how those of us who are not channeling at this time, how we may better prepare ourselves for future contacts, for future workings with you.

I am Hatonn. My brother, we are pleased that you are interested in these matters, for meditation itself is a path toward growth for you and as insignificant as our efforts and advice may be, we welcome the opportunity to share what little we have to offer with you as frequently as you request.

To answer your questions, my brother, the purpose of our contact with you was simply a refinement of our communication with you, for although we would not attempt to force you to channel, as you term it, we would share as—correction—share in as well-balanced a state as possible our own atmosphere with yours, so as to acquaint you with our presence without forcing ourselves upon you. In your case, the balance was near to being concise and therefore did not require much adjustment. As to facilitating your contact with any member of the Federation, the most important discipline for you to undertake is that of consistent, daily meditation, for there is no other tool, as this instrument would say, that will suffice to do the job. There are many disciplines that possess great value in their ability to facilitate an entity to teach himself, but the tool must be appropriate for the job. In this case, the tool for the job is consistent, daily meditation.

May we answer you further, my brother?

D: No, thank you very much and thank you for your unusual contact.

As always, my brother, the pleasure through the service is ours. Is there another question?

S: I have a question. I've experienced a great deal of discomfort this evening. Can you tell me the cause of it and what I can do to alleviate it in the future?

I am Hatonn. The discomfort that you experience is due partly to our own inadequate control of our attempt to share our presence with you and for this we humbly offer our apology, for our intent is not to cause discomfort. We would ask that you understand that the unity of contact within this group ebbs and flows as various individuals are distracted, become tired, or suddenly recall the purpose for which they came and return full force to the energy field of this group. All of this requires a constant tuning and balancing for us and we regretfully are not always adept at this.

In your case as well there is a strong request for our presence and communication but it is hindered by a reluctance which results in a sort of a participatory tug of war between yourself and yourself. As we attempt to step up our signal to you, so to speak, in response to the intensity of your calling, the increased presence at some times meets a repulsion that itself waxes and wanes with the intensity of our signal.

May we answer you further?

S: No, thank you.

We would suggest, if we might, that through further meditation, both with groups such as this one or by yourself away from this group, that you will gradually overcome the fears and reluctance that are affecting your development of your talents, for just as the sudden exercising of unused muscles can cause pain and difficulty, so also can the new flexing, so to speak, of your psychic muscles.

Is there another question?

S: No. You've been very helpful. Thank you.

As always, we thank you. Is there another question?

E: I have another question and that is it seems as though the mode of communication that we're using now would be called telepathy and what I'm wondering is—that is, whether in communicating with you this way we become any more sensitive telepathically to each other and to others on this planet. In other words, are there any changes in our brains as a result of this kind of communication?

I am Hatonn. My brother, in any spiritual striving that results in the individual more closely approximating his or her potential there is an increase in those skills or characteristics that the perfected individual would find inherent.

May we answer you further?

E: So, are you saying that we are in this communication improving our telepathic skills, so to speak?

I am Hatonn. That is correct just as—correction—that is correct, but just as one might limit one's perception to a single area and say, "I improve my telepathic skills," and not see that one is improving simultaneously on all sides, then in another area of research might say, "I am improving my levitational skills," without realizing simultaneously, simultaneous improvement of telepathic skills.

May we answer you further?

E: No, thank you.

C: Hatonn! When I asked a similar question—I may have read the answer wrong, but I thought I was told that although our telepathic skills improve, that on this level there are so few entities capable of sending a powerful enough thought that our ability to pick up thoughts from our fellow entities really didn't increase appreciably. Is that right?

I am Hatonn. My brother, the term appreciably is somewhat confusing, however, if we may attempt to clarify the communication problem we would say that growth occurs—correction—when growth occurs, it occurs in all directions. However, this is not to say that a surge in one area is accompanied by a dramatic surge in a different area. The key to the understanding of this problem is in viewing growth as the ability to accept and make use of the energy inherent in light. To be quite skillful in manipulating energy, to levitate for example, does not imply the same skill acquired through practice in such an area as telepathy. There are, in a sense, limitations to what may be accomplished in the third dimension in the area of telepathy simply because to become as adept with the use of light energy as is necessary to make major displays of telepathy—such as those communications accomplished by some of this group through mechanical devices—would be a level of development far in excess of that requiring an extended stay in the third dimension.

May we answer you further?

C: No. I see what you mean.

Is there another question?

C: Hatonn, when an entity gets a glimpse of future events, a premonition, what source is that entity tapping for this information? Is he, for a moment, open to a higher density negative source, for most future predictions are specific information, or is there, for a brief period, a strengthening of the link between the lower and the plan that the higher self has conceived for his experiences in this density or is it neither of?

I am Hatonn. My brother, there are many possible answers to your question for there are many potential causes to the effect you describe. Obviously, there are ramifications to informing you what the specific cause of the specific event is and for that reason we will not attempt to define a specific cause or a specific event. However, we would also suggest that you examine the creation that you refer to as time, for time itself is a tool created to serve and not to be served. It is malleable and as your higher self is familiar with this malleability and is also in direct communication with you, it is distinctly possible at times that your higher self will choose to give you a glimpse of what you refer to as the future, although in actuality all futures and all pasts are the present.

May we answer you further?

C: No thank you, for the moment. I'll have to think about this for a while.

We thank you. Is there another question that we may attempt to answer?

(Pause)

I am Hatonn. I am again with this instrument. We of Hatonn are grateful for the extended opportunity of service that you have presented us and desire that you be aware that we are available to each of you individually at any time, for however brief a period of time, if we may be of some assistance, for even the occurrence of a stoplight or as instrument describes as "being on hold," are opportunities for a brief but effective effort to establish a link between your selves and ours, if such is your desire and if so, simply address your mental or verbal calling to us and we will be enthusiastically responsive.

At this time we bid you adieu. I am Hatonn.

(Carla channeling)

I am Latwii, and I greet you in the love and in the light of the infinite Creator. We thank you for the opportunity to speak as briefly as possible at this time, for we know that you have had a long meeting. We have been exercising this instrument and causing her to twitch about on the couch for some time. We wanted to tell you how grateful we were to be with you this evening. My friends, we will only speak a few words and answer no questions. We wish to share with you a few thoughts.

We first would like for you to think of the oyster. My friends, when an oyster gets sand inside it, do you think that the oyster says to itself, "Ah, sand! I will now make a pearl." No, my friends, the oyster tries as hard as it can to remove the sand, but the sand is part of the oyster's experience and somehow, as the sand remains and the pain of its remaining is borne, something of great beauty among your peoples comes to be.

The sand within your existence, my friends, is there, not to cause you to swear, although you do, but to create the opportunity for you to create those things of beauty in your nature which shall be of eternal worth. We call you, my friends; we call you. What do you desire? Not yesterday, not tomorrow. At this moment, desire you the joy …

(Tape ends.) ♣

The Law of One, Book III, Session 70
September 9, 1981

Ra: I am Ra. I greet you in the love and in the light of the one infinite Creator. We communicate now.

Questioner: Could you please give me an indication of the condition of the instrument?

Ra: I am Ra. We are gratified to say that it is as previously stated.

Questioner: Why do you say that you are gratified to say that?

Ra: I am Ra. We say this due to a sense of gratitude at the elements which have enabled this instrument to maintain, against great odds, its vital energy at normal vibratory strength. As long as this complex of energies is satisfactory we may use this instrument without depletion regardless of the distortions previously mentioned.

Questioner: The instrument has complained of intensive psychic attack for the past diurnal period, approximately. Is there a reason for the intensification of this psychic attack?

Ra: I am Ra. Yes.

Questioner: Can you tell me what this reason is, please?

Ra: I am Ra. The cause is that with which you are intimately involved, that is, the cause is the intensive seeking for what you may call enlightenment. This seeking upon your parts has not abated, but intensified.

In the general case, pain, as you call this distortion and the various exaggerations of this distortion by psychic attack would, after the depletion of physical complex energy, begin the depletion of vital energy. This instrument guards its vital energy due to previous errors upon its part. Its subconscious will, which is preternaturally strong for this density, has put a ward upon this energy complex. Thus the Orion visitor strives with more and more intensity to disturb this vital energy as this group intensifies its dedication to service through enlightenment.

Questioner: I have an extra little question that I want to throw in at this time. Is regressive hypnosis on an individual past birth in this incarnation to reveal memories to it of previous incarnations a service or a disservice to it?

Ra: I am Ra. We scan your query and find you shall apply the answer to your future. This causes us to be concerned with the first distortion. However, the query is also general and contains an opportunity for us to express a significant point. Therefore, we shall speak.

There is an infinite range of possibility of service/disservice in the situation of time regression hypnosis, as you term this means of aiding memory. It has nothing to do with the hypnotist. It has only to do with the use which the entity so hypnotized makes of the information so gleaned. If the hypnotist desires to serve and if such a service is performed only upon sincere request, the hypnotist is attempting to be of service.

Questioner: In the last session Ra stated that "the path back from sixth-density negative time/space revolves, firstly, about the higher self's reluctance to enter negative time/space." Could you explain the higher self's position with respect to positive and negative time/space and why it is so reluctant to enter negative time/space that it is necessary for the mind/body/spirit complex to incarnate in negative space/time to find its path back?

Ra: I am Ra. In brief, you have answered your own query. Please question further for more precise information.

Questioner: Why is the higher self reluctant to enter negative time/space?

Ra: I am Ra. The higher self is reluctant to allow its mind/body/spirit complex to enter negative time/space for the same basic reason an entity of your societal complex would be reluctant to enter a prison.

Questioner: What I am trying to understand here is more about the higher self and its relationship with the mind/body/spirit complex. Does the higher self have a sixth-density mind/body/spirit complex that is a separate unit from the mind/body/spirit complex that is, in this case, displaced to negative time/space?

Ra: I am Ra. This is correct. The higher self is the entity of mid-sixth-density which, turning back, offers this service to its self.

Questioner: I think I have an erroneous concept of the mind/body/spirit complex that, for instance, I represent here in this density and my higher self. This probably comes from my concept of space and time. I am going to try to unscramble this. The way I see it right now is that I am existing in two different locations, here and in mid-sixth-density, simultaneously. Is this correct?

Ra: I am Ra. You are existing at all levels simultaneously. It is specifically correct that your higher self is you in mid-sixth-density and, in your way of measuring what you know of as time, your higher self is your self in your future.

Questioner: Am I correct in assuming that all of the mind/body/spirit complexes that exist below levels of mid-sixth-density have a higher self at the level of mid-sixth-density? Is this correct?

Ra: I am Ra. This is correct.

Questioner: Would an analogy for this situation be that an individual's higher self is manipulating, to some extent shall I say, the mind/body/spirit complex that is its analog to move it through the lower densities for the purposes of gaining experience and finally transferring that experience or amalgamating it in mid-sixth-density with the higher self?

Ra: I am Ra. This is incorrect. The higher self does not manipulate its past selves. It protects when possible and guides when asked, but the force of free will is paramount. The seeming contradictions of determinism and free will melt when it is accepted that there is such a thing as true simultaneity. The higher self is the end result of all the development experienced by the mind/body/spirit complex to that point.

Questioner: Then what we are looking at is a long path of experience through the densities up to mid-sixth-density which is a function totally of free will and results in the awareness of the higher self in mid-sixth-density, but since time is illusory and there is a, shall I say, unification of time and space or an eradication of what we think of as time, then, all of this experience that results in the higher self, the cause of evolution through the densities, is existing while the evolution takes place. It is all simultaneous. Is this correct?

Ra: I am Ra. We refrain from speaking of correctness due to our understanding of the immense difficulty of absorbing the concepts of metaphysical existence. In time/space, which is precisely as much of your self as is space/time, all times are simultaneous just as, in your geography, your cities and villages are all functioning, bustling, and alive with entities going about their business at once. So it is in time/space with the self.

Questioner: The higher self existing in mid-sixth-density seems to be at the point where the negative and positive paths of experience merge into one. Is there a reason for this?

Ra: I am Ra. We have covered this material previously.

Questioner: Oh yes. Sorry about that. It slipped my mind. Now, if a positive entity is displaced to negative time/space I understand that the higher self is reluctant to enter the negative time/space. For some reason it makes it necessary for the mind/body/spirit complex to incarnate in negative space/time. Why is it necessary for this incarnation in negative space/time?

Ra: I am Ra. Firstly, let us remove the concept of reluctance from the equation and then secondly, address your query more to the point. Each time/space is an analog of a particular sort or vibration of space/time. When a negative time/space is entered by an entity the next experience will be that of the appropriate space/time. This is normally done by the form-making body of a mind/body/spirit complex which places the entity in the proper time/space for incarnation.

Questioner: I think that to clear up this point I will ask a few questions that are related that will possibly help me to understand this better because I am really confused about this and I think it is a very important point in understanding the creation and the Creator in general, you might say. If a Wanderer of fourth, fifth, or sixth-density dies from this third-density state in which we presently find ourselves, does he then find himself in the third-density time/space after death?

Ra: I am Ra. This will depend upon the plan which has been approved by the Council of Nine. Some Wanderers offer themselves for but one incarnation while others offer themselves for varying lengths of your time up to and including the last two cycles of 25,000 years. If the agreed-upon mission is completed the Wanderer's mind/body/spirit complex will go to the home vibration.

Questioner: Have there been any Wanderers on this planet for the past 50,000 years now?

Ra: I am Ra. There have been a few. There have been many more which chose to join this last cycle of 25,000 years and many, many more which have come for harvest.

Questioner: Now here is the point of my confusion. If, after physical death, a Wanderer would return to his home planet why cannot the same entity be extracted from negative time/space to the home planet rather than incarnating in negative space/time?

Ra: I am Ra. As we stated, the position in negative time/space, of which we previously were speaking, is that position which is preincarnative. After the death of the physical complex in yellow-ray activation the mind/body/spirit complex moves to a far different portion of time/space in which the indigo body will allow much healing and review to take place before any movement is made towards another incarnative experience.

I perceive a basic miscalculation upon your part in that time/space is no more homogenous than space/time. It is as complex and complete a system of illusions, dances, and pattern as is space/time and has as structured a system of what you may call natural laws.

Questioner: I'll ask this question to inform me a little about what you just stated. When you came to this planet in craft 18,000 and 11,000 years ago, these craft have been called bell craft and were photographed by George Adamski. If I am correct these craft looked somewhat like a bell; they had portholes around them in the upper portions; and they had three hemispheres at 120° apart underneath. Is this correct?

Ra: I am Ra. This is correct.

Questioner: Were these constructed in time/space or in space/time?

Ra: I am Ra. We ask your persistent patience, for our answer must be complex.

A construct of thought was formed in time/space. This portion of time/space is that which approaches the speed of light. In time/space, at this approach, the conditions are such that time becomes infinite and mass ceases so that one which is able to skim the, shall we say, boundary strength of this time/space is able to become placed where it will.

When we were where we wished to be we then clothed the construct of light with that which would appear as the crystal bell. This was formed through the boundary into space/time. Thus there were two constructs, the time/space or immaterial construct, and the space/time or materialized construct.

Questioner: Was there a reason for the particular shape that you chose, in particular a reason for the three hemispheres on the bottom?

Ra: I am Ra. It seemed an aesthetically pleasing form and one well suited to those limited uses which we must needs make of your space/time motivating requirements.

Questioner: Was there a principle of motivation contained within the three hemispheres on the bottom, or were they just aesthetic, or were they landing gear?

Ra: I am Ra. These were aesthetic and part of a system of propulsion. These hemispheres were not landing gear.

Questioner: I am sorry to ask such stupid questions, but I am trying to determine something about space/time, time/space, and this very difficult area of the mechanism of evolution. I think it is central to the understanding of our evolution. However, I am not sure of this and I may be wasting my time. Could Ra comment on whether I am wasting my time in this particular investigation or whether it would be fruitful?

Ra: I am Ra. Since the concepts of space/time, or physics, and time/space, or metaphysics, are mechanical they are not central to the spiritual evolution of the mind/body/spirit complex. The study of love and light is far more productive in its motion towards unity in those entities pondering such concepts. However, this material is, shall we say, of some small interest and is harmless.

Questioner: I was asking these questions primarily to understand or to build a base for an attempt to get a little bit of enlightenment on the way that time/space and space/time are related to the evolution of the mind/body/spirit complex so that I could better understand the techniques of evolution. For instance, you stated "the potential difference may be released and polarity changed after an entity has learned/taught the lessons of love of self" if the entity is a positive entity that has found itself in negative time/space and has had to incarnate into negative space/time. What I was trying to do was build a base for an attempt to get a slight understanding of what you meant by this statement that potential difference may be released and polarity changed after the above step. I am very interested in knowing, if placed in a negative time/space, why it is necessary to incarnate in negative space/time and learn/teach love of self and develop—I guess—a sixth-density level of polarity before you can release that potential difference. Could you speak on that subject?

Ra: I am Ra. This will be the last full query of this working.

The entity which incarnates into negative space/time will not find it possible to maintain any significant positive polarity as negativity, when pure, is a type of gravity well, shall we say, pulling all into it. Thus the entity, while remembering its learned and preferred polarity, must needs make use of the catalyst given and recapitulate the lessons of service to self in order to build up enough polarity in order to cause the potential to occur for reversal.

There is much in this line of questioning which is somewhat muddled. May we, at this point allow the questioner to rephrase the question or to turn the direction of query more towards that which is the heart of its concern.

Questioner: I will, at the next session, then attempt to turn more toward the heart. I was attempting in this session to get at a point that I thought was central to the evolution of spirit but I seem to have gone awry. It is sometimes very, very difficult for me to question wisely in these areas.

I will just ask if there is anything that we can do to enhance the contact or to make the instrument more comfortable?

Ra: I am Ra. You are most conscientious and the alignments are especially good. We thank you, my friends, and have been glad to speak with you. We are attempting to be of the greatest aid to you by taking care not to deplete this instrument. Thus although a reserve remains we will attempt from this working onward to keep this reserve, for this instrument has arranged its subconscious to accept this configuration.

I am Ra. You are all doing well, my friends. We leave you in the love and in the light of the one infinite Creator. Go forth, therefore, rejoicing and glorying in the power and in the peace of the one infinite Creator. Adonai.

L/L Research

L/L Research is a subsidiary of Rock Creek Research & Development Laboratories, Inc.

P.O. Box 5195
Louisville, KY 40255-0195

www.llresearch.org

Rock Creek is a non-profit corporation dedicated to discovering and sharing information which may aid in the spiritual evolution of humankind.

ABOUT THE CONTENTS OF THIS TRANSCRIPT: This telepathic channeling has been taken from transcriptions of the weekly study and meditation meetings of the Rock Creek Research & Development Laboratories and L/L Research. It is offered in the hope that it may be useful to you. As the Confederation entities always make a point of saying, please use your discrimination and judgment in assessing this material. If something rings true to you, fine. If something does not resonate, please leave it behind, for neither we nor those of the Confederation would wish to be a stumbling block for any.

CAVEAT: This transcript is being published by L/L Research in a not yet final form. It has, however, been edited and any obvious errors have been corrected. When it is in a final form, this caveat will be removed.

© 2009 L/L Research

Sunday Meditation
September 13, 1981

(Carla channeling)

I am Hatonn, and I greet you, my friends, in the love and in the light of our infinite Creator. It is a great privilege to speak with you this evening and we greet the one known as M, who is new to this group.

This evening we would like to share with you a small story. It is the story of a person who was seeking. This person was seeking, not for food, nor for labor, nor for rest, nor for companionship, for this young man was weary of the ways of the world and sought only one thing—the knowledge of the Creator. He spoke to many, for many are the teachers among your peoples and many are the opinions that they hold. From one great teacher he would hear that the Creator is that which is within a great vastness apart from this little life, which is called heaven. From another great teacher he heard that the Creator lurked in the running water and was in fact a state of nothingness. He continued seeking. Another great teacher—and a very convincing one—sought to teach the Creator is honor, righteousness and a graceful way of life. This seemed to make more sense to the young man and yet, the young man was not satisfied.

He looked to the stars, to the forests, to the seas and to all of nature, for he could not, in any case, find any man, no matter how wise, who could tell him about the nature of the Creator. One day, as he was sitting, looking into a still pool, a very old man approached him. Little hair had he and little height. He was apparently poor, for his clothes were tattered. He smiled as he sat next to the young man and inquired after the young man's health. "I'm quite well, stranger," replied the young man, "But my heart is heavy. The things of this world do not satisfy me, and yet I cannot find that which is more permanent. I cannot understand the Creator."

The old man nodded and pointed to the still pool. "Have a look into the water," said he, "For there is the beginning and the end of your search."

And lo! The wizened old man had fled, leaving the young wanderer to gaze at his own face in the calm, clear waters of the forest pond. My friends, in the illusion which you now enjoy, there is every reason for you to believe that the truth will come to you from outside yourself. Your peoples have believed this for a great span of your years, as you call them, and all those about you believe that all things come to you from the outside. There are some items which are available to one who wishes to purchase knowledge. One may learn how to make the illusion work. What one may not purchase for any price from outside oneself is the knowledge of why things are as they are, why we are here, and what is the nature of our being.

To look in the mirror is to see an infinitely small part of the creation. This, my friends, is to the best of our knowledge, a creation made entirely of love. As you view yourself, you may see a tiny portion of an infinite love and yet, within that image in the mirror, there lie depths through which you may only see given a great deal of desire, time and discipline, for that which you seek within yourself, that which is the true heart of love, is locked within you like a seed within the earth or a babe in the womb, and it is through quietness, confidence and meditation that you may let this plan germinate, this babe be born. This entity is that part of yourself that is more fully the original Thought of the Creator—the original Thought of love.

At this time I would transfer this contact. I am Hatonn.

(L channeling)

I am Hatonn. I am now with this instrument and I greet you again in the love and the light of that which has caused our existence in service to one another.

It is a novel situation on your planet that so many who, in their higher self, seek numerous opportunities for service to one another find that on your planetary surface they are able only to seek opportunities for [helping] others to serve themselves. It is disappointing for them to find that their energies were so misdirected. For upon passing through that portal which you describe as death, and gazing back in reexamination of those life experiences, they discover that in one sense they were extraordinarily successful, for against their own higher will and against the natural flow of service that permeates the universe, they were successful in attempting, for their brief period of time, to shove the river of service upstream. Their accomplishment was to, against all help offered by the universe, find themselves opportunities to absorb service instead of projecting service.

It is not often that a planet upon which this is so prevalent is encountered, yet such notoriety is not particularly advantageous, my brothers. It is for this reason that we seek to spend more and more time in communication with the occupants of your planet, such as yourself, for this misdirection of energy, although unpolarized, does not achieve any variation in the individual's attainment. The uncontrolled scattering of energy that this represents is similar to an unharnessed electrical engine which generates sparks, and fires them randomly throughout the arc of its circulation. This random expulsion of energy acts, in its own way, as a summons for the type of help which we may offer if there is a defined calling for our help calling as well.

So, although the situation which we have described greatly validates, so to speak, our efforts, we would prefer that our presence were less intensely demanded. The opportunity for service within the individual consciously oriented toward service is intensified in this situation, for the individuals directing their energy at random on a higher level seek assistance in attaining their focus and for this purpose many of those you describe as wanderers have sought the opportunity for service on your planet.

If those of you present will seek the opportunity for service to your fellow occupants, we would suggest that you not attempt to describe your particular form of communication with those of the Federation—for many are not open to this type of communication and should be allowed to introduce their own calling—but rather attempt to assist your brothers and sisters in attaining a focus for their energies. It is possible, for example, to suggest that an afternoon might be more effectively spent in assisting a friend or relative in a form of necessary labor rather than whiling away the afternoon being entertained by electromechanical devices.

It is not necessary to convey to the individual the entire philosophy offered by members of the Federation to accomplish this suggestion. Rather, offer what is needed to plant the seed and allow it to grow without over-fertilization. We do not intend to imply that the communications you receive should be kept secret, for this is not our purpose, but rather that service is independent of philosophy, may be offered without an awareness of the philosophy we offer and may, in some cases, be inhibited by an awareness of our philosophy. It is for you, in service, to evaluate the situations before you and act accordingly.

At this time we would transfer our contact to another instrument. I am Hatonn.

(Jim channeling)

I am Hatonn, and am with this instrument and greet you once again in love and light. At this time it is our privilege to be joined by our brothers and sisters of Laitos for the purpose of offering the conditioning vibration to those of this group who wish to become more familiar with this vibration in order to deepen their meditation and perhaps at a later date, to take part in the channeling process.

At this time we will pause to allow our brothers and sisters of Laitos to pass among this group and to condition those who mentally request the conditioning vibration. I am Hatonn.

(Pause)

I am Hatonn. I am again with this instrument. At this time we would offer ourselves in the answering of questions which those of this group may find the value in the questing. Are there any questions at this time?

L: I have a question I'd like to ask, Hatonn. Recently I've been experiencing some visual or mental flashes of what seem to be a picture or a memory. As it's only present for a split second and then it's gone, it's not something I can retrieve and it has nothing at all to do with what I was thinking about or seeing at the time. Could you explain to me what this is?

I am Hatonn, and am aware of your question, my brother. To answer it in full, we are afraid, would be an infringement upon your future and your free will. We may only say in this case that this phenomenon which you are experiencing is that which is, shall we say, a trigger for that which is the harbinger of more to come. It is to tickle your curiosity and to incite further seeking. This you have already surmised yourself; this we may confirm. To say any more of a specific nature would be to travel that road of seeking for you. This we cannot do, for that road is the road which contains the learning you seek and this learning we would not take from you.

May we answer you further, my brother?

L: Yes. Within the limitations that you operate, is there any advice you are able to offer that would assist me in determining the direction to turn to develop this particular phenomena?

I am Hatonn. My brother, of these suggestions we may say you are already aware of that path which is most beneficial for the seeking. We may only say that to seek and to persevere is the most efficacious solution.

May we answer you further, my brother?

L: No. Thank you very much.

As always, we thank you. Is there another question at this time?

L: I have one other question, Hatonn. A while back I was involved in a practice session for astral projection that was fairly successful. Is this phenomena fairly significant as an accomplishment or is it simply another phenomena that can be developed, on the order of telekinesis or something like that that is no particular value of its own?

[I am Hatonn.] On this matter, my brother, may we say that the answer has two parts. Indeed, such an ability is a sign of great achievement, for it is not usual among your people to be able to project the astral body at will. It may also be said that it is not usual among your people to be able to, as this instrument might say, juggle five balls simultaneously. The value of either activity depends upon the desire and the purpose of the one so seeking the skills.

May we only suggest that in any seeking which you may undertake, if you should wish to evaluate its effectiveness as regards your own spiritual evolution, you may simply ask yourself the question, "How may I serve others through this activity?" If you can find ways to share the love of the Creator with those brothers and sisters who are one with you upon this planet, then you have done that which is of great value and you have accomplished a feat that few upon your planet can name as their own.

May we answer you further, my brother?

L: No, you've answered my question. Thank you.

We thank you. Is there another question at this time?

(Side one of tape ends.)

(Jim channeling)

I am Hatonn. It is a great pleasure to share in your meditation, but we feel somewhat remiss in our duties to only meditate at this time with you. May we ask if there is another question which any entity present might wish to ask at this time?

L: Is there a service you are capable of offering beyond that of communication?

I am Hatonn. Our services at this time are few in number, but include, as we have mentioned before, joining each entity in meditation wherever that entity might be at whatever time we are asked, the asking being the only requirement. When asked to join an entity in meditation we are most privileged to be allowed to do so. This service combined with the service which we now render in the form of telepathic transmission of thoughts is the service which we are allowed by Confederation guidelines, shall we say, to offer those entities who call for our services upon your planet.

May we answer you further, my brother?

L: Is this a service that is common to all members of the Federation?

I am Hatonn. There are some within the Confederation of Planets in the Service of the Infinite Creator who have varying skills and therefore, varying services to offer. This group is aware of the entity known as Nona who has the skills and services of the healing vibrations. There are others in the Confederation who have the task and the service of contacting various entities upon your planet while they are in states of what you call sleep and dreams and who, in this contact, are able to inspire by image or dream the entity so contacted to perform what the entity has decided before incarnation that it shall perform. These contacts are of an inspirational nature and are, in general, agreed upon before the incarnation of the entity contacted.

Others in the Confederation have, in that which you call your past, been able to make direct contact with various entities upon your planet for the purpose of providing information of a certain nature. In general, such direct contacts have not proven useful in the long run, so to speak, and thus this type of service is no longer offered by Confederation members for such services have proven to have mixed results.

May we answer you further, my brother?

L: No. You've answered me sufficiently. Thank you.

Again we thank you. May we answer another question at this time?

D: Hatonn, this past week during my meditations I've mentally called upon you to meditate with me and during those times I sensed or I felt no added presence to me at that time. Am I doing something wrong or are my spiritual senses just not sharp enough yet to detect that, or is there something that you could suggest I could improve on my technique?

I am Hatonn. In this regard, my brother, may we say that we are aware of your calling and we have indeed joined you in your meditations. We deem it a great privilege to do so. To those who are new to this group and who are in effect calling for our assistance for the first few times, so to speak, we are quite careful to join such an entity by using, shall we say, the light touch. We have, in this group's recent past, not been quite so able to use this light touch and have caused some inconvenience and discomfort, which we once again apologize for. It is not always an easy task to be able to blend vibrations of one density with those vibrations of another density.

As you continue in your meditations to request our presence, we will, hopefully, be able to blend our vibrations in such a manner that you will indeed be aware of our presence, but shall not experience the discomfort of a heavy hand, shall we say.

May we answer you further, my brother?

D: No, I appreciate that answer, Hatonn. Just always be aware that in my understanding of what you're saying, that if at any time you happen to slip and knock me off the couch—that or anything—I'll certainly understand.

I am Hatonn. We sincerely appreciate the range of possibilities which you have provided us. We shall attempt to remain within that range.

May we answer another question at this time?

S: Hatonn, I have a question. When I was experiencing discomfort, is that a result of what you were just speaking of—a heavy hand?

I am Hatonn. My sister, we are apologetically required to answer "Yes." We shall attempt to be more light in our touch in the future.

May we answer you further?

S: No, thank you.

Again, we thank you. May we answer another question at this time?

L: Hatonn, there was an individual on our planet that we called Mahatma Ghandi. What can you tell me of previous incarnations of this individual?

I am Hatonn. On this matter, my brother, we are somewhat limited in speaking to the present activities of this entity, but may say that this entity was one of those whom you have called the wanderer who came among your peoples at the time that you are familiar with as this last incarnation, and who came among your peoples also at a previous time approximately two hundred years earlier, and also this entity walked among your peoples a number of times in your distant past as one who sought to raise the vibrations of this planet by its very beingness and also through the activities afforded to it by each successive incarnation. The incarnation which you are most familiar with was, shall we say, a great triumph for this entity and allowed this entity to complete the mission which it had agreed to complete many thousand of your years ago, when it first offered itself as a wanderer.

May we answer you further, my brother?

L: Yes. Is the individual's current incarnation still involved with working on our planet?

I am Hatonn. Yes. May we answer you further, my brother?

L: No. I thank you.

I am Hatonn. We thank you, as always. Is there another question at this time?

(Pause)

I am Hatonn. At this time we shall transfer this contact and close through another instrument. I am Hatonn.

(C channeling)

I am Hatonn, and I am with this instrument. My friends, tonight as always, it's been a great privilege to speak a few humble words. We of Hatonn do deem it, as always, very pleasing to join with this group, and feel the love that is present in this group. And we always enjoy each opportunity to speak to those who become as part of the entity of your planet who seek, as do we all, the love and light of the one infinite Creator.

We especially enjoy the sounds that are present, in what you call nature, of this time of your year and wish you also to, at times, listen. Open yourselves to your planet. Hear, feel yourselves as one in meditation with your planet and all those entities upon it, for while we all seem to be isolated within ourselves, there's always kindred spirits seeking and willing to share and aid each of those who seek. We are known to you as Hatonn and leave you now in the love and light of the one Creator. Adonai, my friends. Adonai vasu borragus.

The Law of One, Book III, Session 71
September 18, 1981

Ra: I am Ra. I greet you in the love and in the light of the one infinite Creator. We communicate now.

Questioner: Could you first please give me the condition of the instrument?

Ra: I am Ra. It is as previously stated with the exception of a slight improvement in the vital energy distortions. One may note to the support group, without infringement, that it is well to aid the instrument in the reminders that while physical complex distortions remain as they are it is not advisable to use the increased vital energies for physical complex activities as this will take a somewhat harsh toll.

Questioner: In this session I hope to ask several different questions to establish a point of entry into an investigation that will be fruitful. I would first ask if it is possible to increase polarity without increasing harvestability?

Ra: I am Ra. The connection between polarization and harvestability is most important in third-density harvest. In this density an increase in the serving of others or the serving of self will almost inevitably increase the ability of an entity to enjoy an higher intensity of light. Thus in this density, we may say, it is hardly possible to polarize without increasing in harvestability.

Questioner: This would probably be possible in the higher densities such as the fifth-density. Is this correct?

Ra: I am Ra. In fifth-density harvest, polarization has very little do to with harvestability.

Questioner: Would you explain the concept of working with the unmanifested being in third-density to accelerate evolution?

Ra: I am Ra. This is a many-layered question and which stria we wish to expose is questionable. Please restate giving any further depth of information requested, if possible.

Questioner: Define, please, the unmanifested being.

Ra: I am Ra. We may see that you wish to pursue the deeper strata of information. We shall, therefore, answer in a certain way which does not exhaust the query but is designed to move beneath the outer teachings somewhat.

The unmanifested being is, as we have said, that being which exists and does its work without reference to or aid from other-selves. To move into this concept you may see the inevitable connection between the unmanifested self and the metaphysical or time/space analog of the space/time self. The activities of meditation, contemplation, and what may be called the internal balancing of thoughts and reactions are those activities of the unmanifested self more closely aligned with the metaphysical self.

Questioner: As an entity goes through the death process in third-density it finds itself in time/space. It finds itself in a different set of circumstances. Would you please describe the circumstances or properties of time/space and then the process of healing of incarnative experiences that some entities encounter?

Ra: I am Ra. Although this query is difficult to answer adequately, due to the limitations of your space/time sound vibration complexes, we shall respond to the best of our ability.

The hallmark of time/space is the inequity between time and space. In your space/time the spatial orientation of material causes a tangible framework for illusion. In time/space the inequity is upon the shoulders of that property known to you as time. This property renders entities and experiences intangible in a relative sense. In your framework each particle or core vibration moves at a velocity which approaches what you call the speed of light from the direction of supraluminal velocities.

Thus the time/space or metaphysical experience is that which is very finely tuned and, although an analog of space/time, lacking in its tangible characteristics. In these metaphysical planes there is a great deal of what you call time which is used to review and re-review the biases and learn/teachings of a prior, as you would call it, space/time incarnation.

The extreme fluidity of these regions makes it possible for much to be penetrated which must needs be absorbed before the process of healing of an entity may be accomplished. Each entity is located in a somewhat immobile state much as you are located in space/time in a somewhat immobile state in time. In this immobile space the entity has been placed by the form-maker and higher self so that it may be in the proper configuration for learn/teaching that which it has received in the space/time incarnation.

Depending upon this time/space locus there will be certain helpers which assist in this healing process. The process involves seeing in full the experience, seeing it against the backdrop of the mind/body/spirit complex total experience, forgiving the self for all missteps as regards the missed guideposts during the incarnation and, finally, the careful assessment of the next necessities for learning. This is done entirely by the higher self until an entity has become conscious in space/time of the process and means of spiritual evolution at which time the entity will consciously take part in all decisions.

Questioner: Is the process in positive time/space identical with the process in negative time/space for this healing?

Ra: I am Ra. The process in space/time of the forgiveness and acceptance is much like that in time/space in that the qualities of the process are analogous. However, while in space/time it is not possible to determine the course of events beyond the incarnation but only to correct present imbalances. In time/space, upon the other hand, it is not possible to correct any unbalanced actions but rather to perceive the imbalances and thusly forgive the self for that which is.

The decisions then are made to set up the possibility/probabilities of correcting these imbalances in what you call future space/time experiences. The advantage of time/space is that of the fluidity of the grand overview. The advantage of space/time is that, working in darkness with a tiny candle, one may correct imbalances.

Questioner: If an entity has chosen the negative polarization are the processes of healing and review similar for the negative path?

Ra: I am Ra. This is correct.

Questioner: Are the processes that we are talking about processes that occur on many planets in our Milky Way Galaxy, or do they occur on all planets, or what percentage?

Ra: I am Ra. These processes occur upon all planets which have given birth to sub-Logoi such as yourselves. The percentage of inhabited planets is approximately 10%.

Questioner: What percentage of stars, roughly, have planetary systems?

Ra: I am Ra. This is unimportant information, but harmless. Approximately 32% of stars have planets as you know them while another 6% have some sort of clustering material which upon some densities might be inhabitable.

Questioner: This would tell me that roughly 3% of all stars have inhabited planets. This process of evolution is in effect throughout the known universe then. Is this correct?

Ra: I am Ra. This octave of infinite knowledge of the one Creator is as it is throughout the One Infinite Creation, with variations programmed by sub-Logoi of what you call major galaxies and minor galaxies. These variations are not significant but may be compared to various regions of geographical location sporting various ways of pronouncing the same sound vibration complex or concept.

Questioner: It seems to me from this that the sub-Logos such as our sun uses free will to modify only slightly a much more general idea of created evolution so that the general plan of created evolution then seems to be uniform throughout the One Infinite Creation. The process is for the sub-Logoi to grow through the densities and, under the first distortion, find their way back to the original thought. Is this correct?

Ra: I am Ra. This is correct.

Questioner: Then each entity is of a path that leads to one destination. This is like many, many roads that travel through many, many places but eventually merge into one large center. Is this correct?

Ra: I am Ra. This is correct but somewhat wanting in depth of description. More applicable would be the thought that each entity contains within it all of the densities and sub-densities of the octave so that in each entity, no matter whither its choices lead it, its great internal blueprint is one with all others. Thusly its experiences will fall into the patterns of the journey back to the original Logos. This is done through free will but the materials from which choices can be made are one blueprint.

Questioner: You have made the statement that pure negativity acts as a gravity well pulling all into it. I was wondering first if pure positivity has precisely the same effect? Could you answer that please?

Ra: I am Ra. This is incorrect. Positivity has a much weaker effect due to the strong element of recognition of free will in any positivity approaching purity. Thus although the negatively oriented entity may find it difficult to polarize negatively in the midst of such resounding harmony it will not find it impossible.

Upon the other hand, the negative polarization is one which does not accept the concept of the free will of other-selves. Thusly in a social complex whose negativity approaches purity the pull upon other-selves is constant. A positively oriented entity in such a situation would desire for other-selves to have their free will and thusly would find itself removed from its ability to exercise its own free will, for the free will of negatively oriented entities is bent upon conquest.

Questioner: Could you please comment on the accuracy of these statements. I am going to talk in general about the concept of magic and first define it as the ability to create changes in consciousness at will. Is this an acceptable definition?

Ra: I am Ra. This definition is acceptable in that it places upon the adept the burden it shall bear. It may be better understood by referring back to an earlier query, in your measurement, within this working having to do with the unmanifested self. In magic one is working with one's unmanifested self in body, in mind, and in spirit; the mixture depending upon the nature of the working.

These workings are facilitated by the enhancement of the activation of the indigo-ray energy center. The indigo-ray energy center is fed, as are all energy centers, by experience but far more than the others is fed by what we have called the disciplines of the personality.

Questioner: I will state that the objective of the white magical ritual is to create a change in consciousness of a group. Is this correct?

Ra: I am Ra. Not necessarily. It is possible for what you term white magic to be worked for the purpose of altering only the self or the place of working. This is done in the knowledge that to aid the self in polarization towards love and light is to aid the planetary vibration.

Questioner: The change in consciousness should result in a greater distortion towards service-to-others, towards unity with all, and towards knowing in order to serve. Is this correct, and are there any other desired results?

Ra: I am Ra. These are commendable phrases. The heart of white magic is the experience of the joy of union with the Creator. This joy will of necessity radiate throughout the life experience of the positive adept. It is for this reason that sexual magic is not restricted solely to the negatively oriented polarizing adepts but when most carefully used has its place in high magic as it, when correctly pursued, joins body, mind, and spirit with the one infinite Creator.

Any purpose which you may frame should, we suggest, take into consideration this basic union with the one infinite Creator, for this union will result in service-to-others of necessity.

Questioner: There are, shall I say, certain rules of white magic. I will read these few and I would like you to comment on the philosophical content or basis of these and add to this list any of importance that I have neglected. First, a special place of working preferably constructed by the practitioners; second, a special signal or key such as a ring to summon the magical personality; third, special clothing worn only for the workings; fourth, a specific time of day; fifth, a series of ritual sound vibratory complexes designed to create the desired mental distortion; sixth, a group objective for each session. Could you comment on this list please?

Ra: I am Ra. To comment upon this list is to play the mechanic which views the instruments of the orchestra and adjusts and tunes the instruments. You will note these are mechanical details. The art does not lie herein.

The one item of least import is what you call the time of day. This is important in those experiential nexi wherein the entities search for the metaphysical experience without conscious control over the search. The repetition of workings gives this search structure. In this particular group the structure is available without the need for inevitable sameness of times of working. We may note that this regularity is always helpful.

Questioner: You stated in a previous session that Ra searched for some time to find a group such as this one. I would assume that this search was for the purpose of communicating the Law of One. Is this correct?

Ra: I am Ra. This is partially correct. We also, as we have said, wished to attempt to make reparation for distortions of this law set in motion by our naive actions of your past.

Questioner: Can you tell me if we have covered the necessary material at this point to, if published, make the necessary reparations for the naive actions?

Ra: I am Ra. We mean no disrespect for your service, but we do not expect to make full reparations for these distortions. We may, however, offer our thoughts in the attempt. The attempt is far more important to us than the completeness of the result. The nature of your language is such that what is distorted cannot, to our knowledge, be fully undistorted but only illuminated somewhat. In response to your desire to see the relationship betwixt space/time and time/space may we say that we conducted this search in time/space for in this illusion one may quite readily see entities as vibratory complexes and groups as harmonics within vibratory complexes.

Questioner: I see the most important aspect of this communication as being a vehicle of partial enlightenment for those incarnate now who have become aware of their part in their own evolutionary process. Am I correct in this assumption?

Ra: I am Ra. You are correct. We may note that this is the goal of all artifacts and experiences which entities may come into contact with and is not only the property of Ra or this contact.

We find that this instrument has neglected to continue to remind its self of the need for holding some portion of energy back for reserve. This is recommended as a portion of the inner program to be reinstated as it will lengthen the number of workings we may have. This is acceptable to us. The transferred energy grows quite, quite low. We must leave you shortly. Is there a brief query at this time?

Questioner: Is there anything that we can do to improve the contact or to make the instrument more comfortable?

Ra: I am Ra. You are conscientious. Remain most fastidious about the alignments of the appurtenances. We thank you. I am Ra. I leave you in the love and in the glorious light of the infinite Creator. Go forth, therefore, rejoicing in the power and in the peace of the one infinite Creator. Adonai.

The Law of One, Book V, Session 71, Fragment 40
September 18, 1981

Jim: The time/space or metaphysical portion of ourselves is not apparent to any of us most of the time, yet it is the place or realm of our truer being. This is true for anyone. It is the essence from which that which we know of as our conscious selves manifests as a portion of our true selves. Our space/time, physical selves are a reflection or shadow of our true selves which those who have eyes that can see behind illusion see when they behold our time/space beingness. It was this metaphysical self which Ra observed when first considering our group as a potential group for contact.

Carla: Don, Jim and I had a common interest in spiritual community before we ever got together. When we did join households at Christmas in 1980, we consciously joined together as a light group. We wanted to live a spiritually directed life with each other, and serve as we might. Much was sacrificed for this joining on both Jim's and Don's parts, for they were both loners, fond of their own company and not much fond of society, although they were both excellent hosts when guests did come by. But the sacrifices were gladly made, and we felt very blessed to be together. When the Ra contact began three weeks later, we felt very happy that we had gone ahead on faith and joined forces.

What we had together was that clear, pure, unmuddied love and fellowship that stems from there being no fear between us, or needs that were not met. For a golden few months and years, this remained so. I have long felt that Don's decline and death were the result of his becoming fearful that I might leave him for Jim. I would never have done such a thing, and had no idea he was concerned. But I believe that this fear, which he never expressed, and which I knew nothing of, led to his woeful last months, in which he suffered so greatly.

Session 71, September 18, 1981

Questioner: When you say you searched for this group what do you mean? What was your process of search? I ask this question to understand more the illusion of time and space.

Ra: I am Ra. Consider the process of one who sees the spectrograph of some complex of elements. It is a complex paint sample, let us say for ease of description. We of Ra knew the needed elements for communication which had any chance of enduring. We compared our color chip to many individuals and groups over a long span of your time. Your spectrograph matches our sample.

In response to your desire to see the relationship betwixt space/time and time/space, may we say that we conducted this search in time/space, for in this illusion one may quite readily see entities as vibratory complexes and groups as harmonics within vibratory complexes.

L/L Research

L/L Research is a subsidiary of Rock Creek Research & Development Laboratories, Inc.

P.O. Box 5195
Louisville, KY 40255-0195

www.llresearch.org

Rock Creek is a non-profit corporation dedicated to discovering and sharing information which may aid in the spiritual evolution of humankind.

ABOUT THE CONTENTS OF THIS TRANSCRIPT: This telepathic channeling has been taken from transcriptions of the weekly study and meditation meetings of the Rock Creek Research & Development Laboratories and L/L Research. It is offered in the hope that it may be useful to you. As the Confederation entities always make a point of saying, please use your discrimination and judgment in assessing this material. If something rings true to you, fine. If something does not resonate, please leave it behind, for neither we nor those of the Confederation would wish to be a stumbling block for any.

CAVEAT: This transcript is being published by L/L Research in a not yet final form. It has, however, been edited and any obvious errors have been corrected. When it is in a final form, this caveat will be removed.

© 2009 L/L Research

Sunday Meditation
September 20, 1981

(Carla channeling)

I am Hatonn, and I greet you, my friends, in the love and in the light of our infinite Creator. It is a great privilege to greet each of you and we especially welcome those new to this group. It is our hope that we may be of service to you and we are grateful that you have opened your ears to what humble thoughts we may have to share. Let us say to you who are new, before we speak upon any subject whatsoever, that ours is not the path of sure knowledge. We may give you the benefit of our experience, but we cannot give you answers that are without any equivocation, for we ourselves are still learning and still growing in the service of the infinite Creator, and that which we share with you is merely the fruit of our experiences. Thus, we ask that you take what you will from us. Discriminate in your hearts as to what you will keep and what you will leave behind, and if we may be of any aid to you whatsoever, then so be it, for this is our one desire—to aid those upon your planet who are at this time seeking to know the love and the light that surrounds them, that begat them, and that is their existence.

This evening, my friends, we would speak to you upon the subject of the love which you may manifest towards yourself and your fellow beings. This is a difficult subject. It is easy to speak of meditation and of the love that created you but as those upon a path of seeking begin to enter the domain of the meditative life, each seeker finds the daily practice, which this meditation engenders, to be the greatest challenge.

It is not, my friends, that the challenge was not there before. The same challenge always awaits the seeker. However, there comes a point in each entity's incarnation when the entity chooses to release all responsibility for that incarnation, or to take responsibility for that incarnation, for that experience, for the manifestations of the being which the entity is undergoing, for existence, my friends, is an activity, not a state. As you meditate this becomes apparent. Therefore, as you meditate you begin to see yourself and those about you in quite, quite a different light than you previously saw them. Not vanished, but quite faded, becomes the desire to actively manipulate those about you and to manipulate your own feelings and your own beingness because of those things which you believe to be acceptable in the terms of your culture. You begin to measure yourself by a yardstick that you find within yourself. It is this yardstick about which we speak.

In your holy works, my friends, there is a parable. This parable describes the vineyard. In this vineyard the grapes are ready for harvest and men are hired. Early in the morning they trudge to the vineyard to begin to earn their day's pay, but the owner is not satisfied and wishes to harvest more, and sends to the marketplace to discover if there might be more laborers to increase the harvest, and [the owner] admits them. Those who have worked all the morning are joined by those fresh from a lazy siesta upon the street. The afternoon passes. The heat of the day begins to vanish and the pleasantness of a cool evening breeze begins to signal the near end of the working day, and yet, the harvest is not complete. Again, the owner sends to the marketplace asking for workers, and more come and work for a very brief period harvesting the grapes of the owner.

Finally, twilight sends its violet rays along the soft lines of the hills and it is time for the workers to gather their day's pay and wend their way homeward. Behold! Those who have worked through the heat of the morning and the glare of the afternoon, those who have worked only in the afternoon and those who have worked very briefly in the cool of the evening are all paid the same.

My friends, is this the yard stick by which you measure yourself and others? Do you feel that you work longer or harder than others and so deserve more pay? Do you find the services which you attempt to offer to others, in offering to them seeds of thought upon love and light, slightly tainted because you know that you are offering to an entity who has slept the morning and wasted the afternoon the chance to gain the same reward as you?

In your illusion, my friends, it is inevitable that you will judge and that you will be judged by those about you. This, my friends, does not make the phenomenon a well thought out experience. Would you judge yourself? Would you judge others? Nay, my friends. Whatever the behavior that you exhibit, whatever the behavior of those to whom you wish to offer the opportunity to work in the harvesting, let one thing be uppermost in your mind and that is that we are all the Creator. The Creator is in us all and we in the Creator.

Go, therefore with a free and joyful heart, lifting yourself up with cheer when you feel yourself to have fallen, offering your love and your light to any who may ask, be they saint or wastrel. This way lies a great realization. That, my friends, is compassion.

Many times we speak to groups such as this—who are seeking to serve others—about this service, but you must understand that the first entity whom you serve is yourself. To know that you are a part of the Creator, that whatever errors you make, whatever missteps you may take, you may always move back to a perfect portion of yourself. To know this is to become able not to judge.

We encourage you in the disciplines of meditation and in the attempts to be of service, but let these things flow with the freedom of the joy of your participation in the Creator. Those who harvest are under a merciful protector. Harvest yourself, and offer yourself with love and in light to others as they ask and as they wish.

We are pleased to have spoken through this instrument and would, at this time, like to transfer this contact. I am Hatonn.

(Jim channeling)

I am Hatonn. I am now with this instrument and greet you all once again in love and light. At this time it is our privilege to be joined by our brothers and sisters of Laitos for the purpose of offering our conditioning vibration to those in this group who would wish to experience it and to be aided in deepening their meditation by so doing. If each who would wish to experience our conditioning vibration would simply mentally request such, our brothers and sisters of Laitos will pass among you and aid as requested. We shall pause at this time. I am Hatonn.

(Pause)

I am Hatonn, and am with this instrument once again. We thank each in this group for allowing us to join them in their meditations. We would at this time ask for the permission to contact the one known as C so that we may speak a few words through this new instrument. It is our privilege to offer this service to new instruments and those wishing to become instruments in the transmission of our thoughts. If he would relax, we would now transfer this contact. I am Hatonn.

(C channeling)

I am Hatonn, and am with this instrument. As always, it is a privilege to work with any who seek this form of service. We of Hatonn always bring a simple message of love and always welcome new voices with which to speak. On your planet there are many desires that many do not quite yet understand. They seek, but sometimes lack one small push, you might say …

(A line of text is missing in the transcript.)

… choose to follow. Those who choose to serve others by the means of what you call channeling are of great assistance to us to aid those that seek, but not yet have the knowledge, the experience to feel our vibration.

We, as all Confederation members, are always willing to aid any who seek, who desire our assistance in their chosen path. We are always available to you in your meditations at any time that you ask us to join you. We are honored, privileged that we have so many who have chosen channeling as a means of service within this group, and are more than happy to work with the new ones as well as those more experienced, and we assure those within this group who seek also to channel our words—concepts, that we will work with them.

It may seem at times, my friends, that so many within a group may seem a luxury at times, but we assure you that once a channel has learned and exercises the ability, the ability will be there, and when the entity who has gained ability is needed, he or she may be of great service to other entities who seek, for you know that on your planet, that within the illusion many times groups have a way of finding harmony within them, but your various means of existence often pull groups physically apart while they may be mentally, spiritually, always attached.

That is one reason why it's always pleasing to us that many begin a group, seek similar ability, for they can aid others after the original group has begun to go, as you would say, their own ways within the illusion. We always thank this group and all others who listen, for we seek to serve, as do you, aiding in our humble way, your seeking. We also learn in experience through you and by interacting to the extent that we can, with you.

We would, at this time, transfer our contact to another instrument, for we would like, if we may, to exercise others within this group who seek to channel our humble words. I am Hatonn.

(L channeling)

I am Hatonn. I am with this instrument, and again I greet you in the love and the light of the Creator of all that is vast and small, infinite and finite. It is amusing to us in using these descriptive terms to perceive the implausibility of these terms, for they denote the contrast between that which is of reality and that which is of the illusion. For example, the terms infinite and finite both are constructed to attempt to define that which is beyond comprehension, for while you may quickly and readily acknowledge from past experience that the term "infinite" is without picture within your mental construction, has it occurred to you that the term "finite" is of equal caliber?

Is there, within your world or any other, that which is finite? The substance of your illusion is the result of creative efforts by each of you, both individually and collectively, for your illusion is constructed—tailor-made, as you say—to support your quest for knowledge and growth. As the details of your illusion are of this same fabric, each is a facet of a particular lesson and, therefore, a fragment of your experience, that experience which continues as you do yourself

Thus, we perceive the nebulous quality of the term "finite," for what can be finite, yet continue in existence throughout that which we label "infinite"? The term "infinite," on the other hand, although readily acknowledged as incomprehensible, is equally finite, for that which exists, exists only in the now, for in reality now is the future, now is the past, now is.

My brothers and sisters, we do not wish for you to be alarmed, fearing perhaps that we have chosen to embark upon lengthy philosophical discussions without reference to your present situation, for there is, as you might say, a method to our madness. The temptation exists to regard your efforts towards service as money placed within a bank, drawing sufficient interest to pay for a ticket out of this illusion when the harvest time arrives. My brothers and sisters, today is the day in which the rent comes due, as this instrument would say, for the attainment of your service could be regarded as compounded …

(Side one of tape ends.)

(L channeling)

I am Hatonn. I am with this instrument and we find your own instruments humorous.

The interest compounded upon your savings of service, so to speak, are not stored up, but rather returned to you instantly that you may use your gains to further your own efforts toward the development of your ability toward selfless service. Do not be disheartened that your efforts toward service seem tainted because of your awareness that your efforts result from a desire to improve yourself sufficiently to attain harvestability, for this process is within the order of the universe.

The interest gained is the establishment of a path which through habit will more and more smoothly and assuredly guide your efforts toward a selfless form of service. Have you noticed, my brothers and sisters, that although the initial acts of service to others may come with difficulty and only after lengthy forethought and argument with one's more selfish nature, after a sufficient number of these experiences occur, you may suddenly realize that the path toward service to others, while still motivated by service to self, has become more easily acquired as your nature, your vibration, has been adjusted through your efforts toward an automatic choice or orientation toward service to others without tremendous amounts of lengthy forethought and planning.

For this reason, do not be disheartened by the selfishness which exists within all of us, for this characteristic being of negative or selfish polarization acts as a catalyst which results in selfless performance of service to others. We would encourage, therefore, all efforts toward service to others, however motivated, and would comfort those who find their own selfish nature disquieting.

At this time we would attempt to answer questions that you might desire to offer. I am Hatonn.

M: Hatonn, how do chemicals bridge the gap between our physical illusion and our spiritual reality?

I am Hatonn. I am aware of your question. My brother, the chemical substance is of a nature that is unpolarized, yet, as a key, is capable of unlocking synaptic blocks which are used to prevent the subconscious mind from overriding the wishes of the conscious mind. These synaptic blocks are of the substance of your physical illusion, yet one of the rules, so to speak, of your illusion gives dominance to the conscious mind over the subconscious mind, thus allowing you, within the illusion, to refuse communication from your higher self, if such is your choice. The chemical key, or drug, acts to dissolve temporarily those blocks constructed by the conscious mind, allowing the subconscious mind's receptions to be transmitted directly to the conscious mind. The quality of the reception is the result of the orientation of the conscious mind during the period of time in which the synaptic block is removed.

For this reason, the same individual may, with the same key, receive either enjoyable and encouraging or unpleasant and discouraging experiences.

May we answer you further?

M: Yes. Essentially, you remove the chemical inhibitors in the brain to allow the subconscious to come to a conscious level. The images that we then become conscious of, are they a creation of our own—or the spiritual type things that are experienced, are they real spiritual experiences? Are they experiences we are creating for ourselves, or is it a perception of reality that we're then capable of seeing?

I am Hatonn. My brother, all experience is real. For this reason, we suggest that you may desire to rephrase your question.

M: OK. Are you actually having a spiritual experience or are you creating a mental illusion?

I am Hatonn. I am aware of your question. The receptions of the conscious mind from the subconscious mind are similar in nature to that which is referred to by your people as radio or television. The quality of the image received is solely defined by the source of the image which can be of numerous transmitters, so to speak. The image may be the result of a seeking conveyed by the subconscious mind for a specific experience or communication. However, it may also be of the nature of a seeking for an unusual or exciting created experience to entertain.

The subconscious mind can only convey that which is desired and can only attain that which is earned. The spiritual experience, as you refer to it, is the result of a calling within the individual for a specific type of contact or experience and as all vacuums are filled, this calling is answered. However, we would caution you that a calling for an experience which may be characterized by the description, "I want to see God, but not have it really count," will result in a form of entertainment that is characterized by a pervasive aura of goodness.

May we answer you further, my brother?

M: One last part. You mentioned that [if] the subconscious has made a calling for an experience and you are in tune to do that, the drug will help you bridge that gap. How can it be [done] more easily without the assistance of the chemical promoter?

I am Hatonn. My brother, the drug, or key, cannot provide that which has not been earned. For example, the key cannot acquire for one the skills of the adept without the learning or discipline. Conversely, the learning and discipline themselves are sufficient to dissolve the synaptic block if such is your desire. Often this occurs during times of meditation or sleep or prayer, for these are times in which the persuasive contact of the conscious mind with the illusion ebbs and the individual is less convinced of the reality of the illusion within which he or she functions.

To most easily activate—correction—deactivate the synaptic block is through prayer or meditation, for at these times the orientation of the individual's calling is firmly established and the nature of the desired experience controlled by the individual. The chemical synaptic key, conversely, is subject to the whims and changing moods of the individual and thus may cause the entry of both angels and dragons, so to speak. For this reason, we strongly recommend the paths of prayer or meditation over the use of chemical substances.

May we answer you further?

M: No thank you, Hatonn. You've been very helpful.

As always, my brother, we thank you for the opportunity to serve in our small manner. Is there another question.

Carla: I'd just like to clarify something. You mentioned several times that you only get those things which you earn in the drug experience and I was trying to link that up with other material with which I'm familiar and also with my own experience, and it seems that in Ra's terminology, the conscious use of the polarization towards service to others and the desire to worship or praise seems to aid in the experiencing of, as you put it, the angels, rather than the dragons, which would suggest that one were not at the mercy, shall we say, of a drug, but rather had a cooperative effort with it, given that enough energy centers were activated and aware of the seriousness of the experience to use it.

I have no desire to advocate the use of drugs. I just wanted to clarify that. Is this concept correct, that it is the opening of the energy centers, the desire to polarize, etc., that you mean when you say you get what you earn?

I am Hatonn. This is correct. If we may reiterate more clearly our words upon the subject. To give an example—if an individual who has not chosen a direction of polarization consumes a chemical substance designed to dissolve synaptic blocks, the individual is at the mercy, so to speak, of his or her own fluctuations of polarization, which tend to fluctuate more uncontrollably in the absence of your contemporary illusion. Therefore, our statement concerning the angels and dragons.

The individual who is polarized, however, has established a consistent nature within the subconscious mind which acts as a controlling influence on the nature of the receptions transmitted to the conscious mind. Therefore, that individual which has earned his stripes, so to speak, has the ability to receive a consistent quality of perception, whereas that individual [who] is undecided will find the quality varies wildly. The intensity of the experience is also affected in the same fashion.

May we answer you further?

Carla: No thank you, Hatonn. Your clarity is exceeded only by your prolixity.

I am Hatonn. If it were possible, we would blush. We thank you. Is there another question?

(Pause)

As always, the music of the spirits pervading the night draw us closer as we long to share more fully the incredible beauty of your home. We thank you deeply for sharing with us. I am Hatonn.

L/L Research

Monday Meditation
September 21, 1981

(Carla channeling)

I am Latwii. Ho, ho, ho. This was intended to come through another channel, however, we needed to begin with this channel in order to give confidence to the one known as Jim. We greet you through this instrument in the love and in the light of our infinite Creator. We are at the same time extremely glad and extremely sorry to be speaking to you instead of the brothers and sisters of your special teachers, the ones of Hatonn. However, this group entity has again returned to its duty, working in the Far East, as you would call it, working against the spread of disharmony upon your planet. We have been conditioning the one known as Jim while we have been speaking through this instrument and we would again attempt to speak through the one known as Jim. We leave this instrument in gratitude for her quick senses of inner listening and in hopes of speaking through her many times in the future. We thank this instrument. I will now leave this instrument. I am called by your group Latwii.

(Jim channeling)

I am Latwii, and am with this instrument. We great you once again in the love and the light of the infinite Creator. We are please to be able to make this contact through this instrument, for we are aware that this instrument shall be away from this group in the near future and he desires being able to continue this service as he embarks upon his journey and it will be necessary for this instrument to be able to initiate contacts with the Confederation and with our vibration when he is on his own.

We would speak a few words this evening upon the subject of harmony, for the vibration and condition of harmony is one which is not frequently found upon your planet, as is evidenced by the condition of your world situation at the present.

Harmony is that state of being in tune with the infinite Creator which is achieved by desire. A desire for unification, a desire for knowing and experiencing that fullness of being which is the Creator within. Harmony is that force which helps to unite people in the relationships with each other, but it must be sought before it can be found and it is unfortunate but it appears that few upon your planet seek harmony for it is an endeavor that includes the welfare of those around you and most of your people are pointed in the direction of their own interests and meeting them as best they can, fearing there will not be enough to go around.

The state of being within the individual which leads to harmony is the same state that opens doors to any step of growth within the individual and that is the receptivity, the openness, and the desire for attaining such a state. It is often too easy to think only of the personal needs, desires, wishes, beliefs and other codes which we set up for ourselves as we judge our lives. It is far too easy to consider only what one wants for oneself, instead of how to blend one's being with another in the state of harmony.

We would suggest to those who are desirous of attaining that state of harmony to consider that it is a state which is achieved with others, a state which is achieved in cooperative effort as individual entities blend their energies with each other, a task which usually entails a type of compromise of positions so that each may share with the other a common position and the sharing of the position, the belief, or the place is that which is harmony within that concept.

We would suggest to those seeking such a balance point with themselves and with those around them that the first step is to give, to recognize the needs, rights and position of those close about you and that this state of giving and accepting and recognizing will be reciprocated by those with whom you are in close contact. For the state of giving is based on the concept of love, that to give is to share that which is love and that which is love is recognized by the inner being of those to whom it is given, even though it may not be given directly as a gift of love but may begin in more modest ways by the simple recognition of another person's needs.

We would suggest that harmony is that process whereby people in close communication join their beings even closer by agreeing to accept each other as they are and to work from that beginning point in a constant balancing of the needs, ideas and beliefs of each party.

We would at this time pause for a moment as our brother Laitos passes among each in your group and makes his vibration available to those who are in need of deepening their meditation and of becoming familiar with the vibrations of the Confederacy. We speak specifically of the one known as L who has expressed this evening a desire to become a channel. We pause for a moment as our brother Laitos passes among you.

(Pause)

I am Latwii, and am once again with this instrument. We would at this time like to open this meeting to any questions. If any present would have a question, we would do our best to make an answer. Are there any questions?

Carla: I've been reading some cosmic communication ideas which have been run down by some people in the East and I really have no doubt as to the truth of it, but I know they are not precisely in the same company with you guys and I was wondering what your view was among your particular branch of the Confederation of what's happening here? What about the great concern for the survival of leaders? Does that have some kind of implication as to what will happen at the beginning of the new age vibrations with a lot of old vibration people surviving?

I am Latwii, and am aware of your question and would answer you, my sister, simply by saying that the most appropriate phrase for this particular phase which your nation and those individuals who lead it are going through would perhaps be, the first shall be last and the last shall be first. For those who would seek to gain the whole world and yet lose their souls, what in truth and in spirit have they gained? For to hold on to that which is of the material world, that which has up to this point in the evolution of human history been unable to completely fulfill human entities upon your plane, to hold on so tightly to that which is of the material is to focus the energies of one's being in a direction which is likened unto building a house upon sand, and we would suggest that those who engage in such activities and have no concern for the welfare of those whom they are governing, or those whom they have been chosen to serve, those whom it is a privilege to serve, these shall find that not only shall they not be serving such people or be in such high positions, but shall find themselves at the bottom of the pit of their own being which they have dug with their own hands.

And we would suggest that the new age shall see many different responses to the flow of energy which is now sweeping over your planet and you may expect to see the most absurd of dramas appearing upon your world stage, for all the energies of the universe, it would seem, shall be sweeping across the stage of your planet. And you shall see many wonders, but those energies may be channeled and focused into creative elements and centers by those who are truly concerned with serving those who are their brothers and sisters. And to focus in the direction of the spirit is the means by which true survival shall be attained.

May we answer you further, my sister?

Carla: Well, I had a couple of other questions which you may answer at your discretion, of course. I've been very impressed by the Cosmic Awareness things that I've read and I was wondering what your relationship in the Confederation was with this particular source? Is it a planetary source within the Confederation? Is it another source? What is the relationship between the two?

I am Latwii, and am aware of your question and can answer best by suggesting that the source of which you speak is a source which is most well known to those who are familiar with the works of Edgar Cayce. The source which is known as Cosmic Awareness appears to be simply that: an awareness of the state of being which is described as cosmic or of the consciousness of all being, and this source of information is now proceeding to reveal unto those of your people who are concerned about the new age, the pathway or process by which each may attune to these universal forces which we have spoken of as proceeding into your reality with such great speed at the present time, so to speak.

We cannot say whether the information revealed by this source is correct or incorrect for it can never be known at the moment information is given whether it is correct or not, for the mere giving of information alters the situation which is being described. We would suggest with all sources of information, including especially our own, that those who are contacted with information of this nature consider carefully within themselves what they themselves believe, to evaluate carefully on your own concerning what you are reading or hearing and to make those judgments in light of competing or opposing information. For within your world you will discover there are infinite sources of information and it is your task as entities upon your planet to sort and sift through the infinite variety of information available and to chose that which speaks within your own being.

May we answer you further?

Carla: Yes, my brother. Then I see that confirms what I thought about Cosmic Awareness, was that it did seem to be a planetary vibration in that, like the Cayce vibration, it comes from a much higher plane, inner plane of our own planet, close to the Akashic Record. I had pretty much of an idea in my head as to the type of information that they were giving and why they gave that type of information, as opposed to the philosophy that you give, and I just wondered if you would care to say anything on that subject in confirmation or changing of what I had basically thought?

I am Latwii, and would add only that information of a specific nature is most difficult to express clearly for the future, as you know is never fixed. Direction, propensities, tendencies and likelihoods of directions of energy are the most easily pinpointed and transmitted information, but to say where an infinite variety of energies will eventually coincide is very difficult and is a task that we of the Space Confederation do not attempt with these types of contacts for the distortion factor would soon cause the information to become nearly worthless. It is for this reason that we attempt to give the basic groundwork and philosophy of love and light which we feel are so important to your people at this time. We do not feel that the revealing of specific names and dates and places and events is most beneficial to those within your meditation group for this information can be obtained elsewhere and we would be most pleased if we could, in our effort, plant the seeds of meditation, of love, of light, and of the seating of the divinity within each of your people's being. We would suggest that those sources which are focusing in the area of more specific information can be of great value, but must be carefully evaluated upon their performance and we would suggest being very cautious in the area of accepting, without further investigation, any specific information which is obtained, wherever it might be obtained.

May we answer you further, my sister.

Carla: Well, just a little bit. I would like to thank you, because I think you do work with the basic things and teach us love and light, but I wanted to check out the Cosmic Awareness people because I was just interested in them at this point. I made a few basic assumptions. Number one, that they were planetary; number two, that they were giving more precise information because, being planetary, they had a right to do so; and, number three, that they were able to put their probability guesses through because of the particular configuration of one channel, Paul Shockley. A lighter trance, the type of contact we have with you would never work for that information. It would take a different vibration. If you want to confirm any of those three. You confirmed the first one, I just wondered about the second two.

I am Latwii, and we would conclude our comments upon this subject simply by saying that the particular type of trance which is used in this contact of the Space Confederation is most beneficial to the type of message which we have to offer and are also appreciative of the efforts of those who would use the trance medium, for such an entity is indeed able to transmit information of a much different frequency or nature to that which we are able to transmit through our light trances, as you have spoken of them. We would suggest to those who wish to become more familiar with the contact situation to investigate the nature of meditation on their own, so they may themselves discover what variety and types of information are available within their own being.

Are there any other questions?

Carla: No, thank you.

Questioner: I have a question. You are aware of my desire to learn more about channeling and to serve as a channel. I ask how you would advise me to proceed in this matter?

I am Latwii, and, my brother, we would answer you simply by saying that to desire this type of service is the most important ingredient for those who wish to become channels. For it is indeed a service that you render and within your own being it is necessary to search and to seek that you might be made an instrument and might kindle within yourself that desire to share the love and the light of the infinite Creator which resides within your being. We would suggest as well a daily system of meditation of your own design. We would suggest meditating at the same time each day so that you might develop a pattern of relaxation and communication within your own being, so that you might find that point of centering from which you might be of service. We would also suggest that a simple prayer might be used to ask that divine guidance be with you as you serve and that you might be made an instrument of that service of the infinite Creator. We would also suggest that frequent experiences with a channel who has experience, such as those present this evening, may be of use in making the vibration of the Confederation more familiar to you.

May we be of further service?

Questioner: You've answered my questions, thank you.

We thank you. Is there another question?

Carla: No, thank you.

We are very pleased to have been able to speak these few words and to share our thoughts through this instrument with you this evening. We would at this time take our leave of this instrument and, as always, we leave you in the love and in the light of the infinite Creator. I am Latwii. Adonai, my friends. Vasu borragus.

Intensive Meditation
September 22, 1981

(Unknown channeling)

I am with this instrument. I greet you, my friends, in the love and light of the infinite Creator. Tonight we enjoyed listening with you to the music, and we are, as you, sometimes sad when the sounds come to the end. But we say that what we seek has *(inaudible)* you see as convinced are really only starting points of new beginnings as things in your natural world now begin to die or lay dormant with the coming of your fall, they really are only in a *(inaudible)* state where they shall begin anew after this rather bare period of your fall and winter. But even as they cease to be green they still are beautiful and still look to the sunlight though they may seem weak. New times will seem to fade to use your *(inaudible)* you still have sparked a light in themselves at will. You will blossom. *(Inaudible)* that ending are an *(inaudible)* in your existence in your illusion and that as you go you will see past the *(inaudible)*. They will no longer seem as real you *(inaudible)* come ever closer to the light to the Creator.

We are known as *(inaudible)* to you. We are always available to you and your search for love and light. We are now *(inaudible)* we would ask the instrument if he would relax and *(inaudible)* analysis and repeat the words. We are now trying to jump ahead. We *(inaudible)* speak only as the words come to him. So often new instruments they tend to try to get ahead of themselves and will at times lose parts of concepts we are attempting to speak and will find themselves, as you say, "grasping for a limb" when, in reality, the limb is right there under them, and they have a hold of it. So we say to this instrument that he need not rush or try to get ahead, but to simply speak as words comes to him.

We have a new *(inaudible)* and will note that our contact with this instrument is improving. We say once again that your world and its seeming ending are illusion as are many—correction—as are the situations you face in as what you see as your day-to-day existence. The problems that each illusion presents, that each illusion—correction—each situation that is there to learn from is [for] you to see, examine, learn so that you may grow with the use of meditation. The lessons will oftentimes become easier to see and to grow beyond in your seeking an awareness of the rough life that is you and all things.

We are known to you as *(inaudible)*. We will leave you now in love and light of the one infinite Creator. Adonai, my friends.

(Pause)

I am Hatonn, and I am with this instrument. We have some trouble contacting this instrument, for he has begun to channel more the way in which he feels are initial contact attempts has become milder and he at this point [is] sometimes unsure if the contact is being *(inaudible)*. But [we] assure him that he will grow in confidence as he exercises more and he will more easily more recognize the contact attempt.

We are Hatonn. *(Inaudible)* is ever calling for truth or love. Your people will often think of themselves in hopeless situations where they are unable to move in any direction, for they are forever being pulled by various groups who try different methods and philosophies, [seeking] at times the same thing. In your world it is common to find most people seemingly unable to know which way to turn. What they should do to help themselves out of the rut that has been worn in the road … not nearly as many can see that it is easier to be in the light when one has pulled themselves out of the little rut. So many do not want to try to climb in order to see, but blindly *(inaudible)*.

We are Hatonn, [and] are aware of the great difficulties within your vision. We can see the horror it is to pull oneself up and keep from falling back, but when one truly seeks the light no matter if one falls back they may rise again stronger with eyes that they more clearly see the direction [from] which the light shines, and more *(inaudible)* light as it radiates within *(inaudible)*. We of Hatonn are ever ready to aid any to climb from the rut into the light. We shall be with you in your meditation, seeking with you, in [the] love and light of the infinite Creator. I am Hatonn. I will now leave this instrument. Adonai, my friends. ✧

Sunday Meditation
September 27, 1981

(C channeling)

I am Laitos, and I am with this instrument. We greet you in [the] love and light of our infinite Creator. We are most privileged to be with you this evening. We have but a brief message and that is that we are *(inaudible)* we are with each who wish to experience more fully that channeling vibration *(inaudible)*.

l am Laitos. I am Laitos, and am once again with this instrument. We are only too happy and feel privileged to work with those who seek to be of service *(inaudible)* known as channeling to you and tell you that we will be with those who call to us in their meditation *(inaudible)* to serve others is a very—correction—is a positive step toward your own growth in your seeking to become ever more aware of the Creator and we say that the activity you call channeling is but one humble means of service within your everyday lives.

You are constantly exposed to situations in which each makes his own conscious decisions as to whether that individual will serve others or only partially help others or to shut the others out. In your search to become aware you find that ever increasingly so in the situations you will less and less refuse others but will become more in tune with the feeling and needs of others in relation to your dealings with them. But we say that to aid, serve the others, we say that it occurs only as you begin to know self or to know oneself is to know the other, for it ultimately boils down to the awareness of that we all are one.

In groups or as individuals, you seek and we of Laitos again say that we will aid your seeking for we seek to serve, for as you, we seek to know ourselves and seek to grow as do you and your peoples. We are known to you as Laitos. We are your friends and we are your fellow travelers on a road that you have begun to tread. We thank you for the opportunity to speak briefly and will at this time leave this instrument. We are known to you as Laitos. Adonai, my friends.

(Carla channeling)

I am Hatonn, and I greet you, my friends, in the love and in the light of our infinite Creator. We were attempting to contact the one known as L, both previously and before we spoke through this instrument, but we find that this instrument's mind is somewhat preoccupied with the recent experiences which it has undergone and therefore, we happily will speak through this instrument.

We thank each instrument for the service that it provides in allowing us to share our thoughts with you for whatever worth they may be. My friends, these are the ways and the parables of service. As we have said to you before—to those who are present—speaking of meditation, of seeking, and of the love that unified and creates us all, is speaking of those things which are known. Therefore, it is possible for us to continue.

Each of you present in this domicile is at this time seeking to become aware of the ways of service. Thus we would ask you to visualize the flower—the flower who decides that it will not be of service and will not accept service, but will remain independent. Sun shines upon the flower and before the flower thinks, it opens and receives light. Rain falls upon the flower and before the flower can realize it, its roots have drunk and retained health and growth. The bud opens and becomes the blossom. And before the flower has time to think, that animal which you call the bee has taken from it and given to it the propagation of its life that it may continue. And the services that it has given, why, it has forgotten. It has inadvertently been beautiful, giving to each passerby a vision of perfection, of radiance, and of beauty. It has given to the bee who gave it life, the honey which sustains the bee, and has breathed out into the atmosphere that which the humans need to survive—the oxygen which those of your planet who are your peoples, must have.

My friends, there is no way that you can refrain from accepting service and being of service. You are interlocked and meshed in the tapestry of giving and receiving and it takes a great deal of effort to refrain from the realization of all that you receive and all that you may give. We are sad to report that among your peoples it is not uncommon for people to realize that they are receiving gifts from others, but it is very common for people to refrain from the realization that they have many gifts to give and that they are giving those gifts without effort, without trying, with their very existence.

For each of you, my friends, like a flower, is beautiful and radiant and perfect and although you may not see yourself in this [light], there are those who do, and who find in each of you an inspiration of thought, of feeling that that person needs and realizes, although you have no consciousness of being of service.

My friends, the beginning of service comes before you are even aware of the process, as each of you are inevitably of service to others in your behavior, in your actions, in your thoughts. Thus, perhaps, before you try so very hard to learn the ways of service, it may be a good beginning to give thanks to the love that is within you, that unifies you with all that there is and that creates in you a heart that receives and gives back that love in so many ways, with so many devices, that your life is a flowing tapestry of the giving and the receiving of service. Never, my friends, are you out of touch with the life of service. In your most selfish or secluded moment, you are but pausing and learning, adding your sums wrongly and thinking again, for the essence of your life is love and it is out of your hands. You, like the flower, will glow, according to your nature and those about you will realize the love within you, without effort, without trying, without pain.

My friends, there is much that we could say about the kind of service that is conscious, consciously chosen, consciously pursued and at another time we shall speak these things in as many ways as we feel might be helpful, but at this time we wish to give you a bedrock of understanding about your nature. My friends, you are love. You are a part of the original Thought of the Creator. There is not any variation from this simple understanding of yourself, and thus, if your feelings about your efforts in this incarnation are that you could be trying harder, that you could be doing better, that you could be more loving, more giving—lay these thoughts to rest. It is well to have a will to be of service, but it is first well to know your nature, to feel the bedrock of love, to feel your unity, your harmony, your interdependence, the meshing of your lives with all your brothers and sisters. You are all that you seek.

Thus, my friends, bloom as you will and remember to give thanks, for the nature of the Creation is one of great joy and there is much thanks to offer that we may experience living in such a creation. Step out of the illusion at any time this bedrock strays too far from your feet, for it is quite central to your progress that you remain aware of your identity.

We would at this time transfer the contact. We thank you for allowing us to share these thoughts and ask you to take what you will from them. I am Hatonn.

(Jim channeling)

I am Hatonn, and am with this instrument and greet you all once again in love and light. It is our privilege at this time to offer ourselves in the answering of any queries which those present might have the use in the asking. Are there any questions at this time?

D: Hatonn, the entity known to us as Jesus, on his leaving our planet, told us that he would leave what he called the Holy Spirit behind to guide and direct us through our daily lives. Would you, or could you classify yourself as part of this Holy Spirit?

I am Hatonn. My brother, in response to this query, may we say that many are those who are numbered among the legions of light, the same light sources and messengers which the one known to your peoples as Jesus of Nazareth was also a member. When this entity known to you as Jesus spoke the words that you have just recited he was speaking of many such as ourselves and others of the Confederation who offer themselves as the most humble of messengers.

We and our brothers and sisters of the Confederation offer our messages of love and light as a comfort and an inspiration to those of your planet who call for our service. In joy do we offer this service; in love do we send our thoughts; in light do we experience the oneness of the Creator. All of this we offer as a service to your peoples.

There is also another source which you may find that may also be described as the Comforter, spoken of by the entity called Jesus. This source may be found by each entity so seeking in meditation, for as you still your mind, as you open your heart and as you open your innermost being to the Creator in love, there shall you find that small, still voice within, which shall also be of great comfort to you as you proceed on that path of spiritual evolution.

We of Hatonn have through many instruments and in many of your meditations spoken of the necessity for meditation for those who wish to seek the Creator. Within meditation shall you find the Creator. Within meditation shall you find the fruits of your labor of evolution.

May we answer you further, my brother?

D: I would like for you just to maybe to expand on what part of that—that my own desire for finding this still, small voice within is extremely great and through my meditation recently the … I've had a difficult time stilling my mind and realizing the fruits of opening myself up to the Creator. Am I being too impatient? Do I need to just stick with it or do you have any comment on that?

I am Hatonn. My brother, it is often the case with those expressing great desire to seek the Creator that the meditative state will at first resound with this great calling and this great desire. It is not unusual and should not be given too much emphasis or concern. Remain steady in your seeking and know that at each moment that you seek in the manner of meditation, that there is a work that is being done within your being, whether you are aware of its fruits or not.

The art of meditation, stated most simply, is that the seeker becomes more and more aware and conscious of this work that is done while meditation is undertaken. If at first you have few glimpses as to the nature of this work and in fact feel that little work could be accomplished amidst such clamor, rest your concerns and your mind will also rest.

May we answer you further, my brother?

D: No. Thank you very much.

We thank you, as always, for allowing us to serve. Is there another question at this time?

L: Yes. I've been trying to do my meditations early in the morning and have been having considerable *(inaudible)*. Is there any suggestions you could make to improve my contact?

I am Hatonn. My brother, we could only add in your case to that which we have just spoken, that your desire to seek the Creator in your meditations is your strongest ally and that this desire shall open new means for you to experience this contact. We cannot make specific suggestions as to when or how you might structure your meditative periods, but can only suggest that any time which you feel a desire for such contact might be utilized, no matter how short.

May we answer you further, my brother?

L: Yes. Who was the source of the writings by one known here as Saint Paul?

I am Hatonn. Unfortunately, my brother, information of this nature we may not divulge, for there are those who would be, shall we say, adversely affected if a full disclosure of this information was made. We do not wish to appear to evade questions of a serious nature, but we are unable to give this type of information concerning entities who are well known, shall we say, and much revered by your peoples.

May we be of further assistance, my brother?

L: No, you've answered my question. Thank you.

Again, we thank you. Is there another question at this time?

(Pause)

I am Hatonn. As always, it has been a great honor to join this group in meditation. We would at this time transfer this contact and close through another instrument. I am Hatonn.

(L channeling)

I am Hatonn, and I greet you once more in the love and the light of that which you refer to as the Creator. It is a singular pleasure to experience the presence and the intensity of striving of those within this room tonight. My brothers, my sisters …

(Side one of tape ends.)

… we are unable to express fully the gratitude we feel for the opportunity to share what little we can contribute with those who strive that they may contribute so very much. We thank you for this honor and for the service you render us in patiently listening to our feeble efforts. In the love and the light, we of Hatonn bid you adieu, "to God." I am Hatonn.

(Carla channeling)

I am Nona. I greet you in the love and the light of the infinite Creator. We are called here for healing vibrations at this time. We thank you for the opportunity to be of service.

(Carla channels a melody from Nona.)

Sunday Meditation
October 4, 1981

(Jim channeling)

I am Hatonn, and I greet you, my friends, in the love and in the light of the infinite Creator. We are especially pleased to be able to speak to this group this evening. We pause for a moment while an adjustment is made.

(Pause)

I am Hatonn. We are again with this instrument. As we were saying, we are always honored to be asked to join your meditations and are privileged to speak our words, humble though they be, to those whose ears and hearts are opened to the message of love.

My friends, this evening we would say a few words about the perception of love by entities upon your planet. We would begin by saying that there is no shortage of that commodity, shall we say, of love. Many times each of this group, we are certain, has wondered if such a thing as love might actually exist upon this planet, for much seems to be of an inharmonious nature. There seems to be much in the way of contention and strife between peoples, between groups and between nations, and this contention and its manifestation is apparent to all. Many there are among your peoples who seek in one way or another to speak of love and seem stifled to seek for love and seem to come away empty. Many there are among your people who seem to experience nothing of the fruits of love. Many there are among your people whose knowledge of love seems to begin and end with the self.

My friends, we do not deny that this illusion of contention and strife is quite heavy upon your planet. We see, as we look from our vantage point of the density of love, and we see each of your peoples engaged in activities which may be seen from various levels. These activities appear to most on your planet to be struggles for survival and gain for self, but, my friends, we must emphasize that this is an illusion in which you dwell. It is an illusion which has a very important purpose. Each activity, each situation, indeed each thought an entity encounters, serves as catalyst, an ingredient which of itself has no polarity, has no charge, shall we say, but when interacted with by an individual has the capability of allowing that individual to perceive in a variety of manners.

Each individual has certain lessons to learn. These lessons will be expressed and pointed out by the reaction which the individual makes as a result of catalyst. Each entity has available to it the full range and power of love as a response to each situation. You might see each situation with a range of possible responses. At one end we have the concern of the individual for self. At the other end we have love. An individual will place itself at the proper position within this range of responses: there may be strife; there may be confusion; there may be frustration; there may be momentary acceptance and lapses into anger and then acceptance; there may be indifference; there may be a loving acceptance of the situation and all entities within it.

Always is this acceptance and love a possibility, and you may yourself look at each situation which you find yourself in and you may observe in retrospect your response to each situation and you may observe as you consciously seek for love, understanding, compassion and forgiveness, that you indeed are slowly, but surely, ever so surely, proceeding along the path of love. For it has been truly said, that those who seek shall find, that those who knock upon the door of love shall find that door opened unto them and shall find the bounty of love pouring forth from their very being, for that door upon which you knock is within your heart of hearts, may we say, and as you seek for love and understanding, each seeking is as a knock upon this door.

Each time that you find one more ounce, shall we say, of love added to the scales of your own response you shall find the balance tipping towards love. It is not often in your illusion that one finds love at every turn. It is most often the case that entities discover another part of the range of responses available, but, may we say that love does make itself available at every turn in your activities, for it is within your own being and therefore, your own grasp.

(Pause)

I am Hatonn. We allowed this instrument to pause for a moment. We shall continue.

We are aware that there are a number of entities present this evening who wish to exercise their beginning abilities to serve as channels. We pass among this group of entities exercising each in turn and making our vibrations available for the familiarizing and vocalizing, if this is acceptable to each entity. We would remind each new channel that the relaxing of the mind and the refraining from analysis is most important in this endeavor.

We would, at this time, begin with the one known as R and attempt to speak a few words through this new instrument. We will now transfer this contact to the one known as R. I am Hatonn.

(Pause)

(Jim channeling)

I am Hatonn. I am with this instrument once again. We feel that we have a good contact with the one known as R. If he would simply speak our words which are present in his mind we would then continue the message that he does perceive. We shall attempt this contact again. We now transfer once again to the one known as R. I am Hatonn.

(Pause)

(Jim channeling)

I am Hatonn. We thank the one known an R for his attempts in transmitting our message. We shall be with him in the future for renewed attempts.

We now move to the one known as S, and if she would relax we shall now transfer this contact to this instrument. I am Hatonn.

(Pause)

(Jim channeling)

I am Hatonn, and am with this instrument once again. We feel we have quite a strong contact with the one known as S and would suggest the relaxing once again by the expelling of one or two deep breaths for this new instrument. We will attempt once again to make our thoughts available to the one known as S. I am Hatonn.

(S channeling)

I am Hatonn. I am …

(Jim channeling)

I am Hatonn. We thank the one known as S for her efforts in speaking our words. We assure this entity that the words which it was perceiving in its mind were indeed our thoughts and the simple speaking of the words would continue their flow through this new instrument's mind. We thank this entity for its great desire and we shall now pass to the one known as D1. If she would relax and refrain from analysis, we would attempt to speak a few words through this new instrument. I am Hatonn.

(Pause)

(Jim channeling)

I am Hatonn. We are quite pleased with our contact with this new instrument and shall attempt at a future time to renew and improve this contact. We are aware of the difficulty of vocalizing our thoughts in a large group. We move now to the one known as D2, and shall attempt to transmit our thoughts through this new instrument. If he would relax and refrain from analysis we shall now transfer this contact. I am Hatonn.

(Jim channeling)

I am Hatonn. We are aware that there is some degree of analysis that is interfering with this contact with this new instrument. We would assure this instrument that our thoughts are being correctly perceived and need only be spoken. We shall attempt this contact once again. We now transfer to the one known as D2. I am Hatonn.

(D2 channeling)

I am Hatonn, and I greet you through this new instrument. We are pleased with the progress of the instrument. I am Hatonn.

(Jim channeling)

I am Hatonn, and am once again with this instrument. May we thank the one known as D2 for his efforts in transmitting our thoughts. We are most pleased with this new instrument's progress this evening and look forward to making our contact available to each of the new instruments at what you would call future meditations.

We are always most gratified by those of your peoples who seek to serve in this manner, for thusly do we find more and more entities willing and able to share our message of love and light and by this service to the one Creator are all lifted into that love and light. We also wish to express our gratitude to each of those in this group who have given the service of patience while we work with the new instruments. We cannot thank each here enough for this service.

We would now open this meditation to the questions if any present would have the queries that are seeking an answer which we may humbly provide. Are there any questions at this time?

D: First of all, I'd like to thank you for your patience with us who try to channel and my first question is the obvious one, it being my first channeling experience. Was the contact I was receiving—or were the words I was vocalizing a genuine contact or was I making those up as I went along?

I am Hatonn. My brother, may we say your vocalization of our words was completely correct. It may seem to new instruments that the thoughts which are perceived within the mind are the thoughts of the instrument itself. We are aware of this phenomenon and assure each new instrument that though it may seem the manufacture of words comes from the instrument, there is indeed a transmission taking place and it is of a fine or ephemeral, shall we say, nature. This transmission shall become more easily accomplished as the instrument is exercised time and again and shall become much easier to, shall we say, perceive as a transmission of our thoughts in your future.

May we answer your further, my brother?

D: No, that subject *(inaudible)*. Thank you very much. I have one other question and I'll stop taking up your time. Our scientists have discovered a great void in the Universe as is visible from this planet, a void—an area of the universe totally void of any apparent galaxies, of stars, of anything at all. It's highly unusual, at least for the way that we visualize the universe. Could you comment on this?

I am Hatonn. My brother, there are many, shall we say, unusual situations throughout the one infinite Creation of the Father. Unusual to many upon your plane, but not so unusual to those who have expanded, shall we say, their field of vision from microscope and telescope to the vision within. The area of which you speak of as a void may also be looked at with other eyes.

Each area or part of the creation is as a being and may be looked upon as a living being of one kind or another. Such voids, as they have been described by your scientists, may be seen to be quite advanced beings existing in the octave density, shall we say, and existing in a manner which we ourselves do not completely understand or even approach in understanding. That all such areas are beings is without a doubt, in our own way of thinking. Just what the nature of the existence of such beings is, we may say we share your ignorance.

May we answer you further, my brother?

D: No, thank you.

We thank you, as always. Is there another question at this time?

M: Yes, I have a question. Perhaps, Hatonn, you can teach me something. In the Ra works, we look at service to self versus the service of others and how an entity grows on each path. I see some conflicts for the service-to-others type forming in a competitive leadership role. I see a very strong service-of-self influence in that type of situation. Is there anything you can teach me that would help me avoid the service-of-self influence and a leadership role?

I am Hatonn. We are aware of your question, my brother, and would attempt to be of service by saying that the range of opportunities available to such an entity in what you might call a leadership role is quite wide and does include that which may be called the service-to-self possibility, but does also include, as we mentioned in our opening message, the possibility of service to others and the full reflection of the experience of love.

It is, my brother, quite the decision of the entity in this position—may we correct this instrument—position to decide what the purpose and the means of putting the purpose into motion shall be for leadership—for leadership of itself does not necessarily imply contention with others against others or in any way imply a disharmonious being within the entity expressing and exercising the leadership. Each position, each role that an entity finds itself in upon your planet has this full range of possibilities available in its exercise. We would simply suggest that to focus upon the role alone is to focus upon the mechanics of the experience and not the heart of the experience. The heart of the experience lies within the entity, within the experience. It is up to each entity to determine what shall be the purpose of the action, what shall be the purpose of the being. How shall love be sought? How shall love be expressed? How shall love be shared? There is no experience upon your planet that does not offer the possibility of the expression of love.

May we answer you further, my brother?

M: No, thank you.

Again, may we thank you. Is there another question at this time?

L: Hatonn, I had an experience several years ago where while sleeping I received some very, very vivid images that I had assumed were recollections of past lives here on this planet. Is that or is that not correct?

I am Hatonn. My brother, we must apologetically refrain from answering this query, for we find that by so doing we would be, shall we say, robbing you of your own efforts in the seeking for the answer. May we aid you in another way, my brother?

L: Within the limitations of your service could you give me information on the following problem? I seem to have recollections of previous lives on this planet, yet during a recent regression, recollected an immediately prior existence on a different planet. Can you give me any information that might help me balance this?

I am Hatonn. My brother, in this area, we may speak in general and say that it is not unusual for an entity who seeks a certain type of information to experience in what you call regressive hypnosis an experience of a lifetime in which this type of information was contained. The lifetime may or may not have been the immediately previous ...

(Side one of tape ends.)

(Jim channeling)

I am Hatonn, and am with this instrument once again. As we were saying, the nature and the strength of the seeking of a certain type of material within the mind are the determining factors for what shall be recalled upon the experience of that known to you as regressive hypnosis. You have had an experience of this nature and you have received a certain type of information. You may ascertain by the efforts of your own seeking in this area whether you have recalled that which was previous to this life or which was more removed.

May we answer you further, my brother?

L: Yes. In either of the situations I described, is it possible I received input from another individual's experiences?

I am Hatonn. My brother, we are somewhat fettered by the reality that all things are possible. We can only say in this instance that the possibility is somewhat slight.

May we answer you further?

L: No, and I thank you for your service.

I am Hatonn. We are most grateful, as well, for your own. Is there another question at this time?

Carla: I'd like to ask a question which you may not be able to answer. In doing the Ra contact work we've run up against an anomaly and, to the best of our intuition, it seems that we need to add an aspect of a sacramental ritual of some sort to the preparation for contact and for protection. Can you in any way confirm this?

I am Hatonn. My sister, we can speak in no way upon this matter. Can we be of service in any other way?

Carla: It's nice having you around.

I am Hatonn. Our pleasure is immense at the invitation to join this group in any manner and we thank you as well. May we answer another question at this time?

(Pause)

I am Hatonn. We shall at this time transfer this contact to another instrument for a closing thought. I am Hatonn.

(L channeling)

I am Hatonn. I am with this instrument. It is our pleasure and our privilege to be of service to those who strive for greater awareness. We are humbly grateful for this opportunity, for unlike many of our brothers of the Federation who serve, we have been blessed with the opportunity to serve those aware of our presence and able to share with us their love of one another and of the universe which contains them, and being a portion of the latter, we are the grateful recipients of that immense gift. My brothers, my sisters, we of Hatonn thank you and ask only that if there be a situation in your daily lives in which we may be of service, however small, however brief, however insignificant, that you would call upon us that we may, with gratitude, in some way return the wonderful gift that you have given us.

In the love and the light of the Creator, I am Hatonn.

(C channeling)

I am Nona, and I am with this instrument. We come tonight in answer to a strong calling for our specialty of healing.

(C channels a song from Nona.)

L/L Research

L/L Research is a subsidiary of Rock Creek Research & Development Laboratories, Inc.

P.O. Box 5195
Louisville, KY 40255-0195

www.llresearch.org

Rock Creek is a non-profit corporation dedicated to discovering and sharing information which may aid in the spiritual evolution of humankind.

ABOUT THE CONTENTS OF THIS TRANSCRIPT: This telepathic channeling has been taken from transcriptions of the weekly study and meditation meetings of the Rock Creek Research & Development Laboratories and L/L Research. It is offered in the hope that it may be useful to you. As the Confederation entities always make a point of saying, please use your discrimination and judgment in assessing this material. If something rings true to you, fine. If something does not resonate, please leave it behind, for neither we nor those of the Confederation would wish to be a stumbling block for any.

CAVEAT: This transcript is being published by L/L Research in a not yet final form. It has, however, been edited and any obvious errors have been corrected. When it is in a final form, this caveat will be removed.

© 2009 L/L Research

Sunday Meditation
October 11, 1981

(L channeling)

I am Hatonn, and I greet you, my brothers, in the love and the light of the infinite Creator. We of Hatonn are pleased and grateful that this assemblage should call upon us, should share with us the love and the unity which pervades this room this night. My brothers, my sisters, we are blessed beyond words at the service you do us in requesting our presence at your gathering. We of Hatonn would like to exercise the various instruments present, if such is within the will of those who have previously sought such contact. At this time our brother Laitos will move among you and if you will but request, he will attempt to share with you his conditioning vibration. We will pause at this time and, for those who request it, our brother of Laitos will perform this function. I am Hatonn.

(Pause)

I am Hatonn. I am again with this instrument. At this time we would attempt to contact the instrument known as C. I am Hatonn.

(C channeling)

I am Hatonn, and I am with this instrument. We once again greet you in the love and light of the one infinite Creator. It is a great privilege to have so many who wish to channel our humble words and messages. Tonight the energy is strong and we will work with various instruments, if you will be patient with us.

Those here seek to advance closer to a greater awareness of the love and light of the infinite Creator. Each here has a method, or as you might term it, a style of growing. Each is different, yet each seeks, each takes of the most powerful tool available to them. The tool is meditation, the quieting of random thought patterns and opening to the love and the light. We of Hatonn share with you your search. We shall aid when called to help you deepen your meditations and to simply be with you, for we are one in the love and light of the infinite Creator. We of Hatonn know that in your illusion that growth is difficult to maintain, for you are sorely distracted by what you would call your everyday hand-to-mouth trying to simply survive. But, my friends, remember that each situation in your lives is an opportunity and a chance to learn, gain insight on yourself and others, and to aid you as a catalyst in your journey.

We are known to you as Hatonn and will at this time transfer this contact to the one known as Jim.

(Jim channeling)

I am Hatonn, and am with this instrument. We greet you once again in love and light. At this time we would attempt to exercise the instrument known as D1. If she would relax and refrain from analysis we would attempt to speak a few words through this new instrument. I am Hatonn.

(D1 channeling)

I am Hatonn, and I am with this instrument. It is a pleasure to be able to speak our thoughts through this new instrument. We are aware of some discomfort and are attempting to adjust our vibration. If she would relax …

(Jim channeling)

I am Hatonn, and am with this instrument. We are very pleased with the progress of the one known as D1 and would assure her that we shall be with her in her meditations to familiarize her with our conditioning vibration so that the experience of channeling might be less discomforting in the future.

We would move now to the instrument known as R and attempt to speak a few words through this new instrument. If he would relax and refrain from analysis we shall now transfer this contact. I am Hatonn.

(Pause)

(Jim channeling)

I am Hatonn. We are aware of some analysis which the one known as R has allowed to create doubt and would once again suggest the refraining from analysis and the relaxing as much as possible, and we would attempt once again to contact the one known as R. I am Hatonn.

(Jim channeling)

I am Hatonn, and am with this instrument. May we assure the one known as R that the thoughts which he was perceiving in his mind were indeed our thoughts and the contact with this instrument is good and we shall attempt at a future date to speak a few words through his channel.

We move now to the one known as S and shall attempt to speak a few words through this new instrument. If she would relax and refrain from analysis and speak the words which she perceives in her mind, we shall now transfer this contact. I am Hatonn.

(S channeling)

I am Hatonn. I am with this instrument. It is a pleasure to greet you through this instrument. We of Hatonn will now attempt to use this instrument in the near future. We are pleased with the progress of this instrument. I am Hatonn.

(Jim channeling)

I am Hatonn, and am with this instrument. May we say we are most pleased with the progress of each of the new instruments and would now move to the one known as D2 and attempt to speak a few words through [his] instrument. If he would also relax and refrain from the analysis, we shall transfer this contact at this time. I am Hatonn.

(D2 channeling)

I am Hatonn, and I am with this instrument. We of Hatonn are most privileged to speak through this new instrument. I am Hatonn.

(Jim channeling)

I am Hatonn, and am with this instrument. We would now move to the one known as E and attempt to speak a few words through this instrument. If he would relax and refrain from analysis, we shall now transfer this contact. I am Hatonn.

(E channeling)

I am Hatonn, and I greet you with this instrument. We are glad to work with any who seek our services. We have a simple message which you all have heard before. It is mainly of love and is all there is. We are very pleased to have gone this far with this instrument. We will now transfer to the one known as Jim. I am Hatonn.

(Jim channeling)

I am Hatonn, and am once more with this instrument. May we take this opportunity to express our extreme gratitude for the patience which each within this circle of meditation has shown this evening as we have attempted to exercise those entities wishing to serve as instruments. We have found quite fertile ground within this group this evening and are most pleased to discover that the desire to serve as instruments of love and light is quite strong within this group. We assure each new instrument that the contact which it experienced this evening was our contact. We are aware that each instrument experienced varying degrees of doubt, unsure of whether the words perceived in the mind were our transmission or were merely thoughts running through the mind of the instrument's own manufacture. We have said before and now reiterate that each instrument shall experience this phenomenon in varying degrees. The doubt shall be diluted as practice is begun again and again within this group.

We suggest to each new instrument that the opening as a channel for our thoughts is both quite simple and quite difficult. It is simple for those who are willing to appear quite foolish and to allow our thoughts to be spoken by their own voices as they appear within their minds. It is quite difficult for those who would wish to maintain a certainty that they shall not appear foolish, for my friends, upon your planet at this time it is the experience of any who seek to love that this experience shall render one quite familiar with the feelings of foolishness. For upon your planet it is quite foolish, it would seem, to love without the expectation of return, to give for no reason other that to give to one who needs and it is true also that for those who seek to be of a specific type of service, that which you call the channeling, that the experience of foolishness shall also be reflected, for it is, apparently, it would seem, to new instruments not a particular energy associated with that instrument which is being allowed to pass through the channel.

We of Hatonn are your brothers and sisters on the search and the journey for love and unity with the Creator. Thus, we are none other that your other selves and that which we transmit through your instrument is none other than the love and the light of the one infinite Creator which exists within your very being. Therefore, it is not something which is alien to you, but which you are most intimately acquainted [with] when you open your being to the experience of the love that resides within.

May we thank each in this group for the patience and the desire to be of such service. At this time we would transfer this contact to another instrument so that we might offer ourselves in the service of answering questions. I am Hatonn.

(C channeling)

I am Hatonn, and I am now with this instrument. We wish at this time to further exercise this channel by offering [otherselves'] questions to him, which shall be for him a new experience and we seek to deepen our contact with this instrument by this means at this time.

Are there any questions?

R: Hatonn, the entity called Sadat—was this entity a wanderer and, if so, from where?

I am Hatonn, and I am aware of your question. My brother, the entity known to you as Sadat was a entity seeking as do you. We cannot, due to the Law of Free Will, tell you whether or not any in your density is or is not what you term a wanderer, but we may say that the one known as Sadat was aware of love and light and was very oriented toward service to others. He was an open receiver and he did much.

As an example [of] one who has begun to strengthen his polarization towards light, he was however, toward the end of his physical existence, subject to the same influences that have affected others of your world who have or had begun to be an example for others, open to both aspects of love and light, and was having difficulties with his polarization, but he is an aware individual such as you seek—correction—are and seek to come more so.

May we answer you further, my brother?

R: No, thank you.

We thank you, my brother. Are there any other questions?

E: I'd like to ask you about something that you were just talking about. When people open up to selfless love, they can appear foolish and it struck me that there was something very sad about Sadat's death in that, as an example, when Nasser died, millions of people were mourning in the streets and there was a tremendous show of sympathy and respect for him, but when Sadat died the ceremonies were closed to the public and there didn't appear to be more than a few thousand real mourners for his death, and I would like to know if that might be an example of the foolishness that you were talking about?

I am Hatonn, and I am aware of your question.

(Side one of tape ends.)

(Jim channeling)

… but were waiting for the clicking of the tape to be …

(The recording tape is blank for a few seconds.)

(Jim channeling)

… the mourning, for it is a step that all must take and, in this case, it would seem that the man known as Sadat was a—how you might say—an individual in an area where many are seeking to be collectively one in a territorial type of behavior. He was a man unafraid to do those things that flowed within and throughout him. He was, for the most part, isolated by choice from many of what you would call his countrymen and fellow entities.

In this particular area of your planet there is great fear and apprehension on many people's parts to fully express their feelings, for in this area—as it seems throughout your planet—people attempt to influence and dominate others through violence and threats thereof. We can assure you that the feelings of many were suppressed because of fear and say that the mourning, as you term it, was much greater than what you were able to see through your information gathering sources. His was for many people of your planet a great loss, for he was an example to them of what one can accomplish by doing that which is flowing within them as manifested by physical actions. In this case the actions were far-reaching, for he occupied a position on your planet of leadership that affected many. But we wish once again to say that death is not necessarily the time to mourn, for as is taught in many of your religions, it is the next step.

May we answer you further?

E: No, thank you. Thank you.

We thank you. We wish to say that one need not affect many by allowing oneself to flow with that light within them, but we say that as one shines, that they are seen and that they, by flowing within themselves, touch others, whether they actively seek to do so or not, for we all are love and light and the flowing of love and light touches all those around those who become aware.

Are there any other questions?

R: Yes. The material that I've been hearing tonight is very similar to material that I have heard before. Perhaps the main reason why I came tonight was because of my interest in the new material that is included in the new book, *The Law of One*, from the social memory complex described as Ra. So, I would like to know what the connection is between what we have been listening to and what is documented in that book?

I am Hatonn, and am aware of your question. My brother, ours is but a simple message and will many times seem repetitious, for we deliver a message of love and light and seek to encourage the use of meditation as a means of becoming more aware. The material in the book, *The Law of One*, comes from a source, though part of the Confederation, a different density with somewhat different guidelines which they follow.

While we both are limited by the Law of Free Will, or distortion, as it is referred to in the *The Law of One* book, the source known to you as Ra seeks to compensate for what it sees as mistakes that it made in previous contacts with your planet. The aim of both the book, the *The Law of One* and our contact is basically the same. While the approach is different, both seek to make those entities of your planet who seek growth more aware of the love and light of the one infinite Creator. Material that is presented by Ra or the message we seek to convey are aimed at the same end—to aid your planet and the entities upon it in their seeking.

May we answer you further, my brother?

(Inaudible)

M: Hatonn, I'm interested in a concise answer as to how one can protect themselves from being drained when sending energy to others.

I am Hatonn, and I am aware of your question. My brother, sending of light to others need not be to you physically draining, for as you know, light may be conveyed to other entities while in meditation, which is a non-draining activity, for while in meditation the light flows more freely and a great effort is not necessary to convey light to another.

May we answer you further?

M: Perhaps. Often in meditations with a group, I will leave a group feeling very, very charged, but in meditations alone I will sometimes come out of a meditation feeling very, very tired. I feel sometimes drained. Is this just my imagination or is there a way to be drained of energy in meditation?

My brother, I am Hatonn, and am aware of your question. For many who meditate alone, for that matter, within a group, there are times when one may sometimes temporarily, partially, separate themselves from their physical body. This activity, though not necessarily done, as you would say, deliberately, may occur and is draining upon your vital energies. This experience may be avoided, as well as the draining effect, by beginning one's meditations with some form of centering of your energies, by, in some cases, praying or just the performing of some small ritual to center one's energies for the purpose intended. By doing this one may avoid the draining that occurs sometimes in meditation.

May we answer you further, my brother?

M: No, you've answered me now. Thank you.

Thank you, my brother. May we answer another question?

L: Yes. Hatonn, earlier this evening and on a number of other occasions, I've felt, I guess you'd call it, access, to a high intensity energy that seemed to be directable. Could you explain to me the source of this energy and how it is I'm tapping into it?

I am Hatonn, and I am aware of your question. My brother, energies that you feel are simply yours flowing and are energies which are always present and available to you. As you have developed and grown through your meditations, these energies are becoming more available to you.

May we answer you further?

L: Yes. As these energies have been dormant for the majority of my life, it seems to me that they're not necessary for my physical existence. What purpose do they serve, or to what purpose can they be used?

My brother, those energies that you may tap may be used as you wish them to be used, for as with any energy source, he who taps them determines what he shall do with them. Those energies which you are becoming more aware of are there as a means of achieving those things which you wish to achieve.

May we answer you further, my brother?

L: No, I thank you for your help.

We thank you. Is there another question?

(The sound of a cat choking in the kitchen is heard.)

Although the sounds tonight are not quite as pleasant as those of your creatures in nature, we would again be amiss if we merely hung around to listen. So, we will, at this time transfer this contact to the one known as D2 and attempt to end with a few words through him. We are known to you as Hatonn. Adonai, my friends.

(D2 channeling)

I am Hatonn, and I greet you with this instrument. We of Hatonn are …

(W channeling)

I am Hatonn. I am now with this instrument. We are greatly pleased with the progress of the new instruments in the room. We encourage each of you to continue in your meditations as often as it is possible for each of you to do so. We bid you adonai, and leave you in the love and light of the infinite Creator. ♣

THE LAW OF ONE, BOOK III, SESSION 72
OCTOBER 14, 1981

Ra: I am Ra. I greet you in the love and in the light of the one infinite Creator. We communicate now.

Questioner: Could you first give me an indication of the instrument's condition?

Ra: I am Ra. This instrument's physical energy distortions are as previously stated. The vital energy level has become distorted from normal levels, somewhat downward, due to the distortion in this instrument's mind complex activity that it has been responsible for the, shall we say, difficulties in achieving the appropriate configuration for this contact.

Questioner: Was the banishing ritual that we performed of any effect in purifying the place of working and the screening of influences that we do not wish?

Ra: I am Ra. This is quite correct.

Questioner: Can you tell me what I can do to improve the effectiveness of the ritual?

Ra: I am Ra. No.

Questioner: Can you tell me what caused the instrument to become in a condition toward unconsciousness in the last two meditations prior to this one to such an extent that we discontinued them?

Ra: I am Ra. We can.

Questioner: Would you please tell me then?

Ra: I am Ra. The entity which greets this instrument from the Orion group first attempted to cause the mind/body/spirit complex, which you may call spirit, to leave the physical complex of yellow-ray in the deluded belief that it was preparing for the Ra contact. You are familiar with this tactic and its consequences. The instrument, with no pause, upon feeling this greeting, called for the grounding within the physical complex by requesting that the hand be held. Thus the greatest aim of the Orion entity was not achieved. However, it discovered that those present were not capable of distinguishing between unconsciousness with the mind/body/spirit intact and the trance state in which the mind/body/spirit complex is not present.

Therefore, it applied to the fullest extent the greeting which causes the dizziness and in meditation without protection caused, in this instrument, simple unconsciousness as in what you would call fainting or vertigo. The Orion entity consequently used this tactic to stop the Ra contact from having the opportunity to be accomplished.

Questioner: The instrument has scheduled an operation on her hand next month. If the general anesthetic is used to produce the unconscious state will this or any other parameters of the operation allow for any inroads by the Orion entities?

Ra: I am Ra. It is extremely improbable due to the necessity for the intention of the mind/body/spirit complex, when departing the yellow-ray physical complex, to be serving the Creator in the most specific fashion. The attitude of one approaching such an experience as you describe would not be approaching the unconscious state with such an attitude.

Questioner: We have here, I believe, a very important principle with respect to the Law of One. You have stated that the attitude of the individual is of paramount importance for the Orion entity to be able to be effective. Would you please explain how this mechanism works with respect to the Law of One and why the attitude of the entity is of paramount importance and why this allows for action by the Orion entity?

Ra: I am Ra. The Law of Confusion or Free Will is utterly paramount in the workings of the infinite creation. That which is intended has as much intensity of attraction to the polar opposite as the intensity of the intention or desire.

Thus those whose desires are shallow or transitory experience only ephemeral configurations of what might be called the magical circumstance. There is a turning point, a fulcrum which swings as a mind/body/spirit complex tunes its will to service. If this will and desire is for service-to-others the corresponding polarity will be activated. In the circumstance of this group there are three such wills acting as one with the instrument in the, shall we say, central position of fidelity to service. This is as it must be for the balance of the working and the continuance of the contact. Our vibratory complex is one-pointed in these workings also and our will to serve is also of some degree of purity. This has created the attraction of the polar opposite which you experience.

We may note that such a configuration of free will, one-pointed in service-to-others, also has the potential for the alerting of a great mass of light strength. This positive light strength, however, operates also under free will and must be invoked. We could not speak to this and shall not guide you, for the nature of this contact is such that the purity of your free will must, above all things, be preserved. Thus you wend your way through experiences discovering those biases which may be helpful.

Questioner: The negatively oriented entities who contact us and others on this planet are limited by the first distortion. They have obviously been limited by the banishing ritual just performed. Could you describe, with respect to free will, how they limit themselves in order to work within the first distortion and how the banishing ritual itself works?

Ra: I am Ra. This query has several portions. Firstly, those of negative polarity do not operate with respect to free will unless it is necessary. They call themselves and will infringe whenever they feel it possible.

Secondly, they are limited by the great Law of Confusion in that, for the most part, they are unable to enter this planetary sphere of influence and are able to use the windows of time/space distortion only in so far as there is some calling to balance the positive calling. Once they are here, their desire is conquest.

Thirdly, in the instance of this instrument's being removed permanently from this space/time, it is necessary to allow the instrument to leave its yellow-ray physical complex of its free will. Thus trickery has been attempted.

The use of the light forms being generated is such as to cause such entities to discover a wall through which they can not pass. This is due to the energy complexes of the light beings and aspects of the one infinite Creator invoked and evoked in the building of the wall of light.

Questioner: Everything that we experience with respect to this contact, our distortion toward knowledge in order to serve, the Orion entity's distortion towards reducing the effectiveness of this contact, all of this is a result of the first distortion, as I see it, in creating the totally free atmosphere for the Creator to become more knowledgeable of Itself through the interplay of its portions, one with respect to the other. Is my view correct with respect to what I have just said?

Ra: I am Ra. Yes.

Questioner: In the last session you mentioned that if the instrument used any of the increased vital energy that she experiences for physical activity that she would pay a "harsh toll." Could you tell me the nature of that harsh toll and why it would be experienced?

Ra: I am Ra. The physical energy level is a measure of the amount of available energy of the body complex of a mind/body/spirit complex. The vital energy measurement is one which expresses the amount of energy of being of the mind/body/spirit complex.

This entity has great distortions in the direction of mind complex activity, spirit complex activity, and that great conduit to the Creator, the will. Therefore, this instrument's vital energy, even in the absence of any physical reserve measurable, is quite substantial. However, the use of this energy of will, mind, and spirit for the things of the physical complex causes a far greater distortion in the lessening of the vital energy than would the use of this energy for those things which are in the deepest desires and will of the mind/body/spirit complex. In this entity these desires are for service to the Creator. This entity sees all service as service to the Creator and this is why we have cautioned the support group and the instrument itself in this regard. All services are not equal in depth of distortion. The over-use of this vital energy is, to be literal, the rapid removal of life-force.

Questioner: You mentioned that the large amount of light that is available. Could this group, by proper ritual, use this for recharging the vital energy of the instrument?

Ra: I am Ra. This is correct. However, we caution against any working which raises up any personality; rather it is well to be fastidious in your working.

Questioner: Could you explain what you mean by "raises up any personality"?

Ra: I am Ra. Clues, we may offer. Explanation is infringement. We can only ask that you realize that all are One.

Questioner: We have included "Shin" in the banishing ritual, "Yod-Heh-Vau-Heh" to make it "Yod-Heh-Shin-Vau-Heh." Is this helpful?

Ra: I am Ra. This is helpful especially to the instrument whose distortions vibrate greatly in congruency with this sound vibration complex.

Questioner: We will in the future have group meditations. I am concerned about protection for the instrument if she is once more a channel in these meditations. Is there an optimum time or limiting amount of time for the banishing ritual to be effective, or if we continued daily to purify the place of working with the banishing ritual would this carry over for long periods of time, or must the ritual be done immediately prior to the meditations?

Ra: I am Ra. Your former assumption is more nearly correct.

Questioner: Is there any danger now, with the precautions that we are taking, of the instrument being led away by the Orion entity?

Ra: I am Ra. The opportunities for the Orion entity are completely dependent upon the instrument's condition of awareness and readiness. We would suggest that this instrument is still too much the neophyte to open its self to questions since that is the format used by Ra. As the instrument grows in awareness this precaution may become unnecessary.

Questioner: Why is there no protection at the floor or bottom of the banishing ritual, and should there be?

Ra: I am Ra. This will be the last full query of this working.

The development of the psychic greeting is possible only through the energy centers starting from a station which you might call within the violet-ray moving through the adept's energy center and therefrom towards the target of opportunity. Depending upon the vibratory nature and purpose of greeting, be it positive or negative, the entity will be energized or blocked in the desired way.

We of Ra approach this instrument in narrow band contact through violet-ray. Others might pierce down through this ray to any energy center. We, for instance, make great use of this instrument's blue-ray energy center as we are attempting to communicate our distortion/understandings of the Law of One.

The entity of Orion pierces the same violet-ray and moves to two places to attempt most of its non-physical opportunities. It activates the green-ray energy center while further blocking indigo-ray energy center. This combination causes confusion in the instrument and subsequent over-activity in unwise proportions in physical complex workings. It simply seeks out the distortions preincarnatively programmed and developed in incarnative state.

The energies of life itself, being the one infinite Creator, flow from the south pole of the body seen in its magnetic form. Thus only the Creator may, through the feet, enter the energy shell of the body to any effect. The effects of the adept are those from the upper direction and thus the building of the wall of light is quite propitious.

May we ask if there are any shorter queries at this time?

Questioner: I would just ask if there is anything that we could do to make the instrument more comfortable or to improve the contact?

Ra: I am Ra. This instrument has some increased distortion in the region of the neck. Some attention here might provide greater comfort. All is well, my friends. The forbearance and patience observed by Ra are commendable. Continue in this fastidiousness of purpose and care for the appropriate configurations for contact and our continuance of contact will continue to be possible. This is acceptable to us.

I am Ra. I leave you, my friends, glorying in the love and the light of the one infinite Creator. Go forth, then, rejoicing in the power and in the peace of the one infinite Creator. Adonai.

Intensive Meditation
October 15, 1981

(Carla channeling)

I am Laitos, and I greet you, my friends, in the love and the light of the infinite Creator. It is a great pleasure to be able to use this instrument once again, and also a pleasure to be able to work with each of you at this time. May we say to you that as you come into this place of peace and dedication to service, let all those things slide from you that cause you to be caught in the world of illusion where it is difficult to see the one infinite Creator, for here, as you are banded together to seek to be of service, is the Creator. There is a spirit of which we are messengers and of which you wish to be messengers also. As you offer yourselves to this service, my friends, know that you are among the great many friends of we of Laitos, and those of the Confederation of Planets in the Service of the Infinite Creator and many of those whom you call angels are all of a single wish, and that is to be of aid to those who wish to offer themselves as channels of the love and the light of the infinite Creator.

We would pause for a few moments to work on the group as a whole and then we shall begin exercising each individual. I am Laitos.

(Pause)

I am again with this instrument. I am Laitos. We would like to begin by working with the one known as R. We would like to carefully repeat a single phrase through this instrument so that this instrument may begin to feel a sense of what this type of contact may be experienced as being like. If the instrument would relax and refrain from analysis, we shall at this time transfer to the one known as R. I am Laitos.

(Pause)

(Carla channeling)

I am again with this instrument. We are adjusting the contact. There is some slight care which we must take with this instrument in order to avoid activation which is undesirable, therefore, we shall narrow our communication and again attempt to speak the name by which you know us through this instrument. I am Laitos.

(Carla channeling)

I am Laitos, and am again with this instrument. We find a good deal of blockage due to some, shall we say, concern on the part of the instrument that such contact may not be controlled and may be false. May we suggest for the first fear that the instrument, in meditation, visualize a deep violet shade surrounding, in particular, the rear and sides of the portion of the body known as the head, but extending more generally throughout the *(inaudible)*. For the second fear may we suggest the imaging of the opening of the pea pod—as one pea rolls away from the pod, the rest follow. There is an inevitability about this particular process which is felt by the finger or thumb as this is done. So it is with a phrase as we give it. We give a phrase which is easily spoken, then the pod is tossed away, shall we say, and another ready to be given forth.

We thank the one known as R and shall at the end of this session attempt once more to speak through him. At this time we would exercise the instrument known as S by giving a few thoughts through this instrument if she would also relax and speak those things which flow easily into the mind. I am Laitos.

(S channeling)

I am Laitos, and I greet you through this instrument. We are pleased to be speaking through this instrument once more. We are attempting to reach …

(Carla channeling)

I am Laitos, and am again with this instrument. We gratefully thank the one known as S for her service and confirm that the phrase which was given was "reach as many of those upon your planet as it is possible to reach at this time." We offer this confirmation that the instrument may grow in confidence and therefore cease any analysis that may keep the process which you call channeling from being experienced with *(inaudible)*.

We are hopeful that the attempts which we have made in the past few days to cause a comfortable but noticeable experience of our presence has been somewhat successful. May we offer to the instrument the suggestion that with this instrument also there is a visualized color which may be somewhat helpful. If it is desired that the meditation be pointed towards communication and the deepening of the contact to include the conditioning of the Confederation, as the request is mentally sent for our presence the golden color may also be sensed as that which is about the instrument, for this is compatible with this instrument's meditative state.

At this time we would like to exercise the instrument known as D1. We shall offer words slowly and ask that the one known as D1 speak with peace in her heart knowing that we are indeed offering these words. I am Laitos.

(D1 channeling)

I am Laitos, and I am with this instrument. It is a pleasure to greet you through this instrument. We feel that there is a good contact and wish to express our gratitude for the opportunity to work with this group. I am Laitos.

(Carla channeling)

I am Laitos, and am again with this instrument. Again we greet you in love and light and thank the one known as D1. We are extremely happy with the progress which has been made and wish to assure the one known as D1 that we shall at all times be available for the conditioning work. We feel in this particular case there is no advice, shall we say, which we might offer since the instrument has a great desire to serve and is, to the best of her ability, doing those things which we might suggest. Thus, we can only encourage the one known as D1 to continue in faith and in love and to realize that we are always at her disposal.

We would now transfer to the one known as D2 to speak a few phrases. We ask this instrument to refrain most rigorously from analysis and assure the instrument that we shall not be attempting to speak any but those words which are those of the Creator. We would now transfer. I am Laitos.

(D2 channeling)

I am Laitos, and I greet you through this instrument. We of Laitos know of …

(Carla channeling)

I am Laitos. I am with this instrument. We are attempting to make adjustments so that the instrument is more comfortable and can perceive our contact more clearly. After a brief pause, we shall again transfer to the one known as D2. I am Laitos.

(D2 channeling)

I am Laitos. I am once again with this instrument. We are pleased with the contact with this instrument. We will always try …

(Carla channeling)

I am Laitos. I am again with this instrument. We realize that we have some careful adjustment to do with the instrument known as D2 in order to make the contact with him comfortable and clear, and we shall be glad to work with this instrument in conditioning whenever it is requested. We cannot thank this instrument enough for the service which he attempts to provide.

We would now again attempt to vibrate our name as you know it through the instrument known as R, if he will allow our thought to come into his mind and then be spoken. I am Laitos.

(Pause)

(Carla channeling)

I am Laitos. I am again with this instrument. We had a better contact during this second attempt to speak with the one known as R. However, there is a great deal of analysis and this inhibits the clear functioning of such a contact as this. This contact is the result of the free will of each entity offering himself or herself in service to the infinite Creator. There are many things which those who wish to serve wish to offer to all of mankind and in particular to those whom one knows. This is one of many forms of service and we thank each for sharing in this work of service.

We would at this time attempt to exercise the instrument known as D3. I am Laitos.

(D3 channeling)

I am Laitos. I am with this instrument. It is a very great privilege to be able to work with this group at this time. We of Laitos are always pleased when our contact and aid is sought. We will attempt to give through this instrument some simple instructions. It is only necessary that you desire our contact for our contact to be given. Desire, my friends, is the key to the contact. The greater the desire, the more we are able to work with you. If the desire is sufficient we will be there. We will be there at any time, any place, when you have the desire for our contact.

Sometimes it is difficult to establish what we would call the original contact. This is understandable, for quite often the individual who is receiving our contact analyzes that which he receives and quite often interprets that to be thoughts of his own generated from within his own being. We suggest, my friends, that you do not try to discriminate between our contact and those thoughts generated within your own being, but simply say what is available for the saying.

My friends, it matters not whether those thoughts are generated within your own being or from us, known to you as Laitos. Relax and simply speak those words that are available during that period of meditation when you desire our contact. After you have gained same experience in simply letting flow that which is available, regardless of its source, whether it be yourself, whether it be us, or whether it be another source, you will then begin to realize that all sources are one. The information, my friends, is information. It is information of the Creator. It *is* the Creator. It is our understanding, and you will receive it; the greater the desire, my friends, the more the understanding.

I will leave this instrument at this time and transfer this contact. Please be available for our contact, for we shall now, at this time, attempt to contact each of those in this room. I am Laitos.

(Jim channeling)

I am Laitos, and am with this instrument and greet you all in love and light once again. We have been able to make our presence known to each within this circle and with practice we are certain that each entity in time shall be able to speak our words when they are perceived within the mind. We thank each entity within this room for the service which has been offered to those of our group known as Laitos.

We would, at this time, offer ourselves in the attempt to answer any questions which those present might have. Are there any questions at this time?

R: How deep of a meditative state is necessary for contact?

I am Laitos. My brother, it is not necessary that one enter any great depth during the meditation in which contact is sought. The necessity, rather, is for the clearing of the mind and not in the deepening of its perceptive ability. The clearing of the mind, as we have mentioned, consists of removing the tendency towards analysis, which is natural for your peoples and for any new instrument which is attempting to perceive thoughts transmitted from any other source than its own being.

May we answer you further, by brother?

R: No, thank you.

As always, our gratitude is with you. Is there another question at this time?

S: Yes. How can one be certain when a contact has been made?

I am Laitos. My sister, we do not deal in certainty, for this is a phenomenon which has no proof, proof as you know being the greatest of infringements upon your own free will. But we may suggest to you that if you should desire some simple sign that contact has been made, you may ask for conditioning in whatever degree you deem appropriate prior to the contact, and upon receiving this conditioning, this shall be your signal to yourself that the contact is about to be initiated.

Of course, you may also note that any entity who wishes to persist in the analysis may also decide that the signal was not the proper signal. This is why we say there is no certainty, but you may, yourself, during the time that contact is sought, be assured as much as we can assure you that if you desire our contact, it is our contact which you shall perceive.

May we answer you further, my sister?

S: Yes. Why was I not able to perceive the rest of the message? Was there a bad contact? I became somewhat anxious. Is that responsible for not being able to receive the contact?

I am Laitos. My sister, we would confirm your discovery and assertion that the anxiety does indeed serve as an inhibitor to the perceiving of our contact. It is much likened unto what you might—we correct this instrument—much likened unto what you might perceive as the static upon the radio. Anxiety within your mind does block that further perception of the contact. That is why we suggest the relaxing of the mind …

(Side one of tape ends.)

(Jim channeling)

I am Laitos and am once again with this instrument. This is why we have previously suggested the taking of deep breaths and the simple speaking of the thoughts as they are perceived within the mind, without analysis or doubt.

May we answer you further, my sister?

S: No, thank you.

As always, we are most grateful for this opportunity to serve. Is there another question at this time?

D2: Yes. I'm seeming to have more trouble with the contact this afternoon (than) I have had previously, although I did not perceive any difference in my own particular mental state today than I have had before. Are there any adjustments that you would suggest that I could do just to make contact better?

I am Laitos. My brother, in this regard we may simply reiterate those suggestions which we have made in the past, those being the relaxing as much as possible, the clearing of the mind of all extraneous thought and the refraining from analysis. These are the basics which any new instrument must be able to master before the contact can be clearly perceived. We feel, in your case, these are quite sufficient and are being accomplished to a sufficient degree by your own efforts and any other advice at this time would simply be extraneous to the process which is occurring within your own being. We are pleased with the contact which we have through your instrument and may assure you that your meditations in the future will be much more successful in the attempt to perceive our contact, for we feel we have quite a good contact through your instrument.

May we answer you further, my brother?

D2: No, thank you.

We thank you. Is there another question at this time?

(Pause)

I am Laitos. My friends, it has been a very great honor and privilege for us to speak to your group this afternoon and to utilize each of the instruments which we have been able to contact. We are always grateful for any opportunity to speak to any of your people who wish our service. To be able to address a group such as this which is devoted to the specific service of serving as instruments for messages which we humbly offer as our interpretation of the love and light of the one infinite Creator is a joy which cannot be spoken. We assure each entity within this group that we shall be most honored to join each in his or her private meditation and a simple (request?) is all that is necessary.

We would now leave this group, rejoicing in that love and in that light which flows through all of our beings and joins us in the clear light of the one infinite Creator. We are known to you as those of Laitos and we leave you now in that love and in that light. Adonai, my friends. Adonai vasu borragus.

Sunday Meditation
October 18, 1981

(Carla channeling)

[I am Hatonn,] and I greet you, my friends, in the love and in the light of the infinite Creator. It is a great privilege to speak through this instrument this evening. We were attempting to initiate contact with the one known as C and we will transfer to him later in the meeting. We wish to confirm that we were indeed attempting to contact him. We will speak now a few thoughts through this instrument.

We would speak to you this evening of an aspect of love that is seldom understood among your peoples. It is an aspect of love that is one if the most creative and offering the most freedom of all the aspects of love. And that, my friends, is endurance. In the vicissitudes of each of your lives as you experience them at this time, there are many peaks and many valleys and when you reach the peaks you feel that the experience that you have gained, the high points that are the equivalent of the soaring of the eagle or the rejoicing of the angels, will surely carry you through all that may lie ahead of you, but, my friends, this is not to be. There is no mountain high enough to bridge the valleys, and when you are in those valleys, the difficult and dreary times, times when it seems that it is impossible to find a positive reason for your existence and being, it does not seem possible that there will ever come to you again the euphoria of the experience of the empyrean heights, bliss, thankfulness, joy and shared laughter, and yet again this is not so, for there is no valley deep enough to keep you from scaling the next height.

The changes of your life experience are intended to give you cause for thought and reason for action. It is not intended that you should have an uneventful life. It is, rather, intended that your life offer you whatever peaks and vales that you may need in order to experience the joy and the sorrow of your humanity to such an extent that you learn how to endure. How easy it is, my friends, to love and to be loved upon the peaks of your life. How easy to express the graceful phrase, the caring thought, the heartfelt deed. And when you have once again walked into the vale and are locked in the cage of sorrow, how then can you reach through the bars and offer up love and offer yourself to be loved? For you are a prisoner of your sorrow, and know not how to do these things, and yet, my friends, if you experience the alternation of joy and sorrow to a great enough extent and with a great enough clarity of perception, you may discover in this very cycle one enduring thing.

That, my friends, is yourself. Your mind finds peaks and rejoices in freedom. Your mind creates valleys and imprisons itself in sorrow, but there is always your mind, your consciousness, your beingness, the totality of which never changes, never alters and does indeed endure. And who are you, the being experiencing these changes, seasons and cycles of life, of love and sorrow? We suggest to you, my friends, that you are part of an original Thought, part of that which we might call love and as long as your consciousness endures, so shall love.

Love is not a property of the heights of joy, nor are you bereft of it in the utmost depths of despair, for you are love. It is always with you, for it is here, no matter how distorted your perception of yourself and of your experience, how separated you feel from the warmth and the safety of love, yet you cannot deny or ignore your being. You cannot escape your thoughts or your nature. Therefore, my friends, it is well, from time to time, to imagine yourself as one who watches a picture that moves upon the *(inaudible)*. This picture is yourself as you act from day to day, moving as the winds of experience move you, that you yourself, my friends, are the watcher and, as the watcher, you may see, not only the folly of this illusion, not only the missteps, the grand moments and the failures that you fear, but something far deeper, for the watcher sees the reality behind all of these actions. The watcher sees love.

At this time I would transfer this contact. I am known to you as Hatonn.

(C channeling)

I am Hatonn, and I am with this instrument. In your lives, within this illusion, each and every of your days you will face various situations which may at times be pleasant or troubling or just seem to pass. Each moment [and] situation that you face is an opportunity for each to examine, feel, for each moment offers a chance to grow, to become more aware. Each moment offers a lesson which will provide opportunities. Whether you take the opportunity or not is totally a matter of your free choice, for each of you well knows that a lesson unlearned repeats itself or is manifested in similar situations. To grow, each lesson must be learned, although some you will find most difficult and within this illusion may even be a physically or mentally unpleasant experience due to your having to deal with others in this illusion, for those who are aware and seek are often misunderstood. As they become more aware, quite often you will see distances appear between you and those who would shun the lessons that they are faced with, though you may, as you grow with patience, bridge the gap and can make the difference small and even through your love bring you and others closer after a time.

You, as you become more aware, can endure all seeming blindness of others which so often stems from ignorance, for in your illusion many who do not understand or consciously seek turn their eyes away from the light and love of which we all are a part. You need not be ever discouraged by others as you seek more love and light that is within, and as you, will shine and touch others and aid them to begin their own journey.

We would at this time ask if there are any questions which we might attempt to answer? Is there a question?

(Pause)

My friends, it is always a pleasant experience to sit, quietly listen, to hear various vibrations that surrounds, for even in what you would term a silence, there is energy and peace which, not heard, is felt and experienced. We enjoy sitting silent, but we would also enjoy the sounds of your questions and would ask once again if we may be of service to you tonight within this capacity?

(Pause)

I am Hatonn. Since there seems to be no pressing questions upon your minds of the ones within this group, we shall, at this time, transfer this contact to another instrument. I am Hatonn.

(Jim channeling)

I am Hatonn, and am with this instrument. We greet you once again in love and light. At this time we would offer ourselves in the capacity of exercising new instruments. We would begin with the one known as R and, if he would relax and refrain from any analysis, we shall attempt to speak a few words through this new instrument. We shall now transfer this contact. I am Hatonn.

(Pause)

(Jim channeling)

I am Hatonn, and am with this instrument once again. We find that we have some blockage within the one known am R. Our contact enters just above the eyebrows, and if the one known as R would imagine in imagery this area being clear of all thought, and relax the body, we will once again attempt contact with this new instrument. I am Hatonn.

(Pause)

(Jim channeling)

I am Hatonn. We find that we have somewhat a stronger contact with the one known as R, but this new instrument feels not only a hesitance for speaking those thoughts which it finds within its mind, but also feels a good deal of pleasure in the sitting quietly within our vibrations. We appreciate the efforts of the one known as R and shall be with this new instrument in the future meditations and we look forward to being able to speak our words through this instrument, and assure this instrument that the desire to experience our contact, to speak our words, is all that is necessary to do so.

We would at this time attempt to contact the one known as S. If she would relax and speak the thoughts which appear within her mind, we would attempt to speak a few words through this new instrument. We will now transfer this contact to the one known as S. I am Hatonn.

(S channeling)

I am Hatonn, and I am with this instrument. We are pleased to be speaking to you through this instrument once more. We feel we are able to contact this instrument more comfortably now. We have, in the past, caused some discomfort. We are adjusting our … We have had to pause to make a minor adjustment, as this instrument was experiencing discomfort. We feel she is now more comfortable. We of Hatonn wish to speak …

(Jim channeling)

I am Hatonn, and am with this instrument once again. We are most pleased with the progress made by the one known as S in the reception in transmission of our contact. We look forward to meditations at which time we might be asked once again by this instrument to exercise its channeling abilities. May we say that it is a great honor to be able to utilize a new instrument at any time in any manner and we appreciate the desire which each of these new instruments has expressed and demonstrated in working with our conditioning vibrations. We assure each that we shall be with each of them in their meditations and a simple request is all that is necessary for us to join in meditation.

My friends, it has been a great privilege to be able to speak to your group this evening. We of Hatonn …

(Side one of tape ends.)

(Jim channeling)

I am Hatonn, and am once again with this instrument. We have spoken many times to this group. Our subject has always been some aspect of the love of the one infinite Creator. This is our area of specialization. This love which goes quite beyond words is that lesson which we of Hatonn labor to learn. Our learning is greatly enhanced by the opportunity to share our humble learnings with those of your peoples such as are gathered here this evening.

In the sharing of our learning do we thus learn yet more and penetrate further the mystery of being and that which is known as love. We of Hatonn do not claim any certain knowledge. We recognize the mystery of all creation. We know many of your people feel great confusion at this time in their evolution. It is with the hope of alleviating some of that great confusion that we share our simple learnings of love with your people. We cannot express our gratitude at the opportunity to provide this service. But, we assure this group that we shall treasure each future opportunity to speak and thusly serve. We leave you now in that love and in that light of the one infinite Creator. Adonai, my friends. Adonai vasu borragus. ☙

The Law of One, Book III, Session 73
October 21, 1981

Ra: I am Ra. I greet you in the love and in the light of the one infinite Creator. We communicate now.

Questioner: Could you please give me an indication of the instrument's condition?

Ra: I am Ra. It is as previously stated with the exception of the vital energy level which is distorted more nearly towards that which is normal for this entity.

Questioner: Has the banishing ritual that we have performed been helpful for this contact?

Ra: I am Ra. The ritual described has gained with each working in making efficacious the purity of contact needed not only for the Ra contact but for any working of the adept.

Questioner: Thank you. I would like to thank Ra at this time for the opportunity to be of service to those on this sphere who would want to have the information that we gain here.

You stated that free will, one-pointed in service-to-others had the potential of alerting a great mass of light strength. I assume that the same holds precisely true for the service-to-self polarity. Is this correct?

Ra: I am Ra. This is incorrect but subtly so. In invocation and evocation of what may be termed negative entities or qualities the expression alerts the positively oriented equivalent. However, those upon the service-to-others path wait to be called and can only send love.

Questioner: What I was trying to get at was that this alerting of light strength is, as I see it, a process that must be totally a function of free will, as you say, and as the desire and will and purity of desire of the adept increases, the alerting of light strength increases. Is this part of it the same for both the positive and negative potentials and am I correct with this statement?

Ra: I am Ra. To avoid confusion we shall simply restate for clarity your correct assumption.

Those who are upon the service-to-others path may call upon the light strength in direct proportion to the strength and purity of their will to serve. Those upon the service-to-self path may call upon the dark strength in direct proportion to the strength and purity of their will to serve.

Questioner: I will undoubtedly make many errors in my statements today because what I am trying to do is guess at how this works and let you correct me. In considering the exercise of the Middle Pillar I have thought it might be wrong in that in it the adept sees or visualizes the light moving downward from the crown chakra down to the feet. Ra has stated that the Creator enters from the feet and moves upward, that this spiraling light enters from the feet and moves upward. It seems to me that the adept alerting the light strength, in visualizing the use of this, would visualize it entering the feet and energizing first, the red energy center and then moving upward through the energy centers in that fashion. Is this correct?

Ra: I am Ra. No.

Questioner: Could you tell me where I am wrong in that statement?

Ra: I am Ra. Yes.

Questioner: Would you please do that?

Ra: I am Ra. There are two concepts with which you deal. The first is the great way of the development of the light in the microcosmic mind/body/spirit. It is assumed that an adept will have its energy centers functioning smoothly and in a balanced manner to its best effort before a magical working. All magical workings are based upon evocation and/or invocation.

The first invocation of any magical working is that invocation of the magical personality as you are familiar with this term. In the working of which you speak the first station is the beginning of the invocation of this magical personality which is invoked by the motion of putting on something. Since you do not have an item of apparel or talisman the gesture which you have made is appropriate.

The second station is the evocation of the great cross of life. This is an extension of the magical personality to become the Creator. Again, all invocations and evocations are drawn through the violet energy center. This may then be continued towards whatever energy centers are desired to be used.

Questioner: Then will you speak of the difference between the spiraling light that enters through the feet and the light invoked through the crown chakra?

Ra: I am Ra. The action of the upward spiraling light drawn by the will to meet the inner light of the one infinite Creator may be likened to the beating of the heart and the movement of the muscles surrounding the lungs and all the other functions of the parasympathetic nervous system. The calling of the adept may be likened to those nerve and muscle actions over which the mind/body/spirit complex has conscious control.

Questioner: Previously you stated that where the two directions meet you have a measure of the development of the particular mind/body/spirit complex. Am I correct?

Ra: I am Ra. This is correct.

Questioner: It would seem to me that the visualization of the invocation would be dependent upon what the use was to be of the light. The use could be for healing, communication, or for the general awareness of the creation and the Creator. Would you please speak on this process and my correctness in making this assumption?

Ra: I am Ra. We shall offer some thoughts though it is doubtful that we may exhaust this subject. Each visualization, regardless of the point of the working, begins with some work within the indigo-ray. As you may be aware, the ritual which you have begun is completely working within the indigo-ray. This is well for it is the gateway. From this beginning light may be invoked for communication or for healing.

You may note that in the ritual which we offered you to properly begin the Ra workings the first focus is upon the Creator. We would further note a point which is both subtle and of some interest. The upward spiraling light developed in its path by the will, and ultimately reaching an high place of mating with the inward fire of the one Creator, still is only preparation for the work upon the mind/body/spirit which may be done by the adept. There is some crystallization of the energy centers used during each working so that the magician becomes more and more that which it seeks.

More importantly, the time/space mind/body/spirit analog, which is evoked as the magical personality, has its only opportunity to gain rapidly from the experience of the catalytic action available to the third-density space/time mind/body/spirit. Thus the adept is aiding the Creator greatly by offering great catalyst to a greater portion of the creation which is identified as the mind/body/spirit totality of an entity.

Questioner: Desire and will are the factors in this process. Is this correct?

Ra: I am Ra. We would add one quality. In the magical personality desire, will, and polarity are the keys.

Questioner: Many so-called evangelists which we have in our society at present have great desire and very great will, and possibly great polarity, but it seems to me that in many cases that there is a lack of awareness that creates a less than effective working in the magical sense. Am I correct in this analysis?

Ra: I am Ra. You are partially correct. In examining the polarity of a service-to-others working the free will must be seen as paramount. Those entities of which you speak are attempting to generate positive changes in consciousness while abridging free will. This causes the blockage of the magical nature of the working except in those cases wherein an entity freely desires to accept the working of the evangelist, as you have called it.

Questioner: What was the orientation with respect to this type of communication for the one known as Jesus of Nazareth?

Ra: I am Ra. You may have read some of this entity's workings. It offered itself as teacher to those mind/body/spirit complexes which gathered to hear and even then spoke as through a veil so as to leave room for those not wishing to hear. When this entity was asked to heal, it oft times did so, always ending the working with two admonitions: firstly, that the entity healed had been healed by its faith, that is, its ability to allow and accept changes through the violet-ray into the gateway of intelligent energy; secondly, saying always, "Tell no one." These are the workings which attempt the maximal quality of free will while maintaining fidelity to the positive purity of the working.

Questioner: An observation of the working itself by another entity would seem to me to partially abridge free will in that a seemingly magical occurrence had taken place as the result of the working of an adept. This could be extended to any phenomenon which is other than normal or acceptable. Could you speak on this paradox that is immediately the problem of anyone doing healing?

Ra: I am Ra. We are humble messengers of the Law of One. To us there are no paradoxes. The workings which seem magical and, therefore, seem to infringe upon free will do not, in themselves, do so, for the distortions of perception are as many as the witnesses and each witness sees what it desires to see. Infringement upon free will occurs in this circumstance only if the entity doing the working ascribes the authorship of this event to its self or its own skills. He who states that no working comes from it but only through it is not infringing upon free will.

Questioner: The one known as Jesus accumulated twelve disciples. What was his purpose in having these disciples with him?

Ra: I am Ra. What is the purpose of teach/learning if there be no learn/teachers? Those drawn to this entity were accepted by this entity without regard for any outcome. This entity accepted the honor/duty placed upon it by its nature and its sense that to speak was its mission.

Questioner: In the exercise of the fire I assume the healer would be working with the same energy that we spoke of as entering through the crown chakra. Is this correct?

Ra: I am Ra. This is correct with some additional notation necessary for your thought in continuing this line of study. When the magical personality has been seated in the green-ray energy center for healing work the energy then may be seen to be the crystalline center through which body energy is channeled. Thus this particular form of healing uses both the energy of the adept and the energy of the upward spiraling light. As the green-ray center becomes more brilliant, and we would note this brilliance does not imply over-activation but rather crystallization, the energy of the green-ray center of the body complex spirals twice; firstly, clockwise from the green-ray energy center to the right shoulder, through the head, the right elbow, down through the solar plexus, and to the left hand. This sweeps all the body complex energy into a channel which then rotates the great circle clockwise again from right—we correct this instrument—from the left to the feet, to the right hand, to the crown, to the left hand, and so forth.

Thus the in-coming body energy, crystallized, regularized, and channeled by the adept's personality reaching to the green-ray energy center, may then pour out the combined energies of the adept which is incarnate thus offering the service of healing to an entity requesting that service. This basic situation is accomplished as well when there is an entity which is working through a channel to heal.

Questioner: Can you tell me how this transfer of light, I believe it would be, would affect the patient to be healed?

Ra: I am Ra. The effect is that of polarization. The entity may or may not accept any percentage of this polarized life-energy which is being offered. In the occasion of the laying on of hands this energy is more specifically channeled and the opportunity for acceptance of this energy similarly more specific.

It may be seen that the King's Chamber effect is not attempted in this form of working but rather the addition to one, whose energies are low, of the opportunity for the building up of those energies. Many of your distortions called illnesses may be aided by such means.

Questioner: As a general statement which you can correct, the overall picture, as I see it, of the healer and patient is that the one to be healed has, because of a blockage in one of the energy centers or more— we will just consider one particular problem— because of this energy center blockage the upward spiraling light which creates one of the seven bodies has been blocked from the maintenance of that body, and this has resulted in the distortion from the perfection of that body which we call disease or a bodily anomaly which is other than perfect. The healer, having suitably configured its energy centers, is able to channel light, the downward pouring light, though its properly configured energy centers to the one to be healed. If the one to be healed has the mental configuration of acceptance of this light, the light then enters the physical complex and re-configures the distortion that is created by the original blockage. I am sure that I have made some mistakes in all this. Would you please correct them?

Ra: I am Ra. Your mistakes were small. We would not, at this time, attempt a great deal of refinement of that statement as there is preliminary material which will undoubtedly come forward. We may say that there are various forms of healing. In many, only the energy of the adept is used. In the exercise of fire some physical complex energy is also channeled.

We might note further that when the one wishing to be healed, though sincere, remains unhealed, as you call this distortion, you may consider preincarnative choices and your more helpful aid to such an entity may be the suggestion that it meditate upon the affirmative uses of whatever limitations it might experience. We would also note that in these cases the indigo-ray workings are often of aid.

Other than these notes, we do not wish to further comment upon your statement at this working.

Questioner: It seems to me that the primary thing of importance for those on the service-to-others path is the development of an attitude which I can only describe as a vibration. This attitude would be developed through meditation, ritual, and the developing appreciation for the creation or Creator which results in a state of mind that can only be expressed by me as an increase in vibration or oneness with all. Could you expand and correct that statement?

Ra: I am Ra. We shall not correct this statement but shall expand upon it by suggesting that to those qualities you may add the living day by day and moment by moment, for the true adept lives more and more as it is.

Questioner: Thank you. Could you tell me of the number of possible energy transfers between two or more mind/body/spirit complexes. Is it very large, or are there few?

Ra: I am Ra. The number is infinite, for is not each mind/body/spirit complex unique?

Questioner: Could you define this statement "energy transfer between two mind/body/spirit complexes"?

Ra: I am Ra. This will be the last full query of this working. This entity still has transferred energy available, but we find rapidly increasing distortions towards pain in the neck, the dorsal area, and the wrists and manual appendages.

The physical energy transfer may be done numerous ways.

We shall give two examples. Each begins with some sense of the self as Creator or in some way the magical personality being invoked. This may be consciously or unconsciously done. Firstly, that exercise of which we have spoken called the exercise of fire: this is, through physical energy transfer, not that which is deeply involved in the body complex combinations. Thusly the transfer is subtle and each transfer unique in what is offered and what is accepted. At this point we may note that this is the cause for the infinite array of possible energy transfers.

The second energy transfer of which we would speak is the sexual energy transfer. This takes place upon a non-magical level by all those entities which vibrate green ray active. It is possible, as in the case of this instrument which dedicates itself to the service of the one infinite Creator, to further refine this energy transfer. When the other-self also dedicates itself in service to the one infinite Creator, the transfer is doubled. Then the amount of energy transferred is dependent only upon the amount of polarized sexual energy created and released. There are refinements from this point onward leading to the realm of the high sexual magic.

In the realm of the mental bodies there are variations of mental energy transferred. This is, again, dependent upon the knowledge sought and the knowledge offered. The most common mental energy transfer is that of the teacher and the pupil. The amount of energy is dependent upon the quality of this offering upon the part of the teacher, and regards the purity of the desire to serve, and the quality of information offered and, upon the part of the student, the purity of the desire to learn and the quality of the mind vibratory complex which receives knowledge.

Another form of mental energy transfer is that of the listener and the speaker. When the speaker is experiencing mental/emotional complex distortions towards anguish, sorrow, or other mental pain, from what we have said before, you may perhaps garner knowledge of the variations possible in this transfer.

The spiritual energy transfers are at the heart of all energy transfers as a knowledge of self and other-self as Creator is paramount, and this is spiritual work. The varieties of spiritual energy transfer include those things of which we have spoken this day as we spoke upon the subject of the adept.

Are there any brief queries before we leave this working?

Questioner: Only if there is anything we can do to improve the comfort of the instrument and the contact, and secondly, is there anything that you wish not published in today's session?

Ra: I am Ra. We call your attention to two items. Firstly, it is well that the candle which spirals 10° each working be never allowed to gutter as this would cause imbalance in the alignment of the appurtenances in their protective role for this instrument. Secondly, we might suggest attention to the neck area so that the cushion upon which it is supported be more comfortable. This difficulty has abbreviated many workings.

We thank you, my friends, for your conscientiousness and your fastidiousness with regard to these appurtenances which, as our workings proceed, seems to be increasing. Secondly, your decisions are completely your own as to that material which you may wish published from this working.

I am Ra. I leave you glorying in the love and in the light of the one infinite Creator. Go forth, then, rejoicing in the power and in the peace of the one infinite Creator. Adonai. ✣

L/L Research

L/L Research is a subsidiary of Rock Creek Research & Development Laboratories, Inc.

P.O. Box 5195
Louisville, KY 40255-0195

www.llresearch.org

Rock Creek is a non-profit corporation dedicated to discovering and sharing information which may aid in the spiritual evolution of humankind.

ABOUT THE CONTENTS OF THIS TRANSCRIPT: This telepathic channeling has been taken from transcriptions of the weekly study and meditation meetings of the Rock Creek Research & Development Laboratories and L/L Research. It is offered in the hope that it may be useful to you. As the Confederation entities always make a point of saying, please use your discrimination and judgment in assessing this material. If something rings true to you, fine. If something does not resonate, please leave it behind, for neither we nor those of the Confederation would wish to be a stumbling block for any.

CAVEAT: This transcript is being published by L/L Research in a not yet final form. It has, however, been edited and any obvious errors have been corrected. When it is in a final form, this caveat will be removed.

© 2009 L/L Research

Sunday Meditation
October 25, 1981

(L channeling)

I am Hatonn, and I greet you, my brothers and sisters, in the love and the light of the infinite Creator. It is with great pleasure that we of Hatonn are able to listen to your voices unite in song this evening, for it is our joy and our privilege to share in the upliftment caused by your emotions as your spirits unite in joy and purpose. We of Hatonn are grateful for this opportunity and sincerely thank you for this blessing.

Tonight, my brothers and sisters, we would share with you a small story pertaining, perhaps, to ones such as yourselves. The story concerns a small child abandoned on a sea coast through an accident of his parents. The child left behind was forced to rely upon his own devices and his meager knowledge for survival in that his parents, lost as they were themselves, were unable to retrace their steps or recover the offspring of their actions.

The child wandered the seacoast, his ears and mind filled with the monotonous crashing of the sea, its hypnotic waves at times comforting him, at other times irritating in that they seemed almost able to communicate with him, yet not quite able. As the child grew he became less and less like his parents in that his seeking for food, for drink, for understanding, led him into many new and varied experiences that were not shared by those who had lost and later forgot [him]. Yet, the child never in his travels left the sea coast, for [this] message, although seemingly just beyond his ears, was ever a stimulus that drove him onward.

Finally the time came when the child stumbled across another of his race, although not of the family nor the tribe that had abandoned him. An old man sat quietly on the beach, the crashing waves stopping just short of his feet as he gazed sightlessly toward the horizon. The child was hesitant, for although he remembered the human form, he was disturbed by the serenity of the old man, for this was not familiar to him. As he slowly approached, he waited for the old man to turn his gaze unto his own, yet the old man continued staring out to sea until the boy stood at his feet. Finally the old man spoke.

"Do you know the answer?" was his question.

The boy hesitated, unsure of himself, unsure of this question. The old man again asked. "Do you know, child, what the voices say to you?" The boy, again unsure, shook his head. The old man gestured. The boy sat down alongside and began to listen. As the sun warmed them both, rising higher and higher in the sky, the boy became drowsy, his shoulder and then his head leaning gently against that of the old man. And as the waves continued to crash he began to dream and began to understand. He began to realize that the old man was himself; that the ocean was himself; that all who had gone before, that all who he attempted to rediscover, to meet again, were all himself. Gradually the young boy awakened. The old man was gone and yet the old man, a teacher, a sharer, was still there—for he was himself.

My friends, my brothers and sisters, we share this story with you to underline the importance of that which you do. The acts that you perform, the efforts that you make toward growth, toward understanding, toward the assistance of others, are all acts of service, for as you learn for yourself, you learn for all, for all are yourself. Be not ashamed, then, if your heart directs you in paths of learning as well as those of service, for to understand the mysteries of your universe are to love it and to love a part is to love the all.

At this time I would transfer this contact to another instrument. I am Hatonn.

(Carla channeling)

I am Hatonn. We are with this instrument and we greet you once again in love and in light. May we thank the one known as Don for his gracious acceptance of our humble words said with such humor. We shall continue with a few thoughts through this instrument.

We speak of unity using water as a symbol, not only because your singing offered this image for our use in a tuned manner, but also because water is indeed a very appropriate symbol for the path that each of you, as drops of water, may understand himself to be taking as you seek the infinite sea of the creation. A drop of water may seem to be quite powerless and you as an individual may feel lacking or limited in some way in some situation. But, my friends, water is continuous and is not separated from itself. It may fall in drops in service to the fruits of the earth, but as it gathers and moves towards the great oceans, does it not carve out mighty channels from sheer luck that men could not hew so well with all their might? Water is quiet, and yet when stirred can be the most mighty of avengers, changing physical landscapes in minutes.

In your meditations, then, my friends, take each limitation and lack that you may feel that you have experienced, each disappointment that you feel in yourself or in others and offer them up as drops of water, to see them dissolve in a pure, clear ocean of the infinite Creator. Then, my friends, let the rainbow of sunlight through this water fill your heart and send you forth to serve the Creator, each in your own way and yet each a part of the great ocean of being. You are serving yourself, for all that you meet and all that you seek is yourself. If you love the ocean of the Creator then, my friends, you will learn to love each drop of water, each apparently individualized portion of that ocean, yourself and all others, all circumstances and all times.

At this time we would join with our brother, Laitos, in conditioning those in the room who mentally request it. We shall pause at this time, and continue through another instrument. I am Hatonn.

(Pause)

(C channeling)

I am Hatonn, and am with this instrument. We would at this time ask if there are any questions which we may attempt to answer for you. Are there any questions at this time?

M: Hatonn, can you tell me the purpose of the entity that appeared on the mountain in Guadelupe long ago with a message for the people? What was the purpose of that entity and can they be contacted through channeling?

I am Hatonn, and I am aware of your question. The entity of which you speak was a, what you would call, a wanderer, who incarnated in that particular area to reinforce certain lessons which he felt he was lacking in. The entity, as he became aware of his nature and as he became aware of [the] light of the Creator, sought to be a teacher, or you might say, an example for those entities that were aware of him. The entity may, as with other higher density entities, be contacted if there is sufficient calling for that particular entity.

However, we must warn that to seek a particular entity alone can sometimes be a bit dangerous due to a lack of a proper tuning and protection that is present in a group. To seek a particular entity alone opens one to others who would tend to mislead the one seeking contact. So, he may be contacted, but we would recommend that any attempt be made within the protection of a unified group.

May we answer you further, my brother?

M: That will do for now, thank you.

Carla: Excuse me. I had a question about that because the entity of Guadelupe that I was familiar with is Our Lady of Guadelupe, and I was wondering if what occurs when simple individuals who have been taught a simple—in this case, Catholic—belief system, seek, perhaps what they get is fashioned in part by their expectations, so that the entity of whom you speak, though in incarnation being male, would appear when sought as a stylized version of Our Lady. Would this be possible? Is this the same entity?

I am Hatonn, and am aware of your question. This is possible and, in this case, this instrument's particular biases due to his teaching he received at early stages of his development in this illusion have come out in the answer. We will say that you will find that which you seek. If one has a bias toward a male-dominated type of experience, then that individual will perceive those things which they do not fully understand as male, and same holds true for someone who is biased toward a female orientation.

You will, in this illusion, be often misled by things which you have incorporated into your being due to teaching by others within your society.

May we answer you further, my sister?

Carla: Yes. I have another related question. There have been many "Our Ladies" of various localities and I've wondered about them sometimes and wondered about their connection to the Confederation. Are these entities angelic entities of our planetary sphere, for the most part? Or are they those wanderers who've gone before the Counsel of Saturn and put in for this particular job for a certain length of time—to appear and to give inspiration? Or is it a mixture of the two—some from this planet's inner plane and some wanderers?

I am Hatonn, and am aware of your question. The phenomenon which is referred to as "Our Lady of …" is for the most part a combined calling of various groups which are dominated by an orientation toward Mary. Most often these are a manifestation of the desire of these groups. It is possible that in some cases that these were what you would call wanderers, but these were few, for as most wanderers became aware of themselves and of the lessons that they set for themselves, although they did provide examples for others of your world, [they] soon left to continue on their journey. It is rare that one remains for any length of time to be a teacher, other than by example of their own growth.

So, as we said, for the most part, these manifestations were the product of combined desire, faith and love of particular groups on your planet oriented toward the one known as Mary.

May we answer further?

Carla: No, not on that subject. I have a question about the use of precious metal in healing. If a crystal such as a diamond is worn over the green-ray energy center or the heart chakra, is it any aid to the healing if the chain on which this crystal is held be a precious metal such as gold …

(Side one of tape ends.)

(C channeling)

… apologize for the pause.

The metal which holds the crystal is not important. In any healing attempt the important thing is the one making the attempt and not the chain or the crystal, although the crystal is a focusing aid.

May we answer you further?

Carla: No, thank you, Hatonn.

Is there another question?

M: Is there a guardian of the Americas?

I am Hatonn, and am aware of your question, My brother, there is not one who only guards two of your continents. There are many who aid your planet, its people, but they do not literally subdivide your planet, but aid where needed, for there are no chosen areas.

May we answer you further, my brother?

M: No, thank you.

We thank you. Is there another question?

(Pause)

I am Hatonn, and am always eager and happy to be of whatever aid we can to you in the capacity of answering your various questions. We would ask once again if any have a question for us. I am Hatonn.

(Pause)

My friends, in this time of year you refer to as autumn, many living things upon your planet seem to wither and fade as your weather becomes colder, but as always, the rains fall and the sun shines down to aid, perpetuate those lives upon the planet. They are still nourished by rains. They will be nourished by the oncoming snow that will melt in your spring, refresh, aid in new growth, and once again reach toward light and continue [the] cycle that is characteristic of your planet.

There will be times when faith, in your search, it will seem to wither, and all seems dying and without meaning. But if one is patient, they will once again feel the rain nourishing. They will once again feel the love and the light that is them and is with them and will again grow, blossom and be renewed in their faith and their search.

We are known to you as Hatonn, and will be with you all when requested to aid in what way we can. We will now take our leave. We leave you now in the love and the light of the one infinite Creator. Adonai, my friends.

The Law of One, Book III, Session 74
October 28, 1981

Ra: I am Ra. I greet you in the love and in the light of the one infinite Creator. We communicate now.

Questioner: Would you first please give me the condition of the instrument?

Ra: I am Ra. It is as previously stated.

Questioner: Before we get to new material, in the last session there seems to be a small error that I corrected then having to do with this statement, "no working comes from it but only through it." Was this an error in the transmission? What caused this?

Ra: I am Ra. This instrument, while fully open to our narrow-band contact, at times experiences a sudden strengthening of the distortion which you call pain. This weakens the contact momentarily. This type of increased distortion has been occurring in this instrument's bodily complex with more frequency in the time period which you may term the previous fortnight. Although it is not normally a phenomenon which causes difficulties in transmission, it did so twice in the previous working. Both times it was necessary to correct or rectify the contact.

Questioner: Could you please describe the trance state? I am somewhat confused as to how, in a trance, pain can affect the instrument since I was of the opinion that there would be no feeling of pain by the bodily complex in the trance state?

Ra: I am Ra. This is correct. The instrument has no awareness of this or other sensations. However, we of Ra use the yellow-ray activated physical complex as a channel through which to speak. As the mind/body/spirit complex of the instrument leaves this physical shell in our keeping it is finely adjusted to our contact.

However, the distortion which you call pain, when sufficiently severe, mitigates against proper contact and, when the increased distortion is violent, can cause the tuning of the channel to waver. This tuning must then be corrected which we may do as the instrument offers us this opportunity freely.

Questioner: In a previous session there was a question on the archetypical mind that was not fully answered. I would like to continue with the answer to that question. Could you please continue with that, or will it be necessary for me to read the entire question over again?

Ra: I am Ra. As a general practice it is well to vibrate the query at the same space/time as the answer is desired. However, in this case it is acceptable to us that a note be inserted at this point in your recording of these sound vibratory complexes referring to the location of the query in previous workings.

(Note: This question was the last question asked in Session #67.)

The query, though thoughtful, is in some degree falling short of the realization of the nature of the archetypical mind. We may not teach/learn for any other to the extent that we become learn/teachers. Therefore, we shall make some general notations upon this interesting subject and allow the questioner to consider and further refine any queries.

The archetypical mind may be defined as that mind which is peculiar to the Logos of this planetary sphere. Thusly unlike the great cosmic all-mind, it contains the material which it pleased the Logos to offer as refinements to the great cosmic being-ness. The archetypical mind, then, is that which contains all facets which may affect mind or experience.

The Magician was named as a significant archetype. However, it was not recognized that this portion of the archetypical mind represents not a portion of the deep subconscious but the conscious mind and more especially the will. The archetype called by some the High Priestess, then, is the corresponding intuitive or subconscious faculty.

Let us observe the entity as it is in relationship to the archetypical mind. You may consider the possibilities of utilizing the correspondences between the mind/body/spirit in microcosm and the archetypical mind/body/spirit closely approaching the Creator. For instance, in your ritual performed to purify this place you use the term "Ve Geburah." It is a correct assumption that this is a portion or aspect of the one infinite Creator. However, there are various correspondences with the archetypical mind which may be more and more refined by the adept. "Ve Geburah" is the correspondence of Michael, of Mars, of the positive, of maleness. "Ve Gedulah" has correspondences to Jupiter, to femaleness, to the negative, to that portion of the Tree of Life concerned with Auriel.

We could go forward with more and more refinements of these two entries into the archetypical mind. We could discuss color correspondences, relationships with other archetypes, and so forth. This is the work of the adept, not the teach/learner. We may only suggest that there are systems of study which may address themselves to the aspects of the archetypical mind and it is well to choose one and study carefully. It is more nearly well if the adept go beyond whatever has been written and make such correspondences that the archetype can be called upon at will.

Questioner: I have a statement here that I am going to make and let you correct. I see that the disciplines of the personality feed the indigo-ray energy center and affect the power of the white magician by unblocking the lower energy centers allowing for the free flow of the upward spiraling light to reach the indigo center. Is this correct?

Ra: I am Ra. No.

Questioner: Will you please correct me?

Ra: I am Ra. The indigo center is indeed most important for the work of the adept. However, it cannot, no matter how crystallized, correct to any extent whatsoever imbalances or blockages in other energy centers. They must needs be cleared seriatim from red upwards.

Questioner: I'm not sure exactly if I understand this. The question is how do disciplines of the personality feed the indigo-ray energy center and affect the power of the white magician? Does that question make sense?

Ra: I am Ra. Yes.

Questioner: Would you answer it please?

Ra: I am Ra. We would be happy to answer this query. We understood the previous query as being of other import. The indigo ray is the ray of the adept. There is an identification between the crystallization of that energy center and the improvement of the working of the mind/body/spirit as it begins to transcend space/time balancing and to enter the combined realms of space/time and time/space.

Questioner: Let me see if I have a wrong opinion here of the effect of disciplines of the personality. I was assuming that the discipline of the personality to, shall we say, have a balanced attitude toward a single fellow entity would properly clear and balance, to some extent, the orange-ray energy center. Is this correct?

Ra: I am Ra. We cannot say that you speak incorrectly but merely less than completely. The disciplined personality, when faced with an other-self, has all centers balanced according to its unique balance. Thusly the other-self looks in a mirror seeing its self.

Questioner: The disciplines of the personality are the paramount work of any who have become consciously aware of the process of evolution. Am I correct on that statement?

Ra: I am Ra. Quite.

Questioner: What I am trying to get at is how these disciplines affect the energy centers and the power of the white magician. Will you tell me how that works?

Ra: I am Ra. The heart of the discipline of the personality is threefold. One, know your self. Two, accept your self. Three, become the Creator.

The third step is that step which, when accomplished, renders one the most humble servant of all, transparent in personality and completely able to know and accept other-selves. In relation to the pursuit of the magical working the continuing discipline of the personality involves the adept in knowing its self, accepting its self, and thus clearing the path towards the great indigo gateway to the Creator. To become the Creator is to become all that there is. There is, then, no personality in the sense with which the adept begins its learn/teaching. As the consciousness of the indigo ray becomes more crystalline, more work may be done; more may be expressed from intelligent infinity.

Questioner: You stated that a working of service to others has the potential of alerting a great mass of light strength. Could you describe just exactly how this works and what the uses of this would be?

Ra: I am Ra. There are sound vibratory complexes which act much like the dialing of your telephone. When they are appropriately vibrated with accompanying will and concentration it is as though many upon your metaphysical or inner planes received a telephone call. This call they answer by their attention to your working.

Questioner: There are many of these. The ones most obvious in our society are those used in the church rather than those used by the magical adept. What is the difference in the effect in those used in our various churches and those specifically magical incantations used by the adept?

Ra: I am Ra. If all in your churches were adepts consciously full of will, of seeking, of concentration, of conscious knowledge of the calling, there would be no difference. The efficacy of the calling is a function of the magical qualities of those who call; that is, their desire to seek the altered state of consciousness desired.

Questioner: In selecting the protective ritual we finally agreed upon the Banishing Ritual of the Lesser Pentagram. I assume that these sound vibratory complexes are of the type of which you speak for the alerting of those on the inner planes. Is this correct?

Ra: I am Ra. This is correct.

Questioner: If we had constructed a ritual of our own with words used for the first time in this sequence of protection what would have been the relative merit of this with respect to the ritual that we chose?

Ra: I am Ra. It would be less. In constructing ritual it is well to study the body of written work which is available for names of positive or service to others power are available.

Questioner: I will make an analogy to the loudness of the ringing of the telephone in using the ritual as the efficiency of the practitioners using the ritual. I see several things affecting the efficiency of the ritual: first, the desire of the practitioners to serve, their ability to invoke the magical personality, their ability to visualize while performing the ritual, and let me ask you as to the relative importance of those items and how each may be intensified?

Ra: I am Ra. This query borders upon over-specificity. It is most important for the adept to feel its own growth as teach/learner.

We may only say that you correctly surmise the paramount import of the magical personality. This is a study in itself. With the appropriate emotional will, polarity, and purity, work may be done with or without proper sound vibration complexes. However, there is no need for the blunt instrument when the scalpel is available.

Questioner: I assume that the reason that the rituals that have been used previously are of effect is that these words have built a bias in consciousness of those who have worked in these areas so that those who are of a distortion of mind that we seek will respond to imprint in consciousness of this series of words. Is this correct?

Ra: I am Ra. This is, to a great extent, correct. The exception is the sounding of some of what you call your Hebrew and some of what you call you Sanskrit vowels. These sound vibration complexes have power before time and space and represent configurations of light which built all that there is.

Questioner: Why do these sounds have this property?

Ra: I am Ra. The correspondence in vibratory complex is mathematical.

At this time we have enough transferred energy for one full query.

Questioner: How did the users of these sounds, Sanskrit and Hebrew, determine what these sounds were?

Ra: I am Ra. In the case of the Hebrew that entity known as Yahweh aided this knowledge through impression upon the material of genetic coding which became language, as you call it.

In the case of Sanskrit the sound vibrations are pure due to the lack of previous, what you call, alphabet or letter-naming. Thus the sound vibration complexes seemed to fall into place as from the Logos. This was a more, shall we say, natural or unaided situation or process.

We would at this time make note of the incident in the previous working where our contact was incorrectly placed for a short period and was then corrected. In the exercise of the fire you may see the initial spiral clockwise from the green-ray energy center, through the shoulders and head, then through the elbows, then to the left hand. The channel had been corrected before the remainder of this answer was completed.

Is there a brief query at this time?

Questioner: Is there anything that we could do to make the instrument more comfortable or to improve the contact?

Ra: I am Ra. All is well. The instrument continues in some pain, as you call this distortion. The neck area remains most distorted although the changes have been, to a small degree, helpful. The alignments are good.

We would leave you now, my friends, in the love and in the light of the one infinite Creator. Go forth, then, glorying and rejoicing in the power and in the peace of the one infinite Creator. Adonai.

L/L Research

L/L Research is a subsidiary of Rock Creek Research & Development Laboratories, Inc.

P.O. Box 5195
Louisville, KY 40255-0195

www.llresearch.org

Rock Creek is a non-profit corporation dedicated to discovering and sharing information which may aid in the spiritual evolution of humankind.

ABOUT THE CONTENTS OF THIS TRANSCRIPT: This telepathic channeling has been taken from transcriptions of the weekly study and meditation meetings of the Rock Creek Research & Development Laboratories and L/L Research. It is offered in the hope that it may be useful to you. As the Confederation entities always make a point of saying, please use your discrimination and judgment in assessing this material. If something rings true to you, fine. If something does not resonate, please leave it behind, for neither we nor those of the Confederation would wish to be a stumbling block for any.

© 2009 L/L RESEARCH

THE LAW OF ONE, BOOK III, SESSION 75
OCTOBER 31, 1981

Ra: I am Ra. I greet you in the love and in the light of the one infinite Creator. We communicate now.

Questioner: The instrument would like to know why twice during the "Benedictus" portion of the music she sang in a group concert that she experienced what she believes to be a psychic attack?

Ra: I am Ra. This is not a minor query.[2] We shall first remove the notations which are minor. In the vibrating, which you call singing, of the portion of what this instrument hallows as the Mass which immediately precedes that which is the chink called the "Hosanna" there is an amount of physical exertion required that is exhausting to any entity. This portion of which we speak is termed the "Sanctus." We come now to the matter of interest.

When the entity Jehoshuah[3] decided to return to the location called Jerusalem for the holy days of its people it turned from work mixing love and wisdom and embraced martyrdom which is the work of love without wisdom.

The "Hosanna," as it is termed, and the following "Benedictus," is that which is the written summation of what was shouted as Jehoshuah came into the place of its martyrdom. The general acceptance of this shout, "Hosanna to the son of David! Hosanna in the highest! Blessed is he who comes in the name of the Lord!" by that which is called the church has been a misstatement, an occurrence which has been, perhaps, unfortunate for it is more distorted than much of the so-called Mass.

There were two factions present to greet Jehoshuah, firstly, a small group of those which hoped for an earthly king. However, Jehoshuah rode upon an ass stating by its very demeanor that it was no earthly king and wished no fight with Roman or Sadducee.

The greater number were those which had been instructed by rabbi and elder to make jest of this entity, for those of the hierarchy feared this entity who seemed to be one of them, giving respect to their laws and then, in their eyes, betraying those time-honored laws and taking the people with it.

The chink for this instrument is this subtle situation which echoes down through your space/time and, more than this, the place the "Hosanna" holds as the harbinger of that turning to martyrdom. We may speak only generally here. The instrument did not experience the full force of the greeting which it correctly identified during the "Hosanna" due to the intense concentration necessary to vibrate its portion of that composition. However, the "Benedictus" in

---

[2] It may seem that there is an excessive amount of personal and rather melodramatic material about psychic attack included here. We considered long and hard before deciding not to delete it. Our reason—Ra seems to suggest that any "light worker" will, if successful in this work, attract some sort of negatively-oriented greeting. Therefore, we wish to share our experiences and Ra's discussion of them, in hopes that the information might be helpful.

[3] Ra has previously identified this name as the name of Jesus in biblical times.

this particular rendition of these words is vibrated by one entity. Thus the instrument relaxed its concentration and was immediately open to the fuller greeting.

Questioner: The chink then, as I understand it, was originally created by the decision of Jesus to take the path of martyrdom? Is this correct?

Ra: I am Ra. This is, in relation to this instrument, quite correct. It is aware of certain over-balances towards love, even to martyrdom but has not yet, to any significant degree, balanced these distortions. We do not imply that this course of unbridled compassion has any fault but affirm its perfection. It is an example of love which has served as beacon to many.

For those who seek further, the consequences of martyrdom must be considered, for in martyrdom lies the end of the opportunity, in the density of the martyr, to offer love and light. Each entity must seek its deepest path.

Questioner: Let me see, then, if I understand how the Orion entity finds a chink in this distortion. The entity identifying in any amount toward martyrdom is then open by its free will to the aid of the Orion group to make it a martyr. Am I correct?

Ra: I am Ra. You are correct only in the quite specialized position in which the instrument finds itself, that is, of being involved in and dedicated to work which is magical or extremely polarized in nature. This group entered this work with polarity but virtual innocence as to the magical nature of this polarity. That it is beginning to discover.

Questioner: How was the Orion entity able to act through this linkage of the "Hosanna"? Was this simply because of mental distortions of the instrument at this period of time, because of that suggested by the music, or was it a more physical or metaphysical link from the time of Christ?

Ra: I am Ra. Firstly, the latter supposition is false. This entity is not linked with the entity, Jehoshuah. Secondly, there is a most unique circumstance. There is an entity which has attracted the attention of an Orion light being. This is extremely rare.

This entity has an intense devotion to the teachings and example of the one it calls Jesus. This entity then vibrates in song a most demanding version, called The Mass in B Minor by Bach, of this exemplary votive complex of sound vibrations. The entity is consciously identifying with each part of this Mass. Only thusly was the chink made available. As you can see, it is not an ordinary occurrence and would not have happened had any ingredient been left out: exhaustion, bias in the belief complexes, attention from an Orion entity, and the metaphysical nature of that particular set of words.

Questioner: What was the Orion entity's objective with respect to the entity you spoke of who, in a demanding manner, sings the Mass?

Ra: I am Ra. The Orion entity wishes to remove the instrument.

Questioner: Is this a fourth- or a fifth-density?

Ra: I am Ra. This instrument is being greeted by a fifth-density entity which has lost some polarity due to its lack of dictatorship over the disposition of the instrument's mind/body/spirit or its yellow-ray activated physical complex.

Questioner: You are speaking of this other person now who sang in the Mass? Is this correct?

Ra: I am Ra. No.

Questioner: I think there was a little miscommunication here. I was asking about the other person who sings the Mass in creating this chink that was also greeted by an Orion entity, and my question was what density is the Orion entity who greets the other person who sings the Mass?

Ra: I am Ra. We did not speak of any entity but the instrument.

Questioner: OK. I misunderstood. I thought you were speaking of someone else in the singing group who had been identified with the singing. The entire time we were speaking we were speaking only of the instrument? Is this correct?

Ra: I am Ra. This is correct.

Questioner: I am sorry for my confusion. Sometimes, as you say, sound vibration complexes are not very adequate.

The answer to this next question probably has to do with our distorted view of time, but as I see it, Wanderers in this density who come from the fifth-density or sixth-density should already be of a relatively high degree of adeptness and they must follow a slightly different path back to the adeptness that they once had in a higher density and get as close to it as they can in the third-density. Is this correct?

Ra: I am Ra. Your query is less than perfectly focused. We shall address the subject in general.

There are many Wanderers whom you may call adepts who do no conscious work in the present incarnation. It is a matter of attention. One may be a fine catcher of your game sphere, but if the eye is not turned as this sphere is tossed then perchance it will pass the entity by. If it turned its eyes upon the sphere, catching would be easy. In the case of Wanderers which seek to recapitulate the degree of adeptness which each had acquired previous to this life experience, we may note that even after the forgetting process has been penetrated there is still the yellow activated body which does not respond as does the adept which is of a green- or blue-ray activated body. Thusly, you may see the inevitability of frustrations and confusion due to the inherent difficulties of manipulating the finer forces of consciousness through the chemical apparatus of the yellow-ray activated body.

Questioner: You probably can't answer this, but are there any suggestions that you could give with respect to the instrument's coming hospital experience that could be of benefit for her?

Ra: I am Ra. We may make one suggestion and leave the remainder with the Creator. It is well for each to realize its self as the Creator. Thusly each may support each including the support of self by humble love of self as Creator.

Questioner: You spoke in a previous session about certain Hebrew and Sanskrit sound vibratory complexes being powerful because they were mathematically related to that which was the creation. Could you expand on this understanding as to how these are linked?

Ra: I am Ra. As we previously stated the linkage is mathematical or that of the ratio you may consider musical. There are those whose mind complex activities would attempt to resolve this mathematical ratio but at present the coloration of the intoned vowel is part of the vibration which cannot be accurately measured. However, it is equivalent to types of rotation of your primary material particles.

Questioner: If these sounds are precisely vibrated then what effect or use, with respect to the purposes of the adept, would they have?

Ra: I am Ra. You may consider the concept of sympathetic resonance. When certain sounds are correctly vibrated, the creation sings.

Questioner: Would these sounds, then, be of a musical nature in that there would be a musical arrangement of many different sound vibrations, or would this apply to just one single note? Which would it apply more to?

Ra: I am Ra. This query is not easily answered. In some cases only the intoned vowel has effect. In other cases, most notably Sanskrit combinations, the selection of harmonic intervals is also of resonant nature.

Questioner: Then would the adept use this resonant quality to become more one with the creation and, therefore, attain his objective in that way?

Ra: I am Ra. It would be perhaps more accurate to state that in this circumstance the creation becomes more and more contained within the practitioner. The balance of your query is correct.

Questioner: Could you tell me the musical name of the notes to be intoned that are of this quality?

Ra: I am Ra. We may not.

Questioner: I didn't think that you could, but I thought it wouldn't hurt to ask.

Then I assume that these must be sought out and determined by empirical observation of their effect by the seeker. Is this correct?

Ra: I am Ra. This is partially correct. As your seeking continues there will be added to empirical data that acuity of sensibility which continued working in the ways of the adept offers.

Questioner: Is the exercise of the fire best for the instrument, or is there anything better that we could do other than the things that you have already suggested to aid the instrument?

Ra: I am Ra. Continue as you are at present. We cannot speak of the future as we may then affect it, but there is a great probability/possibility if you follow the path which you now tread that more efficacious methods for the entire group will be established.

Questioner: You mentioned in an earlier session that the hair was an antennae. Could you expand on that statement as to how that works?

Ra: I am Ra. It is difficult to so do due to the metaphysical nature of this antennae-effect. Your physics are concerned with measurements in your physical complex of experience. The metaphysical nature of the contact of those in time/space is such that the hair, as it has significant length, becomes as a type of electrical battery which stays charged and tuned and is then able to aid contact even when there are small anomalies in the contact.

Questioner: Is there an optimum length of hair for this aid?

Ra: I am Ra. There is no outer limit on length but the, shall we say, inner limit is approximately four to four and one-half inches depending upon the strength of the contact and the nature of the instrument.

Questioner: May anyone in third density accomplish some degree of healing if they have the proper will, desire, and polarity, or is there a minimal balance of the energy centers of the healer that is also necessary?

Ra: I am Ra. Any entity may at any time instantaneously clear and balance its energy centers. Thus in many cases those normally quite blocked, weakened, and distorted may, through love and strength of will, become healers momentarily. To be a healer by nature one must indeed train its self in the disciplines of the personality.

Questioner: How does the use of the magical ritual invoking the magical personality aid the mind/body/spirit complex totality? Could you expand on the answer that you gave in the last session with respect to that?

Ra: I am Ra. When the magical personality is properly and efficaciously invoked the self has invoked its higher self. Thus a bridge betwixt space/time and time/space is made and the sixth-density magical personality experiences directly the third-density catalyst for the duration of the working. It is most central to deliberately take off the magical personality after the working in order that the higher self resume its appropriate configuration as analog to the space/time mind/body/spirit.

Questioner: Then you are saying that the act, signal, or key for the invoking of the magical personality which is the putting of something on or a gesture should also be as carefully taken off to reverse the gesture perhaps at the end of the invocation. Is this correct?

Ra: I am Ra. This is correct. It should be fastidiously accomplished either in mind or by gesture as well if this is of significant aid.

Questioner: Now in the invocation of the magical personality it is not necessarily effective for the neophyte. Is there a point at which there is a definite quantum change and that then the magical personality does reside in the neophyte, or can it be done in small degrees or percentages of magical personality as the neophyte becomes more adept?

Ra: I am Ra. The latter is correct.

Questioner: The three aspects of the magical personality are stated to be power, love, and wisdom. Is this correct and are these the only primary aspects of the magical personality?

Ra: I am Ra. The three aspects of the magical personality, power, love, and wisdom, are so called in order that attention be paid to each aspect in developing the basic tool of the adept; that is, its self. It is by no means a personality of three aspects. It is a being of unity, a being of sixth density, and equivalent to what you call your higher self and at the same time is a personality enormously rich in variety of experience and subtlety of emotion.

The three aspects are given that the neophyte not abuse the tools of its trade but rather approach those tools balanced in the center of love and wisdom and thus seeking power in order to serve.

Questioner: Then is it correct that a good sequence for the developing of the magical personality would be alternate meditations first on power, and then a meditation on love, and then a meditation on wisdom and then to continue cycling that way?

Ra: I am Ra. This is indeed an appropriate technique. In this particular group there is an additional aid in that each entity manifests one of these qualities in a manner which approaches the archetype. Thusly visualization may be personalized and much love and support within the group generated.

Questioner: You made the statement in a previous session that the true adept lives more and more as it is. Will you explain and expand more upon that statement?

Ra: I am Ra. Each entity is the Creator. The entity, as it becomes more and more conscious of its self, gradually comes to the turning point at which it determines to seek either in service to others or in service to self. The seeker becomes the adept when it has balanced with minimal adequacy the energy centers red, orange, yellow, and blue with the addition of the green for the positive, thus moving into indigo work.

The adept then begins to do less of the preliminary or outer work, having to do with function, and begins to effect the inner work which has to do with being. As the adept becomes a more and more consciously crystallized entity it gradually manifests more and more of that which it always has been since before time; that is, the one infinite Creator.

This instrument begins to show rapid distortion towards increase of pain.

We, therefore, would offer time for any brief query before we leave this working.

Questioner: Is there anything that we can do to make the instrument more comfortable or to improve the contact?

Ra: I am Ra. You are conscientious. The alignments are well.

I am Ra. I leave you, my friends, in the love and the light of the one infinite Creator. Go forth, therefore, rejoicing in the power and peace of the one infinite Creator. Adonai.

L/L Research is a subsidiary of Rock Creek Research & Development Laboratories, Inc.

P.O. Box 5195
Louisville, KY 40255-0195

L/L Research

www.llresearch.org

Rock Creek is a non-profit corporation dedicated to discovering and sharing information which may aid in the spiritual evolution of humankind.

ABOUT THE CONTENTS OF THIS TRANSCRIPT: This telepathic channeling has been taken from transcriptions of the weekly study and meditation meetings of the Rock Creek Research & Development Laboratories and L/L Research. It is offered in the hope that it may be useful to you. As the Confederation entities always make a point of saying, please use your discrimination and judgment in assessing this material. If something rings true to you, fine. If something does not resonate, please leave it behind, for neither we nor those of the Confederation would wish to be a stumbling block for any.

© 2009 L/L RESEARCH

THE LAW OF ONE, BOOK V, SESSION 75, FRAGMENT 41
OCTOBER 31, 1981

Jim: In Session 75 we were trying to help Carla through her upcoming hand operation in a local hospital. When the Ra contact began the pre-incarnatively chosen arthritic limitations set in more strongly than ever, and Carla's desire to do things for others with hands that were meant to be restricted from mundane work brought more and more pain and damage to the arthritic joints—thus necessitating the operation for short-term repair. The length or success of the surgical repairs would depend upon Carla's growing ability to accept the limitations that she placed upon herself before the incarnation in order that her focus might move inward and prepare her for the possibility of becoming a channel. Her ability to accept these limitations delayed the next surgery for four years.

Since she had been a Christian mystic from birth certain prayers of her Episcopalian Church, and the communion service in particular, were felt by Ra to be of aid to her. The Banishing Ritual of the Lesser Pentagram which we had been using for some time to purify our place of working for the Ra contact was suggested for her hospital room and the operating room. The greatest protective and healing device, however, was seen to be love, whether manifest or unspoken, for all any ritual such as prayer, communion, or the Banishing Ritual of the Lesser Pentagram actually does is alert positively-polarized discarnate entities so that they may provide that quality which we call love from their quarters for whatever the purpose might be. Each of us may also provide that same love as a function of our truly caring for another. As we learn the lessons of love within this third-density illusion we are also learning the basics of healing and protection.

Carla: There are surprises in this material, even after all these years. It was not until this moment (writing in 1997) that Jim and I realized we did not follow one of Ra's suggestions during that hospital experience. Jim, Don and I vibrated the Banishing Ritual twice a day; Jim and I both remember that. Neither of us can recall reading the Mass in any form. We just missed it. Imagine wasting Ra's advice! I know we did not do that on purpose. After 16 years, all we can say is that refrain of bozos everywhere … oops!

As to the hand-holding when I meditated, this was a practice that began after a particularly discomfiting experience during one of our public meditation sessions. These were completely separate from the sessions with Ra. Any and all could come and check us out. I did not go into trance at these sessions as I did with Ra sessions, but channeled from a very light trance state. However, during the question and answer period, someone asked a question to which I had no earthly idea about, and I thought to myself, "I wish I were channeling Ra." Immediately, I began to leave my body, which was absolutely NOT to be done, according to Ra. The source which I was channeling, Latwii, simply kept me channeling—probably pure nonsense—but it sufficed to keep me in the body. After that, someone, usually Jim, always held my hand during sessions. To this day, Jim holds my hand as we meditate during our morning offering, and at all meditation sessions we offer. Better safe than sorry is the cliché which covers this.

I remember with great affection the utter fidelity of love and concern that Don and Jim showed me during this time. It was very hard for Don especially to see me in pain. But he did not flinch or draw away, but rather tried ceaselessly to protect and aid me. The same could be said of Jim, but I think it was light-years harder for Don to bear this than Jim. Jim is a simple, straightforward person. To him what is, is. I remember asking him once if all he was going to say in this life was "yup, nope or maybe." "Yup," he replied. Then, after considering, he said, "Nope." Then more consideration, and he finally settled on, "Maybe!" To Don my pain was his pain, for we were truly one being in that ineffable sense which is beyond space and time. The pain, severe though it was, did not overly distress me, but it foundered Don. His level of concern was profound.

Through the years since this channeling, I have more and more come to appreciate Ra's suggestion that I fully accept my limitations. After my miraculous rehabilitation in 1992, I found myself out of the wheelchair and vertical for the first time in many years. A year ago, I was able to give the downstairs hospital bed back to Medicare. (I still find one helpful at night, for sleeping.) when I first started to rebuild a "vertical" life, I was full of ideas as to what I might accomplish. I tried going back to school to get myself current in my old field of library service. I tried to take a job. I volunteered at church far beyond my actual capacity to serve. And this took its toll, as I collected injuries, broken ankle, sprained knees, and two more hand operations. Finally, about a year ago, I managed to pare down my work to the point where I allowed much rest time within the schedule of the day. I've tinkered with this schedule, finding ways to harmonize my efforts with Jim's, finding how to nurture myself, finding what priorities my life really has. I am hopeful that I have at this point realized these set limits to effort, and have begun to cooperate with my destiny.

I fully respect my pre-incarnative choice to take on these uncomfortable limitations. The experience has hollowed me out and made me an ever better channel. I continue to rejoice as I see little bits of my ego fall away. My prayer these days is "Lord, show me Thy ways." There is much work left for me, a true idiot. But I exult in being upon the King's highway

Session 75, October 31, 1981

Questioner: Could you first please give me the condition of the instrument?

Ra: I am Ra. It is as previously stated with some slight lessening of the reserve of vital energy due to mental/emotional distortions regarding what you call the future.

Questioner: I felt that this session was advisable before the instrument has her hospital experience. She wished to ask a few questions, if possible, about that.

First, is there anything that the instrument or we might do to improve the hospital experience or to aid the instrument in any way with respect to this?

Ra: I am Ra. Yes. There are ways of aiding the mental/emotional state of this entity with the notation that this is so only for this entity or one of like distortions. There is also a general thing which may be accomplished to improve the location which is called the hospital.

The first aiding has to do with the vibration of the ritual with which this entity is most familiar and which this entity has long used to distort its perception of the one infinite Creator. This is an helpful thing at any point in the diurnal period but is especially helpful as your sun body removes itself from your local sight.

The general improvement of the place where the performance of the ritual of the purification is to be performed is known. We may note that the distortion towards love, as you call this spiritual/emotional complex which is felt by each for this entity, will be of aid whether this is expressed or unmanifest as there is no protection greater than love.

Questioner: Do you mean that it would be valuable to perform the Banishing Ritual of the Lesser Pentagram in the room in which she will be occupying in the hospital?

Ra: I am Ra. This is correct.

Questioner: I was wondering about the operating room. That might be very difficult. Would it be helpful there?

Ra: I am Ra. This is correct. We may note that it is always helpful. Therefore, it is not easy to posit a query to which you would not receive the answer which we offer. This does not indicate that it is essential to purify a place. The power of visualization may aid in your support where you cannot intrude in your physical form.

Questioner: I see the way to do this as a visualization of the operating room and a visualization of the three of us performing the banishing ritual in the room as we perform it at another location. Is this the correct procedure?

Ra: I am Ra. This is one correct method of achieving your desired configuration.

Questioner: Is there a better method than that?

Ra: I am Ra. There are better methods for those more practiced. For this group, this method is well.

Questioner: I would assume those more practiced would leave their physical bodies and, in the other body, enter the room and practice the ritual. Is this what you mean?

Ra: I am Ra. This is correct.

Questioner: The instrument would like to know if she can meditate in the hospital without someone holding her hand. Would this be a safe practice?

Ra: I am Ra. We might suggest that the instrument may pray with safety but only meditate with another entity's tactile protection.

Questioner: The instrument would like to know what she can do to improve the condition of her back as she feels it will be a problem for the operation?

Ra: I am Ra. As we scan the physical complex we find several factors contributing to one general distortion experienced by the instrument. Two of these distortions have been diagnosed; one has not; nor will the entity be willing to accept the chemicals sufficient to cause cessation of this distortion you call pain.

In general we may say that the sole modality addressing itself specifically to all three contributing distortions, which is not now being used, is that of the warmed water which is moved with gentle force repeatedly against the entire physical complex while the physical vehicle is seated. This would be of some aid if practiced daily after the exercise period.

Questioner: Did the exercise of the fire performed before the session help the instrument?

Ra: I am Ra. There was some slight physical aid to the instrument. This will enlarge itself as the practitioner learns/teaches its healing art. Further, there is distortion in the mental/emotional complex which feeds the vital energy towards comfort due to support which tends to build up the level of vital energy as this entity is a sensitive instrument.

Questioner: Was the exercise of the fire properly done?

Ra: I am Ra. The baton is well visualized. The conductor will learn to hear the entire score of the great music of its art.

Questioner: I assume that if this can be fully accomplished that exercise will result in total healing of the distortions of the instrument to such an extent that operations would be unnecessary. Is this correct?

Ra: I am Ra. No.

Questioner: What else is necessary, the instrument's acceptance?

Ra: I am Ra. This is correct. The case with this instrument being delicate since it must totally accept much which the limitations it now experiences cause to occur involuntarily. This is a pre-incarnative choice.

L/L Research

L/L Research is a subsidiary of Rock Creek Research & Development Laboratories, Inc.

P.O. Box 5195
Louisville, KY 40255-0195

www.llresearch.org

Rock Creek is a non-profit corporation dedicated to discovering and sharing information which may aid in the spiritual evolution of humankind.

ABOUT THE CONTENTS OF THIS TRANSCRIPT: This telepathic channeling has been taken from transcriptions of the weekly study and meditation meetings of the Rock Creek Research & Development Laboratories and L/L Research. It is offered in the hope that it may be useful to you. As the Confederation entities always make a point of saying, please use your discrimination and judgment in assessing this material. If something rings true to you, fine. If something does not resonate, please leave it behind, for neither we nor those of the Confederation would wish to be a stumbling block for any.

CAVEAT: This transcript is being published by L/L Research in a not yet final form. It has, however, been edited and any obvious errors have been corrected. When it is in a final form, this caveat will be removed.

© 2009 L/L Research

Sunday Meditation
November 1, 1981

(Carla channeling)

I am Hatonn, and I greet you my friends, in the love and in the light of the infinite Creator. It is a pleasure and a privilege to be with you this evening and we would share with you a story.

There was once a young woman whose talent with an instrument you call the violin was so great that all who knew her were aware that this young woman was truly remarkable. She had, in the early days of her childhood, been given a small instrument and had been given lessons by a teacher who was neither bad nor good and this child prodigy learned so quickly that she soon outstripped her teacher. There was no effort in her excellence. It flowed from her as a gift and it was as little thought of. As a young woman this person had quickly achieved great fame and she traveled and played before great audiences and received applause and acclaims for this great gift which she had, yet she did not appreciate it, learn from it nor think of it, for it had always been with her and there was no effort involved in her art.

One day she came to a city thinking that she was to play a certain violin concerto with the orchestra which had hired her. She was informed that her information was incorrect and that the orchestra had practiced a different piece, one which she did not know. It was a piece for a virtuoso and she had only hours to rehearse. The unfamiliar score stared at her like an enemy and she felt fear. She picked up her instrument and began to work as she had never worked.

Each difficult place made her want to weep, for she had so little time to understand the music, so little time to understand the fingerings, so little time to grasp the scope and the feeling of the piece and to play the notes correctly. Much was expected of her by the audience which would surely come. Feverishly, desperately, she worked. Not once could she play the entire piece with no errors.

The young woman's time was up. She dressed, she came to the concert, she took her bows and stood before the full house. The music which she had so feverishly practiced was jumbled in her head and yet she knew she must remember it. She had always made mistakes and yet she knew she must not. And all the faces looked expectantly towards her. The conductor lifted his baton and she played as she had never played before. If notes were missed, they went by so quickly that the reviewer missed them, for the piece was played with passion and with feeling, and she went away, knowing for the first time the experience of joy in her chosen part.

My friends, there are many, many times when in your experience those things about you flow easily. Gifts are given you and you accept them thoughtlessly, for they are not hard won. Then a whirlwind seems to hit you, a dilemma, a difficulty, an argument, and you begin to wonder why you must go through this experience. It is your chance, my friends, for growth. In the situation where you are tried, where you are tested, you are also given a great opportunity and your response, no matter how flawed, will bring you joy if the response contains the best that you can give. It is good to experience the calm times, the quiet times, but to be taken by the whirlwind is a great privilege, one which is given to those in your illusion, that you may make the great choice to love and to be of service.

How easy it is to be pleasant when there is no reason not to be. The world about you, my friends, often seems to be calm. This is an illusion. In your geographical location many are violent, many hungry, many in pain, many in the depths of sorrow, and somehow you find your perceptions those of one led into a quiet cove. Use those times, my friends, in meditation, in appreciation of those things about you which you can so easily take for granted and when the whirlwind takes you, realize that this is most appropriate for those experiencing your density. This is the way that work is done within your understanding. This is the way your experience may be utilized to the utmost by your seeking consciousness. And know always that the whirlwind is of the Creator, and it will place you safe once again in that quiet cove of calm where you may once again seek in meditation to understand, and seek in the giving of yourself to express that understanding of love, for the whirlwind is the Creator

Love is far beyond that which you think of as love. The characteristics of this great creative force include those characteristics of the whirlwind which ceaselessly beat against your life to aid you as you wish to be aided, to change you as you choose to change. Know trouble as your friend, for all things and all qualities are of the one Creator, whose only wish for each is love. The ways of this love are many and varied, but all ways are love, all difficulties lead to calm, to light, to beauty. All the false images of your illusion lead to the one original Thought which is the truth which you all seek.

At this time I would pause so that I and my brother of Laitos may begin to condition each of those in the room and after a brief pause we will transfer this contact to another instrument. I am Hatonn.

(Pause)

(L channeling)

I am Hatonn, and I greet you once again in the love and the light of the Creator. It is important that we are able and allowed to exercise the individuals who would offer themselves as instruments for this service, for in doing so we train not only those who so generously offer, but also ourselves. We, therefore, are grateful for this opportunity by which you, in effect, train us in the proper manner in which to establish contact with each individual. For this reason we would like at this time to transfer our contact to yet another instrument. I am Hatonn.

(C channeling)

I am Hatonn, and am now with this instrument. We of Hatonn are always willing to be a part of your meditations and will aid in any way we can. We wish to say once again that you need but request and we shall be with you. We of Hatonn do appreciate each opportunity in which we can serve you, for we grow as we serve and learn as we attempt to share the knowledge that is available to us which we may impart to you within the guidelines of the Law of Free Will. We bring a simple message of love, the infinite Creator's simple but multifaceted message which, though simple in its whole, has so many aspects in areas which may, as you become aware, seem confusing and at times not what you, in your existence refer to as love, for in your existence you may become aware of the aspects of love without understanding, but with awareness you may begin to accept and develop faith in the love of the one infinite Creator.

We will now transfer contact once again so as to allow another to exercise their ability to receive and vocalize our vibration. I am Hatonn.

(Pause)

(C channeling)

I am Hatonn, and am once again with this instrument. We were attempting to speak a few words through the one known as D, and would ask him to relax if he will and we shall once again attempt to speak a few words through this new instrument. If he would relax and refrain from analysis and speak freely, we will now once again transfer to the one known as D. I am Hatonn.

(Pause)

(C channeling)

I am Hatonn, and am once again with this instrument. We are having some difficulty in our attempts to contact the one known as D. We assure him that a good contact was achieved and that we shall, as well as our brothers of Laitos, work with him at any that that he might request our presence. We would now attempt to contact one known as S, give her a chance to experience our particular vibration. We simply ask that she refrain from analyzing of thought, relax and freely speak those thoughts that she receives. We will now transfer to the one known as S. I am Hatonn.

(S channeling)

I am Hatonn, and am with this instrument. It is a pleasure to greet you through this instrument once more. We of Hatonn are always glad to allow each of you who request it the experience of our conditioning vibration. We would assure each of you that you need only to mentally request our presence in your daily meditations and we would be honored to join you.

We are having some difficulty transmitting at this time and would transfer this contact to another instrument. I am Hatonn.

(C channeling)

I am Hatonn, and am with this instrument. We are greatly pleased by the progress of the one known as S and assure her that through practice her skill as a channel will improve and we shall learn, as we are allowed to aid, how to better make contact with this particular channel, for we also learn as we aid you in your endeavor to be, as you refer to them, a vocal channel for members of the Confederation. We are indeed privileged to have so many in this group, both former and present individuals, who have sought to and have become channels for our simple messages and assure each that in this, that too many cooks shall not spoil the broth, for …

(Side one of tape ends.)

(C channeling)

… for hesitation, but we were allowing for the clicks to subside before continuing.

As we began, though each seems to be seeking to improve in an activity that seems to have became crowded in this case, we assure each that this ability, once learned, is not wasted, for even though you may at a later time at what you refer to as your future leave this particular group, you retain your abilities and hopefully will share that which you have experienced in your seeking.

We indeed feel a closeness to each and all within this group and cannot help but do what you call smile at the sight and sound of the love that radiates from within those with whom we have, over these past few years, been with in this group. We of Hatonn are indeed privileged. We thank you again for the chance to aid in what ways we can.

We would now ask if we may aid any by answering any questions which any may have at this time. Is there a question?

L: Hatonn, I have a question. Earlier this evening a number of us were discussing a newsletter for communicating some of the information you've given us. Are there any comments you'd like to offer on this? Any advice or suggestions?

I am Hatonn, and we are happy that you have chosen to further spread our simple messages. We would not begin to voice our own opinions as to form, for this is not a method that is practiced at Hatonn. We only wish to say that we hope that you and any others who aid you with your project allow the love that is them [to] flow into your work and allow it to guide you in your selections of material and let it allow you to perceive [the] need of those who will have a chance to see your work. We are honored that you have chosen to aid us further by this work, and we wish to thank you, my brother.

May we answer you further?

L: No, and I thank you for your help.

We thank you again. Is there another question?

S: Hatonn, my trouble in receiving your message—could you tell me any way I can help improve it? Was it due to my busy mind or are you having transmitting difficulty or what was the cause of that?

I am Hatonn, and am aware of your question. The ability to receive our vibration and our ability to adjust ourselves to you will improve through meditation and practice. We are aware that your mind is busy due to your activities prior to this group meditation but assure you that this is not due to your mind's activity but to somewhat lower than normal level of energy, for you experienced something that brought forth flowing of emotion and in giving of your emotions, energy was expended and the levels dropped somewhat. This is nothing to really be concerned about, for through your emotions you serve others, whether it is love or anger or any other. It provides opportunity for the other and yourself to look into what brought that particular emotion out of your being. Tonight your freely giving love to the one known as R was indeed [a] beautiful moment—allowed you to see each other from [a] very lovely viewpoint—and this expenditure of emotion was the biggest reason for the difficulty that was experienced with your receiving and our transmitting our vibration to you tonight.

May we answer you further, my sister?

S: You've been more than helpful, thank you.

We thank you. May we aid another by answering another question?

(Pause)

I am Hatonn, and indeed have been privileged tonight to be a part of your meditations, for energy and the love that is present is indeed [a] beautiful and greatly gratifying experience for us to share with you. We are known to you as Hatonn. We shall now leave, but assure you that we shall be with you whenever you request it. Adonai, my friends. Adonai vasu borragus.

Intensive Meditation
November 5, 1981

(C channeling)

I am Laitos, and I am with this instrument. We greet you always in the love and the light of the one infinite Creator. We are privileged today to be able to serve the new instruments by conditioning and working with each one. We would at this time transfer and attempt to speak a few thoughts through the one known as S if she would but relax and speak freely. I am Laitos.

(S channeling)

I am Laitos, and am with this instrument. It is a pleasure, my friends, to greet you in the love and in the light of the one infinite Creator. We of Laitos are pleased to be able to be of service to this group at this time. We would hope that each of the new instruments would be able to speak our thoughts as we are able to contact each, what you call, channel. We of Laitos are privileged to be called upon by those of your group. We feel it is an honor to serve you at this time. We are always happy to be with each of you in your daily meditations if you would but mentally request we do so.

At this time we would transfer this contact. I am Laitos.

(C channeling)

I am Laitos, and I am with this instrument. We are indeed pleased with the progress shown by the one known as S and assure her that with practice the contact which is good shall be improved and the words, the thoughts, will become more flowing and feel more natural to her. We are always grateful for the chance to work with any who seek to serve in this function you call channeling, and shall always aid whenever called.

We of Laitos can't say that ground—that there is fertile ground for the growth and spreading of love and light within all who serve others in the name of the one infinite Creator. Your lessons are as leaves fall, your season for autumn. Your lessons accumulate and must be dealt with. One may do as with the leaves, push them aside or attempt to ignore them, but they are there, and within them is potential for growth. If you attempt to break down and examine each problem much as you would mulch the leaves, then the lessons may be understood and will aid your growth as the leaf mulch aids the soil by making it more fertile and enable it to aid growth of the various plants. Your lessons are ever with you and each will aid you if you would but allow it.

We are known to you as Laitos. We are with you when asked and eagerly await your calling for we seek to be of service to others as do you. We would at this time transfer to another instrument. I am Laitos.

(Jim channeling)

I am Laitos, and I greet you through this instrument once again in love and light. We are privileged to be able to offer our service at this time in the answering of questions. If any have questions, may we be of service at this time?

S: Yes. Does the act of channeling have any lasting physical effect on the body?

I am Laitos, and am aware of your question, my sister. We may note that there is no activity which does not have some effect upon the body. The activity which you call channeling has its effect primarily not upon your physical vehicle but upon your vehicle that is of the spirit and also to a lesser extent upon the vehicle of your mind. For in the process of channeling you are utilizing the meditative state and it is the meditative state which carries the most impact in this instance.

The meditative state in the channeling process is somewhat more finely focused, this being necessary on the part of the one doing the activity of channeling in order to correctly receive those thoughts that are being transmitted. This focusing to a fine degree of the meditative state, of the attention, and of the consciousness, does tend to have a relaxing effect upon the mind and an expansive effect upon the spirit, for the spirit is fed as the mind relaxes. There is some effect of relaxation also upon your physical vehicle which is always of aid. For within your illusion activity and over-activity are in great abundance and their balancing in the state of relaxation is always an aid to your physical vehicle.

May we answer you further my sister?

S: No, thank you.

We are most grateful, as well, to you. May we answer another question at this time?

Carla: Along those same lines, I was wondering if some types of channeling might have some effect on the hair? I seem to have experienced a change in the way my hair grows and the color since beginning the Ra contact.

I am Laitos, and am aware of your question, my sister. We of Laitos cannot offer any great changes in the nature of that appendage to your physical vehicle which you call hair, but may note that in the type of channeling which you have recently become engaged, the overall effect to the one who is serving as instrument is quite varied and in one aspect of this impact it might be noted that the physical vehicle will experience some changes.

You have noticed, as you have noted, a change in your hair, as you call it. This, we might say, is due to the effect of the hair serving, as you have recently been informed, as a battery type of instrument. As the hair receives the charge, which is the physical analog of the telepathic contact in our case, and the trance contact, in the case of the ones known as Ra, the hair then builds up this charge and this charge within the hair serves as a stabilizer to the contact and allows the contact to proceed on a more even basis, even with anomalies in the contact such as the wavering of the contact due, in your case, to pain in the physical vehicle. And over a long period of time this effect, this charging of the hair with the contact in its magnetic form, will allow the hair to grow or flourish. In your case this growth has also been accompanied by the changing somewhat of the color to a lighter or more golden nature.

May we answer you further, my sister?

Carla: Yes, but on a different subject. I will be going through an operation next week and would like to aid myself in the healing process as much as possible. And I've gotten quite a bit of helpful guidance in the form of general suggestions already, but I wondered if there was perhaps one touchstone of thought that you might be able to suggest that I seek out in order to aid in my own healing process or to unblock my own healing process. I would like to be ready for service as soon as possible instead of involved in my own recovery.

I am Laitos, and am aware of your question and your desire to be of service. In this regard we may say one simple thing. That is, that you be ever mindful that you are the Creator, that the healing energy, the love and the light of the Creator resides within your being, that you look upon yourself with humility, with love and with the openness to this experience which you shall undergo and see the energies about you moving smoothly through your physical vehicles, through your mental vehicle, and through your spiritual vehicle, so that your entire being becomes as a channel for the energy which shall heal your vehicles on each level as you open your being to this energy.

Remind yourself daily, even moment-by-moment, my sister, that you are the Creator. That when you seek for healing, for wisdom, for love, that each of these attributes and energies may be found within your own being. To remind yourself that you are the Creator is to develop the respect for your own being that will allow each of your vehicles to be attended to by your own efforts.

May we answer you further, my sister?

Carla: No, thank you.

We thank you. Is there another question at this time?

Carla: Be sure and tell Nona, would you two come to Philadelphia with me, so I don't forget the words?

I am Laitos. We shall relay your invitation, my sister.

Carla: Thank you.

Is there another question at this time?

(Pause)

I am Laitos. We are most pleased to experience the feeling of unity within this group at this time, for it is this oneness of being that is the only true nature of any of our being. To think that we are separate in any way is to approach the one original Thought of the one infinite Creator in a lesser manner than if one recognizes and experiences the unity of all creation at each moment of the experience of it. We of Laitos are humble messengers and servants of that one Creator of which we are a part, in which we dwell with you as brothers and sisters in oneness. We leave you now in the love and in the light and in the oneness of the one infinite Creator. I am Laitos. Adonai, my friends.

(Carla channeling)

I am Latwii, and I greet you, my friends, in the love and in the light of the infinite Creator. You will note that we did not make this instrument yell. We too can remember occasionally.

We are called to this group by the new channels and are most happy to come. We have been spending some of your space/time, as this instrument would call it, studying your underlying color, which is yellow in your illusion, and find it so heavily overladen with orange and red that we are quite amazed that there is a group such as your own which is functioning with some degree of genuine sincerity of seeking in the midst of all this basic confusion of vibration. We are very pleased that you have somehow found a way to step out of this, if only for a few moments at a time, for such is not the case apparently for your peoples in general. We can only say to you it is an interesting array of overlaid colors and one which does not augur well for a rich harvest in numbers. But as long as the light shines in some, we are happy to help those who seek.

We would at this time attempt to make ourselves known to the one known as S. If we hit this instrument like a two-by-four, please may we ask that the one known as S mentally tell us so with some sternness and we will attempt to not be so clumsy. We will now transfer this contact. I am Latwii.

(Carla channeling)

I am again with this instrument. I am Latwii. We observe an error in our direction of entering this instrument's auric field. We hope that the neck and shoulders of the instrument were not uncomfortable. We will enter at a sharper angle, from more to, what you would call, above the instrument. We have good contact but there was blockage due to a strong amount of, shall we say, noise generated by the angle of our entry. We shall again transfer. I am Latwii.

(S channeling)

I am Latwii. I am pleased to have been able to penetrate to the consciousness of this instrument. We are having some difficulty in adjusting ourselves to this instrument. We will therefore transfer our contact at this time. I am Latwii.

(Carla channeling)

I am Latwii. Hah! We were successful. That is very pleasing to us. We are not very experienced with groups such as yours and it is a real kick to be able to speak through another such as the one known as S. We thank our sister and would have at it again with the one known as C. We feel this contact to be already made, so without any introduction or suggestion will simply transfer, as we feel this contact to be in good shape already. Again, we request that if it is uncomfortable the instrument let us know. I am Latwii.

(C channeling)

I am Latwii, and I am with this instrument. We have made contact but can see that there is some doubt within this particular instrument due to expectations he had as to how our contact would physically feel. We assure him, however, that contact is strong and that we were able to modify the intensity of our vibration, for we had made contact prior to the transference from the one known as Carla. We of Latwii do enjoy any opportunity which we may have to join with groups such as this, for it is few and far between when we are specifically requested by groups such as these, for the particular configuration of thought within the group …

(Side one of tape ends.)

(C channeling)

I am Latwii, and will now leave this group grudgingly but will be more than willing to aid whenever we can. You know the number, so feel free to call us. I leave you now in the love and light of the one infinite Creator. Adonai.

Carla: I think there's another entity here, and it's a good one, but I can't make out the signal. Can anybody else?

S: I can feel it when we're …

(S channeling)

I am Hatonn, and have been trying to contact this instrument for quite some time. She requires a great deal of conditioning. We are pleased to be with your group at this time. We are always happy to be of service to this group. We of Hatonn are hoping to reach those entities amongst your peoples who request our services. We are often overwhelmed by the calling we receive and are honored to be of service to those who request our services.

We would at this time transfer this contact. I am Hatonn.

(Carla channeling)

I am Hatonn, and I greet you, my friends, in the love and in the light of the one infinite Creator. Although this is an intensive working meditation devoted primarily to the generation of more proficient channeling in the service of the infinite Creator, we feel in this group at this time the need for the sharing of a simple thought or two and this we are very glad to do at any time. For it is truly written that when several gather in the name of the Creator, those things which are asked will be heard and that which is needed will be given.

At this time we feel the need to share with you the thought of your identity. This identity is very easily lost, for you are strangers in a strange land, as this instrument would put it, dealing with many foolish and petty occasions, words and thoughts generated by yourself for your learning and by those about you for their learning. This is a confusing density, we can make no bones about it. It is a difficult one in which to remember your identity. But there is, shall we say, a master and you are his children. And the mark within you is that as his children, you are children of light. And the light within you marks you as the Creator's own. No circumstance, no thought, no behavior, no error, no difficulty, no limitation can remove this mark from your very being and you rest in the arms of the Creator. There is no moment in eternity when this is not so.

The illusion is strong and ofttimes dark, my friends. But there is a light within you and you are the Creator's own. You shall never be forgotten. You shall never be lost. For all who seek begin to intensify that light more and more. As your light becomes brighter, so shall you yourselves begin to light the way of others and so may it go. Perhaps you cannot see your light—many do not. Others will tell you. Trust no words, no thoughts, no behavior in yourself or others, but be grounded in the knowledge of your birthright, of your identity in the light. Call upon it, speak to it and never fear that you shall be lost from it.

Do not attempt to ask yourself to believe anything. You are what you are. That, my friends, is enough. Seek then to know who and what you are. In your meditation, in your seeking, in your crying and in your laughter, call upon us and we are with you. For we are all children of one Creator and are indeed one being.

In this unity may we take the illusory pleasure of bidding you adieu through this instrument that we may retire into another dimension where we may then seek to hear your call and be with you when you call. We leave you in the love and in the light of the infinite Creator. Adonai, my friends. Adonai vasu borragus.

(C channeling)

(Singing)

I am Nona, and I come to assure one known as Carla that I shall indeed be with her in the coming week and never to be afraid to ask. We are grateful to be of service to her and any who may request us.

(Sung melody, "Ah.")

(Singing)

We are one with you and are happy to have been a part of this meditation and to be with anyone who wishes to serve by sharing our vibrations. ❧

Sunday Meditation
November 8, 1981

(C channeling)

I am Hatonn, and I am with this instrument. We greet you, my brothers and sisters, in the love and light of the one infinite Creator. Tonight we would speak briefly on an aspect of love, a part which allows you to remain open to surrounding experiences without judging, without hiding. As you become more and more aware of the true nature of this illusion in which you live, you will find as growth occurs a greater insight and knowledge of the actions around you. To continue growth one should remain open, for if one judges outside influences, even though a person may have greater knowledge than the outside influence, the act of judging is as though taking steps backwards along the path which an entity has begun to travel, for all within this illusion are part of the One and is no worse, no better, than any other within the illusion.

By remaining open to others and events that surround you in your existence you will find that no matter what person or event is you can benefit from [the] lesson offered if you will but accept it as simply another lesson to be felt, experienced, learned and as one may learn one may also, by example, be of service as one who may teach in what small way they can by their example.

In your illusion example is a most persuasive teaching tool, for many times words cannot reach others and will often confuse, for all are on different levels within the illusion. Each has their own awareness and margin for misunderstanding is often great and many of the basic emotions that you feel in this illusion often block the spoken word by making one feel that they are being, as you in this illusion might say, talked with down to or condemned as we see is often the case, many who seek to preach and evangelize their particular awareness of the Creator.

We of Hatonn hope that as you all grow in your seeking that you may come to be more aware of the need to remain open to all that surrounds you and to refrain from your emotion of hatred, to refrain from trying to judge others from your particular point of awareness. We would, at this time, transfer this contact to another instrument. I am Hatonn.

(Carla channeling)

I am now with this instrument. I am Hatonn, and again I greet you in the love and the light of our infinite Creator. You see, my friends, those who judge are like the man who was convinced of the coming end of this earthly experience, convinced that these were the latter days and that the time was at hand when judgment would be rendered for all. And, so he desperately went about speaking to as many as he could and begging them to change their ways so that in this last judgment they would be able to pass the tests set before the righteous in the day of judgment. He told of many difficulties that would have to be endured and encouraged great prayerfulness and watchfulness that all might be ready when these great latter days occur.

One sunny, mild and pleasant day, quite unexpectedly, this same prophet had a failing of his heart and was struck down. And, as he lay there, he knew that his latter days had come and that all that he had said to others he had in many ways forgotten to apply to himself. Now it was he, he thought, who was under judgment and all too soon. A great fear overtook this prophet of the latter days, for he of all people was the least prepared.

This gentleman of our little story remained in your illusion, recovering from his day of judgment. It was indeed a day of judgment, for he had judged himself and found himself wanting. My friends, to refrain from discrimination is not wise, nor would we offer you guidance, for you were given a tool for use and that tool is your intellect. And within your intellect lies the powers of discrimination and judgment, and when used correctly much may be done with these gifts, but love, my friends, is greater than judgment and wiser, for it knows that no matter what you may see, you see yourself; that no matter what you think about another, you think it of yourself.

As you seek the truth, my friends, rest in a unity, in a sense of the strength of love that binds all things and know that all conditions, all situations, all seeming errors of the heart and mind and spirit, lead ever onward to a final, complete dissolution in love.

At this time we would exercise the instrument known as S. My brother, Laitos, will be conditioning those at this time who may mentally request this conditioning. We now transfer this contact. I am Hatonn.

(S channeling)

I am Hatonn. I am with this instrument. We are pleased to greet you once again through this instrument. We of Hatonn are always honored to answer your calls for our presence. We are hopeful to aid, in some small way, those who seek the truth and the knowledge of the one infinite Creator. We would, at this time, wish to exercise the one known as D1 if he would relax and refrain from analysis. We would transfer this contact at this time. I am Hatonn.

(D1 channeling)

I am Hatonn, and I am with this instrument. We are pleased that he is accepting the channeling vibration at this time. We of Hatonn are pleased at the progress of this instrument. I am Hatonn.

(Carla channeling)

I am Hatonn, and am again with this instrument. We would exercise for a few sentences the instrument known as D2, and may we say we greatly appreciate this opportunity. We would transfer at this time. I am Hatonn.

(Pause)

(Carla channeling)

I am Hatonn, and am again with this instrument. We find a good contact with the one known as D2, but find also that it is much more comfortable for this instrument at this time if we condition her and allow her to remain quiet. We will work with each of the new instruments whenever the opportunity is given us.

My friends, we speak from time to time of the need for instruments such as this one. You are, of course, aware that each of you is an instrument. However, sometimes the poetry of your life, your being, your living, and your actions are not enough for one who comes to you and seeks—seeks in a certain way, my friends, seeks with a certain philosophical bent, a certain desire for inspiration. And for this service channels such as this one are helpful, for our function is to enable the part of your being that is often distracted or distorted by the illusion to open up to what you might call a cosmic influence so that those things which may inspire, those thoughts which may provoke further thought, might flow more directly and more straight to the heart, for our message is to the heart, my friends, not to the mind.

We can talk to you about the key and show you the door to your own heart, for it is in your own heart that you will find all that you seek. Within you, my friends, lies the universe. That which you see with your physical eyes is but an image of that which you contain. Thus, we thank each who seeks to serve with all of our hearts, for to share love is the greatest privilege of which we know and we thank you for this opportunity.

At this time we would leave this group in order that one of our sisters may speak with you through another instrument. We are always with you if you mentally request our presence. I am known to you as Hatonn. I leave you in the love and the light of our infinite Creator. Adonai.

(Jim channeling)

I am Latwii, and greet this group in the love and in the light of the infinite Creator. It is with the greatest of joy that we are able to join this group and we hope that we have a good number of queries which are waiting for us. We would now offer our service, humble though it be, in this capacity of answering questions. Are there any questions at this time?

R: Yes. Hatonn—Latwii. I'm sorry. First off, is that a French name?

I am Latwii, and we assume you mean Latwii for French and not Hatonn. We are unsure of the origin of Hatonn, but may say that Latwii is a name which vibrates with the harmonies of the density of light and we might note further that those of your planet known to you as the people of the French persuasion are often the bearers of light and therein lies any significance which might be correlated with our name.

Might we answer you further, my brother?

R: Yes. Once more thing. I had an experience last night and I was curious if you could comment on it to me because I have been mentally requesting something along those lines and I'm not sure if it happened or if it didn't happen. I know it's vague, but can you answer it?

I am Latwii, and in this regard, my brother, we must also be somewhat vague, for experiences such as the one which you have recently had are of such a nature that the seeking for the substance or meaning of the experience by the experiencer is the most helpful of avenues to pursue. Therefore, we may only say in general that this experience was indeed in response to that which you have sought. The seeking on your part of the meaning and the call which you have made is the avenue of pursuit which we would suggest for you.

May we answer you further, my brother?

R: No, thank you.

We are thankful as well for this opportunity to be of service. May we answer another question at this time?

S: Yes, Latwii. Is that your conditioning I've been experiencing for the past fifteen minutes or do I just have a stiff neck?

I am Latwii, and although we are somewhat hesitant to admit that we are often a pain in the neck, we have indeed been conditioning your instrument and apologize for our over-eagerness in the attempt. May we answer you further, my sister?

S: No, thank you.

We thank you, as always. Is there another question at this time?

D1: Yes. Latwii, I've been, in my own search for the truth, because of my religious background—it's sometimes very helpful to me to study the Bible. Some of the things I've heard and read lately through this group—it's brought some portions of the Bible under question as to the value of that in my own seeking. Would you have any suggestions as to how I should pursue a Bible study type program and if that would be beneficial?

I am Latwii, and in this regard, my brother, we would heartily recommend the continuation of your study of the holy work known to your peoples as the Bible, for as with all works of a sacred nature, there is indeed a great amount of inspirational information which is available through this source, as you are aware and have noted yourself. This particular source also shares the somewhat dubious distinction with all other religious types of writings of your people as having some, shall we say, pollution of the information contained within it. This in itself might seem as somewhat of a deterrent to the intensive study of its knowledge, wisdom and love, but seen from another perspective might also be most beneficial to those who study it, for it is the nature of your illusion that nothing can be known for certain and it is the nature of the quest which you are upon that the seeking is most necessary and the discrimination in the seeking is most helpful in determining that which is of value to the seeker and that which is not. If it be known to the seeker that the seeker seeks from a source that is infallible, then the strength of the seeking for the seeker has been removed, for there is no area which might be questioned and therefore develop the seeker's discrimination.

May we answer you further, my brother?

D1: No, thank you. That's very helpful.

We are most grateful to you as well. Is there another question at this time?

E: I have a question, Latwii, about the sermon on the Mount. I've heard some people say that the sermon on the mount was for the disciples of Jesus and not for the ordinary person and I've heard others say that the sermon on the mount was for everyone. Now, the problem it seems for us is that it's very difficult to follow the sermon on the mount and so a lot of people would like to feel as though it were for disciples and not for the general population. Could you illuminate this matter at all?

I am Latwii, and shall make an attempt to shine some sort of light upon this matter. We of Latwii would suggest that each statement which you have just made is correct, that indeed this piece of work which is referred to by your people as the Sermon on the Mount, is for the disciple, but we might also ask, "Who is the disciple?" for are not all who seek the truth disciples of the truth? It is for those who seek to make of themselves the disciple. This is the choice of the people of your density and of your planet at this time. Those who do not wish to make this choice are most free to do so or not do so. The choice to be the disciple of the truth is a choice which will make one such a disciple when the choice is made. Any teaching which is given by any of those who are known by your people as masters is also given not only to the advanced disciple, but is given in some form to each entity upon your planet, for it is truly said that as above so it is below, and each entity has the capability of becoming that which is known as the disciple.

Might we answer you further, my brother?

E: I think there are probably a lot of questions I could ask, but I will ask one more and that is, if one knows that what is stated in the Sermon on the Mount is true and does not follow it, how does that affect one?

I am Latwii, and in this matter, my brother, we might be of most assistance by suggesting that the refusal to follow the path which one knows is most correct for that entity simply …

(Side one of tape ends.

(Jim channeling))

I am Latwii, and am once again with this instrument. We are most grateful and thankful to each for the patience in our pause. May we be of further assistance, my brother, with this query?

E: No, thank you.

We thank you. Is there another question at this time?

D2: Latwii, I have a question. When Hatonn tried to channel through me earlier I felt uncomfortable to the point that it was distracting and I was unable to speak. Could you explain to me why that was?

I am Latwii. My sister, it is often the case with new instruments that the instrument's desire to serve as a channel will be so great that the instrument's sensitivity will be enlarged, so to speak. It is not always apparent to those of the Confederation as to the nature or strength of the vibration which will work most harmoniously with a new instrument, for the process of channeling is a process which takes place upon many levels and there are many fine adjustments which must be made, and in the case of the new instrument it is especially true for the ones attempting to transmit thoughts that this adjustment is often, shall we say, a difficult target to hit and is often over-shot. And this is the case that was in effect for you this evening.

May we answer you further, my sister?

D2: Not right now. Thank you.

We thank you as well. Is there another question at this time?

T: Yes. I have a question. Every time I come to a meditation here or other classes I've taken where the energy seems to be pretty intense, after a while I sit here and I start to twitch. I feel the energy that's going on in the room and sometimes it becomes uncomfortable, but my question is, do you have any suggestions, I suppose along the lines of kundalini practice, that you can do to further develop your ability to handle this energy so you can use it and also so it's not uncomfortable. How do you expand your capacity?

I am Latwii, and would suggest, my brother, in this case that, as it is true with all experiences of this nature, the exercise of the experience is the situation, shall we say, or the aid which will help one the most to experience a more comfortable feeling. It is often the case with those who have practiced various forms of meditation or what you call yoga or other types of mind and body disciplines that the experience from time to time is quite intense because there has been the opening of a channel and the experiencing of the energy flowing through it, then the closing of the channel for a prolonged period of what you call time and then the opening of the channel again at a later date, this continuing on a sporadic basis for some time, thereby giving the new experiencer or instrument, shall we say, a somewhat less than consistent experience, and this requires the experience of the energy on future dates to be more consonant, shall we say, or more regular.

We would suggest in this case that the continuation of your meditations might be the most aid in this situation, for within this meditative state there is the gradual opening on a consistent basis of those energy centers which are referred to by many of your peoples as the chakras and this will enable each to open on a consistent basis.

Might we be of further assistance, my brother?

T: Yes, then I infer from what you're saying that you probably wouldn't approve of chemical enhancement of this energy flow. Is that true—just comment on things like acid and how they affect—I have an idea how they affect it, but whether this effect is good or bad or counterproductive or whatever.

I am Latwii, and in this situation, my brother, we would suggest that the use of what you refer to as chemical assistance to the expansion of one's awareness is much like the roulette wheel. It is of a random nature and may be on one occasion quite helpful and quite useful for the experience of increased energy flowing through the energy centers. On another occasion it might be most detrimental to this flow, for it might be that one has, shall we say, plugged into an energy source which is not of the highest nature, for we would suggest that it is quite a large and well-populated universe that we share with many forms of life. And we would not suggest either the abstinence or the ingestion, for we feel this is a matter of your own free will and may say that in truth there is no sure way of saying or predicting what the overall effect might be. For as many entities as partake in these substances there are also as many experiences as can be had.

May we answer you further, my brother?

T: No, that's fine. Thank you.

We are most grateful to you as well. Is there another question at this time?

E: Latwii, could you explain why it is so important that the neck be unblocked? It seems like I've felt my neck being unblocked fairly often in connection with this group.

I am Latwii. My brother, we might suggest that the neck area is also correspondent to one of your energy centers and it is quite helpful to have all energy centers unblocked if possible, but more importantly the balance between them is more to be sought and in each entity's case there is a certain pattern of balance that is apparent. Each entity will have certain strengths and certain, what might be called, weaknesses or areas which will be focused upon for further growth. In each entity's case the area which experiences what you would describe as physical sensation during the state of meditation is that area which is experiencing some type of activation or energizing effect.

In your particular instance that you have just noted, we might say that the feeling which you have experienced in your neck region, the fifth energy center, is in correspondence with that density which we inhabit, that being the density of light, numbering five, and it is our conditioning which you are experiencing at these times.

May we answer you further, my brother?

E: Yes. If I understand you correctly, then you have a particular influence on the neck because it does represent fifth density. Is that correct?

I am Latwii. In general, my brother, you are correct. More specifically, we might add that we respond to the call as it is made from whatever level it is made, be it the conscious or subconscious.

May we answer you further, my brother?

E: No, thank you. You've been quite helpful. I would like to say, though, that I thank you for the work you've done on my neck. It's helped me quite a bit.

I am Latwii, and we are most grateful that our light chiropractic practices have been of some service. May we answer you further, my brother?

E: No, thank you.

Is there another question at this time?

D2: I have one more about what—the question that I asked you a moment ago. You said that the desire can be so strong. It seems that at times, can the desire be so strong that it … I perceive it as blocking. It seems it reaches a point where it just blocks, it's so strong. Is there something that I could do to alleviate that?

I am Latwii, and my sister, we would suggest that you are quite correct. That the desire can be so strong as the new instrument seeks [to] receive the contact that the desire can indeed work the reverse and block that contact. We would suggest that there are no great secret rituals which one might perform to alleviate this situation, but the simple relaxation of the mind and the body is the most helpful exercise in this case.

May we answer you further, my sister?

D2: No, thank you.

We thank you as well. Is there another question at this time?

Carla: I have one which you can answer very briefly, but I would like to observe that since you called yourself a chiropractor, perhaps you're Egyptian as well as French!

We've been studying archetypes through the Tarot and I found them very interesting and I was wondering—I know that the Confederation numbers quite a few different planets and the archetypes have been defined to us as those which pertain to one particular Logos or Sun. I was wondering if there was a larger Logos which offers its archetypes for all the members of the Confederation or whether the archetypical nature of mind is third density only.

I am Latwii, and we might say that we also appreciate the Egyptian touch to your puns. In answer to your query concerning the nature of archetypes, we might also add that there are as many natures or types of archetypes as there are creators or Logos, as the one known as Ra has so succinctly put it. We of Latwii have at our disposal the numbering of archetypes which approaches infinity, as do each of the members of the Confederation, for there are as many ways of perceiving the Creator as there are perceivers, and we find there is great benefit in using a great variety of ways of perceiving the one infinite Creator, for the one Creator is all that there is.

May we answer you further, my sister?

Carla: Yes, just to clear up one point. This number of archetypes that approaches infinity, is this due to the number of different planetary logoi, all of which are structured, or is it due to the infinite capacity of the consciousness to create its own archetypes?

I am Latwii, and we might agree with your latter assumption, my sister, for the creators of the various systems which you refer to as the solar system is infinite and it is upon the shoulders of these creators the necessity lies to refine, shall we say, the energy patterns which are provided by the one infinite Creator in the creation of all that is.

May we answer you further, my sister?

Carla: No. Thank you. I think I'll study the ones we have here now and then go on afterwards. Thank you very much.

I am Latwii, and thank you as well. Is there another question at this time?

(Pause)

I am Latwii. We have greatly enjoyed the questions that you have offered us this evening. We are always thrilled at the opportunity to be of this type of service for we learn much during these sessions. And we look forward to such sessions in what you call your future and we shall be working in our spare time, so to speak, to match the punstership of this group. We leave you now in the love and in the light of the one infinite Creator. I am Latwii. Adonai, my friends.

Intensive Meditation
November 12, 1981

(Unknown channeling)

I am Hatonn. I greet all you in the love and the light of the one infinite Creator. We are most *(inaudible)* this afternoon as the new instruments continue their quest for the specific *(inaudible)* to your peoples as channeling. In all such channeling efforts *(inaudible)* may we say that the one certainty is *(inaudible)* is making as clear as possible *(inaudible)* language *(inaudible)* a message [of] which each entity upon your planet is intimately aware, though this awareness may not yet be on the conscious level, for as you know, my friends, each entity is, and each entity has within, its Creator, the means of knowing that Creator and expressing that Creator and, indeed, each entity does so each day of its life, for no matter what expression of any entity within any reality, the expression is of the Creator, for it is the nature of the Creator to wish to experience Its own being in as many ways and varieties of experience as possible. In this way the entire creation is enriched by the knowledge of itself.

When you seek service as an instrument—a vocal channel for the one Creator—you're attempting to condense or crystallize the experience, knowledge, beingness of the one Creator into what your peoples understand as words which form concepts upon the written page, more easily understood at one level when read *(inaudible)* but, my friends, we hope you will also realize that the crystallization of the concepts also distorts *(inaudible)* in some way for there are no words which can fully express the beingness of the one Creator which resides within each *(inaudible)* your beingness.

Yet we of the Confederation of Planets in the Service to the One Infinite Creator continually seek new instruments through which to speak for it is our understanding that this is a most efficient method of imparting some small part of the love and the light of the one Creator to those entities who wish to hear such words for inspiration. *(Inaudible)* also remind those who wish to serve as instruments that this is not necessarily the most efficient way, and certainly not the only *(inaudible)*. We suggest the adding of this technique/method of seeking to one's fully developed repertoire of techniques and methods of seeking that which *(inaudible)* as one such technique and one such source of information. We feel that our *(inaudible)* words might then be most useful to each of those gathered in this room and also most useful to those who might come in contact with this message.

We would at this time exercise the instrument known as D, if he would relax, as always, and refrain from analysis. Speak the words *(inaudible)*. We shall transfer this contact and speak our thoughts through the one known as D. I *(inaudible)*.

Intensive Meditation, November 12, 1981

(D channeling)

(Inaudible)

(Unknown channeling)

I am Hatonn. We are once again with this instrument. We are aware of the distractions which the one known as D has experienced within his consciousness at this time. We assure the one known as D that his progress has been most pleasing to us and we shall continue to make our initial vibrations known to the one known as D at any time in what you call your future in which he might request our presence.

We shall at this time make our initial vibrations known to the one known as *(inaudible)* and shall transfer our contact to this new instrument. Speak *(inaudible)*. We shall now transfer this contact. I am Hatonn.

(Unknown channeling)

(Inaudible)

(Unknown channeling)

I am Hatonn, and am once again with this instrument. We have had some difficulty making our *(inaudible)* vibrations known to the one known as *(inaudible)* by which our *(inaudible)* and attempt to speak a few rules through *(inaudible)* channel if she will relax. We shall now transfer this contact. I am Hatonn.

(Unknown channeling)

(Inaudible)

(Unknown channeling)

I am Hatonn, and am once again with this instrument. At this time it is our privilege to offer our *(inaudible)* attempt to answer questions which each of those present *(inaudible)* minds. Are there any questions at this time?

Questioner: *(Inaudible)*.

I am Hatonn. My brother, in this regard we feel that our best response *(inaudible)* to point in *(inaudible)* direction which you are already pointing *(inaudible)*. We of Hatonn have advised meditation for each entity has heard our words for many years *(inaudible)*. We have advised meditation *(inaudible)* and though it seems a simple activity *(inaudible)* the fineness, shall we say, *(inaudible)* of this activity *(inaudible)* meditation. In the meditative state all is possible. The tuning of the meditative state is accomplished through the desire of the one *(inaudible)*. The desire, whatever it might be, may be more easily manifest in the state of meditation, for in this state you are reaffirming your connection with the one Creator and are in fact *(inaudible)* retracing the steps that you have made from your conscious *(inaudible)*. As you retrace this and enter the state of being *(inaudible)* you will find opening before you any avenue *(inaudible)* which you seek. Therefore, it is your desire which shall tune the state of meditation and shall determine how you shall use that state and the energy *(inaudible)* available in that state.

We can also add to this suggestion of following desire with meditation a more specific use of the state of meditation since each in this group is familiar with the work of the group which is in contact with our brothers and sister of the density of unity, those known to you as Ra. In these communications are given several exercises which are also quite useful to the entity wishing to fine-tune the centers of energy which are known to your peoples as the chakra system. The general concept which is used is that of the balancing and by utilizing the exercises which have been made available through the work of this group and the one known as Ra the balancing process might be undertaken and refined at a future time, shall we say.

We feel that at this time these three suggestions are the most aid *(inaudible)* without infringement upon you free will *(inaudible)*. May we answer you further, my brother?

Questioner: *(Inaudible)*.

We are also quite grateful to you as well. May we answer *(inaudible)*?

Questioner: Yes *(inaudible)*. Does the act of meditation … or can the act of meditation help improve one's memory of previous lives? And I know that different entities of the Confederation specialize in different things. Would there be an entity who *(inaudible)* perhaps be more helpful if called upon than another *(inaudible)*?

I am Hatonn, and, my sister, we must say *(inaudible)* the entities of the Federation are always honored to join any meditation and any entity might *(inaudible)* vibrations which *(inaudible)* be used by the one *(inaudible)* meditation for whatever purpose the one using it would choose. We would suggest that the meditative state can indeed be used for the recalling of previous experiences of *(inaudible)* this life but what you would call previous lives as well, but the use of the meditative state for this purpose is more difficult than the use of what your peoples call the hypnotic state, for in the meditative state the one who meditates is engaged in an activity of solitude and would need in effect to be quite adept at use of the meditative energy to also practice the role of what your peoples call the hypnotist who guides *(inaudible)* true experiences to be recalled.

This is a most difficult feat for in the meditative state you are activating the, shall we say, grossly unused portion of your mind *(inaudible)* being the subconscious and in so doing are also of necessity deactivating the conscious *(inaudible)* portion. This aids in meditation but the conscious portion of your mind or some mind is necessary to serve as a guide, shall we say, through your subconscious so that your journey might be *(inaudible)* comfortably accomplished. Therefore, we affirm the possibility that mediation might be of aid in the recalling of previous experiences in this or another life but might not be as successfully used as other …

(Tape ends.)

Sunday Meditation
November 15, 1981

(L channeling)

[I am Hatonn] … those who are wise, omniscient teachers, but rather *(inaudible)* the advice or relation of *(inaudible)* experience from an older brother or sister within your own *(inaudible)* of existence, for it is not our purpose to provide answers, but rather to provide a stimulus serving to assist you in answering your own questions. As you are aware, those answers come only through meditation *(inaudible)* your experiences, for is this not the purpose of your *(inaudible)*. We of Hatonn desire only to be of service and wish that you feel free to call upon us at any time, no matter how brief, no matter how rushed or hurried you may feel, no matter how *(inaudible)*. It is our desire to serve in any way which we are allowed. At this time we would transfer our contact to another instrument. I am Hatonn.

(C channeling)

(Inaudible)

(Jim channeling)

I am Hatonn, and greet you once again. At this time it is our privilege to offer ourselves in service by attempting to answer questions. Are there any questions at this time?

Questioner: *(Inaudible)*.

I am Hatonn, and am aware of your question, my brother. Healing, basically, is a function of the one to be healed desiring to be healed. Those who wish to aid in this process may do so in a number of manners. For those present in this group we would suggest that the method most accessible and useful be done in the meditative state where the one to be healed is imaged in the mind in the condition which needs healing. This condition is seen in as much detail as is possible for the one wishing to be of service. When it is seen as clearly as is possible, then it is replaced by another image. This image being of the one to be healed in the healed condition, surrounded by love and light, seeing every part of the one to be healed body surrounded by this love and light, a glowing effect. This condition is also imaged in as much detail as is possible for the one wishing to be of service. It is recommended, though not completely essential, that each image be maintained for a number of your minutes. Then, that the images be released so that higher forces, so to speak, might take them over and fill in the flesh on the bone, shall we say, of this image.

The healing process, in general, is a process whereby the one to be healed accepts the healing energy which is ever present within its own being, always entering its being through the feet and the lower chakras or energy centers. The one to be healed, therefore, makes a decision either to accept this energy which is ever present, as well as energy which is transferred or sent from another, and if this energy is accepted then there is a new configuration evident within the one to be healed which is what you call the healed condition or health.

In all cases, we emphasize that the healing is done by the one to be healed. Others may serve as what you might call a catalyst for this action and this acceptance, but there is no possibility of another entity healing the one to be healed unless the one to be healed accepts this offering. In the final analysis, so to speak, it is the Creator who does the healing, the Creator residing within the one *(inaudible)*.

May we answer you further, my brother?

Questioner: *(Inaudible).*

We thank you as well. Is there another question at this time?

Questioner: *(Inaudible).*

I am Hatonn, and am aware of your question, my brother. In this regard we might once again recommend that the meditative state be used for visualization of this anger and the one to whom it is being sent and for whom it is being generated. In your visualization see this entity receiving your anger and see the effect upon this entity of such a reception. See in your mind your own identification with this entity. See this entity as yourself as you receive the anger which you have generated for this entity. See this anger entering this entity's being which is now your own being as well. Feel the effects of this emotion which you call anger within your being. Experience its nature. Carry it to its logical, as you would say, conclusion in your mind and in your visualization. Allow this image to remain within your mind for a period of time. Determine by the intensity of the anger *(inaudible)*.

When you feel that your anger has been spent and has been felt in full, then for a moment in your mind image its opposite. Then let that image disappear and let it be, shall we say, a small beacon which you shall approach by a process of what we will call natural discovery. Remaining in the meditative state, continue to see in your mind the entity for which you feel anger and, seeing this entity still in a dual nature, being the other and being your self.

As you see this image make no attempt to guide it either toward the anger or its opposite, towards love, but allow your being to proceed through this natural discovery, until you feel the love which you imaged momentarily filling your being, which is also the being of the other. Allow this feeling of love to overwhelm your senses in the same manner and degree in which the anger did so. When this has been achieved, see both emotions, the anger and the love, in your mind as imbalance. See the imbalance of anger, but see the balance of anger and love. Then accept yourself and forgive yourself and see yourself as whole and complete as is the Creator, which you are, and see yourself experiencing both emotions as means by which the Creator might know Itself.

May we answer you further, my brother?

Questioner: *(Inaudible).*

We thank you for this opportunity to be of service. Is there another question at this time?

(Pause)

I am Hatonn. We are aware of several unasked questions and will once again allow for their asking, for we feel it is an infringement upon free will to respond to any query which has not been spoken. Are there any further questions at this time?

Questioner: *(Inaudible).*

I am Hatonn. My brother, in this regard we may speak in general by saying that the structures of which you speak had their origin within the minds of a small group of adepts who were of the nature of deep religious seekers and who sought to express the grandeur and richness which was their personal experience through the medium of the architectural design and layout of these structures so that by certain geometric relationships future generations of seekers and worshippers might be inspired by the beauty, the grace, and the richness of design to increase their seeking of the one Creator.

It is true in these cases as it is also true in many such cases of the designs of the places of worship in your ancient of times, that those few seekers who had attained some small part of their goal of union with the one Creator put their findings, the crystallizations of their learning, shall we say, in a geometric or architectural form serving much as what you know as pyramids, to funnel, focus and intensify the ever present instreamings of intelligent energy or that which is known in your eastern philosophies as prana, into certain patterns which would be of assistance in their seeking of union with the one Creator. Many such structures are aiding those who worship inside their walls to this day because of efforts of the few in ancient of times of your peoples.

May we answer you further, my brother?

Questioner: *(Inaudible).*

I am Hatonn, and in this regard, my brother, we might say that you are correct, for it is well known to those who are deep religious seekers of truth who have attained some part of that goal of union with the Creator, that all is one and as it has been said many times in your religious history, "As it is above, so it is below."

There are certain relationships, balances and regularities in the relation of different parts or aspects of the mind to itself and to other minds, expanding outward to the master mind and cosmic mind or the mind of the one infinite Creator. There are certain geometric relationships that might also be seen in a geographical nature as well. In this regard there is upon your planet a knowledge of certain structures or forms which aid the seeking of the religious adopt. These forms may be seen to be of a vaulted or a conical nature, that which is similar to the pyramid, the dome or the arch and such structures have been utilized throughout your history and before your written history for the purpose of increasing the focus of the instreamings of the one Creator in a certain area which is to be used for the seeking or sacred ritual of seekers. In many cases these designs or structures are copied from earlier times and earlier structures and indeed are reproductions of forms which have existed previously upon your planet. In other cases these structures are arrived at by individual or original means of inspiration, shall we say, and though they are similar in design to the previous structure, bear the *(inaudible)* mark of one for their inspiration.

May we answer you further, my brother?

Questioner: *(Inaudible).*

I am Hatonn. The structure which you refer to as the flying buttress is indeed an extension of a design which incorporates the pyramid or arch type of structure and is necessary to complete the funneling or focusing of the prana energy.

May we answer you further, my brother?

Questioner: *(Inaudible).*

We are most grateful to you as well. Is there another question at this time?

Questioner: *(Inaudible).*

I am Hatonn, and in this regard, my sister, we would suggest that your planet is populated with a multitude of entities, each of whom is in the greatest of need …

(Side one of tape ends.)

Sunday Meditation
November 22, 1981

(C channeling)

I am Hatonn, and I am with this instrument. We greet you, my friends, as always, in the love and the light of the one infinite Creator.

We see that you are within your illusion about to enter into a time of your year which is reserved for the worship of the one known as Jesus, this time that you have chosen to celebrate the birth of the one who walked the Earth and became an example that many of your peoples have chosen to use in their seeking for the knowledge of what you term as God, which we would more aptly call love and light. This time of your year has power to bring entities together with common bonds which is many times unattainable during the rest of your year. In this time many of your peoples gain a greater awareness of love and light that is within and that is them, and in this time they reach out and touch those close to them and those who have needs. Although this period of time has become, what you would call, commercialized, feelings between and among your people [are] still the source of the power that makes this time of your year so special to so many of your peoples.

We of Hatonn are with you in the seeking for love/light and are very happy and we feel what you may call warmth with you. It is sad, however, that there are those who at this time feel alone or forgotten, who seek to contain the love within their being or who build walls between themselves and the love and light that's so strong at this time. They who have attempted to shut themselves away do not realize that love and light are with them, that they are love and light. They need but look. They need but open themselves just a small bit and they may see the love and light that is. Your peoples have many stories about this season, about people who have closed themselves to others, to love, but come to realize that they needed but to gain a glimpse—was all they needed.

We know that in this group that there is not a Scrooge, but we also know that many peoples on your planet are not aware and have not allowed themselves to feel the true warmth that is love and light. Though this number is progressively getting smaller, there are still many who need but one small example of which to gain even the smallest glimpse that they may begin their seeking and experiencing an awareness of love. We of Hatonn join with you, as always, in this your people's special time of year. We so enjoy the sounds and laughter, the beauty of each individual's being as they experience and transmit to brothers the love and light they have seen, they have felt—that they have seen and felt the experiences of the one they call Jesus. We of Hatonn say once again that we are one with you and the people of your planet and we hope that in this time of your year that many more will experience and begin their seeking of the one infinite Creator.

We would like now to transfer this contact to another instrument. I am Hatonn.

(Carla channeling)

I am Hatonn, and I greet you once again, my friends, through this instrument, in love and in light. We would continue, briefly, with our thoughts through this instrument.

What is it, my friends, that constitutes yourself? As you sit in this dwelling, feel your body, your feet and your hands. Is that where you are, my friends? Perhaps you do not find your self there. Look in your mind, in your thinking. As you listen to these words spoken through an instrument, as these words impinge upon you, am I speaking to you, to the essence of your self? Not yet, my friends, have we found each other. That which is you is closer to you than your body, more nigh to you than your thoughts, dearer and surer than your breath and just as difficult to recognize.

Where are you, my friends? Have you found yourselves completely? In this illusion it is very, very difficult, in the illusion of your density with all the distractions of body and of mind. It is difficult, indeed, my friends, to know even your self. And it is only, my friends, in knowing the self that you can know another, that you can share with another, that you can rejoice and laugh and give with and to another. Is it any wonder then that your peoples are so often alone in a time when even your culture suggests joy? When your rather forbidding society urges rejoicing?

Indeed, my friends, for many among your peoples it is this very urge of the society from without to pretend to be happy that causes the loneliness, that causes the feeling of sorrow. And in many, my friends, this season is a sadness that ends the incarnation. We rejoice with those who rejoice, but my friends, although we feel sorrow for those who are sorrowful, we can only reach out in joy from ourselves to yourselves. We are all one, my friends.

As you enter this particular season, which is much misunderstood among your peoples, seek to know your own self, find that love which is your true being, for in knowing that one, simple spark which is of the one Creator, you will know every person, each entity that you may meet and there can be no division betwixt you. Then you may truly share the love of the Creator, and let Its light come forth from your eyes. There is nothing, my friends, that you need do, for you already are what you seek. If you seek for a basic method of attempting to find that self of which we speak, as always, we suggest meditation, meditation and meditation. The attempt, persistence and the desire are essential. Your estimate of your success is inessential.

It has been a privilege to speak through these channels and before we leave this group we would like to share our conditioning with each and to exercise the one known as D. Our conditioning is designed to aid each in deepening the level of meditation and also, if desired, it is designed to make our vibration known in some comfortable, physical way to each who requests it mentally. In its more powerful forms we use it to condition those who desire to serve as vocal channels, such as this one.

We would begin with the one known as A and condition this entity.

(Pause)

We move now to the one known as M and send blessings and love to this entity also.

(Pause)

We move now to the one known as B, and send a confirmation which only this entity will understand.

(Pause)

If you will allow us to pause, we will touch the one known as L.

(Pause)

B: This one is not comfortable. It's not fluid with the trancing faculty.

I am Hatonn. We ask that you request adjustment mentally and if you are not comfortable immediately to request that we leave and we will work with you at any time, so that we may, in a more orderly manner, develop a good contact.

B: Thanks. Yes. Let us please work with this conditioning at another time. Thank you.

I am Hatonn, and we thank you. We urge you not to attempt to dip too deeply into the well of consciousness, as we prefer to work with complete free will with our contacts and consequently wish to adjust ourselves to a complete free will light contact so that you may at any time while working with us have complete control over the duration of the contact. We scan you now for comfort. We are attempting now to lift all discomforts, touching the nape of the neck and removing all discomfort.

We would at this time transfer this contact to one known as D, if we might have this privilege, so that we might close through this instrument, as our sister is practically beating our door down waiting for her turn to speak. I am Hatonn.

(D channeling)

I am Hatonn, and I greet you once again through this instrument. We of Hatonn wish to express our gratitude for being allowed to be with this group and we will be with any who mentally request at any time. We would leave you now in the love and in the light of the one infinite Creator. Adonai, my friends.

(Jim channeling)

I am Latwii, and I greet you in the love and in the light of the one infinite Creator. We are most pleased to be able to join this group this evening, as our brothers and sisters of Hatonn mentioned. We have been most anxious to join this group and offer our services in the attempt to answer questions which those of this group might have the value in asking. Are there any questions at this time?

Carla: I'd like to thank you and Hatonn and all the Confederation contacts of which I was aware in the hospital for your presence and comfort. This was much appreciated.

I am Latwii, and, my sister, may we say it was a great honor to join you, even though the location of our joining you was somewhat less than satisfactory. We also did not find the food quite up to par, shall we say.

Are there any questions at this time?

B: Latwii, would you entertain a question of a personal nature?

I am Latwii. We shall do our very best to be of whatever entertainment value we might be. As you may have ascertained by this time, we are of somewhat a light density and do appreciate the levity with which such a meeting as this might be conducted. We cannot promise that we shall answer specifically personal questions, but shall give it our, shall we say, best shot, for the concept of free will must always be kept intact and never abridged.

May we answer a question at this time?

B: Thank you. It's my understanding that I've reached what could be termed a turning point in this incarnation where my attention is being directed now beyond self. My purpose for coming to this location is to better determine the energies and the focus of this group, now in body, as well as the consciousness of Ra, and to develop a sense as to whether I can serve in this direction. Can you comment on this, please?

I am Latwii, and my brother, in this regard we might say that it is indeed a point of turning which you feel. We of Latwii recognize your great desire to be of service, to move beyond the boundaries of the concerns for the individual self, to move into the field of consciousness of this planet itself and to encourage that growth of consciousness within the minds, of the hearts and the spirits of the entities which you share this planet with. We of Latwii cannot point to any specific effort which you might perhaps undertake as your unique means of serving your brothers and sisters on this planet. We can suggest that in this attempt to expand your own boundaries of service and concern that you seek within your own being in the meditative state, as you have already done, for the direction which shall be most meaningful for you.

May we also mention and reaffirm what our brothers and sisters of Hatonn have previously mentioned this evening—that is that each entity is already whole and complete within itself. To expand upon this concept, may we also say that there is nothing but service, for there is nothing but the Creator. How you channel or express this service must be a function of your own searching, your own choice, and in the end, shall we say, the fruit of your labors shall be harvested from the effort which you make in this direction.

We encourage the seeking and the attempt far more than the concern with the result, for the attempt to be of service is likened unto the lighting of a lamp, and where there was darkness now there is light. It is the attempt, my brother, that is most helpful at this time for the peoples of your planet, for so many live in the darkness. As you seek your means of serving your brothers and sisters, keep foremost in your mind the desire to serve. Worry not about the means, for as you seek, so shall you find. Your seeking shall be as the magnet and shall attract unto you the means by which you might serve best.

May we answer you further, my brother?

B: Thank you. That's certainly very well. Thank you.

I am Latwii. We are most grateful to you as well for allowing us the privilege of so serving. Is there another question at this time?

Carla: What color are you in tonight?

I am Latwii. This evening, my sister, we are observing the color of your planet and its spectrum, which might be most accurately described as a fuchsia.

May we answer you further?

Carla: No, thank you. I just wanted to get a feel for you.

I am Latwii. We hope that you have enjoyed this color vibration with us. Is there another question at this time?

Carla: I had a series of odd reactions to medication …

(Side one of tape ends.)

(Jim channeling)

I am Latwii, and am once again with this instrument. We might mention in this regard that your feeling of rapid healing has been the result of many entities pouring their love and light, their healing vibrations, in your direction, for there are many around you who wish to aid you in this manner. In the respect of the reaction which you experienced to the, shall we say, drugs in your hospital used for pain control, you were, shall we say, aided in your distortions of response by the entity which you have become familiar with up to this point, the entity which had been attracted by your efforts in the Ra contact.

Might we answer you further, my sister?

Carla: By this entity do you mean the social memory complex Ra?

I am Latwii, and we do not mean the social memory complex Ra, but the entity who greets you from the Orion group.

Carla: I gotcha. Thank you.

I am Latwii. We thank you, my sister. Is there another question at this time?

(Pause)

I am Latwii. We are aware that there are a number of queries which have not been vocalized. It is our understanding that such queries must be vocalized in order for free will to remain intact. We shall ask once again if there are any further queries which we might attempt to answer.

(Pause)

I am Latwii. My friends, it has been a great privilege and an honor to join your group this evening. We of Latwii seldom find such opportunities offered to us and cherish each with the greatest of joy and glee when so invited to join this group. May we remind each that we shall be available for the conditioning vibration at any time in what you would call your future, should you request our presence and assistance. We of Latwii shall now leave this group rejoicing in the love and in the light of the one infinite Creator. Adonai, my friends. Adonai vasu borragus.

(C channeling)

I am Nona, and am now with this instrument. We are privileged and honored that you have called, that we might share our healing vibrations with those who are in your thoughts. We join with you now in order that we may aid you with your healing requests.

(C channels a vocal melody from Nona.) ✣

Sunday Meditation
November 29, 1981

(L channeling)

I am Hatonn, and I greet you, my brothers and sisters, in the love and the light of the infinite Creator. We of Hatonn thank you for the pleasure we have derived from your joyous music, for all too often, my brothers and sisters, the only sounds that reach our ears are those directed to us from individuals who in their suffering cry out for help and relief. Although we of Hatonn realize that it is both our responsibility and service to respond to these messages of distress, we wish to add that we are deeply touched and pleasured by the sounds of joy and sharing that seem to come from your planet all too seldom.

Tonight, we of Hatonn wish to share with you a small story concerning a child who was able to fly. Perhaps this may seem a rather preposterous beginning, yet we will continue with our story, for there is a purpose in our sharing it with you.

A child was born. The child was not abnormal in any fashion. He had eyes, ears, arms and legs of the correct number. As he grew older, he learned to speak, to walk, to handle the various utensils for eating, for working, for enjoyment; yet, this child was different in one respect. He was aware of the world around him. His awareness of his surroundings was not the result of a sudden inspiration or insight, but rather was simply a continuous perception that he had brought into the world with him and had managed to resist being indoctrinated into disbelieving. In a sense, this child was more a normal child that those about him, for he was not blinded by the stories and half-truths that distort reality.

Naturally, the child's familiarity with the world about him became evident due to his ability to flow in attunement with those energies about him. This was evident in others—correction—this was evident to others in that the child was able to create or dissolve material objects at will; yet this was constantly overlooked as simply a slight of hand or deception, for other children do not question reality and elders who regard themselves as much wiser found their own answers to explain this phenomenon rather than to accept it for its actuality.

The breaking point arrived, however, when the child began to fly. Again, the other children, being less fully indoctrinated, were capable of accepting this practice, for is it not a natural practice for one who is aware of the illusory state of his surroundings to be able to manipulate the illusion? The elders, the adults, those who were wise, however, found the prospect much less enchanting. And, again created, in a distorted fashion, their own understanding of this phenomena. The child, being different, must be evil, and therefore must be destroyed.

The child was captured, if a simple response of approaching when requested can be interpreted as capturing, and was put upon a trial in which he was expected to answer a number of questions dealing with complex theories developed by the elders to explain the process by which he had attained large quantities of a supposedly evil and forbidden knowledge. The child was confused, for he knew nothing of metaphysics, of religions, of theories, of superstitions. He simply knew the substance of which his world was composed. He was simply aware of the malleability of his surroundings and his ability to mold them, to flow with them, as a feather flows on a liquid stream.

Eventually the trial was over. The child, now regarded as both evil and uncooperative, was condemned to death, for such was the only response conceivable to those wise elders who sought to protect themselves from the knowledge they suspected the child bore. We will not dwell upon details of pain. It will suffice to say, the child's physical vehicle was terminated, yet the child joyfully continued to fly, for not bearing the heavy burden of wisdom possessed by those elders, the child was not borne down and crushed to the earth by the fears of a physical death, but simply continued to live and to fly. The child was unaware that this death, as they called it, was to be something frightening, to be avoided, to flee [from] as long and with as much effort as possible. He was but a child, and only knew that his universe was still malleable, was still subject to his own powers of creation, and thus, happily, the child continued to fly.

My brothers, the child in all of us continues to fly. We can load it down with the heavy burdens of this supposed knowledge and wisdom of the worlds we create. We can crush ourselves to the earth with our needs, our possessions, with the heavy burdens which we create for ourselves. Or we can see them in their proper perspective, as malleable conditions that we have created for the purpose of our own learning. We can use them toward that, and relinquish them when we are finished. My brothers, my sisters, if your burdens are heavy, lay them down and come fly.

I am Hatonn.

(Carla channeling)

I am Hatonn, and am now with this instrument. I greet you again, my friends, in the love and in the light of the infinite Creator. We would continue through this instrument.

My friends, we realize that there is always some gap between the concepts or inspirations which we might offer you and practical application of the original Thought of the infinite Creator in your life. We have not drifted so far from your experience of third density that we have forgotten the gravity that holds you down, both physically and metaphysically. We do suggest to you that you might lay aside your metaphysical gravity, and take your birthright as a co-creator of this infinite universe and fly wherever and whenever you wish *(inaudible)* is to invite even the most devoted student to inquire as to the precise nature of the mechanics of flight.

My friends, we do not speak of the mechanical concept of flight. Let us look at the same concept from a slightly different point of view. Say that you are a detective, each of you on the trail of the suspect. This suspect is reputed to be the true self. The most daring, careful and inventive detective shall never discover his own true self, for the self is revealed to the self unexpectedly, as if by chance you walked into a strange room in a strange house and unexpectedly caught sight of your face in the mirror. How startled the person is to see that reflection when it is not expected; [how] different the person suddenly looks.

Within the bleak outline of difficult days, or the rich outline of good ones, something [unexpected] occurs and in the life of the self, a discovery is made by you about yourself. These things cannot be predicted, cannot be planned. They are the revelations of the self to the self. They are the marks of an adventure which each of you has begun in the seeking for the truth, for my friends, the truth lies within your self and within that self which is the true self.

That true self, we submit to you, my friends, is love and the nature of that love is such that it opens to you, in all unity, all the Creation. Here, my friends, is true flight. Here is the capacity and ability to be the essence, to experience all that there is. In meditation, such a search is mounted. The self seeks the self. In meditation, such a thing is considered possible. Your spirit can fly. We have had far less of a heavy—we correct this instrument—chemical illusion to penetrate, are able to see more of the creation, as ourselves, to fly further, to feel love. And in our feeling of unity with you we reach out our hands to you. We cannot do this for you, but we can tell you that it is possible.

We shall be with you, my friends, at any time that you wish to meditate. We are messengers of love and we send you that love at all times. It is a creation of love. Come fly with us, my friends, in a universe filled with the love and the light of the infinite Creator.

Before we leave this instrument we would like to work with each in the room, conditioning those who request it, and working with new channels. We would first spend some of what you call time with the one known as R, that this entity may share with us the vibratory harmonics of our relationship. I am Hatonn.

(Pause)

I am Hatonn, and am again with this instrument. We thank the one known as R and will continue spending time with him an we work with the one known as S. We would like to say a few words through this instrument at this time. I am Hatonn.

(S channeling)

I am Hatonn. It is a pleasure to greet you once more through this instrument. It has been some time since we have been able to speak through this instrument. We are pleased to be able to share our conditioning vibration with this instrument once more. We of Hatonn are pleased, as always, to be able to work with those of you who are attempting, what you call, the channeling process. We are indeed honored to be of service to you in this area.

We would at this time like to make our contact known to the one known as D. If he would relax, we would make contact at this time. I am Hatonn.

(Carla channeling)

I am Hatonn. I am again with this instrument, and confirm that we have good contact with the one known as D and intend to speak through this instrument. The one known as D is somewhat fatigued at this time and has some question as to our contact. We would not wish in any way to intrude upon any question or conflict regarding our channeling, but will once again offer this contact to the one known as D, if this entity wishes to use this energy at this time. I am Hatonn.

(D channeling)

I am Hatonn, and am with this instrument. We of Hatonn are pleased to be working with this instrument at this time. I am Hatonn.

(Carla channeling)

I am Hatonn, and am once again with this instrument. We thank the one known as S and the one known as D for the great privilege of working with each of them. We are aware of many questions in the mind of the one known as D of a philosophical nature, regarding our source and our relationship with energies connected with this planet. It is our sincere hope that we, or one of our brothers or sisters of the Confederation of Planets in the Service of the Infinite Creator may speak and share our thoughts to any questions which any entity might have, if not at this time, at any time that is desired.

We would very much like to close this particular message through the instrument known as W. This instrument desires at this time to offer itself for our service. I am Hatonn.

(W channeling)

I am Hatonn. I am now with this instrument. To greet each of you in the love and the light of the infinite Creator is as a constant reminder that in truth we are all as one, with our entire message and purpose for contact [being] sharing this love and experience, and [it] is that spirit with which we leave you and pray you forever share with all of your brothers and sisters on the face of the planet. We leave you. Adonai, my friends.

(Carla channeling)

I am Latwii. I am Latwii. I am with this instrument. We greet you in the love and the light of the infinite Creator and are sorry to yell, but we forget about this instrument. We would like to talk to you about a small, hard-shelled animal. It is on the ocean bottom. It in a private animal, sifting seawater and gaining food. It values its privacy. One day a grain of sand gets stuck in this animal's jaw. What is this animal to do? It cannot spit. It sits there grumbling to itself, "Why do I have a piece of sand stuck in my jaw? It hurts. It continues to hurt." Its hard-shelled body begins to cover the sand to protect it from hurting. It learns to deal with the pain, and one day some alien sweeps along the bottom of the ocean and scoops up this animal, forces it open and finds a pearl, my friends, of great price.

(Side one of tape ends.)

(Carla channeling)

[I am Latwii.] … this instrument for awhile, and are grateful for the opportunity. At this time we would transfer. I am known to you as Latwii.

(Jim channeling)

I am Latwii, and greet you again through this instrument. We are most honored to be able to join you this evening in your meditation and shall now attempt the answering of questions which those present might have value in the asking. Are there any questions at this time?

D: Speaking of the bottom of the ocean, what can you tell me about dolphins?

I am Latwii, and my brother, we can say many things about dolphins. We, of course, do not suppose to give biology lessons, but may remark in passing that the creatures which are known to you as dolphins are much more than animals which swim in the deep, for these creatures have, for many of your years, possessed the prize of the human form which is called the extension of the brain complex known as the frontal lobes, and, therefore, this creature does have the intelligence that exceeds many of your so-called second-density creatures, and is able to communicate with those of its own kind, and other entities as well, on a level which you may describe as telepathic.

Is there any further specific information regarding this creature which you ask about at this time, my brother?

D: What is their evolutionary track? How did they become dolphins?

I am Latwii, and, my brother, in this regard we may say that the creatures known to you as dolphins have progressed upon a path which is in, shall we say, somewhat of a balance or opposition to the path which the humanoid creatures of your kind have traveled. Those of the homo sapien nature have traveled a path that has, for the most part, been a dusty one and one which has remained upon the land. The creatures known to you as dolphins have traveled a path which has been somewhat more moist. This path has included the single-celled creatures of the ocean which have developed over a period of time the nature of the vertebrate, which has included the knobby protrusion at one end known as the brain.

This continuing evolution of complexity of the nervous system has developed additional parts of this brain which have corollaries to your cortex and thinking processes. The continuing development through various forms of what you would call fishes has progressed to the aquatic form of a mammal, which has reached its zenith upon this planet in the ones which you call dolphins and some forms of the creatures which you call whales, in that these creatures have been able to develop an additional portion of the brain organ which we have referred to previously as the frontal lobes, and in this regard have activated an energy center which has allowed them the communication which might be called telepathic.

Is there any further way which we might be of service to you in this regard, my brother?

D: What's the density of the dolphin?

I am Latwii, and, my brother, we might suggest to you that, as you are aware, many creatures upon your planet now, including the human form, possess the body of the fourth density in activation and this is also the case with the creatures known to you as dolphins.

May we answer you further, my brother?

D: No.

We are most grateful for this opportunity to be of service. Is there another question at this time?

L: Yes. On that same subject of dolphins. Will they go through the same process—of division into the polarized groups—as we will?

I am Latwii. My brother, we might suggest that your assumption is correct to the best of our knowledge.

May we answer you further?

L: Yes. In comparison to our own race's progress in polarization, how would you compare our progress with that of the dolphins?

I am Latwii, and, my brother, we do not wish to make any present feel lesser in their seeking, but your brothers and sisters of the dolphin family have been much more united and centered in their seeking and choosing of a polarity, for their seeking has resulted in the positive polarity choice to an almost unanimous degree.

May we answer you further, my brother?

L: Yes. Is this also true of the group we refer to as killer whales?

I am Latwii. This is correct, my brother. May we answer you further?

L: No, thank you for your help.

We thank you as well. Is there another question at this time?

Carla: While we're on dolphins, do dolphin—does the dolphin race precede the humanoid race and have its own individual and particular genetic trail or did those of Atlantis deal genetically with and become part of the dolphin race at one point many thousands of years ago?

I am Latwii, and, my sister, in this regard, we may note that crossover, shall we say, between the races of your third-density beings, this including those known as dolphins and some forms of those called whales, has been very minimal. The genetic progress of the ones known as dolphins has been, for the most part, a progress of a homogeneous nature, dwelling also within the boundaries of the third-density illusion which you experience. Therefore, this trail which has been traveled by the dolphin is a trail which began at the same time the trail of the humanoid form began upon your planet, approximately 75,000 of your years ago.

May we answer you further, my sister?

Carla: Yes. So that those who incarnated as that type of fish reincarnated as that type of fish and so forth, just as we have incarnated many times as what we call humans. Their path has been one that they followed carefully and they are a breed getting ready for harvest, just as we are? Is this correct? Or have they gone through harvest early and are now living in fourth-density activated bodies, or do they have dual-activated bodies?

I am Latwii, and, my sister, upon this query we might say that these entities of which you speak are, for the most part, inhabiting those bodies which you might call doubly activated, and shall continue in that form upon the completion of that which is called the harvest. And we might also note that you are correct in assuming that they have remained with this form for the entire 75,000 years of this third-density cycle, for their experience in that form and in the medium known to you as water has been unique for their race, and to change forms from that of the aquatic to that of the land creature known as the humanoid, would not be of the greatest value in the seeking of the light and the love of the one Creator, for they have their mode, shall we say, and your people have their own.

May we answer you further, my sister?

Carla: No, indeed. Thank you.

We thank you, as always. Is there another query at this time?

W: Yes. Concerning the unicorns in California and the caretakers and so-called otherwise parents of those unicorns, can you elaborate a little bit as to maybe what sort of density beings that the unicorns are and what sorts of people its human caretakers parents are?

I am Latwii, and, my brother, we do not wish to appear too dumbfounded, but we are unable to determine the thrust of your query. We are unable to find such a creature within the realm of your third-density existence at present. May we ask if there is a further refinement of this query which you might make to aid our understanding of it?

W: Would these creatures be of another density and still nonetheless be able to have appeared on this planet and made themselves aware to third-density beings, and what would be the significance of that?

I am Latwii, and we believe we have somewhat more information upon which to begin our response to this query. There are many beings of many forms which inhabit those planes of your planetary existence, which are known as the astral planes. These planes are not of another density, but are associated with the third-density experience. This is much likened unto the form your people take upon the passing through of the stage of death. The activation of the fourth ray or the green-ray body, also known as the astral body, does take place upon the process of death and may pass through many planes of existence which are contained within the astral and devachanic levels of your planet.

Many of the creatures which you have referred to are inhabitants of these planes of existence and may from time to time become visible to some of the peoples of your planet who have a certain relationship with these creatures. It must be understood, however, that these creatures are not what you might call regular or normal inhabitants of your planetary surface, for their pattern of existence is not within the space/time complex or location of your third density, but is upon a level which is what you might call not visible to the normal third-density eye.

May we answer you further, my brother?

W: How about a different question. How can these beings be photographed and put in a newspaper with otherwise what I would believe to be third density going into fourth density human being types?

I am Latwii, and, my brother, we might suggest several possibilities for this phenomenon of the photographing of such an entity. One possibility is that such on entity might for a moment become more material, shall we say, or become focused within this density so that its reproduction by the photograph would become possible. Another possibility which is much greater in its likelihood, is that such a creature might be, shall we say, falsely inserted into such a photograph so that they appear to exist, when in fact they might not have existed at the time the photograph was made.

May we answer you further, my brother?

W: No.

Is there another question at this time?

L: Yes, one last question on the dolphins. There is a tradition or story that dolphins have a strong enmity toward sharks. Is this strictly the result of a protective effort to protect their young or is there a significance to sharks that brings out this response in dolphins?

I am Latwii, and, my brother, we might note in this regard that the ones known to you as sharks and the ones known to you as dolphins do have their evolutionary history and shared experience and it has been the experience of the ones known as dolphins that the ones known as sharks have been, shall we say, placed in opposition to them in the position of the one which would attack and devour the young of the dolphin herd, and, therefore, the ones known as dolphins have, of necessity, made certain precautionary, shall we say, procedures a part of their pattern of existence with these creatures known as sharks. Each has served the other in their own particular pattern of behavior and the progress of each has been thusly enhanced.

May we answer you further, my brother?

L: Yes. What level of development are sharks?

I am Latwii, and we might say that the one known as sharks remain in the high second density of their particular species. There have been some individual crossovers, shall we say, from the shark line into that which is known as the dolphin, which is another part of their evolutionary history—have shared the experience, and has been a part of the chain of evolution for both.

May we answer you further, my brother?

L: This crossover has taken place through reincarnation and not while in occupation of a physical body? Is this correct?

I am Latwii. This is correct.

L: That answers my question. Thank you.

We are most grateful to you as well. Is there another question at this time?

Carla: I have something I've been wondering about. I've always had a very strong feeling for angels, the traditional Christian angel—Seraphim, Cherubim hosts, etcetera. I have no doubt as to their reality on the inner plane and I wondered what their relationship might be to you and if you work with me.

I am Latwii, and, my sister, we might most succinctly say that we are one with all beings. In specific, we shall remark [on] one particular relationship which we have with these beings which you might describe as angelic. Upon your inner planes, upon the planes known to you as the devachanic planes, reside many of what are most frequently called by your people as the masters. Various brotherhoods do exist here upon the inner planes and we of Latwii do have a communication with some of these brotherhoods, for it is from such entities that have gone through the incarnational cycle of your planet and who by their own individual effort have achieved that known to you as the harvest, that we might discover the nature of your people and thereby make our contact more harmoniously felt by the groups to which we hope to communicate. It has been our great privilege to be able to speak with these entities from time to time in the gathering of information which has enlarged our understanding of your peoples.

May we answer you further, my sister?

Carla: Yes. Just a question about something that has always pleased me about angels, and that is the thought that they are forever praising the Creator. Traditionally, what they're saying is "Holy, holy, holy," etc., that this never stops, that there's an endless praising of the Creator. Is this in fact a part of the vibration in this particular plane of existence? Has this in fact happened?

I am Latwii, and, my sister, again we shall begin our response with a general response, saying that each entity, no matter what the density, does praise the Creator. Many entities do this on an unconscious level, as we are noting there is such praise occurring at this moment. As we progress through the levels of the inner planes, we see that there is a varying degree of conscious praising of the Creator in the fashion which you mention and in other means as well.

As we ascend the planes of the devachanic levels, we find that there is, shall we say, less and less of the communication of these angelic beings with those of your peoples and more of that phenomenon which you have described as the constant praising of the one Creator. It is upon such levels that the light and the love of the one Creator truly shines as a beacon.

May we answer you further, my sister?

Carla: I'll hold it til another time. Thank you.

We are most grateful to you for this opportunity to be of service. Are there any further questions at this time?

(Pause)

I am Latwii. We have been most privileged to be able to join you this evening. We hope that our presence will be requested at future gatherings, for we are coming to be somewhat of a ham, as you might say, and do thoroughly enjoy these sessions of questions and answers, and wish we were able to respond to the query of the one known as Fairchild, but do not feel that our mastery of the feline tongue is yet sufficient to do so. I am known to you as Latwii, and I leave you now in the love and in the light of the one infinite Creator. We shall be with you in your future. Adonai, my friends. Adonai vasu borragus. ✤

Intensive Meditation
December 3, 1981

(Carla channeling)

I am Laitos, and I greet you, my friends, in the love and the light of the one infinite Creator. We have been attempting to contact the one known as D and the one known as S but we find that some time of conditioning would be helpful with both of these instruments as there has been a good deal of activity on this day and retuning of the mind towards seeking, towards the ideals of service, towards the impersonal and objective in life.

It is difficult to find in a moment and yet, my friends, this is what you seek, not an easy thing nor a profitable one among your peoples. You seek the invisible and do not find the visible satisfactory or sufficient. You seek the idea and do not find practicality a reasonable excuse for action. You seek service and do not accept the philosophy that to be self-sufficient is service enough. You are, in fact, those in the minority among your peoples, those who consciously and deeply seek something beyond the petty, mundane round of existence that can be seen and heard and felt and experienced.

We are with you, my friends, to share with you a mystery. That mystery is that you do not seek in vain. That mystery is the mystery of an infinite creation, of an original Thought that has created all that there is, including an infinite array of those things that cannot be seen with the physical eye, that cannot be touched, that cannot be experienced—until one thing occurs, until one door is opened. This one thing, my friends, is the seeking that you are now engaged in. We are with you.

We believe that we have sufficiently conditioned each and would now speak through the one known as D. I am Laitos.

(D channeling)

I am Laitos, and I greet you through this instrument. We realize that the instrument is experiencing some difficulty and she is somewhat fatigued. We would suggest that she take a few deep breaths. We have a good contact with this instrument and would like to say that she has made good progress. We would assure her that she did indeed …

(Carla channeling)

I am again with this instrument. I am Laitos. We hope the one known as D will forgive us for continuing to offer our transmission, but there is a breakthrough which is quite close at this time. The difficulty is as it so often is—the analysis of the contact. We were assuring the instrument that we were offering our thoughts to the instrument. It is only when this point has been trusted that we can begin to offer material of a more advanced nature. Therefore, it is worth spending some of your time on, if you will be patient in sessions such as this one.

We wish to build up the confidence of the new instruments by breaking through the point at which the new instrument becomes aware enough of our vibration and the method of our sharing of concept that we can then begin to share concepts in a less predictable manner and gradually develop the unique channel which is possible with each unique being through whom we may speak. We thank the one known as D very much for the privilege of working with her and feel that we are very close to this breakthrough of confidence. We are most privileged to share in this service.

At this time we would speak through the one known as S. I am Laitos.

(S channeling)

I am Laitos, and I greet you, my friends, through this instrument once more. We of Laitos are always pleased to be able to speak through instruments such as those that we find in this group. It makes us feel happy to know that there is such a calling for our presence in order that we may aid those who are seeking to serve in the manner known as channeling. It is indeed a pleasure to serve the one infinite Creator by being of service to those who call us for assistance in their seeking. We of Laitos are indeed honored at the frequency of the calls we receive from your group. It is, as always, a pleasure to work with each of the new instruments. We find a sincere effort is being made by those in this group. We would at this time like to transfer this contact. I am Laitos.

(Jim channeling)

I am Laitos, and greet you once again in love and light. We are honored at this time to offer ourselves in the service of answering questions which entities in this group might have to ask. May we answer any questions at this time?

S: Yes, I have a question. I am usually unable to note your contact. It is either so very light that I don't feel it or I'm just having trouble recognizing it. Do I just need practice to develop the ability to recognize? I can recognize others easily, but your touch seems so light that I have difficulty knowing when contact has been made.

I am Laitos, and am aware of your question, my sister. We of Laitos attempt to respond to the request of each new instrument in the strength of our conditioning vibration through a series of learning relationships and speaking attempts by each instrument. We are able to provide the conditioning which makes each instrument aware of our presence yet does not overstimulate the instrument.

We would suggest at this time, if it be your desire at this time to be more aware of our conditioning vibration, that you mentally request such before meditation begins after the tuning has been accomplished. In this way it will be more easily perceived by any Confederation member wishing to utilize your instrument with your permission what the degree of conditioning you have requested is.

You are also correct in your analysis that more practice on your part will also be of aid to you in perceiving our contact as we attempt to balance your perception of our contact with a touch which is light enough avoid the overstimulation of your instrument.

May we answer you further, my sister?

S: *(Inaudible).*

We are most grateful to you as well for offering us this great opportunity to be of service to the one Creator. Are there any further questions at this time?

Carla: Well, I wasn't going to ask it, but just in case you might have some thoughts that I hadn't been aware of from previous communications through the Confederation, I'm very interested in healing as quickly as possible, and my healing seems to have been quite accelerated already, and I wondered if you had any thoughts regarding my further acceleration of that by any action or thought that I might do?

I am Laitos, and am aware of your question, my sister. In this regard we find that there is not much new information which we may give upon this subject for your desire to be healed has caused you to seek every possible remedy which is available at this time. Your desire is in itself the greatest aid to your healing process. For your desire does pierce that protective shell which holds your physical vehicle in its configuration, whatever that configuration might be, and does allow the healing energy which many send you to enter through your protective auric shell.

This has been the case thus far and your desire to be healed continues to open your shell to healing love and light energies. We simply reaffirm that which you are familiar with, the visualizing of your arm—

and entire body for that matter—being surrounded by light, this light being the healing love/light of the one Creator. This light entering through your lower chakras and feet and circulating throughout your body, coalescing in those regions which need the most healing. And then, to complete the visualization in your meditation, the seeing of your body and any specific areas as being completely healthy and healed.

May we answer you, my sister?

Carla: No, thank you, Laitos.

We are most grateful to you as well. Is there another question at this time?

(Pause)

I am Laitos. We are most grateful for this opportunity to join your group this afternoon. We of Laitos hope that we shall have this honor many times in what you call your future, for this is our service as members of the Confederation of Planets in the Service of the Infinite Creator—that is, the exercising and conditioning of new instruments. We treasure each experience and thank each present this afternoon for adding another voice to the call of service which we have to offer. ☥

Sunday Meditation
December 6, 1981

(L channeling)

I am Hatonn, and I greet you in the love and the light of the infinite Creator. My friends, my brothers, my sisters, it is with great pleasure that we shared your musical and heartfelt vibrations as you initiated this period of sharing. We of Hatonn are sensitive to those vibrations to which you refer as music and are pleasured deeply at this sensation of harmonious vibrations. At this time we would like the opportunity to work with the various instruments present, if they are willing. I am Hatonn.

(C channeling)

I am Hatonn, and I am now with this instrument. We again greet you in the love and light of the one infinite Creator. As always, it is a pleasure to speak to groups as large as this one, for we do not often get to speak our few words through so many at a time. It is especially a pleasure tonight, for within this group there are so many who have chosen to aid others, us, themselves, by the act that you refer to as channeling. We of Hatonn are always grateful [to] all who would serve in this manner, for it enables us to be in contact with more of your peoples who would listen, but who have not yet gained the ability to hear, to feel our vibration, our love, in our attempt to aid those of your planet who seek, to gain awareness, the love and the light that is the one infinite Creator. We would now like to exercise another channel with whom we have not had contact with for a while. We are known to you as Hatonn.

(H channeling)

I am Hatonn. I am once again with this instrument. It has been a great length of time, as you would measure it. It is always our pleasure to be invited into the heart of your peoples and when you open yourselves to our communication this is indeed what you offer. You offer your trust, your commitment to the seeking of truth, and with this, the inner feeling which many of you would call to be the spirit or the heart of your being.

We of Hatonn wish in no way to bring upon anyone what they do not request or desire. We are only here to share with you at this present time our knowledge, sometimes our advice, but we wish in no way to give you advice that would determine your actions. We only wish to share our knowledge, commune it with yours, and allow you to analyze and to decide which is the great truth that permeates the universe and which is the direction that you should seek, for each of you walks a path which you have chosen prior to your birth. Blindly, you lead yourself through this experience upon Earth. Many take generations—excuse the mistake—many take several incarnations to follow one path, for within your Earth environment there is a great deal of confusion and a great deal of what you would call negative energy. It is here to test the strength of your commitment to the seeking of truth and the Creator.

Your walk upon this plane of existence is merely one lesson in a vast universe of endless classes and experiences. You on Earth are fortunate in that you are now culminating what you might call one of your major courses in spiritual growth. You are here to learn the meaning of love, without prejudice or prejudgment. You are here to learn to accept one another. You are here to learn to become an inhabitant of the Creator's entire creation. Look not only upon that which happens upon your globe, but look into the sky and know that you are not alone. All that you see is inhabited in one form or another. Intelligence permeates the universe, and love overcomes all things. We of Hatonn extend our love to you and await the day that we may walk hand in hand in the love and in the light of our infinite Creator.

I shall now transfer to another instrument. I am Hatonn.

(Carla channeling)

I am now with this instrument. I am Hatonn. Once again, my friends, we greet you in love. Before we leave this group, we would greatly appreciate the privilege of sharing with each of you our conditioning vibration. We shall pass among you at this time and if you request this vibration which will allow you to become more aware of our presence and deepen your own meditative states, we ask that you mentally request that we be with you, and we shall be. We shall now pause in order to be with you.

(Pause)

I am again with this instrument. My friends, we thank you for the great symphony of your harmonized circle of vibration. We ask that if you think of us, you think not of who we are, but of only the Creator. We care not what impression we may offer, nor do we wish authority among your peoples, for reputation is a stranger to meaning. We ask only that you consider the love that is the original Thought of the infinite Creator, and we ask that you consider seeking that love in meditation.

We are always with you if you mentally request. If in any way when we condition any who may be sensitive there is discomfort, mentally request adjustment. If there is continued discomfort, mentally request that we leave. We shall do so immediately. When we work with individual or the preliminary times, as you would say, there is a period in which we are adjusting constantly to the unique vibratory pattern of each. Please have patience with us in order that we may serve you, for that is our only desire.

We leave this instrument in order that another of the Confederation may speak. Thank you, my brothers and sisters, for allowing us to meditate with you. I am known to you as Hatonn. Adonai, my friends. Adonai.

(Carla channeling)

I am Oxal, and I greet you, my friends, in the love and in the light of the infinite Creator. May I say that it is with the greatest of pleasure that we speak to this group this evening. We greet each, and especially those who are new to this group, and the one known as H who has been absent for some time. Your life vibrations are a great blessing to us.

You, my friends, are in exile. All upon your planet are in a strange land. There is no comfort for the spirit in the spirit of your culture. The planet that man has made is a strange and barbarous territory. You are in exile in your bodies. There is within you a knowledge, a remembrance, a memory of the light and the infinite life of your true existence and of your true body. But here you are, my friends, cast away and what have you done, my friends, you exiles of the soul? Have you banded together defensively to protect yourselves against the pain of living? Have you attempted to convince yourselves that exile is home? Examine the actions that you take and the thoughts that you think and you may find in yourself many, many traces of the behavior of a stranger in a strange land.

My friends, there is comfort. There is complete and utter comfort. It is in looking outward that you miss the one source of home, for to find that home you must look within the self. Beneath all those things which you have been taught and all those things which you have rationalized, there lies a homeland and a true being, so deeply fixed within you that you cannot lose it, you cannot forget it. It is not to be earned, but it may be sought.

Seek, my friends, the peace of your true home, balm of your true identity, and in that knowledge, my friends, look out upon this illusion and see it in love and in light. If you seek wisdom you shall not find it in your illusion. In meditation go home, for that home is yours by right of infinite birth.

I would now leave this instrument, but I assure you, my friends, I will continue to meditate with this group as one of our brothers speaks, for it is indeed a pleasure to be with you. I am known to you as Oxal. Let there be no division in yourself, my friends. Cease all confusion and know that exiles think strange things. Seek that which awaits within. I leave you in the love and in the light of the infinite Creator. Adonai vasu borragus.

(Jim channeling)

I am Latwii, and I greet you all in love and light. We are most honored to join you this evening. As always, it in our privilege to add what small bit of light that we might to the answering of queries which those present might have the value in asking. May we ask if there are any queries at this time?

M: Yes. Latwii, I have one that was missed on the tape. You answered while we were changing tapes. If someone who knows a truth or knows a particular sermon to be true, what happens in their growth and development if they do not act accordingly to that truth?

I am Latwii, and am aware of your question, my brother. In this regard we might say that when an entity has ascertained information which it has determined to be of value, to be of a certain degree of truth, shall we say, then if this information is not utilized by this entity, the entity shall discover the means whereby it was brought into contact with this truth being repeated, so that the entity might once again discover that which it seeks, that which it has previously discovered to be of value to it in its seeking, and might, thereby, by repetition discover a use for this truth.

The information which an entity seeks is drawn to it like a magnet draws the filing of iron. When the entity does not use this information, but sets it aside, the seeking mechanism remains in motion, drawing unto that entity the means whereby it might once again discover that which it seeks.

When the information, the truth is made a part of the being's behavior and thoughts, a part of the being itself, then there is that which might be likened unto the closing of a circuit and there is a completion at one level of seeking whereby there might be, following that seeking, seeking of a further truth, for the seeking is endless. It is infinite, my friends, and if the product of the seeking on any level is not utilized, then there shall be generated more opportunities by which the truth might be found.

May we answer you further, my brother?

M: No, thank you.

We thank you as well. We are always grateful for the opportunity to be of service. Is there another question at this time?

C: Yes. I could stand a little advice. I've been, here of late, in an ongoing process of trying to improve the relationship that exists between myself and my son. I went through a period where I was, I know now, I was demanding too much of my small son and was just curious as to whether the steps I'm now undertaking will lead to the bettering of our relationship. It seems to be having some effect now, but I was wondering as if you could comment as to whether the steps I'm taking will continue to improve the relationship between us.

I am Latwii, and am aware of your question, my brother. In this regard we must answer in a general nature, for to give specific advice or judgment of your particular line of action would, in our humble estimation, be infringement upon your free will.

C: General is just fine.

We appreciate your compromise with our position and might suggest that in the relationship with the young entities of your illusion, those children of your being, that first of all there are no mistakes. What you do in relationship with your children will affect them in a manner which will eventually result in their growth, their learning and their unity with the Creator, for there is nothing but service that is possible within this or any illusion. Worry not that you make mistakes, for it is the attention which you give your young child in the attempting to be of service to it that is of the most service to it, for the young entity in your illusion needs the models, shall we say, needs the knowledge that those who are in its care and whose care it rests within, do care for it, do give it attention and do attempt to allow its perceptions to be broadened, its experiences to be increased, so that its great desire to master this illusion might be fed the food of your wisdom and your love and your simple being.

By this constant interplay of attention between your child and yourself, there shall grow a relationship of clear understanding that this is an illusion which has no clear cut answers and that the seeking within the self for each answer is that activity which is of most benefit. In this regard, my brother, you have yourself been of great service and know you that your child does recognize this factor.

May we answer you further, my brother?

C: Yes. Maybe. Here of late I've been putting myself into the situation where I'm interacting with the children of others, and am experiencing very warming emotions and experiencing definite growth. And in this situation I see a profound wisdom, that is not within me or the other adults that I'm working with, but within the children within their simple and very—I'm not sure how to say it—their own little world. They seem to display a wisdom that we tend to forget. I realize that each and every situation which we are involved in is a means for furthering our growth, but I guess—I really don't have a question, I just simply wanted to say that the chance that I've had here of late with children has let me see many things which I'd either forgotten or ignored.

Why is it that so many of us forget the wisdom and simple truths that we know as children? Why do adults forget what they seem to be born with?

I am Latwii, and am aware of your question, my brother. We of Latwii can say little that will be of clear understanding in this regard, for it is our understanding that the entities within your illusion are indeed, as our brothers of Oxal have mentioned previously, in exile. Born into this illusion, each entity comes from a unity with the innocence and the purity of one facet of that unity which might be likened unto the unconscious recognition of all as the self. From this innocence must be made a journey, a journey which will lead into a confusion which will lead into this illusion. The innocence of the young must be tested, shall we say, by the fires of this illusion so that the unconscious knowing of oneness might become as the final fruit of the tree of incarnation, balanced by the conscious knowing of the unity.

On this journey there shall be many experiences, many …

(Side one of tape ends.)

(Jim channeling

I am Latwii. To continue with our story, this journey moves from the unconscious into the conscious realms for the entity, and in this journey the entity does experience that which shall teach it to know with its conscious mind that which it knows with its unconscious mind. For the conscious mind to learn this lesson it must learn through experience and experience somewhat of a forgetting, much as each entity upon entering this illusion does experience a forgetting so that the learnings of this illusion will carry weight.

This process is reflected in the life of each entity within each incarnation. Each entity begins as the young entity, quite aware of unity with all, journeys forth, experiences that which appears to be separation from all as the individuality of each entity is formed. The fruits of this journey, the labors, culminate for each entity in the experience of conscious oneness with all. For this experience to carry weight for the entity, there must be a forgetting.

May we answer you further, my brother?

C: No, thank you.

We thank you as well. Is there another question at this time?

L: Latwii, I've got a bunch of questions. The first one is in reference to my friend, R, who is experiencing an emotional imbalance caused by the death of a near relative. Is there anything we can do in addition to sending light and love that will enable R to find the comfort he needs?

I am Latwii, and am aware of your question, my brother, and in this regard we must also reiterate that we cannot give specific advice but can only suggest that if you wish to be of service to one who is in need of your service that you consider carefully the needs of this entity, and in your meditative state seek you this solution, and as you seek to be of service the way shall be made clear from within [your] own being as to which path would be of most value to this entity.

May we answer you further, my brother?

L: Yes, on a different subject, on the subject of healing. I have reached an understanding of a process to assist in the healing of internal organs recently. Is this the best system that I have available to work with, or would you advise that I seek further?

I am Latwii, and my brother, we do not wish to sound confused in our response, but we would suggest both of your assumptions are correct.

May we answer you further, my brother?

L: Yes. My understanding of my present situation on learning healing is that my greatest success in learning will be obtained, not through study under another individual or a particular system, but rather through attuning myself to what I can learn through meditation and performance. It appears to me that the systems are at best distortion, and are something I should avoid for the time being until I have established some basics in my own understanding. Would you regard this as a correct perception of the situation I'm in?

I am Latwii, and, my brother, in this regard we might suggest that your own discrimination has thus far provided you with the path which has borne fruit, and we would suggest the continued following of your own inclinations in this matter, remaining open to any source which appears to be of value.

May we answer you further, my brother?

L: Yes. It is my understanding that certain physical imbalances are created by the individual for their spiritual progress, and that these should not be interfered with. It is also my understanding that other physical imbalances have served their purpose and are inadvertently maintained by the individual who may be served by assisting them to release themselves from these imbalances. My problem is discerning between the two. How would you advise that I discern between the two?

I am Latwii, and in this regard, my brother, we would attempt to simplify your understanding of the healing process by suggesting that as the healer you offer the one to be healed the opportunity to be healed, but do not, by your own actions, heal. Therefore, if there is one who approaches you and seeks your assistance in the healing process, the seeking is that which is necessary for your decision, for if one seeks to be healed, one is seeking the assistance to do that which the entity to be healed has already decided, therefore there is no infringement upon the will of the entity in such a seeking.

May we be of further assistance, my brother?

L: No, that answer itself is a great relief to me. Thank you very much. I have no further questions.

We are most grateful to you as well for allowing us to serve in this capacity. May we ask if there is another question at this time?

Carla: Which part of our density are you scanning tonight?

I am Latwii, and, my sister, we were wondering when you would ask which particular color of your density we were enjoying and have prepared for you a display of that color which you might call the apple green.

May we ask if there is another question at this time?

Carla: No. That suited me just fine.

We are most grateful to you as well. May we ask if there is another question at this time?

(Pause)

I am Latwii. My friends, may we say that it has been the greatest of privileges to join your group this evening. We look forward to such sessions in what you call your future, for it is of great inspiration to our memory complex of entities to be able to participate in such exchanges of perceptions and the vibration of love and light which this group is known to generate.

We shall leave this group at this time and would in the leaving remind each present that at any time in your future which you would be in the need of our assistance in meditation, that we should be most pleased to join you with the simple request for our presence being all that is required. We leave you now in the love and in the light of the one infinite Creator. We are known to you as Latwii. Adonai, my friends. Adonai vasu borragus.

(C channeling)

I am Nona, and greet you, my friends, in love and in light. We of Nona have been greatly honored by this group for some time now. The desire is present in this group to aid others by the sending [of] healing light. It has been for some time now very strong, very potent. The light generated has been well received by those to whom this group has directed its energies. We of Nona are always extremely glad that we may be of service to you by adding our energies to yours as you seek to aid those around and amongst you.

We of Nona are with you and shall always be, whenever you ask, for our main service in your vibration is to aid healing and always feel honored to aid you at any time. We now leave this instrument, but will still be with you as you send healing light to those for whom you have concern. Adonai. 🌣

Intensive Meditation
December 8, 1981

(Carla channeling)

I am Laitos, and I greet you, my friends, in the love and the light of the infinite Creator. We shall speak some brief thoughts through this instrument while we work with each of the new instruments and share our vibrations with each of those present who asks for the conditioning.

How high the snow is in the winter. How blue the cerulean sky. One lone eagle stalks far above, watching. His cohort, the eagle's mate, watches. The air is crisp, the day is long. The eagle is patient. There is a rush, a sudden emptiness where once the eagle soared. The eagle has found its food. The beauty of the sky, the whiteness of the mountain and crispness of the air do not disturb the hunter, for its seeking is quite specific. In this fair creation of the infinite Creator which you call Earth are not only difficulties but many pleasant distractions, many lovely things. Find then within your being room for the eagle that seeks, keen-eyed and patient for the bread of heaven. Those things which will aid you will not come to you in a moment until that moment comes. Keep awake.

We are grateful to have this opportunity to share some thoughts with you and to join in your meditation and a special *(inaudible)* to be able to work with each instrument. We would at this time transfer this contact to the one known [as] M, if she would relax and realize that there is no effort required for us to transmit our thoughts through the instrument which she has. Merely speak that which is sent. We now transfer. I am Laitos.

(M channeling)

I am Laitos, and I greet you through this instrument. It is difficult *(inaudible)* sharing with [experience] like *(inaudible)* this instrument.

(L channeling)

I am Laitos, and I am now with this instrument. We are pleased and grateful at the success and effort displayed by the one known to you as M. We of Laitos are appreciative of the dedication required and the service rendered to us in training oneself that we may be allowed the privilege of communication with beings of your race.

At this time we would like to speak through another instrument. I am Laitos.

(C channeling)

I am Laitos, and I am now with this instrument. It has been some time since we have been able to work with this instrument, and we are grateful for this opportunity to do so. We of Laitos always [are] eager to assist any who choose to be [of] service, as you call channels. For it is through those who choose this service that the simple message of love/light can be made more available to those of your planet who are seeking or have just begun to become aware of the need to seek [the] love and light of the one infinite Creator. Each one who serves aids others as well as takes further steps themselves on their own journey. We of Laitos also seek, we are also on a journey to further our growth and to further our awareness of the love and the light. We are known to you as Laitos. We are one of many within the Confederation, one of many who would aid; one of many, yet one. We say again we all share the journey.

We would now transfer this contact to another. We are known as Laitos.

(Carla channeling)

I am again with this instrument. I am Laitos, and greet you once again in love and light. We thank you for your patience during this pause but we were attempting to initiate contact with the one known as N without the specific mention of the intention in order that we might as rapidly as possible build up the confidence of this new instrument. We may therefore confirm that the vibrations which the one known as N felt were correctly perceived and would have resulted in the continuation of our message. We shall once again transfer to the one known as N.

(N channeling)

I am Laitos, greeting you in light and in love, which each of us are. The completion of your quests will be experienced as the acceptance of yourselves as all is accepted. The length of the journey is one limited only by each individual's free will. We are Laitos. We leave this instrument.

(L channeling)

I am Laitos, and I am with this instrument despite the contact of the other instrument.

(The telephone had just rung.)

My friends, my brothers, my sisters, we thank you for this opportunity to pass among you. We thank you for being allowed to touch, to immerse ourselves, and to make a part of ourselves the love that passes among you at this moment. It is the will of the Creator that all beings, all races, all facets of creation attain a constant awareness of that love which binds each of you to one another and makes you one with yourselves, with us, with many, with one. Again, deeply, we thank you for this sharing. Adieu, my friends, my loved ones. I am Laitos.

(Carla channeling)

I am Hatonn, and I greet you as do my brothers and sisters in the love and the light of the infinite Creator. We wish to make our vibration known to the new instruments but first, if we may, we wish to share our vibration with one with whom we have been in contact but who does not at this time desire the service of vocal channeling but instead wishes to serve in other ways. May we thank this instrument for allowing us to be companions with him. We pause for a moment to send our love to the one known as Don. I am Hatonn.

(Pause)

We move now, my friends, to another of your group that we may share with him also our conditioning vibration. We pause for a moment with the one known as Don, expressing our great gratitude and love that we may so share in this meditation with this instrument. I am Hatonn.

(Pause)

We would …

(Tape ends.)

Friday Meditation
December 11, 1981

(Unknown channeling)

I am Hatonn, and I greet you, my friends, in the love and the light of the infinite Creator. We have been having some difficulty making contact with this instrument, but wish to begin this session with a short period of conditioning that is, shall we say, directed and focused on the new instruments. We have previously attempted to initiate contact through both of these new instruments, without hand-off, shall we say, and have been most pleased with the rapid progress which has been demonstrated by each new instrument. During this session we would like to spend a few more moments acquainting each new instrument with our conditioning vibration so its recognition might be enhanced when these new instruments might leave this group.

At this time it is our privilege to acquaint the one known as M with our vibrations so that she might reach a comfortable state of the blending and might feel the vibration of our contact increase in small increments and decrease similarly. It is our purpose at this time to fluctuate our vibration in an undulating manner so that the one known as M be aware of how our vibration might be perceived in its full range of possibility within the limits of comfort for her instrument. During this process we again suggest that this new instrument mentally request adjustment that would result in more comfort, but that she also realizes we are attempting to fluctuate our vibration so that she might be aware of our nature more clearly.

We shall now attempt to speak a few words through the instrument known as M. With her permission, we shall now transfer this contact. I am Hatonn.

(Pause)

I am Hatonn, and I am with this instrument once again. We are aware that the one known as M has a desire to rest within our vibrations and to familiarize herself with the intricacies, shall we say, and would at this time be best served by being allowed to do so. It is always a privilege for us to be of service in whatever manner is desired by those who call for our service. We thank the one known as M for so fully opening her channel and very being to our presence and allowing us to blend our vibrations with hers on such a frequent basis.

We shall at this time move to the one known as N and allow this new instrument also to experience the fluctuating range of our vibrations for the purpose of familiarizing this new instrument with our contact in as wide a range as is possible within the limits of comfort.

I am Hatonn, at this time we shall offer ourselves in the service of transmitting our thoughts through the one known as N. If this is his desire, we shall transfer the contact. I am Hatonn.

(N channeling)

I am Hatonn, and I greet you in the love and light of the one Creator. This instrument will be seen as having various frequencies through which you may channel. As he becomes more comfortable with receiving our messages [he] may find himself receiving contacts from our brothers and sisters of the Confederation offering their services. Once *(inaudible)* in preparing yourselves *(inaudible)* might arise we will being the deciding factor. We transfer now. I am Hatonn.

(Unknown channeling)

I am Hatonn, and greet you once again in love and light. At this time it is our privilege in offering ourselves in [answering] queries. Is there a question which we might answer?

N: Yes, Hatonn, over the last few communications which part has been myself and which part has been yours?

I am Hatonn, and, my brother, as we stated at the previous asking, your percentage of contribution has remained at a steady-state shall we say, of 40% of the contact, ours at the 60% level, fluctuating only slightly. We feel the contact is strong and rapidly improving and would only suggest that the continued relaxation during the contact via clearing of the mind of all analytical faculties, and the simple allowing of any thought appearing in the mind to be spoken be continued.

We are most grateful to be of service to you, my brother. Is there another question at this time?

N: In reading the *Ra Material* I came upon mention of a wanderer that was lost, or should we say, a wanderer who became entangled with a negative-polarized entity and was transferred to that reality. Do I have an awareness of this wanderer? Can you tell me without violating the first?

I am Hatonn, and, my brother, we find we cannot give an answer without violation of your free will, or the free will of others. Can we answer in another capacity, another query?

N: Yes. In the future, as questions arise as to the energy centers of our bodies, may we take advantage of our communication with you to gain clarity that we will need as we go on?

I am Hatonn. Indeed, my brother, this is a very strong possibility. As we mentioned previously, we are most honored to join our vibrations, and lend out inspiration to those who seek in this manner. We again remind each new instrument that this does not mean that the seeking shall be clarified beyond a shadow of a doubt. There will always be the necessity for continued seeking and clarification [of] that which is felt from within for each entity on your planet does channel information from the sources from which are [quite] beyond the small self, yet each entity needs to keep foremost in the mind the need for renewed seeking, for never resting upon any information whether it be felt of great inspirational nature or simply that found upon, shall we say, your bubblegum wrapper.

May we be of further assistance, my brother?

N: Thank you, Hatonn.

We are most grateful to you as well. Is there another question at this time?

Carla: I have question but I'm not sure you can speak on it. The last two evening channeling meditations, at the beginning I've gotten a strong sending from my friend encouraging unconsciousness. I've found it more easy to deal with today than yesterday, but it was very strong in both cases. I was wondering if you could comment on how this sending could occur since we have been doing protective work in this house for some time.

I am Hatonn, and we find that we are somewhat limited in our ability to speak in this area, but shall do what we can. There is the need in this particular group to recognize the fact that each of you in your seeking of that one Creator and the law of unity or oneness, that this seeking shall meet that which is, in its appearance, an opposition, a supposed separative factor. Each entity [must] determine that this factor of seeming opposition is a part of the great Self and as part of that one great Self, must be treated [with] the greatest love, care and consideration. The means of protection which compose the care and consideration factors must be determined by each entity from within that entity. The members of this group dwelling in this place have determined certain procedures which have been quite effective in this regard. At this time there is a need for further refinement. The nature of such refinement is that ground upon which we may not tread, for it is that which the group must discover.

May be answer further, my sister?

Questioner: No, thank you.

I am Hatonn. We thank you greatly. May we answer another question at this time?

(No further queries.)

I am Hatonn. As always, it has been the greatest of privileges to be asked to join your meditations to make our contact to the new instruments. We shall leave this group for the present and [look], shall we say, forward to that time when we might once again blend our conditioning vibration with any who requests this service. We leave you now in love and light, rejoicing [in] the once infinite Creator. I am Hatonn. Adonai, my friends.

(Pause)

(Carla channeling)

I am [Nona]. I am with this instrument and with this group. And now in light in service to the infinite Creator. We prefer not to speak, but we offer this vibration which you have experienced to all those who seek to heal. We leave you in the all healing love and light. *(Inaudible).*

Sunday Meditation
December 13, 1981

(C channeling)

I am Laitos, and I am with this instrument. We greet you, my friends, brothers and sisters, in the light and love of the infinite Creator. We would at this time like to pass among you and let each experience our particular conditioning vibration and we pause for a brief moment with those who have been working diligently to improve their ability to receive and channel the humble message of the Confederation. We would now pass among you. I am Laitos.

(Pause)

I am Laitos, and am once again with this instrument. We have been privileged this past period of time you call your week in which we have been called to be of service in our humble way to aid new instruments who wish to serve others in the form of the activity called channeling. We of Laitos, as always, assure all present that we shall be with you whenever you request and we shall be also with you and any who seek love and light. We thank you for allowing us this brief time tonight. We will now leave so that another of our brothers may speak a few words through another instrument. I leave you now in love and light. We are Laitos.

(Carla channeling)

I am Hatonn, and I greet you, my friends, in the love and the light of our infinite Creator. It is a great privilege to be asked to share your meditation and we send each of you a blessing and our love, for, my friends, what else could we do, as there is nothing but blessing in each moment, nothing but love in every iota of the one Creation.

Your streets are crowded. We feel within your group the tensions and the expectations of this season which you call Christmas. We sink into gray evenings, the crowded parking lots, crowded schedules, many concerns. We find, my friends, that you are not alone, but that your people as a whole seem to have a great overdose, shall we say, of civilization. To the simple joys of a season in which the trees are bare and the roots rest deep, so much has been added that it almost seems that it is a gaudier season than the bright colors of June.

My friends, are the thoughts with which you fill your minds as beautiful as flowers, as sweet smelling as the evergreen trees which you use to help celebrate this season? We realize, my friends, that it is easy to lose yourself in the crowded maze of your civilization. And we ask you to remember that this is a season also when the trees are bare, when all has gone to seed and lies quiet in the ground, when the surface of things does not really matter. In the world of the Creator this is the season for true birth, for true nurture, and for that great focused silence which brings new growth.

You will remember also that in your holy work which you call the Bible, detail of the life of the one known to you as Jesus is full of times spent alone. Perhaps, my friends, you cannot find a wilderness in these crowded days, but we would ask that you consider the possible virtue of finding that silence within yourself in which you cease to follow the road of everyday life and find yourself upon the trackless desert where nothing is previously set or known. Allow yourself to listen within yourself. There is a source of love which can only speak to one who asks. The content of that speaking cannot be predicted, but there are qualities that can certainly be shared—clarity and sweetness. As you go into meditation seek for that love which is within. Do not expect the road to be already drawn for you, for the wilderness is trackless, and yet, my friends, from each meditation the way before you becomes less crowded, the road more wide and the possibilities for love more evident.

We ask that you consider these words, not as infallible, but only as words from a friend, from a brother, from yourself, for are we not one, my friends? Is not each of us part of a unity which encompasses all of creation? Take from what we say those things which may be of aid to you. Discard the rest and know that we are with you at any time that you may ask, for this is our one great privilege and honor, to be available to those who would wish to share thoughts with us, using instruments such as this or simply being experienced as a vibration which may aid in clarity.

Before we leave this group we would like to share our vibrations with the one known as M1 and the one known as N. If the group would be patient, we would like to work briefly with each instrument, in order that each may have the best possible sense of the nature and quality of our particular tuning. We also wish to make quite sure that the adjustments which we have made with the one known as M1 are entirely comfortable. We would now pause. I am Hatonn.

(Pause)

I am Hatonn, and am again with this instrument. We thank each of you for sharing with us, and especially the one known as M1 and the one known as N. We leave you now, my friends. As you begin to feel crowded and discouraged in this supposedly happy season, and this will surely happen, look up into the limitless sky and know that there is no true reason to feel anything but love. Adonai, my friends. I am known to you as Hatonn.

(Jim channeling)

I am Latwii, and I greet you my friends, in the love and the light of the one infinite Creator. It is once again our privilege and pleasure to join your meditation group and to offer ourselves in the humble capacity of attempting to answer the questions which those present may have upon their minds. May we answer any questions at this time?

Carla: I'd like to ask some for L. He would like to know, "When doing healing work, what is the purpose of the laying on of hands, and the nature of using proximity rather than physical contact?"

I am Latwii, and am aware of these queries, my sister. We shall begin by saying that the purpose of the laying on of the hands is to provide the one to be healed with the opening of the shell of protection which surrounds each entity and does also provide a means by which the one to be healed might know that there is something happening. This something, the actual physical touching, is that which the one to be healed may look to as many of your entities look to the pill, shall we say, of those whom you refer to as physicians. Many of your psychologists have described this effect as the placebo effect. It is necessary for the one to be healed to know that there is an healing activity which is occurring and which will, if the one to be healed wishes it, have an effect upon that one to be healed.

The actual penetrating of that shell of protection about each entity is the, shall we say, foundation of purpose upon which the touching rests. The proximity to the one to be healed of the one attempting the healing—the healer, shall we say—is necessary for this same reason for most entities. This is not so with those entities who wish to be healed with a very great desire and have, with their own efforts and desires to be healed, traveled that path which shall result in the healing. The proximity of the healer to the one to be healed is, therefore, also connected to that which is known as the placebo effect, for if the one to be healed does truly desire to be healed with enough purity of desire and if the one to be healed has, through its own effort, succeeded in working with that catalyst which has not been previously worked with successfully, then it is not necessary for there to be any other self attempting healing, nor would it be necessary for any laying on of hands, but only necessary for the one to be healed to open the self completely to that love/light of the one Creator which, in the end, does all the healing.

May we answer you further, my sister?

Carla: It seems that there is a type of energy that the healer offers by some funneling of energy through the hands. What you're saying is, that it is not necessary for this energy to actually touch the person, and, furthermore, that if the person desires to be healed with enough purity, the piercing of the protective shell by this power is accomplished by the will and desire of the person themself. Is that correct?

I am Latwii, and this, my sister, is basically correct with one small addition. It is indeed necessary for this energy to touch the one to be healed, but is not necessarily, shall we say, a function of the one known as the healer, for it is quite possible for the one to be healed to provide this energy for the self and to touch the self with it by the purity of its desire to be healed.

May we answer you further, my sister?

Carla: I believe that answers that question. L also would like to ask, "Is it necessary to sleep?"

I am Latwii, and, my sister, we find that for the great majority of entities upon your planet, it is quite necessary to sleep, for those activities of your daily routines which provide the catalyst for the learning of love for each part of the creation and each part of the self do take a toll upon both the mind and the body, most especially the body, and there must be for each entity upon your planet so experiencing this catalyst a rest and a respite, shall we say, so that the body complex might use those nutritious elements of your food nature to rebuild those cells which have been, shall we say, sacrificed, and played their part in the role of consuming and using catalyst.

It is also necessary for the mind to be rested from the daily pursuits so that it might turn, in sleep, to other pursuits of a more balanced nature. It is, we may add, not totally necessary that this recharging of mind and body be done in the sleep process. Meditation does offer a great deal of concentrated energy which might recharge both mind and body. There are other forms of relaxation, concentration and prayer which might also be utilized for this recharging process.

May we answer you further, my sister?

Carla: Well, the rest of that question that L had I think you've already answered, but I'll just check. He wanted to know if it was possible to simply use the energy, the life energy that's all around, instead of sleeping.

I am Latwii, and, my sister, we might say this is indeed possible, but for most entities upon your planet is beyond the grasp, shall we say, for this type of recharging by the utilizing of the cosmic energy which surrounds each particle of your being is that process of the adept or the one who has, through a disciplined and purified form of seeking, been able to make use and to use the contact of this energy for such recharging. It is not common among your peoples, but is indeed possible.

May we answer you further, my sister?

Carla: No, Latwii. Thank you. It's been a pleasure to talk to you.

I am Latwii, and we are most gratified to be able to be of this humble service. May we answer another question at this time?

C: Yes, a question I guess also doing with sleep. I was reading about dreams and that during each sleeping period we go through times during that time of sleep that our minds are active in what we call dreams and that if a person is disturbed during the period in which the dream exists, that in the next sleep period that person will dream that much more. I was wondering exactly what are dreams? What is the purpose of dreams?

I am Latwii, and, my brother, we might say in general upon this very large topic that in your daily activities you experience a variety of experiences. These times seem quite overwhelming, numerous in nature, and never ending. Within your dream state you may also notice that there is a great variety of experiences available here as well. Indeed, the number and types of experiences to be had during the dream state is quite infinite.

As you have yourself noted in your query, there might be certain activities in the dream state which are used much as the activities in your waking state are used, that is, for the learning of a specific lesson. We might say that among your peoples it has been noted by most that the dreams are only dreams. We might say in this regard that those activities which are called dreams by your people might, in one respect, be looked upon as being more, shall we say, real than that activity which occurs during waking hours, for within the dream state the mind is more freed from the limitations of your third density physical illusion and may pursue those lessons of the mind/body/spirit complex which the entity has incarnated to learn, with more fluidity, with a greater freedom, with a perception of that which is limitless, and might more efficiently learn those lessons which have been programmed before this incarnation.

There are a number of types of dream experiences. It would be quite exhaustive to cover each at this time, but we might say that the entity in the dream state might have subconsciously programmed the meeting with other entities of its Earth environment, entities of other astral levels, entities of levels of existence in what you would call the heaven worlds, all for the purpose of enacting a miniature drama much like that which you experience during an entire lifetime, and in this drama, however long or short, might then experience that lesson or attempt that lesson which has not been well learned within the waking activity. And when this lesson has been brought to, shall we say, a point of blooming or point of mastery, then this lesson might be brought forth into the waking consciousness so that the entity might manifest it in the third-density physical illusion and thereby more efficiently utilize the catalyst of that particular lesson.

May we answer in more detail, my brother?

C: No, but I was wondering if humans have forgotten how to use telepathy as a means of communication. In the dream state, is one better able to use the brain's telepathic capacity?

I am Latwii, and am aware of your question, my brother. We might in general say that this is a correct assumption, that in the dream state, that which you know as telepathic communication is quite possible. We might also add that it is a matter of choice of the entity's subconscious mind as to what type of communication is utilized within the dream state. For some type of learning the simple spoken word is quite sufficient. For other more intensive, shall we say, learnings the telepathic communication might more efficiently be utilized.

May we answer you further, my brother?

C: Not at the moment. Thank you.

We are most grateful to you, as well. May we answer another question at this time?

N: Yes. In the distortion I call healing and which I term balancing, I hold the crystal in my right hand. Is that, for me, a proper vehicle for the energy which I allow to flow through me to that one being healed?

I am Latwii, and, my brother, we will quite heartily agree that for your particular distortion of the healing process, this holding of the crystal is quite appropriate and for you quite sufficient. We shall also suggest that upon this path of healing you yourself shall discover other means whereby you might also be of this service in the balancing, as you have called it.

May we answer you further, my brother?

N: Yes. Would you please clarify that last statement as to other methods? Is there a better method?

I am Latwii, and, my brother, we might say that there is an infinite array of methods of utilizing the healing by crystal, and indeed there are many methods which are more efficient, shall we say, and our suggestion was simply that you shall, when the time is appropriate, discover these methods.

N: Thank you. I have a further question. In my distortion of the energy which I channel through, I term it a violet transmuting flame type of energy. Is there any correspondence to that with the energies which we've been studying this week that have come through Ra?

I am Latwii, and, my brother, we might suggest in this regard that it matters not what you call the energy which you are working with, for they do have their effect upon the healing process, and whether you call them violet, green, pink or chartreuse, shall we say, matters not. There are, of course, identifications which are more efficacious and more correct, but these are not a part of the healing process, that is, the naming does not heal. The energies which you utilize and channel through your particular channel do aid in this healing process.

May we answer you further, my brother?

N: Thank you for that clarity. I wonder if you might suggest a way in which I might be a clearer channel for this energy?

I am Latwii, and, my brother, we find in this regard that we can make no specific suggestions other than that general suggestion of the meditation and the deepening of the desire to be of service, knowing that within this state of meditation your desire shall lead you upon the path and bring you to those points of learning which will allow you to become an increasingly more efficient, shall we say, healer. To give you the specific methods would be an infringement upon your own free will.

May we answer you further, my brother?

N: No Latwii. Thank you for your clarity.

I am Latwii. We are most thankful, as well, for yours. May we answer another question at this time?

Carla: What color are you in, Latwii?

I am Latwii, and, my sister, the color which we inhabit this evening might be most correctly described as that of the orangish rust or, shall we say, that which is the citron in nature.

Is there another question at this time?

Carla: Since you mentioned that particular color, I was wondering if it is rather …

(Side one of tape ends.)

Carla: … move into green has then to go back to orange and do some homework, I guess you'd say. Is that particular vibration distorted from the norms this close to the end of a cycle?

I am Latwii, and in response to this query, my sister, we may say that the orange vibration is quite pure in its orangeness, shall we say. The distortion lies not in the orangeness, but in its great prevalence upon your planet at this time. We do indeed now investigate this particular color of the spectrum because it is that color which is most manifest upon your planet, that being the color of the individual focused upon the self, not yet exploring beyond the self, focused upon those concerns which assure the survival and maintenance of the self and of the immediate surroundings of the self.

Eventually, as the progress of evolution proceeds, the self-aware entity does move out into those fields of concern which may be likened unto the field of the consciousness of other selves upon the planet, seeing the needs of the other selves, attempting to meet these needs, attempting to share in some manner with other selves those necessities which the self has found for the self.

At this time many upon your planet do move back into this orange ray for the purpose of reassessing those needs of the self, so that eventually there might be a continued movement outward into the yellow ray and the sharing of those sustenance features, shall we say, of your illusion with the other selves.

May we answer you further, my sister?

Carla: No, thank you.

We are most grateful to you as well. Is there another question at this time?

M1: Yes, Latwii. In reference to what you were just talking about, could you use as an example my coming here as being a movement into orange so that I might move from yellow to green?

I am Latwii, and, my sister, we cannot give you the specific information which you request at this time, for it is in our humble opinion an infringement to reveal the nature of your path to you at this time. It is, we feel, more appropriate for you to discover your own path and its winding ways, shall we say.

May we answer you further, my sister?

M1: No, thank you, Latwii.

We thank you. Is there another question at this time?

M2: Yes, Latwii. Back when the Vietnamese and Chinese were in a very intense situation, you were monitoring the situation closely. Are we having a similar situation in Poland?

I am Latwii, and, my brother, we might say in general that your planet is experiencing a great number of intensities at this time. There are among your people many feelings of mistrust, many feelings of hatred for other groups, many concerns of a worldly nature which concern, as we mentioned before, the survival of the self, the refusal of the self to see the need for the survival of other selves.

Many are the intensities upon your planet at this time. We are monitoring many of the situations and are hopeful that as the entities involved in each become more and more involved in the intricacy of the other selves' situation that there might be seen by all concerned the oneness that binds each to the one Creator, for it is the purpose of such catalysts which your peoples now experience to give to those experiencing them the realization that those things which seem to separate peoples are not of a real substance, but are illusions which do teach certain lessons. The students are in the classroom. The lesson has progressed through most of the semester. The graduation does approach. The final examinations are being prepared. Whether the students shall learn the lessons is not known.

We of Latwii, with our brothers and sisters of the Confederation of Planets in the Service of the Infinite Creator, do respond to those calls for love and light as we perceive them and do lend our love and light where it is called. We are hopeful that the students shall learn their lessons and shall receive the passing grades, for it would indeed be much easier if the students realized that the tests which they are now taking do not need to be taken alone, for the answers are within the hearts of each and it is not, shall we say, cheating to give the answer of love to another.

May we answer you further, my brother?

M2: No. Thank you, Latwii.

We are most grateful to you as well. Is there another question at this time?

N: Yes. Is it possible to experience what I would term fine tuning of balancing by asking an entity such as yourself for that?

I am Latwii, and, my brother, to our best understanding of this term which you use, we cannot give such an experience. It must be given by the self requesting it to the self requesting it.

May we answer you further, my brother?

N: No, thank you.

We thank you. Is there another question at this time?

(Pause)

I am Latwii. We have been most honored to be asked to join your meditation group this evening. We hope that each entity present will take those words which have meaning with them, will leave those words which have no meaning behind. We of Latwii are humble messengers of light and do bring our love to share with this group when called. It is a great honor to be called to this group. We come as brothers and sisters. We come as messengers of the one Creator. We come as Creator to Creator, for are we not all one? We leave you now in the love and in the light of the one infinite Creator. I am Latwii. Adonai. ☥

L/L Research

Sunday Meditation
December 20, 1981

(C channeling)

I am Hatonn, and I am with this instrument. We greet you, my brothers and sisters, in the light and love of the one infinite Creator. We found great pleasure in listening to your music this night. In this time of your year many of your peoples who participate in what you call Christian worship join together to sing songs of praise to the one known to you as Jesus—songs of love, songs of giving, of awakening to love that surrounds us, but that so many turn a cold shoulder to for the most of the rest of your year.

In this season, many do feel a new kindling of the warmth that begins to glow within as they stop the rushing, their selfishness, and begin to look about them and see needs of others, the needs of themselves as they take stock of what and how they acted, reacted during your year. Too often your peoples think that the giving to others of material things in this your Christmas season is an adequate way of expressing what many mistake for love. Many feel that giving in this way will bring them closer to what you call God, but we say that although for some the giving material things is a loving gesture, we say to you that the opening of oneself to the needs of others, be they spiritual, material, mental, as you would term it, is much more important.

For as you begin to genuinely open yourself to receive others, you give not only to others, but to yourselves, for as you open yourself to others, to your world, love and light, it is you [who] begins to glow, to become more and more visible [to] those whom you come in contact with, be it physically or spiritually. For as you slowly open, you take steps closer to awareness of love and light of the one infinite Creator. You, my friends, give so much more by seeking greater awareness than you could ever give with things that you can purchase to give to others.

Your love, your light will, not only in this season, but throughout all the days of your existence on your planet, be of great service to the needs of the others around you. We of Hatonn join with you in this time of your year, and any time, to rejoice with each who seeks awareness of the love and the light, for we, as you, are seeking ever to grow. We know that it sometimes seems difficult to remain open, for in your illusion there are many who do not actively seek and may feel threatened and afraid of that which they do not readily perceive and understand, but when you are faced by such, we say open yourself that much more that they may begin to see beauty—that is, the love and light.

We are known as Hatonn. We would now transfer this contact to another instrument. I am Hatonn.

Sunday Meditation, December 20, 1981

(Carla channeling)

I am with this instrument. If you will be patient with me for a moment, I and my brother Laitos would at this time wish to move among you and share our love and our light with each who may request it on a more personal basis in the form of our conditioning wave. If you wish to feel this wave, please mentally request it and we shall be with you, for a brief period, a bit more intensively. I am Hatonn.

(Pause)

I am Hatonn, and I greet you once again, my friends, in the love and the light. May this time of your year be one in which you may find quiet moments, moments to find that which is the heart of your existence, for beneath all those things which you may do and those things which you may say, the heart of existence lies always near, and yet never quite so near as in the dead of winter, when a new life clean and fresh and untouched may spring from the desires and the love of the soul that waits to be born anew.

I am Hatonn. In new life we leave you—in love, in light, in hope, and in peace and always under the care of all that there is, the great and boundless unity of the one infinite Creator. Adonai. Adonai.

(Jim channeling)

I am Latwii, and am with this instrument, and greet you all in our very best holiday cheer and, of course, we bring our greeting, as always, in love and in light.

We have the honor once again this evening of offering ourselves as somewhat of a Christmas present in the capacity of answering queries which those present might have the value in the asking. Are there any presents which we might open?

Carla: In the spirit of that question, I would like to rap with you.

L: Stop ribbin'!

Carla: M1 in Denver, Colorado has had a series of extremely severe tragedies befall her family that have gone on over a period of years and have mostly to do with illness. Everyone but herself is ill in some way in which she cannot be of much help except by nurturing them. She would like to know what nature this catalyst is for her and if there is something that she could be doing to better use this catalyst, because she feels that at this moment it is about to overwhelm her.

I am Latwii, and am aware of your query, my sister. As for your loved sister some distance from this dwelling, we of Latwii can only speak in general terms concerning this entity, for we are most desirous of maintaining this entity's free will, as this is always our uppermost desire. In such a situation as this entity finds itself in it might be ascertained that there is a lesson which needs to be learned on an urgent basis, for the repeating of catalysts of what your people might call an intense nature is most usually a sign that a specific lesson has not been completely comprehended.

In such a situation as this one where [there is] the continuation of catalyst of an intense nature, especially that dealing with that known as the ill health or the disease, one may find a *(inaudible)* in reviewing each such instance quite carefully, as the surgeon with the scalpel; the viewing the complete nature of each such situation, looking at that which surrounds it, that which fostered it, that which was its genesis; looking also at the response to each situation by those finding themselves within its swirls of energy.

Further inspection would also be suggested into the results of each situation upon the entity. What lessons were learned? What possibilities were not explored? Where did the path of seeking lead from each situation? Looking at each situation in this manner may provide a pattern, a pattern of the catalyst, so that the entities within each situation might become aware—more aware—of those parts of the pattern previously ignored, for these particular types of catalysts do provide certain lessons.

When the lessons have not been completely comprehended, the catalyst must be repeated. We would remind this entity, and each such entity finding itself in a situation which has been repeated, that there is an infinite amount of time in which to learn all lessons. Each lesson within this illusion does carry with it certain responsibilities, certain abilities to respond. There is an infinite range of response possible for each lesson. There is free will, my friends. Lessons may be learned. Lessons may be ignored. Lessons may be postponed. There is no right or wrong way of learning. It may also be the case that an entity shall choose to learn lessons within the period of catalyst provided for the original lesson. All is quite permissible within the plan of the Creator and within the framework laid by each entity before incarnation. It may also be the case that preincarnative choices have been made for the purpose of reminding the entity of certain lessons and their needs for mastery of these lessons within a certain period, therefore requiring the repeating of the providing of the catalyst.

To summarize our somewhat lengthy response, may we say that all such lessons and catalysts reviewed in meditation by the entity finding themselves within these lessons, will provide the entities with the solutions which are necessary for the learning of the lesson and the walking of the path.

May we answer you further, my sister?

Carla: Not on that point, no, and I thank you on the behalf of my friend M1. I would also like to ask a question that was prompted by a friend of mine named S. No matter how much difficulty I have ever been in, mentally or emotionally or physically, since I've been coming to these meetings, no matter how disharmonious I feel, I've always felt very close to the Confederation entities such as yourself that we contact at meetings, but S, who is having a lot of emotional feelings having to do with the feeling that she is not fulfilling her mission in this life, says that she has a feeling that the Confederation entities that she has been calling upon for so long look down upon her, but have put a wall between themselves and her, and she feels very lonely. I wondered if you could comment on this perception?

I am Latwii, and am aware of your question, my sister. In this regard, again we find ourselves able to speak only in general terms, for once again we wish foremost to respect the free will of this entity. This entity has for many of your years pursued the path of spiritual evolution and has, in her own way and manner, been of great service. This entity, as it is well known to your own being, has great potential and does recognize this potential. This entity wishes to be of service in a manner which is equal to this potential. This entity, in its own evaluation of its service, has felt that it does not yet meet its potential.

We of the Confederation of Planets in Service of the Infinite Creator look upon each of your peoples, this entity as well, as having infinite potential for service, each potential unique. We can say that no entity of Confederation affiliation ever puts a wall between itself and those who seek its service. Many we find upon your planet who put walls within their own being, for it might be, shall we say, necessary for a certain time for an entity to build a wall and to contain itself so that it might know what its limits are within that wall, and it might be necessary at a later time for that entity to remove that wall which it has placed within its own being by its own efforts, for its own reasons, so that it might explore yet more means of service, new fields of consciousness, and new depths of its own being.

It is often necessary for an entity to place certain restrictions upon the self so that certain lessons might result from experiencing those restrictions. This entity has chosen to serve in a way which is not yet revealed fully unto it. The wall does keep that revelation from piercing through into consciousness, for reasons which this entity can find within its own being as a result of its continued seeking. We would only suggest to this entity the continued seeking, for the highest path of service shall provide it with the ladder, shall we say, to scale the wall which it has erected.

May we answer you further, my sister?

Carla: I have one more question, and thank you on behalf of S. I think if she wants to ask further on this point she'll probably write me. I have a question of my own. In the past month or so we've had a couple of fairly remarkable healings of people for whom we have prayed and sent light and I was wondering if you could comment on the method that we use to send light in order that we might become better channels for that light, and refine that channel if we possibly could?

I am Latwii, and am aware of your query, my sister. We are quite pleased with the efforts made by this group in the area of healing, and we may add that there is no effort which does not have its positive effects. The technique used by this group—the envisioning of the entity to be healed surrounded by light—is effective to a degree. At this time surveying those present, those a part of this group, in this surveying we feel that there is the possibility of one refinement which those present might add to their current technique. This would be spending more of that which you call time visualizing each entity to be healed, seeing first the diseased nature of the entity as described by the one asking for the healing for the entity. A few moments spent visualizing the diseased nature of the entity would then best be followed by the same amount of time spent seeing the entity to be healed, healed. Do not attempt to see the healing occurring, but see it completed. Again, see the entity surrounded by light.

At this time we feel this is the only suggestion which we might make that would increase the growing ability of this group to do that which [it] is providing of the healing energy.

May we answer you further, my sister?

Carla: No, thank you, Latwii. I really appreciate the time you took.

I am Latwii, and we are most grateful to you as well, and to each in this group for allowing us to spend that which you call time with you. May we answer yet another question at this time?

M2: Yes, please. Latwii, I have some problem with some choices in my life from time-to-time where either of two options look like the positive option, yet either of the two options look like there may be a lot of negativism. I have a problem determining what's right and wrong. Can you perhaps help me?

I am Latwii, and am aware of your question, my brother. We find, indeed, in this particular illusion it is not always easy to travel the paths which are laid before the seeker of spiritual evolution. This illusion does provide many areas which might be considered between the poles of that known as right or good and that known as wrong or bad. Many are the areas of grayness that confuse those who choose to serve others …

(Side one of tape ends.)

(Jim channeling)

I am Latwii, and am once again with this instrument. To continue our response in terms of a general nature, we may say that at any time when you find a choice of paths which is not clear in your own mind, in your own heart, in your own being, that retiring yourself into yourself in meditation is the most helpful avenue of choice. Meditate upon each path, examine all possibilities, feel within your being a choice of yes and no for each path. Travel the "yes" and "no" for each paths in meditation in your own being. Visualize as clearly as possible the results of traveling each path. See in great detail the ramifications of each choice. Experience your feeling about each choice. Allow these distillations of feeling to permeate your being. Imagine each as real.

Find, then, within your being the patience necessary to make no choice until a choice must be made. Then, make your choice when it must be made, from the depths of your being, after having traveled all possibilities in your visualized reality. The response most appropriate for you at each turn shall became evident, for as ye seek, ye shall find. Many times this has been said to your peoples. Again, we repeat, for those who seek there shall be that finding of a new goal, for as the magnet draws the iron, so does the seeker draw the sought.

May we answer you further, my brother?

M2: No, I know that will be very helpful for me. Thank you.

We are most grateful to you as well. May we answer another question at this time?

A: I have a question. For those living in confusion … if one has the knowledge which could be given to others which could either cause them to have a greater understanding or to be in more confusion, is it better to be silent or to try to lift confusion?

I am Latwii, and am aware of your question, my sister. And in this regard we might respond as we are, for we of Latwii seek to be of the service which is requested of us and would suggest to each present that when attempting to assist another self within your illusion, to assist in the highest degree one must be asked for assistance. To give that which is not sought is to add to the confusion of another self. If asked for advice, give that which you feel to be of the highest and best available to you. Allow it to come through your being as you serve as a channel, for all entities are channels of the one Creator. Give that which comes from you naturally when it is requested. Allow the one requesting assistance to digest, shall we say, the food which you have provided for its nourishment. Reply further when requested for more information. Resist the, shall we say, temptation to be that known to your peoples as the teacher when the teachings are not requested. Give that which is requested and which comes easily from your being.

May we answer you further, my sister?

A: Only a question as to whenever answering there is the free will. How do you know when you're going against someone's free will?

I am Latwii, and am aware of your question, my sister. We might say in this regard that as you come into contact with those who request your assistance you do not violate their free will by responding to their requests, for, whatever your response, they are always free to refuse your assistance, for there is nothing special about any entity within this illusion in relation to any other entity which would make any entity believe that which another offers as assistance. There is little chance of infringing upon the free will of another self if you respond to their requests for assistance and do not offer, without the request for assistance, aid which is not sought.

May we answer you further, my sister?

A: No. Thank you, though.

I am Latwii, and we are most grateful to you as well. Is there another question at this time?

L: I have several questions, Latwii. First on the subject of healing. In working with the instrument known as Carla in this area we have found that our efforts can produce temporary effects, but not permanent effects. Have you any advice to offer to assist us in making our efforts more permanent?

I am Latwii, and am aware of your questions, my brother. Again, in this area we find that to maintain your free will we must respond only in general and suggest that the continued, shall we say, balancing efforts of the one known as the healer is the endeavor which shall provide the increased ability to offer the opportunity for healing, for the opportunity for healing must flow through the entity as water through a pipe and the pipe must be cleared of the blockages which do not permit easy flow of the nourishing water.

May we answer you further, my brother?

L: Yes. In our efforts I have been using the process of conditioning diseased parts taking on a healthy aspect. If I understood your comments earlier this evening, you strongly advise against that process. Could you speak on that subject?

I am Latwii, and am aware of your question, my brother. In this regard we might say that certain techniques do work for certain entities, and can repeat our suggestion that seeing the entity becoming healed is an aid to healing, but seeing the entity healed is perhaps more efficacious. This shall be discovered by each entity as the entity practices that known as the healing art. We offer our suggestions as humble advice and would advise further that each entity make these discoveries for the self, for until the self believes such and such a situation to be correct the entity shall not have the faith that such is correct and no amount of, shall we say, correctness shall allow that technique to work for that entity.

May we respond further, my brother?

L: I have a last question on a different, more personal, subject. I have found in myself recently an ambivalence on the subject of emotional relationships, when I find a part of me strongly drawn toward it and at the same time, given the opportunity, often find reasons to avoid it. I realize that this is something I'm going to have to sort out for myself, but I would appreciate any observations of a general nature that you could make on the lessons to be learned from the interactions.

I am Latwii, and am aware of your question, my brother, and upon this subject we may speak a few words, and suggest that the relationships between your peoples, especially those of the male to the female, are somewhat tinged, shall we say, with the coloration of one entity pitted against another, both vying for the, shall we say, emotional satisfaction of owning the affections of the other. Your relationships of the sexual nature, male to female, do suffer somewhat in your society because of the coloration of what has been named, shall we say, the adversary relationship by our brothers and sisters of the social memory complex of Ra. It is not particularly easy for entities within your illusion to join with their polar opposites, for there is the bartering of emotions which does, in the final analysis, hinder the free flow of that known to your peoples in sparing degree as love, for that concept of love does not in its true form know any boundary, does not know any limitation to amount which may be given, does not know that there is the, shall we say, artificial need to be balanced by more of the concept of love given by another in order to balance the scales of the relationship and to complete the transaction of emotions.

The concept of love is the free giving of the self without reservation to another because the other is as it is. The giving of love which demands another be other than it is is a distortion of love which has severe, shall we say, ramifications and does result in that known as the emotional pain and the withdrawal of love from the account of the entity experiencing the pain. In such instances the entity experiencing pain shall then feel an aversion to further experience of the love relationship, for the love relationship has not been experienced in a positive way for the reasons which we have previously enumerated.

Within your illusion each entity must find its way through the confusions of the marketplace of emotions, for that known as love has been colored, has been twisted and contorted by your peoples for many generations upon your planet and has resulted in the misapprehension of love as something which can be divided into parts and traded as a commodity. We would suggest to those who have experienced the pain of the withdrawal of affections, either of self for another self or of another self for the self, that the pure experiencing of love upon your planet is a rare occurrence, but one which we cannot speak too highly of, for even though the one who would love with no expectation of return might be viewed as most foolish, surely it is such foolishness which shall eventually be seen to be the container which knows no limits and can, therefore, contain, shall we say, the concept of love, and where there is love freely given for no reason and with no expectation of return, then there is created within the entity who gives this love in this free manner, there is created a vacuum which shall draw unto that entity that which it gives, for there is nothing truly apart from an entity, for all beings are one and when one is loved, for any reason or no reason, then all are loved and the self also find its love.

May we answer you further, my brother?

L: No, thank you. You've answered me well.

I am Latwii, and we are most grateful to be of whatever service we might be. Is there another question at this time that we might attempt to answer?

(Pause)

I am Latwii. My friends, we are most gratified to have been able to join your group this evening. We know that occasions such as this are most honored by each present and especially in this season of joyous thanksgiving and praise of the one Creator, we know that those present do feel a special bond in the sharing of love and light. We leave you now rejoicing in that love and light and wishing each present a most joyous season of holiday cheering and loving and sharing and we shall be with you as you share your love for the one Creator each with the other. We leave you now in that love and light. We are known to you as Latwii. Adonai, my friends. Adonai vasu borragus.

(Carla channeling)

I greet you in the love and the light of the Father. I am Am Ne Ra. My children, you call to me and I come, but am I not always with you? Is my peace not in you? My incarnation is known to you and still you seek as if I were not here. I am with you always and yet it is not I nor all those things which I say. Ah, but those things given me by the Father, let it be so with all … I am Am Ne Ra. I am with you in the love and the light of the one infinite Creator. ♣

Year 1982

January 3, 1982 to February 14, 1982

Sunday Meditation
January 3, 1982

(Carla channeling)

I am Hatonn, and I am with this instrument. I greet you once more in the love and light of the infinite Creator.

My friends, the nature of the journey that you are on is such that it may bring about periods in which you feel that your pilgrimage is no longer functioning properly. We ask you to consider a small example of such a pilgrimage. Take for example the young man. He is alone, and he seeks to make a journey, and as he seeks, he changes. This young man grows older year by year and experiences various locations, various entities. He is a visitor in homes which seem to him to be oh, so normal and so pleasant, and he asks himself over the years, "Why, if I am like other men, can I not have such pleasantness?"

Still he seeks and still he sheds what light he has upon those he meets and one day he meets an old woman. She is alone but has not always been so. Though her face is wrinkled, her eyes sparkle. The man, no longer so young, asks her, "Why must the seeker always have such a lonely pilgrimage?" The old woman smiles very gently. "There are no rules to a pilgrimage except those that you make for yourself," she says. "Examine that which you think you need. If it stays the same, there is not the beginning of the opportunity for growth. "Why," the young man says, "you were married for many, many years." "Ah, yes," said the old woman, "but we were both pilgrims."

My friends, whatever your path, search it with your mind and your heart in each moment that you can possibly find to obtain in this most important activity so that when you go into meditation you are conscious of your being. Take yourself into yourself, for in meditation the conscious and the unconscious meet, become acquainted and begin to merge into one ever larger beacon of the light.

For those dead spots which seem to be upon the road we can only suggest the balm of meditation while remembering it was your choice to begin this pilgrimage, and that pilgrims are happy as no other entities can ever be when they are changing. In any crucible of transformation joy is an inevitable byproduct.

We would pause at this time and offer our vibration to any who may wish to experience it. We would especially like to exercise in conditioning the one known as D and to assure this instrument that at the appropriate time we will be most happy to work with this instrument. If you will have patience and ask mentally, we will be glad and most grateful to touch each of you. I am Hatonn.

(Pause)

I am again with this instrument. I am Hatonn. We thank each of you for the opportunity of being able to work with each one and would like to confirm at this time that we were attempting to contact the one known as W for the purpose of closing this message, as one of our brothers in the Confederation of Planets is waiting to speak also. We would again attempt to contact the one known as W. I am Hatonn.

(The rest of the tape is inaudible.)

Sunday Meditation
January 10, 1982

(Carla channeling)

[I am Hatonn.] We greet you, my friends, in the love and the light of the all infinite Creator. This evening we have greeted each of you individually throughout the tuning and in the time hence. We are glad to see this group together again in meditation.

There are changes as the seasons pass by the years. New relationships are formed and changes of relationships that are *(inaudible)*, that all is growing. With change there are two directions that a person can face in order to see change that he or that others around him are going through. One may look in the forward direction or one may look in the direction from which one has already been. Both are equally valuable although it is easy sometimes to be caught in the focusing on one of the two directions.

One of the great uses in meditation is the stabilizing or the balancing of the views of the two different directions in looking upon the past deeds of your life and the experiences that you have had that have helped bring you to where you are today and the direction ahead to a new, as yet unrealized, goal that we each have; and that that goal can be controlled, or, shall I say, guided by the will of each individual along their journey.

We all have pictures in the backs of our minds, specific goals or things which we would like to do, which we think that may help us get to wherever that we individually desire to be. Many of these are but glimmers of possible realities and many of these are but modified recollections from our past experiences, in that many such individuals who are on a path and among themselves acknowledge that they are all on similar paths and in trying to understand that they have a similar goal encounter many obstacles or memories, as it were, of seeds which have not come to fruit. And it is sometimes very difficult to see that there are still many more seeds which need to be planted and cultivated to ensure further spiritual growth among you individually and as a small collective of light beings desiring to be of service on the planet.

We shall now continue this contact through another instrument. I am Hatonn. I leave you in love and light.

Carla: Does anybody else feel uneasy? I'm not getting any feelings. Why don't we just meditate silently.

(Tape ends.)

L/L Research

L/L Research is a subsidiary of Rock Creek Research & Development Laboratories, Inc.

P.O. Box 5195
Louisville, KY 40255-0195

www.llresearch.org

Rock Creek is a non-profit corporation dedicated to discovering and sharing information which may aid in the spiritual evolution of humankind.

ABOUT THE CONTENTS OF THIS TRANSCRIPT: This telepathic channeling has been taken from transcriptions of the weekly study and meditation meetings of the Rock Creek Research & Development Laboratories and L/L Research. It is offered in the hope that it may be useful to you. As the Confederation entities always make a point of saying, please use your discrimination and judgment in assessing this material. If something rings true to you, fine. If something does not resonate, please leave it behind, for neither we nor those of the Confederation would wish to be a stumbling block for any.

CAVEAT: This transcript is being published by L/L Research in a not yet final form. It has, however, been edited and any obvious errors have been corrected. When it is in a final form, this caveat will be removed.

© 2009 L/L Research

Sunday Meditation
January 31, 1982

(L channeling)

I am Hatonn, and I greet you in the love and the light of our infinite Creator. My brothers, it is a great pleasure to join our vibrations with your own once again. It has been a long time by your own standards since we have been able to communicate with this group and to share that which we call love with one another. We are grateful for your sincere and joyful invitation, and we hope that we may be of service to you this evening. It is always our pleasure and desire to be of service to those who ask for our vibration. We remind you that whether singly or in groups, you need only ask and we shall be with you. We of Hatonn realize that the demands of your illusion often tempt you to forgo the meditative contact that you might otherwise seek on a more regular basis, for a time once existed in which we shared the same difficulties in our own time of growth. We would lovingly advise you not to be discouraged at your susceptibility to your illusion, for it is an illusion that is designed to press you to the limits of your abilities, for it is at these limits that true growth occurs.

At this time we would like to transfer this contact so as to exercise another instrument, for it has been a period of time since this opportunity has occurred. I am Hatonn.

(D channeling)

I am Hatonn, and am with this instrument. It has been a long time since we have contacted this instrument. We of Hatonn are happy to contact this instrument when he is ready to meditate on a more regular basis. I am Hatonn.

(Carla channeling)

I am Hatonn, and am now with this instrument. May we thank the one known as D for the great opportunity which he offers us in blending our consciousness with his and in transmitting our thoughts through him. These, my friends, must never be considered to be simply our thoughts, for we are, as all members of the Confederation, messengers, not gods. We bring you a message of love. To be able to share this message through instruments such as these is an ineffable privilege, one which we cannot give adequate thanks for, and as these messages continue in a group such as this one, and the members of the group become more and more aware of the fundamental concepts of love and service, we are able to offer many more diverse insights than we could offer at first.

For the work which this group has done consciously and unconsciously, we thank you. We are aware that each in this group considers himself to fall far short of the spiritual mark. We are not here to gauge that mark but only to say that it is the seeking that concentrates, preserves and enlightens the organism of your spiritual self.

You, my friends, are as those who search through days and nights, through clarity and haze, through clichés and misunderstanding, looking restlessly for the inspiration that will be food for your true self. How diversely you look. Were you capable of travel, your desire is such you would seek the Earth over and you would have many strange experiences, and yet we say to you, you have many and strange experiences. It is your discriminatory power which will point the heart of your experiences out to you and make you realize the incredible adventure of experiencing the illusion which you experience. The greatest adventure lies in the microscopic interplay of synaptic connections which lies within the confines of the consciousness and that electrically powered organism which houses it. The adventure of interpretation, discrimination, understanding and self-discovery is such that your greatest explorer could not discover any territory so vast and so uncharted. Took you ship and sailed the globe around you could not go as far as you can go in meditation and in self-discovery

My friends, you are not creatures of your body. You are not bound by time or space. Your birthright is that which you have called Christ-consciousness. You are love. The one known as Jesus said, "I am the way." This consciousness is a path, a path so exciting, so all-encompassing, and so attractive that all those upon your planet will eventually find it, it and no other, for it is the path of truth, of life, of love. The universe, my friends, is one thing. It is within you, both to find that one thing and to be that one thing. We ask your permission to coax you into the consideration at all times, in all decisions, in all situations, of the dimensions of meditation and of seeking. Surely it is well to set aside the time, as you call it, for this marvelous exercise of the joyousness of silence, for this tremendous opportunity to listen to that which has so long been lost among your peoples.

But beyond that, my friends, is the path, and you are not on the path only when you meditate. There is no action or thought that cannot be considered in relation to the path. We are upon it, and we know you seek to be upon it also. Thus, we do ask your permission to say, please, my friends, do not cut any part of your life off from the path, for in all stations of life, in all moods of man, there lies perfection, love and a wonderful surety of step that only come to the mind of one who has begun the practice of being.

We are aware that there are many judgments among your peoples. There are no judgments upon the path. This instrument says to herself, "Many times I am too rowdy. Many times I am in bad humor. How can I be on the path?" My friends, how can you not be on the path? There is only one I AM and all of you are part of it. I AM the way. In laughter and in tears, never fear that you have stumbled. We thank you for allowing us to share these humble thoughts.

At this time we would leave the group in order that our sister may speak. We leave you, my friends, in the love and in the one great illumination of the Father. I am Hatonn. Adonai vasu borragus.

(Jim channeling)

I am Latwii, and I greet you, my friends, in the love and in the light of the one infinite Creator. We are, as always, filled with great joy to be able to speak to your group once again. We offer ourselves also as humble messengers of the one Creator, and offer ourselves, as is our custom, in the capacity in the answering of those question which might be put to us. Is there a question at this time?

D: Yes. Latwii, as I have been meditating recently—of course not enough, as Hatonn pointed out—I've been envisioning myself during meditation as being enveloped in light myself. It seems to create a very interesting sensation. I just wanted to know if that was a proper meditation technique?

I am Latwii, and am aware of your question, my brother. We may say in this regard that such a technique such as that which you have mentioned is most appropriate for those of your people who wish to activate the throat energy center, shall we say, that which is used in the communication of concepts, the inspiration, and the inner understanding, the seating of the learning which the entity meditating has experienced as catalyst. The enveloping of the self in light does have the effect upon the inner planes of the entity utilizing this technique of illuminating the learning that is being assimilated, seating it within the mind/body/spirit complex and making it available for future reference, shall we say, the recalling of the distillations of lessons learned, so that they might be shared with the other selves which the meditator comes into contact with.

The enveloping of the self in the light also has other functions and effects, one of these being the protection, shall we say, so that those concepts and feelings of positivity might be those which are admitted. The enveloping of the entity in light also has the effect upon the inner planes of your planet of creating a beacon, shall we say, which does signal other entities that there is a calling for a certain type of understanding which needs be answered.

In short, may we say this is a most useful technique in meditation and does carry great facility, shall we say, for the practitioner.

May we answer further, my brother?

D: No, thank you. I just want to thank you or Hatonn or Laitos or whoever it was that revealed that to me in meditation. They really helped me along with that.

I am Latwii, and am most grateful as well to you for allowing us to be of this service. May we answer another question at this time?

L: I have a number of questions that I would like to ask with the benefit of your patience. The first one is, an individual named Paul Blighton was once contacted by an entity who claimed to be within a UFO. Was this a member of the Federation and, if so, who was it?

I am Latwii, and, my brother, we fear that the response shall be shorter than anticipated. We cannot give this information for we feel that it would be intrusion upon the free will.

May we answer another query, my brother?

L: Yes. At one point within the past year I described to either yourself or another member of the Federation a visual experience that occurred some time back during which there were two chairs, one on either side of an altar, one of which within I was placed. The other I could sense had an entity but I wasn't able to perceive who it was. Am I correct in my assumption that the occupant of the other chair was the totality of my other selves?

I am Latwii, and am aware of your question, my brother. May we say in this regard that your assumption is, in general, correct. There are, of course, various levels of understanding that can come from any such vision or image. The one which you have described and experienced does hold for you increased, shall we say, levels or intensity of description and distillations of learning. We, therefore, would recommend the continued pondering and meditating upon this particular experience which you have described.

May we answer you further, my brother?

L: Yes. Again I thank you for your patience. Prior to that experience there was an earlier experience in which I was able to sense a—I would not characterize it as heat as such—a perception of my entire spinal column coming down from my head to the base of my spine in conjunction with a religious ceremony that was occurring at the time. Could you describe to me what was actually occurring to cause this sensation besides the physical events that I am aware of?

I am Latwii, and am aware of your question, my brother. In this regard we find again that we cannot be too specific in our response, for the experience which you describe is one which has the purpose of teaching you many levels of lessons. That which you query about at the present is the key to the unlocking of the various levels which are available to you through this particular experience. We would simply suggest the reexamination of the circumstances which surrounded this experience, the symbolic nature of the experience as it has been revealed to you through your own seeking, and the inner levels, shall we say, which have been made available to you as possibilities through, once again, your own seeking. We do not wish to sound too ambiguous or to be shy of words but we do not wish to travel that trail of the teach/learner, if we may borrow a term, that is the proper role of the one who seeks the solution to mystery. If we were to give the solutions, where would come the strength in the seeking and where would the seeker look to within its own being when we were absent from its presence?

May we answer you further, my brother?

L: Yes, again, on a different subject. A number of my learning experiences recently have involved emotional contacts with women. This seems to be increasing as far as frequency and therefore learning experiences. I realize that you are very limited, but I would ask for any advice that you might give to assist me in maximizing my learning experience.

I am Latwii, and am aware of your question, my brother. In this regard, may we suggest that to maximize the learning in any situation, whether it be of the mind, the body, the spirit, or the emotions that are the distortions of the mind and the expression of the feelings, that the entity seeking the learning available look to the moment with an openness, and what you might call a vulnerability which does not seek any reward other than the opportunity of being of service and of learning what love the moment can teach.

The difficulties for many upon your planet come when they attempt to get something in return for that which is given. This particular attitude does then hinder and inhibit the free exchange of energies, shall we say, between the entities involved in the learning situation. This attitude of seeking reward for that which is given does then color the situation so that that love which is available in the moment to each becomes reduced and hidden, shall we say, for each holds on to that which it could give the other until some sign is given that it will receive in a balanced fashion, equivalent reward, or exchange to that which it gives.

To make, shall we say, a long story short, seek ye to [give] freely, seek ye to learn love, and that which ye seek shall be drawn unto you.

May we answer you further, my brother?

L: No. You've given me a great deal to ponder. I thank you for your time and your patience.

I am Latwii, and, as always, we are most grateful to be allowed the opportunity to give freely that which we humbly have to give. May we answer another question at this time?

Carla: I have a question that I hadn't thought of for a while but the message brought it up to me. A friend of mine asked me why she has such an easy life. She's well-situated, married with a very much loved husband who very much loves her. The children of the marriage are much loved. She's very comfortably fixed for supply of all kinds: money, friends, family, all the blessings of the daily life. She is also blessed with a perfectly lovely attitude towards life and kind of a joy and a personality that always meets things with a grace and verve, and she realizes this. She spent quite a bit of time coming to this group a few years ago, and that was one question that I really never could feel had really been answered in my own mind. She asked it and an answer was given that she was indeed serving people in her daily life, but she really wanted to know where were the lessons for her; where were the difficulties that were talked about; where were all the limits that were being pushed towards and that she wasn't feeling? Was she somehow missing the boat by being so happy?

I am Latwii, and am aware of your question, my sister. In responding to this most interesting question may we say once again that each of your peoples inhabits an illusion. The illusion has many lessons to teach. Each entity chooses before the incarnation those lessons which it most needs in order to learn those lessons necessary for the graduation to the density of understanding, the density of love and compassion.

An entity, through many incarnations, such as the sister of whom you speak, may have encountered the difficulties upon difficulties without end, shall we say, and may have learned the lessons which the outer expression of difficulty and the meeting of difficulty have to teach. Such an entity then may determine that there are other types of lessons which are of value in the upcoming, shall we say, incarnation. It may be determined, for example, that the lessons of abundance might need be explored, for what is abundance? Where can it be found? Is abundance found in the life of leisure? Is abundance found only with a family that meets the standards of success described by your culture? Is abundance found in friends who stimulate the mind with conversation? Is abundance found in any part of this illusion other than in the heart of the seeking of the one Creator within the center of the being?

Many are the lessons which your illusion has to teach. It would seem to many entities upon your planet that the life described by your sister is the life which holds the full promise kept, the promise made to each entity within your illusion, and we do not say that such cannot be so, but we do suggest that there might be a much greater difficulty, shall we say, in obtaining the lessons of love for an entity experiencing those material abundances which are so often sought among the peoples of your planet and especially the nation in which you reside.

We might, in closing, suggest that the learning of love might also be quite well supported in such a surrounding which you have described, for the love of the one Creator is available in each moment. The ability to perceive and share this love depends only upon the strength of the desire of the entity seeking this love and experiencing any moment. Your sister may have indeed found the love of the one Creator and may indeed be experiencing it moment by moment. It may also be true that she shall use the illusion in which she lives to deepen that experience by removing the illusion of love to uncover the pearl of great price which resides within the heart of her being, and which no earthly treasure can match.

May we answer you further, my sister?

Carla: No. I thank you.

We are most grateful as well to you. Is there another question at this time?

L: I would simply like to add my thank you for all the information tonight. I feel overwhelmed with the quantity of learning that you've dumped on me.

D: Likewise.

Carla: Ditto.

L: I would simply like to say thank you and compliment you on the performing of your service in a superior manner.

I am Latwii. We are most gratified to have been able to have offered what we consider to be our treasures to this group which has, for some long period of your time, so sincerely sought that which we so humbly offer. We of Latwii do not assume to know all that can be known, but we do, with every fiber of our being, attempt to share all that we have. We thank each of you, for there is no greater service, in our estimation, than the service which you provide by seeking the one Creator and seeking to serve that one Creator.

We remind each entity that we are available upon simple request of our presence during your meditations or during your daily round of activities. It is a great honor for us to be asked to join you at any time. We look forward with great joy and anticipation at being able to answer such requests. We leave you now in the love and the light of the one Creator residing in the heart of each being. We are known to you as Latwii. Adonai, my friends. Adonai vasu borragus. ☥

L/L Research

L/L Research is a subsidiary of Rock Creek Research & Development Laboratories, Inc.

P.O. Box 5195
Louisville, KY 40255-0195

www.llresearch.org

Rock Creek is a non-profit corporation dedicated to discovering and sharing information which may aid in the spiritual evolution of humankind.

ABOUT THE CONTENTS OF THIS TRANSCRIPT: This telepathic channeling has been taken from transcriptions of the weekly study and meditation meetings of the Rock Creek Research & Development Laboratories and L/L Research. It is offered in the hope that it may be useful to you. As the Confederation entities always make a point of saying, please use your discrimination and judgment in assessing this material. If something rings true to you, fine. If something does not resonate, please leave it behind, for neither we nor those of the Confederation would wish to be a stumbling block for any.

© 2009 L/L Research

The Law of One, Book IV, Session 76
February 3, 1982

Ra: I am Ra. I greet you in the love and in the light of the one infinite Creator. We communicate now.

Questioner: Could you first please give me an indication of the condition of the instrument?

Ra: I am Ra. This instrument is in a state of physical complex bankruptcy which has existed for some of the measure you call time. The vital energies are normal with a strong spiritual complex counterpart and will lending substance to the mind/body/spirit complex energy levels.

Questioner: Will our continued communication with Ra be deleterious to the physical energies of the instrument?

Ra: I am Ra. We may answer in two modes. Firstly, if the instrument were thusly dedicated to this use with no transfer of energy of physical complex nature it would begin to call upon the vital energy itself and this, done in any substantive measure, is actively deleterious to a mind/body/spirit complex if that complex wishes further experience in the illusion which it now distorts.

Secondly, if care is taken, firstly, to monitor the outer parameters of the instrument, then to transfer physical energy by sexual transfer, by magical protection, and, lastly, by the energetic displacements of thought-forms energizing the instrument during contact there is no difficulty in that there is no worsening of the instrument's mind/body/spirit complex distortions of strength/weakness.

It is to be noted that the instrument, by dedicating itself to this service, attracts greetings of which you are aware. These are inconvenient but, with care taken, need not be lastingly deleterious either to the instrument or the contact.

Questioner: Of the three things that you mentioned that we could do for the instrument's benefit, would you clarify the last one? I didn't quite understand what you meant.

Ra: I am Ra. As the entity which you are allows its being to empathize with any other being, so then it may choose to share with the other-self those energies which may be salubrious to the other-self. The mechanism of these energy transfers is the thought or, more precisely, the thought-form for any thought is a form or symbol or thing that is an object seen in time/space reference.

Questioner: Has our use of the Banishing Ritual of the Lesser Pentagram been of any value and what is its effect?

Ra: I am Ra. This group's use of the Banishing Ritual of the Lesser Pentagram has been increasingly efficacious. Its effect is purification, cleansing, and protection of the place of working.

The efficacy of this ritual is only beginning to be, shall we say, at the lower limits of the truly magical. In doing the working those aspiring to adepthood have done the equivalent of beginning the schoolwork, many grades ahead. For the intelligent student this is not to be discouraged; rather to be encouraged is the homework, the reading, the writing, the arithmetic, as you might metaphorically call the elementary steps towards the study of being. It is the being that informs the working, not the working that informs the being. Therefore, we may leave you to the work you have begun.

Questioner: Would it be beneficial for us to perform the banishing ritual more in this room?

Ra: I am Ra. It is beneficial to regularly work in this place.

Questioner: I am sorry that we have had such a long delay between the last session and this one. It couldn't be helped I guess. Could you please tell me the origin of the tarot?

Ra: I am Ra. The origin of this system of study and divination is twofold: firstly, there is that influence which, coming in a distorted fashion from those who were priests attempting to teach the Law of One in Egypt, gave form to the understanding, if you will pardon the misnomer, which they had received. These forms were then made a regular portion of the learn/teachings of an initiate. The second influence is that of those entities in the lands you call Ur, Chaldea, and Mesopotamia who, from old, had received the, shall we say, data for which they called having to do with the heavens. Thusly we find two methods of divination being melded into one with uneven results; the, as you call it, astrology and the form being combined to suggest what you might call the correspondences which are typical of the distortions you may see as attempts to view archetypes.

Questioner: Then am I correct in assuming that the priests of Egypt, in attempting to convert knowledge that they had received initially from Ra into understandable symbology, constructed and initiated the concept of the tarot? Is this correct?

Ra: I am Ra. This is correct with the addition of the Sumerian influence.

Questioner: Were Ra's teachings focusing on the archetypes for this Logos and the methods of achieving a very close approach to the archetypical configuration? Is this correct?

Ra: I am Ra. This is correct without being true. We, of Ra, are humble messengers of the Law of One. We seek to teach/learn this single law. During the space/time of the Egyptian teach/learning we worked to bring the mind complex, the body complex, and the spirit complex into an initiated state in which the entity could contact intelligent energy and so become teach/learner itself so that healing and the fruits of study could be offered to all. The study of the roots of mind is a portion of the vivification of the mind complex and, as we have noted, the thorough study of the portion of the roots of mind called archetypical is an interesting and necessary portion of the process as a whole.

Questioner: Is there, in Ra's opinion, any present day value for the use of the tarot as an aid in the evolutionary process?

Ra: I am Ra. We shall repeat information. It is appropriate to study one form of constructed and organized distortion of the archetypical mind in depth in order to arrive at the position of being able to become and to experience archetypes at will. You have three basic choices. You may choose astrology, the twelve signs, as you call these portions of your planet's energy web, and what has been called the ten planets. You may choose the tarot with its twenty-two so-called Major Arcana. You may choose the study of the so-called Tree of Life with its ten Sephiroth and the twenty-two relationships between the stations.

It is well to investigate each discipline, not as a dilettante, but as one who seeks the touchstone, one who wishes to feel the pull of the magnet. One of these studies will be more attractive to the seeker. Let the seeker, then, investigate the archetypical mind using, basically, one of these three disciplines. After a period of study, the discipline mastered sufficiently, the seeker may then complete the more important step: that is, the moving beyond the written in order to express in an unique fashion its understanding, if you may again pardon the noun, of the archetypical mind.

Questioner: Would I be correct in saying that the archetypes of this particular Logos are somewhat unique with respect to the rest of the creation? The systems of study that we have just talked about would not translate quickly or easily in other parts of the creation. This is a very difficult question to state. Could you clear that up for me?

Ra: I am Ra. We may draw from the welter of statement which you offer the question we believe you ask. Please requestion if we have mistaken your query. The archetypical mind is that mind which is peculiar to the Logos under which influence you are at this space/time distorting your experiences. There is no other Logos the archetypical mind of which would be the same any more than the stars would appear the same from another planet in another galaxy. You may correctly infer that the closer Logoi are indeed closer in archetypes.

Questioner: Since Ra evolved initially on Venus Ra is of the same archetypical origin as that which we experience here. Is this correct?

Ra: I am Ra. This is correct.

Questioner: But I am assuming that the concepts of the tarot and the magical concepts of the Tree of Life, etc. were not in use by Ra. I suspect, possibly, some form of astrology was a previous Ra concept. This is just a guess. Am I correct?

Ra: I am Ra. To express Ra's methods of study of the archetypical mind under the system of distortions which we enjoyed would be to skew your own judgment of that which is appropriate for the system of distortions forming the conditions in which you learn/teach. Therefore, we must invoke the Law of Confusion.

Questioner: I am going to ask some questions now that may be a little off the center of what we are trying to do. I'm not sure because I'm trying to, with these questions, unscramble something that I consider very basic to what we are doing. Please forgive my lack of ability in questioning since this is a difficult concept for me.

Could you give me an idea of the length of the first and second densities as they occurred for this planet?

Ra: I am Ra. There is no method of estimation of the time/space before timelessness gave way in your first density. To the beginnings of your time, the measurement would be vast and yet this vastness is meaningless. Upon the entry into the constructed space/time your first density spanned a bridge of space/time and time/space of perhaps two billion of your years.

Second density is more easily estimated and represents your longest density in terms of the span of space/time. We may estimate that time as approximately 4.6 billion years. These approximations are exceedingly rough due to the somewhat uneven development which is characteristic of creations which are built upon the foundation stone of free will.

Questioner: Did you state that second density was 4.6 billion years? B, b-i-l? Is that correct?

Ra: I am Ra. This is correct.

Questioner: Then we have a third density that is, comparatively speaking, the twinkling of an eye, the snap of a finger in time compared to the others. Why is the third density cycled so extremely rapidly compared to the first and second?

Ra: I am Ra. The third density is a choice.

Questioner: Third density, then, compared to the rest of the densities, all of them, is nothing but a uniquely short period of what we consider to be time and is for the purpose of this choice.

Is this correct?

Ra: I am Ra. This is precisely correct. The prelude to choice must encompass the laying of the foundation, the establishment of the illusion and the viability of that which can be made spiritually viable. The remainder of the densities is continuous refining of the choice. This also is greatly lengthened, as you would use the term. The choice is, as you put it, the work of a moment but is the axis upon which the creation turns.

Questioner: Is this third-density choice the same throughout all of the creation of which you are aware?

Ra: I am Ra. We are aware of creations in which third density is lengthier and more space/time is given to the choosing. However, the proportions remain the same, the dimensions all being somewhat etiolated and weakened by the Logos to have a variant experience of the Creator. This creation is seen by us to be quite vivid.

Questioner: I didn't understand what you meant by what you said "as seen by you to be quite vivid." What did you mean?

Ra: I am Ra. This creation is somewhat more condensed by its Logos than some other Logoi have chosen. Thus each experience of the Creator by the Creator in this system of distortions is, relatively speaking, more bright or, as we said, vivid.

Questioner: I am assuming that upon entry into third density, for this planet, disease did not exist in any form. Is this correct?

Ra: I am Ra. This is incorrect.

Questioner: What disease or form of disease was there and why did this exist at the beginning of the third density?

Ra: I am Ra. Firstly, that which you speak of as disease is a functional portion the body complex which offers the body complex the opportunity to cease viability. This is a desirable body complex function. The second portion of the answer has to do with second-density other-selves of a microscopic, as you would call it, size which have in some forms long existed and perform their service by aiding the physical body complex in its function of ceasing viability at the appropriate space/time.

Questioner: What I am trying to understand is the difference between the plan of the Logos for these second-density entities and the generation of what I would guess to be more or less a runaway array of feedback to create various physical problems to act as catalyst in our present third-density condition. Could you give me an indication of whether my thinking is anywhere near right on that?

Ra: I am Ra. This instrument's physical body complex is becoming more distorted towards pain. We shall, therefore, speak to this subject as our last full query of this working. Your query contains some internal confusion which causes the answer to be perhaps more general than desired. We invite refinements of the query.

The Logos planned for entities of mind/body/spirit complex to gain experience until the amount of experience was sufficient for an incarnation. This varied only slightly from second-density entities whose mind/body complexes existed for the purpose of experiencing growth and seeking consciousness. As the third density upon your planet proceeded, as has been discussed, the need for the physical body complex to cease became more rapidly approached due to intensified and more rapidly gained catalyst. This catalyst was not being properly assimilated. Therefore, the, shall we say, lifetimes needed to be shorter that learning might continue to occur with the proper rhythm and increment. Thus more and more opportunities have been offered as your density has progressed for disease. May we ask if there are further brief queries before we close?

Questioner: I have one question that is possibly of no value. You don't have to expand on it, but there is a crystal skull in the possession of a woman near Toronto. It may be of some value in investigating these communications with Ra since I think possibly this had some origin from Ra. Can you tell me anything about that, and then is there anything that we can do to improve the contact or to make the instrument more comfortable?

Ra: I am Ra. Although your query is one which uncovers interesting material we can not answer due to the potential an answer may have for affecting your actions. The appurtenances are carefully placed and requisite care taken. We are appreciative. All is well.

I am Ra. I leave you, my friends, in the love and the light of the one infinite Creator. Go forth, therefore, glorying and rejoicing in the power and in the peace of the one infinite Creator. Adonai.

Intensive Meditation
February 4, 1982

(Carla channeling)

[I am Hatonn,] and I greet you, my friends, In the love and in the light of our infinite Creator. We would like, at this time, to confirm that we have been conditioning the one known as S. If the instrument known as S had wished, it would have been possible for this instrument to initiate contact. This is a desirable ability, for there is not always an experienced instrument present during a time when one who wishes to be of service by offering itself as a vocal channel finds the opportunity to share in our thoughts.

We would speak a few words through this instrument before we work with the one known as S, for we sense the deprivation of some information which may perhaps be of service at this time. This deprivation is not due to any individual's efforts, rather, it is due, my friends, to the culture in which you find yourselves experiencing the great patterns of life which you weave day by day. It was intended by the Creator that you might experience your so-called work as a form of meditation and as an experience of love. It has been many centuries among your peoples since it was possible for many of your peoples to profoundly experience the combination of work and love.

It has been said, "To work is to pray," and for those lucky enough, shall we say, to have found occupations which enable them to supply themselves with the necessities of survival which also feed the spirit, this is in the deepest sense true. You may find these people working with their hands to make beauty, working with their minds as channels of various forms of love, working among people in such a way that their very being is of service in a substantial manner. But for so many, my friends, the connection between the daily life and love, between action and meditation, is not apparent. And in order for you to become able to link in any way the work of empty form which you find yourselves performing and the work which is love, it is recommended that you begin with the meditation rather than with the work.

To move from one consciousness to another is like mounting the great hillside, the bottom of which is vanity, pollution, pettiness and distraction. In your spirit's garment you move in consciousness of this lovely hillside. You can feel that your garment, the garment of your spirit, is soiled from all that touches you that you perceive as being unclean, and so you remove the garment and cleanse yourself in the waters which you find falling down the hillside in a lovely waterfall, brilliant with crescents of *(inaudible)* and iridescent as it sprays the rocks, the moss, and the grass. Leaning into the water, you can begin to see the purity of your true being and you can cleanse yourself with the waters of [the lake.] Taking up your fresh garment, a new washed linen, you move onward until you sit at the top of this hillside. The air about you is warm and redolent with the scent of wild flowers—pinks and roses and whites, all in profusion about you. And as you settle into meditation, this is your consciousness, this is who you are. All of creation breathes with you and desires to be of service to you, and you in turn offer up the rhythms of your body, your mind, and your spirit in service to this beautiful [place you're in,] loving and delighting in its beauty, its purity, and its gentle ever present strength.

Yes, my friends, you come down again into the marketplace where you live the illusion, where your lessons [collect.] But you bring with you an unsoiled garment, a cleanliness of soul, and a new vision that begins to attempt to see the top of the hillside, beneath the soiled garment of all labor, all conditions, and all relationships. You cannot and never shall function as a great [wise] one working in the valley. Within yourselves you must find a place in which in silence you find the creation offered unto you, and offer yourself unto the creation, feeling the great beating rhythm, unity that binds all things together.

We ask that you never be discouraged if you fail to manifest what you have learned in your meditations, for this is the work of your life—to find who you are. That is, my friends, to find the Creator, that one great original Thought which is love and which when *(inaudible)*.

We are pleased at this time to transfer this contact to the one known as S, after pausing for a brief period in order to make our conditioning vibration *(inaudible)*. And to the one known as R, and to the one known as [Don]. I am Hatonn.

(Pause)

(S channeling)

I am Hatonn, and am with this instrument. We greet you, my friends, once more. It has been a pleasure to work with those who have requested our conditioning vibration. We are always pleased to join with those who seek our contact. We are honored to be with this group today, as it is indeed a joy to be of service to the one infinite Creator by aiding those who seek our help. We of Hatonn are always available to these who seek out aid. We ask that you simply mentally request our presence and we shall be with you. We are hoping to be with each of you in the near future, and would attempt to contact another instrument at this time. I am Hatonn.

(Pause)

(Carla channeling)

I am Hatonn, and am again with this instrument. And please excuse the pause, but we were attempting to initiate contact with another instrument, shall we say, an old friend of ours. May we say to the one known as S that her fidelity to our channeled communication is such that the degree of the instrument's own thoughts coming into the contact is very nearly nonexistent. At this point in the training of the new instrument we do the opposite of that with which we start. We attempt to encourage the somewhat experienced instrument to feel more free to speak upon a subject about which the instrument does not have a prior recollection of, a subject matter from another contact.

This type of channeling is the next step and requires that the instrument allow us to present her with images drawn from the treasure trove of her own experiences, recollections and thoughts. We use this framework in order that our extremely simple message may be offered in the greatest possible variety, or kaleidoscope, of patterns, for each various view of love, of the Creator, of the universe, of reality may for the first time inspire one to whom all previous words were naught but chatter and foolishness.

The nature of inspiration is so personal and so unpredictable that we simply cannot expect to create parrots. We hope instead to create those who are able through practice in sessions such as these to recognize our vibrations, and to trust in our contact enough to sally forth into vistas about which they have not thought, and to describe concepts and stories, the gist and outcome of which is not known to the instrument. This is the work of some time, as you call it. We say all this to assure the instrument that she is progressing very well. Well enough, in fact, to consider the possibility of launching forward on the next step at any contact at which she may feel comfortable in so doing.

The knowledge of the instrument, that subjectively familiar material—[it] being integrated into a meditation—causes all beginning channels, except those who are not excellent, to have doubts as to the origin of the channeled information. However, my sister, it is our way of insuring that each message is somewhat fresh. We thank the one known as S, and as always assure her that we and those of the Confederation in general, offer ourselves at any time we may be requested to accompany meditation. I am Hatonn.

We leave you on a hillside, my friends, gazing forth into a world of illusion, a world in which each illusion has a central core of purity and love. As this instrument would say, your mission is, impossible though it may seem, to find it. I leave you in the love and in light. I am Hatonn. Adonai vasu.

(Carla channeling)

I am Latwii, and greet you all in love and light. It is a great honor for us to be asked to join you this afternoon during your meditation. As always, we look forward to such adventures with glee and a happy anticipation. Before we would attempt to answer queries, we would attempt to offer our conditioning to the one known as R, and simultaneously to the one known as S. And then if the one known as S would care to speak our thoughts, we would speak a few words through this new instrument. I am Latwii.

(S channeling)

I am Latwii, and am with this instrument. I greet you, my friends, in the love and in the light of the Creator. We are overjoyed to be speaking to you through this instrument once more. She is indeed a contact that we enjoy. We are happy to be with her at this time. We are always pleased to be able to speak through instruments such as this, for we are not often given the opportunity to do so. We find it a great deal of fun. We are sorry to say that we feel we should close this contact so that we may be of service to those who have questions on their minds. We would therefore sign off. I am Latwii.

(Jim channeling)

I am Latwii, and am with this instrument once again, and greet you all in love and light. May we at this time ask if any present might have a question which we would attempt to answer?

Questioner: Yes, Latwii. How can I, or how is it possible, to increase receptiveness to the conditioning vibration?

I am Latwii, and, my brother, may we suggest that there is nothing in particular to do. Rather, it is that which is not done which is most helpful to the reception of, not only our conditioning vibration, but the conditioning vibration of any Confederation entity. That is, simply the relaxing of mind and body to the greatest degree possible, and the opening of the being as clearly and freely, shall we say, as is possible. This, of course, is predicated upon the assumption that the desire for such a contact is present and we find that desire is quite present in your case. The many methods of relaxing the mind and body which have been written down among your peoples as the various methods of meditation are helpful, but we would also suggest that the concept of not doing and of simply seeking is the foundation stone upon which any technique is based.

May we answer you further, my brother?

Questioner: No, thank you.

I am Latwii. We are most grateful to you as well. Is there another question at this time?

Questioner: Yes. Latwii, during one of my meditations I received what seemed to be very strong conditioning that I didn't ask for and was not able to get rid of for quite some time. It kind of frightened me. Can you give me any information about this?

I am Latwii, and am aware of your question, my sister. May we say in this regard that whenever you might feel a vibration which is not pleasant or desirable, at that time request that it be removed, and if the entity generating that vibration is of the Confederation of Planets in the Service of the Infinite Creator then you may be assured that the vibration shall be removed. If upon such request the vibration is not removed we suggest the ceasing of the meditative state for a moment, the gathering of the self in concentrated thought, and the sending of love and light to all entities present, then the constructing, shall we say, of the shield of light about the self so that meditation may be resumed.

May we answer you further, my sister?

S: No, not on that subject, but I do have another question. Due to my feeling, lately I've had a strong urge to proceed and go further, and against advice from the Confederation I proceeded to try channeling with just R and myself present. It did serve to confuse me as I was warned might happen, but I still feel somewhat compelled to continue so that I may be able to get more practice and therefore move along at a faster pace. Would you strongly advise against this or can I do anything more than I'm doing now to project myself?

I am Latwii, and am aware of your question, my sister. It is always our advice to those …

(Side one of tape ends.)

(Jim channeling)

I am Latwii, and am once again with this instrument. As we were saying, we do not recommend that new instruments attempt to channel from any Confederation source without the presence of at least two other entities, one preferably being an instrument with some experience so that the contact might be, shall we say checked and balanced, so that there is reduced the possibility of the infringement of the contact by those entities which do seek to confuse positively-oriented instruments and do seek to sway such new instruments by giving information of what we might call a questionable and specific nature.

For those entities such as yourself who seek to speed their growth upon the spiritual path in general and the, shall we say, specific part of that path known to you as the channeling phenomenon, we recommend the intensive meditation periods such as this period now occurring with an experienced channel present. Also, we might recommend the additional meditation periods for the new instrument, at which time the instrument would request the conditioning vibration of the Confederation. We would also suggest the lengthier, shall we say, meditation periods during which time the new instrument would attempt to increase the attention span, shall we say, that is, the state of mind which is most receptive to a contact.

This state of mind might be increased in its duration by the visualization technique that is the imaging on the mind during meditation of the new instrument of any symbol which has a particular meaning to that entity, whether it be the cross, the rose, the circle, the Buddha or whatever. This is most helpful for the new instrument who wishes to improve its ability at receiving information as purely as possible.

To close this somewhat lengthy response, may we reiterate we are always available for the conditioning vibration to be experienced by any entity requesting it, and we further remind each present that it is most necessary to be accompanied in meditation that is directed toward the channeling phenomenon by at least two other entities. This is necessary, as we said, to preserve the purity of the contact.

May we answer you further, my sister?

S: No, thank you.

I am Latwii. We are most grateful to you as well. Is there another question at this time?

(Pause)

I am Latwii. We [are] most grateful to each present for inviting us to join this meditation. We of Latwii have a history, shall we say, of being somewhat more humorous in our contacts with this group, but have in recent contacts found the necessity, shall we say, to balance this particular distortion with the giving of information in response to queries of a, shall we say, more serious or intense nature, for we feel the entities within this group who have been seeking our service have sought the guideposts, shall we say, to direct them to the heart of their seeking, and it has been for this reason that we have attempted to deal in a more, shall we say, serious manner with these particular topics and our responses to them.

We do not mean by such gravity to suggest that the lightness and the humor which we are known for does not have a value in such situations but we wish these entities to seek our service, to know without a doubt that we value their seeking, their questions, and their being greatly, and would honor each entity with the most purely formed response. With this qualification made and recorded, we shall look forward to joining this group in the future in our more familiar mode of lightness and joy. We thank each entity for requesting our presence. We shall be with each at any time in the future that our presence is so requested. We are known to you as Latwii, and we leave you now in the light and the love and the humor of the one infinite Creator. Adonai vasu borragus. ☙

Sunday Meditation
February 7, 1982

(L channeling)

I am Hatonn, and I greet you, my brothers and my sisters, in the love and the light of the infinite Creator. My friends, it is with great pleasure that we listen to the gentle sounds of the young child, for we understand its meaning. It shares with you and with us its wonderment at the infusion of love and light into your room this night as your spirits join and become one. It is our pleasure, as well, to be both perceivers and participants in this mingling, and for this we offer you our thanks.

We of Hatonn would like at this time to share with you a story, one in which a child is born, lives and dies in the manner of your density, yet accomplishes a great deal more than is obvious to those who shared his presence. The child of whom we speak was in no way outstanding, either physically or mentally. The child was of inauspicious parentage, having been raised of poor parents in a small village. When the child reached maturity he joined himself with a woman for he sought the comfort that this type of companionship could provide. As things progress in your density, the child grew older, fathered children, grew older again, and eventually died.

Not a very impressive tale of a life, you might assume, yet the child accomplished, in this brief lifespan, that which he set out to do. The learning which the individual had prescribed for himself prior to this incarnation did occur, and although this individual did not attain great wisdom, did not even obtain the realization of choice between service to self or service to others, still the individual attained that which he set out to do.

My brothers, my sisters, there are many in your world today who are like this child. The lessons toward which you strive exist yet for them far in their future, for as one must learn to walk before one may run, one must first learn to crawl. We would suggest to you, therefore, to be generous in your hearts to your other selves, your other brothers and sisters of this world, for although they have not attained your awareness, although the revelations which you seek and hold so dear are not revealed to them, we urge you to realize that their lessons to them are equally important, that their learning is paid for with as many tears and as much pain as your own.

It is often difficult to extend your love to some who fall within this group, for their confusion seems to abrade their lack of awareness, makes them appear almost another species, a duller, dimmer species, somehow distantly related to your own. My friends, they are not merely your own species, these are your own selves. It is not our desire to chastise, for judgment is not ours, rather it is our desire to encourage, that you may, in perceiving your other selves as such, find your hearts less reluctant to share your love with them. Loving is not always an easy task and on some occasions is poorly rewarded, but my brothers, is reward what you seek? Therefore, we would humbly implore that you extend to yourselves that love which you extend to us.

At this time we desire to speak through another instrument. I am Hatonn.

(Carla channeling)

I am Hatonn, and am with this instrument. We offered this contact to the one known as C, but this entity requested that we move on. Therefore, we shall close through this instrument. We greet you once again in love and light. To feel, my friends, that one is a finer example of the species is to find oneself upon dangerous ground, if we may use that term in a spiritual sense. In your holy work which you call your Bible a great king of Assyria made a request to a great king of Israel, that a great Assyrian might be healed of leprosy. The request was made in a grand and formal manner and the gentleman of importance who had contracted this feared contagion journeyed forth to the land of Israel. The king of Israel was about to turn away this gentleman, but one known as Elisha offered instead to heal this man. "Go forth," he said to this fine and important man, "and wash yourself in the river seven times."

Now, this man was important. It was not for him to do such a thing, an unimportant act. He expected his healing to have all the grandeur of his person and at first would not go wash. In the end, desiring to be cleansed, he did indeed wash in the river seven times over and emerged cleansed and healed.

Whenever, my friends, you do find yourselves gazing at a brother or a sister and feeling that feeling of distance betwixt you and he or she, know for certain that your feeling of a great height upon which you stand by reason of intellect or knowledge or spirituality will soon become an opportunity for you to experience humility, and when this happens, my friends, greet this experience with as much enthusiasm as you can muster, for it is a valuable way of learning the ways of love.

Before we leave this instrument we would pause and offer our conditioning vibration to each of those in this circle, to all of whom we send our love. Please request mentally that we be with you and we shall attempt to make our presence known to you. I am Hatonn.

(Pause)

(Carla channeling)

I am Hatonn, and speak once more through this instrument to assure each of you our gratitude for your call to us that we may share our humble thoughts with you. As you go about your daily tasks, know that these feelings which you experience in meditation are with you, are a part of you and are available to you. Let not this beauty fade from your life, for what is there to replace it?

We leave this instrument in the love and the light of our infinite Creator. I am Hatonn. Adonai, my friends. Adonai vasu.

(Jim channeling)

I am Latwii, and I greet you, my friends, in the love and in the light of the one infinite Creator. We are most honored to be asked to join your group this evening. It is always a great privilege to blend our vibrations with this group, for we have many memories of the joyful intercourse, shall we say, with this group in the capacity of answering the queries which those present bring as treasures to us. May we at this time ask if there are any questions which we might attempt to answer through this instrument?

M: I have a question for S. She had a spiritual experience recently and needs an answer, if you can help her, on how an individual can react or respond to her kind of spiritual experience.

I am Latwii, and am aware of the query which you ask for your sister. May we say first of all that the experiences of what you would call a spiritual nature are most private and personal and unique unto each entity. Each entity upon your planet seeks either consciously or unconsciously union with the one Creator and all of Creation. Each entity, by the path it travels, in the beliefs it holds, and the way in which it experiences its life, does create a framework through which each truth shall be revealed unto it. Each entity, therefore, does determine a manner in which it seeks and the manner in which it shall receive that which it seeks.

Therefore, when an entity such as the one known as S experiences that which your peoples call a spiritual revelation, this entity is experiencing a greater portion of itself, because it has asked to know, to receive, and to be answered in such a way as it has been answered. To speak specifically to this particular experience for this entity would not be, in our humble opinion, a service to this entity, for the greater portion of such a spiritual revelation is the seeking of the meaning of that experience within the heart of the being of the entity experiencing it. For another, such as ourselves, to attempt to reveal unto this entity the meaning of such an experience is to travel that path for the entity, and thus remove for the entity the opportunity of gaining further spiritual strength and understanding that would ensue as a result of this entity attempting to assimilate fully the meaning of this experience.

We can only suggest that this entity, and any other in a similar situation, meditate upon the situation preceding the experience, the experience itself and the results in the experience that follow. In this way we feel we might be of most service to this entity.

May we answer you further, my brother?

M: Just a little. I believe she understands your answer and would have expected that. The problem with meditation is an evil presence she feels as she tries to meditate almost makes her afraid to meditate. She wonders if she should, in fact, meditate at all, if she's bringing on that type of vibration.

I am Latwii, and am aware of your query, my brother. In this regard, may we make a simple suggestion to the one known as S, that being that to seek purely the one infinite Creator and to serve the one Creator by serving the other selves that one finds in one's daily round of activities, is a shield, shall we say, that does provide protection from entities of what you would call a negative nature who would seek to infringe upon the free will of another.

To refine this seeking of the one Creator and this service, it may be useful in this instance for this entity to engage in what might be called a fast for purification and protection. This fast to be of the description which is most beneficial to the entity, the most important ingredient being the dedication of the fast, of whatever nature, to the seeking of the one Creator. This fast to continue for a period of approximately three days. During this period the concentrating upon the seeking and the purity is to be recommended. During this period it might also be helpful to include material of a spiritual nature, of an inspirational nature, to be read by this entity periodically as a reminder for the purpose for which it seeks.

At the end of this period of fasting it is suggested that the entity begin a series of what might be called rituals which would consist simply of the shielding of the self in light to begin the meditation, a prayer of supplication, invoking the presence of the guides of this entity, and invoking the love, the light of the one Creator. In this way we feel that this entity might be aided by portions of its own being in the seeking of purity and of service to the one Creator.

May we answer you further, my brother?

M: Thank you for the instructions, Latwii. I'm sure that will be very helpful.

I am Latwii. We are most grateful to you as well. Is there another question at this time?

L: I'd like to ask a couple of questions if I may. Within the last few months—couple of months— I've been receiving some visitations at night from some rather malevolent entities. I'm curious as to who is favoring me with their attention, and why, as far as their choosing this particular time. Is there any information you can give me?

I am Latwii, and am aware of your query, my brother. We may answer in this regard by saying that such instances as those which you experience in your sleeping state may be of many origins. There are those entities, as you have surmised, which are of what you would call a negative nature. That is, they seek to serve their own individuated selves by the gaining of control of some nature over another self. Entities upon your planet who seek to serve the one Creator upon the positive path—that is, the serving of other selves in preference to the serving of the self—in this activity of service do attract unto them, as a function of the balancing nature of all of creation, entities of a negative nature.

The entities of the negative nature are providing a service. They provide, shall we say, a test, a force against which you may move and thereby further express service to other selves. Your response to such an experience is also a service and in remaining steadfast to the positive path of service to others, by sending love and light to these entities while in the dream state if possible, and while awake in meditation if not, is a great service, for, my brother, as you know, the Creation and all of its parts are one thing, one being. The Creator shall know Itself in every possible way. There is, as you would say, no right or wrong and in truth there is no polarity, for all, at some point, shall be reconciled through the dance of the densities and the illusions which you experience.

As you become more convinced or confirmed, shall we say, upon the positive path, you shall experience a greater array of experiences in every part of your life. This is simply a signpost, shall we say, that indicates you are ready for further lessons. These lessons may not always be in conformance with that which you would imagine or desire would lie upon the spiritual path, but, my brother, we may suggest that as you travel this path and meet those entities of a negative nature, whether in dreams, visions, thought forms, or in person, the greatest service which you can provide is to envelop these entities in love and in light, for they are your other selves just as surely as is any other self.

May we answer you further, my brother?

L: Yes. On that topic, my understanding of what is being sought by a negatively oriented individual would lead me to assume that the presentation or response of love and light to the individual would be less than in tune with their desires, their own service to themselves. How am I assisting them in that manner? I don't understand that.

I am Latwii, and am aware of your query, my brother. By sending such an entity love and light, you do radiate unto that entity the core of your being as undistorted and clearly as you perceive it. By revealing that which is the heart of your being, you do serve this other self by expressing your nature without reservation, and do accept this other self without reservation, without demand of any kind. This is the perfect expression of the positive polarity path. The acceptance, the forgiveness, and the loving of all other selves no matter what their dance through the illusion, in this way do you express unto the other self of whatever polarity the heart of your being which is love and acceptance of all, and thereby do you provide catalyst for an other self of a negative polarity to work upon its own perceptions and being.

May we answer you further, my brother?

L: Yes. One last question, then I'll give room for someone else. In previous meetings I had understood that there were certain rituals that could be used to, in effect, exclude the inclusion of unwanted entities into your living space. It's something I'd considered doing. At the same time I'm reluctant to because I feel that it would be reducing the amount of service I could do to one of these entities as well as, in effect, giving them the opportunity to concentrate on me instead of bothering somebody else. I realize this is not a decision you can make for me, but I would be interested in hearing any advice you could offer.

I am Latwii, and am aware of your query, my brother. In this regard we feel we may be of most service by simply referring you to these entities present who have utilized such rituals for this purpose. In this way we feel we might allow the further pursuance of this course of action to take, shall we say, a more natural turn in events.

May we answer you further, my brother?

L: No, I thank you for your patience.

I am Latwii. We are most grateful to you as well. We look forward now to another query which we might attempt to answer through this instrument. Is there another query at this time?

(Side one of tape ends.)

(Jim channeling)

I am Latwii, and would assure each that we are with this instrument once again and are awaiting a further query.

M: How can one best maintain high spiritual and physical energy levels?

I am Latwii, and am aware of your query, my brother. In this regard, may we say that the maintaining of such levels of physical and spiritual nature is that which is the work of, shall we say, the adept, for there are few upon your planet who concern themselves with such matters and are quite content to seek periodically the solution to such problems. In actuality, we would suggest that such matters are of such a simple nature that it almost escapes the sincere seeker, for within simplicity the seeker is usually surprised to find the answers to the questions of a complex nature.

Therefore, we may simply answer you by saying your desire is that which shall assure your maintaining of such levels of energy upon the spiritual, the mental, and the physical complex nature. We could suggest a multitude of exercises, diets, regimens, readings, and other paraphernalia of the spiritual seeker, but we do not feel that specific suggestions such as these are of most service to those who seek upon the spiritual path, for most often such externalities, shall we say, simply dissipate one's energies, when the simple rekindling of the desire to seek the one Creator on a daily basis, no matter how simple or short, is that which shall assure your treading of the path of the pilgrim, the one who seeks union of all with all and through each experience that is encountered.

May we answer you further, my brother?

M: No, that was very nice, Latwii. Thank you.

I am Latwii. We are most grateful for this opportunity to be of service in this manner. May we answer another question at this time?

(Pause)

I am Latwii. We are very grateful to be able to experience the silence and the seeking with each in this group. We are aware that there are yet remaining some questions of an unasked nature. We do not feel it proper to answer queries which have not been vocalized. We would, therefore, ask once again if there is a question which we might attempt to answer?

(Pause)

I am Latwii, and am with this instrument once again. We find that the only queries we have been able to elicit at this time are those of the young, for which we have difficulty in the translation. Therefore, we shall at this time thank each present for allowing us to join our vibrations in meditation. It is a great honor and a privilege which we cannot thank you enough for. We are always grateful for such opportunities and look forward with an anxious *(inaudible)* for the next opportunity of this joining. We remind each present that a simple request for our presence in meditation is all that is necessary for our joining there. We leave this group now in the love and in the light of the one infinite Creator. I am Latwii. Adonai vasu borragus. ♣

L/L Research

L/L Research is a subsidiary of Rock Creek Research & Development Laboratories, Inc.

P.O. Box 5195
Louisville, KY 40255-0195

www.llresearch.org

Rock Creek is a non-profit corporation dedicated to discovering and sharing information which may aid in the spiritual evolution of humankind.

ABOUT THE CONTENTS OF THIS TRANSCRIPT: This telepathic channeling has been taken from transcriptions of the weekly study and meditation meetings of the Rock Creek Research & Development Laboratories and L/L Research. It is offered in the hope that it may be useful to you. As the Confederation entities always make a point of saying, please use your discrimination and judgment in assessing this material. If something rings true to you, fine. If something does not resonate, please leave it behind, for neither we nor those of the Confederation would wish to be a stumbling block for any.

© 2009 L/L RESEARCH

THE LAW OF ONE, BOOK IV, SESSION 77
FEBRUARY 10, 1982

Ra: I am Ra. I greet you in the love and in the light of the one infinite Creator. We communicate now.

Questioner: Could you please give me an indication of the condition of the instrument?

Ra: I am Ra. It is as previously stated.

Questioner: Was the instrument under attack just prior to this session?

Ra: I am Ra. This is correct.

Questioner: Is there anything that we could do to help protect the instrument from these attacks prior to the session?

Ra: I am Ra. This is correct.

Questioner: What could we do?

Ra: I am Ra. Your group could refrain from continuing this contact.

Questioner: Is that the only thing that we could do?

Ra: I am Ra. That is the only thing you could do which you are not already attempting with a whole heart.

Questioner: I have three questions that the instrument asked me to ask which I will get out of the way first. She wants to know if the preparation for her hospital experience could be improved if she should ever have to repeat it?

Ra: I am Ra. All was done well with one exception. The instrument was instructed to spend space/time contemplating its self as the Creator. This, done in a more determined fashion, would be beneficial at times when the mind complex is weakened by severe assaults upon the distortions of the body complex towards pain. There is no necessity for negative thought-forms regardless of pain distortions. The elimination of such creates the lack of possibility for negative elementals and other negative entities to use these thought-forms to create the worsening of the mind complex deviation from the normal distortions of cheerfulness/anxiety.

Questioner: The instrument would also like to know if what we call tuning could be improved during times when we do not communicate with Ra?

Ra: I am Ra. That which has been stated in regard to the latter question will suffice to point the way for the present query.

Questioner: Finally, she wishes to know why several days ago her heart rate went up to 115 per minute and why she had extreme pain in her stomach? Was that an Orion greeting?

Ra: I am Ra. Although this experience was energized by the Orion group the events mentioned, as well as others more serious, were proximally caused by the ingestion of certain foodstuffs in what you call your tablet form.

Questioner: Can you tell me what these tablets were, specifically?

Ra: I am Ra. We examine this query for the Law of Confusion and find ourselves close to the boundary, but acceptably so.

The substance which caused the bodily reaction of the heartbeat was called Pituitone by those which manufacture it. That which caused the difficulty which seemed to be cramping of the lower abdominal musculature but was, in fact, more organic in nature was a substance called Spleentone.

This instrument has a physical body complex of complicated balances which afford it physical existence. Were the view taken that certain functions and chemicals found in the healthy, as you call it, body complex are lacking in this one and, therefore, simply must be replenished, the intake of the many substances which this instrument began would be appropriate. However, this particular physical vehicle has, for approximately twenty-five of your years, been vital due to the spirit, the mind, and the will being harmoniously dedicated to fulfilling the service it chose to offer.

Therefore, physical healing techniques are inappropriate whereas mental and spiritual healing techniques are beneficial.

Questioner: Is there any technique that we could use that we have not been using that would be beneficial for the instrument in this case?

Ra: I am Ra. We might suggest, without fractiousness, two. Firstly, let the instrument remove the possibility of further ingestion of this group of foodstuffs.

Secondly, each of the group may become aware of the will to a greater extent. We cannot instruct upon this but merely indicate, as we have previously, that it is a vital key to the evolution of the mind/body/spirit complex.

Questioner: Thank you. I would like to go back to the plan of this Logos for Its creation and examine the philosophical basis that is the foundation for what was created in this local creation and the philosophy of the plan for experience. I am assuming that I am correct in stating that the foundation for this, as has been stated many times before, is the first distortion. After that, what was the plan in the philosophical sense?

Ra: I am Ra. We cannot reply due to a needed portion of your query which has been omitted; that is, do we speak of this particular Logos?

Questioner: That is correct. I am asking with respect to this particular sub-Logos, our sun.

Ra: I am Ra. This query has substance. We shall begin by turning to an observation of a series of concept complexes of which you are familiar as the tarot.

The philosophy was to create a foundation, first of mind, then of body, and then of spiritual complex. Those concept complexes you call the tarot lie then in three groups of seven: the mind cycle, one through seven; the physical complex cycle, eight through fourteen; the spiritual complex cycle, fifteen through twenty-one. The last concept complex may best be termed The Choice.

Upon the foundation of the transformation of each complex, with free will guided by the root concepts offered in these cycles, the Logos offered this density the basic architecture of a building and the constructing and synthesizing of data culminating in The Choice.

Questioner: Then to condense your statement, I see it meaning that there are seven basic philosophical foundations for mental experience, seven for bodily, seven for spiritual, and that these produce the polarization that we experience sometime during the third-density cycle. Am I correct?

Ra: I am Ra. You are correct in that you perceive the content of our prior statement with accuracy. You are incorrect in that you have no mention of the, shall we say, location of all of these concept complexes; that is, they exist within the roots of the mind and it is from this resource that their guiding influence and leitmotifs[4] may be traced. You may further note that each foundation is itself not single but a complex of concepts. Furthermore, there are relationships betwixt mind, body, and spirit of the same location in octave, for instance: one, eight, fifteen, and relationships within each octave which are helpful in the pursuit of The Choice by the mind/body/spirit complex. The Logos under which these foundations stand is one of free will. Thusly the foundations may be seen to have unique facets

---

[4] leitmotif: *Lit:* leading motive. *In music:* A distinguishing theme or melodic phrase representing and recurring with a given character, situation, or emotion in an opera.

and relationships for each mind/body/spirit complex. Only twenty-two, The Choice, is relatively fixed and single.

Questioner: Then I am probably having a problem with the concept of time since it appears that the Logos was aware of the polarization choice. It seems that this choice for polarization at the end of third density is an important philosophical plan for the experience past third density. Am I correct in assuming that this process is a process to create the proper or desired experience that will take place in the creation after third density is complete?

Ra: I am Ra. These philosophical foundations are those of third density. Above this density there remains the recognition of the architecture of the Logos but without the veils which are so integral a part of the process of making the choice in third density.

Questioner: The specific question that I had was that it seems to me that the choice was planned to create intense polarization past third density so that experience would be intense past third density. Is this correct?

Ra: I am Ra. Given that our interpretation of your sound vibration complexes is appropriate, this is incorrect. The intensity of fourth density is that of the refining of the rough-hewn sculpture. This is, indeed, in its own way, quite intense causing the mind/body/spirit complex to move ever inward and onward in its quest for fuller expression. However, in third density the statue is forged in the fire. This is a type of intensity which is not the property of fourth, fifth, sixth, or seventh densities.

Questioner: What I am really attempting to understand, since all of these twenty-one philosophical bases result in the twenty-second which is The Choice, is why this choice is so important, why the Logos seems to put so much emphasis on this choice, and what function this choice of polarity has, precisely, in the evolution or the experience of that which is created by the Logos?

Ra: I am Ra. The polarization or choosing of each mind/body/spirit is necessary for harvestability from third density. The higher densities do their work due to the polarity gained in this choice.

Questioner: Would it be possible for this work of our density to be performed if all of the sub-Logoi chose the same polarity in any particular expression or evolution of a Logos? Let us make the assumption that our sun created nothing but, through the first distortion, positive polarity. There was no product except positive polarity. Would work then be done in fourth density and higher as a function of only the positive polarization evolving from the original creation of our sub-Logos?

Ra: I am Ra. Elements of this query illustrate the reason I was unable to answer your previous question without knowledge of the Logos involved. To turn to your question, there were Logoi which chose to set the plan for the activation of mind/body/spirit complexes through each true color body without recourse to the prior application of free will. It is, to our knowledge, only in an absence of free will that the conditions of which you speak obtain. In such a procession of densities you find an extraordinarily long, as you measure time, third-density; likewise, fourth density. Then, as the entities begin to see the Creator, there is a very rapid, as you measure time, procession towards the eighth density. This is due to the fact that one who knows not, cares not.

Let us illustrate by observing the relative harmony and unchanging quality of existence in one of your, as you call it, primitive tribes. The entities have the concepts of lawful and taboo, but the law is inexorable and all events occur as predestined. There is no concept of right and wrong, good or bad. It is a culture in monochrome. In this context you may see the one you call Lucifer as the true light-bringer in that the knowledge of good and evil both precipitated the mind/body/spirits of this Logos from the Edenic conditions of constant contentment and also provided the impetus to move, to work and to learn.

Those Logoi whose creations have been set up without free will have not, in the feeling of those Logoi, given the Creator the quality and variety of experience of Itself as have those Logoi which have incorporated free will as paramount. Thusly you find those Logoi moving through the timeless states at what you would see as a later space/time to choose the free will character when elucidating the foundations of each Logos.

Questioner: I guess, under the first distortion, it was the free will of the Logos to choose to evolve without free will. Is this correct?

Ra: I am Ra. This is correct.

Questioner: Do the Logoi that choose this type of evolution choose both the service-to-self and the service-to-others path for different Logoi, or do they choose just one of the paths?

Ra: I am Ra. Those, what you would call, early Logoi which chose lack of free will foundations, to all extents with no exceptions, founded Logoi of the service-to-others path. The, shall we say, saga of polarity, its consequences and limits, were unimagined until experienced.

Questioner: In other words you are saying that originally the Logoi that did not choose this free will path did not choose it simply because they had not conceived of it and that later Logoi, extending the first distortion farther down through their evolution, experienced it as an outcropping or growth from that extension of the first distortion. Am I correct in saying that?

Ra: I am Ra. Yes.

Questioner: Then did this particular Logos that we experience plan for this polarity and know all about it prior to its plan? I suspect that this is what happened.

Ra: I am Ra. This is quite correct.

Questioner: In that case, as a Logos, you would have an advantage of selecting the form of acceleration, you might say, of spiritual evolution by planning what we call the major archetypical philosophical foundations and planning these as a function of the polarity that would be gained in third density. Is this correct?

Ra: I am Ra. This is exquisitely correct.

Questioner: In that case, it seems that a thorough knowledge of the precise nature of these philosophical foundations would be of primary importance to the study of evolution of mind, body, and spirit, and I would like to carefully go through each, starting with the mind. Is this agreeable with Ra?

Ra: I am Ra. This is agreeable with two requests which must be made. Firstly, that an attempt be made to state the student's grasp of each archetype. We may then comment. We cannot teach/learn to the extent of learn/teaching. Secondly, we request that it be constantly kept before the mind, as the candle before the eye, that each mind/body/spirit complex shall and should and, indeed, must perceive each archetype, if you use this convenient term, in its own way. Therefore, you may see that precision is not the goal; rather the quality of general concept complex perception is the goal.

Questioner: Now, there are several general concepts that I would like to be sure that we have clear before going into this process and I will certainly adhere to the requests that you have just stated.

When our Logos designed this particular evolution of experience It decided to use a system of which we spoke allowing for polarization through total free will. How is this different from the Logos that does not do this? I see the Logos creating the possibility of increase in vibration through the densities. How are the densities provided for and set by the Logos, if you can answer this?

Ra: I am Ra. This shall be the last full query of this working. The psychic attack upon this instrument has, shall we say, left scars which must be tended, in our own opinion, in order to maintain the instrument.

Let us observe your second density. Many come more rapidly to third density than others not because of an innate efficiency of catalysis but because of unusual opportunities for investment. In just such a way those of fourth density may invest third, those of fifth density may invest fourth. When fifth density has been obtained the process takes upon itself a momentum based upon the characteristics of wisdom when applied to circumstance. The Logos Itself, then, in these instances provides investment opportunities, if you wish to use that term. May we enquire if there are any brief queries at this space/time?

Questioner: Is there anything that we can do after this contact to increase the comfort as related to the psychic attack, or is there anything that we can do to make the instrument more comfortable and to improve the contact in the present situation?

Ra: I am Ra. The faculties of healing which each has commenced energizing may be used. The entity may be encouraged to remain motionless for a period. As it will not appreciate this, we suggest the proper discussion.

The physical appurtenance called the censer was just a degree off, this having no deeper meaning. We do ask, for reasons having to do with the physical comfort of the instrument, that you continue in your careful efforts at alignment. You are conscientious. All is well.

We leave you, my friends, in the glorious love and light of the one Creator. Go forth, therefore, rejoicing in the power and in the peace of the one infinite Creator. I am Ra. Adonai. ☥

Intensive Meditation
February 11, 1982

(Carla channeling)

I am Laitos, and I am with this instrument. We greet you, my friends, in the love and in the light of the one infinite Creator. It is, as always, a great privilege to be allowed to work with those who seek to serve as channels to speak the humble message of the Confederation. We of Laitos know that for many of those who attempt to serve as channels there come times when the individual begins to regress somewhat in the progress they have made. The ones who choose to serve as channels often find doubts in their minds about their abilities, doubts about whether they are truly receiving, doubts about whether they are speaking randomly or not and soon with the message that the Confederation offers.

As you continue, however, to exercise your abilities these doubts will begin to smooth out and you will once again be able to relax and allow the words to flow freely without attempting to examine each and every phrase, each word. We do not speak of doubts as a handicap, for doubt is a very important part of your seeking. Without doubt one does not question. To find answers, unknowns, one must question not only others but oneself. Questions will aid you as well as we of Laitos.

(Inaudible). Each insight, each thought, offers opportunity to increase one's awareness, one's knowledge of the Creator, of the self. We of Laitos encourage each to be used—the doubts—and not void them. We will aid you in whatever way possible. If you would call and we shall be with you.

We would at this time like to transfer this contact to one known as S. If she would but relax and allow the words to flow without analyzing them. We now transfer.

(S channeling)

I am Laitos, and am with this instrument. We of Laitos are honored to greet you all with this instrument once again. We are happy to be with you all today and appreciate your allowing us to serve by being of aid to you. We are always pleased to be with each of you at any time should you request we do so. We hope to be able to speak through another instrument, so we would transfer this contact at this time. I am Laitos.

(Unknown channeling)

I am Laitos, and I am with this instrument. We greet you all once again in love and light. We apologize for the delay in making our contact known to the group. We were unable to reach the one which we had intended to speak through. We would at this time offer our conditioning vibrations to the one known as R so that he might be able to reach a greater depth in his meditation. We would pause for a moment. I am Laitos.

(Pause)

(Unknown channeling)

I am Laitos, and am once again with this instrument. At this time we would offer ourselves in somewhat of an unusual capacity, i.e. the answering of questions. We feel that at this time we might be of most service in this capacity. Is there a question at this time?

Questioner: I have a question, but first I would like to ask if the drawing of the group energy is acceptable for the channel to remain energized because of the sleeping?

I am Laitos. We are able to maintain this contact at a level which is acceptable at the present though we cannot guarantee, shall we say, this shall be the case for the remainder of the session. We shall do our best, my sister. May we answer you further?

Questioner: Yes, thank you. I got a letter today from a brother who is very, very busy seeking Nirvana of the quickie variety and he would like to know the answer to a question which is difficult for me to fathom. However, I will ask it as he asked it because I would very much appreciate being able to send him a reply. He has studied under a yogic philosophy for many years and would very much like to return to the source. He identifies this source as being at the ninth density. He would like to know if it is possible to bypass all the intervening densities in this lifetime and go back to the source using his yogic practices. Could you comment on these concepts and help our brother, who is truly an earnest seeker, in any way that you see appropriate, please?

I am Laitos, and am aware of your question. We are also aware that entities such as this brother upon your planet at this time seek with great intensity the meaning of their lives and a path which might bring them that which might be called enlightenment. Many are the ways which your peoples have chosen to seek this path throughout the history of your planet. Each path has provided integral pieces of the puzzle, shall we say, which are most necessary for the sincere seeker to utilize in the polarization of the self to a degree which is, shall we say, harvestable. Many such paths have produced those called the saints, the avatars, the gurus, each of which, through disciplined exercises of many kinds, has been able to balance the centers of energy in your mind and body/mind/spirit complex to a degree that is necessary for this harvest into the next density of the illusion of the one Creator. Each discipline, while providing a viable path for the spiritual evolution, also contains those facets which may be considered distortions or misapprehensions of certain spiritual qualities and descriptions.

It is our humble understanding that the path of spiritual evolution must be one which is straight and narrow and of some considerable length, traveling through many illusions and densities with the one goal of becoming one with the Creator. What this means for each entity in any illusion is that the in-streamings of the love/light of the one Creator are available for use by each entity; this love/light or prana being channeled through the energy centers or chakras, if you will, in such a manner that the light is used efficiently, each density providing the seeker of union with a greater intensity of light.

Upon the completion of the cycle of incarnations in any density an entity is given the opportunity to, shall we say, grade itself by being bathed in the light of the one Creator until it is no longer able to withstand or utilize the increasing intensity of light. This light has degrees shall we say, of vibration. When the entity can no longer withstand or use the light, then it stops at that point and that point falls where it may. Wherever it falls it is then the entity's choice, by its own ability to use the light, to continue its study in the appropriate illusion which matches the intensity of light which has been utilized.

Few there are upon your planet at this time who can withstand the intensity of the light of the fourth density. For this light is what might be called a quantum leap beyond that which you now experience within your third density. If any entity were to experience it for but a moment and be able to withstand it, for that moment that entity would feel indeed that it had returned to its Source and would most likely be quite appreciative of that experience. For such seekers as your brother to desire to progress more rapidly than is possible, shall we say, realizing that all things are possible, is a commendable trait, but one which is not likely to be realized, for though your density provides an intense degree of catalyst and opportunity for traveling the spiritual path, to the best of our knowledge, it does not provide enough catalyst to build the polarity necessary to, shall we say, skip any density.

To the best of our knowledge, when this octave of densities is completed the individualized entities will find themselves at the level of the eighth density—one with the Source of this particular creation. But our teachers have not themselves found such union nor have their teachers told them of an end to such progressions.

We shall continue. For an entity to return to the Source does not mean the end to evolution. For an entity to desire to progress spiritually as rapidly as possible is quite commendable, but we would suggest that it is most necessary to learn to walk, shall we say, before one runs or flies or soars beyond the start. Yours is a density in which the child learns to crawl. Rejoice in the opportunities which are thusly presented to you.

May we answer you further, my sister?

Questioner: No. Thank you, for that was very helpful, I am sure, and I am sure that B thanks you too.

I am Laitos. Our thanks be with your brother as well. May we answer another question at this time?

Questioner: Yes, can you give me some information about the technique of unblocking energy centers during meditation, and is this helpful?

I am Laitos, and am aware of your question, my sister. May we say that the balancing and unblocking of energy centers is the single process which each entity upon your planet is now busy with, though most are quite unaware of the process that is in motion. The incarnation offers the entity the opportunity to accept, to forgive, to love all beings, all experiences, all events, including the self. This learning of acceptance and loving is that learning which shall allow the graduation, shall we say, into the next lesson's series or density. The entity throughout a lifetime, therefore, has the opportunity of learning to love that which is unlovable, learning to accept that which is unacceptable, learning to forgive that which is unforgivable.

This process of loving, accepting, forgiving of all might be enhanced in the meditations upon those circumstances, situations, entities or characteristics of the self which are deemed by the self to be unacceptable, unforgivable, unlovable. Such characteristics occurring within the daily round of activities might be beneficially noted within the mind and used as a catalyst for the learning to love, accept and forgive in the meditative state.

It is our understanding that to see the original feeling as it occurred in its natural surroundings and to allow that feeling to be concentrated upon intensifies it until its logical outcome is perceived, is most beneficial. For example, anger at any would be intensified until the logical outcome of anger would be seen. Anger increasing to violence, violence to pain and suffering, pain and suffering to remorse, remorse to a desire to make retribution—leading to a feeling of love and acceptance. Then seeing this range of experience as polarized opposites at the extremes and seeing the self as acceptable for having these facets, for the one Creator within to know Itself through.

This, we feel, is the most beneficial use of the process of balancing that might be utilized at this time. The descriptions of the centers of energy and the behavioral patterns corresponding to them are available from this group.

May we answer you further, my sister?

Questioner: No, thank you.

We are humbly grateful to you. May we answer another question?

(Pause)

(Unknown channeling)

I am Laitos. At this time we would attempt to close this contact through another instrument. I am Laitos.

(Pause)

(Unknown channeling)

I am Laitos. We were attempting to reestablish contact with the one known as S, but we were unable to reach her at this time. We would like to once again attempt to establish contact with her to end our part in this meditation. We would now attempt once again to contact the one known as S. I am Laitos.

(Unknown channeling)

I am Laitos, and am once again with this instrument. We are still working with this instrument to make our contact known to her, as she is still having some problems in recognizing our contact. We would, however, like to speak through this instrument as we leave you today. It has indeed been an honor and a pleasure to be with this group and to be a part of your meditation. We are always grateful to you for allowing us to be with you. And we will end this contact at this time. Adonai, my friends. Adonai vasu borragus.

(Portions of the following recording are inaudible.)

(Unknown channeling)

We are again with the instrument. I am [Latwii]. We thank the one known as C and assure him that as a good instrument would say *(inaudible)* whatever that he must surely get beyond through constant application. We would thank you and each of the others in this group, some of whom desire to be channels such as this one, some of whom desire only to feel our presence and to deepen their own meditation. *(Inaudible)* a sort of carrier of strengthening your own individual vibration. We only therefore at this time attempt to make our presence known to *(inaudible)* to *(inaudible)* to *(inaudible)* and to *(inaudible)*.

Now to the one known as *(inaudible)* I contact *(inaudible)*.

My friends, it is a great privilege to work for this group, and we leave you with the request that you do ask for us to have us there for a few minutes. Never think it is for too short a time. For if you can look carefully at one blade of grass as beauty *(inaudible)* the *(inaudible)* for your own test as your pursue it. As the clock strikes. As a bird sings. As you hear the sound of water *(inaudible)*. Let all things be signals to meditate upon the beauty of the creation of the Father.

We are always with you. You need but ask. I am Latwii, and will leave this instrument now. Adonai *(inaudible)*.

(Unknown channeling)

I am Latwii, and am again with this instrument. We took a *(inaudible)* at the one known as Jim, but he is not yet ready to answer questions for a large group. We think that he is, but he does not think that he is, but we will work that out in the future as you *(inaudible)*. Actually, to us it is a kind of *(inaudible)* to this instrument. May we ask at this time if there are any questions. If you have one please ask.

Questioner: Yes, first I would like to thank you. *(inaudible)* attempting to contact me *(inaudible)*.

We realize, my brother, that that is not precisely the question, however we will make it into one as we know that which you mean. It is a common occurrence with one who has not yet truly vanquished the old habits of the body. We will state that in such a way that you do not feel that because you eat [spaghetti] you cannot channel. The habit of the body is to be active. Unless the body is asleep it is most often active. Even while watching one of your television shows the body will be active and will attempt to feed itself *(inaudible)* or have some sort of pastime. It is very certain that the mind and the body do have some kind of activity.

(Tape ends.)

Sunday Meditation
February 14, 1982

(C channeling)

I am Hatonn, and I am with this instrument. We greet you, my friends, in the love and in the light of the one infinite Creator. Tonight we will speak but briefly. We of Hatonn wish to express our gratitude at being allowed to be a part of this group for what has been in your terms a long time. We feel as much a pupil as do all in this group, for through this group we have also learned and have been aided in our journey. So, we wish to say thanks to you and hope that we may continue to be with you.

On your planet the season you call spring is at hand. As your weather begins a change and as the warmth begins to return, a new cycle is about to begin. New growth will stretch and reach for the light, will bask in the warmth *(inaudible)* will be nurtured and will fulfill its purpose. My friends, you are reaching, stretching, ever attempting to expose more and more *(inaudible)* to the light, to the love of the Creator. In this illusion in which you are now a part, you are slowly, steadily, fulfilling your purpose, attempting to be a part of the whole. You, as you become more and more aware of the love that is within, without and that is you, blossoming, growing, fulfilling, as you are nurtured by the light the radiance of yourself shines increasingly brighter. You cannot hide it, for it is part of you and it is there for others to see; whether they can appreciate or not, whether they will become like it or seek to ignore or destroy, the light that is you shines.

That light, my friends, is most beautiful to us. We are most joyful in being able to see this light grow. We hope that this light, if seen by others, may awaken them and enable them to fulfill their purposes. We ask not for you to make yourselves conspicuous, as do so many who would preach to others but attempt to drag them along and into their particular way of growth, but we hope that each, by example, may start a small spark in others, that they may come to know the love and the light of the one infinite Creator. We ask, we hope, that you will not flash in front of people, but merely allow the love and light that is you [to] shine so that others may see and deal with as is their way.

We would now like to transfer this contact to another. We are Hatonn.

(Carla channeling)

I am Hatonn, and I greet you once again in the love and in the light of our infinite Creator. We would continue through this instrument.

My friends, in expressing our gratitude for being able to share with you in your meditations over a period of what you call your time, we are expressing appreciation of something which has a fundamental function in the spiritual life. Picture, if you will, the creation of our planetary sphere that surrounds you, in some parts towers above you, curves away from you in the far distance, out of eyeshot finally. The creatures of that creation are in many cases so totally interconnected physically that there is no misunderstanding possible of the fundamental truth of unity. The mother, the nurturer, the Earth itself bears the fruit that supports the life, and the creatures of that creation are aware of this, and do not question it. They know that they are a part of one creation and a piece of one unity.

Creatures, such as yourselves, my friends, have reared up on their hind legs and have walked away from the mother, that is, the symbol of a kind of unity that is nurtured *(inaudible)*. It does not often occur to your peoples that you all could indeed be a part of one being, particles of one creation, and yet, my friends, just as the roots of trees intertwine and touch in their search for light, so do all the creatures of your world touch each other. The air circulates among you, the earth is under your feet, even in your domicile, my friends, each of you rests upon some chair, a sitting place, which touches the floor, that touches the next sitting place. The air touches all of you. These words, that this instrument offers itself that we may speak, come to each of you. You are one, my friends, and that is the fundamental function of meetings such as this. We do not suggest that you are in any way better than your fellow man, wiser than your fellow man, or more to be than your fellow man, for you are your fellow man.

However, my friends, each of you has made a simple, but sometimes devastating choice and that is to pursue the path of spiritual seeking, Although it is an adventure, it is one which often causes one to feel immensely alone. Each of you, hearing these words, is now seated in a domicile with a group of like-minded seekers. It matters not what you say or do not say, whether you are jocular or serious or silent. What matters, my friends, is that just as the floor and the chairs and the air physically touch all of you together, so your seeking allows you to feel the touch *(inaudible)* of all the *(inaudible)*, not a touch of the hand, necessarily, but the touch of caring of sharing, of daring the determination, and of a kind of honor which is not the property of those who yet sleep.

So, my friends, it is so far more to feel that light within you *(inaudible)*. Here lies that which in your heart may became a resource. As you move into groups of people who are not necessarily at all of a like mind and to whom it is your desire to be of service, your chief service is to share that light that you feel at this moment and at those times when your meditations allow you magnificent moments of that feeling of sweetness and unity which occur unexpectedly, as roses in the desert. Here is where your own resources may be brought up, to use this instrument's phrase, your batteries may be charged, for there are those who will indeed seek to drain you, and it is important for your own maintenance that you have control over this process so that you are never open when you have been completely drained. Fill, then, your batteries with love and light and then know that nothing can come from you, but only through you. Keep these feelings in your heart and as you attempt to express the manifested love in your daily life attempt only to be.

We could speak to a far greater extent upon this subject, however, for the present, we shall close. If there are questions we shall allow our brother to answer. Again, my friends, we thank you. We wish you the peace of your path, in the company of those who are seeking to know how to love.

I am Hatonn. We leave you in the love and in the light of the infinite Creator. Adonai, my friends. Adonai vasu borragus.

(Carla channeling)

I am Latwii. I am with this instrument, and I also greet you in the love and light. It is a privilege to speak through this instrument as we do not often do so since this instrument does not use question and answer format. We, however, wish to use this instrument in order to comment on the hilarious conversation that three of the instruments present are having at this time. Each of them is saying, "Why don't you go to someone else?" We have been playing round-robin up here for the last several of your what you call minutes and we would be glad to keep doing so except that no one can hear it except us and therefore we cannot answer any questions. We say to the one known as L, we understand, old boy, you are a little lame-brained tonight, therefore, we would, if we might have the honor, work with the instrument known as Jim, if he would allow us to enter into the realm of his energy centers, rather than asking us to try L. I will now leave this instrument. It has been a joy to speak through her. I am Latwii.

(Jim channeling)

I am Latwii, and am with this instrument finally. We greet you all in love and light and do marvel at the ease of moving through a door which has been opened. We especially enjoy evenings such as this, for is it not variety which is the spice of every life? And now for the main course, so to speak. May we answer queries at this time?

L: I have a question, please, in reference to my lame-brainedness. I seem to be having a lot of trouble maintaining concentration tonight. Have you any advice to offer or explanation of what might possibly be causing it?

I am Latwii, and am aware of your query, my brother. In this regard may we say quite simply that when a portion of the physical vehicle is what you might call injured, it is much more difficult to place the concentration at a, shall we say, constant state or a steady state, for there is the natural concern of the body complex for a portion of its being and as your mind, body and spirit are intertwined in quite close fashion, it is only logical to assume that when one part has been injured, there is the taking away of, shall we say, energy and concentration from the whole, so that that part might be healed.

May we answer you further, my brother?

L: Yes. I recently had some trouble in the area of my throat. Considering the proximity of one of the chakras to that area, is there a connection between the physical ailment I've been experiencing and that chakra?

I am Latwii, and am aware of your query, my brother. In this regard we find we are unable to speak specifically, for indeed there is a connection between these two phenomenon—we correct this instrument—phenomena. We are sure the one known as Carla would appreciate this correction.

Carla: Thank you, Latwii.

We continue by saying that there is a connection which is relevant to the current growth of your being. This connection is most beneficially sought for and discovered within your own meditative seeking. We cannot infringe by describing its nature, for that would be to, shall we say, rob the prize from you.

May we answer you further, my brother?

L: No, and I thank you very much for your assistance.

I am Latwii. We are most grateful to you as well. Is there another question at this time?

M: Yes, Latwii, something that may be of interest to our readership. You talked about the new cycle is beginning soon. Can you give us some idea of what soon is?

I am Latwii, and am aware of your query, my brother. We of Latwii are unable, as is each of the Confederation, to specifically delineate time frames. Firstly, we are unable because we cannot compute correctly the frame of time that will elapse between the present and, shall we say, the heart of the beginning of the new cycle, for it is already, in some respects, quite well underway and shall be determined in its specificness and completeness by the combined free will choices of each of the entities upon your planet. Even if we were able to determine all the [initial], shall we say, parameters we could not give specific information as to its inception or date, shall we say, for such information is not deemed proper or pertinent to the spiritual evolution of entities upon your planet.

To summarize, may we suggest that this cycle has begun and shall continue in intensity for some period of your time as you measure years and decades.

May we answer you further, my brother?

M: No. I think I knew that answer before I asked. It was not a wise question. Next one has to do with material I've been reading from back in 1974 and before and concerned as to what changed in the thinking of the Confederation—you talked many, many times about a very broad contact or even a landing that was imminent and I'm curious as to what's changed in your way of thinking about that approach of bringing truth to this planet.

I am Latwii, and am aware of your query, my brother. To this question we may best respond, we feel, by suggesting that the changes have occurred within the instruments and their tuning. To be more specific we may suggest that new instruments or instruments with tuning which is not precisely positive in nature may receive information which is not always accurate or of Confederation origin.

May we answer you further, my brother?

M: Yes. Do I understand you correctly that the Confederation never alluded to a mass landing type contact and that that was only something that came through the instrument's own imagination?

I am Latwii, and would respond to this query by suggesting that this is partially correct. It is also suggested that telepathic contact with entities of origins other than the Confederation might also have been the source of such information in a few instances in the past of this group.

May we answer you further, my brother?

M: One last question. That topic came up many, many times in the past. Were we routinely in contact with entities that identified themselves as Confederation that were not? Back in '74?

I am Latwii, and to respond to this query most generally, we may suggest that the concept of a mass landing by Confederation entities has been a concept which has been widely disseminated among your peoples for a great length of time, by entities of both the positive and negative polarities, for some period of your time. Such a contact with your peoples through the landing of craft has been occurring from both Confederation …

(Side one of tape ends.)

(Jim channeling)

I am Latwii, and am with this instrument once again. To continue our response. This concept of the landing of craft has been widely disseminated for a long period of time as your peoples measure time. Many landings have occurred, landings originating from the Confederation and from other origins. The concept of a mass landing has never been a strong possibility, as far as Confederation sources are concerned. The telepathic contact with various channels has been somewhat hampered, shall we say, when these instruments are aware of the landings which have occurred and are aware of the messages transmitted by other sources which suggest a mass landing, for the various purposes of teleporting, shall we say, entities off of your planetary surface, of giving technological information, of teaching the spiritual laws, and so forth.

Instruments who have become aware of information from other sources have, in their minds, by their own choice, a distortion toward such information quite frequently which allows sources other than the Confederation to eventually infringe upon the purity of their contact and utilize the information and distortions already present in the mind complex so that further information of this nature might be given. It is possible, therefore, that an entity for a period of time may receive a positive contact and through its own distortion towards such and such a type of information thereby distort that information and allow an opening to occur within its own instrument for the further description and dissemination of this type of information.

May we answer you further, my brother?

M: No. Thank you, Latwii, for your patience.

I am Latwii. We thank you as well. Is there another question at this time?

L: Latwii, I have a couple of questions I'd like to ask to ensure my understanding of how this whole thing came about. In discussing this subject with a friend recently, I found I had some questions in my mind as to the purpose that you had for UFOs, so I would like to make several statements and have you either agree with them or disagree and correct them if you would.

The first is that some, but not all, of the UFO occurrences that have occurred in the past have originated with you and that they were for the purpose of drawing attention to the fact that you do exist. Would you say that is correct?

I am Latwii, and am aware of your question, my brother. We assume that when you use the word "you" that you are referring not only to those known as Latwii, but to the Confederation in general, and we would respond by saying that some contacts of the sighting and encounter of the UFO craft, as your peoples call them, have been of Confederation origins and have the general purpose of presenting to the people of your planet the concept of mystery which then produces, hopefully, the seeking for the solution to the mystery.

In specific cases, entities upon your planet who have such contacts with Confederation craft have such contact for the purpose of awakening within their being a knowledge of information which has been seeded within their mind/body/spirit complex before this incarnation having to do with their own seeking and service to the one Creator.

May we answer you further, my brother?

L: Yes. In reference to those you just discussed, what is the necessity of the craft? Why is the craft necessary at all?

I am Latwii, and am aware of your query, my brother. In many cases—in most cases a craft is not necessary. Many such contacts, shall we say, are made in the state of sleep and dreams and may not even be consciously remembered by the entity contacted. The purpose still is the same: to awaken the one contacted to the purpose of its life and mission as determined by it before this incarnation. In some few cases the entity is contacted by the use of a craft of the UFO description, for it is felt by the entity's own higher self, shall we say, that such a contact is most beneficial for the awakening of that entity, as each entity is unique and in some cases the contact by the craft is also utilized for a wider purpose, that being the presentation to your population of the concept of mystery, so that the seeking to its solution might be generated.

May we answer you further, my brother?

L: So, would it be correct to say that the use of a physical craft is simply to take advantage of the individual's or group of individuals' favorable distortion toward such a craft as opposed to a boat from Shangri-La or something similar?

I am Latwii, and am aware of your query, my brother, and may respond by saying that, in general, this is correct, although there is no advantage, shall we say, which is taken, but an opportunity which is presented according to the distortions of the entity receiving this opportunity.

May we answer you further, my brother?

L: No, that should hold me for a while. I'll get back with you when I've had some time to look at it. Thank you very much for your patience.

I am Latwii. We are most grateful to you, and look forward to further queries from you. May we answer another question at this time?

(Pause)

I am Latwii. We have been most honored to join your group this evening. The exchange of love and light with each present has given us great joy. We especially enjoy those moments of laughter, for it is not often that we can partake in such levity, shall we say, for those of our vibration have heard all our jokes. We look forward to future gatherings with this group and shall bring our repertoire of bad puns. We leave this group now, rejoicing in love and in light. We leave each of you in that love and that light, radiating as it does from the one infinite Creator within all beings. We are known to you as Latwii. Adonai, my friends. Adonai vasu borragus. ✦

www.ingramcontent.com/pod-product-compliance
Lightning Source LLC
Chambersburg PA
CBHW080420230426
43662CB00015B/2164